Tiny Rowland

Other books by Tom Bower

Blind Eye to Murder
Klaus Barbie, Butcher of Lyons
The Paperclip Conspiracy
Maxwell The Outsider
The Red Web

Tiny Rowland

A REBEL TYCOON

Tom Bower

HEINEMANN : LONDON

To Veronica, Nicholas, Oliver,
Sophie and Alexander

First published in Great Britain 1993
by William Heinemann Ltd
an imprint of Reed Consumer Books Ltd
Michelin House 81 Fulham Road London SW3 6RB
London Melbourne Auckland Toronto

Copyright © Tom Bower 1993

The author has asserted his moral rights

A CIP catalogue record for this book
is held by the British Library
ISBN 0 434 07339 3

Phototypeset by Falcon Graphic Art Ltd
Wallington, Surrey
Printed and bound in Finland by
Werner Söderström Osakeyhtiö

Contents

Introduction and acknowledgments

The genesis of this book was in May 1973 when, for over one month, Lonrho's boardroom row dominated newspaper headlines in Britain. During that period, as a diligent BBC Television producer, I sat for three days in the hall of Lonrho's Cheapside offices, anxious to secure the first television interview with the mysterious Tiny Rowland. My patience was rewarded then and over the following two years with further occasional meetings. By then, I had interviewed many who had known Rowland since his childhood and during his business career. Those conversations and a continuing interest over the last twenty years are the bedrock of this biography.

The book was commissioned in the wake of Robert Maxwell's death. Although the two men are often mentioned in one breath, their differences outweigh their similarities in foreign parentage, ruthless ambition and pariah status.

Yet both are products of a unique era in Britain's history when the infusion of enormous talent from continental Europe into Britain before the Second World War enriched this country out of proportion to the numbers who were often reluctantly admitted. Hence the life of Tiny Rowland is not merely a biography of an exceptional tycoon but also a story and a reflection of our times.

In writing this book, I owe a great debt to Richard Hall, the first biographer of Tiny Rowland, who by his initial encouragement and donation of his archives and contacts, helped me enormously.

Secondly, I received considerable help from Ian Mills, the

veteran BBC correspondent in Harare who discovered the surviving witnesses of Rowland's early days in Rhodesia.

In the United States, I was, as always, helped by the indefatigable Robert Fink, a researcher without equal.

Other research was undertaken by Brigitta Schübeler in Hamburg; Nicholas Gibson and Christopher Silvester in Britain; Michael Hall and Melinda Ham in Zambia; and Charles Rukuni and Beverley Tilley in Zimbabwe.

By its very nature, much of the information obtained in an undertaking such as this is given only on the strict understanding of anonymity. Of over three hundred and fifty people whom I interviewed, most requested that their assistance should not be acknowledged. The fear of Tiny Rowland deterred not only bankers, brokers and lawyers but also government officials in Britain, the United States and across Africa. Significantly, even multi-millionaires who had clashed with Rowland in the past were prepared, albeit reluctantly, to disclose their troubles with Tiny, but not 'on the record'.

Some of the few who were prepared to allow their help to be acknowledged are: the late George Abindor, Fred Adams, John Addey, Philip Adeane, Eric Armitage, Neal Ascherson, Noel el Assad, Bruce Barclay, William Barclay, Ken Barton, Brian Basham, Susan Baxter, Graham Beck, A.S. Bell of Rhodes House Library, Johnny Bevan, Larry Bickerton, Rt. Hon. John Biffen MP, Les Blackwell, the late Sir Michael Blundell, Bunny Bowles, Colyn Braun, Fred Butcher, the late Andrew Caldecott, Cyril Carton, Elias Chipimo, Richard Cockett, John Coker, the late Jack Cole, Joan Cole, Michael Cole, Bob Contat, Suzanne Cronje, John Cruickshank, Stewart Cumberbank, Peter Davey, Marquand de Villiers, Peter Dobson, J.P. Esterhuysen, Ivan Fallon, Tom Ferguson, Alex Finer, Bruce Fireman, Udi Gecaga, Alves Gomes, Lord Goodman, Rt. Hon. Mervyn Greenway, Dennis Grennan, Joe Hamlin, Rt. Hon. Roy Hattersley MP, Philip Hawley, Ian Hossy, Anthony Howard, Maurice Hynett, Oliver Irvine, Oliver Jessel, Ngethe Jeroge, His Excellency Kenneth Kaunda, Basil Kiplogat, the late Stefan Klein, Verena Klein, Desmond Krogh, Eileen Kruger, Hugh Laughland, Colin Legum, David Leigh, Manus Linklater, Leslie

Lloyd, Jack Lundin, Duncan Mair, Alan Marsh, Ashraf Marwan, Dan Mayers, Wally Milne, Roger Moss, Dr Mathias Mpande, Tom Mtine, Dr Jeno Mungai, John Munthali, Valentine and Flavia Musakanya, Vernon Mwaanga, Richard New, Harry Nieman of Mercedes, Julian Ozanne, Bruce Page, John Patterson, Richard Philips, John Plender, Brian Pottinger, Colonel Johann Prinsloo, Don Prittie, Jenny and Michael Reynolds, Murray Ritchie, the late Derek Robinson, David Russell, Cornelius Sanyanga, the late Sir Basil Smallpeice, Ian Smith, David Spanier, Paul Spike, John Sunley, Brian Thomas, P.K. van der Byl, Dr Keith Viewing, David Wadman, Pauline Wallace, Royston Webb, Basil West, Francis Wheen, Phyllis and Clifford Wilkinson, George Willoughby, Captain Bill Wilming, David Young, Lord Young of Graffham, Arthur Yoyo.

I am grateful to my colleagues at the BBC's Documentaries Department for their tolerance and support, in particular Paul Hamann and Steve Hewlett.

This book required the careful attention of a lawyer and David Hooper of Biddle & Co rose manfully to the task.

At Heinemann I am particularly grateful to Emma Rhind-Tutt and Tom Weldon whose help and encouragement were significant. Jane Moore was diligent and helpful in fact-checking.

One person who deserves special thanks is Michael Shaw of Curtis Brown whose advice, support and friendship was, as always, invaluable.

Finally, as most authors testify, no book which requires so much time, travel and dogged determination can be undertaken, let alone completed, without the support of one's family. The friendship, tolerance and good humour provided by my wife Veronica and my children transformed an undertaking into a lot of fun. For above all, discovering and recording Tiny Rowland's life has been a most enjoyable experience.

Preface

Torrential rain drenched the runway, obliterating the Nigerian lunchtime light. From the doorway of the VIP terminal at Lagos's Ikeja airport, Maurice Hynett peered through the mist as the Gulfstream jet skidded across the tarmac. Two employees, breathing heavily, awaited the signal. As the steps lumbered down from the aircraft, Hynett nodded and the three men raced forward with umbrellas to welcome their boss.

Smiling, suntanned and dressed immaculately, Roland 'Tiny' Rowland emerged with perfect bearing from the doorway. Sheltered from the driving rain, he was escorted towards the venerable building. Uniformed officials, representatives of the military dictatorship, watched motionless as the personality glided past. None considered demanding a passport or a visa. Nor did Rowland anticipate the request. In Tiny's world, the Gulfstream was the passport.

Waiting outside was a fleet of flagged Mercedes limousines. Six motor cycle outriders were impatiently revving their engines. The style suited Rowland's aspirations. This was not a business trip, rather it was a mission, a factor in his unremitting agenda. A visit by the chief executive of Lonrho to the president of Nigeria – a meeting of heads of state. In Rowland's mind, running a country and a company were similar tasks and both were best undertaken by dictators.

As the convoy sped towards town, Rowland uttered a few words reassuring Hynett, a Lonrho trouble-shooter, that he remained 'the blue-eyed boy'. The meeting with General Yacuba 'Jack' Gowon, Nigeria's president, had been arranged with panache and promises by another Lonrho fixer, Tony Lumley-Frank. Rowland required a reprieve from potential disaster. Six months earlier, the Organisation of African States had outlawed any further relationship with Lonrho. Rowland would beseech the general to terminate the humiliation.

Rowland's accommodation, the state guest house, was a good omen. But first, there was a formal dinner. Hynett knew that his employer would savour the frisson on his return to Lonrho's shabby offices in London's Cheapside the following day: 'Interesting dinner in Lagos last night.' The image was cultivated and nurtured.

The prospect of that evening caused the occupant of the third car driving from the airport some unease. Larry Bickerton, based in Nigeria for twenty-six years, was the manager of a trading company which Lonrho, in a phenomenal burst of activity, had just acquired. Amid the greetings at the airport, Bickerton had been studiously ignored by Lonrho's chief executive. The reason would become apparent twelve hours later.

Once ensconced in the guest house, Hynett outlined the arrangements. Dinner for fifty guests had been arranged in Quo Vadis, Mike Segrani's fashionable restaurant in the penthouse of a downtown towerblock. 'It's discreet,' disclosed Hynett. 'The Nigerians are not keen that the press should discover you're here.' The emphasis upon secrecy, as Hynett knew, appealed to Rowland, who equated stealth with power and influence. Publicity for the lone gun was to be avoided except on his own controlled terms. Anything written at that time, in April 1975, was invariably antagonistic. Although among Africans it was different. They displayed respect and friendship.

As Hynett explained, at least five ministers had accepted invitations and the other guests were senior civil servants, military procurement officers and a clutch of influential chiefs. 'The wheelers and dealers who are Lonrho's boys', as Hynett described them to Rowland. 'All the political leading lights will be there and the soft underbelly from whom we're earning.' Nigeria, as Rowland knew, was probably the most unscrupulous nation on the continent. 'Both Nigerian and European food will be served,' continued Hynett.

Rowland was delighted. Unlike other businessmen, Rowland saw marvellous opportunities in black Africa despite its total gross national product being less than tiny Holland's. Under his control, Lonrho's pre-tax profits had soared in the past fourteen years from £100,000 to £63 million. Over the next fourteen years, the pre-tax profits would rise, he believed, beyond his critics' dreams. Convinced that he would build a Goliath equal to Harry Oppenheimer's Anglo American, he genuinely loved Africa and the Africans loved Tiny. Even his critics would be pushed to allege that he had harmed any African country.

Rowland's performance that night was immaculate, confirmation to Hynett of the prevalent narcissism in his character. With grace, charm and wit, the fifty-eight-year-old tycoon treated individual guests in his uniquely self-deprecating style. Seeming or pretending to know everyone, he encouraged his guests to be in his presence and they felt rewarded by the experience.

To Rowland, oil-rich Nigeria was a special challenge. The potential earnings for his trading conglomerate were enormous, although the sheer scale of corruption was daunting and, from his experience in West Africa, provided few guarantees. Within the past year, Maurice Hynett had attempted to overcome that particular hurdle. Those to be 'kept sweet' had been dispatched to London to collect a brown envelope from 'Accounts'. Within Cheapside, they were considered 'seeds well sown'.

Paying bribes did not trouble Rowland although Hynett recalls, 'Tiny didn't want to talk too much about it.' For Rowland, they were 'special payments' or 'an investment in people'. Even his critics would attest that Rowland is not personally corrupt. 'Every man has his price,' he would say. 'The definition of an honest man is when his price is too high.' Dispensing money simply ensured Lonrho's continuing success. The perennial question was whether a corporation which paid bribes could be intrinsically honest. In London, where Rowland had surrounded himself with many nonentities, the answer among City practitioners seemed negative. Even Rowland noticed that his subordinates in Cheapside lacked his competence and brilliance but he ignored that each had been personally selected by himself.

Incompetence at headquarters in Africa, however, could not

be tolerated. The management of Lonrho's thirty-nine subsidiaries employing over 100,000 people producing or trading a bewildering assortment of merchandise from sugar to newspapers, platinum to beer, and motor cars to gold comprised diligent professionals, specially chosen to produce profits without supervision. Rowland, the deal maker, was not a manager. Nothing was bought without Rowland asking, 'Who will run it?' and Rowland prided himself on not visiting the assets he owned.

Larry Bickerton was not a Lonrho type, although Rowland would be pressed to define the typical Lonrho employee. The type was generally defined by negatives rather than virtues. Bickerton epitomised Rowland's antipathies. 'I can't abide their culture,' Rowland told Hynett, 'the old colonial English, drinking G and T at the club bar, who wear shorts and knee-length white socks.' But even Hynett had not anticipated the drama which would unfold at one o'clock that morning.

Everyone agreed that the dinner had been a jolly affair. As the last guest staggered into the lift and headed home, Rowland, half-sitting on the back of a chair, beckoned Hynett, Bickerton and two others. With the debris of the dinner strewn across the horse-shoe table, the four gathered around the man whose activities two years earlier had been castigated by an English prime minister as an example of 'the unpleasant and unacceptable face of capitalism'.

Rowland's topic was Bickerton, an amiable and decent man who understood Nigeria and was liked by everyone. Gently rocking the chair back and forward, speaking in a monotone, polite voice, Rowland accused Bickerton of running an amateur, low-profit and unaggressive show. 'I want a new image here. I want someone who will get under the skin of the local people.' Inexorably, the hapless manager was deflated, denigrated and finally demolished. Bickerton was ordered to return to Britain. 'But my children are at school here,' he spluttered. 'There are schools in England,' smiled Rowland.

'Crushed, he was simply crushed,' recalled Hynett, who during his thirteen years' service in the Royal Navy and the SAS had never witnessed similar cruelty. 'Rowland's mocking voice didn't rise by a decibel. The moving chair was the only sign of tension.' Amid the human devastation, Rowland's calm was a deadly virtue. Lumley-Frank was similarly struck. 'I have a tremendous regard for Tiny but he behaved like an absolute bastard. We were flabbergasted that he could be so brutal to a man.' Bickerton shed tears.

The manager's emotions did not appear to trouble Rowland. Hypersensitive about real or imagined slights to himself, he was not worried about humiliating and manipulating employees – paradoxical in a man who proclaimed the importance of loyalty among members of the 'Lonrho family'. To his victims, his protestations of fidelity sat uneasily with his evident skill in identifying and playing upon weaknesses. Like God, he had passed judgment.

Even his oldest colleagues could only speculate that the source of his vitriol dated back to the 1940s when, as a suspected Nazi sympathiser, he had been interned by the British government. Having buried that legacy, he was later pursued for avoiding payment of taxes. Twenty-five years afterwards, he was outlawed as a pariah by the City. Like a woman, Tiny wanted to be admired and, by the same token, loathed his critics, distrusted their motives and would offer no concessions in the countless vendettas he has waged to secure their total destruction. Invariably, Rowland would complain that he was the victim of prejudice, a conspiracy or dishonesty. Others would remark that, so often, Rowland was himself the initiator or even the aggressor. In Lagos, it was very clear that Bickerton was an object of his displeasure, against which Rowland could prove the righteousness of his case and assert his indomitable ambition to rule.

Bickerton's sentence, seemingly endless in passing, lasted just ten minutes. Quietly and separately everyone left the restaurant. In the guest house, Rowland was satisfied with the first part of his itinerary. He was not a philanthropist and Lonrho was not a charity. He desired money and power. Others might allege that he was running an expensive hobby which had proved profitable for himself and not for his shareholders, but they misunderstood.

Britain, his adopted country, penalised rather than praised initiative and wealth creation. He had to fight for himself and for Lonrho. To most, his agenda was self-aggrandisement, a trait which was particularly disliked amongst the British ruling classes, the very people whose admiration he sought.

In Africa it was different. The stigma attached to him by governments in London disappeared when he crossed the Sahara. Welcomed by governments, he was treated as a hero. Hence his visit that morning to General Gowon, Nigeria's president, would be like a meeting of the Titans.

It was not accidental that Rowland's fortune was not earned in the democracies of Europe but on a continent ruled by a mixture of murderers, corrupt military officers and their puppets.

Intoxicated by the power which Europeans wield in Africa, Rowland delighted in straddling the continent, flying from London to discuss war, peace and money with an assortment of presidents, many of whom had become old friends. Proving himself and occasionally deluding himself that he was a maker and shaker of African governments compensated for the devastating opprobrium he has suffered in Britain. The subtleties of Westminster-style government held little appeal for a man who flourished when dealing with like-minded benevolent dictators. 'A one-eyed king in the land of the blind,' is the judgment of an African and former Lonrho director. 'He deals with some Africans as if they are corrupt or gullible.'

The events in Dodan Barracks the following morning when Rowland called on General Gowon suggest the contrary. Earlier that year, Rowland had manoeuvred Lonrho into bidding for an exclusive contract to supply oil to the whole of black Africa. The audacious ploy had exploded and Rowland needed a mediator to repair the damage. Gowon, an unusually honest leader, seemed willing to assist. Their meeting was planned to last forty-five minutes. At its best, Rowland's performance with his targets is unsurpassable. The charm, the wit, the notable absence of any condescension, the seduction, the evidence of his affection for Africa and his intelligence persuaded the president to extend their conversation for two hours. Cynics would say that Gowon was simply grateful that a white man had flown especially from Europe to see him. But eyewitnesses would confirm the importance of Rowland's network of contacts, developed since 1948, across the continent. 'A player in my league,' was the highest compliment Rowland could pay in his continuing quest to contact the rich and the influential.

Rowland emerged satisfied from the president's office. Standing in the hall was Daniel Gowon. Rowland noticed that the foot of the president's younger brother was deformed, the result of polio in childhood. 'I know a doctor in New York who can fix that,' said Rowland. The remark seemed to be forgotten in the ensuing conversation. Two months later, Daniel Gowon telephoned Lumley-Frank, the Lonrho fixer in Lagos. 'Tiny's a marvellous person,' he sang from a New York hospital. 'He sent a plane ticket and everything's fixed.'

Paying for Daniel Gowon was generous. Two weeks after Rowland's visit to Lagos, the president was removed in a coup. The same night, Rowland dictated a telex for Hynett: 'Why on earth do you waste my time and introduce me to a load of has-beens?' Hynett laughed. Tiny had a wonderful sense of humour. He also had a brutal temper. Hynett would witness both.

For Rowland's life is a story of paradoxes: a man who surrounds himself in mystery and refuses an entry in *Who's Who*, but who yearns for publicity and an everlasting legacy. His is a life of a simultaneous battle within himself and against his adopted country. His rebellion is against history, political reality and, he says, corruption. The course of his revolt, its successes and failures, is a reflection upon Britain over the past fifty years.

One
Metamorphosis

Rebellion and revenge percolated the character of Roland Fuhrhop from the day of his birth. Resentment, exacerbated by the circumstances of his youth, was transformed during Fuhrhop's adulthood into deception. For the past forty-five years, a victim of this century's political turbulence, Roland Fuhrhop, alias Roland 'Tiny' Rowland, has generated myths about his past, distortions about the present and dreams about his future.

The beginning was not auspicious. The Belgaum Detention Camp in Simla, India, a destitute internment centre for undesirable enemy aliens, had been his parents' home for just over two years when on 27 November 1917, Muriel Fuhrhop gave birth in difficult circumstances to her third child, whom she named Roland Walter.

Her husband, Wilhelm Fuhrhop, born in 1885 in Hamburg, Germany, was suffering considerable financial hardship, his trading business confiscated by the colonial authorities. Roland was born to parents who were helpless victims of British arbitrariness.

They had married on 7 March 1906 in a Protestant Church in Richmond, London. Muriel Kauenhoven, the daughter of a Dutch father and British mother, was born in London on 16 March 1883 and remained an Anglophile. Muriel was ambitious and purposeful, while her husband was a quiet, perfunctorily educated and decidedly unimpressive, staunch German nationalist and disciplinarian who described himself as a 'manufacturer's agent'.

Soon after the birth of their first child, a daughter Phyllis in 1907, they sailed to Calcutta where Wilhelm was initially employed by a merchant, A. Janowitzer. By the eve of the First World War, Wilhelm Fuhrhop was a modestly successful, self-employed representative of German insurance companies and a Baden-Baden engineering factory who also exported mica, a form of asbestos used as an insulator, to Europe. Subsequently, there would be stories that Wilhelm was involved in gun running and diamond smuggling but the evidence suggests the contrary. The family lived in a small apartment and were conspicuous by their anonymity.

At the outbreak of war, the British government ordered the liquidation of all German businesses. The family moved to Darjeeling, a cool location south of the Himalayas where a second child Raimund Everest was born in November 1915. Soon after, the Viceroy announced the internment of enemy aliens. The colonial administrators had little affection for Germans and Wilhelm did not disguise his regard for the Kaiser. Belgaum, a malarial region, 2500 feet high and 200 miles inland, was a decidedly unhealthy location where many died. The births of German nationals, like Roland's, were only partially recorded but he was indisputably a British citizen as he was born on British territory.

Even in India, the apocalypse seemed imminent. To the north, Lenin was consolidating the Bolshevik revolution in St Petersburg, and in Europe the Kaiser's army on the Western Front was regrouping for a final attack.

On the subcontinent, Germany's surrender in November 1918 was unexpected and sudden. By the very nature of slow communications and the aggravated xenophobic sentiments of those not directly involved in the war, the Fuhrhops were not released from the camp until 1919 and then, since Wilhelm had displayed disloyalty, were issued with an expulsion order. Consequently, when the family arrived by ship in Britain in August 1920, Wilhelm was refused entry. While Muriel remained temporarily in Britain with her children and her family, who during the war had changed their name to Carton, her husband sailed on to Hamburg, an Anglophile city whose businessmen displayed a marked predilection for Britain.

The Fuhrhops' savings in Europe had remained intact allowing Wilhelm Fuhrhop to settle in a seven-room, ground-floor apartment at 28 Jungfrauenthal, Klosterstern, located in an affluent area of Hamburg. Secluded from the worst of the communist revolts in Munich and Berlin, life in the solidly socialist city was stable. Wilhelm established a new business, India Agentur, importers of mica from India.

The dominant influence on four-year-old Roland's life was his mother, a kind woman who bestowed upon her son love and good humour. By every account, family life for Roland was relatively happy and, within the neighbourhood, his father became prosperous. Mother and son spoke English together and it was only in 1929 that Muriel formally applied for German nationality, although under contemporary British law she had automatically become German by marriage.

Hamburg, unlike most German cities, emerged unscathed from the political and economic turmoil which racked Germany during the Twenties. With the exception of a small communist revolt, quickly suppressed, the city suffered like the whole country from the collapse of the German currency and the hyperinflation of 1923 when the one dollar bought 4200 billion Reichsmarks. Everyone's German savings disappeared but Wilhelm Fuhrhop had deposited sufficient money in Switzerland to avoid penury.

During that intensely political era where no German could ignore the bitter debate and physical antagonism between the communists, democrats and fascists, those apocalyptic events did not unduly influence the Fuhrhop household. When Roland reached the Heinrich Herz Real Gymnasium in 1929, the tall, handsome youth, nick-named 'Tiny' by his mother, showed no special interest in politics, finance or culture.

Among his schoolfriends, Tiny was memorable as an athlete. As a member of the Hamburger Sportsverein, he had won the 100-metre race and the records show that in other events he was either second or third. As a Jugendmeister, he proudly wore his master's badge on a HSV shirt when playing football at the regular Saturday athletic meetings.

Sensitive, slightly emotional and preoccupied by somewhat ephemeral matters, Roland was also remembered by his school friends, especially Jurgen Hilmer, for his appearance. 'He was the best dressed, always in grey flannels without braces.' His

appearance and remarkably fluent English were Roland's noteworthy qualities against his average academic achievements. 'But
he was always helpful and very sociable,' recalls Hilmer. 'Very
different than his elder brother Raimund who was neither sporty
nor sociable.'

On 30 January 1933, Adolf Hitler was appointed Chancellor.
About one third of the twenty boys in the class were Jews. All
left the school at the end of the summer term. Roland, like all
the other non-Jews, showed little emotion. *'Er war ein guter
Kamerad,'* recalls Gunther Walk who walked daily with Roland
for thirty minutes to and from school, 'and just acknowledged
that the Jews had gone but carried on.' As patriotic Germans,
no members of the class showed overt sympathy for the Jews.

Under the new laws, many youth clubs were automatically
affiliated to the Hitler Youth Movement and their members
wore the regulation brown uniforms. Roland, who was photographed in the brown uniform, would later claim that he joined
'as everyone did'. However Hamburg's state archives show that,
between 1933 and 1934, the Hamburger Sportsverein was specifically not included in the Hitler Youth Movement. Therefore
it must be assumed that Roland's membership was voluntary.
Whether that decision was significant for a sixteen-year-old is
debatable, but it does reflect upon Roland's parents, especially
his father, whom Roland would later claim was interned despite
his anti-Nazi opinions.

During 1934, Roland's final school year, as legitimised Nazi
terrorism persecuted opponents, burned the Reichstag and imposed the Nazi ideology throughout the country, Muriel Fuhrhop
decided that after completing his final examinations her younger
son should continue his education in Britain.

In the summer of 1934, Roland travelled with his mother
to London. They were welcomed by her brother Cyril and
his son, also called Cyril Carton. Her selection of a boarding
school, Churchers College near Petersfield, Hampshire, was
logical. Originally established to train young men for the East
India Company's shipping line, it had become popular for the
sons of British military families who served in India.

During his four terms at Churchers, 'Fritz Fuhrhop', who was registered as Ronald Fuhrhop of Hamburg, is remembered on two counts: his response to anti-German taunts and his sportsmanship. 'A great big blond chap,' recalls the Reverend John Pibworth who was surprised when Roland kept his distance from three other German pupils. 'They were Jewish,' recalls the clergyman who believes Roland had 'Nazi sympathies'. Goaded by his class about his Nazism, 'Fritz Fuhrhop' regularly jumped to attention, arm outstretched and shouted '*Heil Hitler*'. In retrospect, some are understanding about Roland's Germanism. 'He was torn in two directions,' comments a former schoolfriend. 'It wasn't easy to come down against your country which was recovering its prestige.'

But the recollections of Philip Brown, another contemporary, are steadfast: 'Fuhrhop justified Hitler's action against the Jews on the grounds that in the Twenties before Hitler came to power, the wheeler-dealing and cornering of markets by Jews had greatly incensed the German people and created hardships for them.' According to Brown, those views caused the headmaster's 'antipathy' towards his pupil who none the less was admired for his sporting prowess.

A fine boxer, a hurdler, a champion shot-putter and a good rugby player, despite the criticism that he 'Must be quicker off the mark', Roland was praised as 'a promising three quarters who will improve with experience'.

In the school holidays, he stayed with the Cartons at their home in Shepperton. 'We played a lot of tennis and cricket,' recalls his cousin. 'He was more English than German.'

Before the end of his schooldays, Roland was remembered for supporting capital punishment in a debate arguing that, 'A life punishment was too dreadful. It reduced criminals to wrecks. Death was far better and saved the country money and trouble.' On leaving, he donated a biography of Hindenburg to the school library, the life of an outstanding general and miserable politician. In 1936, *The Churcherian* recorded that Fuhrhop 'has commenced a business career and is now in a merchant's office. We wish him success.'

Having left Churchers in 1935 without any qualifications, Roland Fuhrhop lived in Richmond with his brother Raimund who was working for his father. It was an opportunity to row with the Thames Valley Skiff Club where he met many girls. His only possibility of work was offered by Cyril Carton, his uncle, as a salesman in the family business. Although Rowland would claim in 1988 in the *Observer* that his first job was at a 'shipping broker called Kittel & Co in Fenchurch Street in the City', in fact he worked for Ryley & Co, a haulage company based in Bethnal Green Road in London's East End.

Ryley & Co were shipping and forwarding agents, specialising in transporting freight to Germany: 'Pheasants to everything,' according to Cyril Carton.

Cyril Carton remembers his unglamorous and poorly paid cousin as 'uninspired, unambitious, somewhat adrift'. Aged seventeen, Roland lacked the connections to establish a social life among the British upper-middle classes whose shoulders he brushed daily in the City, nor did he possess the financial background to build his own business. The social ostracism was mirrored by his critical opinion of the British. Compared to the Germans, they were idle, inefficient and incompetent. Their homes lacked central heating, proper bathrooms and draught proof windows. Their restaurants and pubs compared poorly with those in Europe and their food was inedible. Even their motor cars – Rowland had developed a passion for fast cars – lacked the refinements which the Mercedes Benz boasted.

Yet London was the centre of an empire and the financial capital of Europe. Hamburg compared to London's metropolis was a sleepy village. For a young man anxious to earn his fortune, there was a clear choice between working in democratic Britain or within the German dictatorship where the state increasingly controlled all business. In London, Roland could learn and earn considerably more than in Hamburg and simultaneously use his connections with Germany.

One connection which Roland used delicately but profitably was to help Jews transport their furniture, art, jewellery and money from Germany to Britain. Ryley's trucks travelled regularly to Germany and provided a secure service for persecuted citizens. Roland's possession of two passports and his employment as a freight salesman provided excellent cover.

In 1938, at an expensive lunch in Simpsons in the Strand, Roland regaled an old schoolfriend about the irony that a loyal German, who was not especially keen on Jews, should be earning from that race's misfortune. Roland's boasts were substantiated by his wealthy appearance and the large tip presented to the waiter.

Wilhelm and Muriel Fuhrhop had arrived in Britain in 1936. In later years, their younger son would claim that the father had left Hamburg as a convinced anti-Nazi. The evidence suggests that the pressure to leave Germany was his wife's and was not political. By then, German life was completely dominated by the Gestapo, the discriminatory laws against non-Aryans and the deliberate suppression of all opposition. While Muriel Fuhrhop found the Nazis intolerable, her husband, a humourless and severe man who appreciated the disciplines which the Nazis imposed, could still profit from the German economic expansion while based in Britain. Indeed, importing mica from India would be easier from London, which still ruled India, than from Germany. With his son Raimund, Fuhrhop could supervise his German business quite easily from across the Channel. Accordingly, while Muriel and Phyllis lived in London, Fuhrhop initially commuted to Hamburg. Kurt Achenwall was retained there as manager, on an annual salary of £1500, the equivalent today of £60,000, but all the official correspondence with the German authorities was naturally signed by Fuhrhop.

In 1938, Raimund was conscripted to the German army. Father and twenty-two-year-old son consulted the German embassy about the problem of Raimund's dual nationality since he was born in India. According to Cyril Carton, Wilhelm 'insisted' that his eldest son obey the embassy's advice and return to Germany. The alternative, according to Carton, was the government's confiscation of their business. Rowland would later say that his father was 'furious' that his elder son returned and that his decision provoked an irreconcilable breach. Subsequent events suggest that Rowland's version was untrue. His father was pro-German, with business interests in Hamburg, and he would be reluctant to annoy the authorities.

On 1 October 1938, the day the German army entered

Czechoslovakia, Raimund returned to Hamburg and enlisted in the Wehrmacht. By then, Rowland's sister Phyllis, who in 1932 had married in Hamburg Clifford Wilkinson, an employee of Barclays Bank, was destined to spend the war in Trinidad in the West Indies.

Roland did not consider returning to Germany to enlist, aggravating his relationship thereafter with Raimund. Deeply attached to his mother and by then more British than German, Roland was not tempted politically or emotionally to waste his life in any army. 'He was very easy-going,' says Cyril Carton, 'and enjoyed his comforts and girlfriends.' Self-sacrifice for any ideals other than his own advancement was not on the agenda. Instead, throughout that period, Roland travelled to Germany from Britain, beginning to earn his fortune from the lucrative trade which continued between the two countries.

During one of his last trips, he has recounted, he 'was stopped and questioned by the police'. According to another version by him, after 'association with two well-known anti-Nazis [he spent] eight weeks in a Gestapo jail in Berlin'. The arrest story was retold by Rowland many times in the post-war years, often to the same people, but it is nevertheless an improbable exaggeration to embellish his anti-Nazi credentials. In 1939, few people spent eight weeks in a Gestapo jail and emerged unscathed, especially in the circumstances Rowland described. Persuasively, Cyril Carton says, 'To my knowledge he was never imprisoned in Germany.'

More likely is the story Rowland told in 1946: the 'anti-Nazis' were Jews and a transport operation had run into problems followed by a brush with the police which was resolved forty-eight hours later with the help of a British passport. Here was the genesis of an entrepreneur, sensitive to potential profits earned by avoiding authorities and their regulations, and astute to the realities of winning others' dependence upon him.

When Britain declared war on 3 September 1939, the legalistic choice of allegiance had disappeared. At the age of twenty-two, a British national by virtue of his birth in India, Roland rejected his German passport and applied on 12 October to change his name by deed poll to become Roland Walter Rowland. Cynics

at Lonrho would later quip that he chose the same fore- and
surnames to obscure the embarrassment of a peremptory summons by his surname. Others date this as Rowland's first sign
of creativity.

Since he had no degree or family connection to secure a
posting to a good regiment, Rowland was certain to be enrolled
as a private in the most menial task. To avoid that unpleasant
fate, he returned to Churchers College to beseech his headmaster
for a testimonial which would assist his application for a job with
field intelligence. Apparently the headmaster was unwilling.

Three months later, on 12 December, Rowland was conscripted into the British army and given the service number,
7365586. He would later claim that he volunteered for the Field
Intelligence Service to use his fluent German for the interrogation of prisoners, but was rejected. That is possible. But the
suggestion that he had served with the British expeditionary
force in Norway was untrue. Rowland appeared unwilling to
die for Britain. By his own account, he did not seek to join
a combat unit and fight fascism.

In some circumstances, depending especially upon his own
attitude, Rowland's antecedents, with a brother fighting for the
enemy, would have rendered him in 1939 as unsuitable for a
serious posting. But he was not pleased to be assigned to the
Royal Army Medical Corps and dispatched to Peebles, south
of Edinburgh, the base of the 33rd General Hospital.

James Anderson, a piper and later an employee of Scottish
and Newcastle Breweries, recalls Private Rowland's arrival as
noteworthy because he was placed, contrary to normal practice,
in a surgical ward with tonsillitis. Anderson also remembers
Rowland because he was bound by specific security restrictions.

The hospital cared for personnel at the nearby Rosyth naval
base and the patient records would always indicate the presence
of Royal Navy ships and the location of army units. Both these
pieces of information would be of use to the enemy. Rowland
was specifically forbidden access to those records. Instead he was
tasked to watch the gates or clean the latrines. But Anderson did
observe that 'Rowland was something different because he was
obviously very well educated and to the best of my knowledge

spoke several languages.' Anderson's assumption was based on seeing Rowland speak with Polish patients.

Cooped up with uncultured representatives of the British working class, subject to the mindless routine of the military and wasting his youth in purposeless duties for a country which seemed destined to lose the war, Rowland became increasingly alienated. The canteen for NCOs at Peebles had nothing in common with Simpsons in the Strand. 'He was an oddity,' decided Anderson, 'because of his attitude and his obviously different class.'

The antagonism was not shared by everyone. As the handsome product of a minor public school, he established a relationship with Colonel Malcolm MacKinnon, the company commander, and some of the local gentry. In particular, according to Anderson, the family of Captain Maule Ramsay, the local Conservative member of parliament who was interned as a German sympathiser.

Ramsay's family apparently invited Rowland to their home for meals and he was seen with an attractive, well-dressed woman who was related to the politician. On one occasion, Rowland dined at the Ramsays' with Colonel MacKinnon and his wife.

Rowland's own account of those fifteen months in Scotland concedes that it was the worst period of his life. Understandably, he glosses over those parts which are more unsavoury than those he cares to admit.

Rowland's self-proclaimed crisis began after July 1940 when his father was interned on the Isle of Man as an enemy alien and a potential security risk. It was the second time that Wilhelm Fuhrhop had been imprisoned by the British government and, according to Rowland, was completely unexpected because 'He had spent relatively little of his life in Germany and had come to England because of his dislike of the Nazi regime.'

The Home Office had been refining plans for the internment of enemy aliens ever since the outbreak of war. The targets were suspected spies, potential members of a fifth column and anyone who might be minded to assist the enemy, which included British fascists. All Germans and Italians were to be arrested and to be judged by tribunals whether they were likely to help their own country against Britain. While fewer than one thousand had been interned during the first weeks of war, everything changed amid panic in May 1940 following the German invasion of Holland and France.

News of the British army's evacuation from Dunkirk propelled the Cabinet on 24 May impulsively to accept warnings that 'every German is an Agent' and authorise a wave of arrests. Within one month, 27,200 people had been incarcerated. Since both the police and members of the tribunals were often incapable of distinguishing between foreigners, many of those interned were Jewish refugees, anti-Nazis and even apolitical housewives. Among the remainder was Wilhelm Fuhrhop.

For the Home Office, there were good reasons for his internment. Fuhrhop was a German; he had been interned during the previous war; he had maintained a business in Germany until the outbreak of war which still existed; and his son was serving in the Wehrmacht.

After his arrest, Fuhrhop was dispatched to the Isle of Man, a speck of green fields and sandy beaches in the Irish Sea, where hotels, boarding houses and a holiday camp had been requisitioned for the duration of the war. Despite the image, conditions were relatively good. Internees were well fed, could attend educational classes, concerts, work in private allotments and even walk in the town.

Rowland says that his father's arbitrary plight was tormenting. On 2 July 1940, the *Arandora Star*, a 15,000-ton luxury liner, had been torpedoed and sunk in the Atlantic transporting 1190 internees to Canada. Half of the passengers drowned, provoking a considerable protest, even in the midst of Britain's perils. Rowland says that his mother feared that her husband might also, without notice, have been dispatched to Canada or Australia.

Isolated in Scotland, Rowland was unwilling to accept his fate. Repeatedly and unsuccessfully he asked Colonel MacKinnon for help to secure his father's release. According to Rowland, 'The officer was not unsympathetic, but said "it could not be done".' Rowland then requested permission for leave to travel to Southampton to bid farewell to his mother, who, he said, was sailing to

America. At that moment, his mother was living alone in London also about to be arrested for internment. The officer's refusal was ignored. Rowland disappeared.

A teasing telegram arrived shortly afterwards. In essence, Rowland wrote sarcastically, 'Dear Colonel, I regret you could not see fit to give me leave to see my mother', and ended sarcastically, 'I trust you will keep my job open for me.' Rowland's job was latrine cleaning.

Rowland was arrested after a visit to the Isle of Man and was returned to Scotland. Asked whether he would take 'the colonel's punishment', that is prison, Rowland refused and insisted upon a court martial. Anderson was assigned to guard Rowland. Their relationship became controversial but Anderson's account has not been convincingly denied by Rowland.

The Scotsman says that, while awaiting trial, Rowland gave an alarming account of his life. Admitting that he had been a member of the Hitler Youth, he also claimed that his escape from Germany was thanks to 'Anthony and Winston'. But there was no gratitude because Rowland poured out his hatred of Britain and its working class, 'What bloody good is he anyway, give him a pint and enough for the cinema, that's all he's interested in. You've got him.' Rowland, Anderson concluded, was pro-Nazi, 'Certainly no use to Britain; a fascist and a complete utter sham.'

Eventually, Rowland decided that instead of six months' imprisonment from a court martial, he would accept 'the colonel's punishment'. But instead of the anticipated 'few days', he was sentenced to twenty-seven days in the military wing of Barlinnie prison in Glasgow. Anderson escorted Rowland to the jail, reputedly the harshest in Britain.

While completing the formalities, Rowland complained about his lack of Beecham pills, a common laxative at the time. His thoughts were interrupted by an NCO who, without notice, insulted the prisoner and hit him with his leather-covered swagger cane. A weal appeared on Rowland's face. Sensing the danger, Rowland immediately complied, double marching to the reception and enduring his fate. 'It seemed like 270 days,' he recalled. 'I was bitter and angry with the authorities.'

Shortly afterwards, Muriel Fuhrhop was incarcerated in Holloway prison. Raimund's military service, her husband's internment and Rowland's own behaviour were clearly factors influencing the authorities. According to Rowland, his mother was released but volunteered to join her husband in the Isle of Man rather than live separately. Security officials on the Isle of Man say that she had no choice. She had been denounced by neighbours as a security risk.

On his return from Barlinnie, Rowland was met by James McCulloch, the regimental sergeant major who subsequently became a teacher. McCulloch recalls Rowland arriving 'amid a lot of mystery, possibly under escort, with firm instructions that he was not to be allowed access to any information. Even his mail was to be intercepted.' Soon after their first encounter, McCulloch admits that he was brutally frank: 'Rowland, you're no use to anyone. It's a waste of the convoys to bring your food.'

During 1941, Rowland returned to his menial chores, cleaning latrines and carrying sacks. His version of that year's event contrasts with the sworn recollection of another British soldier, Private Kenneth Calderbank from Lancashire.

Rowland says that on his release from Barlinnie he was posted to the military hospital at Edinburgh Castle. By then, he had lost all sympathy with Britain and its war. His priority was to secure his father's release. Eventually he was told to 'shut up or get out'. As reported in 1981, Rowland told the officer that, 'He could not serve while his father was interned and was told that he would have to be discharged and sent to the Isle of Man.'

Calderbank, who was billeted with Rowland and about seven other privates in Edinburgh Castle, has sworn a different version. Like Anderson, Calderbank recalls Rowland as 'over-confident, even arrogant to the point of being objectionable', paying others to undertake some of his chores.

In the middle of one night in early December 1941, Calderbank lay awake and says that he could hear that Rowland was listening to Lord Haw Haw, the British-born propagandist broadcasting from Berlin. 'Sink the bastards, sink the bastards,' Rowland began uttering. 'He was aglow with joy,' swears Calderbank who soon realised that Rowland had heard about the sinking by Japanese aircraft of the British battleships HMS *Prince of Wales* and HMS *Repulse*. The destruction, causing the deaths of over one thousand British sailors, was the prelude to Japan's epic capture of Malaya, Hong Kong and Singapore.

'I was absolutely outraged,' recalled Calderbank. 'Livid, I jumped out of bed in my pyjamas and shouted at Rowland that he was a Nazi bastard.' Having grabbed the radio, Calderbank had thrown it down the stairs and run to the Regimental Sergeant Major to protest. 'I told him that I would never sleep in the same room as Rowland ever again.' Rowland was arrested and removed from the camp.

On 5 January 1942, Rowland formally left the army. The official reason for his discharge was 'services no longer required'. In the secret report, Rowland is recorded as expressing his incapability of fighting against his brother and was therefore prepared for internment. At that time, many Germans, including Jews, had volunteered to join British combat units and were undergoing training pending their deployment abroad. Although Rowland would later hint that he simply wanted to be with his parents, a more plausible explanation is his belief that the Allies had lost the war. At that moment, the Wehrmacht had advanced to the outskirts of Moscow, the Japanese had just destroyed the American fleet at Pearl Harbor, and Britain had suffered huge naval losses in the Mediterranean, isolating the army in North Africa. Rowland did not need to listen to Lord Haw Haw to become convinced that the Germans seemed on the verge of victory. The Isle of Man would be a good location when Hitler drove down the Mall towards Buckingham Palace. Rowland would back many losers in his career. Those who knew him in Scotland attest that Hitler was his first.

Critically, Rowland was not interned but detained under Regulation 18B as a man likely to endanger defence, public safety, public order or the war effort. The leaders of the British fascist movement were held under the same order and were among Rowland's fellow five hundred inmates when he arrived at Peel camp, a fortified prison on the island. Naturally,

Rowland would subsequently talk about his internment, not detention.

Richard Bellamy, a British fascist, distinctly recalled Rowland's arrival: 'You would have thought he had just strolled in from Savile Row,' he told Richard Hall, author of *My Life with Tiny*. 'He was not very popular because he had such expensive clothes and plenty of money.' Rowland also received plenty of food parcels, often delivered personally by a 'string of damsels'. Robert Row, another detainee, remembers, 'It is remarkable how many visits he received from well-dressed girls – he seems to have had several.'

By summer 1942, most of the internees on the Isle of Man had been released. A regular review of the remaining five thousand, the vast majority non-Jews, gradually reduced the numbers. Most of those remaining were, according to Karl Wehner, one of the inmates, 'friends of Nazism'. Rowland might also have expected release if he was genuinely anti-Nazi. Other internees recall his prediction that Hitler would lose the war, but he was not released. There are three possible reasons. Firstly, because he still posed a security risk. Secondly, because he sought to avoid the possible dangers of actually fighting in the war. Thirdly, Rowland insists that he wished to stay with his mother. 'Security' is the reason given by Jack Cole, the MI5 officer responsible for all inmates at Port Erin.

Rowland's father had been elected the leader of the inmates at Port Erin, a camp for married couples. Rowland would claim that his father was 'regarded as the head of the anti-Nazi section'. But Jack Cole contradicts Rowland: 'Wilhelm Fuhrhop was elected leader by the Nazis in the camp. By then, we barely had any Jews and even fewer anti-Nazis interned.'

Fuhrhop is also remembered by Cole's wife Joan, the camp's billeting officer, as 'a very good and loyal German who did not resent internment. Port Erin was very comfortable and Fuhrhop had nowhere else to go, even if he had been released. And there was no chance of that.' The Coles' recollections sharply contradict Rowland's campaign to secure his wronged father's release.

Muriel Fuhrhop had arrived at Port Erin on a sunny day

in July 1941. Joan Cole had seen the sick woman walk slowly through the gates and inquired about her condition. 'They told me in Holloway that I was healthy, but I'm not,' Muriel Fuhrhop complained. 'I sent her to our hospital,' says Joan Cole, 'and she never came out.' The diagnosis was terminal cancer.

Shortly after his arrival on the island, Rowland was allowed to visit his mother in hospital. Both Coles were struck by the 'quiet, shy, retiring young man', a contrast to the arrogance mentioned by the soldiers in Edinburgh. Since escape was highly unlikely, the atmosphere in the camp was relaxed and the camp commandant agreed that Rowland should be allowed to live at Port Erin rather than at Peel.

Noticing his aimlessness, Joan Cole recruited Rowland as a school teacher to four boys aged sixteen. On the first day, a smokebomb exploded in the classroom cupboard. Rowland was embarrassingly apologetic. 'He was afraid that we'd send him back to Peel,' laughs Joan Cole, 'but we understood it was a prank.'

Joan Cole, like everyone in the camp, found Rowland's deep affection for his mother remarkable. She and others, including her husband, were also convinced that Wilhelm Fuhrhop was a stepfather. 'Jack saw it in the files,' she says.

The 'illegitimacy' theory about Rowland finds its source in his detention on the island. It suggests that on conscription Rowland revealed neither his original name, nor that his German parents were in Britain. Instead, he volunteered that Rowland was his surname at birth and he mentioned his uncle Cyril Carton as next-of-kin. Effectively, Rowland, who would undertake strenuous efforts after 1945 to conceal his origins, is said to have embarked upon his subterfuge in 1939. His concealment would be exposed in 1961 by an MI5 source with access to those files. It is now apparently impossible to verify the original content of the army's file. The folder, stored by the Home Office at Hayes, Middlesex, is apparently empty.

The Coles's certainty about Rowland's relationship with Wilhelm Fuhrhop stems from the events surrounding his mother's death in 1944. Muriel's painfully slow death was

watched by her son. Sitting by her bed as she uttered her last
breath were Rowland and the hospital sister. The medic was
'shocked' as the twenty-seven-year-old son began 'pulling at the
corpse' displaying 'extravagant grief which faintly embarrassed
everyone'. In the midst of a war when millions were dying in
appalling circumstances, Rowland's violent reaction to the
death of a sixty-year-old woman was unexpected, but their
relationship was clearly unique and influenced Rowland throughout his life. Others who worked with Rowland in later years
could never quite reconcile his extreme emotions.

Muriel was buried on the island. Although Rowland has
said, 'he was told that there was no reason for him to remain'
and he could leave the camp 'returning every few weeks to see
his father on the Isle of Man', he in fact remained interned
in Port Erin until nearly the end of the war. For security
reasons, Jack Cole would not release Wilhelm Fuhrhop until
July 1945.

Rowland returned to London aged twenty-eight, comparatively
impoverished and without a foreseeable future. His savings had
been spent, his pre-war contacts had disappeared and, because
of his status, he was compelled to accept any work ordained by
the government's Labour Exchange.

One job, at the direction of the government, was working as a
porter at Paddington railway station. 'He wasn't pleased,' recalls
Cyril Carton, 'but he had no choice.' Although Rowland would
later embellish the notion by suggesting that he telephoned the
signal box at Reading to ascertain where the first-class compartments were situated on the incoming trains, the reality was that
he knew precisely who had the money to pay tips and how to
ingratiate himself to earn bonus amounts. 'He simply walked into
first-class compartments and picked up the luggage regardless of
the passengers' requests,' recounts one post-war acquaintance.
'They were so overwhelmed by his charm and accent that they
gave bigger tips.'

On his release, Rowland had lodged with Paul Hunger,
a German-born salesman and fellow internee whose English
wife had remained in London during his imprisonment. Among

the benefits of his relationships in the Isle of Man were the endless discussions with other internees about their lives and ideas for earning money. Unlike common prisoners, Rowland's companions included intelligent and successful businessmen who revitalised his interest to find business opportunities.

There was one substantial obstacle. London was filled with surviving heroes; men who, in Britain's fight for survival, had excelled either in actual battle or in the ministries and military headquarters. Intoxicated by victory and survival, they would enjoy for a limited period a unifying freemasonry which excluded those who had languished while others suffered. Rowland recognised that, by contrast, he had endured a 'bad war'.

Rowland assessed his predicament realistically. As the horrors of the extermination camps in Poland and elsewhere were exposed and countless accounts of German brutality were published, tidal waves of anti-German sentiment spread across Britain. The country, which had voted for a socialist government, would not regard Rowland's past other than unfavourably.

His solution was to disguise his first twenty-eight years. Like a chameleon, he would shed in certain company any suggestion of his German background and his internment. 'If I know who your father was,' Rowland once explained, 'where you went to school, what you studied at university, who you worked for, then I'll know all about you. I'll know how you'll behave, how you will react. You become an open book to me.' In a country which judged individuals by accents and appearance, Rowland felt confident that his beguiling charm could overcome his actual lack of social standing. But he could not immediately identify the opportunity and finance to use his business acumen to exploit the enormous possibilities in London in the aftermath of war.

In May 1945, England was plagued by shortages of absolutely everything yet hampered by the delusions and incompetence of its inhabitants. Convinced that 'British is Best', the country's understanding of the inefficiencies of its industry and economy was deflected by the military victory. The government imposed rationing and allocated meagre amounts of available food, fuel, furniture, clothes and motor cars. Yet amid the dislocation, for the minority willing to trade and produce vast fortunes could be earned, not least by overcoming the avalanche of regulations imposed by the Labour government. Rowland possessed the instinctive expertise to profit from circumventing regulations but lacked the finance to lubricate his ideas.

At the end of the war, released from compulsory employment, Rowland lived with his father in Brook Street, Mayfair. Wilhelm Fuhrhop was, according to Carton, 'too mean' to give his son any money, and accordingly Rowland set out to seek his own deals. One lucrative venture was selling chickens to nightclubs, an erratic but natural business for a trader. More reliable employment was driving a taxi for London & Aero Motor Services, based in Elstree, which was managed by Eric Smith, a cautious, dour Scotsman, who was occasionally helped by his wife Irene, an attractive but not particularly intelligent woman. The Smiths became Rowland's close friends.

One night in spring 1946, Rowland was driving Robert Cleminson, a trader and engineer who among his businesses imported cloth from India. Among Cleminson's contacts was Krishna Menon, the Indian politician. In later years, Rowland would claim a friendship with Menon.

By the end of the journey Cleminson, struck by the unusually well-spoken and elegant driver, agreed that the two should meet the following day to discuss the possibility of a joint business. Rowland, it seemed, had already formulated a proposition linked with Reg Ingham. Before the war, Ingham, an engineer, had been a works manager at Lagonda cars and had established himself as a manufacturer of nail files and trouser stretchers. Rowland suggested that Cleminson join Ingham and himself to deal in metal products.

By summer 1946, Rowland, Cleminson and Ingham were joined by Maurice Clements, another trader, all working from offices in Maddox Street, in London's West End. Their initial deals would be in trading army surplus material, such as irons and scissors, but they had other ambitions. During their journeys to Sheffield, then the home of Britain's metal manufacturing industry, the four also realised the possibility of producing refrigerators.

Before the arrival of the American army during the war, few Britons owned or were even aware of the advantages of refrigerators in their own homes. Like television sets, they were a luxury and even a novelty. With the demilitarisation of industry, there was both metal and factory space available for such domestic products to satisfy the enormous demand. But, consistent with the era, there were shortages and the few appliances available were subject to strict rationing.

The four partners had discovered a manufacturer in Sheffield producing a refrigerator called Artic Air. On 21 November 1947, Rowland and Clements incorporated a company called Articair Refrigerators, bought the factory's total production and sought other local factories willing to produce the appliance. Since the factories and the machinery could be rented cheap from the government, the outlay was low. A second matter to be addressed was to secure Articair's right to purchase the refrigerators from the rationing authority.

To overcome government rationing regulations, the partners established a succession of seemingly independent companies, each of which applied for an allocation from the factories.

The third hurdle was to avoid payments of tax which in that era mounted to a confiscatory 98 per cent and occasionally over 100 per cent. Labour, creating a planned socialist economy, was set upon penalising the rich and redistributing their wealth. To avoid those draconian controls, the partners established a simple ruse. Their refrigerators were bought cheap from the factories and 'resold' for a handsome profit as second hand. The taxation problem seemed solved. Articair bought its own premises in Stoke-on-Trent and began manufacturing refrigerators with plans to begin production of washing machines, another American luxury unknown in British homes.

Once Articair was established, conditions in Britain markedly deteriorated. The winter of 1947, one of the most severe in history, paralysed the nation. Without fuel, there was limited electricity and even foods available during the war were rationed. Britain's status as a world power crumbled as the reality of its bankruptcy undermined its economy. The fuel crisis was followed by the sterling crisis which, while common in later years, profoundly shocked Britons still basking in their military success.

The national gloom did not affect Articair's four directors. Through hard work they had become seriously rich. Although Rowland's claim in 1981 that 'he was earning £5000 a day' is an exaggeration [the present equivalent would be £60,000 per day or £16 million annually], their individual income during two years was £100,000, the equivalent today of over two million pounds. A sign of their new wealth was their move to expansive, plush offices in Upper Berkeley Street.

Rowland's life had been transformed. Regularly he was seen in London nightclubs where, because he worked late, he could be sure of a meal and drink after normal hours. Over his drink, he talked to Cleminson about the war. 'He was certainly pro-German,' recalls Cleminson, 'and said that Hitler was not "totally wrong". But he showed no interest in politics.' Significantly, in the formal incorporation document for Articair, the column requesting disclosure of Rowland's former surname was completed with the word 'None'.

Occasionally Rowland dated beautiful women but he was not known to his partners as a womaniser. His greater passion was for cars. Bentleys and Mercedes were bought and sold quite regularly, in Rowland's account, 'to get petrol' which was also rationed. They would be traded for another car with a full tank. None of his cars would excel the convertible Mercedes 540K. Built in 1937 for a British army officer, the white/silver car, with running boards and exhaust pipes emerging through the body work and fenders, could speed at nearly 100 mph, one of the fastest motors then built.

With money, Rowland also travelled, especially to America, to find new ideas and to enjoy freedom from Britain's socialist austerity. In later years, he would flash a photograph of himself with a beautiful blonde on his lap. 'Marilyn Monroe and myself at Las Vegas,' he smiled. Criss-crossing America and travelling even to Mexico, an unusual adventure for a Briton in that era, he realised the enormous potential for an ambitious businessman but did not leave Britain despite the opportunities.

By then he had constructed a palatable obfuscation of his past.

Hiding his background had become part of life, especially about his family. In 1981, Rowland suggested that there had been two brothers, 'One was killed on the Eastern Front, the other was made chief of police for northern Germany after the war but later died from the effects of wounds he had received.' In fact Raimund, the only brother, survived the war as a lieutenant in artillery and returned to Hamburg. Rather than becoming a police chief at the age of thirty as Rowland suggested, he had sought to recover the family business from Achenwall, the wartime manager.

Until late 1946, Wilhelm Fuhrhop would have been barred from entering Germany by military government restrictions. Accordingly, he sent his son a power of attorney to appeal to a court for recovery of the business on the grounds that Achenwall was too old. The court, ignoring allegations of Achenwall's Nazi past, transferred the company to Raimund. Wilhelm Fuhrhop never returned to live in Germany. In 1947, with Rowland as a witness, he married another internee from Port Erin. With his son's help, Wilhelm patented a carpet-weaving machine and earned a small income. Rowland was also helpful to his father's friend Friedrich Schmitz, a designer and another former internee: 'Tiny introduced me to a cosmetic company which needed packaging. It rebuilt my career. He was very good to people.'

Britain staggered into 1948 amid hopes that the worst was over. Although the government's nationalisation of industries, rationing and state controls continued, there were signs of prosperity. Articair's production was increasing and Reg Ingham proposed that the partners, instead of pocketing all the profits, invest in improvements of the factory. Rowland disagreed: 'I want the profits. I'm not interested in long-term investment.'

The two engineers opposed the two traders. At issue was how four men who had avoided paying taxation would be able to invest money in a factory without declaring their profits. The disagreements became irreconcilable and a battle began over control of the company. Injunctions were issued and argued in court without resolution before everyone agreed to a divorce.

The collapse of Articair was naturally noticed by the Inland Revenue. Rowland was summoned and asked to explain the company's accounts and particularly, the apparent 'trade in companies'. On Rowland's own admission to Cleminson, the investigation 'broke me'. Until that summer, unable to undertake any further business, he spent his days in the Revenue's offices discussing a settlement. Later, he would boast that he was even accorded a desk and became an ad hoc consultant to others who were trapped by officialdom.

Under the eventual settlement, Rowland repaid approximately £200,000 in taxes. Effectively, in any further business enterprise, he was marked for special surveillance by the Revenue. Any future income would be heavily taxed. In future, he would seek to avoid that special attention by establishing his formal residency outside Britain.

But in 1948, exhausted and dispirited by Britain's socialism and austerity; degraded, prosecuted and imprisoned by the government, Rowland, among many other Britons, began considering a new life.

Cleminson also decided to emigrate. Government controls on the export of money restricted his movements to those countries within the empire which were categorised as scheduled territories within the sterling area. One country which offered a particularly attractive lifestyle was Southern Rhodesia, a landlocked, naturally rich but sparsely populated British colony. The local government was offering generous enticements for new white settlers from Britain.

Rowland's interest was galvanised by the decision of two other friends to emigrate to Rhodesia. Eric and Irene Smith, the managers of the London & Aero Motor Services who had employed Rowland to drive taxis, had spoken enthusiastically about southern Africa.

Irene Smith's grandfather, a stockbroker, had retired to Salisbury, Rhodesia's capital, in 1947 and encouraged his children to escape Britain for the sun and a land of plenty. Irene, her sister and their husbands had left for Africa. Rowland decided to follow. Just to have a look.

Two
A New Beginning

Rowland arrived in Southern Rhodesia in suitable style. On 4 November 1948, driving his convertible Mercedes 540K, he crossed Beit Bridge, the border with South Africa. Travelling on British passport number 1042389, which had been issued two months earlier, Rowland declared his total assets as £4000 in Rhodesian currency; £5000 worth of shares and £10,000 in cash deposited in Britain. Although thirty years later he would say that he left Britain with £200,000, the evidence suggests that Rowland did not arrive in Africa as a wealthy man.

From the border, the road journey to Salisbury, the capital of Southern Rhodesia, was 370 miles. As he drove in the sunshine along the striped tarred road through lush green hills and unpopulated pastures, he could not fail to perceive the contrast to Britain. Rhodesia was paradise.

The self-governing colony had become a mecca for disgruntled Britons, weary of socialist austerity and Britain's social claustrophobia. Ex-servicemen, especially former RAF personnel who had trained in Rhodesia, were enticed to settle in a country that offered a lifestyle which only the very rich in Britain could afford. Unlike in Britain, the 200,000 settlers could be sure of ample food, a car and some land. Friendly servants drawn from the three and a half million Africans cost £1 per month plus food and the provision of a hut in the garden. There was unlimited sport, partying, big game shooting and fishing. The settlers, in what was called 'the Garden of Eden', were often the black sheep of the family, or so-called remittance men. Each immigrant could choose, with government help, either to farm or to mine.

Compared to South Africa's alien environment which was embracing apartheid, Salisbury's segregation was hidden behind the tidy streets and cultivated parks which resembled a small English country town whose rural atmosphere was perceptibly changing as a new breed of aspiring entrepreneurs arrived from England.

Rowland stayed at Meikles, a family-owned, luxury hotel, overlooking Cecil Square, Salisbury's beautiful gardened centre where the pioneer column dispatched by Cecil Rhodes halted in September 1890 to celebrate the occupation of Mashonaland. Standing in the sunshine, which enhanced Rowland's appearance and mood, breathing pure and refreshing air, and seeing colourful bougainvillaea swaying over a manicured lawn in the midst of Africa, Rowland felt a frisson of excitement. The African bug is infectious but understood only by those who venture into the continent. Rowland's immediate awareness of his liberation from a decade of hardship and pressure was palpable.

Dressed in his immaculate suits, monogrammed silk shirts and highly polished shoes, Rowland gave the impression of the quintessential, manicured, perfectly accented Englishman. No one suspected that the would-be immigrant was German-born and, rather than fighting the hated Nazis, that he had spent the war in an internment camp. Considering the Rhodesians' recent sacrifices in defeating Nazism, his concealment was wise.

Near Meikles was the office of Guest & Tanner, the leading estate agents. Rowland's inquiries led to a kaffir truck store in a village called Eiffel Flats, eighty miles outside Salisbury on the main road towards Rhodesia's second largest town, Bulawayo. An option had already been sold on the farm there.

Rowland took a second option. In the Meikles hotel lobby the following day he was told by the agent that the original buyer had withdrawn. Rowland now had the option to buy and wanted to consult the Smiths who lived in Hartley, a small farming community near Eiffel Flats. But before he inspected the shop, there was a new twist. The first purchaser, having secured his finance, asked Rowland to resell the option. Rowland's price, £2000, was accepted.

The alacrity of the acceptance surprised Rowland. Fearing that he had sold too cheap, he drove out to Eiffel Flats. The

400-kilometre road to Bulawayo lacked a complete tarmac cover. Rowland's car drove along two strips laid across the sand. To pass, on-coming cars both pulled to the side.

The countryside, farmed by English settlers, was similar to the pastures of Buckinghamshire and Berkshire with hills rising in the distance. But after one hundred miles, the road was surrounded by bush – an impenetrable shield to the hinterland. Eiffel Flats was just off the main road, near the Cam and Motor gold mine which was owned by one of Southern Rhodesia's biggest companies, the London and Rhodesia Mining and Land Company, subsequently known as Lonrho. The property which he had just passed over was satisfactorily unappealing. He had struck an easy and good deal. But nearby, a 4000-acre farm with two small, primitive, corrugated roofed houses called Shepton seemed interesting. The owner was Bill Bartlet, a Scottish stockbroker who soon afterwards began quietly buying shares in Lonrho which he dubbed 'a bagful of unreleased gems'.

Rowland bought Shepton with Eric and Irene Smith, taking the larger house called Rondavale for himself. Neither Smith nor Rowland knew about farming but were encouraged by the easy availability of cheap labour. About a dozen natives were obtained from the chief of a local tribal reserve and lodged with their families in simple, round huts built of the traditional mixture of mud, manure and grass two hundred yards from the house, near the main road.

Rowland showed little affection for the farm. To neighbours he seemed more of a gambler than committed to growing maize, cotton, tobacco and raising cattle. Besides his Mercedes, his only ostensible luxury was a swimming pool which was built soon after his arrival. Most Sundays, he would lie by the pool, sustaining his suntan.

The local police in Gatooma were however aware of an unusual local farmer. One night, Rowland, clearly upset, arrived to complain that one of his suits had been stolen. 'It was very expensive,' he told Derrick Robinson, the local CID officer. 'It was made in England.' The loss was registered. The police decided to look for a well-dressed African and make an arrest. The two men would meet in very different circumstances twenty-five years later.

In Salisbury too, Rowland struck the authorities as unusual. Together with Smith, he had applied for permission to grow opium poppies for the manufacture of medicinal drugs. Their scheme was rejected.

The arrangement with the Smiths, which began in high spirits, soon soured. Compared to Rowland, Eric Smith was lifeless and unimaginative. Irene fell in love with Rowland and, six months after the purchase, Eric left Shepton and his wife. Irene, five years older than Rowland and by no means the epitome of sex appeal, became Rowland's mistress but did not live in the house.

Instead, Rowland lived alone at Shepton surrounded by dogs, ducks, a monkey, a parrot and his African servants. The few visitors were struck by the image of a seemingly lonely bachelor, no longer dressed in his immaculately monogrammed silk shirts but in khaki shorts and shirt, living in unkempt, even squalid conditions, chain-smoking a hundred Star cigarettes every day, lighting one from the butt of the last. Farming had proved unprofitable and his supply of money was dwindling. His visitors included a small number of fellow German ex-internees, especially Billy von Stranz, all classified by the British government as 'dangerous'.

In October 1950, he was aroused from his torpidity by the arrival of Robert Cleminson and his younger brother Benjamin who had flown from Britain in a Rapide, a wooden bi-plane, bought from the RAF for £750, which had been recanvassed and refurbished. The Cleminson brothers, equally anxious to find their fortunes beyond Britain's bleak austerity, had landed in Umtali and telephoned Rowland. Surprised and thrilled, Rowland drove the 400 miles by truck in record time. 'He was full of charm, laughing and talking about the old times,' recalled Robert Cleminson whose first venture in Rhodesia was to lend Rowland money to finance the season's crops at Shepton. In November 1952, Rowland bought out Smith's share, incorporated the farm as Shepton Estates, and began living with Irene. On the official registration form for the particulars of incorporation, Rowland entered 'Nil' in the column requiring disclosure of 'any former names'. Roland Fuhrhop was forgotten.

Rowland's declining fortunes had been saved during that year. One of the original companies manufacturing washing

machines for Articair in England was declared bankrupt. Among
the creditors, Rowland was owed £2000 and he used the pretext
to return to London. Bill Bartlet would later say that he lent
the money for Rowland's airline ticket. The visit inspired a fundamental change in thirty-five-year-old Rowland's life.

Churchill's new conservative government had rapidly discarded the last of wartime rationing and was pledged to reverse
some of Labour's nationalisation legislation. Capitalism was no
longer taboo. The stock market was active and profits were
enriching a new breed of entrepreneurs. Compared to the docile
backwater where he lived, London was booming. Although
there was no inclination to remain in Britain, Rowland returned
to Shepton having 'emerged from his hibernation', noticed
Cleminson. 'He was galvanised to start again.'

Farming in Rhodesia offered a reasonable income to the
proficient, but was not an attractive proposition for an impatient, ambitious deal maker. An alternative source of income
was mining. As the world's economy expanded, the demand for
minerals was insatiable and Rhodesia possessed an abundance
of minerals – coal, chrome, emeralds and especially gold.

Gatooma, the local town, was bursting with ex-servicemen
who had taken government loans to ease their resettlement and
were seeking their fortune underground. Gold fever gripped the
area as mines which had been worked and then abandoned over
previous centuries were, with the benefit of new technology and
especially the provision of electricity to extract water, re-opened
to excavate in directions and depths inaccessible to earlier prospectors. On Tuesdays and Saturdays, the Grand and Specks
hotels in Gatooma were crammed by raucous and drunken
prospectors who had returned from their small workings in
the bush for supplies and fun while, in their absence, Africans
on pittance wages continued digging. With little thought to the
future, the bloodhounds, searching for instant and spectacular
wealth despite the world price of gold being fixed at $35 an
ounce, were partying in an atmosphere which resembled the
American Wild West.

Although Rowland did not contemplate descending into a
black hole, he was infected by the fever. For more than a

century, Europeans had been enticed to Africa because of its abundance of raw materials and cheap labour. Fortunes were made when the two were harnessed and the product was transported to a seaport where the ore could be shipped to the industrialised world.

The first step to his fortune, as Rowland knew, was to find the deal and hire others to carry out the work. In Salisbury, he met a geologist who had discovered a chrome deposit near Balingwe on land owned by Tassilo Rukovina, a German baron. Rukovina was frustrated because he was unable to exploit his rich find. Rhodesian railways, suffering an acute shortage, had refused to allocate any wagons to transport the ore from the Polo mine to the Mozambique port of Lourenço Marques where the Portuguese pleaded that the docks were full. The chrome was therefore worthless.

Whether Rowland actually understood the mining and sale of chrome is unlikely, but he did understand that profits were being earned by its excavation and sale. What he lacked in expertise was compensated by enthusiasm, energy and ingenuity in the construction of a deal with an ability to persuade others of the benefits of his offer.

The essence of Rowland's offer to Rukovina was classic: 'If I can arrange the rail transport and obtain the cash to develop the mine, will you give me a half interest in the mine?' Rukovina did not refuse.

For Rowland, the challenge was to secure a booking for an ore carrier at the port in Lourenço Marques and obtain the rail trucks. The situation was a Catch 22. Both the Rhodesian and Portuguese authorities blamed the deadlock upon each other. Flying to Lourenço Marques, Rowland called on the governor and port authorities. Claiming that he had secured an allocation of rail trucks in Salisbury, he persuaded the officials to grant him space in the port.

Once he had returned home, among his first appeals was to Ian Smith, then the member of parliament for the Selukwe constituency, 250 miles from Salisbury. On a Saturday afternoon, the former RAF pilot and politician was working on his farm when a huge estate wagon halted on his track for what the future Rhodesian prime minister would recall as a 'hilarious occasion with a penniless farmer from Norton'.

'I'm a constituent of yours,' said the tall English-speaking visitor, 'and I need your help.' Rowland explained his transport problem and complained that all he requested was equal treatment with the 'big boys' like Union Carbide who seemed to enjoy a monopoly of wagons to export their chrome. 'He told me that he had secured port space in Lourenço Marques,' says Smith who invited his unusual guest into the house for a cup of tea.

Janet Smith was struck by the 'strange man' in her living room. Unmarried and strikingly handsome, he explained that he owned fifteen dogs whom he had to remove from his bed before he could go to sleep: 'If one of them barks in the night, it takes hours to get them all quiet again so I can go back to sleep.'

'I've made my life in Rhodesia,' said their visitor, 'and I just want an opportunity to make an income.' Smith agreed to accompany his constituent to the federal minister of transport, Roy Welensky, a tough, Jewish, former engine driver whose father had emigrated from Russia. At that time, Southern Rhodesia was a member of the three-nation Central African Federation. The colonial governments of Nyasaland [Malawi], Northern Rhodesia [Zambia] and Southern Rhodesia [Zimbabwe] were subject to the federal government which was located in Salisbury. 'I don't see why we shouldn't help our friend,' agreed Welensky. Rowland's friendship with the minister, which included financial support, lasted for the remainder of the politician's lifetime.

Rowland's next hurdle was to finance the development of the mine. Flying from Salisbury to Nairobi on the so-called 'puke run' because of the many stops en route, he called on Jack Carvill, a friend from London. Carvill's company, Engineering and Industrial Exports, both secured the money and simultaneously sold the chrome ore to Derby & Co in Britain.

Under the deal, Rowland would receive staggered payments for the ore, but 90 per cent would be paid by the time it was loaded on to a ship. There were penalties if the ore was sub-standard and, to protect their interest, Derby & Co sent a 'checker' to live at the mine. Richly entertained by Rukovina, he seemed to overlook the ore's low purity which became apparent soon after extraction began.

Rowland understood the predicament. With Carvill's help, he began extricating himself. Northern Mercantile, a Tyneside company with interests in shipping and mining, was offered the mine. Northern Mercantile's surveyor wrote a favourable report, convincing his British client to buy the mine. By the time that the first shipment of ore had reached Britain, nearly one year after its excavation, Rowland and Rukovina were no longer the mine's owners. The mine was closed down shortly afterwards although Rowland was not blamed. As he had already discovered, in the mining industry the risks, like the profits, were enormous and *caveat emptor*, let the buyer beware, was the accepted guiding principle. The only complainant was Rukovina who threatened legal proceedings, alleging that he had not received his share from Rowland. Eventually, the baron was placated.

Rowland's funds were still limited. Shepton was proving an unimpressive investment which was losing money, although he had found the ideal manager. Lionel Taylor, who had worked at Lagonda motors with Rowland's former partner at Articair, had emigrated from Britain with his wife Mary and two children to manage a plywood project financed by the Cleminson brothers. In 1953, Taylor became sick and the project failed. Although he had no farming experience, Taylor was hard working, honest and methodical. The family moved into the empty house.

Silent and apparently friendless, Lionel Taylor invariably wore leather gloves and was reputed to dress formally for dinner every night. 'He and Mary would drink champagne with candle-lights under a corrugated iron roof,' according to Ken Barton who owned the adjoining farm. 'He was weird, although he learned how to farm.' Those qualities suited Rowland who relied upon his employee's discretion, loyalty and obedience to his whims. If Rowland left his pen on the desk, its position was to remain unaltered, even if he returned six months later. Rowland, Taylor discovered, was a creature of habit.

That trait was not apparent to Josie Taylor, the seven-year-old daughter, who became enchanted by their handsome and charming neighbour on the isolated farm. According to apocryphal legend, Rowland had changed Josie's nappies and pushed her pram. In Gatooma, there are eyewitness accounts of Rowland holding Josie on his knee. Some speculated that Rowland wanted children but that Irene had refused on account of her age. Irene's relations blame Rowland's all-consuming ambition which at thirty-six distracted him from any commitment to a relationship which did not advance his commercial objectives. But there is no doubt that Rowland showed genuine affection for the Taylors' daughter, who eventually became his wife.

With the farm's management settled, Rowland sped daily along the strip road to Salisbury in the convertible Mercedes. During one of those journeys, the car developed an engine problem. A local car mechanic, Gisa Vaga, the German manager of Norton Motors in Gatooma, was asked by Rowland to repair what he would describe as 'my first and last love'. Vaga had been transported to Rhodesia as a prisoner of war and remained in 1945, employed by a group of eight tobacco growers who jointly owned shares in Norton Motors, the owners of the Mercedes franchise in Rhodesia.

The relationship between the two Germans flourished and Rowland quickly fastened on to his compatriot's complaints. The 'tobacco boys', as Rowland later dubbed Norton's shareholders, had been persuaded by Vaga of the advantages of Mercedes's diesel engines but could not be tempted to exploit their franchise and sell the whole range of cars. Their sole interest was to obtain their own cars and spares at cost.

Rowland saw his opportunity. Like many Rhodesian settlers, the eight tobacco boys were hard working on their farms but otherwise interested only in sport and social life. The potential wealth of the Mercedes franchise was unimaginable to them. Indeed, most Britons, seeped in the chauvinism that 'British is Best' would not have understood, even in the late 1950s, that the British motor industry, at that time one of the largest in the world, was doomed to irreversible decline. Only a non-British sceptic like Rowland could appreciate the inherent superiority of

German engineering and production, and appreciate the possibility of challenging British domination of the local motor market. Considering the era, it was visionary to see the potential of the Mercedes franchise although even Rowland could not have imagined that owning a model would become the aspiration and symbol of success for every African politician and businessman.

Rowland schemed with Vaga to buy the Norton shares. The tactic was separately to buy the shares of each of the eight owners, which needed time and some subtlety, and simultaneously to secure the support of Mercedes in Germany. His approach to Mercedes's headquarters was aided by Günter Weitz, the company's manager in South Africa.

Once in Stuttgart, Rowland found an easy rapport with his fellow Germans, not least in their common antipathy towards the British. In his fluent German, Rowland told the Mercedes executives that, under Norton's present management, there was no hope of increasing their sales. 'Norton's board meetings,' he explained 'ended after three hours with everyone drunk from whisky and without taking any decisions.' The solution, he suggested, was to transfer the franchise. 'Let me get rid of those folk,' Rowland urged. 'I love Mercedes. Give me eight to ten months to buy up all the shares.'

With Weitz's support, Rowland returned to Gatooma with the gloomy news that Mercedes had decided to withdraw the franchise. Buying up the shares proved easier than he expected although one shareholder, Jack Smeaton, the owner of the Coq d'Or, one of Salisbury's favourite cabaret restaurants, was more reluctant than others. But even Smeaton, to his everlasting anger, was persuaded by Rowland who, noticing that he needed money to finance his restaurant, offered a satisfactory solution. Just two months after his return, Rowland cabled Stuttgart, 'Sorry for keeping you waiting, but it took a bit of time to chase these baboons out of the garden.' The Mercedes franchise in Rhodesia belonged to Rowland. In gratitude, in 1957 he would donate his 540K to the Mercedes museum, 'A fitting end for such a faithful friend . . . who has given me nothing but joy . . . It is a wrench to be parted from her . . . I could not bear the thought of her passing into any other hands but yours. Please excuse my expressing these feelings to you, but I cannot let the car go without paying tribute to her.' Ingrained within Rowland was not only a love of motors, but also the skills and temperament of a car salesman.

Norton Motors was Rowland's first substantial business in Rhodesia. Based in Hardwick House, an office block on Jameson Road near Rhodesia's Reserve Bank, Rowland shared four rooms with Cleminson and Carvill. Through the windows they could see Charter House, the headquarters of the giant and pervasively powerful Anglo American Corporation, which Rowland, whose appetite for mining was aroused, would pledge his ambition to overtake.

Rowland's major ally was Harry Jefferies, the manager of the Standard & Chartered, Rhodesia's biggest bank. Since both Rowland and Jefferies were bachelors, they spent evenings in each other's company and, it was said, even travelled in Europe together. Theirs was a founding relationship endorsed by Sir Cyril Hawker, the bank's chairman, guaranteeing Rowland lifelong support from the bank. Forty years later, Lonrho had outstanding loans of over £500 million to Standard & Chartered.

The relationship between Rowland and the bank began with intimate conversations between Rowland and Jefferies. 'I'm going to make a million,' Rowland told Jefferies, 'just lend me enough to start.' Among the first loans by Jefferies was the finance for the journey to Germany to obtain the Mercedes franchise. During that visit to Europe, an intelligence agency noted that Rowland met Krishna Menon, the Indian foreign minister, in Monte Carlo. The agency noted that Rowland had concluded an arms deal with the Indian. Although the details remained unspecified and were unverifiable, the intelligence agency eventually became convinced that the agreement provided Rowland with some of the funds which facilitated his first major mining deal in Rhodesia.

In the course of his conversations with Jefferies, Rowland would occasionally hear hints about which of the bank's clients was successful and who was facing some difficulties. Among the latter was Peter Goosen.

Peter Goosen was probably Gatooma's most successful gold prospector. An unsophisticated, roughneck, Second World War returnee, Goosen possessed a fortuitous talent for finding gold reefs which had been lost before the war. Ostentatiously indicative of his skill was the Cadillac which he drove regularly through the town on Tuesday and Thursday, Gatooma's shopping and drinking days, when the miners emerged from the hills and bush around the town to celebrate in noticeable style. Dressed like all the other prospectors in khaki shorts and shirt with a bush hat, Goosen stood at the Cam Hotel's bar, generously dispensing his new wealth. Among the beneficiaries were his family who were bought houses and his friends who were invited on hunting expeditions for which Goosen even paid to have tracks cut through the bush. For Goosen, life was a mixture of hard work and expensive fun. Still prospecting gold in the Zimbabwe bush in 1992, aged eighty-four years, he simply believed that 'finding a bit of gold is like winning a beautiful girl'. Akin to a bloodhound, Goosen spent his life looking for the 'big strike'.

Among Goosen's successful strikes was at the Kanyemba mine, a typical Rhodesian small working, which was twenty miles from Gatooma, just off the main Salisbury road. In 1957, Goosen had sold an option on Kanyemba to the Rhodesian Selection Trust [RST] for £120,000 and he was certain that it would be exercised. Goosen needed the money because, as Rowland heard from Jefferies, the prospector was under serious pressure from the Inland Revenue for unpaid taxes.

Rowland was known in the Gatooma area as a money lender. Occasionally, he had advanced loans to local farmers on the security of their next crop, borrowing the money himself from the bank. Rowland was therefore not surprised by Goosen's approach to borrow £120,000. The security for the loan was half the Kanyemba mine which Goosen was convinced RST would soon be buying.

RST, in the meantime, had dispatched Keith Viewing, its consulting geologist, to survey the Kanyemba mine. Born in Surrey, England, Viewing knew that RST's chairman, Sir Ronald Prain, was ambitious to develop the corporation into a blue-chip rival of Anglo American. Initially, Viewing was told to report on Kanyemba's pyrites deposits, an ore used in the production of fertilisers. Within a short time, Viewing became 'amazed' that

RST had taken an option on the mine. 'I became very unpopular for my opinion,' he recalls.

After some discussion, Viewing was told to survey Kanyemba for gold but at the end of six months he reported that even his deep drilling revealed 'an ore channel but only nugget effect'. In his report, Viewing concluded that there were 'bluish quartz type reef deposits' but, most critically, that the Kanyemba was 'unsatisfactory' for RST's purposes. In 1958, Prain decided not to exercise his option.

Goosen was naturally disappointed, especially since he would have to transfer the mine to Rowland whom he now sought to persuade that Kanyemba was worth more than Rowland's original loan. Rowland also had a problem. If the mine was worthless, he had lost a lot of money which he had borrowed from the bank. The alternative was to believe Goosen's valuation.

Thirty-two Africans and one Rhodesian settler were working at the Kanyemba mine. The settler was Ken Adams, a courageous, honest and dedicated workhorse who had fought the war in the British navy. For Adams, it was just another hot day in the unchanging dry bush when he saw a Rolls Royce Silver Cloud manoeuvre over the dirt track 'road' towards the mine. Unable to avoid the potholes, the Silver Cloud stopped. What followed was a rare if unprecedented sight in the Rhodesian bush. From the car, a tall man in a City-style tweed suit, waistcoat and monogrammed silk shirt emerged and walked towards the house. Momentarily, Adams and his wife were mesmerised. To their surprise, their visitor was charming and asked to see the mine.

Still dressed in his tweeds, Rowland descended with Adams and Lionel Taylor down the shaft, inquiring about the Kanyemba's prospects. To the miner it was obvious that neither of his visitors knew anything about gold mining but they obviously trusted Adams's assurances. For confirmation, a German mining engineer based in South Africa was hired by Rowland. He valued Kanyemba at £250,000. Rowland took a further option from Goosen to find the additional money.

Three months later, Rowland owned his first gold mine. Adams, invited by Lionel Taylor to remain and work for Shepton

Estates, soon understood that his new employer was of a very different breed from Goosen.

Adjacent to the Kanyemba plot was the Hepworth mine. The owner, Cecil Sheard, agreed to sell his mine to Rowland for just £40,000. When asked by Adams, quite astounded by the low price, to explain, Sheard could only mutter, 'Rowland hypnotised me.'

Adams was not just hypnotised by Rowland but also bullied: 'All hell broke loose' under the new management. But he was also impressed. Despite the immaculate clothes, Adams discovered a 'very strong man'. During one of his visits, Rowland challenged the local welder, 'Tys' Rabe, who could crush beer bottle tops between his fingers, to a contest. 'Tys' visibly flinched as Rowland proved his strength. Over the following years, Adams would never cease to be impressed by Rowland. His lifestyle was so exceptional. The Rolls Royce, his regular sunbathing by the pool at Shepton and his apparently spontaneous solicitations about Adams's son or the warm greeting to Mrs Adams at the Christmas party at Meikles hotel, guaranteed Adams's unstinting, lifelong dedication. Adams was among the first of an army of future employees who discovered that Rowland was unsurpassable in cultivating, nurturing and valuing others' admiration of himself.

Of course, there was a motive. Rowland intended to sell shares in the Kanyemba and Hepworth mines to the public through the Johannesburg stock exchange. His partner was Graham Beck, a twenty-eight-year-old South African businessman who had invested in coal mines.

'Rowland was very plausible when he approached me,' recalls Beck. 'His lifestyle and appearance suggested that he had lots of money. I thought he was a down-the-middle guy.' Rowland explained to the South African that he needed money to exercise the Kanyemba option and assistance on its flotation.

Rowland's sympathisers claim that what then followed was organised by Beck. But the South African rejects the accusations. 'It was all Rowland. I only realised later that he was a Jekyll and Hyde guy.'

The key to any successful public flotation of a mine is the

report by an independent consulting engineer. Potential share-holders depend upon the engineer's report in the prospectus but should beware of Mark Twain's homily: 'A gold mine is a hole in the ground with a liar at the top and a fool at the bottom.'

The prospects in gold mining are particularly hazardous. The unpredictability of the course which the reef containing the gold will follow under the ground automatically jeopardises any assessment of a mine's potential. To overcome that hazard, engineers drill boreholes at regular intervals to monitor the path of the reef and, depending upon their ability and experience, are able to assess to some degree of accuracy the amount of extractable gold. That was the process which Keith Viewing had pursued on RST's behalf before reporting that Kanyemba was not a viable gold mine. Clearly, Viewing's report would not have enticed many prospective shareholders to part with their money.

But Rowland was fortunate. With Beck's help, in Johannesburg he found Roelof Rademeyer, a South African mining engineer and former inspector of mines, who was unknown both in Rhodesia and in his own homeland. A small, bespectacled and ineffectual personality, Rademeyer had developed a particular expertise in surveying coal mines but was not known as an expert in small gold workings. Nevertheless, he was eager to survey and report on Kanyemba's prospects.

Rademeyer was asked by Rowland and Beck to report on Kanyemba's provable reserves, the possible reserves and the quality of the gold content in the ore. Rademeyer's brief was precisely the same as Viewing's but his conclusions were surprisingly different.

Rademeyer's survey, delivered in July 1958, was peppered with optimistic phrases about Kanyemba's 'reasonable prospects'. If some operations were successful, he advised, the mine's 'life would be substantially increased'. No uninformed reader would have noticed that Rademeyer's report even quoted Viewing's borehole results but omitted Viewing's conclusions. Instead Rademeyer concluded that, 'Taking a very conservative view' which was based on fifteen years' exploration, the investors would earn handsome profits. But he went even further and postulated that the mine would have a life 'in the order of twenty-two years' – and probably more. Rowland was delighted to have a positive report from a professional.

Armed with Rademeyer's report predicting that the mine would profitably produce gold for at least the next twenty years, Rowland and Beck turned to Beck's father, a stock-broker, both to float the mine and to recruit two prestigious names, the Honourable Thomas Boydell, a South African politician, and Sir John Rowland, a director of several small mines and a former administrator on Indian railways, as directors to ensure the flotation's success.

The new company issued 1.5 million shares worth £450,000, practically double the amount Rowland had paid for the mines. The public were offered 600,000 of those shares at 37.5 pence, making a total of approximately £225,000, but they would be denied control of the company. Rowland received 900,000 shares, a 60 per cent stake which he would divide with Beck. Effectively, Rowland kept control of the company and also received £225,000, his original investment, in return for the promise of rising profits as gold production increased. To achieve his prediction, twenty-two Europeans and over four hundred Africans were hired. Under Adams's direction, new plant was bought to increase production from about 300 ozs to 450 ozs per month, and occasionally more.

Not everyone in Salisbury was convinced about the probity of the Kanyemba sale. Sir Cyril Hatty, the minister of mines, was warned by his officials, 'it's a bit odd'. Rumours that Keith Viewing had doubted the mine's viability were already circulating and Rademeyer was unknown. Hatty, also a recent settler from England, realised that Rowland was, 'very different from the others. He just didn't mix very well.' Rowland, the minister knew, was not 'part of the Government House set' although locals believed him to be an Englishman born in India. But the minister cast aside his officials' caution when Harry Jefferies, the manager of the Standard & Chartered Bank, assured the politician that Rowland was 'quite remarkable'.

Rowland's other admirer was Josie Taylor, his manager's daughter. Josie was attending Arundel, Rhodesia's elite girls' boarding school. To the snobs, it was a centre for the creation of 'young ladies'. Her contemporaries at Arundel, including Susan Baxter, a classmate, found Josie, from the outset, 'very odd'.

A very private girl, uninterested in sport and not outstanding in any academic pursuit, Josie would withdraw from the natural girls' banter about boys and marriage. Her only contribution at the age of fourteen was, 'I'm going to marry Tiny,' then aged forty. To her schoolfriends it seemed that Josie was being groomed to be Tiny's wife. When Josie arrived at the school in Rowland's Bentley or Rolls Royce, 'they looked like father and daughter', Susan Baxter recalls.

No one has ever extracted from Rowland the nature of his sentiments towards the schoolgirl at that stage. Most have assumed that Rowland, apparently enjoying a stable relationship with Irene Smith, was more concerned with becoming seriously rich and, in 1958, soon after the Kanyemba flotation, another attractive opportunity to do so arose.

The offer was brought to Rowland by Michael Reynolds, a small farmer who was born in 1921 in Gwelo. Like so many white Rhodesians, Reynolds was dedicated to and even obsessed by his desire to discover his fortune underground when he began prospecting in 1950.

Reynolds's farm was in the remote Doma area where he grew buffalo beans. At night there was little entertainment and occasionally Reynolds would sit by the camp fire to talk with his African workers. Over many months, the elder natives spoke about the rich copper mines in the area which their forefathers had worked. Despite the occasional foray, Reynolds's searches for the abandoned workings were unsuccessful. That changed one night when the 'boss-boy' came running to Reynolds. Walking over the hills, he had noticed the startling green light of solid malachite, or copper oxide. 'It couldn't be missed if you saw it,' recalls Reynolds. The site, sixty miles north-east of Karoi, near the Mozambique and Zambian borders, was pegged and registered in Reynolds's name. It was called Shamrocke by Reynolds on account of its colour.

Hastening to Salisbury, Reynolds excitedly sought the advice of his brother-in-law. Like so many prospectors, Reynolds had no capital, no expertise and, it must be said, insufficient knowledge to handle the development of his discovery.

'There's only one man who can handle this,' Reynolds was told. 'He's Tiny Rowland who just floated the Kanyemba mine.' An early morning meeting was arranged for Reynolds with Rowland at the Ambassador hotel. The roughneck was impressed, as intended, by Rowland's appearance. Compared to most Rhodesians, Rowland was dressed impeccably, spoke fluently and displayed unusual self-assurance. Reynolds was seduced into remarkable honesty: 'It's too big for me. Can you handle the negotiations and sale?' Rowland agreed.

Their agreement seemed straightforward. The mine would be owned by a company called Nyaschere Copper, named after the nearby river. In return for £1000 which Rowland paid Reynolds, the prospector handed over 50 per cent of the company and mine to Rowland. They were equal partners with one exception. According to their agreement, Rowland was appointed the 'sole selling agent' in negotiating the company's mining claims. Reynolds was so impressed with his new partner that he even agreed to grant Rowland the exclusive right to decide the terms of any agreement. 'I was buying Tiny's skills,' confirms Reynolds. 'He was a brilliant negotiator.'

Initially, Reynolds's trust in Rowland's negotiating skills seemed justified. Through Graham Beck, Rowland was introduced to a subsidiary of Rand Mines which paid £100,000 for a three-year option to exploit the Shamrocke plus a share in any successful strike. Similar to the Kanyemba deal, Beck received a half share of Rowland's interest in Nyaschere.

During that period, Reynolds believed that the two were becoming firm friends. 'He gave me that impression,' recalls Reynolds. At regular lunches at the Coq d'Or, Reynolds even endured Rowland's critical lecture about his own lifestyle. 'Rowland was that type of man,' rues Reynolds who returned to the outback in the expectation that he would soon be rich.

At the age of forty, Rowland had recovered the zeal and pace which he displayed in London. Combined with his previous experience, he was unique among Salisbury's traditional businessmen who could not conceive of the opportunities which

Rowland contrived. In a country of farmers, miners and the ancillary trades working in a village atmosphere, deal makers like Rowland, buying and selling to earn a profit on the turn, were rare. Since his finances were limited, when a major opportunity arose, he realised the need for an alliance with an international. The Cam and Motor gold mine, a publicly quoted mine near Shepton, was such an ideal proposition. Operations at the deep and productive mine were managed by the London and Rhodesia Mining and Land Company Limited whose fortunes were declining.

Founded on 13 May 1909 by a solicitor in Mincing Lane, London, on behalf of seven people described either as gentlemen or merchants, the London and Rhodesia Mining and Land Company Limited was managed by Julius Weil to invest its £1300 founding capital to buy mining rights in Rhodesia.

At that time, the British South Africa Company, founded by Cecil Rhodes, was offering stakes to pioneers who were enticed to Rhodesia to develop the country's agriculture, cattle, crops and gold in what they hoped would repeat the recent boom in South Africa's Rand.

In 1912, Weil bought a tranche of land and mines from Sir Abe Bailey, a formidable but unsuccessful South African politician. But disease, drought, the fluctuating price of gold, and the First World War undermined Weil's fortunes. In 1920 Bailey, revitalised and re-educated in modern agricultural and mining techniques, began reinvesting in Rhodesia. Systematically, his agents scoured the bars searching for small and disillusioned landowners, plying them with drink, until they sold their land and mining rights at bargain prices. He bought the approximately one million-acre Rhodesdale estate, and eventually also repurchased control of Julius Weil's company which by then owned three gold mines, 41,600 acres of farmland and was capitalised at £300,000. Befitting its aspirations, the company's headquarters were sited in an impressive, purpose-built mansion overlooking Cecil Square, opposite the Salisbury Club and the prime minister's office.

To manage all his mines, Bailey hired Sir Digby Burnett, a bullying, ruthless mining engineer, trained in the Gold Coast, who eventually would be dubbed 'Rhodesia's Uncrowned King'. Piloting his own aeroplane around the country, Burnett transformed the company's fortunes, balancing mining and agriculture to support each other as their fortunes fluctuated. By 1945, Lonrho had become Rhodesia's biggest company, having bought the Rhodesdale estate and Willoughby Consolidated, another mining and agricultural conglomerate.

During the 1950s, the company's management was led by Joseph Ball, a former senior MI5 officer, a racist, arch-appeaser and close confidant of Neville Chamberlain. Ball failed to sustain Lonrho's fortunes. To survive, Ball and his son Alan, a depressive who suffered from his father's domination, began selling parcels of land. By 1957, they had reduced Lonrho's assets to four gold mines, 835,000 acres of cattle ranch land, some property in Salisbury, an air charter company and a range of frustrated involvements in a diversity of other mineral industries. The share price had fallen to a third of its peak when the Glazer brothers, two South African financiers based in Johannesburg, began aggressively buying Lonrho shares, calculating that the company's assets were worth more than the market price.

The Glazers' activities prompted alarm among Lonrho's three principal shareholders. Among the trio was Harley Drayton, the big, cigar-smoking chairman of a well-known conglomerate and investment trust called '117 Old Broad Street', later known as the Drayton Group. Collaborating with Drayton was Sir Robert Adeane, a socially well-connected, aggressive investor who was a leading benefactor of the arts in London.

The second principal shareholder was Lord Robins, an American-born businessman and chairman of the British South Africa Company, which had owned most of Northern Rhodesia and had become a finance and investment company in Africa's mines, railways and agriculture.

The third investor was the legendary Harry Oppenheimer, chairman of Anglo American which had become Africa's dominant mining corporation.

Bolstered by Ball's forecast that Lonrho's profits would double in the coming years, the three counter-attacked in concert in the expectation of either profiting because the

Glazers would be compelled to pay more for Lonrho's shares, or because they might win control of the conglomerate for themselves. Oppenheimer, in particular, considered Lonrho to be just one of several British mineral companies based in Africa to be added to Anglo's rapacious empire.

By the end of their buying spree, Drayton, Robins and Oppenheimer owned 25 per cent of Lonrho and, having frustrated the Glazers' bid, also bought the South Africans' Lonrho shares, raising their own stake to 51 per cent. Inevitably Lonrho's share price rose and the three eagerly anticipated the fruits of their investment.

Lonrho's plight and the need to sell assets was of course known in Rhodesia. On the network, Rowland heard also that Rio Tinto Zinc, a British mining company which originally operated in Spain, was aggressively seeking new investments in Africa. The Cam and Motor gold mine was a suitable proposition. The skill for Rowland lay in brokering the deal and earning a fee from RTZ for arranging the purchase from Lonrho.

Clearly, if Rio Tinto's geologist asked to inspect the Cam and Motor mine, the company's interest would be registered and the price would increase accordingly. Rowland's plan was to persuade Rio Tinto to support his pretence that he was negotiating with Lonrho on his own behalf. Accordingly, he visited the mine and discussed the idea with the manager, Ronny Walker. The next step was to fly to London to suggest the deal to Val Duncan, Rio Tinto's percipient managing director.

Reluctantly Duncan agreed that Rowland could visit his country home on a Saturday morning: 'I'll give him fifteen minutes. No longer.' The meeting lasted two hours. Standard & Chartered were instructed to guarantee Rowland the necessary money.

On Monday morning, Rowland presented his offer to Sir Joseph Ball, his son and Brigadier Keith Thorburn, Drayton's representative, in Lonrho's offices in Cornhill. The three made little attempt to hide their mocking incredulity: 'For a start, you haven't got the money, Tiny.'

Rowland smiled, 'Why don't you telephone my bank and ask?'

The negotiations began. There was every reason for the

Balls to reject Rowland's bid. The Cam and Motor mine was providing a substantial percentage of Lonrho's profits and was also employing many Lonrho metallurgists, geologists and mining engineers. Yet the Balls were persuaded to sell. The price was not the determining factor. Rather, it was the compensation which Rowland promised that they would personally receive for 'loss of office'. The Balls would pocket £35,000. Their venal, selfish interest overcame their obligations to the shareholders and their employees. It was an inducement which Rowland would proffer many more times in his career.

Once the option was signed, Rowland revealed, to the Balls' surprise, that he was acting for Rio Tinto. There was also a shock for Ronny Walker, the mine manager. Alan Ball instructed Walker to consider his position in the corridor for fifteen minutes. Either he could go with the mine to Rio Tinto or stay with Lonrho. Walker left Lonrho deeply resentful. To this day, he still suffers the humiliation which he claims Rowland inflicted.

For Rowland the deal was a fundamental breakthrough. Paid an estimated £100,000 finder's fee, he was appointed to Rio Tinto's board in Rhodesia initially as a consultant and later as a commercial director. Automatically his status in Salisbury rose. 'He was over the moon,' recalled Cleminson. His joy was augmented by the award by Rio Tinto of a further £140,000 'for other services'. But his relationships suffered. 'People hated him for getting the better of everyone in deals,' recalls David Russell, a South African mining expert.

The third and most important consequence was that Lonrho, without the Cam and Motor mine, was significantly weakened. The company's geologists, metallurgists and managers who had just moved into the new offices in Salisbury were seriously underemployed. Inevitably, Lonrho's finances deteriorated further just as Rowland's fortunes were flourishing.

Rowland was proving a godsend to Rio Tinto. Among his 'other services' was the purchase of the Empress gold mine and, more importantly, hearing about the new Sandawana emerald mine, east of Bulawayo.

The tip came from Herman Stern, a gem dealer. Two men,

Rowland was told, had discovered and claimed an enormous deposit of emeralds. According to Stern, both were incapable of realising the Sandawana's potential. One was only semi-literate. Stern suggested that his young associate, Dan Mayers, who was the world-wide agent for selling emeralds, could introduce Rowland to the two prospectors.

Mayers, who would become involved in a controversial amethyst deal with Rowland in later years, was an American gem expert whose personality and character were in diametrical contrast to Rowland's. Born in 1922 in New York, Mayers had studied at the College of Mines at the University of Arizona and worked in South America before travelling to Africa.

In return for a commission, Mayers agreed to assist Rowland in convincing the prospectors to sell the mine. After quick negotiations, Rowland paid £150,000 for a mine which would earn millions over the ensuing years. There was a celebratory lunch at Salisbury's New Club where the semi-literate prospector, Cornelius Oosterhuisen, complained about depositing his money in a bank, 'because I want to get at it'. His signature, according to folklore, was a simple 'X'. The same day, Rowland resold a 50 per cent interest to Rio Tinto and agreed that RTZ would operate the mine.

With his new wealth and to avoid the inconvenience of commuting from Gatooma, Rowland had been searching for a home for himself and Irene in Salisbury. In 1960 he found High Noon, a beautiful two-storey villa at 27 Dacombe Drive in the suburbs, set in fourteen acres of cultivated lawns and flowerbeds which were tended by twelve garden boys. Rowland bought the house for £28,000 and established a friendship with the owner, Wally Milne, a former Battle of Britain pilot, who had emigrated when Labour won the 1945 election to become a successful property developer. Significantly, Milne would remain for years unaware of Rowland's German background or the existence of any Fuhrhop family.

An undemanding, sociable character, Milne did however notice the strain in Rowland's relationship with Irene. Irene was both domineering and possessive, 'constantly demanding to know about Tiny's whereabouts'. Since Rowland thought only about his business and would fly or drive away at any moment to pursue the next deal regardless of any social or emotional commitments, Irene nagged Rowland to make him account for his movements. 'She wanted to own Tiny,' recalls Milne, 'and he wasn't going to be owned by anyone.' Invariably, Rowland was unresponsive to her questions: 'Tiny was too absorbed in business to care about her,' comments Milne who sat for hours listening to Rowland's monologue on 'how I'm going to beat the competition'.

Even when they chartered a private plane to fly for a week-end's barracuda fishing on the *Melody*, berthed at Paradise Island off the Mozambique coast, Irene would demand an account of her partner's past movements. Marriage and children were not an option, Rowland confessed to his friend as he swung his American rod: 'With all my travel, it wouldn't work.' Not with Irene, and especially not in the midst of his most ambitious deal – to build a 184-mile pipeline to carry oil from the Mozambique port of Beira to Umtali, just inside Rhodesia.

Rowland had read in the *Reader's Digest* about pipelines under construction in Russia and the Middle East, carrying not only oil but even coal. For Rhodesia, whose oil was transported by a constant shuttle of expensive and unreliable trains, the advantages were considerable. Ownership of the pipeline, Rowland envisaged, would be a ceaseless profit machine.

Although Rhodesia's government records suggest that a pipeline had been considered a decade earlier, no one in the country had the expertise or initiative to transform the idea into reality. But for that matter, Rowland also lacked money, technical knowledge and relations with the Rhodesian and Portuguese governments before he embarked upon the project. It was a genuine green-field project which instantly attracted considerable opposition. 'No one had heard of pipelines before,' explains a lawyer who negotiated on Rowland's behalf, and there were vested interests, especially the oil companies, who instinctively opposed independent ownership.

In 1957, Rowland incorporated Associated Overseas Pipelines with three partners including Jack Carvill and began negotiations with four governments: firstly, with the Southern Rhodesian government whose prime minister was Edgar Whitehead; secondly, with the federal government whose leader was Roy Welensky; thirdly, with the governor of Mozambique, a Portuguese colony; and fourthly, with Dr Antonio Salazar, the Portuguese dictator in Lisbon.

Prerequisite to persuading these four administrations was the securing of a source of finance and the presentation of a realistic technical survey. Another hurdle to overcome was the opposition from Shell and BP, the two oil giants who would use the pipeline. Both saw the advantages of building and owning their own supply route. Finally, Rowland needed to win over those Rhodesian politicians who opposed the project on account of its complexity – in Rhodesian terms the proposal was unprecedented – and because of Rowland's own recent record.

On Rowland's side were his energy, his commitment and his persuasive manner. Since the pipeline would run in Mozambique, he sought first the approval of the Portuguese authorities. Finding the men of influence in a dictatorship is easier than in a democracy but in both systems, to succeed, the applicant needs to gain access to the decision maker.

In Mozambique, Rowland first called upon the Bishop of Beira and the Archbishop of Lourenço Marques. A donation to their favourite charities secured favourable access to the governor and won a relationship with Jorge Jardim, a local politician, a successful businessman and, most importantly, a close friend of Salazar.

In a lesson which would guide his activities for the remainder of his life, Rowland appreciated that Salazar considered dealing with a self-employed and certainly discreet businessman such as Rowland to be preferable to meeting a committee of oil executives who were required to report back to superior committees, with a consequent uncontrolled profusion of paperwork and indecision. Rowland would claim that, within three years, he flew sixty-eight times to Lisbon to win Salazar's support and then occasionally on to London to convince Lord Godby, the chairman of Shell, and the directors of John Brown, the construction company, that his venture would materialise.

On 25 July 1960, Rowland briefed the federal Rhodesian

government about progress. At the Carlton hotel in Johannesburg and later in Lourenço Marques, he had negotiated compensation to Mozambique railways for the loss of revenue for transporting the oil. He had agreed that the pipeline would be owned in proportion of 51/49 per cent by the Portuguese on Mozambique soil and 51/49 per cent in his favour in Rhodesia. Finance, he assured the Rhodesian federal government, could be raised. But Rowland had not dispersed the hostility. After he had left the government offices, the minister ordered that the Rhodesian government rather than Rowland should be the pipeline's owner and told Frank Owen, a wayward travel agent turned politician, to pursue that course.

Rowland faced similar problems with the government of Southern Rhodesia. Rubridge Stumbles, the minister of transport, also opposed the pipeline. In the parliament he was supported by the more parochial members who were 'disturbed' and suspicious of Rowland's motives. William Harper muttered his concern about 'a certain individual' who arrived in Gatooma 'without any resources' but overnight was rich. Harper had been informed by Rhodesian intelligence that Rowland's source of funds was Krishna Menon, the Indian politician, and demanded careful monitoring over Rowland and the pipeline.

But in early 1961, Roy Welensky, by then the federal prime minister, intervened and the opposition began to melt. Rubridge Stumbles was unexpectedly replaced by a minister who wholeheartedly supported the pipeline, and in the federal government, Frank Owen became minister of transport and a convert to Rowland's proposition. Rowland also found support from Dennis O'Donovan, the federal secretary for law, and two members of parliament, Peter Staub and Saul Udwin. When the Federation collapsed one year later, all four politicians would be employed by Lonrho, while Welensky would be granted free office facilities in Lonrho's building. Rowland had mastered the nature of relationships with politicians. Within Rhodesian society, the short pipeline had transformed Rowland from merely another deal maker into a notable personality just as his resurrection was being consummated.

In April 1961 Angus Ogilvy arrived in Salisbury. Aged thirty-three, the second son of the Earl of Airlie had followed a classic career for that era. After Eton and Oxford and two years in the Scots Guards, he had decided to 'do something in the City' despite his father's warning, 'They're all crooks.' Ogilvy's employer was Harley Drayton, the self-made millionaire who ran a conglomerate of twenty-three companies. Lacking a son, Drayton had 'adopted' Ogilvy and dispatched his protégé to South Africa to report on the company's investments. At the last moment, Drayton mentioned that, on his return journey, Ogilvy should stop in Salisbury and 'have a look at Lonrho'.

Contrary to Alan Ball's prediction, Lonrho's performance had declined ever since the trio had intervened to stop the Glazers' bid. Its £17,000 trading losses were covered by further property sales to raise £163,369 but the share price had fallen from 75 pence to 12.5 pence. Ball's palliative had been the appointment as Lonrho's chairman of Sir Peter Bednall, the recently retired paymaster-general of the British army who was ignorant about Africa, farming and business. Bednall had flown to Salisbury to celebrate with Welensky the opening of Lonrho's new headquarters, an ugly concrete block whose grey exterior matched the internal laminated, light brown plastic walls and plastic ceiling tiles.

That unprepossessing scenario was straining the union between Drayton, Oppenheimer and particularly Lord Robins who, at a lunch in London, had proposed to liquidate Lonrho. Drayton however was convinced that the company, with stated assets of £1.7 million, was undervalued. If properly managed, it could produce rich profits. 'A new man is required to run London Rhodesian if you find one,' he told Ogilvy.

Ogilvy's first call in Salisbury was on C.G. Rogers, the new manager of the Standard Bank, to whom he explained that Lonrho needed revitalisation. Rogers suggested that Ogilvy meet 'the man who has earned more in commissions from RTZ than all the board of directors combined'.

The following day, at Rogers's invitation, Ogilvy and Rowland met for lunch in the bank's dining room. Ogilvy admits that he was smitten by the sheer charisma of the Rhodesian farmer. 'He proposed so many ideas,' Ogilvy recalled later, 'that I was fascinated.' Enthusing the Englishman about his pipeline, his mines and his conviction that Africa was 'the future', Rowland amazed Ogilvy, who was unsophisticated about the hidden nuances of a balance sheet, above all by his mastership of financial jargon and technicalities.

Within two days, Ogilvy decided that Rowland could save Lonrho. During a six-hour session in Rowland's office in Hardwick House, they typed out a draft agreement for Rowland to join Lonrho. Instead of becoming simply Lonrho's Rhodesian manager, Rowland proposed that his assets in Shepton Estates, Rowland's holding company, should be exchanged for shares in Lonrho and he would become a director based in Salisbury. Rowland would later boast to Dan Mayers, the gemstone dealer, 'I cleaned the pants off Ogilvy. I had him eating out of my hands.' On his return, Ogilvy persuaded Drayton that to save Lonrho he should accept the agreement.

Rowland was summoned to London and was taken by Ogilvy for lunch with Robins, Drayton and Oppenheimer. It was an awesome introduction for a man who only four years earlier had bought his first gold mine. The three shareholders were divided about their strategy. Drayton favoured Rowland; Oppenheimer was ambivalent because he wanted to buy Lonrho cheap; while Robins, according to an aide, was 'suspicious about Rowland and outrightly opposed the appointment'. Nevertheless, on Drayton's insistence, the negotiations started between Rowland and Lonrho. The company, then based in Cornhill, was represented by Alan Ball, Ogilvy and Andrew Caldecott, a solicitor. All three were Old Etonians, enhancing the trust between them but leaving them lacking in business acumen compared to their proposed partner. Rowland assessed their strengths and weaknesses. The latter easily outweighed the former.

Lonrho, Rowland told the three, was worth less than £1 million despite its £1.7 million valuation in the accounts. The pre-tax profits in 1961 were a mere £157,000. The Mazoe Consolidated gold mines [later renamed Corsyn] which incorporated the Connaught and Bucks mines near Salisbury, like the farmland, were, he said, inefficiently managed; while Colyn Braun, Lonrho's current general manager in Salisbury, had, he claimed, contracted Lonrho to clear part of the Zambezi river on terms which would bankrupt the company. 'In retrospect it's clear that he deliberately talked Lonrho down,' recalls one participant.

In contrast, Rowland extolled the virtues of Shepton Estates. Its assets were Norton Motors, the owner of the Mercedes franchise; Consolidated Holdings, which supplied car parts; his shares in the publicly quoted Kanyemba gold mine; the Mashaba gold mine; the Shamrocke copper mine which he owned jointly with Reynolds, and the prospect of the pipeline. Although the official value of the assets was £375,000, Rowland argued that once the pipeline was built, his dowry would be worth nearly £1 million, similar to Lonrho's.

Both Joseph and Alan Ball, who were already enriched after Rowland's negotiated purchase of the Cam and Motor mine, were again vulnerable to Rowland's seduction and salesmanship. If there was to be a deal, said Rowland, it needed rapid resolution while he was in London. A telex was sent to George Abindor, Lonrho's South African consulting engineer, to produce an 'immediate valuation' of Rowland's three mines. Abindor, a professional of indisputable repute, questioned Alan Ball's haste. 'We've got no time,' replied Ball who seemed to Abindor to desire favourable reports. 'I had four days to look at the three mines,' recalled Abindor. 'I needed three months.' Lionel Taylor, who knew nothing about mining, accompanied Abindor.

The two men first visited the Shamrocke mine. By March 1961, Rand Mines had spent nearly £300,000 in exploration but because the price of copper was falling, Rand decided that commercial exploitation was uneconomic and had allowed their option to lapse. The rights reverted to Reynolds and Rowland. To their advantage, they were now better aware of the mine's potential but the handicaps remained. The mine was ninety miles from the nearest smelter, the tracks towards the area were impassable even for heavy trucks, and some details of the preliminary exploration would still need to be completed. Abindor concluded that the mine's commercial exploitation was 'decidedly risky'.

Abindor next visited the Mashaba gold mine. 'It's valueless,' he reported and advised that it be closed immediately.

Finally Abindor visited Kanyemba. A proper survey would take two months, but on Ball's instructions that was impossible. 'I had to rely on Rademeyer's survey,' recalls Abindor, 'and information from the mine workers, including Adams, the manager, and from Graham Beck, the joint owner. Everyone was rushing me.' On that basis, Abindor agreed with Rademeyer's assessment that Kanyemba would be productive for twenty years.

Yet he remained concerned. Only one of the three mines was worth exploiting and furthermore his valuation of Kanyemba was speculative. In handing over his report to Colyn Braun, who would carry the report to London, he told him, 'I don't know how important the mines are to Lonrho's deal with Rowland. If the whole deal is based on the motors and pipeline, and Kanyemba is just an appendix, it won't matter. But if the value of the mine is important to Lonrho, then I want to be in London to qualify my report.' Braun agreed. Later he would tell Abindor, 'It was all discussed so quickly that there was no time to call you.' Rowland's valuations, despite Abindor's report, were accepted.

Since Rowland was thinking many times faster than Ball and seemingly offered Lonrho's only hope of salvation, he initially demanded majority control of Lonrho. Even Harley Drayton, aware that Oppenheimer and especially Robins opposed the deal, cautioned against greed: 'That would go down very badly with the public.' Rowland, who recognised in Drayton a prototype of himself, agreed to modify his demands. Shepton Estates was to be issued with 1.5 million Lonrho shares with an option to buy a further 2 million shares over the following five years [in the first three years for 30 pence and thereafter 35 pence]. To safeguard the value of Rowland's stake, Ball agreed not to issue any more shares. Rowland was guaranteed ownership of 43 per cent of the company.

Under the agreement, which became controversial in 1973, Rowland [on behalf of Shepton Estates] would inject into Lonrho Norton Motors, Consolidated Holdings, his shares in two mines, Kanyemba and Mashaba whose annual profits were estimated respectively at £178,000 and £36,000, and the prospect of the pipeline. After some discussions and misunderstandings between Rowland and Lonrho's managers in London, the Shamrocke mine was not included in the final deal and remained Rowland's private interest, controlled by Shepton Estates. Rowland was receiving Lonrho's shares for 47 pence each when the stock market price was 20 pence but the asset value was 57.5 pence. Effectively, the terms of the deal nearly doubled the value of Shepton Estates from £375,000 to £700,000.

The prospect of Rowland as the company's new manager was not welcomed by everyone in Salisbury. Still irked by his cunning purchase of the Cam and Motor mine and uneasy about the Kanyemba flotation, some members of the Salisbury Club began questioning the precise background of a man known locally as an Englishman born in India. Since Lonrho's management in London was clearly unsympathetic, they sought the help of Robins and Oppenheimer. Both were responsive.

The South African, keen to block the advance of any competitor and launch his own bid for Lonrho, began criticising the valuation of Rowland's assets. Robins, whose distrust of Rowland had intensified, began inquiries about Rowland's past.

A contact in the Home Office briefed Robins about Rowland's German background and about his wartime record. Robins added, wrongly, that Rowland's imprisonment had been for fraud. Surprised, Drayton asked Ogilvy to discover the truth.

The revelations, that the gentleman farmer from Shepton was in fact Fuhrhop from Hamburg, had already been sent by MI5 to the Federal Intelligence and Security Bureau, Rhodesia's intelligence service. In a special appendix attached to a cabinet paper about the pipeline and restricted to a few ministers, Rowland had been described as a 'Nazi sympathiser'. A brief and sanitised version was leaked to Ronny Walker, Lonrho's former manager.

Rowland heard the news of the exposure in London. 'His face was white as a sheet,' recalled Stefan Klein, a successful German entrepreneur who had worked for MI5 during the war. 'He didn't know how to deal with it.' It was one of the few occasions when Rowland faltered. Klein's advice was blunt: 'Tiny, I've done all right despite my name and background. Brazen it out.'

Rowland turned to Drayton for support and found a mutual benefit. Drayton was trying to sell his stake in Halls Holding, a loss-making motor distributor in Nyasaland. Rowland proposed to Drayton that Lonrho buy Halls in return for Drayton's support. By then Drayton had heard that the allegations about Rowland's financial irregularities involved only his dispute with the Inland Revenue. Since Rowland's only sin was to conceal his past, Drayton telephoned Oppenheimer to express support for the deal against the South African's proposed counter bid. 'Oppenheimer was told to lay off,' recalled Cleminson. Halls was bought in 1963 for £550,000 worth of Lonrho shares. The 'mutual deal' became Rowland's hallmark and the shorthand for praising his 'genius' as a negotiator. The technique was also Drayton's. In an explanation of changing City morals at that time, Drayton exemplified his rise from office boy to owner of Britain's biggest independent television franchise, Associated-Rediffusion: 'In the old days they helped you out of kindness. Nowadays they all want their cut from you.'

But not only Drayton was receiving secret favours. At the same meeting where Drayton smoothed the final wrinkles of opposition, Rowland turned to the veteran city operator and asked, 'Do you mind if Angus and Alan get part of the action?'

'Not at all,' replied Drayton, understanding precisely Rowland's intention. 'I hope you boys stick together.' Both Ogilvy and Ball received an option to buy 200,000 and 400,000 Lonrho shares respectively. But Rowland's gift would remain a partial secret. During the finalisation of the deal between Rowland and the Lonrho board, three of the eight directors were unaware of the arrangement. In Rowland's view, it was his display of gratitude. Others would believe that Rowland had identified the weakest members of the board and rendered them beholden to him. For the public, Rowland's arrival was hailed as a victory.

Joseph Ball, just prior to his death in July 1961, was euphoric. 'I have the greatest respect for Mr Rowland's business capabilities, particularly in the field of negotiation – and I think that I am in a good position to judge, having carried out these somewhat extensive negotiations with him over the past few months.' The justification for the merger was Ball's prediction that Lonrho's profits would double.

If in retrospect the deal proved to be brilliant, then even at the time Rowland realised that he had won an astonishing coup. Over the following thirty years Rowland would earn more than £100 million in salary and dividends from Lonrho. In return for a Mercedes car franchise, two dubious gold mines and an unbuilt pipeline, the uncertain businessman, who was not even a member of the Salisbury Club, was taking control of Rhodesia's most venerable, company which was quoted on the London stock exchange.

At forty-four, Rowland was enjoying a transformed status. His visiting card as joint managing director with Alan Ball in London guaranteed him entry into corporations, ministries and banks across the world. He also retained a position as financial adviser to Rio Tinto in London. That reality was the realisation of a dream, albeit that Lonrho's pre-tax profits that year were a mere £157,000.

There was another dream now: to build an empire across Africa. Rowland was in a hurry since he was of an age when most men had achieved their best. No barrier would be big enough to halt the fulfilment of his ambition to construct an empire which would rival Rio Tinto or Anglo American. Like Val Duncan or Harry Oppenheimer, he could sit as a colossus to be consulted and considered by his peers, prime ministers and presidents. Drayton's creed was apposite for Rowland: 'You don't have to worry about being popular. You have to take risks and stick your neck out.' The only foreseeable obstacles to Rowland's ambition were his fellow directors and Lonrho's finances.

In his previous twenty-five-year career, Rowland had rarely been answerable to anyone, even to those with whom he was collaborating. By nature conspiratorial, on joining Lonrho he did not consider changing his habits.

Rowland had already assessed Lonrho's directors. Andrew Caldecott, a solicitor and Ball's schoolfriend, was friendly;

Forbes Davies lived in Rhodesia and took little interest in the company's affairs; John Whitehouse, a seventy-six-year-old mining engineer was equally uninterested; while Jack Kiek, a dull investment manager with the British South Africa Company in Salisbury, suspected by some of having 'given Lonrho to Rowland' in return for a Lonrho directorship, nevertheless reflected Rhodesian society's antagonism towards the newcomer. Collectively and individually, they were unimportant. Instinctively Rowland trusted only Alan Ball, who remained as chairman, and Angus Ogilvy. Both were socially acceptable, pleasant Old Etonians who were susceptible to Rowland's tendency to embrace passionately those whose friendship he sought. Both found in Rowland a father-like figure, which was ironic because Rowland seemed occasionally to be searching for a similar totem. Observing the relationship between the three men develop, Andrew Caldecott, the solicitor, remarked how Rowland's 'cardinal policy' was to keep 'people on a string'.

The final element linking the board was Fred Butcher, described as the 'group chief accountant'. Significantly, Butcher was not qualified as an accountant although he understood the essentials of bookkeeping. A devout Christian, Butcher survived and prospered within Lonrho because he performed as an efficient business manager and displayed complete subservience initially to Ball and later to Rowland, which resembled the reasoning of a Jesuitical Catholic who could convincingly reconstruct any facts within his mind to justify his actions as truthful and honest. His trait ideally suited Rowland's business style.

Only Sir Robert Adeane refused to join the board. 'Tiny's too fast and too risky,' he told his son and admitted that he was 'quite pleased' for Ogilvy to represent the Drayton Group while he would keep abreast of developments at dinner parties for the three at his home in Cheyne Walk.

But in those early months, the centre of Rowland's operations were the company's offices in Salisbury. On his desk he placed a photograph of himself, aged about twenty, standing with his mother in a park. Only gradually would his anger against the British for their treatment of his devoted mother become apparent. His brief return to London had sparked mixed memories, a good reason to discard the possibility of ever returning to Britain. He did not contemplate leaving Rhodesia.

Like Field Marshal Montgomery's exclusive and unqualified trust in soldiers with desert sand in their shoes, Rowland gathered around himself in Salisbury a group upon whose loyalty, diligence and commitment he could rely. None was more important than Nic Kruger, a thirty-nine-year old South African and practising Christian, who joined Lonrho six months before Rowland. It was a sign of Rowland's need to be superior that he would always insist that Kruger arrived six months after him.

To some, Kruger seemed an unlikely friend for Rowland. Sensitive, his modesty easily interpreted as indecision, and with a propensity for whisky, he would subsequently reveal to a Lonrho director, 'I would pay for the privilege of working for Tiny.' The framed photograph on his bedside table was not of his family but of Rowland, smiling victoriously at a board meeting.

Kruger's weaknesses and loyalty made him especially attractive to Rowland. The two would often breakfast and dine together on the same day. 'It's the first million that's hard to make, Nic,' Rowland would repeat. 'But if I lose it, I'll make it again.' Some would blame Rowland for Kruger's transformation into a lifelong alcoholic, which rendered him apparently incoherent by mid-morning. When Alan Ball also became an alcoholic, the charge against Rowland's peculiar treatment of those directors who were close friends gained strength. 'He could treat Nic abominably,' recalled Eileen Kruger. Others could only recall that Rowland would telephone both Ball and Kruger daily from any part of the world to ensure that they were not drunk. Rowland's peculiarly variable relationships with his close associates reflected his own contrasting moods.

The surfeit of loyalty and indefatigability among Lonrho's staff was offset by the perilous deficit in the company's bank account, a perennial problem for Lonrho and a constant handicap for Rowland's imperial ambitions. Ever the optimist, Rowland would dismiss concerns about Lonrho's finances with, 'Don't worry, something will turn up.' Some would condemn the financial irresponsibility while others admired his cool bravery. In 1961, his audacity fixed upon finalising the contract for the pipeline.

The shuttling between Salisbury, Lourenço Marques and Lisbon recommenced. Gradually, an agreement materialised which allowed Lonrho a minority ownership of the pipeline in return for Portugal retaining control, receiving compensation for their railway's loss of revenue, an annual rental, and winning a share of the construction contract. In December 1961, Rowland signed the contract in Lisbon.

On his return to Salisbury, Rowland faced the obstacle that conservative politicians, quoting security reasons, would argue illogically against dependence upon the Portuguese. He began to organise a lobby to strengthen Welensky's existing support.

Returning home somewhat drunk at two o'clock one morning, Rowland was discussing with George Abindor how to break the log-jam. 'Let's phone the mayor of Umtali and get him to lobby Welensky,' shouted Rowland with sudden vigour. Ignoring the time, Rowland telephoned the official. 'I'll dictate what you've got to say in your petition to Welensky,' said Rowland. There was a pause as the drowsy mayor explained his needs. 'What,' exclaimed Rowland, 'do you mean that you don't go to sleep with a pencil in your pyjamas?' The mayor's newly discovered complaint to the federal prime minister about the 'tardiness of your decision' concerning the pipeline was telegraphed to Salisbury later that day. On 16 February 1962, the pipeline agreement was signed by Rowland and Frank Owen, the minister of transport, on behalf of the Rhodesian government. 'Owen can merely look out of his ministry's windows and wave to Mr Rowland in his offices,' wrote a critic, suspicious of Owen's relationship with Rowland. Without disclosing the full terms, Welensky obtained parliament's approval. The pipeline, whose daily capacity was 600,000 gallons of crude, was due for completion by the end of 1964.

Rowland's euphoria was shortlived. In the midst of dealing with prime ministers, presidents and bankers about the pipeline, he had probably all but forgotten the Kanyemba mine. After all, it had become a minor element in what Lonrho's directors understood to be 'Tiny's Grand Design'.

Ken Adams, working in the bush near Gatooma, was reporting declining production. A consultant, appointed to find the missing gold, was groping through Kanyemba's deep shafts, following Rademeyer's survey to identify where the gold could be found. Sitting in the office on the surface reading the Kanyemba prospectus, the consultant was 'puzzled and curious'. Adams, conscious both of the contradictory conclusions of Rademeyer's and Viewing's reports and of 'what side my bread was buttered', remained tactfully silent.

A confrontation was organised in the bush. George Abindor was summoned from Salisbury and Rademeyer from South Africa. The latter arrived without his plans. 'I sent them by post,' Rademeyer explained to his incredulous audience. Adams produced a set. Abindor listened to Rademeyer's explanation with mounting anger, 'You misled me.'

Rademeyer looked at Adams: 'You agree with me don't you Ken?' Adams had become strangely unsupportive. Rademeyer was crestfallen, 'I'm sorry.' Instead of twenty years' production, Kanyemba would be exhausted within two years.

Shortly afterwards, Adams was approached near the mine by a stranger. Unsuspecting, the miner admitted that Kanyemba's prospects were blighted. The stranger revealed himself to be a shareholder who was investigating rumours.

The news was passed to Wilfred Brookes, the publisher of *Rhodesian Property and Finance*, Rhodesia's only financial newspaper. Born in Essex in 1915, Brookes had grown up in South Africa and served with the Royal Tank Corps during the war before settling in Salisbury. An astute journalist, for a brief period Brookes had been among Rowland's enthusiastic supporters. Soon after his return as Lonrho's managing director to Salisbury, Rowland had bought control of Willoughby's Consolidated, a cattle ranching business with 752,000 acres of land managed by Major Colin MacKenzie, a Highlander who had spent the war in a German POW camp and was married to the Duke of Grafton's daughter.

Brookes described the cash deal as a 'fabulous bargain' and tipped Lonrho's shares as 'a good purchase'. The souring of Brookes began after the Cam and Motor deal and when he noticed the coincidence that Ogilvy was a director of both Willoughby's and of Halls, the Nyasaland motor distributors, which Lonrho bought. Since Lonrho's financial position was precarious, Brookes, an increasingly xenophobic nationalist, began questioning the source of Rowland's money.

The Kanyemba prospectus, in Brookes's opinion, was clearly dishonest and became the grounds for a ceaseless campaign against a foreigner. Brookes's first report, simply mentioning a 'discrepancy', provoked Rowland's alarm.

In a quick attempt to limit the damage, Sir Peter Bednall, by then the chairman of the Rhodesian Unit Trust, was recruited as an independent arbitrator. On 19 February 1962, Bednall met Adams and 'persuaded' the miner not only that he had endorsed Rademeyer's fictitious statistics but that he still considered them valid. Six days later, in a statement which was published in *Property and Finance*, Bednall claimed that he had 'several interviews' with Rowland and had visited Kanyemba, with Rowland's co-operation. The arbitrator concluded that the difference in the estimates of ore reserve was 'due mainly to differences of opinion in methods of calculation' and that Adams agreed with Rademeyer. 'The words were put in my mouth,' Adams later admitted.

Kanyemba was symptomatic of something worse. On 12 April 1962, Rowland told the Lonrho board that he was 'extremely concerned' about the failure of the Mashaba gold mine. Despite Lonrho's engineers having been given 'every facility' to complete their survey, explained Rowland, the mine was less productive than anticipated. In fact, it was as worthless as Abindor had predicted. Within just eight months, the value of Rowland's contribution to Lonrho, for which he had received a potential 43 per cent share in Lonrho's assets worth over one million pounds, had halved.

In normal circumstances, Rowland would have been under pressure for an explanation. Instead, he knew that he could rely upon Alan Ball and Angus Ogilvy. Both had been promised 'a part of the action' and were convinced that only Rowland could save and rebuild Lonrho. Accordingly, during the board discussions about the disastrous performance of the mines, neither director disclosed their private interest in keeping Rowland in charge. Both were by then firmly under Rowland's spell –

not only of his charm, but also of the favours which he organised.

A newly acquired flat at Avenfield House in Park Lane, ostensibly for the use of Lonrho's overseas visitors and visiting directors, was available for Ogilvy, whose gratitude was effusive: 'I wish I felt able even to begin to thank you for all you did . . . the option, the cases, the flat – everything – but it's impossible. I only hope you realise how grateful I am. It'll make a tremendous difference to my personal life.' Ogilvy's letter ended, 'Don't stay away too long – life gets boring.' Ogilvy also apparently asked for his share of the 'action'. Rowland accordingly transferred an option on 200,000 shares out of the two million which he owned.

Uncensured in London, Rowland was nevertheless criticised in Salisbury. Trumpeting the details of what he called 'the hush-hush pipeline concession' which allowed the Portuguese 'financial and physical control over the country's oil artery', Wilfred Brookes also attacked Rowland's suspicious profiteering at Kanyemba. Fearful of professional criticism, George Abindor searched Lonrho's files for his original report. It was missing and there was no duplicate. Abindor's concern was heightened by the first of many financial crises affecting Lonrho under Rowland's stewardship.

By August 1962 Lonrho's cash reserves were depleted and the bailiffs were threatening to seize office furniture. Rowland received board approval for the sale of some 440,000 acres of land to the government for the use of Africans, a common palliative for the company. In the course of that sale, Rowland told the board that he had paid a commission of £15,000 to finalise the deal.

The news of the commission triggered Jack Kiek to complain about Rowland's unauthorised activity and submit his resignation from the Lonrho board, later withdrawn. Although Rowland promptly dispatched a cringing apology, the incident marked an important milestone in Rowland's stewardship of Lonrho. Firstly, Rowland would thereafter seek to prevent other independent spirits from joining the board, especially non-executive directors. Secondly, many decisions were thereafter taken informally with Ball and Ogilvy. The other directors would be asked to rubberstamp a short 'minute' circulated before board meetings.

Thirdly, unlike any other Rhodesian company, Rowland decided to start investing in Nyasaland. Unlike any other British businessman in that region, Rowland was not totally dismayed by the political turbulence which threatened the Central African Federation's future.

Harold Macmillan's speech in February 1960 forecasting the 'Winds of Change' blowing through Africa had signalled Britain's refusal to fight for the continuation of white Rhodesian rule over Northern Rhodesia and Nyasaland through the artificial federation. The two nationalist leaders in those countries, Kenneth Kaunda and Dr Hastings Banda, imprisoned following riots and massacres of African civilians, had been released and began agitating for independence. Their campaign mirrored the threat to white rule throughout the continent. Amid horrendous incidents of rape and murder against whites, the neighbouring Belgian Congo had plunged into chaos, prompting the conviction and alarm that Africa, like South East Asia and Berlin, had become a Cold War battleground.

In February 1962, Duncan Sandys, the Commonwealth secretary, flew to Salisbury and told Welensky over lunch, 'We British have lost the will to govern.' Since British troops would not be committed to enforce colonial rule, the minister reported to Macmillan that there was no alternative but to accede to Dr Banda's demand for Nyasaland's independence. The Federation's demise and the prospect of independent Malawi and Zambia shattered the hopes of white Rhodesians, prompting their demand for independence, 'without negotiation and without conditions'. Unperturbed by the prospect of turmoil, Rowland pursued the wily entrepreneur's favoured adage: to move in the opposite direction to the one taken by his competitors. Unlike others who rejected Africa as insecure for investment, Rowland reasoned that, like the army surplus deals in post-war Britain, there were opportunities for quick profits.

To the curious, Rowland would quip, 'Africa is down. It can only go up.' Critics would allege that Rowland treated the continent like a commodity, but Rowland later explained that he was an idealist sharing the vision of its new leaders about a Utopia harnessing its vast mineral resources. The truth was somewhere in between.

As the Federation collapsed, Rowland began secretly buying the shares of Nyasaland's railway and the Trans-Zambezi railway which included the ownership of the bridge stretching two miles across the river. The 600-mile, single-track network linked Beira to all three countries in the Federation to southern Tanganyika [Tanzania]. Like most settlers, Rowland believed that ownership of the railways would be crucial to white Rhodesia's survival when nationalist governments eventually ruled the neighbouring countries. As his stake grew, Rowland was rightly suspected of undertaking the initiative by secret agreement with Welensky. The federal prime minister, aggrieved by Britain's betrayal of the settlers, greeted Rowland's part in the conspiracy as 'vital to Southern Rhodesia's [ability] to control the economic policies of Nyasaland in the future'. Welensky continued, 'Mr Rowland assures me that there is nothing that can be done by the Territorial government to prevent a deal of this nature being undertaken.'

The former train driver feared that a future black Nyasaland government would divert its rail traffic away from Rhodesia to another East African port. With control of Nyasaland's railways in Salisbury rather than in London or Blantyre, the possible loss of revenue, he believed, was avoided. Instead, enthused Welensky, thanks to Rowland, white Rhodesia was the 'real controlling force'. As they discussed his achievement, Rowland also revealed his ambition to buy the railway which ran from Zambia through the Congo [renamed Zaïre] to Benguela, the Angolan port. For Welensky, Rowland had become 'the best thing to happen to Rhodesia since Cecil Rhodes'. Others with less enthusiasm would say that Rowland was 'like Rhodes but without the vision'. With the politician's flattery, the hitherto insignificant businessman became convinced that he had both vision and determination. When asked, soon after, to comment upon Welensky's praise, he replied, 'Who cares about the vision as long as I build the empire?' Noticeably, there was no suggestion that Rowland was motivated either by love of Africa or commitment to the black government. That would have been injudicious in Salisbury. The public announcement of the takeover of Nyasaland's railways was made by Frank Owen, the minister of transport, speaking, according to some, 'virtually as Lonrho's public relations officer'.

The ownership of a rail network was prestigious for Lonrho and a commercial coup. Political uncertainty had drastically reduced the value of the shares. For £140,000, Rowland had bought a minority but controlling interest in a company with valuable assets and over £5 million cash deposited in the bank to pay for new locomotives ordered from Britain. The tactic was well known and adopted by Rowland throughout his career. Control had been bought without the company's agreement for a minimum amount which, considering Lonrho's financial predicament, was important. In Nyasaland, the sufferers were the remaining shareholders including the government, who could neither sell their shares at a profit nor prevent Lonrho stripping the company of its assets or loading expenses on to its accounts. Control also allowed Lonrho to include a proportion of the railways' assets within its own accounts, so bolstering Lonrho's apparent value.

Shortly after the takeover, Rowland cancelled the order for the railway's rolling stock, complaining that the locomotives supplied by AEI were inadequate. The cash was used to buy shares in Henderson's Transvaal Estates, a South African company with investments in coal and gold mines. Lonrho continued to take a management fee from the railway company but the users noticed that the service became unreliable.

In the midst of that manoeuvring, on 22 March 1962, Rowland was summoned to meet Dr Hastings Banda. 'Why are you buying these railways?' asked the prospective prime minister. Rowland, according to Banda, was momentarily silent, conjuring an overpowering air of innocence and hurt before replying, 'Because I think that this country has a future. This is the only country in Central Africa where the political situation is solved.' The theatrical performance was entwined with his commercial ambition. Like many merchant adventurers before him, Rowland recognised that governments were the principal source of power and money.

Rowland's relationship with Banda, a former general practitioner from Willesden, north London, and a reputed expert in the treatment of venereal diseases, was another keystone in transforming Lonrho from its moribund bankruptcy. Unlike Africa's other new leaders, Banda was not a doctrinaire socialist but understood the limitations which dictated Malawi's prosperity. Landlocked and deprived of investment during the colonial era, the politician was searching for European expertise.

There was never any doubt that Banda would rule as a dictator, which simplified Rowland's task. Compared to his problems in Salisbury in reconciling conflicting ministers to the merits of the pipeline, Rowland appreciated that in a dictatorship one man took the decision. The coincidence of two men embarking upon their careers, anxious to manage their respective empires unfettered by challenges, appealed to Rowland. The businessman also indicated his own importance. Days earlier, he told Banda, he had met Krishna Menon at the Dorchester in London and received a message from Pandit Nehru whom he had met the previous year in Delhi. At a time when the Third World wielded influence between the two rival superpowers, the prospective leader of a tiny and irrelevant African nation could only be impressed by Rowland's contacts.

Moreover, Banda liked Rowland's style. His politeness, Banda noticed, was natural and not condescending. He used the word 'sir' with charm. Subtly, Rowland hinted that he shared a bond with Banda and understood the black man's struggle. Like Banda, he too had been imprisoned by the British and suffered the sense of outrage, injustice and grievances of liberty denied by arrogant and heartless officials. This empathy appealed to Banda who watched as other white businessmen, in anticipation of black rule, sought a fast exit from his country. Nevertheless, Rowland told Welensky that he had urged Banda to avoid confrontation and negotiate with the white government.

The relationship with Banda was noticed by Salisbury's intelligence service who foolishly identified Rowland as a 'communist', a conclusion which they supported by his £50,000 donation to Welensky's political party. Rowland, an intelligence officer reported, was 'utterly unscrupulous in business affairs; although a brilliant financier, Rowland's sole intent in life is the making of money and the enjoyment of power that results from holding vast business interests.' Regardless of its validity, that judgment influenced politicians who queried Rowland's relationship with Owen, Staub and Udwin the former federal politicians, who by then were employed by Lonrho. 'He'll turn anyone's silver in his pocket,' commented Donald McIntyre, a minister of finance. McIntyre and others believed that Rowland's rejection by Government House had 'driven him to the blacks'.

To Banda, Rowland's self-promotional rhetoric was credible, and he found that Rowland was unencumbered by the ingrained prejudice against the natives. For his part, Rowland trusted Banda to allow Lonrho to earn profits while discouraging his countrymen from assuming that independence bequeathed the right to ignore the law and seize any attractive land.

The purchase of assets in Malawi, regardless of price, was unproblematic, but concomitant with businesses being sold cheap by fearful whites was the exodus of trained manpower, further damaging an economy which, unlike Southern Rhodesia, lacked roads, water, electricity and telephones. No one else but Lonrho was a buyer in that uninspiring netherland. But in contrast to other settlers, Rowland had seen that profits could be earned even in Nazi-occupied Europe and socialist-controlled Britain. While the gamble was favourable, the challenge was exhilarating. Rowland wanted to be rich and there was little to lose by investing a little more in Malawi. In early 1963, he bought for about £140,000 the British Central Africa Company. Essentially, Rowland bought BCA to own more shares in the railway. But with the purchase Lonrho inherited BCA's two tea factories, a 3500-acre tea plantation, and small sisal and coffee estates. Practically by accident, Lonrho was becoming a conglomerate. The notion was appealing and Banda was welcoming. Lonrho now required a manager in Blantyre for the empire's new outpost.

Gerald Percy, an Old Etonian, cousin of the Duke of Northumberland and a direct descendant of Hotspur, had first seen Rowland through a keyhole. Employed for five years by the British South Africa Company, Percy had been working in Lusaka. Before entering a director's office one day, he had checked to see whether there were any visitors in there already. 'I bent down and saw a handsome, fair-haired man lounging in an armchair.' Like Rowland, Percy was infected by a love of Africa but was more committed to the inhabitants' rights. In 1961, he resigned from the British South Africa Company to campaign with Garfield Todd, the liberal politician, in a forlorn attempt to defeat Rhodesia's white extremists. Percy had called on Rowland to contribute to the party's funds but was spurned. Rowland was supporting Welensky. Two years later, Percy's social connections in Rhodesia's white society, liberal credentials among the African nationalists and his commercial experience rendered him ideal for Lonrho.

At their confirmatory lunch at the Jameson hotel in Salisbury, Percy would hear the classic self-deprecatory remark posed by Rowland to assert his authority: 'I think we should decide, will you work for me or will I work for you?' The ascendancy was never in doubt although Rowland's instinctive charm created a close relationship. Three months after Percy joined Lonrho, his wife Jennifer gave birth to a son. Rowland agreed to become his godfather and during the first years would always remember to send a birthday present and fond wishes.

Within two months of arriving in Blantyre, Percy had spotted the opportunity which transformed Lonrho into Malawi's principal foreign investor and exporter and, more important, provided Rowland's essential passport to approach every other African prime minister as a friendly investor.

Booker McConnell, one of the world's major sugar producers, had refused Banda's request to build a sugar plantation and refinery. In July, Lonrho, without any experience in sugar production, offered to undertake the venture. Eighteen months after the bush was cleared, the first sugar cane was harvested. In gratitude, Banda hosted what the president described as a 'peculiar dinner' in honour of Alan Ball and Rowland. The guests included every ambassador assigned to the new nation. Sitting on either side of Banda, the two Lonrho directors were incredulous of the politician's praise. 'These two men have faith and confidence and trust in the future of this country,' said Banda as a prelude to a vitriolic attack against the 'Welensky gang' who had deprived Nyasaland of investment and threatened its future. Rowland smiled about the attack on his friend Welensky and smiled again when Banda disclosed that he only recently realised that Alan Ball, Lonrho's chairman, was the company's 'real boss'. His host's *naïveté* was amusing.

Five months later, Rowland would be less amused. Encouraged by Alan Cameron, the only white minister in the Malawi government and a critic of Rowland, Banda demanded an increased return from the railways. Ironically, Rowland complained to his friends that he was 'thoroughly fed up' with Banda's demands which were 'criminal exploitation of the masses. Let him look for suitable suckers elsewhere.' He chuckled when told that at a public dinner, 'Banda sounded more like Peter Sellers imitating Adolf Hitler than ever.'

'If you think that I like sitting on the couch with Banda close up to me,' Rowland told George Abindor on his return to Salisbury, 'spitting into my face as he talks, you must be mad. But it's business.'

The gentle charm concealed the consuming ambition. Within the Salisbury office, an emotional web had embraced Lonrho's employees, who willingly attached themselves to a rising star. Kruger was not alone in blessing his fortune in working for a dynamic financial mind. Ian Hossy, a thirty-six-year-old South African mining engineer, recruited in 1962, counted his blessings that he was part of 'an exciting, inspired period'. Flying ceaselessly in a twin-engined Beechcraft between Salisbury and the neighbouring countries, Rowland's unlimited energy and remarkable humour provoked a unanimous chorus: 'There's no deal too big for Tiny.'

Completing the deals was reserved for Rowland. When Colyn Braun, the South African-born general manager, returned from Blantyre having signed a contract for the railways, Rowland exploded: 'How dare you!' Nic Kruger understood. 'Tiny always had to do the deals. He couldn't stand being upstaged.' Colin MacKenzie, the manager of Willoughby's who joined the Lonrho board in 1963, discovered the same. Lonrho's directors could not challenge Rowland's negotiations and decisions: 'Tiny was the boss.'

Rowland's egotism rubbed shoulders with his sensitivity. Arriving in the Lonrho office one morning, George Abindor passed Rowland rushing down the corridor towards his car. Braun explained that the plane for Blantyre was waiting at the airport especially for Rowland. Minutes later, Rowland burst into the office: 'Why didn't you say hello to me, George? I'm being ignored.' Astonished, Abindor realised that the giant wanted to be loved. 'Why do you people from Johannesburg always look down on us?' asked Rowland. Rowland had good reason to be wary of Abindor. At Lonrho's annual general meeting in London, Alan Ball had disclosed that the development of Kanyemba was proving 'unexpectedly and consistently poor'. Ball blamed 'adverse factors' and admitted that there was 'concern' about the whole mine. The original prediction one year earlier that 211,000 tons of ore would be mined had been substituted by an estimated 69,000 tons. Gold production was less than a quarter of what Rademeyer had calculated. The price of Kanyemba shares fell from 37.5 pence to under 15 pence.

Similarly, Ball disclosed that another part of Rowland's dowry to Lonrho was less profitable than anticipated. Eight months after Rowland's engineers at the Mashaba mine had forecast a glowing future, they now cautioned that the mine was practically worthless, having lost £10,000 rather than producing the forecast profit of £36,000.

Finally, contrary to Rowland's predictions, the pre-tax profits at Norton Motors were £53,000 instead of £84,000.

Naturally, the annual report disguised the bad news by reporting 'record profits' without emphasising that the money was obtained by selling off cattle and land to cover soaring expenses which included the move to new offices on the fifth and sixth floor of Cheapside House. At least some money was saved on the decoration by retaining the brown linoleum and not painting over the grey walls.

The fall in the share prices, noticed particularly by investors in Rhodesia and South Africa, was highlighted by Wilfred Brookes: 'For the first time the question "Who is this man Rowland – and what is his background?" is being asked.' Suspiciously, Brookes anticipated a crash from the 'risk and speculation' and the 'confused and breathless' expansion because there was no obvious source of money.

The criticism infuriated Rowland. As he explained to his friend Wally Milne: 'I would be happy to buy all the Kanyemba shares back but that's been forbidden by Ball.' Ball reasoned, according to Rowland, that if Kanyemba were subsequently profitable, the shareholders would complain of being cheated.

Rowland's anger was compounded by his inability to bring similar pressure upon Brookes to that he exercised upon other journalists. The previous year, he had become associated with the Corner House Group which controlled Rhodesia's principal newspaper publishers, the Argus Group. Using that association, Rowland had enjoined the owners to suppress any critical comment. Only Brookes was beyond his orbit.

Brookes remained unconvinced and was invited to Lonrho House. In a style which would be repeated for the next thirty years, Rowland, with Sir Peter Bednall at his side, delivered a three-hour monologue explaining his dedication to business and the country and asking his audience to ignore 'a little mine like Kanyemba'.

'Look how much I'm doing for Rhodesia and to rehabilitate Lonrho,' he challenged the unimpressed journalist. 'You should apologise for your criticism.' Brookes again challenged Rowland about the real losses suffered by the shareholders and subsequently wrote, 'Events have so far justified the refusal to publish such a withdrawal.' After all, Rowland cleared £225,000 in cash and retained 60 per cent of the company plus the profits of any shares sold at the top of the market.

Brookes and other white supremacists, recalling Rowland's origins, began noticing his associates, in particular, Peter Staub, the member of parliament, and Freddie Hoffman, a businessman. Both supported Africans' rights and were classified as communists. The three were dubbed 'Berlin Jews'. To counter Brookes and the adverse propaganda, Rowland recruited Archie Levin, a financial journalist, for £5000 per annum, to feed favourable stories to the newspapers.

Simultaneously, Rowland stepped back. Quietly he dropped his scheme to build another pipeline carrying either maize or coal from Rhodesia to Beira and sought a cosmetic solution to remove the accusations of dishonesty over Kanyemba.

Rowland had already sold many of Lonrho's mining interests in Rhodesia for cash. The remainder, including Kanyemba, were grouped in one Rhodesian company, Corsyn, which in turn was wholly owned by the publicly quoted South African company, Coronation Syndicate.

Shareholders in the Kanyemba mine were offered shares in Coronation Syndicate at a specially low price. It was a blatant but successful public relations exercise to save Rowland's reputation whose cost was not borne by Lonrho but by the other shareholders. Lonrho, the principal shareholder, managed Coronation Syndicate as if it was wholly owned. The ruse eventually brought Rowland to the precipice of disaster.

Although Rowland was well known in Salisbury, he markedly and, many believed, deliberately withdrew from social gatherings. Kanyemba had tarnished his reputation and his name no longer evinced simple neutrality. The social chatter which was such an unavoidable element of the garden parties and cocktail evenings in colonial Salisbury bored Rowland. 'He wasn't socially shy,' observed Percy, 'he just wasn't interested in people if they were no use to him.' His disdain was probably a reaction to the absence of any invitations to Government House. Rowland was not welcome. By nature he was not an insider. Inevitably, Rowland harboured resentment towards those who were invited to Salisbury's social events, including Percy: 'He couldn't tolerate that an employee had influence in circles where he was unknown.' On one occasion, Rowland telephoned Percy from London: 'Meet me tomorrow in Nairobi.'

'I can't,' replied Percy. 'I'm having dinner with the Governor.'

'Cancel it,' said Rowland.

'I can't. It would be impolite.'

'Cancel it,' snapped Rowland, 'or consider your position with Lonrho.'

Percy cancelled the invitation. Rowland's control over an employee was total.

But Rowland was not averse to using social connections when it seemed appropriate. Lonrho's board was dominated by Old Etonians, and on 24 April 1963 Ogilvy married HRH Princess Alexandra of Kent, a first cousin of the Queen. In an era when the royal family was still unreservedly revered, the wedding was a newsworthy social occasion. Rowland was invited to the glittering national event and offered to give the couple a Bentley as a gift. 'Tiny is spontaneously generous,' Ogilvy explained, 'but so naive. I persuaded him that it was impossible.' Instead, Ogilvy received a carpet. The celebration was the closest Rowland would ever come to hospitality provided by the royal family although the genuine friendship between him and Ogilvy embraced the princess. Rowland was always delighted to be invited for tea to the family home, Thatch House in Richmond Park, and, not surprisingly, was quick to recognise the commercial advantages. Thereafter it was not rare for Lonrho's employees in Africa to hear the managing director extolling the company's special connections with the royal family. 'Tiny made it his task to know all the very rich,' Ogilvy would tell a friend. 'Later he managed to quarrel with most of them.'

Rowland's ambitions cost him his relationship with Irene. Increasingly, instead of returning to High Noon and arguing with his partner, he would arrive at Wally Milne's home to eat scrambled eggs or drive with them in his Rolls Royce to Meikles hotel to eat snails with brown bread and coffee. Even his forty-sixth birthday was celebrated at Milne's home. The two men and Greta Milne ate scrambled eggs. Milne gave his friend an English gold five-guinea piece. 'I'll keep that as a lucky token,' said Rowland who, as always in high spirits, kept his companions amused with accounts of his exploits and plans. 'Why don't you go into politics?' asked Greta. 'Oh, it's too dirty for me,' replied Rowland, who well understood the power of the organ grinder. At the end of the evening, Rowland often returned to Lonrho House to sleep in the small flat on the ground floor.

On those occasions when he slept at High Noon, Rowland did not share a bedroom with Irene. The arguments were becoming too distressing. Several times, Kruger was telephoned in the middle of the night to intercede between the quarrelsome couple until, in mid-1963, Rowland telephoned at 2 a.m. 'How long will it take you to get here?'

'Thirty minutes,' replied Kruger.

'That's too long.'

Kruger arrived to find Rowland in an emotional state. His employer jumped into the car. 'That's it. It's all over. I'm leaving forever.' Everything was abandoned, including a Rolls Royce and a Mercedes. 'Tiny was too emotional to drive,' recalled Kruger. It was to be a complete break with the person and the past. To his credit, after Irene resisted all requests to leave the house, Rowland agreed that she remain rent free in the house. Through Kruger, all her bills were paid, including nursing care when she became geriatric in the late 1980s. Unencumbered by any personal ties, Rowland dedicated every moment to creating his empire.

The close relationship with Hastings Banda had bestowed on Rowland and Lonrho useful credibility in neighbouring countries, albeit that Banda, a non-socialist, was neither an ally of Julius Nyerere in Tanzania nor of Kenneth Kaunda in Zambia.

Zambia, rich in copper, gemstones and other minerals, was a particular magnet for Rowland who, soon after Percy's recruitment, flew to Lusaka to meet the future prime minister in Percy's house.

Kaunda was born in 1924 near the Congo border and his father was a Church of Scotland missionary. A teetotaller, a former scoutmaster and a practising Christian whose deep religious beliefs convinced some that he was naive and others that he was an honest and popular politician, Kaunda was leading the campaign for his country's independence.

Rowland's style established the nature of their future relationship which would be critically supportive of Rowland's career. Quietly ingratiating, listening rather than speaking, Rowland encouraged the future prime minister to believe his interest in the politician's opinions and understand the mutual advantages of cooperation between Lonrho and Zambia. Kaunda requested a donation for his election fund, and graciously Rowland complied, sealing the rapport between the two men. Naturally, on Rowland's part, there was an unspoken agenda.

Convinced that the newly independent Zambia would expropriate the British South Africa Company's mineral rights, Rowland proposed to Kaunda that Lonrho would take over and manage the assets in co-operation with the new government. Rowland's salesmanship, which would be endlessly exercised throughout the continent, was initially persuasive: 'Use our expertise to help Zambia get the benefits of these companies which previously you lost.' The opportunity of undermining the British corporation appealed to Rowland. Percy continued the negotiations but eventually Kaunda perceived his own interests. During Zambia's independence celebrations, Kaunda issued an ultimatum to the BSA chairman: if BSA did not surrender all its assets voluntarily to Zambia in return for some compensation, everything would be nationalised.

Rowland, bursting with prospective deals, found Kaunda's rejection of one proposal a surmountable disappointment because there were so many others. Percy was dispatched to Livingston with two letters, written by Rowland and addressed to Rowland, for Kaunda to sign. The first invited Lonrho to present its terms for building an explosives factory in the copper belt; while the second asked Lonrho to prepare a feasibility study for a rail link between Zambia and Tanzania. After hours of discussion in a dusty townhouse, Kaunda signed. Ecstatic about Percy's success, Rowland hired a private plane to collect his manager and awaited the hero of the hour on the tarmac in Salisbury. Like everyone else employed by Lonrho, Percy was enthralled by the sheer exhilaration of working with Rowland, a quality hard to find with other businessmen.

The glossy, leather-bound feasibility study of the 500-mile railway line which Rowland and Percy presented to Kaunda in November 1963 extolled the advantages for Zambian copper of using the shorter route to the Indian Ocean rather than relying upon the Benguela railway through Zaïre. The plans for the proposed £17-million railway were ink lines crudely drawn on an old ordnance map. 'It's amateurish but it will do,' Percy laughed. The charge to the Zambian government was £150,000.

By any measure, it was an ambitious project for a small private company to undertake but Rowland's enthusiasm was infectious. 'We shall keep our surveyors only 100 miles ahead of the track layers,' he told Kaunda. 'Then as soon as the track has settled, the locomotives will start running. That way, you don't waste any time, and the railway makes money as fast as it advances.'

Optimistically, Rowland called upon Elias Chipimo, the acting permanent secretary at Zambia's Ministry of Transport to 'push every button and shove on every door' to win the contract. Chipimo was unimpressed by his frequent visitor because, despite Rowland's humble approach, 'seeking to fit in wherever he could', he was 'aggressively simplistic'. Rowland, according to the official, did not understand the political environment in which he was touting for work.

That view was shared by Harry Grenfell, an Old Etonian who had lost his legs during the war and was an employee of the British South Africa company, Lonrho's competitor: 'If decisions involving large sums of money are going to be taken by African politicians without proper consideration of the economic merits of the project, then I can only forecast that the poorer will get poorer.' Blind to his own miscalculation, Rowland commented that Grenfell was 'amusing'.

Like so many African nationalists, Kaunda's policy was anti-imperialist and anti-West. Regardless of the financial package which Rowland could assemble, Kaunda was attracted to the Soviet bloc, prepared to pay any price to secure Zambia's allegiance. 'Rowland couldn't understand the African political scene,' recalls Chipimo with prejudice. 'No one even wanted to know what he proposed. He was politically wiped out.'

Rowland's *naïveté* was pinpointed by Dennis Grennan, a British socialist who served as Kaunda's personal adviser. 'Rowland was a Rhodesian with a chequered background, a chancer with an aggressive reputation, and that irritated Simon Kapwepwe, [the future vice president].' Like many who had campaigned for Zambia's independence, Kapwepwe was sceptical of any white man's conversion to decolonisation. Rowland's good relations with the whites in Rhodesia proved to Kapwepwe that Lonrho was as untrustworthy as any other British company. Kaunda rejected Lonrho's proposal. The railway was eventually built by the Chinese government for an estimated £3 billion.

Non-prestigious businesses, similarly discounted by the political turmoil, were easier targets for Lonrho. Settlers anxious to raise any money and flee from nationalist rule, reminiscent for Rowland of the Jews' stampede from Nazi Germany, gratefully accepted any price in their bid to escape. In Zambia, Lonrho opened branches of Consolidated Motors, which owned the Mercedes franchise, while in Tanzania the company took over sisal and tea plantations and Riddoch's Motors, which owned the Ford franchise, at comparatively low prices reflecting the buyers' market. Victor Milward, the country's major road hauler, was offered to Rowland for £400,000. Rowland paid £90,000, two thirds in South Africa. Others were paid in Lonrho shares, an astute method to overcome the new exchange regulations and to protect Lonrho's depleted cash reserves.

Characteristic of those deals was Rowland's purchase of a 55 per cent interest in the Kundalilla mine producing rich purple, semi-precious amethysts.

The mine, which in reality was a hill of pure amethyst ore, lay 250 miles south of Lusaka. It was opened in 1959, and the owner, Kenneth Horden, had proven the mine's riches but had failed to sell the gems. His finances exhausted and fearing expropriation by the new government, Horden granted Dan Mayers, the American gemstone dealer who tipped Rowland about the Sandawana emerald mine, an exclusive distribution agreement in return for financial guarantees.

Rowland's relationship with Mayers had developed during the weeks after the Sandawana deal. Appreciating that Mayers' expertise was of value to his ambition to challenge Anglo American's gem empire, Rowland had travelled with Mayers to Bogota, Colombia, and ridden on mules high into the mountains to inspect other emerald deposits. Mayers, who considered that he had 'made Tiny' because of the Sandawana deal, recalled the journey as 'interesting' despite Rowland's adamant refusal to 'speak about women or his tax status'. Rowland, he believed, 'possessed the most brilliant mind I've ever met. But he's like a child, using his intellect to achieve what he wants and he wants to get his way.' Rowland was less flattering about Mayers although the American said that 'we were best of friends'. After one week in the Colombian mountains they abandoned their quest, but personal preferences were irrelevant when Mayers proposed a deal on the Kundalilla mine.

Ian Hossy, Lonrho's mining expert, was dispatched secretly to survey the mine. He concluded that Kundalilla was 'unique in the world with regard to quantity, quality and ease of working' since the stones lay just inches beneath the surface. With Mayers' agreement, Rowland approached Horden's sons [the father had died] with a bid to take over 55 per cent of the mine for £51,500. 'Rowland told them,' recalls Mayers, 'that there was a good chance that when Kaunda became president he would nationalise the mine. Rowland's friendship with Kaunda would prevent that confiscation.' Rowland subsequently described those recollections as 'absolutely balderdash'. In the event, they accepted Rowland's proposition, retaining 25 per cent of the shares and Crystals S.A., Mayers' company, taking the remaining 20 per cent.

Rowland's conduct thereafter was noticeably strange. Instead of placing the 55 per cent interest in the mine's holding company, Northern Minerals [Zambia] Limited, directly into Lonrho, 30 per cent was assigned to Northchart, a Rhodesian company, and 25 per cent to Coronation Syndicate, the South African publicly quoted company whose mines were located in Rhodesia. The apportionment, to reduce taxation payments, was confusing. The mine was in Zambia, the ownership was divided between Rhodesia and South Africa and the only people aware of the whole operation were in Britain. Eventually, the mystery would cause an explosion.

For the moment, Rowland would have no further involvement in the mine's management, finance or distribution of the amethysts. That responsibility was assigned to Fred Butcher who watched approvingly as Mayers developed annual sales from a paltry $1000 per month to nearly $100,000 five years later. Rowland was simply content that another deal had been completed while, like a Hoover, he sought other opportunities beyond Lonrho's mining, cattle ranching, motors, sugar, explosives, matches and textiles, railways, road haulage and pipeline businesses.

In January 1964, Rowland flew to Mexico for one week's

holiday complaining of 'fatigue'. Gradually, he was realising that the crude arithmetic of business in nationalist Africa showed peculiar advantages which others seemed to ignore. His formula was to limit severely investment of hard currencies *into* Africa but ensure the remittance of maximum dividends in hard currencies *from* Africa to London. His soothing commitment to the African leaders, he hoped, glossed over the reality.

As Lonrho's debts increased, purchases in Africa were completed by the issue of more Lonrho shares. To maintain the value of those shares, Lonrho's profits were, with the help of creative, albeit legitimate accountancy, forecast as 'record highs'.

Once purchased, all Lonrho operations were, on Rowland's orders, self-financing. All costs and expenses inside the African country were paid in local currency while profits, paid as dividends, were converted into hard currency and sent to London. When inflation then ravaged those African economies, the internal costs were minimal compared to the income earned from the exports. The conundrum was then how to hide the hard currency income from the African governments. The unusual ownership of the Kundalilla mine was evidence of Lonrho's avoidance of Zambia's exchange controls.

Yet Zambia was becoming the kernel of Lonrho's expansion. The breakthrough was the purchase of Max Heinrich's brewery. The gnome-like German had become rich creating Chibuku, the most popular beer in Zambia's copperbelt, but his wealth was imperilled.

On the eve of independence, Heinrich had been persuaded to invest some of the beer profits into a new newspaper which would serve the black miners who were otherwise dependent upon the South African-owned *Northern News*.

In his ignorance, Heinrich bought a defunct, twenty-five-year-old printing press in South Africa which after a 2000-mile voyage was haphazardly reassembled in Kitwe. Those recruited to write and edit the new *Zambia Daily News* and *Sunday News* were not the finest of the journalists' profession, producing unintelligible and unreadable newspapers.

Convinced that it was politically impossible for the newspaper to be closed, Heinrich's depression accumulated with the losses.

Exhausted he sought a buyer for his whole company which included a modern hotel and some property. Rowland, the only deal maker in the region, flew in October 1964 to Ndola and paid £800,000 for a profitable brewery and an albatross.

The deal, which coincided with Zambia becoming independent, on 24 October 1964, was Rowland's breakthrough in Zambia and eventually, with Kaunda's help, in black Africa. The most senior black Zambian employed at Heinrich's brewery was Tom Mtine, a thirty-eight-year-old of limited business acumen but who had just been elected Ndola's first mayor and was close to Kaunda. Recognising that some of the new president's entourage were ill-disposed towards him, Rowland flattered and recruited Mtine to become Lonrho's chairman in Zambia, the first of Lonrho's African 'runners'.

Mtine, who fell in and out of favour with Rowland over the following decades, believed that Rowland came to Zambia 'to help the country. He didn't only want to earn profits.' The evidence was Rowland's tactful treatment of his first newspaper.

Unable and unwilling to close the newspaper, he sought to cover his costs by expansion. His target was the *African Mail* which was founded in 1960 by Richard Hall, an energetic and devoted supporter of African nationalism. Hall had secured the financial support of David Astor, whose family trust owned the *Observer* in London. Long before it was either fashionable or a natural progression, Astor was dedicated to decolonisation and black majority rule and, as the *Mail*'s debts increased, continued to subsidise a pro-African newspaper against the white colonialists.

Since the newspaper's circulation could not rise above 30,000 because of the primitive printing presses, Astor, who could no longer afford the subsidy, was keen to sell. The price was £100,000, his total subsidy over the previous four years. Rowland resisted the offer. Instead, he bought the *Northern News*, merged it with Heinrich's *News* and named the new newspaper *The Times of Zambia*. Dick Hall was hired as editor. 'Tiny was a nervous editor,' recalls Hall. 'He had little experience of newspapers and hadn't learnt yet how to put the screws on an editor.' Kaunda bought Astor's *Mail* for just £40,000, an unwelcome insight into nationalist gratitude for the liberal white.

By the new *The Times of Zambia*, Hall's major concern was whether the thrusting capitalist who had no proven record as a supporter of black nationalism would interfere in his editorship. 'You must not think about that,' exclaimed Rowland. 'Put it right out of your mind. You must run the paper as you wish. We shall never interfere. Never.' Hall claims that Rowland's assurance remained unbroken: 'Rowland kept his distance'. Others dispute Hall's conviction.

At the end of 1964, the foundations of Rowland's influence in Zambia had been established, while simultaneously he had created a source of genuine profits in South Africa by increasing Lonrho's ownership of coal mines.

On 22 December 1964 the £3.5 million pipeline opened. Although the triumph was muted by the failure to complete the refinery, Rowland's achievement was considerable. The 49 per cent stake had cost Lonrho only £500,000 while its exclusive contract with Shell and BP not to deliver oil to Rhodesia by any other route seemed to guarantee uninterrupted profits.

Ogilvy's confidence in Rowland had been proven. Lonrho's profits had doubled, the company employed 20,000 people in sixty-three subsidiaries and Rowland's ceaseless travels through southern and eastern Africa promised another record year. The only doubts were in the political crisis developing in Salisbury.

The breakup of the Federation and the independence of Zambia and Malawi had prompted the British settlers in Rhodesia to demand their complete sovereignty. The legislation granting self-rule in 1923 protected the rights of the Africans but had never been invoked, encouraging the settlers' conviction of self-government. Whitehall's refusal to grant independence to a minority government when the Federation collapsed swept aside moderate politicians. Throughout 1965, Ian Smith, the new prime minister, threatened to unilaterally declare independence and resist the mediatory attempts by Harold Wilson, the British prime minister, to find a compromise.

By October, only the possibility of a British military invasion was deterring Smith's declaration of a formal break. On 8 October, Wilson, under pressure from lobby groups in London, publicly rejected the use of force to prevent or suppress any anticipated rebellion, but warned Smith that if he dared to declare independence, many countries would impose sanctions. Smith was unimpressed. On 25 October, Wilson flew to Salisbury and renewed his warning of the inevitability of oil sanctions. Smith showed little concern. Since the possibility of direct intervention had been excluded, Smith believed that the only requirement to Rhodesia's survival was a guarantee by Rhodesia's two neighbours, South Africa and the Portuguese government in Mozambique, to continue the supply of oil to the landlocked country.

From both Pretoria and Lisbon, Smith received messages of positive neutrality. As Wilson publicly dithered, Dick de Bruyne, Shell's co-ordinator for Africa, arrived secretly in Salisbury to reassure the government that oil sanctions were unlikely since Zambia would automatically also become a victim. But de Bruyne also knew that there was a contingency plan with Total, the French petroleum company. In the event of oil sanctions, a swap arrangement with Total guaranteed Rhodesian oil supplies, while Shell would fulfil the French company's contracts. Simultaneously, a Portuguese emissary reassured Smith's ministers that oil supplies would be guaranteed from Mozambique. Smith's final hurdle was to secure a supply route. Anticipating that Lonrho's pipeline might be closed as a target of sanctions, Rhodesia's civil servants planned for oil supplies by road and rail. In the meantime, the country accumulated an unprecedented stockpile, sufficient for one month's consumption.

As the tension in Salisbury grew, Rowland flew to Lusaka. Huge profits could be earned in a crisis and Lonrho needed, more than ever, to diversify.

Entering from the president's private door, Rowland appeared in the office of Valentine Musakanya, the secretary to the Cabinet. Musakanya, Zambia's most important civil servant, was even more impressed when his unexpected visitor strode up to the wall map of southern Africa and drew a line in pencil from

Dar es Salaam, on the Tanzanian coast, to Ndola in Zambia's copperbelt.

'I can forget my Rhodesian pipeline,' Rowland said to Musakanya. 'I want to build one here.' The Zambian, who would become quite close to Rowland during the following years, considered the idea 'mad and preposterous' but was persuaded of its feasibility. Yet the official was not sympathetic towards the financial package which Rowland said the British government would fund. Especially because Rowland was in alliance with BP and Shell.

Recently Musakanya had visited the Commonwealth Office in London to enlist their support in an important venture. In anticipation of the Unilateral Declaration of Independence [UDI], Zambia needed road tankers to transport essential oil supplies from Tanzania. Shell and BP had fifteen unused tankers in Nigeria. Musakanya wanted their transfer to Zambia. But consistent with their supine tradition, the British civil servants refused to approve the proposal. 'It will provoke the Rhodesians,' Musakanya was told.

'I was angry,' recalls Musakanya, 'and when the Italians offered a cheaper pipeline which would be built in sixteen months rather than Rowland's three years, I supported giving the contract to the Italians.'

Three
A Decade of Dreams

Ian Smith's Unilateral Declaration of Independence was announced on 11 November 1965. In his lunchtime radio broadcast, bringing the country to a halt, Smith spoke of striking 'a blow for the preservation of justice, civilisation and Christianity'. Black majority rule, said the leader of the new rebel regime, was to be deferred for one thousand years. Harold Wilson portrayed UDI as 'the greatest moral issue which Britain has had to face in the post-war world', and announced limited sanctions which did not include oil.

In Lonrho House, Rowland was dejected. 'British paratroopers', he told Kruger as he sank into an insuperable depression, 'will be landing by lunchtime. There'll be violence. It's all over. A total disaster.' Rowland even predicted that Ian Smith would be taken away in chains.

Later that afternoon, David Wadman, a legal adviser, discovered Rowland in tears. 'I'm ruined,' he sobbed, his head covered by his hands. 'My business is destroyed.' Among the fictions which later gained currency was an account that Rowland, at the end of that day, staged a public protest and was imprisoned. Of course, nothing of the sort occurred but UDI was another watershed in Rowland's life.

There is no reason to doubt that Rowland's emotions were genuine. Politically, he opposed racism and, commercially, Lonrho's annual pre-tax profits which had nearly doubled again to £1.8 million were jeopardised. But there was an amusing paradox. In the previous four years, Lonrho had been speculatively acquiring businesses across the borders at discounted prices because of political uncertainty. Yet when similar instability hit his own country, Rowland's reaction was as distraught as that of the settlers whose valuations he had mercilessly squeezed. Similarly afflicted, he could not see the potential profits in Rhodesia's crisis. The substantial portion of Rowland's wealth, held by Shepton Estates, was deposited in Rhodesia and automatically blocked by sanctions. On the eve of his forty-eighth birthday, Rowland risked, for the third time, losing his fortune. Opposed to Smith's regime, he saw no reason to sacrifice his new wealth.

On the second day of UDI, Rowland made a clean and public break from Rhodesia. Flying to Lusaka, he obtained a new British passport, number 675087, and registered as a resident of Zambia. Simultaneously, to prove his break from Rhodesia, he registered his Zambian residency in Malawi. There is no evidence that he applied in Salisbury to deregister as a resident of Rhodesia. But ironically, despite all his protestations of love for Africa and its peoples, Rowland had no intention of living in a black African country.

Based in London, he began to calculate how to manage the whole company from Britain, while seeming to isolate Lonrho's profitable Rhodesian operation from his emerging empire in the black states. Even the company's name, he reasoned, should be jettisoned. However, hours of speculation to forge a new corporate name proved unfruitful.

Unlike the major oil corporations and established pan-African giants such as Inchcape, Anglo American, Consolidated and Rio Tinto whose indispensability compelled African governments to ignore their political allegiances, Lonrho was small, still irrelevant and vulnerable to the hysterical anger sweeping black Africa against the Rhodesian settlers. Proving Rowland's pro-African credentials had become essential. Kenneth Kaunda, about to become the direst victim of the undeclared war, seemed to be a natural ally. But Rowland's approaches to resume their early relationship were blocked by Dennis Grennan, his personal assistant: 'I just told Rowland that KK had no time.' The early days were not easy for Rowland.

On his arrival in London, Rowland met Sir Burke Trend,

the secretary to the Cabinet. According to Rowland, he urged upon the civil servant, 'a very workable and painless solution . . . which in part depended upon the swift action of the British government in slicing Britain's financial links with Rhodesia'. Claiming support from 'some of the most influential non-racial Rhodesians', Rowland was assured that his plan would be passed to Harold Wilson. 'You can leave this little man [Smith] to us – God bless his little heart,' said Trend who, like most Whitehall officials, subscribed to the notion that the rebellion would be speedily crushed. Rowland was reassured.

In mid-November, the unequivocal success of UDI and the evident unwillingness of the Wilson government to topple the illegal government provoked the African states to demand more effective sanctions. On 20 November, the United Nations approved an embargo of all oil supplies to Rhodesia. By then, the Smith regime had accumulated a three-month stockpile. One month later, after winning Washington's support, the British government issued an Order in Council forbidding all British registered companies to supply oil to Rhodesia. Reflecting the deep divisions in Britain, some members of the Conservative Party voted against the embargo while others abstained. With characteristic hyperbole, Wilson reassured the world that the efficacy of the oil sanctions spelled the inevitable doom of the Smith regime 'within weeks rather than months'.

The British legislation however was nebulous. Under British law, it was criminal for British companies to trade with Rhodesia but this did not prevent their foreign-registered subsidiaries supplying goods and services to the illegal regime. British companies could retain their Rhodesian subsidiaries although, in an undefined manner, their relationship was to be broken. Apparently, neither Wilson nor Whitehall wished to recognise the inconsistency.

The credibility and efficacy of sanctions depended upon Shell and British Petroleum. Without oil supplies, Rhodesia would grind to a halt. Yet the oil corporations' management in London, in the absence of firm instructions from Whitehall, were content to be guided by the South African government and permit their South African subsidiaries to supply refined oil products across the border. As the flow, first by road and later by rail, increased, MI6 alerted the government that the oil sanctions were being blatantly ignored by British-owned companies. Their warnings were similarly ignored. Petrol rationing in Salisbury was soon relaxed. The sanctions were only affecting impoverished Zambia. 'We were misled,' Harold Wilson later rued, blaming bad advice from his officials and self-delusion. Others accused Wilson of lying to protect himself.

The legislation naturally was of utmost importance to Lonrho. As sanctions were announced, Andrew Caldecott, the solicitor, formally advised his fellow directors that they should consider separating Lonrho and themselves personally from the company in Rhodesia. Caldecott did not take his own advice seriously. Nor did Rowland. No one believed that UDI would last and Lonrho's directors, like everyone else in London, were not contemplating the sacrifice of the company's major assets, especially since the legislation did not outlaw the continuation of Lonrho's businesses in Rhodesia. The illegality was to trade with Rhodesia. Caldecott shared his fellow directors' attitude: 'People turned a blind eye' to sanctions breaking 'and I perhaps did nothing to discourage it.'

In contrast to other British companies, however, Lonrho suffered an irreconcilable conflict. The company was expanding in black Africa yet owned Rhodesia's visible source of lifeblood, the oil pipeline. Rowland's predicament was unenviable. Building the pipeline had been a Herculean effort and investment, while its revenue, 10 per cent of Lonrho's income in the first year, was important to the company's prosperity. Losing that income was unavoidable. Off the Mozambique coast, a British navy patrol was posturing to prevent oil tankers docking at Beira. *De facto*, the pipeline was already closed.

Lonrho too needed to be seen publicly in Africa as an opponent of Smith, especially since Rowland believed that UDI would end within five months. On 4 January, Caldecott, Ball and Rowland flew to Lisbon to vote for the closure of the pipeline. Technically Lonrho could be outvoted by the Portuguese majority, but their hosts were persuaded that, if only to safeguard their own country's oil supplies from the international embargo, the pipeline's closure should be announced formally. For Rowland, it was a resounding success. To the British public, Lonrho was obeying the law and the Smith regime had suffered a grievous blow. Reflecting upon his good conduct, Rowland began negotiations with the British government for compensation. Monthly payments of £54,000 began in April 1966 to bribe Lonrho not to pump any oil which might be delivered. Five months later, once a naval patrol was established, the payments ceased.

Rowland and his directors had by then realised that the government's oil sanctions were an expensive charade. Telephone conversations with Salisbury confirmed that oil supplies were normal. From Lusaka, where he had just negotiated the takeover of Smith and Youngson, the country's principal road hauler whose trucks were indispensable for Zambia's struggle to survive sanctions, Rowland decided to return to Salisbury to reassess Lonrho's strategy.

Lonrho's operation in Rhodesia was run by Nicholas Kruger, the South African accountant from the Transvaal. Like Rowland, Kruger opposed UDI but was committed to the company's survival which, at that stage, was not assured. Within two years, Lonrho's debts had tripled from £3.4 million to £9.6 million. Rowland's heady expansion across the continent, buying breweries in Botswana and Swaziland, more coal mines in South Africa and Smiths in Zambia had depleted the finances. Kruger had been warned by the Reserve Bank to reduce Lonrho's borrowings. In the Rhodesian Treasury, the minister ordered officials to 'let Lonrho stew a bit. They backed the wrong horse.' But the company was too important to ignore and, with Kruger as 'the acceptable face of Lonrho' in charge, a working arrangement was established whereby Lonrho observed the requirements and laws of the rebel regime.

During that visit, on 8 March 1966, Rowland was summoned to Ian Smith's office in Salisbury. Their mutual antagonism had erupted before UDI when Rowland purposely employed General 'Jock' Anderson, the commander of the Rhodesian military forces, who had resigned rather than obey Smith. Anderson, to Smith's irritation, was employed managing Lonrho's match factory in Zambia. According to Rowland, Smith 'ordered' the reopening of the pipeline by the construction of a new connection in Beira. Rowland alleges he was threatened that his refusal would result in imprisonment, and claims that at the end of 'this unpleasant meeting', he was escorted under guard and later released. Ian Smith denies the melodramatic account.

Their political disagreement did not prevent Rowland's visits to Rhodesia. Arriving at night, his drive from the airport to meet Kruger at Lonrho house was concealed from other employees. 'Sometimes he'd only spend a few hours there,' recalled Colin MacKenzie although the subterfuge would be dropped in later years.

Sitting in his office, a single white telephone and the framed photograph of himself standing with his mother on his desk, Rowland agreed with Kruger that Lonrho, like many other British corporations, would ignore sanctions. He would maintain overall control by telephone and telex, using codewords to describe personalities, countries and commodities. Kruger would be responsible for the detailed daily management.

The decision to flout the law inevitably inhibited open discussion in the Cheapside board room. For Rowland, naturally reluctant to consult all the directors, the progression to greater secrecy was not intractable. But running Lonrho, as Rowland desired, required subterfuge and deviousness. That dishonesty would spread beyond the need to conceal Lonrho's Rhodesian activities into the very nature of managing the corporation. To outsiders, however, Rowland seemed to have distanced himself from any transgressions.

Amid the hiatus of UDI, Rowland knew that his valuable share options were endangered. Under the original 1961 arrangement, Rowland could buy 2 million Lonrho shares for 35 pence per share. That amounted to 45.3 per cent of Lonrho's share capital. The option, granted to Shepton Estates, expired in August 1966. As a Rhodesian company, Shepton was subject to sanctions. It was neither in Rowland's nor Lonrho's interest that nearly half the company's shares should fall under the control of the illegal Rhodesian government.

Rowland was personally beset with further problems. Although Lonrho's share price was quoted at about 35 pence, he did not possess £700,000 to purchase the shares. All his assets, including the 1.5 million Lonrho shares which he had originally been given in exchange for his own assets, were held by Shepton Estates. Even if he were to borrow £700,000, he was disinclined to abandon his wealth to Rhodesian control or bring it within the grasp of the British Inland Revenue.

Accordingly, in the aftermath of UDI, Rowland began to conceive a plan to accommodate his interests: firstly to extend the period of the option and secondly to reduce the price. Those changes required the board's agreement but Rowland was increasingly confident that his fellow directors, albeit officers of a publicly owned company, would agree.

Rowland's relationship with other men was certainly idiosyncratic. His charm, natural but certainly controlled, offered a unique intimacy which appealed to weaker men such as Alan Ball, who sought comfort for his congenital misery in increasing consumption of alcohol. 'Alan was like a rabbit in headlights whenever Tiny was around,' recalled Percy. Around Christmas 1965, Rowland began discussing his needs with Lonrho's chairman.

Rowland had not only proven his enormous value to Alan Ball but had converted the majority of his fellow directors to his gospel. Caldecott had observed how Rowland had transformed 'a sleepy dozy company into something dynamic' but within an atmosphere where natural excitement occasionally developed into frenzy. In accepting Rowland, who was so persuasive and evidently successful, the directors had to tolerate a man who often teetered on the verge of emotional outbursts if he feared that his decisions were being challenged. 'A sort of tyrant and part madman', Caldecott realised in later years when Rowland's prolonged sojourns in London allowed his true nature to emerge.

At that stage, Caldecott's unspoken reservations were exceptional. Rowland was admired by those who had witnessed Lonrho's astonishing evolution within four years from a Rhodesian mining and ranching company to a conglomerate operating in ten African countries. Ball was instinctively accommodating to Rowland's needs and was supported by Sir Robert Adeane, the associate of Harley Drayton who also owned various interests throughout Africa.

Out of his friendship with Rowland arose Adeane's curiosity about the latter's apparent lack of interest in women. One night in Johannesburg, when Rowland was a guest at Adeane's house, Rowland had refused to accept an invitation to dinner at Harry Oppenheimer's. 'I won't accept his hospitality,' he told Adeane, who was accompanied by his friend Pauline Wallace, the Irish owner of the Apron Strings club and later Mayfair's Casanova gambling club. After the dinner, Adeane invited Wallace back to the house. 'Meet Tiny,' urged Adeane, 'and tell me why he doesn't like women. But be on your best behaviour.'

Rowland was in bed when Wallace entered. Papers were strewn everywhere. 'So you're the woman hater,' she laughed. Rowland, she realised as they sat talking, was simply interested in beating the challenge and amassing power. Yet Wallace's opinion inherently contradicted the popular image of Rowland: 'Money alone didn't mean anything to him,' believes Wallace. 'His ambition was to prove himself. Women could get in his way.' Wealth, he believed, should not be flaunted, especially when the grandee possessed more wealth than himself. Rowland, she discovered, hated the deference which Oppenheimer automatically commanded from the Establishment. To snub the South African, Rowland had abruptly refused to join the South African coal cartel, spurning Oppenheimer's request 'not to rock the boat'. Rowland, it appeared, was happier speaking to an African dictator than the chairman of a multinational, unless he was an equal or, even better, wealthier.

In the developing friendship – Rowland, Adeane and Wallace – the trio flew around southern Africa in Lonrho's Beechcraft. Rowland's humour and disdain for displays of ostentatious living revealed an uncommon chemistry. Consumed by an ambition to build an empire, he was equally dedicated to enjoying himself.

Regularly, late at night in London, he called at Wallace's Casanova Club and dealt the cards at the blackjack table. 'Let's see Robert's face,' he told Pauline Wallace as they entered a casino and moved to the roulette wheel. Rowland placed £500, the equivalent today of nearly £5000, on red. He won. The normally unflappable Adeane was nonplussed.

In recognising Rowland's talents, Adeane noted that, as

Lonrho's deals became technically more complicated, his friend would need advice. There was no one in London better suited to provide that help, Adeane decided after consulting Angus Ogilvy, than Eric Koerner of Warburgs.

Among merchant banks in London, Warburgs was exceptional. Founded in 1946 by a German refugee, the bank, through skill and diligence, had established its reputation amongst the best in the City's premier league. Sigmund Warburg, his peers agreed, had achieved nearly the same in twenty years as the Rothschilds in a century.

There was a natural sympathy between Koerner, a seventy-three-year-old Viennese who had been employed in Austria's Central Bank, and the young Anglo-German who would regularly visit the bank to discuss his plans. In his prime, Koerner had been an exceptional dealer in shares and currency with a particular talent to sell securities. But the old banker lacked any experience in the management of commercial or industrial organisations. Rowland did not notice that handicap. To be accepted by Warburgs had the kudos of a commoner marrying into the British royal family.

Therefore, while Lonrho was fortunate to have the prestigious bank as their adviser, Rowland was less fortunate in that Koerner accepted his new client as a vehicle for resuming his own career rather than recognising that Rowland, essentially a dealer, required careful guidance.

Rowland was also admired by Koerner's young associate, Ian Fraser, an Oxford-educated former journalist who was destined to become one of the City's most respected bankers and regulators. Fraser felt a bond towards Lonrho. In the 1920s, his father, working with Joseph Ball, had been a manager of Coronation Syndicate, the South African mining company.

To both Koerner and Fraser, the potential new client was unusually intelligent and 'full of good ideas'. The aspect of Rowland's attitude which the two bankers found particularly attractive was his 'hit list' of targets in unfashionable areas. His predator's hyperactivity generated excitement and the prospect of profits not only for himself but also for the bankers.

As a final check on Rowland's probity, Fraser visited Cyril

Hawker, the chairman of Standard & Chartered Bank. 'Is he trustworthy?' asked Fraser.

'In all my experiences,' replied Hawker, 'I've never been misled.'

With Warburgs' seal of approval, Lonrho had finally emerged from the backwater. Formally, the bank's role was to act as Rowland's adviser based on a relationship of mutual trust and honesty. Acting like a family doctor, the bankers would expect Rowland to confide in them about his most sensitive intentions and decisions. No one seems to have considered that Rowland would need to effect a change of character to comply.

At an introductory dinner hosted by Fraser at White's – a venue which Rowland would particularly enjoy over the years – the new client spoke for over three hours about Africa and his ambitions. 'We were fascinated,' recalled Arthur Winspear, the deputy of Ian Fraser. Rowland had been accepted by one City institution which, unlike its competitors, did not look askance at the businessman who dealt with the same 'nig nogs' who only months earlier were branded as murderous terrorists by the British government. Bribery, Rowland told his hosts was, contrary to British prejudice, not necessary in Africa: 'They'd be offended if you offered them a bribe.'

During his absences in Africa and hectic pace in Britain, neither of the bankers was troubled that their client was unwilling to compromise to win acceptance in the City. Although Rowland would often talk to Arthur Winspear for hours about the City's prejudice, his instinctive scepticism of a tribe who enjoyed endless alcoholic lunches, afternoons on the golf course and weekdays shooting pheasant, naturally prevented him from joining the club. Indifferent rather than resentful about his exclusion, Rowland judged that the mere fact that Lonrho shares were quoted on the Stock Exchange did not imply his need to become an insider. Those personalities and their institutions had been responsible for his family's misery. There was every reason to avoid contact. The tribes in Africa were more to his taste. 'A freelance vagabond,' concluded Winspear, 'who would have been happier in Wall Street in 1900 when the rail barons ruled without any controls.'

'He didn't know the City and didn't want to become part of it,' comments Fraser. Rowland's prime concern was to generate profits and, as Lonrho's share price rose, he could buy companies in Africa for shares rather than cash. But Fraser is certain that in those early days there was 'never any suggestion that Tiny would play against or outside the rules'. The presence of Ogilvy and MacKenzie as Lonrho directors seemed reassuring.

Although the idea of shareholders' power was still unknown, Lonrho's small annual meetings of about forty shareholders attracted a number of blue-rinse widows who admired Rowland and enjoyed their association with a flying entrepreneur who dealt with black presidents. The attraction was magnified because Rowland watched silently, even mysteriously, while Ball, Lonrho's chairman, read the report. Rowland's silence at public meetings, initially motivated by shyness, became a useful device to encourage speculation and later to avoid hostages to fortune. At the customary reception after the meeting, the women struggled to engage the handsome bachelor in conversation. 'Tiny made them swoon,' laughs Fraser. 'He loved the attention.'

Against such a backdrop, the accomplished performer required limited effort to persuade Ball that if the terms of his options on two million Lonrho shares were not varied, he might reconsider his future with the company.

There was a conclusive temptation on Ball's part to agree. Four years earlier, Rowland had promised both Ball and Ogilvy 'a part of the action'. While Ogilvy had concluded a secret agreement with Shepton Estates for 200,000 Lonrho shares, Ball always knew that he would receive a greater benefit. 'Sink or swim together, we'll go down together,' gritted Rowland to the puppy-like Ball. Rowland was naturally generous, especially to those dependent upon him. Business was fun and it was important that everyone enjoyed the perks and pleasures. Ball was therefore reassured of his share of the action. While Rowland had promised Ogilvy 10 per cent, Ball would receive 20 per cent of Rowland's options.

Ball therefore agreed that Rowland's option should be transferred from Shepton Estates to a company which would be incorporated in the Bahamas, a taxhaven. They made two further decisions which they hoped would remain unknown beyond the boardroom. Both were beneficial to Rowland.

Firstly, the terms of the option were to be altered to allow Rowland more time to take up the shares. Secondly, the variations would allow Rowland to receive the dividend even if he bought the shares after the dividend had been declared. Critically, the 35 pence price per share would remain practically unaltered.

Since the variations directly benefited Rowland and not Lonrho, Caldecott needed to be persuaded. Mindful that Lonrho's share price had doubled during the first six months of 1966, reflecting the rise in profits over five years from £112,000 to £1.8 million, Caldecott's approval was hardly in doubt. The performance of Lonrho's stock was quite exceptional as the Labour government struggled to maintain the parity of the pound and the stock market plunged to unexpected lows. Like Ball and Ogilvy, the lawyer was concerned to keep Rowland satisfied. At that moment, Caldecott was unaware of the 1962 agreement to give Ogilvy 200,000 Lonrho shares.

On 6 March 1966, the Lonrho board ratified the modified agreement with Rowland. Shareholders would be told that because of developments in Rhodesia and 'abnormal factors thereby created' Rowland should be granted 'revised terms' over the option. The shareholders were not told about the two variations concerning date and price which allowed Rowland to receive dividends before he owned the shares. With the approval of the board and shareholders, Rowland believed he had satisfied the legal requirements.

By August, Lonrho's share price was 70 pence, double the price of the options which would lapse within one month. Ball, Ogilvy and Butcher flew to the Bahamas to initiate the creation of a company called Yeoman Investments to which all Rowland's private interests, including the Lonrho shares, would be transferred from Shepton Estates. The first stage of implementing the revisions had been accomplished.

In London, Rowland apparently hesitated about completing the arrangement. Writing to Caldecott Rowland asserted, 'It seems sad but I have suddenly realised that unless Alan stops drinking there can be no great future for our company.' Caldecott knew the truth of Rowland's allegation and feared dire repercussions for Lonrho if Rowland's threat, voiced on previous occasions, materialised. To outsiders it might seem odd that Rowland should threaten resignation, but the lawyer had already grasped the unpredictability of Rowland's emotional gyrations. Yet Caldecott was unaware that the ultimatum was a ploy to win time.

Rowland was immersed in uncompleted negotiations to avoid British taxation. During 1966, Africa's primitive communications facilities had necessitated prolonging his visits in London to run Lonrho's operations. Although he was still registered as a resident of Zambia, the British Inland Revenue could argue that he was living in Britain and subject to local taxes. Rowland's object was to be registered off-shore, yet, to his consternation, officials at both the Zambian and Malawi Reserve Banks were reluctant to allow his escape from their net so easily.

Negotiations in London had also proved complicated. Officials at the Bank of England were scrutinising his application to take up his share options tax free in the Bahamas, while remaining a resident in Britain. It had needed considerable effort to persuade the officials that he was no longer a resident of either Zambia or Rhodesia.

The intensity of the British officials' interrogation had surprised Rowland. 'Copious notes were made and I confess it left me feeling lonely and naked at the end,' reported Rowland pessimistically as if he had emerged from an exam. Rowland was even more surprised when, just before Christmas, his application was approved subject to his agreeing that Lonrho's headquarters remained in Britain. 'They say that Lonrho is now of national importance. Seems odd to me, I must say.'

Yeoman Investments Limited was formally incorporated on 30 January 1967. Three months later, Lonrho shares were about 75 pence. For one year, Rowland had hedged his bets about the wisdom of buying the Lonrho shares but, on the eve of declaring the dividend, Rowland decided that it was opportune. To beat the deadline, at the end of February, Ball and Rowland began a hectic race.

The board was due to declare the final dividend on 3 March 1967. Without explanation, Ball delayed that meeting for three days. While Rowland flew to Africa to obtain the formal clearances to satisfy British officials, Ball rushed to the Bahamas to finalise the tax arrangements. Both returned on 3 March and successfully presented their scheme to the Bank of England.

That weekend, having borrowed £725,000 from the Standard Bank, Rowland formally bought the 2 million Lonrho shares at 36.5 pence. As a bonus, he received the dividends which Lonrho had paid in the previous two years – a total of £154,219. Effectively, Rowland was paying 28 pence for the shares and owned 45 per cent of Lonrho.

On 6 March 1967, Lonrho's board met. Half the directors were ignorant of the hectic activities in the preceding days. The dividend was approved and Rowland benefited by £62,000 of dividends. Four weeks later, on 4 April, the same board approved a bonus scheme, granting shareholders one extra Lonrho share for each share held. Rowland now owned 7 million Lonrho shares. Colin MacKenzie knew that Ogilvy and Ball were benefiting from the exercise. 'It meant that Tiny was certain of two votes,' he recalled. 'One recognised the fact that he had a complete hold.'

Understanding that his allies should be rewarded and, cynics would subsequently suggest, silenced, Fred Butcher and Gerald Percy were thanked by Ball and appointed directors, joining Rowland's inner circle. A third new director, Sir Peter Youens, a former government service officer in Africa, was also appointed director. As a token of Lonrho's prestige, he was distinctly left on the outer rim.

By then, Rowland had affected a style in Cheapside which, while seemingly casual and unintimidating, did display his considerable authority. Immaculately dressed in suits tailored by Anderson & Sheppard, he sat in his plain, small sixth-floor office, the door notably always open, his feet often propped up on his polished desk, and held court. The other directors, who were the only occupants on that floor, hovered like courtiers around the emperor. Their presence was a palliative to his inherent loneliness. There were no women among them. Lonrho was and remains a company where only men are welcome. Sex was never discussed since everyone knew that Tiny disliked philanderers.

Occasionally, Rowland sipped a glass of white wine, often mixed with soda, enjoying the competition which he generated among his 'office boys' anxious to attract his attention. Some even arrived early to be the first in his office. Relaying his first thoughts of the day could be a sign of power and a source of envy. Most raved about their boss's remarkable intellect and retentive memory. But that was often a reflection upon their own inadequacies rather than his capabilities. Rowland did not suffer equals easily and shunned as a potential employee anyone who might be superior.

'I have an instinct, a deep animal instinct for the chemistry of people,' he explained. 'I would be aware of everything that flowed out from you when we met, from your eyes and your voice, and I would know whether we were likely to be able to work together.'

Like a woman, Rowland thirsted after admiration and attention. Those who satisfied that lust were generously rewarded and saw little hint of malice. By the same token, he reacted wildly to any admonition. Critics discovered that, castigated as disloyal and untrustworthy, they would become targets of his emotional venom. Without explanation, courtiers and associates would be cut off with at best an icy stare from his blue eyes. Enemies could never be forgiven, unless they were needed.

Visitors would come, discuss their business and depart while the courtiers continued to hover or were dispatched on an errand. Telephone calls from Europe, Africa, America and Asia were connected to Rowland who would delight in not permitting the surrounding mêlée to interrupt the conversation. Those in the room might hear what Rowland was saying but Rhodesian sanctions had prompted his adoption of code words for personalities, countries and commodities. Increasingly fearful of exposure by intercepts, Rowland began to minimise commitment of his thoughts to paper, preferring meetings and telephone calls.

To the small group of insiders, Rowland's management style guaranteed constant excitement and unexpected challenges. To the Old Etonians, it was a refreshing break from tradition. This was a rebel they adored. Tiny, they felt, could be so kind and generous. 'Leverage', a favourite Rowland expression, implied, as everyone understood, the prerequisite of Tiny's tolerance of people: they had to be susceptible to his pressure. The Old Etonians were willing to provide respectability and subservience.

There was a reverse side of taking favours from employees in London, namely, giving favours to Africans to obtain business. Paying bribes, it would be later said, was a natural and expected practice in Africa. The ignorant would disapprove, but for those seeking licences, contracts and permits there was a simple choice: either pay or cease business.

'Tiny doesn't pay bribes,' explains one of his African directors, Les Blackwell who managed Lonrho's twenty-two companies in Malawi for twenty-five years, 'he invests.' Blackwell remained unsure whether Lonrho's 'investments' were beneficial.

In Malawi, Lonrho's bribery started soon after the Sucoma sugar refinery began. Dr Hastings Banda, delighted with Lonrho's performance, asked Rowland to build a Heinrich's beer hall in the town of Limbe to serve as a social centre for the Women's League. 'Mr Rowland promised it to me as a present,' Banda told Percy. £14,000 of shareholders' funds had disappeared. Banda also refused to pay a £6000 account for Land Rovers supplied to his political party. The expectation of bribes was introduced to Lonrho by the African dictator. Lonrho's benefit was that Banda ceased monitoring for some weeks the compulsory acquisition of the railways.

'Lonrho paid out huge bribes and it wasn't necessary for business,' says Blackwell. 'We just got the reputation as a soft touch. When Africans wanted money we were in the front line and got hit first.' Other international companies in Malawi, he discovered, 'could operate quite normally without paying into Banda's charities'.

Rowland was becoming fixated that Lonrho's growth depended upon the favours of local politicians. Unlike the established giants, Anglo American and Rio Tinto, Lonrho needed to fight for every advantage which was within the gift of the presidents. He rationalised that the payments were examples of his generosity and, because it is impolite and immodest to mention gifts, the payments remained undiscussed.

Within the company, only those few directors involved knew about the developing payment of bribes. Several deliberately sought to avoid all knowledge and the board was never consulted. The so-called 'special payments', classified as 'General Expenses Africa', were entirely Rowland's responsibility. His payments would be drawn on a personal account at the British Linen Bank, off Piccadilly. In the first ten years, he paid at least £836,000 in unreceipted 'special payments' which even Lonrho's accountants would only occasionally discover by accident. But no one dared challenge the architect of Lonrho's fortunes.

The cool, buccaneering panjandrum criss-crossing Africa in his new Mystere Falcon jet was consumed by an insatiable appetite for acquisitions. As he sped through time zones, Rowland declared 1968 as his annus mirabilis. Lonrho had grown the previous year into a conglomerate operating in seventeen countries with fixed assets valued at £20 million compared to £1 million in 1961, and pre-tax profits of £3.6 million compared to £0.1 million six years earlier. During 1968, Lonrho's auditors would certify that profits had jumped 97 per cent to £7.1 million.

He had reached a new peak. While his contemporaries battled to stem the student revolts, the demands for socialism in Europe and the turmoil in America in the wake of military defeats in Vietnam, Rowland became inspired by the very political uncertainties which paralysed his competitors. In a blitz of activities across Africa, he quietly proved himself one of the world's most consummate capitalists, prepared to take unique risks which placed him firmly in what he called 'the big league'. 1968 would be his most productive, frenetic and awesome year, temporarily silencing potential critics about the company's debts which escalated from under £1 million in 1961, to £19 million in 1967 and zoomed to £44 million in 1968.

The acquisitions were straightforward, doubling Lonrho's assets. In Kenya and Uganda, Rowland bought a controlling interest in Consolidated Holdings, a conglomerate of about twenty subsidiaries in property, printing, paper production, shipping, road haulage, tourism and 'tent and chair hire'. In Ceylon, he bought Anglo-Ceylon, a tea estate; in Swaziland, Lonrho bought a sugar plantation from Adeane; in several African countries, Lonrho bought David Whitehead, the continent's biggest textile producer; in South Africa, the same country which he so vehemently condemned north of the Zambezi, Lonrho bought more coal mines and deftly hid the contradictions. Most of the purchases were financed by Lonrho shares which rose during 1968 from 90 pence to 190 pence and then towards £3. As Ball would proudly tell shareholders, every £100 invested in 1961 was worth £950 in 1968.

The vision was an empire of profit-making businesses producing record 'doubled' results, but Lonrho's accountants had allowed the inclusion of 'extraordinary' profits in the 'trading' column which gave the impression that earnings per share had risen by 5 per cent when in fact they had fallen by 18 per cent. Financial prudence was not the priority.

Even the reality of the empire occasionally lacked coherence. Asked by Winspear what a factory which he was buying actually made, Rowland replied, '2.4 per cent after tax'. The product was not even considered. For any other corporation or individual, those acquisitions in the course of one year would be exhausting and indigestible, but for Rowland it was just part of his activities.

The overriding ambition was to rival Anglo American, Harry Oppenheimer's seemingly unassailable mineral empire. The fast route, Rowland understood, was by winning the support of individual African presidents who wielded the patronage. Securing personal introductions to those presidents was essential and, accordingly, Rowland sought Africans whose personal connections could pave his access.

Gil Olympio, the son of a murdered president of Togo in West Africa and the representative of the International Monetary Fund in that region, was Rowland's first recruit. In the course of his IMF duties, the Francophone African had negotiated directly with many heads of state in a region which hitherto had been inaccessible for British companies. Rowland proposed an attractive package. In return for introductions and contracts, he would help the Togolese fulfil his own ambitions to become an 'African Tiny'. The mutuality of interest was sealed with Olympio's receipt of a good salary, a car and a flat in Grosvenor Square. Olympio was 'thrilled' and proved his value.

Through a family connection, Olympio introduced Rowland to the president of the Ivory Coast, Felix Houphouet-Boigny, the ruler of six million people. Despite intense and well-orchestrated French opposition, Rowland sold Houphouet- Boigny a sophist- icated $80 million sugar complex, financed by bank loans to the Ivory Coast government, although the plant would be managed by Lonrho. Lonrho's 'ownership' was purely cosmetic.

It was a trail-blazing formula which Rowland attempted to rep- licate throughout the continent. Principally, Lonrho negotiated finance for an African government in return for earning a man- agement fee of the completed project. Outsiders would believe that the plantations were wholly Lonrho owned. Olympio's reward included a $1 million fee from the American builder of the plant.

Rowland would also sell Houphouet-Boigny Ivory Coast's first insurance company, La Sécurité Ivoirienne, as a joint venture with the Guardian Royal Exchange.

In world terms, Houphouet-Boigny's economy was unimpor- tant but as Rowland's relationship with the president developed, he sought, as a minor service, an effusive letter of introduction to a neighbouring dictator, General Joseph Mobutu of Zaïre, formerly the Belgian Congo.

Rowland's target was the interests of Union Minière, the giant Belgian mineral corporation. Under Belgian rule, the Congo's huge mineral wealth had been mercilessly exploited by the conglomerate, extracting annually 350,000 tons of copper, and by a British company called Tanganyika Concessions, alias Tanks, which transported the ore on its railway to the port of Benguela in Angola. Substantial shareholdings in both compa- nies were owned by two international giants: the Belgian Société Générale and Anglo American. All four corporations conducted their businesses as laws unto themselves. In 1966, Union Minière had been nationalised by Mobutu but allowed to retain a management contract. Compensation remained unsettled. Rowland saw the mineral-rich country as an ideal foundation from which to challenge Anglo American.

In his carefully planned strategy, Rowland had understood that a blunt offer from Lonrho, an upstart among the mining giants, would be derided. Instead he bought a Trojan horse, Cominière, a Belgian company registered in Luxembourg and a rival, albeit smaller, to Union Minière. Owning buses, electricity and water utilities, an insurance company, a travel agency and a shipbuilding yard in Zaïre, Cominière had been created by Martin Thèves, a carpenter's son who, like so many white businessmen in Africa, wanted to extricate some money for his retirement. Thèves had agreed to Rowland's offer, paid in Lonrho shares, in April 1968 on a single condition: that the sale would remain secret so that he could retain his social position in Belgium. Rowland agreed and the purchase was executed through Loncom, a nominee company registered in Luxembourg. Since the purchase had to be disclosed to Lonrho shareholders, the condition was soon broken. 'After Tiny bought Cominière,' recalled Gil Olympio, 'he broke the secrecy agreement and told Thèves to go to hell.'

Rowland arrived in Zaïre with Gil Olympio to meet Mobutu bearing an offer to provide the management of Union Minière's former assets in conjunction with the government, and a plan to construct a new railway across the jungle from Katanga's copperbelt to the Atlantic Ocean.

Among those outraged by Rowland's bid to usurp Union Minière were the Belgian government, Baron de Spirolet, the president of Union Minière, Harry Oppenheimer and Lord Colyton, the chairman of Tanks. Unitedly, they were pressuring Mobutu to pay compensation as a warning to other African dictators that confiscation would be shortsighted and fiercely resisted. Their combative strategy risked evisceration by a rebel's gambit. Rowland soon found himself outclassed.

Spurred on by Baron Spirolet's and Lord Colyton's denigration of Lonrho, Mobutu, in a volcanic display of outrage about the secret acquisition, nationalised Cominière and, as a second blow to Rowland, granted Union Minière a twenty-five-year management contract. Rowland was shattered and, seeking an intermediary to Mobutu, recruited Thomas Kanza, a Zaïrean diplomat.

Like Olympio, Thomas Kanza was an exceptional African for that era. Educated, erudite and politically sophisticated, Kanza, aged twenty-eight, was serving in 1961, in the midst of the civil war, as the country's ambassador at the United Nations. Seeking allies, he had asked the advice of Sir Alec Douglas Home, then the British foreign secretary. 'Don't bother with our government,' counselled Home, 'they won't give you any help. Try businessmen instead.' Home's advice was not totally welcome. To Kanza, businessmen were stereotype villains uncaringly content 'to destroy my country'.

But Home suggested that one businessman was different: 'Talk to Tiny Rowland. He's a "no good", but he's a clever buccaneer.' Kanza was soon sitting in Rowland's office. Like so many Africans, Kanza was attracted to Lonrho's executive because, 'Rowland was exceptional. He knew and liked Africa. He wanted to challenge the established mining houses who had exploited us.' The emotional appeal won Kanza's support and eventually his cooperation to recover Cominière.

In a published interview which Kanza arranged with a Belgian newspaper journalist, Rowland begged Mobutu's forgiveness, pleading that he had been misunderstood. Kanza ensured that the publication was read by the dictator.

By then, Mobutu had arrived in Geneva and shortly afterwards Lonrho's Mystere landed in the Swiss city with Rowland and Alan Ball on board. This was an occasion to which Rowland could rise. Using his charm and self-salesmanship to win favours from a limited reprieve, he struck a deal with Mobutu to recover 70 per cent of Cominière's empire, forsaking only the utility companies. There were two conditions. Mobutu's uncle, Joseph Litho, was to become deputy chairman of the company; and there was to be a donation to the president's favourite charity. Rowland was grateful to Kanza for the assistance and embraced the African as part of his close entourage.

In the midst of saving his cashless investment in Zaïre,

Rowland had flown to Ghana to negotiate another deal with Silvan Amagashi, the minister responsible for mines and Gil Olympio's uncle. Rowland's goal was the Ashanti gold fields where, unlike Rhodesia, one could see the veins of gold in the ore and occasionally extract a lump of pure metal. In retrospect, Ashanti, one of the world's richest gold mines, had been a plum just waiting to be picked. Rowland's genius was to realise the possibility.

Ashanti, an established British public company, was managed by Sir Edward Spears, aged eighty-two, who, as a child before the turn of the century, had followed his father 'around Belgrave Square shooting snipe'. During the First World War, Spears had been decorated four times for bravery, and during the Second World War, having rescued de Gaulle from France in 1940, he remained an adviser and friend to Churchill. By any account he was a remarkable character whose final career, managing a gold mine famed as 'the richest square mile in Africa', had afforded him the luxury of eating frozen grouse flown from Britain.

Rowland's intrigue, unknown to Spears, began in Accra, Ghana's capital. In a succession of long but seductive monologues, Rowland persuaded the Ghana government that the Africans, rather than the Europeans, should control the nation's most valuable resource. 'Of course you need European managers and technical assistance,' expounded Rowland, 'but you should earn more of the profits and you, and not the old colonials, should be the owners.' Lonrho, he continued, was their natural ally against the imperialists. With its expertise and trusted dedication to African nationalism in Malawi, Zambia, Kenya and elsewhere throughout the continent, Lonrho was an ideal partner for Ghana. Rowland proposed that the Ghana government should terminate Ashanti's ninety-year lease granted in 1897 and award Lonrho a fifty-year lease in return for immediately granting 20 per cent of the new company to the government with an option of a further 20 per cent. Lonrho would earn an annual management fee in Ghanaian currency. If the government exercised its option, it was to pay Lonrho £1 per share. His terms were accepted and the completion of the purchase took place in London.

At the beginning of the day on 20 October 1968, Arthur Winspear, the Warburgs' banker, arrived at Morgan Grenfell, Ashanti's merchant bankers, to deliver a bid for the company. The bid was rejected as derisory because it grossly undervalued the company. Winspear departed to observe what he told colleagues was an 'unimaginable, flabbergasting pincer movement' which destroyed Spears's control over the mine.

Days later, the news was leaked that the Ghana government had terminated Ashanti's lease. As the value of Ashanti's shares crashed, Winspear returned to Morgan Grenfell proffering a letter obtained by Rowland from Amagashi affirming that the lease would not be renewed. Winspear repeated his bid for the worthless lease. The company, whose board included Duncan Sandys the Conservative politician, capitulated and received just £15 million for the mine. To soften their sentiments, Rowland invited the company's four African directors to London and hosted their holiday at the Dorchester hotel. 'Special payments' of £35,000 were also made on cheques drawn from the British Linen Bank and debited to 'General Expenses Africa'. Three further payments of £31,250, £80,000 and £16,500 were made by Henderson Transvaal Estates, a Lonrho company, through the British Linen Bank during December 1968. General Spears was not amenable to similar generosity. As Rowland had told Percy: 'Every man has his price. The definition of an honest man is when his price is too high.'

Infuriated by Rowland's coup, Spears considered hindering the transition until Rowland began a charm offensive. Rioting Ashanti miners, complaining about conditions, jeopardised the takeover. Only Spears was capable of placating the employees and Rowland solicited the general's assistance. Travelling with his 'poisonous' wife, Spears returned to the company's imposing residence near the mine, but then stubbornly refused either to undertake Rowland's requirements or to relinquish the house. Eventually, Rowland seconded General 'Jock' Anderson, higher-ranking than Spears, to 'order' compliance with Rowland's orders, but Spears's resentment lingered. In Rowland's defence, Ian Fraser, the Warburgs' banker, believes that 'Tiny was generous towards Spears. He made him a director of Lonrho and gave him more money than necessary.' Indeed, the banker was surprised that Rowland bothered even to see the general. He misjudged Rowland's intentions.

Seeking friends and allies, Rowland was deliberately avoiding the antagonisms which had clouded his life in Salisbury. The widening circle of reputable personalities and institutions who responded to his call in London reflected Lonrho's growth and his own enhanced reputation. Although he did not boast his own table for lunch at the Savoy Grill with the major City players, but ate rather with the parvenus at the Dorchester or Grosvenor House, he was still a trusted outsider. After all, his bankers were Warburgs and among his fellow directors was Angus Ogilvy, a member of the royal family.

While Rowland would later quip that the other directors, who in his view played secondary parts, 'were sort of Christmas tree decorations', Ogilvy and Ball were trusted lieutenants and friends, tied to his interests through their common and secret ownership of Lonrho share options vested in Yeoman Trust in the Bahamas.

Such was Rowland's conviction until on Sunday morning, 25 February 1968, the trio were sitting by the swimming pool of Gerald Percy's house in Nairobi. Their usual good-humoured banter was broken by Ogilvy who revealed that he was keen to sell his 10 per cent interest in Lonrho. Ogilvy explained that he needed money and the tax avoidance scheme to settle the Yeoman income in trusts for the benefit of his children was on the verge of an irrevocable settlement.

Rowland was shocked. In an extraordinarily frank letter, written as he flew from Nairobi, which he described as 'the most important' in his life, Rowland urged Ogilvy to desist from selling any of his interest in Yeoman. Owning the shares, he explained, 'helps to give the three of us the effective means to control Lonrho' reducing the other directors to 'secondary parts'. Yeoman's intrinsic worth, he added, 'is sacrosanct'.

'I am in character', Rowland confessed, 'far more reckless than you are, Angus, for obvious reasons. However it would be foolhardy in the extreme if Yeoman's position were put in jeopardy.' If Ogilvy sold, their total control over Lonrho would

be weakened and his own interest would 'decrease'. Their domi-
nance, which he described as a 'shadow of the largest number
of shares' would diminish disproportionately. Even though, he
admitted, the company might be 'more profitable' if someone
else took control, that scenario would be 'tragically sad'. Their
own power, he urged, should remain inviolate and should be
reduced only if unanimously agreed by the trio. Rowland concluded with emotion: 'Perhaps, Angus, if you have a moment
and would consider my thoughts and apprehensions, would you
let me know whether you feel I have overstepped the mark by
being too personal and direct?' The iron fist within a velvet
glove persuaded Ogilvy to bow to his friend's wishes.

Rowland's relationship with Ogilvy, critical to both his survival
and threatened downfall over the ensuing five years, reflected the
delicate balance between Rowland's unpredictable emotions and
capricious aspiration to create an empire. The unstable chemistry of Rowland's personality was manifest as he flew, later that
spring, with Ogilvy and Robert Adeane to Mauritius to buy the
island's biggest sugar producer.

Rowland had just bought Adeane's sugar plantation in Swaziland and anticipated that the Mauritians, reluctant sellers, could
be persuaded of similar advantages. Ogilvy listened, impressed
with Rowland's calm assurance. 'Of course,' continued Rowland,
'it's all thanks to Angus that Lonrho will soon be the biggest
company in Africa.' Adeane watched Ogilvy bridling with pleasure, unaware of the cat-and-mouse antics. Adeane, a shrewd
businessman, knew that Ogilvy was being publicly brought into
line, reminded that only thanks to Rowland was he a millionaire.

To Rowland's friends, the Mauritian deal seemed a hopeless venture. Yet for two days Ogilvy and the others observed
Rowland with his self-deprecating manner, posing questions to
which he surely knew the answers, bestowing upon the owner
unaccustomed self-importance, and they grasped his carefully
laid enticement: the promise of personal wealth if Rowland's
offer was accepted. The trap was sprung and Rowland owned
another company.

As the Mystere flew towards the northern hemisphere, crossing a continent where the existence of any modern facilities

was thanks to the white settlers whose compulsion to abandon their life's work was fuelling Lonrho's expansion, Rowland delivered his homily to Ogilvy, 'Lonrho only buys. It does not sell.' Ogilvy understood that he was not to dispose of 'his part of the action'.

Rowland of course understood that Ogilvy's desire to extricate himself from Lonrho was not entirely motivated by money. Membership of the royal family had imposed obligations upon Ogilvy which included compliance with the law. Lonrho's activities, instinctively shrouded in mystery by Rowland's style, were contravening British sanctions against Rhodesia.

After the Nairobi poolside fracas, Ogilvy announced his resignation from directorships of Lonrho's Rhodesian based companies. The public, understanding his desire to avoid embarrassment to the royal family, assumed the directorships he was forsaking involved the oil pipeline. But beyond the Lonrho board, the Foreign Office and the intelligence service knew that the company was actively breaking sanctions. The unpublished issue was Ogilvy's awareness of all the developments.

The futility of oil sanctions had become apparent by early 1966, yet Harold Wilson had publicly dedicated his government to their enforcement. Irritated by the hypocrisy which deprived Lonrho of considerable profits by the closure of the oil pipeline, Rowland decided on 22 May 1967 to discuss his predicament with the government.

In the course of a discussion with James Bottomley, a deputy under-secretary of state in the Commonwealth Office, Rowland presented evidence which proved, he claimed, that 300 railway tank wagons were shuttling Shell's and BP's oil from Mozambique to Rhodesia. Rowland's evidence was not unknown in the Department. Identical reports about the oil companies' illegal deliveries from Mozambique and South Africa had been supplied by the Portuguese, French and Zambian governments to British diplomats. Bottomley – 'at all times most courteous', remarked Rowland – thanked his visitor for the information but his colleagues were less polite.

Martin Le Quesne, a deputy under-secretary responsible for Africa, and Denis Greenhill, then the deputy under-secretary of state, having consulted the Department's lawyers, were assured that the oil companies in Britain were not acting illegally. Nor were their subsidiaries in South Africa. 'They are just fulfilling orders,' they consoled themselves. Foreign Office officials, sceptical about sanctions, chose to ignore the truth.

Like all his colleagues, Le Quesne nevertheless understood the importance of pretence to Britain's credibility throughout the world. Sanctions was an emotional issue, especially amid the Cold War's ideological battle. Rowland's intervention, thought Le Quesne, was 'distinctly unhelpful' in that struggle for survival. 'Whose side is he on?' he asked a colleague. 'A maverick, out for himself,' was the reply. The officials' disdain was encouraged by the oil companies who even ten years later would claim that Rowland's evidence was 'absolute rubbish'. Rowland's understandable outrage was exacerbated by the politicians' endorsement of the falsehoods.

Labour ministers had accepted the reports from BP and Shell executives and from civil servants who blamed the French for breaking sanctions. To the companies' good fortune, George Thomson, the Labour minister responsible for Commonwealth Affairs, did not expose their dishonesty.

The first conspiracy ended on 21 February 1968 when the two chief executives of Shell and BP arrived in Thomson's office and confided the secret of their oil deliveries. Thomson passed on the news to Harold Wilson and senior ministers. His note coincided with a government crisis following the resignation of George Brown, the foreign secretary. Thomson was transferred to another ministry and absolved of further responsibility. In the aftermath, Wilson decided to avoid a costly confrontation with South Africa about the oil supplies, which would endanger British industry and banks. Instead, the prime minister perpetuated the cover-up. In public, Wilson claimed that sanctions were having a 'crippling effect' upon Rhodesia.

Considering the losses from the pipeline closure and the halt to compensation payments, Rowland's fury was considerable. 'Let's sue the British government,' he suggested to Ogilvy. His friend was alarmed. Fearing embarrassment to the royal family, he sought the advice of Sir Michael Adeane, the Queen's private secretary. The message was passed back to the Foreign Office. 'He's being very unhelpful,' said Le Quesne, the Office's expert on sanctions. Rowland was, he believed, a 'major nigger in the woodpile who is singlehandedly trying to undermine the oil embargo'. Irrationally, Rowland became the epitome of what was making life difficult for the diplomats. A response was sent back via Adeane to Ogilvy. If Lonrho embarked upon legal action, Ogilvy would be expected to resign.

The Foreign Office saw Rowland's refusal to join the conspiracy as his intention to embarrass Britain. Their response was to investigate Lonrho. An MI6 operation, using a secretary inserted into Lonrho's office in Johannesburg, produced incriminating evidence that Lonrho was breaking sanctions. The word within the Foreign Office became indelibly cast: 'Lonrho is the most notorious sanctions buster.'

As all other British companies, Rowland zealously sought to protect Lonrho from sanctions. Ostentatiously, he had distanced himself from the Smith regime, volunteering that Lonrho in London was fully complying with the British government's laws.

As a consequence, there was little affection for Rowland in Salisbury. Ian Smith was irritated that Lonrho's newspapers in Zambia were critical and that Rhodesia's supply of Mozambique hardwood was owned by Lonrho. Similarly, his Treasury officials complained about Lonrho's finances and supported the suggestion by the economic adviser to the Central Intelligence Organisation that Lonrho should be nationalised. 'Lonrho was a company without integrity,' summarised the secretary to the Treasury of the illegal regime. Rowland was an enemy. His offer to Smith in June 1968 to act as an intermediary was spurned.

But amid the personal antagonism, everyone knew that Lonrho was breaking sanctions. British laws did not require companies to divest themselves of their Rhodesian subsidiaries but merely to break any contact. Despite Caldecott's formal advice, Rowland and most of the directors remained in constant communication with Kruger, Lonrho's office manager. Dubbed 'His Master's Voice', Kruger struggled to comply with the formal orders from London to withhold Lonrho's resources from the regime, while simultaneously obeying London's instructions to maximise Lonrho's profits in obedience to the Smith government. 'The lies drove him to drink,' recalled his widow. Major Colin MacKenzie flew, albeit circumspectly, to Salisbury to 'wave the flag' at Lonrho's ranches while Rowland's flits through the country confirmed his own involvement, especially in profit from the Sixties boom business – copper production.

Mandatory sanctions approved by UN Security Council on 16 December 1966 and incorporated by British legislation forbade the purchase of Rhodesian copper. The new law, passed twelve days after Harold Wilson's unsuccessful negotiations with Smith on board HMS *Tiger*, outlawed 'any act' which promoted the export of copper from Rhodesia. At that moment, Kruger and Ian Hossy, the consulting engineer, had embarked upon a valuable copper extraction programme which neither they nor Rowland intended to abandon.

The Inyati copper mine, situated one hundred miles east of Salisbury in the Headlands area, had been surveyed by Hossy in December 1965. Excitedly, Hossy had recommended the acquisition of mining rights within a sixty-four-square-mile area. On 6 April 1966, Rowland flew to Salisbury, agreed the purchase, and approved £143,000 expenditure to develop the mine.

On 6 January 1967, two weeks after British legislation forbade 'any act' promoting Rhodesia's copper production, Lonrho in London telexed an order to the Inyati mine manager to stockpile the output until further notice. Ostensibly, Kruger and Hossy obeyed but their compliance was swiftly countermanded by the Rhodesian government who appointed an agent to oversee the continuance of the mine's operations. The Lonrho directors seemed unperturbed. Within one year, the mine's milling facilities were increased from 7,500 tons to 36,000 tons. On 28 April 1967, Hossy telexed Rowland, 'I'm pretty sure we have our big one.'

Hossy however feared that his secret El Dorado would be discovered. The boreholes, he told Rowland, were uncomfortably close to the neighbouring land. 'We must keep this result quiet,' he told Rowland – who agreed.

Over the following months, Hossy planned Inyati's exploitation to increase from 36,000 tons to 120,000 tons and double by

1971, but was frustrated by lack of finance. Rowland's solution, apparently deft, would eventually lead to charges of corruption.

Ever since he had mitigated the Kanyemba débâcle by grouping all Lonrho's mines in a company called Corsyn, controlled by Lonrho, but whose ownership was obfuscated through a succession of public- and private-owned companies registered in South Africa, Rowland had sought to disguise Lonrho's involvement in Rhodesia from nationalist governments in Africa. UDI had compounded the problems, quashing any prospect of raising money for industrial developments inside Rhodesia. To overcome that obstacle, Rowland used the complicated ownership structure of Lonrho's mines to finance Inyati's development.

On Rowland's orders, Corsyn sold to Lonrho a stake in Inyati for £350,000. That investment would not be revealed to Coronation Syndicate's other shareholders. Indeed, over the following months, Rowland further complicated the ownership of Corsyn to disguise the company's activities beneath a web of interlocking share ownerships and agreements of various companies who would suddenly transfer their assets from one to another. Finally, in April 1968, to make absolutely sure that other shareholders would not discover the truth, the directors of Coronation Syndicate obtained official permission in South Africa to discontinue issuing quarterly reports 'in the interests of Rhodesia's security'.

In May 1968, Rowland arrived in Salisbury to pledge a further £1 million in exchange for a half share in the mine. The money would be supplied by Lonrho in Rhodesia. In every sense, he was breaking sanctions imposed by the British government and committing a criminal offence.

Rowland's self-justification, quite correct in the circumstances, was the knowledge that his decisions were no different from those of other major British companies since most, especially in industry and the Conservative Party, opposed sanctions. The distinctions however were Ogilvy's presence on Lonrho's board and that Rowland was volubly complaining about others' sanctions busting. His defence however was credible. He had opposed Smith and supported sanctions until he could no longer risk Lonrho's fortunes. On 13 October 1968, when Harold Wilson's second attempt to persuade Ian Smith to end the rebellion failed, on board HMS *Fearless* moored in Gibraltar, and UDI seemed destined to continue into the foreseeable future, he decided irrevocably to settle in Britain, which by implication committed him to abide by British laws.

Josie Taylor, the daughter of Rowland's manager on Shepton Estate, Lionel Taylor, had arrived in London in 1965 to attend a finishing college. Both her fees and her flat in Princes Gate, South Kensington, were paid by Rowland. In the following months, Josie was occasionally seen at Rowland's home in Park Lane or in her own flat, acting as an unofficial hostess for Rowland, whom visitors remember her calling 'uncle'.

Reformed since his days in London after the war, Rowland was not an overt womaniser. Some suspected that it was self-protection – not emotional cladding, but wariness that his enemies might seek to control or blackmail him through women or parties. Others just assumed that Lonrho was his life and love. Jokes were made about his only luxury in Avonfield House, the Park Lane flat, being his enormous double bed covered in swagged silk. 'A boudoir', recalled one visitor who also noticed the solitary picture of a bull elephant by David Shepherd. To avoid Rowland qualifying as an official resident in Britain, the apartment was owned by Tweefontein Collieries of South Africa.

Josie was in London just when Rowland, aged fifty, needed company and a family. Since her childhood, she had never hidden her affection for her hero and father figure. 'My knight in shining armour', she confided to her few friends. A foil to Irene, twenty-four-year-old Josie understood precisely what Rowland needed. No controls, unqualified affection, unlimited support and no questions. 'They had a lot in common,' recalled Eileen Kruger, 'especially Rhodesia and their shyness. Tiny liked Rhodesian women.' Josie accepted the generation gap without complaint. Rowland appreciated her unqualified adoration of him. 'I had held her in my arms,' Rowland told Gil Olympio, 'and decided to marry her.' Their untroubled relationship was based upon a common sentiment: the fulfilment of Rowland's ambitions. Gradually, Rowland came to rely upon his wife's judgment, especially of people.

The first evidence of the relationship was their inspection together in summer 1967 of Bourne End, a house at Hedsor Wharf on an arm of the Thames near Cliveden, the Astors' family home. The house was bought by Lonrho in October and architects were commissioned to embark on considerable alterations. One side of the Kentish farm house was demolished and rebuilt with a Georgian façade. The tributory was slightly diverted and a bridge costing £40,000 was built across the water. On completion of the bridge, Rowland was so taken by the idea, he ordered a second one.

Caldecott arranged the conveyance but recommended delaying the contract until after 5 April 1968 to protect Rowland's tax status as a non-resident in Britain. Paid for by Sucoma, Lonrho's sugar company in Malawi, and costing £73,500, Josie's original improvements had been priced at £25,000. The work would be completed in 1971 costing £323,589. Rowland never asked the Lonrho board to consider or approve the increased expenditure.

They married on 1 July 1968 in a Westminster registry office. Neither Lionel Taylor nor Josie's mother knew of the wedding. When told, they refused to comment and displayed no pleasure. There was neither a party nor an apparent celebration. The noteworthy feature of the wedding was the manifestation of Rowland's continuing concern to conceal his background. On the marriage certificate, Wilhelm Fuhrhop was recorded as William Rowland. Rowland's critics would later point to his commission of perjury. For her part, Josie appeared irritated by Irene Smith. On the latter's occasional visits to London, financed by Rowland, 'Josie's annoyance was real', recalls Dan Mayers the gemstone dealer. On one visit Irene broke a limb. Rowland generously paid for Irene's care. 'Josie did not like that,' says Mayers who was in regular contact with Lonrho's directors about their amethyst operation in Zambia.

It might be harsh to assert that, in 1968, Rowland was untroubled by transgressing the law but the evidence seems compelling. Having infringed the sanctions laws and the rules about disclosure to Coronation Syndicate shareholders in South

Africa, he had ignored the need of approval of Lonrho's board for the expenditure at Hedsor Wharf, had approved a false entry on his marriage certificate and now became involved in a deal in Zambia which also provoked allegations of wrongdoing.

The issue was the Kundalilla amethyst mine, 250 miles from Lusaka. Under Dan Mayers' direction, the mine's high-quality gems had established a near-monopoly across the world which in turn had stimulated expansion of production. Under the agreement between Northern Minerals and the Zambian government, the monthly $10,000 profits which Crystals, Mayers' Swiss-registered company, earned on the amethyst sales were reported to Lusaka. That amount, minus a sales commission, was remitted to Northern Minerals in Zambia which filed accounts in Lusaka. But a delicate problem had arisen. A by-product of the huge expansion of production, contained in the ore exported to Europe for processing, was literally tons of inferior-quality amethysts. Mayers' dilemma was the disposal of the inferior, so-called B and C material. If the latter were sold on the open market, the price of the high-class gems would collapse. Alternatively, if he sold a small amount of the B and C material, and reported those sales to Lusaka, the Zambian government would assess the total surplus tonnage at that price. Taxes would be imposed on that whole amount, ignoring the reality that the tonnage was unsaleable and there was no money to fund the payments. Those taxes would have bankrupted Crystals and destroyed the whole operation. Mayers consulted Rowland.

Zambia had become the hub of Lonrho's expansion in Africa and Rowland's developing relationship with Kaunda was pivotal. His affection for Africa was genuine as were his public utterances of devotion to the African cause. But that could not interfere with the real business of earning profits.

Mayers and Rowland therefore agreed upon a scheme which eventually defrauded the Zambian government. Rowland would claim total ignorance of the intent and the details, having assigned all responsibility to Mayers and Fred Butcher. Mayers would insist that Rowland was party to the conspiracy.

Under the new procedure, Northern Minerals would in future export all its production at a nominal price, sufficient to cover the

a takeover bid by Rowland in October 1968. Instead of paying cash, Rowland proposed to offer Lonrho shares whose price was heading towards £3 per share.

Naturally he wanted to buy John Holt cheaply. An advantage would be to start the bid with the 20 per cent of Holts owned by Jessel Securities, founded and managed by Oliver Jessel, a well-known 'Go-Go Boy' of the Sixties. On Thursday, 14 February 1969, a broker acting on Rowland's behalf inquired whether Jessel's shares were for sale. The cold approach disarmed any suspicions which Jessel should have harboured instinctively. Surprisingly, Jessel did not ask the suitor for his reason. Nor did he query Rowland's request to have the share transfer carried out by a number of different companies and people. Jessel was simply delighted to earn a good profit. Rowland intended to announce his bid on the following Monday morning.

But Rowland's offer was flawed. Throughout 1968, his hectic deal-making schedule across Africa had been undertaken amid the bravado of Rowland's own rules. Dictators were charmed and established institutions had been challenged. Yet his offer for Jessel's shares was subject to the City's rules on takeovers which differed considerably from those in Zaïre, Ghana and Nigeria. In London the rule for takeover bids was simple. Every shareholder had to be offered the same deal. For Rowland to buy Jessel's shareholding except as part of the general bid made to all shareholders was prohibited.

During Friday, Jessel's shares were transferred to Rowland's control. On Friday night, Rowland told Winspear at Warburgs about his intention to bid for Holts after the weekend and asked that the bank should, as usual, act for Lonrho. It was the first inkling of Rowland's intentions which the bank had received. The brief notice was unusual but not spurious. Yet Rowland's revelation that he had bought Jessel's shares caused panic.

'You've got to stop this man,' Henry Grunfeld, Warburgs' senior director, told Angus Ogilvy in a heated telephone call on Friday night. 'If you don't, we'll all be in court.' Ogilvy, having just returned from abroad, was in bed listening to the furious banker. 'Do you realise what's happening? The front page won't be big enough if this gets out.' Ogilvy spluttered ignorance. 'And you're Princess Alexandra's husband,' fumed the banker. 'Bring him to my office at 9 a.m. tomorrow!'

In Grunfeld's office on Saturday morning, Rowland acted contrite. 'So sorry, I thought there was no problem.' By then, Grunfeld had arranged with Jessel and his banker that the deal was nullified and the paperwork cancelled. Warburgs formally announced the bid and Lonrho digested another company in return for more shares. Even Rowland's show of remorse was expunged by what he believed was a further endorsement of himself and Lonrho by the British Establishment.

In November 1968, Nicholas Elliott, the son of a renowned headmaster of Eton, himself an Old Etonian and the director of MI6's section responsible for Eastern Europe, met Rowland for lunch at White's. As MI6's former director for Africa, Elliott had become intrigued by the businessman who regularly featured in his subordinates' reports about his relationships with the African heads of state. During their meal, Elliott impressed Rowland sufficiently for the businessman to offer his host a directorship at Lonrho. The intelligence officer was not displeased by the suggestion. 'I satisfied myself about Rowland and Lonrho before accepting the job,' Elliott told friends who queried his judgment, suggesting that he had relied upon colleagues in the security service. At a subsequent lunch at the Savoy, Elliott agreed to start on 1 April 1969.

Elliott's directorship of Lonrho, combined with Joseph Ball's service with MI5, reinforced the impression of the company's links with the British government, particularly because of Elliott's high-profile career in the intelligence world.

In 1956, as head of MI6's London station during the visit of Nikita Khrushchev to Britain, Elliott had dispatched Commander Lionel Crabb, a frogman, to investigate the hull of the cruiser which had brought the Soviet leader to Britain. The discovery of Crabb's headless corpse in the Plymouth waters and Moscow's vehement protest, provoked a diplomatic crisis between the two nations but Elliott survived because he had obeyed orders.

Elliott's second public appearance was his visit to Beirut in 1963 to confront the former MI6 officer Kim Philby with conclusive evidence that he was a Soviet spy. Elliott returned to London with a confession. Philby soon after fled to Moscow.

Some interpreted Elliott's appointment to Lonrho as another astute tactic by Rowland to build links with African leaders and receive the benefit of MI6's network of relationships. Rowland admitted that he hoped the former MI6 officer would be 'very useful for introducing us to ambassadors in Africa'.

Accompanying Rowland in the Mystere as translator, companion and personal assistant extraordinary, Elliott's genial presence as they stepped on to the tarmac of an African airport emphasised Lonrho's importance. Every tinpot dictator envied the legendary if uncertain British intelligence agency and Rowland was travelling with a former director as his employee. In Kinshasa, for example, Rowland and Elliott would stay at the British Ambassador's residence. Others imagined something more sinister: Rowland, the 'head of state' travelling with his chief of intelligence.

The impression of Lonrho acting as a cover for MI6 developed when Elliott recruited Godfrey 'Paul' Paulson as an aide at Lonrho. Paulson, also a former MI6 officer who had served in Beirut simultaneously with Philby's residence, travelled occasionally to Africa for Lonrho, reinforcing the impression, cultivated by Rowland, that the company was inimical to Britain's establishment.

One other incident suggested to outsiders Lonrho's relationship with British intelligence. Soon after joining Lonrho, Elliott asked Rowland's new pilot, Captain Bill Wilming, about a recent journey. Wilming wrongly interpreted the question as a hint that Elliott's old 'office' might be interested in his services. But the pilot's colourful account fuelled the rumours. An MI6 African specialist would dismiss the notion as 'ridiculous'. The truth lay in the beholder's perception. Rowland liked the notion of a relationship with intelligence services and governments; while Elliott neither dismissed Rowland's impression nor resisted, over a drink at White's, passing his assessments, gleaned while hopping around Africa, on to old friends.

Wilming's recruitment in 1968 had completed the image of Rowland as a tireless, buccaneering jet traveller. Born in in 1930, Wilming was trained as a pilot in Biggin Hill and Fort Worth, Texas. Having ferried supplies by air in both the Biafran and Congo wars, he became a demonstration pilot for Dassault of their Falcon Mystere executive jets.

In May 1968, Dassault in Paris was telephoned by Rowland. He had dismissed his British crew in Salisbury for refusing to fly extra hours and returned to London on a commercial air-liner. Could the manufacturer, asked Rowland, send a pilot to Rhodesia to repatriate his Falcon to London? On his arrival at Cheapside, Wilming was made an offer he could not refuse. In return for an enormous salary and generous expenses, Wilming was guaranteed an exciting life. Rowland requested only that Wilming ignore the regulations limiting flying hours, a choice that was open to the pilot since the Lonrho Falcon was registered in Switzerland which at that time did not impose any restrictions.

Over the next twenty years, Wilming became Rowland's closest if not only friend and a partner in some of his most daring escapades. Based either in Bremen or Paris where the Falcon could be serviced, the pilot was on instant call to return to Heathrow, one hour's flight time, to fly anywhere in the world. Included among his many passengers would be Princess Margaret whom he flew, at Lonrho's expense, to Sardinia.

Rowland's style of travel was frugal. Neither champagne nor caviar was ever allowed on Lonrho's jet; only wines and water. Wilming arrived from Bremen with loaves of German rye bread and ordered by radio one day's supply of food from British Airways. Smoked trout and cuts of cold meat were supplemented with tins of soups, ravioli and vegetables. Conscious of his weight, Rowland favoured lots of vegeta-bles and banned gourmet dishes. Extra, fresh food would be bought each day at hotels in Africa where the plane landed.

On long journeys, Wilming would erect a couch in the cabin for Rowland to read before falling asleep. Occasionally, his pas-senger would ask for a tape of classical music or Dean Martin songs. In later years, he also watched video films and television documentaries, especially, the twenty-six parts of *The World at War*. Stowed in the cabin was Rowland's red leather brief case.

Invariably locked, it contained up to £100,000 in dollar, Swiss franc and Deutschmark notes to pay for incidental expenses, including aviation fuel. Rowland was never known to carry a credit card or pay by cheque.

On the ground, the pilot and the businessman sat and played together in hotels from Cairo to Cape Town while waiting for appointments to materialise. Chatting about the business and the past, Wilming noticed that his employer never spoke about his family. Indeed, Wilming never even knew that Rowland's father was alive and remained unaware when he eventually died. The past was as mysterious as the present. Wilming would never understand Rowland's ambition or the legacy he wished to create. 'Is it all worth it?' he asked Rowland in the midst of one particularly hazardous journey across jungles and deserts, from country to country, at breakneck speed. 'Yes,' replied Rowland, but never explained the purpose of his dream of empire. Was their unique lifestyle merely for money, wondered Wilming, who enjoyed the routine of a girlfriend at every airport.

Wilming's most frequent stop was in Salisbury. Despite the sanctions imposed by the United Nations on 29 May 1968, the Falcon quite unashamedly – routed via Malawi with Dr Banda's personal approval – returned repeatedly to allow Rowland to oversee Lonrho's operation. Although Rowland would later say that his visits were rare and furtively at night, Wilming is adamant that despite the fear of compromising his status among nationalist Africans, until 1973 Rowland regularly visited Lonrho House to discover that increasingly his friend was suffering from the pressure of deceit. 'Nic found it very difficult to continuously lie,' recalls his widow Eileen, 'and sanctions busting required constant deceit.' Kruger's salvation was alcohol. Many would express surprise that Rowland did not dismiss Kruger and interpreted his loyalty as self-interest.

A by-product of their visits was to allow Nicholas Elliott an opportunity to meet Ken Flower, the director of Rhodesia's Central Intelligence Organisation (CIO). Believing that Lonrho was helping MI6 collect information understandably reinforced Rowland's self-confidence about the future.

Four
Eve of the Storm

Rowland's ninety-minute meeting in Mayfair in April 1969 with Jim Slater, then the arch-priest of the new capitalism, provided a clear outline of Rowland's image. Slater, a forty-year-old industrial accountant had become a renowned 'money-maker', initially by speculating in shares, then as a fund manager investing in the manufacturing industry, and later by asset-stripping.

When the two men met in Slater's office, they found they had much in common. Both were mavericks, had realised their ambitions to become rich, were disdainful of Britain's financial establishment and yet anxious for City recognition. With the help of Ogilvy and Harley Drayton, Slater had joined with the model Conservative politician, Peter Walker, to form Slater Walker, which, temporarily, was a widely publicised model for the profitable management of unit trust funds and the astute takeover of undervalued corporations and conglomerates.

Slater Walker's growth had been more phenomenal than Lonrho's. Between 1966 and 1969, the share price had risen nearly 1300 per cent while the company's equity capital increased from £4 million to £135 million. Slater Walker was a high-profile team on the threshold of explosive growth, winning plaudits as Britain's great hope for the regeneration of its industry. Lonrho, by contrast, was an apparently successful but unknown company whose manager chose to remain in the shadows. Considering the common opprobrium which tarnished both Rowland and Slater for their dubious business practices shortly after that meeting, it was to Rowland's credit that his fate was remarkably different from Slater's.

Slater approached his first negotiations with Rowland with characteristic caution: 'Avoid talking first because it's expensive. Let the other person show his mind.' Slater was offering a wattle business in East Africa, called Forestal Land; Timber & Railways, a recently purchased conglomerate; and Motor Mart, which owned the franchise to sell Massey Ferguson tractors, Bedford trucks and General Motors cars.

In Slater's view, 'Rowland was arbitraging my ignorance. I knew nothing about Africa. He was a one-eyed man in the Kingdom of the blind. It was an area where no one else would want to go.' In fact, Slater was ignorant about the value of his assets. The wattle plantation covered 150,000 acres of prime agricultural land in Kenya's Rift Valley and was the area's biggest enterprise. Motor Mart supplied about 50 per cent of Kenya's cars and the country was built on Bedford trucks. The showrooms were based at Bruce House, Nairobi's prime property site. For Rowland, it would be his major introduction to Kenya, opening the way into the whole of East Africa.

In the event, Slater stated his price and Rowland not only paid less than Slater wanted but infinitely less than the assets were worth. Even better, Rowland paid in paper – Lonrho shares which were then priced at £3.25. They parted on good terms. 'What is wattle?' asked Rowland. 'Where's East Africa?' replied Slater who suspected that Rowland was playing a different game from the other Boys in London. 'I knew that I could gradually sell the shares in the market,' recalled Slater. In the event, Slater had five months to sell the Lonrho shares before their price began to slide and the first serious questions about Rowland's operations were posed. The cause of the problem was the Inyati copper mine in Rhodesia.

Inyati's profits depended upon exporting the copper by avoiding sanctions. A devious export route was discoverd by Kruger who, in July 1968, bought the Edmundian copper mine which was situated just hundreds of yards across the border in Mozambique, still a Portuguese colony. Edmundian was derelict but was situated on the Umtali to Beira railway line, precisely the route Inyati copper was transported. Ken Adams, Kanyemba's manager, was dispatched to the Edmundian mine to commence limited activity. Inyati's production would be relabelled, 'ex-Edmundian'. The plan, agreed with Rowland, was to sell the copper in Japan.

Inyati's ownership was confused. The Rhodesian operating company which owned the mine was called Corsyn. In turn, Corsyn was owned by Coronation Syndicate, the South African public company. Lonrho was the majority shareholder in Coronation Syndicate. That fractured ownership caused problems.

Since Lonrho was financing Inyati's development and the expected profits were enormous, the Lonrho directors decided they wanted to retain all the profits. Their chosen method was to make an offer to buy out the minority shareholders of Coronation Syndicate. Instead of cash, the minority shareholders would be offered Lonrho shares.

Initially, the Lonrho directors were faced with two problems. Firstly, if they revealed Inyati's expansion, the value of Coronation Syndicate shares would rise. Secondly, if the link between Coronation Syndicate, Inyati and Lonrho became known in Africa, the nationalist governments whom Rowland was wooing would realise that, contrary to his protestations, Lonrho was actively involved in racially segregated states. The solution was to embark upon a policy of deceit.

The first step to disguise the mine's prospects had already been taken. On 26 July 1968, the Corsyn board decided to discontinue issuing reports about the mine's development. The decision was endorsed by Butcher who asked Clifford Bentley, Coronation Syndicate's South African chairman, to consider 'remoulding [Corsyn's annual] report to avoid the giving of too detailed information about Inyati.'

Over the following months, the offer to exchange Lonrho's shares for Coronation Syndicate's was formulated. Rowland's agreement to the undertaking was explicit but he constantly feared the repercussions, especially in Ghana where the Ashanti deal had just been completed. Ball and the old Rhodesian hands, thought Rowland, did not understand the delicacy and the need to disguise Lonrho's southern African connection. But eventually he cast aside those doubts. The Inyati profits, reasoned Rowland, were too good to lose.

On 24 December 1968 Rowland approved the terms of the offer and flew for his traditional Christmas holiday to Acapulco, Mexico, leaving Ball and Butcher to finalise the remaining details. An application was dispatched to the Johannesburg stock exchange to offer the exchange of shares and a formal announcement was published on 27 December.

The basis of the offer document, written by Kruger and Bentley, was an artifice of disguise. The unwitting Coronation Syndicate shareholder would not realise Inyati's true value. The details to distort Inyati's value were plotted by Kruger in Salisbury and Bentley in Johannesburg who referred their decisions to Lonrho in London. In a substantial exchange of telexes, later discovered by the South African police, Bentley told Kruger on 21 February 1969 that the auditors in Johannesburg were 'adamant' about some disclosure which would be embarrassing and counter-productive. Bentley wanted to fly to London to consult Butcher on text which would avoid being honest. Kruger agreed. 'It is a pity,' he telexed to Bentley, 'but agree fully that you put it over to Fred as there is nothing we can do this side.'

Kruger was therefore admitting that Butcher and in turn Rowland would have to approve any deceit. Bentley therefore telexed Butcher explaining, 'We have deliberately avoided reference to increased production' but the auditors insisted on some disclosure.

In London, Butcher was unimpressed with the attempted cover-up. He needed to know the nature of the auditors' 'pressure'. As Butcher knowingly explained, auditors were malleable: 'Auditors will very often insist but revise their opinion if the appropriate sounds are made and it is in Nic's place that the pressure must be exerted.' Butcher's proposal was stark: 'Suggest all reference to Inyati be eliminated.' Too many people in Johannesburg were already involved to accept that option.

Bentley and Kruger therefore adopted another solution. The accounts, they decided, should be completely rewritten. Time however was pressing. It was Friday afternoon and Kruger would need to deploy his entire staff over the weekend. Bentley had an additional problem, 'Please endeavour to come back to me this afternoon as my wife is away and I have an appointment with the girlfriend tonight.' But that proposal also collapsed when Kruger failed to persuade the auditors in Salisbury to underwrite the proposed dishonesty. It was Bentley who finally invented the solution. A new statement had been written, incorporating a submission by Hossy. According to Bentley, Lonrho's mining engineer had 'deliberately tried to make the review as dull as ditchwater and difficult reading'. On that basis, over the weekend, two sets of accounts were prepared. One presented the company's financial state as worse than the other.

There was no doubt that Rowland was aware of these manoeuvres. Regularly, Hossy commuted to London to brief Butcher, Rowland and Gerald Percy about Inyati's developments. 'I was against giving any information to the shareholders,' he admits. He won agreement that it was best to disguise the rapid developments at the Inyati mine.

Accordingly, in contrast to Coronation Syndicate's 1967 annual report where Inyati activities were explained in detail, the accounts for 1968 disguised Inyati's results. The profits were grouped with three other Rhodesian mines, all moribund or about to close, under the heading, 'Base Metal Mines'. The price of Inyati's copper was also distorted. Instead of 1039 rand per ton as earned for Messina, Inyati's price was stated to be 930 rand per ton. Subsequently, it was believed that there was transfer pricing.

Bentley's personal statement to Coronation Syndicate's shareholders was equally misleading. Compared to the detailed information about Lonrho's gold mines, Bentley merely explained under the heading that Inyati's production was 'encouraging' although 'lower' than the previous year. Ore production had in fact more than doubled. Expenditure was said to be 'substantial' whereas in fact the profits had risen six-fold. Finally, Bentley concealed Lonrho's plan to double Inyati's production within two years.

According to Hossy, the architect of that deception was, 'Butcher, in a moment of idiocy'. Few believe that Butcher acted on his own initiative.

Coronation Syndicate's annual general meeting was due to be held on 27 May 1969. Just before flying to Johannesburg, Kruger feared that he might be vulnerable to accusations of suppressing information. He decided upon a realistic cover story, namely, that under the prevailing conditions in Rhodesia, the disclosure of increased production of copper would infringe security. To obtain official cover for that deceit, Kruger wrote to the minister of mines requesting that he issue an order that Lonrho should withhold information.

Kruger arrived in Johannesburg anticipating problems. The document's publication had provoked criticism that the offer was too low and rumours that Lonrho's motives were suspicious. The principal instigator was a Johannesburg stockbroker, Jacobus Esterhuysen.

In March 1968, Esterhuysen had read a mining engineer's report which described Inyati as the 'jewel in Pandora's box for Corsyn'. Intrigued, Esterhuysen flew to Salisbury to inspect the mine and visit Lonrho House. Kruger, suffering from the constant deceit, was as usual inebriated. Esterhuysen was told that the government's security regulations forbade visits. But, without any problems and to Kruger's embarrassment, Esterhuysen obtained the minister's permission to visit the mine: 'I saw a lot of activity. I knew then that the mine was worth a lot more than they claimed.'

One year later, at Coronation Syndicate's 1969 annual general meeting in Johannesburg, Esterhuysen accused Kruger of producing a 'false' offer document. Forlornly, Kruger sought to persuade Esterhuysen that Lonrho was not concealing anything. That night, Kruger reported to Rowland about the shareholders' 'dissatisfaction'. Ball replied, ordering the manager to keep Esterhuysen unaware of 'London approval' for the policy. Lonrho's chairman sincerely believed that they could deceive the South African shareholders.

The following day, 525 tons of Inyati copper concentrates were impounded in Japan. Although identified as emanating from the Edmundian mine in Mozambique, the true provenance had been leaked weeks earlier to a British diplomat by a disgruntled shipping clerk in Beira. The exposure was published by the

United Nations sanctions committee. Momentarily, everyone at Cheapside feared that Lonrho would be identified as a sanctions buster. But there was a temporary reprieve. The metal's source was merely stated to be Hochmetals, a Rhodesian company operating in South Africa.

Esterhuysen's campaign continued. Initially, he protested to the minister of mines in Salisbury but was rebuffed with excuses about the needs of security. But since his criticisms were reported by South African newspapers, the Rhodesian government, sensitive to the country's vital ally, relented. Lonrho was ordered to issue more information about Inyati.

Kruger was aghast and pleaded on 10 June 1969 that the release of information was 'not in the interests of shareholders'. Regular shipments of copper were sent to Japan, Kruger wrote, and if their source was known, there would be 'a degree of embarrassment' ultimately forcing the mine's closure. Spurred on by Wilfred Brookes in *Property & Finance*, the government knew that Kruger was lying. Lonrho's conspiracy was beginning to unravel.

On 30 June 1969, Esterhuysen contacted the Central Merchant Bank, Lonrho's representatives, and Charles Friedman, the company's lawyer. The stockbroker requested an opportunity to produce his evidence of deliberate deception. To both the bankers and the lawyer, this was the first indication that their clients were being accused of deceit. Contrary to popular belief in Britain, South Africans, despite their country's sympathy for Rhodesia, were not always prepared to compromise their individual principles and profits by joining all Rhodesia's conspiracies to avoid sanctions.

Friedman summoned Kruger, Bentley and Hossy. At that meeting on 9 July, the Lonrho experts dismissed suggestions that the mine was productive. Kruger told the lawyer that, 'development has not come up to expectations.' Promising to hand over a detailed mining report, Hossy and Kruger gathered their papers and rushed to catch a plane for Salisbury. Left behind, Bentley unwittingly handed Friedman his unexpurgated copy taken from his desk. Within the file was Hossy's four-page report predicting huge profits from Inyati.

The following day, Kruger was told that both the bank and the lawyer had no alternative but to inform the regulatory authorities that the offer document was inaccurate and that the Rhodesian government would be informed.

Kruger could no longer cope alone. Rowland, Ball and Butcher flew to Johannesburg. During the ensuing discussions, the bankers and lawyers discovered that there were more complications than they imagined. The duplicity had started earlier when Lonrho had created a company called Eastern Minerals to take over Inyati from Corsyn. After operating the mine for sixteen months, Eastern had retransferred the mine back to Corsyn. In the process, by a technical manoeuvre, Corsyn's $1.5 million profits had 'disappeared' by nullifying Eastern's capital. [The ruse however would come unstuck. Eastern told the High Court that the transfer back occurred in October 1969 but that was untrue because at the March 1970 annual general meeting, Eastern still owned Corsyn.]

Stunned, the bankers advised the Lonrho directors to withdraw the offer documents. There would be no need for publicity. It could all be done quietly. Rowland and his friends agreed. In a terse statement, the Lonrho directors blamed 'the recent Rhodesian referendum and other political difficulties'. With the exception of Esterhuysen, the financial community in Johannesburg remained unenlightened and uninterested about the background of the statement.

Rowland returned to London to cope with a more serious problem. Lonrho's accounts for 1968 were two months overdue and rumours had depressed Lonrho's share price from 316 pence in March to 175 pence in June. Five days after their dash to Johannesburg, on 16 July 1969, Rowland sat silently beside Ball for the annual general meeting as the chairman reassured everyone about Lonrho's past 'record year' and predicted that the 1968 pre-tax profits of £7.1 million would increase to £13.5 million in the following year. The Coronation Syndicate offer was brushed aside as irrelevant. Shareholders were told that the offer had been withdrawn 'very reluctantly' because of the 'evident lack of enthusiasm' among shareholders. It was a lie which Bentley called 'a tragedy', because an overwhelming number of Coronation Syndicate's independent shareholders had enthusiastically accepted the offer.

Temporarily Lonrho's shares recovered to 230 pence but in August they began falling again. Their erratic decline reflected developing suspicions about the value of the company's glamour projects. Sceptics for the first time queried Rowland's strategy. Embracing nearly 400 companies in Africa, Lonrho suddenly appeared as a ragbag of assets spread over a large, high-risk area rather than concentrated like Anglo American on a few, guaranteed profit earners. For the first time, Rowland's grandiose ventures seemed to be soured dreams. His proposed oil pipeline from Tanzania to Zambia was awarded to an Italian company; his proposal to build a railway from Katanga to the Atlantic coast was rejected; his bid for a diamond mine was frustrated; his announcement that Lonrho would buy a platinum mine in South Africa was mocked by other companies which had tried and failed in the same area; Lonrho had failed to win the Katanga copper contract; the statistics of gold production in Ghana had been delayed; and some copper mines in Zambia had been nationalised. Lonrho's whole edifice, built upon the goodwill of African politicians and the efforts of one man, was questioned. Lonrho was perceived to lack any financial management to balance its risks in Africa. Rowland, it was rumoured, was running a public company in his own interests. Confidence was slipping fast. To combat the criticism, Ball predicted, 'We'll make £19 million profits for 1970.' Just weeks earlier, he had promised profits of £13.5 million. Talking up the profits did not stabilise Rowland's faltering star. By autumn, the share price was down to 130 pence.

The cause of the fall was an examination of the 1969 annual report. Lonrho's profits had been stated as £14.44 million, more than double the previous year. However the figure contained £9 million of pre-acquisition profits of the newly absorbed companies, a revelation that excited doubts.

As the share price fell, Rowland's and Ball's public pronouncements about Lonrho's good health became volubly shrill. Realising that Lonrho's credibility was low, Rowland had tried to recruit 'stars' as directors to the board. One approach to Winston

Churchill, the grandson of the former prime minister, had been rejected on the grounds that it would clash with his journalistic career; others had shied away on more spurious grounds.

The problem was more substance than image. Philip Hunter, a new Lonrho director, complained to Ball in September 1969 about the financial chaos inside Cheapside: 'I was always thumping that there was a lack of financial information.'

Rowland, as Hunter knew, was renowned for literally compiling Lonrho's accounts on the back of an envelope. 'He would forecast the following year's profits,' explained a Lonrho director, 'and then pronounce the figures above the line which added up to his predicted total.'

For the first time, Rowland's limitations were exposed. He was a deal maker, outrightly indifferent to the intricacies of management. His overriding interest was the statistics proving Lonrho's size. He had no sympathy for accountants. 'They're paper merchants,' he scoffed. 'I know what's going on.' The truth was the opposite. Events would prove that Lonrho's finances were doomed by Rowland denying himself regular, accurate accounts from every subsidiary. On Rowland's own admission, he was unable to cope with the critical disciplines required to sustain the empire he desired. To those who had not heard his loathing for independent accountants, Rowland told the joke about a balloonist landing in a field and asking, 'Where am I?' A passer-by answers: 'You're in a wicker basket beneath a balloon in a ploughed field.'

'You must be an accountant,' replies the balloonist.

'How did you know?'

'Because your information is totally accurate and totally useless.'

Nevertheless, Rowland agreed to the appointment of an accountant on condition that he remained out of sight on the fifth floor.

Eric Armitage, recruited from Hoover as the chief accountant, arrived to find little sympathy from his supervisor, Fred Butcher. 'He was a pen pusher who didn't know how to use a calculator,' is one of Armitage's more flattering assessments of the unqualified finance director. Armitage had been introduced to Rowland by

Butcher as 'the best of a bad bunch'. Besides Armitage, Lonrho
employed one other accountant and two secretaries to manage
the group's finances from the fifth floor. Accountants were not
a valued commodity in Cheapside. Indeed, Rowland himself
admitted that in ten years, 'I have been down to the fifth floor
once or twice.'

The repercussions of the delayed accounts had not evaporated. The fault, Armitage soon concluded, was Lonrho's use
of Fuller Jenks, a small firm of accountants. The firm's senior
partner Leonard Pratley was a solitary, weak character with a
passion for collecting coins. Pratley was prepared to pretend
that all Lonrho's earnings in Africa were in genuine hard
currency and hid the reality that much of the so-called profits
were unremittable and worthless. That Lonrho had employed
Fuller Jenks as its auditors was, 'quite deliberately to present
the accounts to suit Rowland', concluded Armitage. Armitage
believed that his task was to distinguish between real and blocked
earnings from Africa but he found no sympathy from Butcher.
'Rowland had given him a Rolls Royce with a chauffeur,' says
Armitage, 'and he was totally beholden to Rowland. It wasn't a
good beginning.' Armitage was dispatched to Africa to examine
the empire.

Lonrho's financial problems were compounded by an approach
to Ogilvy concerning Lonrho's activities in Rhodesia. The issue
was the copper seized in Japan which had originated from
Lonrho's Inyati mine. During September 1969, the Foreign
Office was told by the United Nations sanctions committee
about Lonrho's use of the Edmundian mine. The presence of
Ogilvy on the Lonrho board made the information particularly
sensitive and was eventually considered by Sir Denis Greenhill,
the newly appointed senior civil servant at the Foreign Office
and Sir Burke Trend, the secretary to the Cabinet.

Greenhill's predicament was unusual. As the head of the
Foreign Office, he had read the minutes of the meeting in
Whitehall between George Thomson and the executives of Shell
and BP on 6 February 1969, where the government had effectively
condoned arrangements for the British companies' delivery of oil
to Rhodesia. Greenhill was not shocked. He had no sympathy for

the sanctions policy but he understood the sensitivity of Ogilvy's dilemma. The royal family's connection with Lonrho could not be ignored.

On 19 November, Greenhill and Trend met Ogilvy in the Cabinet offices. The two civil servants outlined their incontrovertible evidence based upon reports from MI6 stations in Pretoria and in Salisbury that Lonrho was breaking sanctions. 'We are only concerned with the risk of scandal rubbing off on the Crown,' said Greenhill who added that Lonrho's reputation for bribery did not help matters.

At the best of times, Ogilvy was indecisive. Ever since his marriage and his consequent appointment to over forty prestigious directorships, there had been whispers about the unsuitability of Lonrho. Some would say that Ogilvy feared Rowland. Others suggested that Ogilvy adored his friend who was also a neighbour in the Park Lane apartment which Lonrho provided. Rowland would say that the two families were the 'closest of friends, often breakfasting together in our dressing gowns'. For good or ill, the relationship was sufficiently close for Ogilvy to defend Rowland to the two Whitehall emissaries.

'Old wives' tales,' he said dismissively. 'There's no way,' he told them, 'that I can check whether Lonrho is bribing officials or breaking sanctions.' At that time, so far as Ogilvy was concerned, Lonrho was obeying the same rules as every other British company like BAT, the tobacco company, and BP, the oil giant.

Ogilvy seemed to be discounting the civil servants' information. After all, if he were to follow the officials' argument to its conclusion, he would need to resign and that would be expensive, bad for his reputation and damaging to Lonrho. As Greenhill returned to the issue of the problem for the Crown, Ogilvy countered with his loyalty to Rowland. 'I can't just walk out on him. He's a friend and he would be harmed. And for what? I've never heard of this Edmundian mine.' Both officials became impressed with Ogilvy's concern for the shareholders. But neither was aware that Ogilvy counted himself among the shareholders who would suffer if he resigned.

Ogilvy proposed a solution. 'How would it be if I got an

assurance from the chairman that these stories were untrue?'
Greenhill was not completely enthusiastic but two days later
scrutinised Ogilvy's draft letter to Ball requesting confirmation
of Lonrho's innocence. Greenhill's amendments eradicated the
source of Ogilvy's initiative.

Ogilvy's letter to Alan Ball mentioned that he was 'still
rather fussed' about the rumours 'flying around the City in
which Lonrho is alleged to have been involved in bribery and
corruption, sanctions breaking etc.' Ogilvy asked his friend for
an assurance that 'there is absolutely no truth in them'.

Ball could hardly have taken the letter seriously. Ogilvy, he
believed, knew that bribes were regularly paid in Africa and
approved the practice. Indeed, Ogilvy was not against the principle of bribery in Africa. It was part of doing business like paying a merchant bank an underwriting fee. He knew that Lonrho
had paid a Ghanaian diplomat in Kenya £6122 for arranging
the contacts to build a brewery in Ghana. The cash was handed
to the Chief's wife in a briefcase. Ogilvy also knew that Lonrho
had sought to destigmatise their 'special payments' by making contributions to 'charities'. In Kenya, Lonrho's favoured charity
was the Agricultural Development Fund which had received one
donation of £7500 while Kenyan Breweries had received two
payments of £10,000 and £5000.

Ball, normally the epitome of ineffectual mildness, responded
violently to Ogilvy's letter. Since the rumours were true and he
would need to lie, he chose to launch an intemperate attack on
Ogilvy's suspicions as the best defence. Claiming that he was
'astonished' that any executive director should have requested
such assurances, Ball alleged that Lonrho was 'caught up in the
middle of a vicious smear campaign'. The directors' duty, he
claimed, was to run a successful company and 'devote far less
valuable time to worrying about these absurd rumours'.

Ogilvy was satisfied. The letter, he believed, was protection
if events soured and his conduct was queried. Ball's reply could
be produced to show that 'even if he had been a fool, he had
not been a knave'. In the meantime, he would feign to ignore
all discussions within Lonrho about Rhodesia.

At the heart of the deception was Ogilvy's apparent participation in the development of the Shamrocke mine in Rhodesia, another secret operation, in breach of sanctions, which was financed by Lonrho's money but for private gain.

Within Rowland's tight circle, there was excitement about the rising price of copper. During 1969, copper prices would climb steadily from £532 to £720 per ton, stimulating the same speculation as the oil boom of the 1970s. With every expectation that the trend would continue, Rowland reconsidered the prospects of exploiting the deposits at the Shamrocke mine whose ownership, although still formally a joint venture with Michael Reynolds, was in some dispute.

Rowland's original agreement with Lonrho in 1961 had not included the Shamrocke mine. During the years after the initial option had expired, Reynolds had urged Rowland to consider other investors or buyers, including one which Reynolds had found. Rowland had refused, leaving Reynolds powerless since under their agreement Rowland possessed the sole power to decide the terms of any sale.

In Reynolds's opinion, Rowland had embarked upon guerrilla tactics to undermine his partner. During late 1965, their disagreements had climaxed when Reynolds discovered that Rowland had charged a visit to London against Shamrocke. Reynolds had objected and subsequently discovered that, 'I had resigned from the board and Rowland had accepted my resignation.' The minutes of the meeting recording Reynolds's resignation had been authenticated by the auditors, Peat Marwick and Mitchell. Reynolds none the less disputes their authenticity.

In the ensuing confrontation, Rowland had allegedly told Reynolds, 'Mike, you are a comparatively poor man and I am a comparatively rich man. As long as I am alive, Shamrocke will remain a hole in the ground.'

In March 1966, Reynolds lost all his money when his hotel, the victim of UDI, ceased trading. He was declared bankrupt. The following events revealed Rowland's methods of operation but, more importantly, would lead him, Ogilvy and Lonrho into a scandal which tainted them for ever.

Reynolds's interest in the Shamrocke mine was controlled by

the bankruptcy trustee in the interests of the creditors. Naturally, Rowland was offered Reynolds's share. Rowland proffered
£250. Reynolds was outraged and soon found another bidder
who offered £10,000 for the whole mine. Rowland rejected that
solution and in turn decided, in March 1967, to pressure the
trustee to sell by issuing new shares for which the trustee would
have to pay £1000 or lose his interest. With Reynolds's help, the
money was found but the following month Rowland again tried
to force Reynolds to sell by demanding that more shares worth
£16,000 be issued. On that occasion, his ploy was defeated. Five
months later, Reynolds produced a £60,000 bid from Japan for
the whole mine. Again Rowland rejected the offer. Unknown
to Reynolds, Rowland had dispatched Gerald Percy to Japan
to negotiate the financing of Shamrocke with Nisho Iwai. The
introduction had been arranged by Jack Kato, a contact of
Rowland's.

Two years earlier, Ian Hossy had judged that Shamrocke's
development would be economic if the world copper price was
above £400 per ton. A strike in America had forced copper
prices to zoom within five months from £413 to £720. Percy was
reporting 'intense interest' in Japan to conclude a long-term deal
for Shamrocke's copper.

Suddenly, in April 1968, that interest evaporated. The
American strike was settled and the copper price began sinking.
Despite that collapse, in July 1968, Rowland paid Reynolds's
trustee £18,500 to obtain total ownership of the mine. But the
money, under a private arrangement between Rowland and
Kruger, was paid by Lonrho in Salisbury and Reynolds's shares
were owned by Lonrho. At that stage, Rowland claimed that
the mine was worth £1 million.

Shamrocke's ownership was unusual. Half the mine belonged
to Lonrho Investment Company Ltd (LIC), Lonrho's main holding company in Rhodesia [having passed through Corsyn], while
the other half belonged to Shepton Estates, Rowland's personal
company, subject to his 50 per cent partnership with Graham
Beck, his original South African partner.

Significantly, Rowland had tried in November 1967 to sell his
own interest to Corsyn. The attempt was blocked by Reynolds.

Rowland did not renew the transfer after Lonrho had bought Reynolds's share.

One year later, in July 1969, just as production at the Inyati copper mine was increasing and the Coronation Syndicate furore was attracting attention, Rowland told Kruger and Hossy to commence production at Shamrocke. Copper prices, Rowland believed, were about to rocket, justifying the large investment needed to develop both mines. Critically, Rowland arranged for all the costs of the development of the Shamrocke mine to be paid by Lonrho. For Rowland, it was an ideal position. Any losses would be paid by Lonrho while he would share half of any profits. Significantly, the arrangement was not discussed by the Lonrho board. According to Ball, Lonrho agreed to finance only the 'initial development'. In contradiction, Rowland claimed that Lonrho agreed to pay all the costs. That was not the only misunderstanding.

Rowland's original contract with Lonrho in 1961 stipulated that he could not undertake any work for any other company which was similar to Lonrho's. In previous years, he had often argued quite violently with John Mills, Lonrho's transparently honest general manager, about whether Shamrocke should be owned by Lonrho. 'They used to annoy one another to such an extent,' observed Ball about their disputes at board meetings, 'that it invariably broke up in disarray.' Unlike Mills, Ball said that he never regarded the issue as 'serious'. He had good reason. Unknown to Mills and the other members of the board, both Ball and Angus Ogilvy had received from Rowland a secret interest in the Shamrocke mine and hoped that with the rising price of copper, they would earn a tax-free bonus. 'Tiny was much more interested in the development of Shamrocke than Inyati,' recalled Percy. 'He had a personal interest.'

By February 1970, Lonrho had spent over £140,000 on Shamrocke's development and Rowland feared that any profits would be stuck in Rhodesia. Although the Labour government's sanctions policy was discredited and there was every indication that in the imminent elections the Conservatives, eager to negotiate a settlement with Smith, would win, he wanted to protect his investment against any investigation. In February 1970, Rowland flew with Fred Butcher and Alan Ball to South Africa. Their purpose was to transfer ownership of the Shamrocke mine from Nyaschere, the Rhodesian company, to a new company called HCC Investments, registered in South Africa. The purpose of HCC Investments was to overcome sanctions. Either the development of the Rhodesian mine could be financed with money from Britain passing through South Africa or dividends could be paid from Rhodesia to South Africa and then to Britain.

Once HCC was established, the company received both Lonrho's and Rowland's shares in Nyaschere and the Shamrocke mine. By that stage, Rowland's shares had been transferred by a complicated route to Switzerland, and the mine's ownership was divided between Rowland, Ball and Ogilvy. Hence, Ogilvy was personally a part owner of a copper mine in Rhodesia contrary to the British sanctions laws. Ogilvy would blame Rowland for placing him, without his knowledge, in that embarrassing position.

The complication started when Rowland, returning from South Africa, decided that he needed some money. He wanted to use the 5.7 million Lonrho shares which were held by Yeoman Trust in the Bahamas as security to raise a US$2 million loan. Rowland asked Ogilvy for help to raise the loan.

Among Ogilvy's directorships at that time, was that of the Midland Bank and of the Canadian Imperial Bank of Commerce. Ogilvy's recollection was that Rowland said, 'We need it to develop our mines in South Africa', and wanted to borrow £2.5 million.

Ogilvy's relationship with Rowland had changed substantially over the previous eight years. While his admiration remained, he had become gradually concerned about Rowland's style and manner. Essentially a gentleman businessman, Ogilvy's mind could not cope with Rowland's recent deals which seemed to be of increasing complexity.

Nevertheless, Ogilvy arranged for two representatives of the Canadian bank to meet Rowland on 12 March 1970 at Lonrho's headquarters. Rowland, according to the bank's own record, mentioned that the money was needed to develop both South African mines and 'a copper mine in Rhodesia'. Ogilvy would later claim not to have heard that part of the conversation which he asserted was contrived by Rowland. Rowland however, emphatically contradicted Ogilvy: 'There was not a single thing he did not know.' Rowland says that Ogilvy 'wanted money'. In the event, the bank agreed to lend $2 million.

Under Rowland's orders, the $2 million was channelled into a labyrinth of companies. Half a million dollars was transferred to London, of which Rowland kept for personal use about £100,000. The remaining $1.5 million was transferred in July 1970 to Switzerland. Firstly into a company called Mines and Minerals AG and from there into another company called Borma – which not coincidentally was later interpreted as an acronym for 'Ball Ogilvy Rowland Mutual Association'. Borma's registered address was at the Swiss Bank Corporation in Zurich and was later transferred on 7 July 1970 to c/o Dr Oscar Menz in Zug, Switzerland. Alan Ball would subsequently describe these arrangements as 'very involved' but it was consistent with Rowland's habit of depositing his funds beyond the scrutiny of the British government.

Borma used the $1.5 million to buy the 50 per cent interest in the Shamrocke mine owned by Shepton Estates. Borma then 'sold' its interests to HCC. Two curious calculations then followed.

The three men agreed that Rowland's interest in Shamrocke was worth $1.36 million [£590,000], nearly the total sum deposited in Borma. Yet originally Rowland had paid £18,500 for Reynolds's share, when he claimed the real value was £1 million. The Rhodesian government estimated the value when its ownership was transferred to South Africa at £46,000.

The hubris was now concluded. Rowland paid Ogilvy £60,000 and Ball just under £120,000 which represented their 10 per cent and 20 per cent interest in the original agreement to have 'part of the action'. Both men, to avoid paying tax, had placed their interest in trusts for their family. In theory, they were not able to decide personally how their interest could be used. Nevertheless, Ogilvy believed at the time that the money was either a gift or a loan. 'I had no idea that I was now a part owner of the Shamrocke mine,' he would later claims which contradicted others present at the meetings to raise the loan. Ball could not explain why he received the money other than as a gift or a loan; while Rowland pointedly refused to explain why his two friends received the payments. Eventually Ogilvy interpreted that money as Rowland's future stake for 'blackmail'. At the moment he received the money, Ogilvy later claimed that he was considering resigning from Lonrho. The decision was deferred both then and on seven separate occasions thereafter.

The final situation therefore was that the Shamrocke mine was half owned by Lonrho, and the remaining 50 per cent was owned by Rowland, Ball and Ogilvy in a 70:20:10 split. Significantly, Graham Beck, who owned 50 per cent of Rowland's original interest, had been ignored.

News of the new arrangements in Switzerland were withheld from the other Lonrho directors who also remained unaware of Rowland's private interest in the mine. Moreover, more than half the board were unaware even of Lonrho's detailed financial commitment to develop the mine. That was known only to Rowland, Ball and Butcher.

At that moment, the price of copper had fallen to £568 per ton from its peak of £731 per ton in March. By the end of the year, copper prices would fall to £436, close to Hossy's cut-off point where the mine would be commercially worthless. None the less, by the end of 1971, Lonrho would have paid nearly £3 million to finance the mine's development and no profits were earned.

Rowland's use and abuse of Lonrho, a public company, was evident on a train journey to Liverpool. Travelling with Ball and Percy, he told his two companions, 'Most senior company chairmen and directors have company flats or houses. It seems ridiculous that you two don't.' By then Rowland had used Lonrho's money to buy Hedsor Wharf and the apartment in Park Lane. Ogilvy's adjoining apartment had been renovated, decorated and furnished by Lonrho. Nicholas Elliott also enjoyed a Lonrho flat in Belgrave Square. Not surprisingly, Ball replied, 'It sounds a very nice idea.'

Percy bought a house in Chelsea Square while Ball took a flat in Kensington. A Lonrho subsidiary, African Investment Trust

[AIT], bought the houses without disclosing the purchase to the board. AIT was described by Ball as Lonrho's 'Group "Banking" company' to handle discreet payments.

To Rowland's irritation, Andrew Caldecott the solicitor opposed both the use of Lonrho's money and the subterfuge in the properties' purchase. The money of a public company, he protested, was being used for the directors' personal benefit. Percy and Ball, he insisted, should not receive rent-free accommodation: 'I don't approve of buying these expensive houses.'

Peremptorily, on 11 September, Ball wrote to Caldecott asking for his resignation from AIT and also questioned his continuation as the group's legal adviser. Irritated, Caldecott raised the issue at Lonrho's board meeting. To divert attention, Ball agreed that a special committee of Rowland, Butcher and Caldecott should investigate the complaint, but the committee never convened. Caldecott's replacement was Fred Butcher, who was inclined to sympathise with the opinion that Rowland was generously rewarding those building the company. Others placed a more sinister interpretation on Rowland's designs to secure his directors' tolerance of his idiosyncratic style.

The fuse which would eventually fracture Ogilvy's and Rowland's reputation was at that moment being set in South Africa. William Barclay, a stockbroker, had been tipped in January 1970 by a client that the shares of Coronation Syndicate, the part owner of the Inyati copper mine, were unusually 'lively'. Thirty-five-year-old Barclay was not a particularly experienced broker but, working as a partner in his father's firm, he always diligently pursued the information which he received. Critically, he was unaware of Esterhuysen's interest and activities the previous year.

Barclay contacted a mining analyst and was shown two aerial photographs of the Inyati mine. The contrast between the first in 1965 and the second in 1969 confirmed that serious developments had been undertaken. Barclay concedes that it was, 'a speculator's dream' and he advised his clients to buy Coronation shares. Simultaneously, he too began buying shares on his own account and watched as other speculators, aware of the rumours, also began buying. By the end of January 1970,

Barclay had increased his holding to 153,000 shares. It was an enormous commitment and Barclay was becoming distinctly nervous: 'It was our firm's biggest deal.'

At that moment, Clifford Bentley, the chairman of Coronation Syndicate, wrote to the Johannesburg stock exchange passing on a statement which he had given to Reuters, the news agency. 'This company,' Bentley stated, 'has made no new major mining discoveries in Rhodesia which it has not already announced to its shareholders.' Since Coronation Syndicate had until then never announced a 'new major' discovery, Bentley's statement was, as he intended, at best ambiguous.

Nervous about his financial commitment to an uncertain proposition, Barclay decided to inspect the mine. In what Barclay describes as a 'cloak and dagger' operation, he drove out of Salisbury to the Inyati mine and discovered, hidden behind surrounding hills, an 'unexpectedly huge' mining operation which included a smelter and a refinery which was under construction. Lonrho's deception was indisputable but Barclay was uncertain about the reasons. Having seen the smelter and refinery, Barclay believed that the most obvious cause was to overcome sanctions. The finished copper was either to be used in Rhodesia or was for export. He returned to Johannesburg, however, intent on eliciting more information from Bentley and Kruger at Coronation Syndicate's annual general meeting which was due on 26 March 1970. Across Johannesburg, Clifford Bentley, Coronation Syndicate's chairman, having heard about Barclay's visit, feared that the meeting might become a débâcle.

In a telex to Rowland and Ball on 6 February, Bentley warned that Esterhuysen and Barclay had obtained sufficient evidence to prove that Lonrho was lying. He warned that if the criticisms emerged at the annual general meeting, the shares could be suspended and Lonrho's attempts to raise loans would be 'disastrous'. Rowland was unpersuaded and remained adamant even when Bentley telephoned three days later. Instead, Bentley was ordered to pacify the opposition.

To Barclay's surprise, on the day before the annual general meeting, he was invited to meet Kruger and the other directors. 'We'd like to keep tomorrow's meeting brief so let's settle any questions you might have now,' explained Kruger.

Ostensibly, it was a cosy meeting in Lonrho's offices. Sipping a Scotch, Barclay set out his estimate of Inyati's worth but carefully did not reveal that he had visited the mine. His predictions provoked Kruger and Bentley to laugh. 'We couldn't afford a smelter at the mine,' smiled Bentley, feigning ignorance of Barclay's having seen the smelter and the Lonrho refinery under construction. 'When I realised that they were being blatantly dishonest,' recalls Barclay, 'I shut up.' But Barclay still believed that Lonrho was attempting to avoid sanctions, and not involved in a bid to deceive the shareholders.

At 10 a.m. on 26 March 1970, the annual general meeting convened at the Barclays Bank building in Johannesburg with Bentley in the chair. His report, written six weeks earlier, announced that Inyati was producing 10,000 tons of copper per month. But at the meeting, Bentley admitted that the mine's production had doubled to 20,000 tons per month and predicted an increase to 24,000 tons. Yet Bentley insisted that 'no payable orebodies have been discovered'. To avoid alerting the shareholders to the deliberate deception, Bentley did not mention the new refinery. Both Barclay and Esterhuysen, who correctly estimated current production at 30,000 tons, voted against adopting the report.

One week later, Barclay confronted Bentley: 'Why did you distort the figures?' he asked. 'We don't want publicity,' explained the Lonrho employee. 'We could be jailed for sanctions busting.' The broker accepted the explanation.

In July, Barclay published a pamphlet urging investors to buy Coronation Syndicate shares because he predicted that production would rise to 40,000 tons annually compared to the company's prediction of 24,000 tons. Barclay admitted that he had a stake in the company. The value of Coronation Syndicate's shares did not increase. Traditionally, the investing public would only trust information officially provided by the company. Once again Barclay travelled to Rhodesia to see the mine. In his absence, to his surprise, the price of the shares fell from 2 rand to 1.4 rand. It was the first of what he calls, 'three unexpected and mysterious falls'.

By August 1970, Barclay had borrowed 770,000 rand to buy the Coronation Syndicate shares, many of them on 'long' contracts. In the previous weeks he had become convinced from conversations with other brokers that there was a shortage of the shares and hence the price would rise. Instead, the price fell once more and a sudden flood of shares materialised to satisfy Barclay's contracts. He suspected but could not prove that they came from nominee companies in the Cayman Islands. The effect upon Barclay was devastating. As the deals became payable and the quoted share price was below his contract price, he needed to borrow more money.

By December, Barclay was despairing. Lonrho still refused to authorise the publication of accurate information and the price of the shares was stuck. Technically, the Barclays' firm became insolvent.

The Barclays hoped that their predicament would remain a secret but on a Friday afternoon, Tom Adams, a partner of the firm's auditors Aitkin & Carter arrived with devastating news. 'Your liabilities are greater than your assets,' said Adams. 'The stock exchange council must be told.' South Africa's laws forbade Adams to allow the firm any time to raise the money to cover their debts. In what Barclay would subsequently call, 'an unfortunate coincidence' Adams did have an apparent conflict of interest. He was also the auditor of Coronation Syndicate and all Lonrho's companies in South Africa. Subsequently, Adams became a director of Lonrho, South Africa but the auditor is adamant: 'I never discussed Barclay's investment in Coronation Syndicate with Lonrho.'

Barclay's hope for a reprieve was dashed. The following Monday, his firm was hammered and Barclay was declared bankrupt. The epitaph was sour. His Coronation Syndicate shares were bought by a bank representing a nominee account based in the Cayman Islands. Moreover, compelled by the stock exchange during 1971 to reveal the mine's activities, Bentley and Kruger published the first true account of Inyati's development. Coronation Syndicate shares, which Barclay's trustee sold for 1.1 rand, rose to 9 rand. Both Barclay and Esterhuysen were set upon revenge. On the fifth floor of Johannesburg's John

Vorster police headquarters, they presented their complaint to Captain Johann Prinsloo, an officer in Commercial Branch.

Unsuspecting, Rowland relegated Coronation Syndicate as a problem of the past. Perhaps there was little choice. South Africa, the biggest source of Lonrho's remittable income in Africa, was Rowland's ideal location for continued expansion. His latest and biggest gamble was the development of a platinum mine which lay in the Bophutatswana homeland at Merensky Reef. Platinum, initially used like gold and silver as a precious metal for jewellery, was increasingly used as a catalyst in petroleum refineries and in motor cars. Initially, Rowland had been reluctant to buy the interest. Merensky Reef, he feared, was a risk beyond Lonrho's experience. The enormous capital investment required would stretch Lonrho's finances too far. But Lonrho's geologists, engineers and Alan Ball had combined to overcome his reservations. Those who questioned Rowland about the repercussions of Lonrho investing in South Africa were treated after a moment's reflection to a display of pragmatism: 'We are buying because we are anti-apartheid and we will sell only to another company which is against apartheid.' Once the contracts were signed in 1969, Lonrho was committed to begin extraction of the platinum by 1971. The prospect of the staggering investment puzzled Eric Armitage, the accountant in London. 'I was becoming sceptical about the company's arrangements,' he explained.

In April 1970, Armitage had flown to Africa for a tour of Lonrho's offices. His first stop in Nairobi confirmed that Cheapside's financial control over its African subsidiaries was practically non-existent. Unpaid debts, rising costs and inadequate controls over the conglomerate Consolidated Holdings were aggravated by the low quality of the accountancy personnel. 'There is little doubt,' he reported after meeting Paul Spicer, Lonrho's East Africa chief, 'that the cash situation will become critical unless something is done.' Armitage was unimpressed by Spicer whose recent recruitment to Lonrho was, he believed, based upon all the wrong reasons.

Born in 1928, Spicer had attended Eton, but not university. After four years in the Coldstream Guards, he had only reached the rank of lieutenant. Unsuccessful in the army, he joined Shell in 1949 and, despite family connections, over the next twenty years was shifted through a succession of assistant posts which culminated as Shell's managing director in Tanzania. 'He was just dumped there,' comments one of his friends about the institutional abandonment. Frustrated by his failure to win promotion, the result of his natural inabilities, he had asked Gerald Percy, an Old Etonian school friend, about his prospects in Lonrho. Percy passed his friend on to Nicholas Elliott, also an Old Etonian who eventually arranged an interview with Rowland. Since there was a vacancy in East Africa, Rowland approved Spicer's appointment.

Spicer would soon understand the idiosyncrasies of his new employer. At Christmas 1968, Jennifer Percy and June Spicer decided to host a black-tie dinner for friends in Nairobi. The invitations were sent to seventy people. News of the party reached Rowland, who was outraged. 'Cancel the party immediately,' he telexed, 'or consider your position.' Rowland's excuse was that no Africans had been invited and it would seem that Lonrho's directors were racist. In reality, Rowland needed to prove his control over everything and everyone.

In Nairobi, Armitage observed Spicer's abilities. 'The accounts are in a shambles,' the former grammar schoolboy told the Old Etonian polo player. 'Produce a budget which reflects your losses and produce a solution.' It was an inauspicious introduction.

In Lusaka, Armitage discovered worse muddle. Internecine warfare among the Lonrho employees had aggravated what the junior manager, John Price, described as 'bad management'. Prestige projects like the African match factory were losing money. Rowland had refused to heed the experts' warnings that Zambia's timber was unsuitable and the unsaleable matches had piled up in the factory while, according to Price, 'the accounts are in chaos'. Little money was being remitted to London and, according to Price, the 'forecast forms', which Armitage had sent from London, had only recently been found, untouched in a corner of an office. 'That's why we've been guessing your figures in London,' grumbled Armitage.

Lonrho's internal problems were compounded by the use of

poor auditors, unchallenged thefts from stores and the refusal of local government officials to pay bills for cars and garaging in Lonrho's garages.

As Armitage's tour continued, the picture worsened. In Malawi, the local manager asked if he could borrow £100,000 to survive; in Rhodesia, Lonrho was suffering a 'mild cash shortage'; in Mauritius, Armitage provoked a ferocious confrontation with the local managers by condemning the 'appalling state of accounts' and demanding 'clean audited accounts'; while in South Africa there was a 'state of turmoil'.

Even the range of businesses was odd. In Choloka, Malawi, Armitage visited a rope maker and tobacco grading plant owned by Lonrho which was a 'quaint relic from the past; there was a Lonrho subsidiary renting deck chairs in Kenya; an insolvent hotel chain in Mauritius; and at Riddoch motors in Tanzania, the stores boasted 'a liberal coating of dust'. The reality contrasted oddly with a press release under preparation which glorified Lonrho interests in twenty African countries in 'gold, copper, coal, diamonds, tea, sugar, textiles, newspapers, real estate, brewing and motor trading. In Europe its principal activities are shipping, insurance, motor trading and wine.' Lonrho did control an enormous range of businesses but Armitage returned to London mystified by the philosophy which propagated the belief that such a ragbag collection of assets could be profitable. His report to Butcher suggested that he would begin establishing financial controls across the group.

On the sixth floor, Rowland was not enamoured of Armitage's work. Indeed, he found the accountant distasteful. In his view, Lonrho's record spoke for itself. By 1970, Lonrho's assets, worth £198 million, were spread over twenty-nine countries and employed more than 100,000 people. His company would boast pre-tax profits of £16.2 million which, if not quite the £19 million predicted by Ball, were another record. In his bid for glory, Rowland had no patience for the regulations and controls which accountants wanted to impose. That sentiment naturally influenced Butcher, but provoked some suspicion in the City.

Lonrho's debts, £117 million, were too high for some City practitioners to accept unquestioningly Lonrho's self-serving promotions. No one could quite understand how profits in Africa were measured and were unimpressed that Lonrho's accounts suggested the company was earning a mere 8 per cent return on its capital. Rowland was caught in a dilemma.

Increasingly, to protect the company from criticism in nationalist Africa, he was minimising that Lonrho's best earnings were in South Africa. The alternative, admitted Ball, was Lonrho being 'thrown out on its ear'. But that disguise fuelled suspicion about a company identified in the City with a continent which epitomised confiscatory socialism, revolutionary nationalism and endemic corruption. Lonrho's share price whose 1970 peak was 165 pence, fell towards 90 pence.

Rowland's attitude towards Lonrho's shareholders and the City, which would assume enormous importance in 1973 was, by any measure, unique. Since 1967, Lonrho's broker had been Myers & Co whose senior partner, Erland d'Abo, was a good passport to City investors. The brokers were converts to Rowland's genius and undertook a 'crusade' to persuade the City to invest but 'the shares never moved'.

Despite his constant concern about the share's price movement, Rowland refused to play the required role at the broker's lunches and often refused even to leave Cheapside. 'He refused to stand in the front line,' recall the brokers. Instead, Percy was dispatched to explain the unremittability of Lonrho's African earnings.

The broker's task was complicated by the evident instability of Lonrho's business in Africa. The government of Zaïre, in July 1970, formally announced its refusal to have 'any further dealings' with Lonrho and denied that the company possessed an option worth £170 million to build a railway to the coast. It was the latest twist in the saga between Rowland, Mobutu and Cominière.

At a lunch in Cheapside, Martin Thèves, who was suffering because Rowland had broken his promise to keep the original transfer secret, raged at his host about the duplicity. 'I'm not speaking to you any more,' said the Belgian as he pushed back his plate and stood up, 'You're not a gentleman.'

'And you're not a gentleman either,' smiled Rowland, 'You're the son of a carpenter.'

Thèves had returned from Africa in summer 1970 after organising the continuing opposition of Anglo American, Union Minière and others against Rowland, and then died of a heart attack. His success coincided with another publicised humiliation for Rowland.

In his bid to challenge the giants, Rowland had sought to oust De Beers, the South African diamond producer and trader, from Sierra Leone, a former British colony in West Africa.

As with many other minerals, the diamond trade was and remains concentrated among a cartel dominated by De Beers. Even the Soviet Union, itself a substantial diamond producer, had avoided a confrontation with the cartel and instead, despite the Cold War and its declared antagonism towards apartheid, sold its stones by arrangement with De Beers whose operations spanned Africa.

Eighty-five per cent of Sierra Leone's foreign revenue was earned from diamonds. The stones were mined by Consolidated African Selection Trust, a British company, and sold through De Beers. In its newly independent state the Sierra Leone government was vulnerable to any suggestion which rectified the legacy of colonial exploitation, especially Rowland's eloquent sermon that British policies in Africa had been despicable.

Introduced by Olympio, Rowland shuttled to Freetown seeking to persuade the government to expel Consolidated. According to one eyewitness, 'Tiny spent so much time pouring scorn and dripping poison on British policies in Africa that I became quite unhappy.' Even Ball was shocked by Rowland's approach. 'Everyone was unhappy about Tiny's methods,' recalled a fellow Lonrho director and eyewitness. As an ally, Rowland even recruited Aki Stevens, the prime minister's son, then studying in Moscow. Stevens was in direct contact with a Russian diplomat serving in Freetown who would support Lonrho's proposition. 'Tiny was very patient in Freetown,' recalls Captain Wilming.

Patience was the overriding virtue on those occasions and when Rowland arrived for the first time in 1970 with a fellow director, he resigned himself to a lengthy wait. During the course of those days in Freetown, Rowland startled the Lonrho director by his commitment towards his company. 'I'm ready to be buggered,' said Rowland, without any trace of irony, 'if it helps Lonrho. Would you?'

'No, Tiny,' came the reply with alacrity. 'I don't own 20 per cent of the equity.'

In June and July 1970, cash payments totalling £13,500 were paid by Rowland from the British Linen Bank account to help his cause. Initially, he was successful. Consolidated and De Beers were informed that their contracts were to be revoked.

Rowland's initial proposal to the Sierra Leone government was for a 51:49 per cent share with all control vested in Sierra Leone and subject to local laws. In a memorandum written by Nicholas Elliott and marked 'Top Secret', Lonrho proposed that the government's offer of compensation to RST should start at book value, which would inevitably be artificially low. RST, according to Elliott who travelled with Rowland to Freetown, had paid 'practically nothing' for the original concession and initially was exempted from all rents, taxes and other charges. Payment, he suggested, should be on an ungenerous sliding scale from future dividends to compensate for what Rowland had characterised as 'an outrageous position which no effective government should tolerate'. The government, Rowland suggested, should take over RST's 'entire organisation' without payment.

Rowland's credentials for managing Sierra Leone's diamond industry were questionable. Lonrho's expertise was limited to a £300,000 hunt for the stones inside a snow-covered mountain in Lesotho. The result, Rowland was told by the geologist, was 'We've found enough brown diamonds to fill a thimble.' Rowland would eventually sell a 50 per cent stake to Newmont for £300,000 and the remaining share for £600,000. His flair to sell a loser was impressive but was used by RST and De Beers to counter his offensive in Freetown. Amid embarrassing publicity, Stevens's government abruptly spurned Rowland's offer without explanation.

To be outplayed in Zaïre and Sierra Leone would not in normal circumstances have influenced a company's status in London. At

worst, both were ambitious gambles in distant places which most
would have difficulty spotting on a map. Hitherto Lonrho's image
had depended upon its overall accounts, its high dividend and
upon Rowland as the trusted expert in Africa. In normal circumstances, it would not have been judged by the few interested City
stockbrokers by individual feats. But Lonrho had exceeded the
bounds of normal comprehension. During the summer of 1970,
the setbacks provoked closer examination of Lonrho's excessive
debts and prompted the conclusion that the blame rested upon
the investment in platinum, a speculative commodity riding at
the top of a boom.

As the archetypal polemicist for the theory that 'something
will turn up,' Rowland's solution to the predicament evolved
from his greatest quality: self-salesmanship. Rowland is a master
of presentation and keenly aware that within the British financial
community image could disguise reality. He judged that Lonrho's
problems could be overcome by selling a minority interest in
Western Platinum. Gerald Percy was dispatched to Canada and
sold a 49 per cent stake to Falconbridge, a mineral specialist
managed by Howard Keck, a tough and brash Texan. Rowland
would not meet Keck until the deal was negotiated. Their relationship could enjoy only limited possibilities. 'Both', observed
Percy, 'had similar personalities.'

Percy's negotiations were rushed to be finalised just hours
before a shareholders' meeting on 27 August 1970. The announcement of the sale, accompanied by a news release describing Lonrho as 'heading a 10-year growth league of British
companies' added that the company was 'listed in *Fortune*
magazine's top 200 industrial corporations outside the United
States.' Since Rowland knew that the presentation of an ever-
rising graph to shareholders was valuable for the company's
well-being, Butcher was allowed by the auditor to backdate the
agreement with Falconbridge by four days to allow the initial £2
million payment to be included in the 1970 accounts.

The effect was beneficial. In the City, despite Rowland's nonchalance that Lonrho's accounts were not 'understood', Dickie
Birch-Reynardson of Myers & Co, Lonrho's brokers, successfully enticed institutions to buy Lonrho's shares on Rowland's

assurance of the company's satisfactory performance, which was certain to improve. Rowland's salesmanship overcame the critics and for the first time Hambros and other institutions invested in Lonrho. There was no mention that Lonrho's agreement with Falconbridge contained a clause requiring the development of the mine to be financed in representative proportions by both companies. Rowland ignored the problem that, since Lonrho had no cash reserves, it might be a problem to finance the mine's development.

The long-term salvation, Rowland believed, lay in improving Lonrho's image. As Ball's infirmities became more apparent, Rowland renewed his search for personalities who could better represent Lonrho's interests, especially towards governments.

In January 1971, Rowland heard that Duncan Sandys, whom he occasionally met at Ashanti board meetings, was planning a tour of southern Africa. The sixty-three-year-old Conservative politician and Winston Churchill's son-in-law enjoyed a reputation as an 'elder statesman' of the party despite antagonism from the new prime minister, Edward Heath, who objected to Sandys's vocal opposition to immigration and his support for the right wing of the party. Yet Rowland regarded these credentials as ideal for promoting Lonrho's interests in southern Africa.

Considering Rowland's attitude towards nationalist Africa, especially his constant public criticism of apartheid, Sandys would seem an odd choice. But to draw such a conclusion would be to misunderstand Rowland's priorities. Lonrho and its profits were his sovereign principles. Commuting between African presidents and witnessing the hypocrisy of sanctions against Rhodesia, Rowland understood the *realpolitik* of international trade. Moral principles were for politicians to utter and for everyone to ignore. Rowland had however also grasped two corollaries. Politicians hated exposure of their hypocrisy and they rejected the connection between business and politics. To Rowland's delight, Sandys was not tainted by those false pieties and had recently, on Lonrho's behalf, visited Libya.

Rowland had flown to Libya soon after Colonel Muammar Gadaffi had overthrown the country's corrupt monarch. Among Gadaffi's earliest edicts was to augment the price of Libyan oil and engage in increasingly abrasive negotiations with oil companies, especially British Petroleum. Irritated by the continued losses incurred by the closure of the Beira pipeline while BP and Shell transported their oil by rail to Rhodesia, Rowland conceived that a relationship with Gadaffi would gain him entry into the lucrative oil market. If that failed, the accumulation of money in Libya offered Lonrho an opportunity to supply its 'expertise'.

Rowland found the revolutionary officer charming but irritated by the British government's refusal to renegotiate an unsatisfactory contract for radar which had been concluded with the deposed monarch. Acting as a self-appointed intermediary between the Libyan and British governments was precisely the 'service' which appealed to Rowland and could pave the way to secure a contract for an oil refinery from Gadaffi. Sandys had engaged in the initial negotiations with the Libyan government to build the installation.

In London, Rowland visited Anthony Parsons, the Foreign Office official responsible for the Middle East. Rowland began their meeting, arranged by Elliott, by relaying Gadaffi's threat to nationalise British Petroleum's assets if the British government refused to remedy the defective radar equipment. Rowland then outlined a grandiose scheme to combine Zambian minerals, Egyptian manpower and Libyan money. The lynchpin was the British government's settling of Libya's complaint to secure the release of the Arabs' funds for Lonrho's project. The essence of Rowland's message was, 'If you don't do what I tell you to do straight away, disaster will follow. I promise you.' Rowland's attitude confirmed Parsons's scepticism. Faced with a man who would not accept 'no' as an answer, Parsons realised that Rowland completely misjudged the nature of British government. Even a senior Foreign Office official was subject to his own departmental superiors, the Cabinet and popular sentiment. Parsons would be among the first to experience Rowland's conviction that countries were governed in an identical fashion to his management of Lonrho. 'You don't understand realities, Mr Rowland,' said Parsons.

But according to Rowland, Parsons's manner – 'You don't

know the Arabs as I do' – was condescending and patronising, typical of the style for which his Office has become an international byword. Rowland cursed Parsons for censuring Gadaffi's threats as unrealistic and his revolt as unacceptable to Britain. 'Well, Mr Rowland,' concluded Parsons. 'You've spent twenty minutes being offensive to me. When we next meet, you must allow me to tell you what I think of you.' BP's assets were eventually nationalised and Rowland blamed Parsons for arrogantly dismissing the credibility of the Libyan threat

'I think I've got a moral blind spot,' wrote Rowland years later. 'I don't like being told what my opinion ought to be. Governments renege on their opinions and alliances at the drop of a hat, and are unreasonable in expecting their citizens to fervently follow their latest ideas . . . Today's enemies are tomorrow's friends.'

Those maverick notions about governments' morality and hypocrisy encouraged Rowland to invite Sandys to become a consultant to Lonrho on his return from South Africa. Every country, including the nationalist government in Zambia, was trading with South Africa and Rhodesia despite the international campaign against apartheid. Lonrho's highest earnings emanated from South Africa and the company needed to establish a relationship with the government. Since Rowland wanted to avoid any conspicuous approaches, Sandys would be the perfect representative. He offered the politician an annual salary of £10,000, a substantial sum for those days.

The offer appealed to Sandys, not least because Lonrho ignored sanctions against Rhodesia. Anticipating his retirement from politics at the next election, Sandys welcomed the protection of his income, destined to inevitable decline in the future. But to protect his windfall, he sought generous expenses, first-class travel and payment 'overseas' to avoid paying tax. As Sandys was a British resident, the operation would be strictly unlawful yet Rowland showed no hesitation in accepting the condition. Sandys would be under his control. To create a tax avoidance scheme, the politician would be employed by Lonrho South Africa at £10,000 per annum, to be paid into a Jersey account, and receive an annual salary of £1000 from Lonrho in

London.

Sandys's acceptance of a scheme to avoid paying tax would attract much criticism when it was eventually exposed but, in that period, with the highest tax band at 98 per cent, it had become customary for all international traders like Unilever, BP and Bookers to pay part of their executives' remuneration abroad to cover the alleged services outside Britain.

'I am much looking forward to our association,' Sandys wrote when the agreement was concluded on 1 May. 'As I have told you, I greatly admire your adventurous spirit and I shall be glad to make any small contribution I can to the successful progress of your wide-ranging enterprises.' The trio – Butcher, Ball and Rowland – did not tell the other directors about the arrangement.

In tandem with strengthening his links with South Africa, Rowland had established a close, personal relationship with Kenneth Kaunda, the president of Zambia. Thanks to Tom Mtine, Rowland's 'runner' in Zambia, appointed because of his friendship with the president, Rowland had won easy access to the most important nationalist politician in southern Africa. In the view of the British diplomats, the relationship was certainly based upon Rowland's personal qualities but cemented by his generous bequests to the president's favourite charities.

Among Kaunda's close intimates whom Rowland frequently met was Andrew Sardanis, a Greek Cypriot who had arrived in Zambia as an impoverished youth in 1950. While working as a ticket collector on the buses in the copperbelt and managing a shop, Sardanis had educated himself and become involved in the African nationalist movement. In the period before Zambia's independence, Sardanis had supplied food to Kaunda during his imprisonment and, in recognition of his allegiances, was appointed by Kaunda as the manager of Zambia's industrial development corporation, earning himself the epithet 'The Golden Greek'.

Travelling around Africa on Kaunda's behalf, Sardanis established a network of relationships with African leaders which rivalled Rowland's. Simultaneously, he proved himself to be an astute businessman.

After independence, Zambia began nationalising some European companies and Sardanis, on behalf of the government, negotiated the compensation. Among those deals was Lonrho's disposal of Smith & Youngson, the transport company, which was losing money. Lonrho was compelled by Sardanis to pay the government to take over its company.

Rowland could see that the management of Lonrho's African interests would benefit considerably from Sardanis's qualifications and contacts. With Kaunda's blessing, Sardanis, who wanted to earn his fortune rather than remain a bureaucrat, was recruited to join Lonrho in London. His arrival at Cheapside in February 1971 was hailed throughout Africa as a considerable coup. Like a monarch in ancient times, it was said, Kaunda had passed on a favourite son. Among the cognoscenti, the status of both Lonrho and Rowland rose appreciably.

Within his first weeks in Cheapside, Sardanis began to have doubts. Eric Armitage, the accountant, was relieved to confide in someone his doubts about the company's financial health. The accounts of Lonrho's subsidiaries in Africa, Armitage explained, were chaotic. Creative accountancy, he believed, was inflating Lonrho's African profits and asset valuations, and disguising remittances. To Sardanis, who had seen the problem from the government's side, Armitage's confessions were not surprising but raised doubts whether Lonrho's financial health was as secure as the published annual report suggested.

The Greek Cypriot had further doubts, fired by Rowland's behaviour. Despite the promise that Sardanis would be Lonrho's manager in Africa, Rowland resisted delegating sufficient authority to his new appointee. Rowland in London, thought Sardanis, was different from the man he knew in Lusaka. Eventually, he confided to Armitage that their employer was a megalomaniac.

Among the sceptical minority in Cheapside these disparate strands of unease coalesced, and the worry intensified on 12 May 1971 when a telephone message from Lonrho's office in Johannesburg reported that Captain Johann Prinsloo, the police officer of the Commercial Branch, had arrived at 9.30 that morning accompanied by a sergeant to search the premises.

Prinsloo, having studied Esterhuysen's complaint, had convinced himself and his superiors that there were good reasons to believe that Lonrho of London had perpetrated a fraud against the shareholders of Coronation Syndicate. 'They were shocked when I walked in,' recalls Prinsloo, an Afrikaner, 'and they quickly began calling lawyers and London.' Three and a half hours later, the two detectives returned to police headquarters carrying every Lonrho file which bore the name Coronation Syndicate.

Eyewitnesses say that Rowland seemed unconcerned when told the news from Johannesburg. Coronation Syndicate was in the past. Others describe the frenzy on the sixth floor. If Rowland was sincerely calm, it was a reflection of his confidence in the realisation of his latest vision of Lonrho's future.

Among the many introductions smoothed by Gil Olympio, few were more important for Rowland at that time than meeting Khalil Osman, a Sudanese vet who, while practising in Kuwait, had befriended Sheikh Nasser Sabah al Ahmed, the son-in-law of the ruler of Kuwait. Sheikh Nasser owned Gulf Fisheries, an averagely rich company, owning 180 sophisticated shrimp trawlers operating throughout the world. Within a short time, Osman had become Sheikh Nasser's friend and trusted business adviser and developed Gulf's extensive interests in Sudan. When Olympio had met Osman in West Africa, the Sudanese was scouting on Sheikh Nasser's behalf for investment opportunities for Gulf Fisheries.

It is in the very essence of international wheeler-dealers like Rowland and his protégé Gil Olympio that whenever a chance encounter presents an individual who either possesses or controls wealth, the relationship becomes of interest. On that occasion, Olympio suggested that when Osman next visited London he might be introduced to Rowland.

During the dinner, held shortly afterwards at the Dorchester, Olympio and Rowland patiently endured Osman's monologue. They had rightly judged that the diminutive but amusing Arab could bring them business and deliver oil money. For his part, Osman was enthusiastic about Rowland and Lonrho. Having suffered from British imperialism and British condescension, he found it a pleasure to sit with business executives who avowedly supported the development of Third World countries like Sudan.

By the end of the evening, Osman agreed to introduce Rowland to Sheikh Nasser but on condition that they flew first to the Sudan to assess development opportunities in his poor country. Two visits ensued. 'This is a great opportunity,' said Rowland touring the vast emptiness. 'They need everything.' One project which Rowland judged he could immediately construct was a sugar industry. Half of Sudan's annual consumption was imported. Rowland calculated that his success in West Africa with sugar schemes made them an ideal blueprint for similar development in the Sudan. Except that this venture would be bigger. 'Lonrho's expertise would be of great value,' Rowland assured his host.

Osman was enthusiastic and also suggested textile, pharmaceutical and bottle-making factories. Finance was not a problem. Sheikh Nasser would surely support Rowland and Lonrho. For his part, Rowland cast himself as the merchant banker, putting a package together while Lonrho earned a fee. The technical 'expertise' was included. Osman was delighted.

On 25 May 1971, the second anniversary of his revolution, Rowland was introduced to President Ja'afar Numeiry. The Sudanese president, dependent upon Soviet military equipment, had nationalised British assets. But with the celebrations blaring in the background, Numeiry hinted that he was reconsidering his ideological allegiance. Lonrho's sugar scheme appealed to him.

The chance for Rowland to prove his unique value occurred sooner than expected. Osman's status, like that of all Third World businessmen, depended upon Numeiry. The general had seized power in 1969 with the support of the left wing but thereafter had asserted dictatorial powers against his erstwhile allies. By June 1971, when Rowland had returned to Khartoum to continue his negotiations, he found Numeiry to be nervous. One month later, on 19 July, Numeiry was in prison – the victim of a coup launched by left-wing officers.

On the night of the coup, Rowland and Olympio were dining at the Carlton Tower with Osman and a large group of Sudanese generals and ministers who were negotiating loans and purchases with the British government. The news was broken at 10 p.m.

Naturally concerned about his business and fortune, Osman pleaded with Rowland that he needed to return immediately to Cairo to organise a counter-coup. Contacted at the Skyline hotel at Heathrow, Wilming filed a flight plan and took off in the early hours for Belgrade carrying Osman and five other Sudanese including General Khalid Abbas, the minister of defence. Two other generals were waiting for the plane at the Belgrade terminal. 'The KGB didn't want to let us go,' recalled Wilming. 'We argued for five hours and then I just taxied to the runway and took off.'

From Cairo, Wilming flew General Abbas to Tripoli, Libya, where Gadaffi, a supporter of Numeiry, allowed Abbas to broadcast an appeal for a counter-coup. On his return to Egypt, Wilming, based at the Hilton hotel, watched as Osman began negotiating the collapse of the coup. Like a taxi service, flying between Cairo, Khartoum and military bases at Osman's behest, Wilming takes credit for providing the logistical service which outmanoeuvred the rebels: 'They even put a bomb in my plane to kill some Sudanese military who were passengers. I was warned and returned in time by the radio tower.'

By coincidence, when the coup was announced, two of the rebel leaders were in London. Both, with British government agreement, boarded a BOAC plane bound for Khartoum. As the VC-10 flew through Libyan airspace, it was ordered to land. Initially, the captain refused and turned back towards Malta but later, with the British government's approval, he returned and landed in Libya. The two Sudanese left the plane and were subsequently executed. For a brief moment, Rowland and the British government were supporting the same side.

On 23 July, Egyptian soldiers were flown to Sudan and reinstated Numeiry. Osman was a hero and, grateful for Lonrho's jet, proffered the rewards to which Rowland was rightfully entitled. In their re-embrace of Sudan within the western sphere of influence, the British government granted the country export credits worth £10 million. Lonrho's reward was to be appointed, on a commission basis, the 'sole purchasing agents' in Britain for the Sudanese government. Even more valuable was Numeiry's agreement that Lonrho, with Gulf International [a consortium including Gulf Fisheries] and Osman, should mastermind the development of Africa's biggest sugar scheme.

Rowland's second reward was the fulfilment of Osman's promise to introduce Lonrho to his Kuwaiti employers. By temperament and physical presence, Rowland could excel on such occasions. A huge animal, crafted in fine silver from Aspreys, was packed into the Mystere jet before they took off for the Gulf. Just as heads of state customarily exchange gifts during official visits, the chief executive of Lonrho observed the common courtesy.

Rowland, Olympio and Elliott were greeted as statesmen at the international airport. Driven by cavalcade to the Hilton, each of the Lonrho executives was assigned a suite which even Rowland admitted was 'vast'. After a formal presentation to Sheikh Sabah, the foreign minister, Rowland was invited for lunch. His hosts were Sabah's two sons Hamed and Nasser.

Twenty sheep were being cooked for 150 guests housed under a huge tent. The hospitality was traditional and the Arabs' suspicions were undisguised. Rowland knew that winning their trust would be time consuming but among his strengths was determined patience. Osman watched his new friend relaxing. 'This is fun,' Rowland smiled to Olympio. His relationship with Osman and the Kuwaitis seemed more than promising. Ever since he had completed the pipeline, Rowland had sought new opportunities to earn the millions which the oil industry offered. This was the best chance since the pipeline's completion ten years earlier. With delicate handling and the provision of special services, Rowland could hope for an unprecedented quantum of business and finance. 'Lonrho's expertise is at your service,' he repeated fondly. No one could deny that, in Africa, Rowland could dream of standing among the giants. Rowland's weakness was failing to distinguish between dreams and reality. Aspirations abroad were deemed fulfilled even if events taking place in London were ominous.

On 28 July, five days after Numeiry returned to the presidential palace, there was a meeting of the Lonrho board. These were occasions where Rowland's unease was tempered with contempt for those directors who were not his unquestioning sycophants and allies. Even his friends knew that Rowland disliked hearing bad news and indeed created barriers to protect himself from criticism and frowned upon the messengers of gloom. He could not however ignore the company's financial problems, already widely known. Lonrho's shares were down to 91 pence against a high of 316 pence in 1968.

Everyone in the boardroom had read a short article two weeks earlier in the *Daily Telegraph* 'strongly' advising readers to sell Lonrho shares because of 'numerous and alarming' rumours in London and Johannesburg.

For the first time, the board was given a properly drafted financial statement. Its author was William Wilkinson, who had joined Lonrho in November 1970 from a merchant bank to institute a group planning system. Wilkinson, another Old Etonian, had been recruited by Elliott.

After completing the African tour, Wilkinson returned like others convinced that the potentially good businesses needed better management. Rowland, he believed, just did not understand planning or enjoy management and therefore terrified those who proposed changes.

According to Wilkinson, Lonrho's income in some businesses was falling and problems remained in finding its share of the finance needed to develop Western Platinum. Rowland's confidence that the First National City Bank was committed was misplaced, said Wilkinson.

Not least of the problems identified by Wilkinson was that Lonrho's annual expenditure in Britain exceeded its income by £1 million and could worsen if the African subsidiaries required bigger subsidies. In a draft document, Wilkinson had proposed selling off some Lonrho interests selected from its gold, copper or platinum rights. 'Action', he had written, 'needs to be swift.' Not least of his problems as he worked through the accounts was that, 'I saw cash flowing out but I didn't know where. On the other hand, I saw all the profits which we told the public that Lonrho had earned, but they weren't remittable from Africa. Finally, all the money involved in Rhodesia and South Africa didn't impinge on me. I was just working on consolidated accounts which meant that I didn't know much.' Wilkinson predicted that Lonrho's deficit would reach about £6 million by the end of that year.

Other directors warned Wilkinson that Rowland would 'explode' if he was presented with that advice. Accordingly, in his final report, Wilkinson advised that Lonrho should just sell the Ceylon tea estate and borrow more money. His second proposal addressed Lonrho's 'credibility' problem. The City, he wrote, had lost confidence in Lonrho's auditors Fuller Jenks whose capacity to serve Lonrho was 'outgrown'. Lonrho needed a 'top flight firm' followed by 'a policy of full disclosure to one's financial advisers'.

Until that moment, Rowland had enjoyed an unbroken record of success. His mind was unreceptive to any suggestion of problems. The sale of assets was unacceptable to him because it would restrict his ambition and, similarly, raising money by issuing more shares was anathema because it would reduce his power.

On his instructions, Butcher, who had denied Wilkinson full access to the financial records, did not reveal to his fellow directors that the consequence of the drain of money was their company 'bleeding to death'. Like Rowland, Butcher did not trust the board to protect their fearful secret from the stock market.

Notwithstanding, when Rowland summoned Wilkinson and asked: 'What's our position?', Wilkinson replied, 'You're going to be bust by Christmas.' Rowland, not expecting that reply, was shocked and furious. 'He considered the warning a personal attack on his ability,' testified Wilkinson. His whirlwind expansionism, bereft of accountants' advice, had plunged Lonrho into a dire financial predicament. But instead of heeding Wilkinson's warning, he had embarked on yet another deal which he had decided to conceal from the board that day.

Five
Deception

The *Zeitgeist* dictated expansion, not caution. Rowland's contemporaries were expanding on a boom set off by Edward Heath ordering that controls on credit should be abandoned. In that giddy era dubbed 'Slater Walker government', when the stock market surged 75 per cent in fifteen months, Jimmy Goldsmith and Jim Slater were capitalising on the government's 'dash for growth'.

'A seething pyramid of escalating paper,' commented the *Sunday Times* as punters flocked to profit from Slater's golden formula of buying companies, raising more loans on the collateral of the new purchases, and churning shares around the globe. Dreams, in that brief era, swept aside reality.

Rowland, a sage compared to the youth who plunged into the market, perceived the flimsy nature of Slater's operations but was none the less infected by the heady atmosphere where capitalists, after six years of Labour government, were again respectable. Taking risks in secrecy and without controls embodied Rowland's style. Normally his decisions would be casually referred to the board for formal ratification but at the board meeting of 28 July, he withheld information about the deal of the year, the purchase of a car engine's patents.

The saga had started in autumn 1970, when Stefan Klein telephoned and promised 'the big one'. Austrian-born Klein, an engineer and pilot who had worked for British intelligence during the war, was a commission agent who earned fees for introducing deals and matching personalities. His allure and fund of anecdotes won him friends and admirers throughout the world.

Some felt he was an irresponsible rogue with plausible style, but to Rowland he was a friend whose range of contacts had been invaluable.

Klein's latest proposition concerned the Wankel engine, a rotary motor which, unlike the conventional four-cylinder piston engine used by motor cars had five rather than forty-two moving parts. Theoretically, Felix Wankel's invention reduced the cost of replacements and ran on lower octane petrol. Rowland, always fascinated by cars and the earnings from motoring, was convinced that, having sold cars in Rhodesia, he understood better than the world's motor manufacturers the potential of a revolutionary engine.

A Wankel-powered motor car, the Ro80, produced in Germany by the car manufacturer NSU, had been applauded at the Frankfurt Motor Show in 1967. But contrary to the inventor's promises, the engine consumed a gallon of petroleum every ten miles and the five moving parts required constant replacement. Those however were pioneering days and Rowland, after a half hour's ride in the Ro80, declared that it was more comfortable than his Rolls. It was the future.

When Klein introduced Rowland to the idea, the Wankel engine had already attracted interest among twenty-one motor manufacturers in Europe, Japan and America. Volkswagen seemed anxious for the rights and General Motors had signed for the patents, guaranteeing annual payments over the following five years. General Motors's agreement however was subject to their right to renege with just one day's notice and with no penalty. Wankel was a possibility of riches but not a promise.

Felix Wankel and Ernst Hutzenlaub, a former architect who specialised in selling patent licences, were offering to sell the Wankel patents for DM100 million, the equivalent in 1972 of about £12 million. Klein proposed that Rowland and Lonrho buy the patents. On 28 October, Rowland met Hutzenlaub in Munich and congratulated Klein on producing another winner. The Austrian's reward, confirmed in a letter from Rowland written without any authority from the board, was to be either £100,000 or 2 per cent of the price which Lonrho would pay.

There was one stricture. Nothing, Rowland told Klein, was to be mentioned to his fellow directors at Lonrho.

Decisive action was hampered by Lonrho's lack of money. Rowland therefore took his idea to David Scholey, a director at Warburgs. By then, Rowland's relationship with the bank had altered. Ian Fraser had become the director general of the Take Over Panel. Until his departure, Fraser saw himself as 'the orchestra's conductor' where Rowland followed the banker's advice. That relationship did not continue with Fraser's successor Arthur Winspear who acted under the elder banker Koerner's interference and Scholey's supervision. The previous warmth between Rowland and Fraser had been replaced by a purely professional relationship with Scholey.

Rowland suggested to Scholey that the bank should invest its own funds in a joint venture with Lonrho to buy the Wankel patents. Scholey's response was conditional. He required more information and would want to meet the two Germans. The absence of automatic enthusiasm announced the beginning of the schism between Rowland and Warburgs, a decisive moment in his life.

Fraser recalls Rowland's contemporaneous complaint that he was receiving no help or advice from Warburgs about the deal and would blame the breakdown in his relationship with the bank upon individual Warburg directors. Scholey would claim that instinctively Rowland was unwilling to allow anyone to interfere in his deal: neither the bank nor the Lonrho board. Others described Rowland's behaviour as deception.

In normal circumstances, the lack of money would have terminated those plans. But Rowland was determined and, ignoring Lonrho's chronic financial plight aggravated by the purchase of Western Platinum, he wrote on 17 December 1970 to Hutzenlaub, 'I can now confirm to you that the Board of Lonrho Limited has formally authorised me to continue discussions with you, with a view to concluding the purchase.' Since that was not true, to protect himself, Rowland urged upon the German complete secrecy. Three weeks later, on 6 January 1971, Hutzenlaub gave Rowland an option until the end of the month to buy the Wankel patents for DM150 million. Rowland was euphoric. The finance, he believed, could still be raised from his friend Val Duncan or Kleinworts, the merchant bank.

Within two weeks, Rowland's mood cooled. The engine, he heard, had been touted for some time. Car manufacturers were unsure of Wankel's potential. Even General Motors's commitment was uncertain. Some offers had been as low as DM60 million. Val Duncan was uninterested and British Leyland had rejected the idea. Klein's 'unique deal – just for you' was obviously less than exclusive. There was an additional complication.

The Israel-British Bank, then a credible investment institution based in Tel Aviv with links to Swiss banks, owned 25 per cent of the engine. In the late Sixties, the bank's lawyer, Elihu Miron, an Orthodox Jew, had skilfully fought in the German courts to assert the Bank's rights to NSU, the car manufacturer, and then agreed with Hutzenlaub to buy the 25 per cent stake in Wankel.

Hutzenlaub's offer to Rowland was therefore subject to the rights of others. It also suggested that Hutzenlaub was desperate to sell. The offer seemed messy to Scholey and he would recall a parting shot from Rowland: 'If Hutzenlaub isn't more co-operative about the price, we'll pull out.' In the event, Warburgs were not interested and Rowland failed to find other potential partners.

On 20 January 1971, the Lonrho board held its regular weekly meeting. For the first time, Alan Ball told the directors about Rowland's negotiations for the Wankel. Ball added that there was 'no commitment' by Lonrho and the option agreement was allowed to lapse.

By April, Rowland had regained his confidence about the Wankel deal and flew with Nicholas Elliott to Tel Aviv to meet Max Bunford, a motor dealer who had also bought an interest in the engine. The two met a representative of the Israel-British Bank which by then had become involved in a legal dispute with Hutzenlaub. Instead of walking away from the mess, Rowland had become so mesmerised by the potential profits which the engine would surely earn that he was willing to buy off the two potential competitors.

Rowland's plan was to encourage the bank to pursue their

case against Hutzenlaub in the expectation that the price for the Wankel patents would fall. Then the three parties – Rowland, Bunford and the bank – could divide the spoils. In exchange, Rowland granted the others a 20 per cent interest for their rights, later called, 'a 20 per cent free ride'.

Enraptured by the deal rather than querying the detailed substance, Rowland recommenced his negotiations with Hutzen-laub. On 13 July 1971, he concluded a preliminary agreement to pay DM100 million. Lonrho also paid a DM1 million non-returnable deposit as proof of Rowland's good will and reshuffled the agreement between the three parties.

So far, Ball, Butcher and Elliott apart, the other seven Lonrho directors knew little about Rowland's activities. Even the three directors involved were often unable to follow Rowland's discussions, which were conducted in German. Elliott, for exam-ple, had only travelled to Israel for the ride to see old friends. Namely Mossad officers, with whom he worked during the Six Day War. Josie had joined the trip for sightseeing.

The opportunity to rectify the board's ignorance presented itself on 28 July 1971 but the Wankel negotiations were bare-ly mentioned. Rowland was not minded to confide his commit-ments beyond mentioning the DM1 million payment. He would later claim that his fellow directors 'allowed me to play with Wankel'.

The mood at that board meeting was sombre. Rowland had just returned, in a fury, from a dash through Africa. In Lusaka, just as the Mystere had landed, a radio message announced that Andrew Sardanis had resigned. Armitage and Elliott had stood on the tarmac waiting for Rowland. 'He won't come out,' sighed Captain Wilming. Rowland was sulking, outraged and humili-ated. Six months after accepting a job with Lonrho, Sardanis claimed, 'I found myself in basic disagreement with Lonrho's objectives and style of management.' Sardanis criticised Lonrho's acquisition of companies without adequate money or managers to invest. He did not publicise the discovery that Lonrho, to overcome the financial pressures, was revaluing some assets, including those in Tanzania and Ceylon which were candidates for nationalisation. Rowland's public explanation that Sardanis was simply 'homesick' for Zambia concealed his discomfort and his claim that he had been deceived.

According to the Zambian official Valentine Musakanya, 'Sardanis wanted to establish himself as a competitor to Lonrho. He made himself very rich and made Rowland mad.' But Sardanis's explanation and judgment upon Lonrho remained on the public record. Few gave any credence to Ball's declaration that the company 'has never been in better shape'. Instead, the resignation again suggested Lonrho's troubled fortunes. Sardanis, however, would not comment publicly about his departure. He feared Rowland's retaliation.

A combination of other stories was further depressing Lonrho's share price. In Johannesburg, newspapers reported that South African police were investigating the company. Initially, Ball retorted that the investigation was completed, which was untrue. Then he blamed 'malicious complaints', which was partially accurate. At that moment, Fred Butcher was in Johannesburg immersed in complicated negotiations with the First National bank to finance Lonrho's share of the development of Western Platinum. The acquisition had highlighted Lonrho's huge debts which were exacerbated by the purchase. By the time Captain Prinsloo was told of his presence, Butcher, unaware that the policeman was waiting for an opportunity to arrest at least six Lonrho and Corsyn directors, was at the airport returning to Britain.

In London, Lonrho's share price was falling from 80 pence towards 60 pence. Rowland's behaviour suggested that he was unaware of the crisis. 'He was inscrutable,' recalled Wilkinson. 'He just conveyed the mood which suited him at that moment. Namely, that there was no problem. Some of us, however, were tense.'

On 2 August, Hutzenlaub arrived at Cheapside with an unusual request. Felix Wankel wanted to avoid paying tax on the DM100 million. Hutzenlaub asked Rowland to split the payment so that DM64 million would be paid by Lonrho and the remaining DM36 million by Rowland personally. [DM18 million by him and DM18 million from General Motors] and over the following two days concluded a binding agreement on Lonrho's behalf with Hutzenlaub and Wankel for the patents. On his own behalf, Rowland wrote a letter stating, 'I bind myself personally to an additional payment of DM36 million.' Later he claimed that the DM36 million represented the anticipated payment by General Motors, although there was no formal contract.

That day, 3 August, Butcher and Wilkinson spent several hours with Arthur Winspear at Warburgs. The issue was how Lonrho would finance the £6 million deficit needed to fund Western Platinum whose whole development since May had become endangered. Wankel was not mentioned. 'I was writing a report,' recalled Winspear, 'about Lonrho's debt reduction. I had no idea that Rowland was intending to increase borrowings.'

The following day, the Lonrho board read about their company's Wankel agreement in the *Financial Times*. The report from Bonn was their first inkling that Rowland had gone further than paying DM1 million for an option and was committed to a £12 million deal. 'We were very upset,' Percy said soon after. Rowland had ignored Warburgs' advice. The pace of events suddenly accelerated.

Twenty-four hours later, Butcher heard that First National would not provide a $15 million loan for Western Platinum. The company's financial position was deteriorating by the hour. 'The publicity about the Wankel deal is very damaging,' complained Winspear when Butcher and Wilkinson called, 'out of the question now.' Butcher agreed but urged that since Rowland's mind was set on the deal, it would be better to steer him gently away rather than issue a command. 'He knows how serious it is,' said Butcher with apparent sincerity. The three agreed that the Wankel deal was off.

That night, Angus Ogilvy flew back from Canada and telephoned Scholey at home. In addition to the problems concerning Wankel and South Africa, the news from Canada, reported Ogilvy, was 'not good'. The relationship with Falconbridge was near breaking point.

Soon after their marriage, disagreements had erupted between Lonrho and Falconbridge about the financing, extracting and marketing of platinum. While Howard Keck wanted to sell the platinum through the established cartel, Rowland wanted to buck the system and use the free market. In turn, Keck insisted that the company use Falconbridge's processing plant in Norway, which added to costs, already distorted by a worldwide slump in demand for platinum. Overriding all those problems was Falconbridge's failure, according to Lonrho, to find the loans to finance the mine's development.

The policy disagreements encroached on a mean personality clash between Keck and Rowland reflected in rows about the location of the last board meeting.

'I'm not crossing the Atlantic for this board meeting,' grunted Keck.

'And I'm not crossing the Atlantic either,' chipped in Rowland, suggesting Johannesburg as a compromise. A succession of capitals in Europe, South Africa and America was named by both sides, to be rejected. Finally, Paris was agreed. A complete floor was booked at the Ritz.

Rowland arrived at Orly in his Mystere. Wilming was directed to park near Keck's aircraft. To Rowland's dismay, the American had flown the Atlantic in the larger Grumman Gulfstream 11. Rowland would order one on his return.

The board meeting lasted two days. Rowland lost the argument about marketing and was bridled by Keck's demand, contrary to their original agreement, that Lonrho supply 51 per cent of the cash for the mine's development. Procuring that finance would propel Lonrho towards a crisis.

Keck's suspicions that Lonrho would renege on the commitment to produce the money fed rumours about Lonrho's solvency. In Toronto, he had issued Ogilvy with an ultimatum that Lonrho produce its share of the development finance.

To meet that demand, Lonrho, in a succession of intercompany loans, invested money already provided by Falconbridge to Western Platinum. Initially Keck, believing that Lonrho was investing fresh capital, was mollified but under South African law that arrangement could be illegal.

On his return from Canada, Ogilvy sensed Scholey's disapproval of Lonrho's management. In particular, the banker suspected that his advice about the Wankel engine was being ignored. 'Lonrho's predicament,' said Scholey, 'is acutely embarrassing but it is possible to meet the liabilities if we pursue the right course.' The banker knew that Ogilvy feared an outburst from Rowland if anyone sought to exercise any control. 'Terrified' seemed to be the best description of the impressionable Lonrho director on the telephone: terrified both of Rowland staying and terrified of Rowland resigning and walking away. The company's survival, at that moment, hung on a thread provided by the Standard & Chartered Bank.

At the boardroom lunch in Cheapside, Rowland revealed his desperation. Howard Keck's ultimatum had been bitter. Scholey was irritating. But the worst was Rowland's despair about his unsupportive fellow directors. 'I'm going to give up,' wailed Rowland theatrically. 'Resign. I'll leave all you people to run it on your own.' The embarrassed silence was broken by Rowland looking at Percy: 'What would you do if you were in charge, which you still might be?'

'We've never had a policy, so why should we have one now?' replied Percy.

Ball interjected, 'Oh yes we have: shit or bust.'

'And here we are,' laughed Percy, 'after ten years, regarded as shits and nearly bust.'

That week, Rowland visited Ian Fraser at the banker's house in Roehampton. By acting against Warburgs' advice, Rowland had found himself isolated and 'naked'. For the first time he was short of money, bereft of friends in the City and Lonrho's shares were again falling. Somewhat overwrought, shedding 'real tears', Rowland despaired about the lack of advice from Warburgs. 'Change your bank,' suggested Fraser.

'Would you become our chairman?' asked Rowland. Fraser refused. Although he 'liked and trusted Rowland completely', Fraser had chosen a different career.

At that moment, Rowland could have chosen to escape from the Wankel proposition and devote his energies to securing Lonrho's future. Instead, he ignored reality, convinced himself that 'something will turn up' and, believing that the engine was a certain future source of millions in profits, plunged further into the negotiations.

Rowland's assessment of himself as the consummate and outstanding deal-maker, an opinion conveyed and confirmed to him by so many acolytes and employees, made no allowance that anyone else could negotiate more consummately than he. But in the Wankel deal, he had given Klein and the Israel-British bank personalities a 20 per cent stake for nothing and he had personally promised Hutzenlaub a DM18 million tax-free payment. Hutzenlaub had proven to be a master salesman.

During that week, the German announced that he had received a higher offer for the patents and asked whether Rowland would be prepared to release Felix Wankel from the deal. Rowland's response was at best naive. Swallowing the story, he committed Lonrho to the DM100 million purchase subject only to the board's endorsement.

At 3.30 p.m. on 9 August 1971, Nicholas Elliott was summoned to a special board meeting. Only Rowland and Butcher were present. Elliott, who had assumed the mantle of 'political adviser' and was on his own confession inexperienced in business, sat bemused by the proceedings. Within fifteen minutes, the three men granted Rowland powers to conclude the Wankel agreements. The sum agreed was DM64 million. Rowland's personal commitment for DM36 million and the '20 per cent free ride' deal with Klein and the Israel-British bank were not mentioned in the formal minutes.

Twenty-four hours later, the three directors met again for five minutes and granted Rowland 'absolute discretion' to negotiate the Wankel deal. Rowland later described that meeting as the directors 'allowing me to play with Wankel'.

On 11 August, the following day, Rowland flew to Zurich and signed further holding and agreements with Hutzenlaub. Scholey and other Lonrho directors again first read about the agreements in the *Financial Times* on 12 August. 'They were shocked,' says Wilkinson. Over the previous days, the bankers and Lonrho's limited financial team had discussed solutions to the company's financial predicament, only to learn unexpectedly that Rowland had committed Lonrho to spend non-existent funds. That morning, Rowland was summoned to meet Koerner and Grunfeld at Warburgs. 'He was euphoric about Wankel,' recalled

Winspear, 'and was barely aware of Warburgs' anger at not being told anything about the Wankel deal.'

The unease had leaked into the City. Lonrho's share price was falling towards 50 pence. Concerned for the first time, Rowland was hunting for finance. Wilkinson, Butcher and Percy were dispatched to Switzerland while Rowland and Robert Dunlop, unkindly named by some colleagues, 'Dennis the Menace', his personal assistant and a former machine salesman, whose wife was Josie's friend, flew to Kuwait. In Zurich, Wilkinson presented his projections to the Union Bank of Switzerland showing that if all the motor companies with options continued their interest the engine would be profitable. He concealed his apprehension that Rowland 'didn't understand the management and technical resources needed for this difficult project'. All three gave assurances that DM36 million was Rowland's private commitment. The bank agreed to provide DM64 million. Publicly, no one questioned why the bank should advance so much without collateral other than the patents but, unknown to Wilkinson, Lonrho had pledged Ashanti gold as the security. The team returned to London convinced that the Wankel deal would not be a drain upon Lonrho.

In euphoric mood, the Lonrho board met on 15 September 1971. First National had after all agreed to finance Western Platinum and combined with the Swiss bank loan for Wankel Wilkinson's presentation of the financial predicament was positive. 'They were all cheering like anything,' recalled one director.

At that meeting, Rowland had asked Wilkinson to present the status of the Wankel deal, 'as someone who knew the position'. Dependent upon Rowland's information, Wilkinson suggested that Lonrho would buy 100 per cent of Wankel for DM64 million. In fact, Rowland intended that Lonrho should pay DM100 million for an 80 per cent interest. 'I was wholly and utterly misled by Rowland,' testified Wilkinson subsequently. 'He just sat at the meeting silently and watched me give a false account. One week later, Rowland himself gave the same version to the board.'

On 23 September, Rowland and Ball flew to Zurich finally to buy the Wankel patents. The previous day, the two men and

Butcher had held another 'special' board meeting bestowing the necessary powers. The contract price was DM64 million. Among the conditions, Rowland agreed to pay Felix Wankel an additional DM36 million on 1 October. Wilkinson queried the source of that money. 'If I die,' Rowland reassured Wilkinson, 'my estate will be liable for the DM36 million.' Five days later, Wilkinson claims that he realised that he had been misled. His intention to challenge Rowland was interrupted, as was all Lonrho's business, by unexpected news from Johannesburg.

Unannounced, on 8 September, Captain Prinsloo had obtained seven arrest warrants on charges of fraud. Among those named on the warrants were Rowland, Angus Ogilvy, Ball, Butcher and Caldecott. Prinsloo need only await news of their arrival in South Africa. The information would be supplied by a Lonrho employee.

The call came through on 27 September. Prinsloo rushed to Lonrho's offices on the tenth floor of the Trust Building and into the offices of Sidney Newman, Lonrho's South African managing director, a well-respected international rugby player and a former manager of Rand Mines. Butcher looked up from his chair. 'He was very surprised,' remembers Prinsloo with some satisfaction. Both Butcher and Newman, who would be charged with other offences, were taken to police headquarters to take finger prints and then to the chief magistrate. In a closed session, Butcher's bail was set at 5000 rand. He was allowed to keep his passport. Officially, there was no mention that arrest warrants had also been issued against Ogilvy. The police had been warned about the consequences of a warrant to arrest someone directly linked to the British royal family.

Cheapside was stricken by shock. Only a handful knew about Coronation Syndicate yet most assumed that there 'could not be smoke without fire'. Butcher, despite his unstinting devotion to Rowland, was considered a man of moral scruples and firm religious conviction. 'A nice man taken hostage', recalled Wilkinson who believed that Butcher went through private hell working for Rowland. 'It's very embarrassing,' Ogilvy told a friend. 'Lonrho looks crooked.'

In retrospect, Rowland identified the arrest as the birth

of the opposition to him within the boardroom. In the previous ten years there had been 'unqualified support from everybody' but after Butcher's arrest 'people shied away'. It was the genesis of Lonrho's hugely publicised problems and not surprisingly Rowland placed a smokescreen over the reason for the arrest and investigation.

Publicly, Ball explained that the arrests were motivated by the spiteful revenge of a disgruntled shareholder. 'Esterhuysen's a crook out to make trouble,' raged Rowland. Esterhuysen, he shouted, suffered a poor reputation in the financial community while Barclay blamed his bankruptcy upon Lonrho. The headlines in Johannesburg spread opprobrium. The charges against Newman, a popular personality, were followed by the arrest of Clifford Bentley on board a cruise liner which had just berthed in Cape Town. The news prompted First National to terminate their promise to finance Western Platinum. Lonrho's cash crisis was compounded by a *Götterdämmerung* in London.

On the direction of Sir Siegmund Warburg, the bank resigned as Lonrho's financial advisers. Blaming the Wankel deal as a 'voluntary and gratuitous' additional burden, the bankers complained that their advice had been rejected 'completely and without discussion'. Scholey and Winspear would later explain their 'relief' in parting with the uncontrollable Rowland. 'He hated sophisticated controls,' recalled Winspear. 'We couldn't do business with him.'

For Rowland, Warburgs' resignation was a disaster, the equivalent of expulsion from Eton or conviction at the Old Bailey. Regardless that he neither understood nor wanted to be a part of the City, he knew the consequences of the public humiliation. 'It was a blow in the kisser,' smiled Winspear, 'and it stuck in his memory.' Rowland's bitterness, particularly directed against David Scholey, never waned. His anger against the bank influenced his career thereafter.

For his part, Ball, who understood the damage to Lonrho's image in the City, replied robustly that he too was relieved by Warburgs' resignation because Lonrho shared 'a loss of confidence in the value of your advice', a memorable riposte when Rowland later accused Warburgs of waging a vendetta against him.

The crisis snowballed. The following day, 28 September 1971, Andrew Caldecott and Philip Hunter resigned from Lonrho's board blaming the Wankel deal. For some time, Caldecott had delayed his departure in the hope that Rowland would be ousted. Lonrho's management, he believed, had not changed since the Sixties. The dispensation of Lonrho's money for Rowland's private use was, he believed, immoral, as was the £1 million expenditure for Rowland and Dunlop to fly around the world. When the possibility of removing Rowland had evaporated, Caldecott hoped that he could extricate Ogilvy. But finally he complained that he was in an 'impossible position' because Lonrho was 'run more as Tiny's private empire than an important public company' and it would never change.

Rowland heard the news in the Sonesta Tower hotel while visiting Flavia Musakanya, the wife of Valentine Musakanya, the governor of Zambia's Central Bank. Flavia was recovering from a serious illness. At Rowland's insistence, Lonrho had paid for her treatment at the Royal Free hospital in Hampstead. The telephone rang as Rowland sat in the sick woman's room. Flavia Musakanya watched Rowland listening to Angus Ogilvy. Tears began flowing down Rowland's cheeks. 'I looked at him, but he didn't explain anything.'

Ogilvy's position was critical. Ever since his marriage to Princess Alexandra, Lonrho's status in the City had risen because of the association with the royal family. That association also brought obligations upon Ogilvy. He would later claim that four days before Butcher's arrest, he had consulted Sir Leslie O'Brien, the Governor of the Bank of England, who advised that he should not offer himself for re-election as a Lonrho director. Butcher's arrest had undermined his strategy. 'Tiny felt quite reasonably that pals should support you. We'd built it up together,' he explained. Torn by his friendship for Rowland but also mindful that he owned 'part of the action', Ogilvy prevaricated. Later, he would say that he was blackmailed. 'Tiny was acting like a desperate man in the jungle,' he told a friend. For the moment, speaking to Rowland in the hospital, Ogilvy left the impression that he was considering his position. 'I was out of my depth,' he would later confess.

Rowland was outraged. Disloyalty, regardless of the circumstances, was unforgivable. 'I wish you would all resign,' he sneered at Percy early the following morning. 'Are you going too?' By the afternoon, the volatility had swung in the opposite direction. Ogilvy, who knew more about Lonrho than Caldecott, had not resigned. Questioned by a newspaper journalist about his intentions, he affirmed that he would remain a director. 'That was unfortunate,' he later confided, 'but it was too late to reverse.' That night, Rowland sent his friend a brief note, 'My dear Angus, I don't know what to say, except THANK YOU SO MUCH ANGUS – FOR EVERYTHING'.

With the resignation of bankers and directors and the arrest of other directors, Lonrho's share price fell further. Inside Cheapside the anticipated pandemonium was restrained by Rowland's calm manner. 'Tiny's not at bay,' said Percy who did not contemplate resignation.

Wilkinson, however, was worried. Butcher had revealed that Rowland had charged the extra DM36 million for the Wankel engine to Lonrho. Rowland had also worsened Lonrho's financial predicament by unilaterally drawing DM6 million from other Lonrho bank accounts, and destined for other debts, for the Wankel deal. Wilkinson was 'very upset'. Only Butcher's arrest prevented his immediate resignation. 'I do feel Tiny,' Wilkinson wrote on 3 October 1971, 'that you have let your colleagues down badly over this.' He would stay only, he added, 'to help clear up the mess'. A sense of duty prevented Wilkinson's resignation. Rowland had not protested against Wilkinson's admonition. Perhaps, thought Wilkinson, Rowland realises his errors. Wilkinson was mistaken. Rowland was preoccupied with Lonrho's fate in South Africa.

On 30 September, accompanied by Ball, Rowland had met Hendrik Luttig, the South African ambassador, at the embassy in Trafalgar Square. To the ambassador's bewilderment, Rowland showed an uncharacteristic lack of self-restraint. 'Prinsloo is not an impartial investigator,' fumed Rowland, 'it is scandalous that this sinister, politically motivated officer should be allowed to hound an innocent businessman.' Rowland continued that it was quite clear that Prinsloo, exploiting Esterhuysen's vendetta, was seeking to destroy a company because it traded with black Africa. 'In the past,' continued Rowland, 'I have wished South Africa well but I no longer feel inclined to.' The ambassador, recalling Rowland's attacks on his country, raised his eyebrows. Rowland threw a piercing glance. Both knew that John Vorster, the South African president, was seeking to end his country's isolation by establishing better relations with black Africa. Vorster had targeted in particular Houphouet-Boigny of the Ivory Coast. 'I will use my close ties with Houphouet-Boigny,' said Rowland with menace in his voice, 'to stop the dialogue with South Africa.' He allowed a pause for the diplomat to realise that this was not an ordinary businessman or an ordinary matter. 'And I might use my close relations with presidents Banda, Kaunda and Numeiry to further influence South Africa's situation.'

'You had better tone down your attitude, Mr Rowland,' snapped Luttig. Rowland recoiled. 'I'll report your message to Pretoria,' concluded the ambassador. 'Thank you.' The Lonrho delegation left with little confidence that their threats had made any impression. 'Tiny was unhappy that he'd failed at the embassy,' recalled Percy.

At the end of September, Lonrho's overdraft had reached £13 million, its ability to borrow had evaporated, and there was no merchant bank to help relieve the liquidity crisis. Lonrho's costs in Britain exceeded its income. Huge amounts were being spent under the headings 'Salaries' and 'General Expenses – Africa' [£138,000 out of a total £468,000] which were disproportionate to the company's earnings in Britain. Eric Armitage, out of touch with the tension on the floor above, had discovered that under the heading 'General Expenses' was a palatial house for Doctor Banda which was, 'clearly a bribe'.

The culture within Lonrho was that only the directors directly involved in making special payments would know any details. Armitage would not know that Fred Butcher was paying money to Africans through two Swiss banks or that a telex sent by Spicer listing the dispatch of antique furniture to an African leader was a gift. Any discovery of a payment could only be accidental but this isolated exposure was sufficient to alert even the naive to be suspicious about the unexplained mysteries.

The generosity had become ingrained within the company. At that very moment, despite the company's problems, Flavia Musakanya was about to leave London. At Rowland's insistence, a Rolls Royce had driven her son to school in Bath and another chauffeur drove her to Asprey in New Bond Street. 'I looked around and said to the chauffeur, "I can't afford this." He replied, "Don't worry. Just choose what you want. It will all be taken care of." '

Flavia Musakanya refused the gifts: 'I couldn't see why anyone should pay so much money for me.' Her surprise was compounded on her return to the hotel. The driver handed over an envelope. Inside were British banknotes. She handed the money back. 'From that time,' Flavia Musakanya recalls, 'our relationship with Tiny was never the same again.' If asked, Rowland would explain that his friends had misunderstood his generosity.

In Cheapside, Armitage would know nothing about these payments. He was absorbed by the need to balance the books. The African businesses needed white managers who refused payment in worthless local currency demanding instead pounds or dollars. But since the African subsidiaries were either losing money or alternatively were prevented by local exchange controls from converting the worthless African money into pounds, Lonrho in London had to pay the managers their salaries without receiving any compensating income. Lonrho was subsidising African subsidiaries and, contrary to the information provided to shareholders, the dividend could not be adequately covered by the remittances from Africa. 'Butcher,' according to Percy, 'was pulling his hair out. But Tiny was magnificent. He just wouldn't admit defeat. Whenever the news got worse, he just became more active and more aggressive.'

Armitage had a different interpretation. The accounts which he prepared for that month's board meeting were ready and stapled on his desk in the morning. Rowland appeared: 'Well Eric, what does it look like?'

'Not good.'

'Right, I'll tell the board that the accounts aren't ready.'

Armitage was unused to the ways of an entrepreneur. 'It was constant worry with calls, letters and telexes demanding money.' Nor could he cope with Rowland's moods; or when Rowland told his accountant, 'My marriage means nothing to me. I only live for my work,' and ordered Armitage to fly to Africa one night without going home to see his five children.

Armitage's complaints were forgotten after a phone call from Johannesburg. On the morning of 6 October, Prinsloo and the Rhodesian police had raided Lonrho's office in Salisbury. Kruger was 'upset and scared' as the police, with a warrant issued with the agreement of the Rhodesian government, began searching for the Coronation Syndicate files. After a fruitless hunt, Prinsloo feared that the papers had been destroyed. Then he looked at Kruger, fidgeting in his chair. The policeman looked under the desk. Kruger's feet were planted on top of a file. 'Thank you sir,' smiled Prinsloo.

In London, Rowland could only hope that the Smith government would prevent the documents leaving the country. Although the news from Salisbury would not be publicised in London, he was, on one of those rare occasions, concerned with Lonrho's public image. He issued a press statement. Circulated on 8 October, it extolled Lonrho's great success in securing the Wankel patents but it contained three distortions. Firstly, it claimed that the Wankel deal was executed 'with the prior approval of the entire board'; secondly, it wrongly asserted that all 'the necessary finance' had been arranged in Switzerland; and thirdly, it did not reveal the secret 20 per cent deal with Klein and the Israel-British bank. No Lonrho director objected to the circular's publication because none yet knew the exact position. 'Rowland's irresponsible behaviour and lack of frankness', said Wilkinson, 'had led to the financial crisis.' Lonrho's financial plight was worse than Wilkinson had imagined in April when he warned Rowland that the company would be 'bust by Christmas'.

Surveying the 'empire', Wilkinson concluded that with the exception of Swaziland Sugar, the Western Platinum mine, a French vineyard and one ship, which if sold would produce cash, Lonrho's empire was unsaleable and therefore worthless.

If its assets were sold, the company's income would be simultaneously crippled. Lonrho was an unprofitable shell. 'The situation is urgent,' he told the directors. 'It is very serious.' The profits from the much vaunted Ashanti goldfields had evaporated beneath Ghanaian taxation and they were therefore temporarily worthless. The company was losing annually nearly £2 million in Britain; £11.5 million of its £15 million profits for 1971–72 were from Nigeria, Zambia and Rhodesia, which were all blocked. Wilkinson recommended curtailing the payment of the interim dividend. 'It would be unfortunate,' he advised, 'if Lonrho declared a dividend without the money to pay.'

Ogilvy, by now struggling to understand how Rowland could accurately predict profits on the back of an envelope, groped for a palliative. Later, Ogilvy would say that he had introduced Rowland to Lonrho and 'felt a responsibility to stay and sort out the mess'. Accordingly, he told his friend, 'I insist that we call in Peats to investigate Lonrho.' On 14 October 1971, the accountants were appointed to investigate the company.

Leading the investigation was Sir Ronald Leach, the company's senior partner, currently investigating for the Department of Trade the affairs of Robert Maxwell and Pergamon Press. He was assisted by James Butler, later an admirer of Rowland's. Over the following twenty years he undertook to persuade the entrepreneur to become more acceptable. 'Both were happy to take the fees,' recalled one senior director. 'To our surprise, we soon realised that they weren't going to pull the plug on him. Tiny's charm did the job.'

Publicly, Rowland explained that Peat Marwick had been summoned to prove that there were no skeletons in the cupboard. Wilkinson hoped that the accountants would impose a modern financial structure on the company. But remarkably, throughout the Peats investigation, Rowland did not alter his style or activities.

On 26 October, the Lonrho board met. The pressure to avoid paying the interim dividend had grown although Standard & Chartered had lent Lonrho £4.5 million subject to strict conditions which stipulated the prerequisite of major sales. Rowland had accepted the money but the sales failed to materialise.

At the board meeting, James Butler vetoed the dividend payment but was opposed by Rowland. Lonrho's consistent high dividends cemented the cornerstone of the company's share price in which Rowland had an interest, although his personal shareholding by then had been diluted to 20 per cent. Everyone around the boardroom feared that failure to pay a dividend would be commercial suicide. In the chair, Alan Ball sat speechless, petrified by Rowland's silence. Everyone looked to Rowland, who had assumed the presence of a godfather, to provide a solution. For once he sat despondent. Ogilvy, who arrived understanding better than the others the financial crisis, broke the deadlock: 'Tiny, could we have a word?' The two disappeared into a neighbouring office. Five minutes later they returned.

'Tiny has agreed to lend the company £1 million to pay the dividend,' announced Ogilvy.

'That's remarkably generous of you Tiny,' gasped Ball.

Critically, no terms were discussed and few questioned where Rowland had accumulated £1 million in the previous year; or asked whether he was borrowing against his shareholding. The meeting ended in relief.

In the aftermath of his impulsive decision, Rowland recognised his own generosity. The £1 million was lent without any security to a company which was on the verge of insolvency and he might be dismissed during an effort to organise its salvation. Summoning Ball, Rowland persuaded his chairman that he needed two guarantees for the loan. It was to be backed by collateral and the stipulation that he could not be removed from the board nor anyone else effectively appointed as a director while he was owed the money.

On 8 December, Ball circulated a letter from Rowland which set out those two conditions ostensibly suggesting that they merely repeated Rowland's conditions uttered at the board meeting. Butler, having specifically refused to sanction dividends based on any conditions, was the first to protest. With Butler in his office, Rowland summoned Percy. 'Gerald, wasn't it agreed that the loan was secured?'

'Nothing was agreed Tiny.'

Rowland blanched and left the office. From his Park Lane flat, where he remained for some days, he dictated his resignation. Percy's naive honesty was depressingly incomprehensible. It fell to Alan Ball to assuage Tiny's tempers. Eventually, Lonrho's joint managing director was enticed back to Cheapside.

Rowland harboured a natural contempt for most of his senior staff in London. With reason, he judged that true competents would be his competitors not his employees. He never considered the corollary. They were all his appointments chosen because of their weaknesses.

On the fifth floor, Eric Armitage, an exception, chosen for his probity, was among those who resisted Rowland's manipulation. According to Armitage, 'I no longer had any faith in Rowland's capabilities.' Too much, Armitage believed, was hidden from him. Butcher was unsupportive, and one discovery had caused an unbridgeable chasm between himself and the directors.

After a five-week investigation into Riddoch Motors in Dar es Salaam, Armitage concluded that the management had overvalued in the accounts. 'Everything was rusty,' he recalls. 'The local auditors hadn't even visited the garage.' Spicer, based in Nairobi but responsible for Riddoch, was jolted by Armitage's criticism, as were other directors when Spicer's version reached London. 'Rowland wanted yes-men,' rues Armitage, 'and couldn't accept unpleasant facts.'

Butcher, Rowland's faithful servant, a 'white cuffs' man as some unkind employee would observe, had, according to Armitage, 'perfected the art of picking up Tiny's pieces after Tiny made a deal and knew when to ignore unpleasant facts as his master required.' Butcher ignored Armitage's report.

Eventually, Rowland summoned Armitage and, according to the accountant, falsely accused him of adultery in East Africa. 'He went beserk and fired me,' says Armitage who is a devout Christian. 'He said that he would ruin me and that I would never work again.' Indeed, Rowland's threat was fulfilled. Lonrho's references for the forty-seven-year-old were so bad that Armitage's career was nearly terminated: 'They made me unemployable.' Armitage's departure drew a line across the bad news for Rowland. Life in Cheapside resumed its accustomed pace.

The replacement as accountant, Roger Moss from Bass Carrington, was unimpressed with his inheritance from Armitage. The controls over Lonrho's 484 companies, he discovered, were 'non-existent'. Wilkinson, disenchanted that Rowland ignored his financial plans, told Moss, 'We need some professionalism here.'

Like Armitage, Moss flew to Africa to inspect the empire. Like his predecessor he saw businesses which, if properly managed, would earn profits. Like Armitage, he introduced stricter financial controls and prided himself on telling staff, 'I want you to do well for Lonrho, for your country and for yourself, in that order.' His strictures would make a limited impression. Rowland, Moss soon observed, disliked accountants, the paper merchants who fettered his style and brought only bad news. 'Mrs Moss,' Rowland would once say, 'your husband travels all around the world doing the most irrelevant things.'

Rowland, in contrast, was satisfied by Lonrho's activities in Africa. Most of Lonrho's staff relished the opportunity to live on the continent which they loved and understood. Rowland was a shrewd judge of those who were proven professionals in mining, ranching, agriculture and industry. In a formula which never altered, Rowland assigned to the professionals the task of managing the businesses profitably, which suited Lonrho's staff, while he struck the deals and smoothed the politicians. Since Rowland was convinced that in Africa so much depended upon his relations with politicians, he was acutely sensitive to any weaknesses in his personal network. In autumn 1971, Rowland realised that his ambitions in Kenya were threatened and his immediate weakness was Paul Spicer, Lonrho's manager in East Africa.

Lonrho's potential profits in Kenya were promising. Well organised during the colonial era, the British settlers had transformed the wilderness into a rich agricultural society. Since independence in 1963, unlike most other African nations, Kenya had neither espoused socialism nor discriminated against Europeans. On the contrary, despite the unpleasant Mau Mau campaign which won independence, Jomo Kenyatta, the country's first president, had encouraged the large white community to remain. The alternative, Kenyatta had been persuaded, would be similar collapse into chaos which had destroyed neighbouring Congo when the Belgian settlers fled. Among the British settlers who supported Kenyatta and successfully encouraged fellow Britons to remain was Bruce McKenzie, an able but unscrupulous buccaneer loyal only to his self-interest.

Elected to the first parliament, McKenzie swiftly assumed enormous influence by ingratiating himself, in a purring manner, to the tribe and family which ruled the country. In the purest sense, Kenya had become a 'Godfather' society. Jomo Kenyatta ruled absolutely while his divided family battled among themselves for power, influence, money and the eventual succession. Success, as elsewhere in Africa, depended upon access to the president.

McKenzie was Kenyatta's link to the white community, the guarantors of the country's prosperity. With a view to his own future well-being, McKenzie sought business opportunities and spotted Lonrho as a candidate for his attention. After Rowland had bought the conglomerate Consolidated Holdings in 1967 and Jim Slater's Motor Mart in 1969, McKenzie noted that Lonrho had become the country's key foreign investor. McKenzie presented Rowland with a simple proposal: in return for favourable influence with Kenyatta, he required a large interest in Lonrho's business.

Recognising a 'battle for turf', Rowland began negotiating. He was prepared to pay a reasonable price but would not respond to extortion. Lonrho's position in Kenya opened the door to the rest of East Africa: Tanzania and Uganda, and at that time Uganda's economy was booming.

McKenzie and his partner David Dobie owned a wide range of businesses which included the Mercedes franchise, but were minnows compared to Lonrho. Both however knew that selling cars in Africa was easy and profitable. In their discussions, McKenzie demanded from Rowland that in return for merging his and Lonrho's businesses in Kenya, he and Dobie, as chairman and managing director respectively, would become the largest shareholders.

The crunch was delivered to Rowland near Mombasa, Kenya's

main port on the Indian Ocean. Walking along the fashionable beach at Diani, McKenzie turned to Rowland: 'Kenya is my turf.' Rowland had little inclination to disagree. McKenzie's great friend was Charles Njonjo, the attorney general and the president's confidant.

As the waves crashed on to the sand, McKenzie continued with the scenario: Kenyatta was considering banning most car imports. Instead there would be assembly plants. 'He will give us,' continued McKenzie, 'the exclusive rights to the remaining imports and favour us for licences to assemble.' Rowland could only acknowledge that he understood.

Lonrho would not only lose profits in Kenya but also the secret payments on the 'B invoices' paid into its Swiss bank account. To ensure that the profits on car sales were in hard currencies, the importers of cars into all African countries were given two invoices by the European and Japanese motor manufacturers. The 'A invoice', with the higher price, was for the African government. The 'B invoice', with the lower amount, was the real price. The Kenyan government released sufficient US dollars to pay the higher amount on the 'A invoice' and the extra was deposited by the car manufacturer in a Swiss bank account. It was a simple method of avoiding Kenyan exchange controls and building tax-free profits.

McKenzie now struck home. The name Lonrho, he said, was associated with Rhodesia and South Africa: 'That's a problem in Kenya. In some quarters, you might be seen as an agent of apartheid.' Rowland anticipated the next move. Lonrho had proposed to the Kenyan government that it build an oil pipeline from the coast to Nairobi. McKenzie wanted an equal share in the business which Rowland had dubbed 'a licence to print money'. McKenzie turned. 'You've put all this money into Kenya. If you want to continue, you'll have to do business on our terms.' Their stroll ended.

Rowland understood blackmail. The alternative was to lose everything. Barred from access to Kenyatta by McKenzie, Rowland perceived no solution other than compliance with McKenzie's demands. He was irked by the excessive greed, but Paul Spicer, Lonrho's manager, was incapable of playing politics. Indeed, for Rowland, Spicer had become a grave disappointment, one Etonian too many. His selection reflected on Gerald Percy's judgment and cautioned Rowland in his reliance upon his deputy, the first step towards a major confrontation.

During those months, Rowland had confided his problems to Ngethe Njoroge, the Kenyan high commissioner in London since 1970. Njoroge had been introduced to Rowland by Thomas Kanza, the Zaïrean, in the Dorchester Grill. Like most Africans, Njoroge was impressed by his host. Although he was eating roast beef, Yorkshire pudding and cream spinach and appeared to be quintessentially English, Rowland was so different from the settlers in Kenya and all the other Englishmen whom the diplomat met in the course of his duties in London. Rowland loved and understood Africa and, unusually for a white, made the African welcome, even inviting him to Hedsor Wharf for Sunday lunch.

Rowland's principles for success in business also appealed to Njoroge: 'Abstain from alcohol to think clearly; always be honest to survive a crisis; and don't get involved in politics unless you are sure of winning.' Njoroge certainly noticed that Rowland did not drink. So when Rowland, lamenting about his problems with McKenzie, questioned Njoroge on whether there was a solution, the ambassador was pleased to mention his nephew Udi Gecaga, a twenty-six-year-old banker in Nairobi.

Similar to Gil Olympio, Rowland's fixer in West Africa, Gecaga was intelligent, internationally educated [Princeton, Trinity Cambridge and the Sorbonne] and exceptionally sophisticated. Like Olympio, Gecaga was a putative Tiny Rowland.

Gecaga had another advantage. He was related to Kenyatta. His uncle, Dr Njoroge Mungai, Kenya's foreign minister, was Jomo Kenyatta's nephew. Mungai had appointed Njoroge, his brother, as Kenya's high commissioner in London. Critically in that Godfather society, Mungai, Njoroge and Gecaga were opponents of McKenzie's protector, Charles Njonjo. Rowland saw a path to Jomo Kenyatta. 'Fly him to London immediately,' suggested Rowland.

Within hours of arriving, Gecaga was being seduced in the '007' bar at the Hilton hotel. Njoroge, his uncle, was also present.

'Call me Tiny,' said Rowland, 'Can I call you Udi?' Gecaga felt at ease, glad of Rowland's treatment of Africans as equals. 'Spicer is failing to manage the business profitably and failing to beat off McKenzie,' complained Rowland. 'Would you be prepared to take over Spicer's job?'

Gecaga was overwhelmed. 'You can write your own cheque,' added Rowland sensing that Gecaga was unconvinced. Rowland's offer was more than three times his current salary. Gecaga accepted on condition that, to avoid embarrassment, he become Spicer's deputy. The arrangement was kept secret for three months. When they returned to Cheapside, Rowland led the way into his office. Opening a desk drawer, he withdrew his personal cheque book of the British Linen Bank. 'Is this enough?' asked Rowland, writing a five-figure sum. 'It's for you and your family. Take care of the political problems.'

'I was blown away,' Gecaga told his relatives. 'He is making the right noises.'

The announcement of Gecaga's appointment infuriated McKenzie. The signal was clear. Rowland had abandoned their negotiations and, to save his investments, had aligned himself with McKenzie's enemies. McKenzie's revenge was immediate.

On Vice-President Daniel arap Moi's instructions, the work permits for Lonrho's European staff were cancelled. Rowland's Kenyan businesses faced ruin. Two days later, Gecaga arrived in Jomo Kenyatta's office. The president listened and telephoned the Director of Immigration: 'Cancel the order.' Rowland had won the first round.

McKenzie's next move was to organise the cancellation of all transport licences for Lonrho's haulage business. Again, Gecaga appealed to the president. Kenyatta revoked the order. McKenzie's revenge was to secure an order declaring Spicer a prohibited immigrant. Amid sniggering speculation, the insipid Etonian was compelled to leave with barely any notice.

Gecaga was now solely responsible for fighting Lonrho's battles. The rewards flowed quickly. With Gecaga at his side, Rowland was finally granted an audience with the president. A photo of the two smiling men duly appeared in Lonrho's

Nairobi newspaper, the *East African Standard*. Rowland had beaten McKenzie.

Appreciative of his own judgment in appointing Gecaga, Rowland posed as a close friend and mentor. 'Udi will be my successor,' he told friends in Gecaga's company. Aside, Rowland whispered advice: 'Udi, make sure that you're always dressed like the best white man. Not just to impress, but correct for the occasion.' Cultivating an image, Gecaga recognised, was inimical to Rowland's act. Money was not a source of corruption but a measure to score one's success. Gecaga quickly learnt that Lonrho had no political or philosophical agenda to transfer technology but was simply a vehicle to make money. Rowland was impressed with his latest student. When, shortly afterwards, Gecaga married Jomo Kenyatta's daughter, Rowland and Josie joined the newly weds for the second week of their honeymoon in Acapulco. Lonrho's assets in Kenya, Rowland reassured himself, were secure.

In Johannesburg, Captain Prinsloo had finally received the Coronation Syndicate files from Lonrho's office in Salisbury. Prompted by Rhodesian intelligence, whose officers were unsympathetic towards Lonrho and especially Rowland, the government had rejected Kruger's objections. Rowland's flights into Salisbury with Elliott baffled Ken Flower's staff. Either Rowland was working for British intelligence or, alternatively, his activities in nationalist Africa suggested that he was a communist sympathiser. A CIA report passed to Flower in 1970 had assessed the two possibilities and concluded that Rowland was working for MI6, especially in Nigeria where, in the wake of independence and the Biafran war, the agency had failed to establish a network. The CIA report speculated that Lonrho's purchase of John Holt had been to provide a cover for MI6 operations. The likelihood that Lonrho was being used by British intelligence, and the Smith regime's dependence upon its neighbour, directed the decision to pass the Coronation Syndicate file to Pretoria.

To Prinsloo, the evidence of fraud in the files was overwhelming. 'A baboon could win this case,' a lawyer in the attorney general's office told Prinsloo. Butcher's trial was set for 17 July 1972. It was expected to last ten days. Since the arrest, neither Rowland nor any other Lonrho director had dared to set foot in South Africa. Aware of the repercussions if Butcher's prosecution went ahead, Rowland searched for solutions.

Among the possible lifebelts was Duncan Sandys. Of all British politicians, Sandys was well respected in South Africa and enjoyed the connections which, if properly used, could save Lonrho. Approaches to Sandys had started before Butcher's arrest when Rowland, aware that Ball sat behind the only closed door on the sixth floor drinking, decided that the company needed a replacement for its discredited chairman. 'Alan Ball was no longer able to hold that job,' said Rowland.

In November 1971, Rowland offered Sandys £50,000 per annum if he devoted himself exclusively to Lonrho as a roving ambassador. Initially, Rowland wanted the agreement to run for one year but Sandys insisted upon six years. The politician explained his fear that since Rowland wanted his exclusive services, he might, once the arrangement ended, be unable to get other directorships. At sixty-four, he wanted security. In truth, Sandys had barely any City experience but saw the opportunity to exploit his status.

In addition to a six-year agreement, Sandys wanted a lot of money. Rowland and Sandys briefed Ogilvy and Butcher. The negotiations were not revealed to the other directors. Rowland's request for reticence was understandable. Jim Butler of Peat Marwick had already cautioned that a one-year agreement for £50,000 was 'excessive' and Rowland had gone further. Moreover, to help Sandys avoid paying tax, payment was to be made abroad.

Under British tax laws, salaries of British residents paid abroad were not subject to UK tax if the duties were carried out abroad or for a foreign company. Tax was payable only if the money was remitted to Britain, not if it was spent abroad. The usage was common among multinational companies.

To keep their secret, Sandys would be paid by London and Overseas Services, a new company established in the Cayman Islands, a centre for tax avoidance. The new company was not a Lonrho subsidiary but was owned by Rowland who paid local Cayman Islands lawyers to be the shareholders. Initially, the funds would be taken from the secret commissions which Lonrho received from European suppliers to Lonrho's African businesses and accumulated in Switzerland. Later there was a remittance of £50,010 from the British Linen Bank. As a pretence, Sandys received an official payment of a further £1000 from Lonrho in Britain for serving as a consultant. Even that payment and the relationship was unknown beyond Lonrho.

Rowland was paying a lot for a man whose prime was past but there was a sublime mischief in it for Rowland. Born in British internment and having spent his early manhood in British internment, he was corrupting a member of the British Establishment. Some Old Etonian directors were less enamoured of the arrangement. 'Duncan was bent ever since he was a lower boy at Eton,' recalled one of the Etonian directors. 'He was arrogant, born with a silver spoon and dishonest.'

The first result of Sandys's new arrangement was a letter which the politician wrote on 11 November 1971 to Dr Hilgard Muller, the South African foreign minister, pleading that he use his influence to waive the prosecutions. 'The recent arrests,' Sandys wrote, 'are extremely puzzling and disturbing. . . In the absence of any precise information about the alleged offence, the company is unable to make any reply.' Having explained how the arrests had 'cast a dark shadow' over the company and were 'gravely affecting' its business, Sandys volunteered that he had 'the fullest confidence' in its directors. All they wanted was the opportunity, without the fear of arrest, to come to South Africa and 'clear up this whole unfortunate business'. Muller took note of the letter.

On 17 February 1972, Peats delivered a 1566-page report on Lonrho, completed within four months. The raw statistics revealed Lonrho's poor performance. The return on capital was not, as previously suggested, 8 per cent, but 6.5 per cent, low for a high-risk investment. Moreover, no less than 96 per cent of Lonrho's profits were earned in Africa and 45 per cent of those profits were frozen by the local governments. If those circumstances had been disclosed to outsiders, Lonrho's share price would have suffered. It was a testament to Butcher's and Rowland's silence that Armitage, Wilkinson and Fuller Jenks,

Lonrho's accountants in London, had been unaware of the complete truth.

Yet while critical of some accountancy practices and suggesting the sale of some African businesses to increase Lonrho's earnings of hard currency, Leach and Butler had accepted most of Rowland's personal representations and parried his critics. On the Wankel engine, for example, both accountants discounted Wilkinson's complaints and accepted Rowland's version that the 'project appears to have good potential'. Their trust of Rowland also embraced accepting his version of the Nyaschere mine's financing.

The accountants reported that Rowland had arranged for Lonrho to acquire its 50 per cent share in the copper without any payment although, in his view, the mine 'had a value of approximately £1 million'. Peats reported that, in exchange for arranging that deal, Lonrho agreed to finance the mine's entire development. That was not accurate. There was no formal agreement.

While Butler did not probe Rowland's reply, the accountant had approved Butcher's request to minimise Lonrho's debts. In an accounting exercise which Butcher admitted was 'window dressing', Butler agreed that a £1.5 million loan from Lonrho to Nyaschere which was financing the mine's development could be disguised as an asset. Other accountants would condemn that practice as 'misleading and . . . wrong'. Butcher's subsequent admission was honest: 'It would just be one of those weaknesses which somebody would catch on to.' Butler's acquiescence was judged by some as unprofessional. Rowland's critics among the directors felt that Butler had permitted a 'whitewash'.

Peats's major criticism was directed at Lonrho's management structure which had not changed since the early Sixties. In Leach's and Butler's judgment, it was 'now unsuitable for administering the complex and diversified group that Lonrho has become'. To strengthen the management, Ball and Butcher were to be demoted and a new chairman and finance director appointed. Wilkinson and Dunlop were to be promoted to the board to be joined by two new independent non-executive directors. Rowland would become chief executive with Percy as his deputy. Peat Marwick were to become Lonrho's new auditors, a welcome boost to the partnership's income.

Considering the ensuing revelations, the two accountants' benign criticism of Rowland seemed to many peculiar. Sir Ronald Leach's explanation is revealing. 'I liked his non-pomposity. When I arrived in Cheapside, I could go in and see him unannounced. His office door was always open, he was usually talking on the telephone to Africa. There were never any refreshments other than a cup of tea. He was always so polite.' For Leach, Rowland compared so favourably with Robert Maxwell, 'a wall of fat always suing us'. The worst Leach can say is that Rowland was possibly 'unreliable, secretive and there were some grey areas'. On reflection, Leach realised that Rowland 'talked too much' but their relationship was not adversarial and the auditors were not investigating suggestions of dishonesty. Rather, they were providing help. Therefore they were willing to believe everything their client reported, and their client appeared to be helpful.

Nevertheless, the auditors' proposal for a more structured company and the appointment of non-executive directors irritated Rowland and his acolytes since it limited what Robert Dunlop called 'Mr Rowland's span of control', hindering his 'undoubted and exceptional capabilities'. But for the moment, Rowland was too weak to resist the accountants' limited strictures.

Without merchant bankers, and facing a liquidity crisis and the imminent South African prosecutions, Rowland made it a priority to find a new chairman before the next annual general meeting. Lonrho's reputation repelled the cast list of the 'great and the good'. The names put forward, including Lord Shawcross, the former Labour minister and advocate, Sir Roy Welensky and Sir Hugh Weeks, a retired civil servant, were rejected by Rowland. Heading the criteria Rowland required of a good chairman was the certainty of no interference in his business and the candidate's susceptibility to his manipulation. No names matched that description until, on 24 February 1972, Ogilvy met Sandys at a dinner party.

Ever since Peats's appointment, Ogilvy's family trusts had been selling Lonrho shares. During that dinner, Ogilvy confided his fears about Lonrho's problems to Sandys, including their hunt for a new chairman. 'They've got a lot of problems,' said Sandys. According to Sandys, Ogilvy brushed those problems aside. 'Ogilvy spoke with admiration of Mr Rowland's remarkable flair for business,' he recalled, 'and said that he was someone in whose honesty and loyalty he had complete confidence.' Ogilvy mooted the possibility of Sandys's candidature. The politician was noncommittal. Ogilvy found the absence of an outright rejection encouraging.

That night, Ogilvy telephoned Rowland to report the conversation. The following day, the Lonrho directors would meet for the first time to consider Peats's report. The critical meeting would last the whole day. Since the report demanded a new board and especially a new chairman, the possibility of Sandys's acceptance was seized upon by Rowland.

To have Winston Churchill's son-in-law and a senior Conservative politician on Lonrho's board would surely improve the company's image. Sandys had already proved invaluable when he had assured Sir Leslie O'Brien, the governor of the Bank of England, that Lonrho was not breaking sanctions. Sandys's assurance had been given 'as a Privy Councillor'. Yet considering Rowland's attitude towards Africa and business, Sandys would seem an odd choice. He was a tired man bereft of any business experience or acumen. As commonwealth secretary, he was identified with the anti-black nationalist, pro-hanging wing of the Conservative Party. His 'reactionary' reputation had been proven by his good relations with Hilgard Muller, the South African foreign minister. It was hardly the background to win friends among Africa's new leaders. Yet Sandys suited Rowland's requirements.

Before the board meeting, due to start at 10 a.m., Rowland and Ball visited Sandys in Vincent Square. If Sandys could be persuaded to become chairman, there were still serious obstacles to overcome, not least the inevitable opposition to his appointment by some directors. But the advantage of Sandys, as Rowland understood, was that the politician was easily manipulated, greedy and already compromised. With Sandys as chairman, Rowland saw that he would have little difficulty in continuing to run the company unimpeded. Early that morning,

Sandys reacted positively to the offer but was explicit that his remuneration was crucial.

Rowland brushed the problem aside: 'I will do everything Duncan to let this agreement go for the full five or six years.' Rowland promised that half of the £40,000 annual fee could be paid into the Cayman Islands. They parted with the agreement that Butcher would visit Sandys to negotiate the salary. Possibly Rowland was attempting to avoid personal involvement but his intent was clear: Sandys was to be secured at any price.

At Cheapside, the reconstruction of the board was approved and it was agreed that Sandys would be invited to become chairman. Significantly, there were no discussions about his pay. With that settled, Rowland raised the dividend, the most critical factor in his view owning 20 per cent of the stock. Butler had insisted that since Lonrho had no money to pay the dividend, it could be paid only if the company could secure a satisfactory loan. Fearing that without a healthy dividend Lonrho's share price would fall further, Rowland suggested that Fred Butcher be empowered to negotiate a £10 million loan with the Kuwait Investment Co. A vote approved the proposal and Butcher drove immediately to Heathrow to fly to the Middle East.

Three days later, on 28 February 1972 at 9 o'clock in the morning, the board reconvened. Butcher had returned with a Kuwaiti offer of £5 million on unattractive conditions. After forty-five minutes, Ogilvy and Butler left Cheapside and drove to the Standard & Chartered Bank. Two hours later they returned having successfully negotiated an £11.5 million overdraft to be repaid by 30 September. Lonrho had won a seven-month breathing space. There were cheers. A dividend could now be paid.

With the annual general meeting in seven weeks, Butcher visited Sandys on 8 March. Convinced by Rowland that Lonrho's recovery and survival depended upon Sandys agreeing to become chairman, Butcher steered the conversation in an amicable but businesslike tone.

Together they sat at a table, Butcher writing figures on two sheets of paper calculating Sandys's potential loss of tax-free earnings if his annual £50,000 consultancy had been, under the contractual terms, cancelled with one year's notice. 'What did you have in mind as compensation?' Butcher asked aware of Rowland's attitude: 'If you want something, do not quibble about the price.'

Effortlessly, Sandys dominated their discussion, leaving Butcher in no uncertainty that despite his maximum contractual legal entitlement of £88,000, he would not accept less than £130,000. 'There was no need for me to bargain,' Sandys would subsequently explain. 'I was not neck craning for this job.' Having heard Sandys's basic demand, Butcher reported to Rowland: 'God, I offered him £60,000 and he had made up his mind he wanted £130,000.' Sandys was greedy.

For Rowland, there was little to consider. Lonrho needed a chairman and the secret payments to Sandys were no different from Lonrho's payments to keep its businesses working in Africa. He was prepared to pay £250,000 to 'avoid the holocaust' of Lonrho without a chairman. Butcher returned to Sandys the following day to confirm the agreement.

Paying Sandys £130,000 compensation in the Cayman Islands proved less easy than anticipated. Since there were insufficient funds in secret accounts in Switzerland, Butcher began scouring Lonrho's 480 companies to find the cash, undermining from the outset the plot to hide the payments. Eventually sufficient money was found in the accounts of the tea producer, Anglo-Ceylon. To disguise the transfer to the Cayman Islands, the money was funnelled through a newly formed subsidiary to the specially created London and Overseas Services.

Nothing would be disclosed to the Lonrho board or in the company's accounts. Rightly sensing that the deal would provoke criticism, Rowland decided the best course was to keep it secret. The 'Christmas Tree decorations' did not need to know. Butcher understood the intention. Not so much, he would later say, to 'mislead' Lonrho's directors but rather 'not to inform them'. The paper trail, however, could not be destroyed. The deal was completed on 9 March. A letter dated 17 March informed Sandys that his consultancy would be terminated on 19 March 1972 and confirmed the £130,000 compensation.

Parallel to the overt reconstruction of the board and Rowland's intent to buy respectability in the form of Sandys, was Butcher's removal of the traces of any hidden arrangements whose exposure could add to Lonrho's embarrassment. Among those was the secret agreement with Dan Mayers to conceal the profits on the sale of Zambian amethysts through Blorg, the Liechtenstein company.

In March 1972, Butcher confided to Mayers that Lonrho intended to liquidate Blorg. According to Mayers, he was told, 'In the climate of investigations, Lonrho simply could not stand such disclosures.' Among the embarrassments which the Lonrho director feared was the discovery by the South African police that Coronation Syndicate had an interest in Blorg. Butcher's new arrangement with Mayers was that the amethysts, mined in ever greater amounts, would be shipped direct to Mayers's company, Crystals. That company would trade on behalf of all the partners, informally named 'The Consortium'. Rowland therefore totally trusted Mayers to reimburse Lonrho's share of the profits. Mayers was also bequeathed the responsibility to dispose of the forty-ton stockpile of inferior-grade stones. Contango, the Liechtenstein company which secretly received Lonrho's share of the profits from Blorg, was not liquidated. With that housekeeping chore completed, Butcher hoped that the manoeuvre could be forgotten.

The board meeting to approve Sandys's appointment was convened on 22 March. By then, a sanitised and abbreviated version of Peats's report had been published but it understated many potentially embarrassing disclosures about the source and remittability of Lonrho's earnings. Similarly, the public did not read any reference to the accountants' demand that Rowland, Ball and Percy should cease living rent free in their houses.

The directors attending that board meeting arrived with different degrees of knowledge about the contract with Sandys. Rowland, Ball and Butcher knew everything. Ogilvy knew about the £51,000 consultancy agreement but says that he did not know about the compensation agreement. Percy and Elliott knew that Rowland was considering offering Sandys the chairmanship but knew nothing about either the original consultancy agreement or the negotiations to terminate the agreement. The other three directors knew only that discussions with Sandys were underway. Rowland was not inclined to enlighten them further.

Just before the board meeting, Butcher showed Percy and Elliott a minute of the board meeting held on 25 February 1972. Butcher asked them to give their formal approval. As the two directors read the bland typescript, they became agitated. Initialled by Ball, it summarised the board's approval of Sandys's £51,000 consultancy contract.

In unison, the two directors protested: 'We agreed to invite Sandys to join the board,' said Percy, 'but we had no idea about the consultancy agreements.' The board meeting began in unusual commotion. 'What happens to the consultancy agreements,' asked Percy, 'if Sandys accepts the chairmanship?'

'They fall away', replied Rowland.

'Are there any extra payments?' asked Percy.

Rowland said nothing. There was no mention of the signed compensation agreement for £130,000 and there was no reason for anyone to believe that the issue arose. Significantly, neither Leach nor Butler contributed to the discussion.

Aware of the growing tensions among the directors, Rowland urged his board to agree to the £51,000 consultancy fee. 'We must have a unanimous vote,' he urged, 'to show we are friends.' Since Rowland and Ball had already signed the agreement to appoint Sandys as Lonrho's chairman, five directors agreed but Percy and Elliott abstained. 'It's too high for a consultant,' criticised Percy. 'It will prove embarrassing for us. I want my abstention recorded in the minutes.' Butcher, who was keeping a record, agreed that the abstentions should be recorded in the private minute book.

'Loyalty to Tiny' was both Percy's and Elliott's explanation for their reluctance to pursue their opposition. Their admiration for Rowland's achievements and their attraction to his magnetic personality overrode any instinctive suspicion of his duplicity. 'Tiny was fun. Working at Lonrho was exciting. We'd got over the crisis, it was best to let things settle,' recalls a director.

Although Lonrho was Rowland's private fief, he encouraged everyone to feel part of the team, a comforting mystique for Old Etonians.

Sandys was officially appointed chairman on 4 April 1972. Two thirds of his £38,000 annual salary plus £2000 expenses was to be paid abroad to avoid tax. Sandys's functions, everyone agreed, were restricted to being a figurehead – presiding at board meetings and at the annual general meeting.

Leach and Butler meanwhile had been summoned to the Bank of England. Both accountants admired Rowland and were prepared to earn Lonrho's fees on Rowland's assurance that he would implement their recommendations to install financial controls. A finance director was to be appointed and two more non-executive directors. Their discussions with Sir Leslie O'Brien, the Governor of the Bank, concerned the appointment of the independent directors. Ogilvy's position on the board was sensitive to the royal family and O'Brien suggested that one of the independent directors should be Sir Basil Smallpeice who included among other appointments the position of administrative adviser in the Royal Household, counselling on investments and financial matters.

In every respect, Smallpeice's nomination reflected the City's maladroit understanding of Rowland, Lonrho and international commerce. Both physically and intellectually, Smallpeice was unlikely to appeal to Rowland. A small man with pebble glasses, his myopic sight, seriously impaired by cataracts, was a reflection of his personality. His long business career was marked in public opinion by failure. Fired by a Conservative government in 1963 for his stewardship of British Overseas Airways [BOAC] and blamed for the losses at Cunard, Smallpeice's career was symptomatic of the British business scene where failure evoked sympathy while success provoked anger, a phenomenon which Rowland despised. Yet Smallpeice was an acceptable Establishment figure who could protect Ogilvy.

The formal invitation came from Sandys, but Smallpeice was urged by O'Brien and Leach to accept because, while Lonrho was sound, someone was needed to control Rowland. 'I was asked to ensure that he observed the requirements and disciplines in running a public company,' recalled Smallpeice. 'It was essential for there to be people on the board such as myself to reassure the City. . . The good name of the City of

London was at stake.' Smallpeice became deputy chairman and a non-executive director. He was to be paid £12,500 of which £2500 was paid abroad. While Rowland held over 10 million Lonrho shares, Smallpeice, the watchdog, owned 1200 shares.

Two conditions provided by Peats to secure Smallpeice's agreement were immediately broken. A second independent non-executive director was not appointed after Rowland cast a veto. Secondly, Butcher was not replaced as finance director. Rowland blamed his inability to find a suitable candidate but according to Percy one year later, 'We didn't try because Tiny didn't want Fred to go.' Butcher was a master of creative accountancy and Butler, bedazzled by his abilities, ignored his own requirement.

But, for the first time, Lonrho directors were to receive the agenda of board meetings one week in advance. Accompanying the agenda, there would be, also for the first time, monthly financial, budget and forecast reports produced by Moss. In theory, Lonrho seemed destined to become similar to other corporations. There would also, for the first time, be a personnel department.

The final appointment to complete Lonrho's refurbishment were the new merchant bankers. Elliott had tried to interest friends at Schroeder Wragg but failed. Others tried Hambros as they vainly trawled the Square Mile. Finally, only one bank was willing to accept the chalice, Keyser Ullman. The bank was managed by Roland Franklin and its chairman was Edward Du Cann.

Born in 1924, Du Cann had earned a reputation both in Westminster and in the City. In 1956, he had been elected Conservative member of parliament for Taunton and in 1957 he had invented and successfully launched Britain's first Unit Trust, the Unicorn, eventually sold to Barclays Bank. A potentially successful ministerial career had started in 1962 as economic secretary to the Treasury. In 1963, he was minister of state under Edward Heath at the Department of Trade. But his appointment as chairman of the Conservative Party after the election defeat was terminated abruptly by Heath in 1967. Du Cann had not supported Heath in the 1965 elections for Party leader. There was also a slight cloud over Du Cann's reputation, exemplified by the quip, 'You've got to take the smooth with the smooth.'

After the 1970 election victory, the Party leader's antagonism precluded ministerial office and Du Cann was voted chairman of the 1922 Committee, representing backbenchers in the Commons. He then became chairman of Keyser Ullman.

By any measure, Keyser Ullman, although founded in 1853, was a second-division merchant bank. Roland Franklin, the senior partner, was technically competent but not respected among the City scions. His talents during the Sixties, challenging the orthodoxy of the self-preening City establishment, had aided James Goldsmith's rise to fortune. Yet in 1972, Goldsmith abandoned Keysers in favour of a more reputable bank just as Keysers was lending huge sums to property developers.

Lonrho lacked an alternative. Any reservations among directors were not voiced. Sandys insisted that Du Cann, an ally from the House of Commons, also be appointed a director. He was supported by Jim Butler following a visit to Du Cann. The bank was to be seen by the world, said Du Cann, to be helping Lonrho. In those circumstances, Franklin extracted a profitable deal. In return for the bank's services, Lonrho gave Keysers 1.5 million low-cost options for Lonrho shares over the following three years. The deal proved to be Lonrho's salvation. The bank's priority, to raise £10 million to cover Lonrho's debts by a rights issue, was accomplished within record time: 'We saved the company,' Du Cann would justifiably claim. 'We won the confidence of bankers and newspapers.'

Rowland, a master of pulling victory from the jaws of defeat, had once again instilled confidence among Fleet Street commentators. Among the chorus whom he persuaded that Lonrho's future was safe was Patrick Sergeant in the *Daily Mail*. 'Booming' wrote the journalist describing the company's record fifteen pence dividend, the profitable warrants from the Wankel engine, and the rise in price of gold and platinum. Lonrho, enthused Sergeant, had 'solved their liquidity problem and could enjoy a profitable future'.

Smallpeice agreed that the City had shown a 'handsome vote of confidence' although Lonrho clearly could not survive without the public's money. The issue was whether Rowland would acknowledge his responsibilities towards directors and shareholders.

During his first weeks, Smallpeice had diligently attempted to disentangle Lonrho's finances, establishing which profits in Africa were remittable, and to rectify the directors' use of company funds as their own pocket money. Having Cunard and BOAC as a comparison, Smallpeice was particularly struck by the lack of controls over expenses and Rowland's ability to commit the company to huge projects without the board's approval. 'The way you manage the company,' Smallpeice told Rowland, 'it will be impossible to recruit suitable accounts staff.'

On the fifth floor, like his predecessor, Moss was attempting to impose financial controls. He was not helped by Rowland's exhortations as he flew around Africa advising local accountants, 'Don't bother to fill in Moss's reports.' Bigger deals, not management organisation, remained Rowland's priority. Moss was intrigued by items charged to 'General Expenses Africa'. Butcher was unforthcoming: 'I can't tell you, but it's got Bank of England approval.' The codes were eventually broken. '202' was Zambia, '404' was Kaunda, '405' was Banda, while '203' was Malawi. Moss would eventually discover one charge was a donation to Mrs Anwar Sadat's hospital.

Inevitably, Lonrho's cash crisis again worsened, but Rowland seemed preoccupied with sustaining his own control over the company. The appointment of the new directors spurred him to limit even further the number of directors he could trust. Isolating the newcomers reflected Rowland's anger that these new Lonrho directors, not selected by himself, were making decisions about his company. They needed to be neutralised. Robert Dunlop responded. 'With a part-time chairman,' wrote Dunlop, 'it is proposed that his role as executive be confined to chairing board meetings and both annual and extraordinary general meetings.' Sandys was agreeable but Smallpeice was not co-operative.

Smallpeice was certain that his duty was to clean up Lonrho and reform Rowland. The opportunity to demonstrate his authority and purpose occurred on 22 May, just one month after his appointment. Two American banks, Exim and First National City, had agreed to loans of $63 million to build the sugar refinery in the Ivory Coast. That morning, Rowland was planning to fly to West Africa with Sandys and Olympio.

Just before their departure, Smallpeice cornered Sandys. Explaining his concerns about Lonrho, Smallpeice asked the chairman to persuade Rowland during the journey that Lonrho was committed to the conditions laid out in Keyser Ullman's prospectus. These were that Lonrho was to invest outside Africa, especially in Britain; and that it would cease supporting or sell off its unprofitable African subsidiaries. Sandys seemed receptive. Two days later they met again at a meeting of the newly constituted Lonrho board. Smallpeice was agitated.

The deputy chairman had been prying through the directors' offices. On one desk he had seen Dunlop's memo referring to the limitation of Sandys's powers. Rowland had scribbled 'OK', showing his approval. His fellow directors, concluded Smallpeice, were not independent minds, but Rowland's placemen. Everything crystallised during that board meeting.

The reforms promised by Peats and Keyser Ullman, Smallpeice concluded, were being ignored. Everyone was inferior to Rowland, making 'frank discussion impossible'. Rowland, he observed, refused to delegate or consult, still running the company as his personal fiefdom. The requirements of the Companies Acts were being flouted.

After that board meeting, Smallpeice complained to Sandys. 'I am far more disquieted than I was – this is an understatement: I am in fact very disturbed by what I have witnessed and learnt.' The businessman warned the politician that his reputation could in the future be 'tarnished' by 'a major financial fiasco' because of intentional concealment by Rowland, Ball and Butcher.

Sandys was irritated, both by the burden of Smallpeice's information and by Smallpeice himself. The latter, patently suffering both from ill-health and the death of his wife, was a nuisance. Everyone believed in Tiny and only Smallpeice, a niggling Jeremiah, was carping about Lonrho's future. Sandys acknowledged and ignored the complaint.

In turn Smallpeice confided his dismay to Wilkinson. In the

course of their afternoon conversation, Wilkinson disclosed the board's post-dated ratification of the £50,000 fee for Sandys's consultancy. Smallpeice was 'shattered' by the information.

The deteriorating relationship between Rowland and Smallpeice exploded in argument on 7 June. Once again, Rowland was about to fly to Africa. On that occasion, his destination was the Sudan to sign an £80 million deal for the sugar scheme despite Lonrho's continuing liquidity crisis. Nothing had been discussed at the board meeting, a reflection, Smallpeice believed, of Rowland's unfettered expansionism.

Ian Fraser had discouraged Rowland from investing in the Sudan. Rowland, the banker believed, knew too little about the Arabs' and was vulnerable to the regime's instability. 'You won't be able to use your usual charm,' he had warned Rowland before leaving Warburgs. Rowland however was convinced of the similarity between Africans and Arabs. Moreover he was convinced that growing sugar in Africa would earn millions. By then, Lonrho owned sugar estates in Malawi, Mauritius, Swaziland and South Africa. Using the management blueprint in the Ivory Coast scheme, Rowland enthusiastically proposed similar plantations in Guyana, Togo, Pakistan, Kenya, Uganda, Iran, Liberia and Mauritania. At that moment, Lonrho's expertise was concentrated in precisely two people: René Leclézio, and René Noel, both Mauritians. Even Gil Olympio was bewildered by the expansion. The international trade in sugar, he told Rowland, was minute and, like all commodities, vulnerable to volcanic price fluctuations. Domestic consumption in African countries was as small as Lonrho's resources. To those who had advised caution, Rowland replied, 'The more the merrier'. Only Smallpeice could not be charmed into acquiescence. Stubborn and crusty, he stood fixed in Rowland's office, demanding to inspect the terms of the Sudan agreement. The chief executive was irritated by this meddlesome midget who understood neither swashbuckling politico-business nor the African way. 'It is not the concern of a non-executive deputy chairman,' scoffed Rowland departing for Heathrow.

Smallpeice did not give up and made an appointment to

meet Rowland and remove what he called 'misconceptions about my role'.

Rowland had just returned somewhat elated from the American embassy. In a meeting with Julius Walker, responsible for the Africa desk, he had expounded his ideas for Africa's development. Walker recalls that he was 'flattered' by the visit of a man who is 'attractive, magnetic and brilliant. When he entered my room he filled it with his presence.' Rowland had been urging the American administration to close its Salisbury consulate. Unbeknown to Rowland, the decision had been delayed for intelligence purposes. 'I was surprised by his progressive position,' recalled Walker.

On his return to Cheapside, Rowland's emotions had not adjusted for a confrontation about management practices. With emotion and passion which embarrassed and perplexed Smallpeice, Rowland recounted his conversation in the American embassy – his love for Africa, for Lonrho and how a political solution in Africa would increase Lonrho's profits by '£100 million a year'. For Smallpeice this was 'a flight of fancy' which was irrelevant to the overriding issue of Lonrho's credibility in the City.

Looking down at the diminutive representative of the Establishment, Rowland was blunt. 'I will not tolerate interference by a non-executive deputy chairman.'

'I just want to make Lonrho acceptable to the City,' countered Smallpeice.

'If you want to limit my freedom to run Lonrho then I'd prefer to sell my shares and depart. I'll only stay on my terms or not at all.'

Rowland's agitation and ultimatum spurred Smallpeice to confide to both Sandys and Du Cann that he thought that they should accept Rowland's implicit offer of his resignation. 'I think he would find altogether unbearable the financial and organisational harness that we would require him to wear. He would obviously be much happier pursuing his own ends. . . I have come to feel very strongly that, in the interests of the other 80 per cent of Lonrho shareholders, it would be wrong not to accept Tiny Rowland's offer of resignation.' Both politicians were appalled. 'Lonrho without Tiny is inconceivable,' said Du Cann. Sandys agreed.

Rowland ignored the warnings. Lonrho's shares were rising as the prices of gold and platinum increased. Butcher's trial was also temporarily resolved. On Rowland's instructions, a doctor had been procured who would certify that the Lonrho director was 'too ill to travel'. In the meantime, Butcher flew to Johannesburg and, as Prinsloo heard from his informant, was working in Lonrho's offices. The policeman would only become aware of Butcher's 'illness' on the morning of the trial. 'I was surprised,' he confesses with Afrikaan understatement. The judge postponed the hearing until 30 August to allow Butcher to 'recuperate'.

Rowland even scorned the pressure to cease using a public company for his own profits. Among Peats's principal complaints was his joint ownership with Lonrho of the Shamrocke mine. Like others, Sandys was perplexed about the mine's ownership: 'Tiny, do you own 50 per cent or not?'

'Mr Chairman,' replied the fox, 'I plead the Fifth Amendment.' No one realised that Lonrho in Rhodesia was totally financing the mine's development or that Rowland's interest was shared with Ball and Ogilvy.

To allay the pressure, Rowland ostensibly sold his 50 per cent share to Lionel Taylor, his manager at Shepton Estates and his father-in-law. 'As I told you last month,' he wrote to Taylor, 'Peats's report is the final straw, and I must get rid of my interest in Shamrocke.' The alleged price, without any formal contract, was $1,822,000. Since Rowland's interest was owned through a succession of three offshore companies and Taylor neither possessed that amount of money nor was expected to pay, the transfer was, as Rowland intended, a sham. Inadvertently, Rowland had admitted that the mine was worth $3.6 million. The massive increase in value could only be accounted for by Lonrho's investment, to which he was not contributing while claiming half the benefit.

There was another unannounced problem. Graham Beck, Rowland's former South African partner, had issued a writ in the High Court to recover his 50 per cent share of Rowland's interest in the mine. 'Rowland totally ignored me,' recalls Beck.

'He thought I would let him off the hook. He took me out to lunch and tried to buy me off but I wouldn't agree.'

Rowland's behaviour and the charges of fraud against the directors including Ogilvy in Johannesburg fed suspicions of dishonesty. Hearing rumours 'on the circuit' that Scotland Yard might be investigating allegations concerning fraud at Lonrho, Colin MacKenzie and Nicholas Elliott visited Peter Brodie, an assistant commissioner of police. Among those who joined their discussion was Kenneth Etheridge, a senior officer in the Fraud Squad. Their suspicions confirmed, the directors agreed to deliver copies of identified files from Lonrho. 'If I agree to lunch with you in two weeks,' said Brodie, 'it will show the all clear.' The three would meet for lunch.

The atmosphere of discontent permeating Cheapside was pervasive. To Rowland's irritation, he could see across the corridor Smallpeice and Wilkinson, supported by Moss, writing and dispatching a succession of thick documents describing Lonrho's new scheme of organisation, the defined responsibilities of individuals and how budgets were to be prepared and submitted to London. The recipients in Africa, Rowland realised, would conclude that, in the wake of the past crisis, the new chief executive was no longer in total control.

In retaliation, Rowland sent out a short memorandum to seven executive directors effectively banning any communication with the non-executive directors without his permission. 'It has come to my attention,' he wrote on 19 July, 'that in recent weeks a number of papers have been circulated to non-executive directors containing proposals about which I had neither been consulted nor indeed had any prior knowledge.' Rowland insisted that he be consulted before any more proposals were circulated to avoid 'misunderstandings'.

Smallpeice now joined war with Rowland. The results for 1971 were due to be published on 30 September and Smallpeice was determined to neutralise what he called 'the pressures at work underneath the surface' to protect both the Palace and Duncan Sandys.

Sandys's consultancy fees and his chairman's salary would, by law, have to be mentioned in the accounts. Smallpeice believed that Sandys's £40,000 salary as a figurehead chairman would provoke 'a public scandal'. Legally, Sandys was entitled to that remuneration but Smallpeice, a puritan, thought the amount was simply excessive and needed to be 'saved'.

Writing as 'a friend' who was 'concerned with protecting you from walking into a trap', Smallpeice told Sandys on 21 July 1972, 'You yourself are in great potential danger . . . from the personal financial arrangements made for you.' Prompted by his admitted intention to 'put the fear of God' into Sandys, Smallpeice added that the arrangements would convince people that Rowland had 'bought' Sandys's allegiance with the consequence that the politician was 'riding for a most almighty fall'. Smallpeice suggested that the two might need to resign.

Understandably, Sandys was alarmed. He knew that Rowland and the trio held Smallpeice in contempt and that they would withhold from him details about his secret contract, especially the £130,000 compensation payment which was known to only four of the fifteen directors. He sought advice from Du Cann. Could the salary be justified? Sandys alleged that Du Cann had been told by Butcher about the £130,000 compensation. Sandys would also claim that he mentioned the compensation to his friend. Du Cann would subsequently deny all knowledge but he suspected that Smallpeice was beginning to 'blackmail' the chairman. He adjusted his allegiance accordingly. The fuse was set for the biggest boardroom dispute in British corporate history.

To intensify the pressure, Smallpeice underlined Rowland's alleged failure to fulfil the conditions listed in Keyser Ullman's prospectus. Advising Sandys that they both faced prosecution as criminals under the Companies Act and a possible Board of Trade inquiry for issuing a fraudulent prospectus for the rights issue, he urged the politician to 'take this whole question very, very seriously'. Sandys should not, he concluded, 'make the mistake of allowing yourself to be lulled into a sense of false security by anything Rowland may say to you'.

After forty years in public life, Sandys was robustly unintimidated by the warnings of a comparative nonentity and insensitive, despite his own illness, to Smallpeice's ailments. He shared the view that small-minded Smallpeice was unable to grasp that Lonrho was not a sweetshop but a bold, enjoyable, risky adventure in Africa. Du Cann's advice that the salary, contrary to Smallpeice's complaint, was within the norms settled the question. In a lengthy reply, Sandys dismissed all the complaints and queries, apparently terminating Smallpeice's campaign. But deliberately, the politician did not reveal the £130,000 compensation which he had received. 'I did not consider [it] his business,' he explained.

As the deadline of 30 September crept closer, encompassing the need for agreed accounts and an agreed directors' report, Smallpeice's complaints could not be ignored. As Rowland leant back in his chair in a board meeting calculating Lonrho's profits, literally on the back of an envelope, Smallpeice grimaced. 'I want proper tabulations, not figures plucked out of the air.'

'It's all a waste of time,' fumed Rowland. 'Oh for God's sake, what's the next item on the agenda?'

'I've got some figures here,' continued Smallpeice. His artificial serenity was interrupted by Rowland's impatience: 'I don't have to listen to this.' Simulating anger, Rowland moved towards the door, 'I don't need accountants meddling in my business. I'm going off to Africa to make lots of money and I'll be successful.' Turning on Smallpeice, Rowland added, 'I know how to make money. I can't understand people who can't make money.' But the two politicians, with an instinct for survival, invited Roger Moss for a private briefing.

The invitation to Vincent Square for Saturday lunch on 'exquisite' china was for the whole Moss family. Sandys, the consummate politician, sought to win the sceptical accountant's sympathy. In his study, surrounded by red ministerial boxes, Sandys asked some relevant questions. 'Solid ivory behind the ears,' thought Moss as the financial jargon left no impression on the politician's face. 'His diligence just reflects lack of comprehension,' concluded Moss who failed to notice any evidence of Rowland's secret arrangement with Sandys.

Drinking Earl Grey tea with Sir Edward Du Cann seated beneath a Unicorn at Keyser Ullman was a marked contrast. Impeccably dressed and wearing a Royal Yacht Squadron tie,

Du Cann understood precisely Moss's analysis: 'You're sitting on a time bomb,' said Moss. Du Cann's expression remained unchanged. 'Well done, dear boy, you're clearly doing so well.' He would not interfere in Lonrho's management. 'It was a mistake to trust Sandys,' said Du Cann shortly afterwards to explain his reluctance to interfere.

Smallpeice's terrorism had however galvanised Rowland to undertake some housekeeping chores. On 29 August, Butcher flew to Jersey to organise the purchase of Hedsor Wharf and Ball's flat in Kensington through a firm of Jersey lawyers. Effectively, the transaction would protect Rowland from qualifying as a British resident liable to pay income tax. Percy's wife had already bought their house.

In the Johannesburg courthouse the following day, a doctor's certificate was again produced asserting that Butcher, then just returning from Jersey, was 'too ill' to travel. The trial was postponed until January 1973. Captain Prinsloo was 'not very happy' but did not suspect that what he believed to be his 'cast iron' prosecution was vulnerable.

Not surprisingly, Butcher was considering whether Lonrho could break its link with Rhodesia, which was having a 'bad effect on the Lonrho image' not least because 'it is known that certain offences under Sanctions Legislation have been committed by officials of subsidiaries in Rhodesia.' But other than simply abandoning the mines and farms, an alternative opposed by Rowland, Lonrho's options were paralysed.

To repair Rowland's counterproductive protest at the South African embassy one year earlier, Duncan Sandys, possessing the right connections and manner, had embarked upon quiet diplomacy. His contact was Hilgard Muller, the South African foreign minister. In September, Muller was due to fly to New York to attend a United Nations session. En route, he would stop in London where he would meet his friend Sandys.

In the previous weeks, South African diplomats, in utmost secrecy, had been negotiating with Kenneth Kaunda a prospective meeting with John Vorster, the prime minister, in a train on Beit Bridge. South Africa, desperate to break out of its isolation, sought Kaunda's friendship to mitigate the threat of African terrorism. To win over the leader of the Front Line States, every potential obstacle needed to be removed.

One obstacle, as Sandys explained to Muller on the telephone, was the prosecution against Butcher. 'Tiny is very close to KK,' said Sandys, 'and Lonrho is very important in Zambia. Don't underestimate Tiny's ability to influence KK's attitude towards South Africa.' Muller trusted Sandys's judgment.

On 12 September, Captain Prinsloo was summoned to the Union Buildings in Pretoria, the seat of federal government. Accompanied by General Christoffel Buys, the head of South Africa's CID, K. D. Moodie, the attorney general of the Transvaal, and the secretary for justice, Prinsloo was ushered into Muller's office. Muller had asked for a briefing about the Lonrho case. Moodie was well prepared.

'We are acting on the advice of both our internal lawyers and Laurie Ackerman, one of our most eminent private counsel,' reported Moodie. 'Both agree that there is a prima facie case.' Moodie then read Ackerman's opinion. None of the five men who left Muller's office, including Moodie, harboured any doubts that the prosecution would go ahead. Yet exactly four months later, just days before the postponed trial was due to begin, Moodie announced that the prosecution was withdrawn. He gave no explanation. 'It's the biggest miscarriage of justice,' charged Prinsloo. The politician was unmoved. Subsequently, Rowland would claim that the government of the Transvaal had 'apologised' for issuing the warrants. That was untrue. The Palace's relief that the charge against Ogilvy was withdrawn was passed to Sandys.

There was also relief when the accounts were settled on 30 September. The annual report was characterised by admissions of mistakes, caveats about the future and promises of rectification of past errors. Although agreed by Butler and Leach, neither accountant had elicited the several beneficial but still secret arrangements enjoyed by Rowland and Sandys.

In Cheapside, the visible wounds were still real. Two directors had resigned; another had been charged with fraud; Warburgs had departed; the share price had fallen; and a final dividend had not been paid. Within the boardroom, Rowland had been exposed as deceptive, some would argue as a liar. Company minutes had been falsified. So far, all those transgressions were excused on the grounds that Rowland had earned enormous benefits for Lonrho, epitomised by Wilkinson's assessment on 15 November of Wankel's 'challenging opportunities'.

The engine, predicted Wilkinson, would 'capture' 40 per cent of the market by 1980 and 70 per cent by 1985. Profits before tax would, by 1985, be £23.8 million. 'The economic trends', he wrote, 'are increasingly in favour of the particular advantages afforded by the Wankel engine.' Even Rowland's critics believed in his genius. Tiny was never wrong. It was the lull before the storm.

Six
Conspiracy

Rowland spent Christmas and the New Year in Acapulco. During his three-week holiday, a satirical ballad circulated in Cheapside about 'Tiny clicking his balls together', a skit on the two steel balls which signalled Captain Queeg's stress during the Caine mutiny.

In Rowland's absence, Jim Butler, finalising the 1971–72 accounts, summoned Fred Butcher. For some time Butler had been puzzled by a £75,000 loan from Anglo-Ceylon deposited in the Cayman Islands' account of Consultancy & Development Services Ltd. 'What is this account?' Butler repeatedly asked Butcher over three weeks. The deadline was a board meeting on 15 February. Butcher prevaricated until the last moment. The money, explained the unqualified executive, funded a £44,000 payment to Sandys.

'That should have the board's approval,' said Butler, unaware of the agreement, yet not eliciting further details. Butcher disagreed: 'Only a few of the directors know about the arrangement.' That afternoon, Butler invited Sandys to visit Peats's offices.

At Cheapside, without explanation, approval of the accounts had been delayed but two items of housekeeping, ordered by Butler, were discussed. Feigning innocence, Butcher had recommended in a memorandum that Lonrho should pay Rowland £750,000 for his 50 per cent stake in the Nyaschere mine, either in sterling or Swiss francs. Percy erupted. 'The most unpleasant board meeting I ever had in my years with Lonrho.' Even Sandys could not understand why Lonrho should buy a blocked Rhodesian asset for sterling. 'Tiny was furious when we turned it down flat,' recalled Percy.

Rowland's temper worsened when Peter Dalgleish, a non-executive director, complained that Rowland's purchase of Hedsor Wharf from Lonrho was still uncompleted. The ill-humour was symptomatic of Rowland's refusal to accept any constraints upon his personal authority. For the first time, Rowland's control over his directors was uncertain. As Dalgleish confided to the other directors, so much depended upon Leach's and Butler's attitude towards Rowland. To the directors, the accountants seemed critical but supportive of Rowland.

The mood in Cheapside was already sombre when Sandys met Butler and Leach. The two accountants explained that any compensation payments needed board approval. '£44,000 is not unreasonable,' said Leach, 'but it must be approved.' Sandys looked blank, concealing his own participation in the duplicity. 'The £44,000 is the first payment for the total of £130,000.' The two accountants were 'astounded'. As Sandys left, Butler was summoning Butcher: 'Come immediately and bring any documents concerning the termination of Sandys's consultancy.'

'Why did you tell us that the compensation was £44,000 and not £130,000?' asked Butler. 'It was possible that the difference would be paid by Mr Rowland and not Lonrho,' muttered Butcher lamely. 'Rowland was very naughty about that,' said Leach who was nevertheless prepared to be accommodating.

Smallpeice was briefed by Leach the following day. Surprisingly, the accountant proposed to conceal the payment if there was formal approval retrospectively by the board. Hurrying back to his office in Park Lane, Smallpeice summoned directors whom he believed to be trustworthy. 'We've come to the end of the road,' sparked Smallpeice. 'We must get rid of Rowland.'

Late that afternoon, Butcher joined Elliott for a drink at White's. 'You'd better know the truth,' confessed Butcher. 'We had no choice if we wanted to save the company.'

'I'm not surprised,' smiled Elliott. 'I knew I was dealing with a merchant adventurer.' The former MI6 director, said friends, had even consulted a psychiatrist to provide an analysis. Rowland was diagnosed as suffering from a condition which provoked

Rowland was known at school in Hamburg for his smart appearance, his fine athletism and his ability to speak fluent English. In class in 1932 aged fifteen, centre of the second row.

Rowland carried his reputation for athletic prowess to Churchers College in Hampshire, where he was also remembered for his strong German nationalist opinions. Shown here in 1934, second row, fourth from left.

Peter Goosen (*top left*), still prospecting for gold in 1992, sold Rowland the Kanyemba gold mine in 1957. After Rowland floated the mine on Salisbury's stock exchange on the basis of twenty-two years' productive life, George Abindor (*top right*), Lonrho's consulting engineer, declared that it was near worthless. According to Cyril Hatty (*right*), Rhodesia's minister of mines, 'People were angry. They felt ripped off.'

Rowland rode with Dan Mayers on mules to inspect Colombia's emerald deposits hoping to replicate his biggest financial coup – buying the Sandawana emerald mine in Rhodesia.

Rowland travelling with Alan Ball and Angus Ogilvy. When negotiating his 'takeover' of Lonrho in 1961, Rowland had secretly promised both directors 'a part of the action' of future profits.

Rowland flew with Pauline Wallace and Sir Robert Adeane around Africa on the Lonrho Beachcraft. Adeane asked Wallace to discover Rowland's attitude towards women.

Rowland met Irene Smith in London in 1947. After her divorce, they lived together in Rhodesia until he fled their Salisbury home in the middle of the night.

Rowland's founding relationship with Dr Hastings Banda of Malawi was critical to his success throughout Africa.

Tom Mtine, Lonrho's chairman in Zambia, is typical of Rowland's African 'runners'. A local politician, Mtine smoothed Rowland's access to President Kaunda (*below*) whose friendship secured profitable advantages for Lonrho.

Lonrho's success in Kenya depended upon Jomo Kenyatta's patronage. Lonrho's local manager, Paul Spicer (*far right*) was expelled from Kenya. Nicholas Elliott, formerly of MI6, travelled extensively with Rowland.

In gratitude for Rowland's gift of maize seed, Samora Machel, president of Mozambique, gave Lonrho nearly 80,000 acres of farmland. Machel's successor, Joaquim Chissano, (*far right*) was less enthusiastic about Rowland. Les Blackwell (*second from right*), Lonrho's manager in Malawi, was sceptical about the investment.

J. 50.

Warrant of Apprehension, or of the further detention of a person arrested without a Warrant.

To all peace Officers Empowered by Law to Execute Criminal Warrants.

*Delete whichever is inapplicable.

WHEREAS from *written application subscribed by Senior Public Prosecutor, Johannesburg * or from information taken upon Oath before me, there are reasonable

grounds of suspicion against Roland Walter ROWLAND, alias

TINY ROWLAND, alias FURHAP.

of Cheapside House, London E.C.2, United Kingdom

that he did on the During period 1.1.1969 to 11.7.1969

commit the crime of FRAUD

THESE are therefore to command you that immediately upon sight hereof you

{ apprehend or cause to be apprehended
{ detained or cause to be detained } the said ROLAND WALTER ROWLAND

and brought before Magistrate Johannesburg

to be examined and to answer to the said information, and to be further dealt with according

to law.

Given under my hand at JOHANNESBURG

this 8 -9-1971 day of

†Signature and capacity of officer issuing Warrant.

Description of Accused:—

White male,

Joint Managing Director of

LONRHO LIMITED, Cheapside House,

LONDON, E.C.2, United Kingdom.

MAGISTRATE'S OFFICE JOHANNESBURG

LANDDROSKANTOOR

ADD. LANDDROS, MAGIST. BEHEERBEAMPTE—STRAF...., CONTROL OFFICER—CRIMINAL COURTS, JOHANNESBURG.

The warrant issued in South Africa in 1971 for Rowland's arrest on fraud charges provoked Lonrho's first public crisis. The charges against all the Lonrho directors were dropped in 1973 as a result of lobbying by Duncan Sandys.

Lonrho's crisis in 1971 exposed Rowland to public attention for the first time.

Among his close supporters were Stefan Klein, (*left*) an Austrian middleman, and Nicholas Kruger, Lonrho's manager in Rhodesia, who sought unsuccessfully to conceal the evidence of the alleged Inyati fraud.

The 'Straight Eight' who sought Rowland's resignation from Lonrho for unacceptable behaviour in 1973. Sir Basil Smallpeice (*left*), Lonrho's deputy chairman, and Gerald Percy, the deputy managing director, led the revolt. They were joined by (*clockwise from left*) William Wilkinson, Nicholas Elliot, Sir Edward Spears, Stanley Dalgleish, Dr Alfred Gerber and Colin MacKenzie.

The attack upon Rowland's 'perks' focused on his house, Hedsor Wharf, which was purchased by Lonrho, and his Mystere jet. One of Rowland's key supporters was Edward Du Cann, the Conservative politician and banker who subsequently became Lonrho's chairman. Angus Ogilvy's resignation outraged Rowland who sought to establish his friend's knowledge of Lonrho's illegal activities.

deep depressions if plans, calculated on intuition, went awry.

Others' reactions were less controlled. Wilkinson was 'horri-fied. Sandys was meant to be an impartial not a compromised chairman.' Rowland had been disloyal and dishonest. 'Tiny's gone too far,' said Colin MacKenzie. Percy was 'shocked'. Half the board voiced their anger. Immediate resignation from Lonrho was precluded on the legal advice that shareholders could complain about directors' dereliction of duty.

By then, Lonrho's preliminary profits had been published. To avoid embarrassment, Leach suggested that if the compensation was reduced to £75,000 they could avoid a public statement. For five directors, settling the accounts had become academic. In the past months, they had discussed the possibility of Rowland's departure. He had crossed the boundary, they agreed, into the realm of 'financial recklessness and management inadequacy'. They accepted Smallpeice's warnings: 'If we're not careful, we could all end up in the Old Bailey.'

Smallpeice met Sandys later that day. 'I believed that the board had approved the payments,' uttered the chairman. Smallpeice and other directors accepted Sandys's protestations. The politician's plight was less important than Rowland's finan-cial irresponsibility and lack of integrity. But most crucial for Smallpeice was his own status in the Palace and City.

Rowland remained unbowed. With Leach's and Butler's acquiescence, the secret payment could be contained. After all, it was water under the bridge. Sandys would be asked to accept a 50 per cent reduction and granted time to con-sider the position. Rowland acted as if nothing had occurred. Those who were not unquestioning admirers were derided by Rowland. William Wilkinson was a 'financial pygmy' of whom he thought 'the more I saw him the less I thought of him, and the less I saw him the better I was pleased'.

At the next board meeting, ineffectually chaired as usual by Sandys, Smallpeice struggled to assert authority. In the midst of his survey of Lonrho's finances which showed that Lonrho's deficit was again escalating uncontrolled from £1.5 million towards £9 million, Rowland entered the boardroom. Wearing a cashmere coat, he sat, to display his contempt, at the back of the room. Around the table sat fifteen men whom he slotted into three categories: those whom he could break; those whom he had compromised; and those who were beyond his control. The latter, his foes, needed to be humiliated. With his chin resting on his hand, his forefinger on his cheek, Rowland listened apparently impassively to Smallpeice. Then he rose and the distinctive voice interrupted the monologue: 'Mr Chairman, if I may?' Sandys made no attempt to halt Rowland. He was paid to perform as required.

'Sir Basil,' continued Rowland whose pronunciation of 'Basil' was especially contemptuous, 'is talking about a company I own. My business. And yet I simply don't understand what he is saying.' There was silence. Sandys was baffled. Smallpeice was furious and the others were embarrassed. The meeting broke up. This was, Smallpeice felt, another example of Rowland's determination to override and disregard decisions of the board. 'He has a total inability to collaborate in any form of team effort. Almost every action he takes seems designed to destroy rather than engender team effort,' he complained.

The accountants' attitude puzzled Smallpeice. Butler had witnessed the calibre of Rowland's veracity and refusal to reform the company. The dishonesty had infected even the chairman. Smallpeice, unlike the other directors, was not a stranger to the City's personalities. Quietly, he agreed with Percy and Wilkinson that they should consult Kleinwort Benson, the merchant bankers, and Slaughter & May, the solicitors. He personally would visit Sir Leslie O'Brien, the Governor of the Bank of England.

In the amateurish fashion which marked the regulation of the City's financial markets, the Governor represented the judgment of Solomon regarding ethics in the market place. In an era when the practitioners' boast 'my word is my bond' was still believed by outsiders while insiders profited from unauthorised dealings, the Governor was more concerned about image than substance.

Smallpeice however trusted O'Brien's adjudication and, having confided his fears, received the wisdom for acting as his conscience dictated. On his return to Cheapside, Smallpeice approached Percy: 'If we are convinced that we must demand Tiny's resignation, we've got the grounds.'

Percy was certainly outraged by Rowland's behaviour. But, unlike the others, he had spent nearly all his professional life in Africa, returning to Britain only two years earlier. Although he did not realise it at the time, he was naive about the consequences of the course which Smallpiece was proposing.

Yet there was an issue of principle, reinforced when he glanced at the record of past board meetings. One year ago, Percy had pointedly abstained rather than approve Sandys's contracts. The minutes omitted any mention of his abstention. The private minute book was also 'inaccurate and incomplete'. Both entries had been falsified by Butcher who, Percy assumed, was acting on Rowland's behalf.

Smallpiece urged revolt but others feared a public scandal. Sir Peter Rawlinson, the Attorney General, was consulted by Percy. The lawyer and politician listened to the catalogue of crimes: Sandys's secret payment, Shamrocke and the company perks. 'Oh dear,' moaned Rawlinson. 'The shit is going to hit the fan! Why don't you unburden yourself to Du Cann? He is a wise man.'

Sandys's agreement to repay his compensation did not prevent a majority of the sixteen directors from voting on 14 March, contrary to Rowland's wishes, to establish a subcommittee under Du Cann to investigate the Sandys agreements. But, by then, it was a sideshow. Percy, propelled by his conscience and by Smallpiece, had cast the die. Percy's relations with Rowland, the godfather of his son, were barely civil. Compromise and peace was ruled out by Rowland's temper, threatening like Samson to destroy the company.

The conspiracy, which had been hatched in Cheapside in full view of all the other staff walking along the sixth floor, was, despite the openness, unsuspected by Rowland. Lonrho's chief executive did not consider the possibility that Smallpiece, Wilkinson, Elliott and Percy sitting in an office could be plotting his downfall.

Slaughter & May had produced a resolution which could be presented at the next board meeting. 'We, a substantial

proportion of the Directors of Lonrho Limited believe that, in
the best interests of the Company, Mr R. W. Rowland should
cease to hold the offices of managing director and chief executive.' Since Rowland owned ten million shares, about 20 per cent
of Lonrho, he would be offered a directorship without executive
responsibility. The resolution also demanded the resignation of
Butcher and the appointments of Percy as managing director and
Basil West, an accountant, as finance director. Secrecy, the conspirators agreed, was essential to forestall Rowland influencing
any doubters.

The execution of the plot commenced on Friday 16 March.
Nine signatures were required for an outright majority of the
sixteen directors. That morning, Smallpeice, Wilkinson and
Percy signed. MacKenzie was telephoned in Scotland: 'Just
give me the document. I can't wait to sign.'

Early on Saturday, Wilkinson flew for the day to Zurich to
obtain the signature of Alfred Gerber, the representative of Wankel. Treated like a stuffed shirt by Rowland during their frequent
rows instead of the respect merited by a Swiss professional,
Gerber signed with glee. On Sunday morning, the same document bearing four signatures was taken to Newcastle. Dalgleish
signed. Returning to London that afternoon, Smallpeice called
on Sir Edward Spears. 'This gives me the greatest pleasure,'
said the General, finally tasting revenge for Rowland's usurper's
purchase of Ashanti. 'His conduct is uncontrolled, his language
is immoderate, he becomes so hysterical when contradicted that I
wonder whether he is responsible for his actions.' The resolution
bearing six signatures was passed to Wilkinson.

The next call was on Nicholas Elliott at his Lonrho flat in
Belgrave Square. The former intelligence officer, accustomed
to manipulating *coups d'état* from the shadows, was uncertain
about a debut in the spotlight. The two directors walked several
times around the square while Elliott decided his course. But
their plot was already unravelling.

Spears, too excited to remain silent, had telephoned Ogilvy.
'Have you seen the document? You should sign it.' Ogilvy was
stunned. He had just returned from Hedsor Wharf where
Rowland had also invited Ball, Du Cann and Sandys to discuss

the reconstruction of the board. All had pledged their support to Rowland, including Ogilvy – despite his later claim to the contrary.

Aged forty-four, Ogilvy had at best a difficult and compromised position. His demeanour according to those at Hedsor Wharf was 'all over the place'. Just days earlier, Roger Moss, the accountant, had warned Ogilvy that trouble was brewing. Revealingly, Ogilvy had replied, 'The trouble with this man is that he will destroy everybody.' Four years earlier he had spurned the advice of Whitehall's most senior civil servants to break his links with Rowland. Since then, there had been several occasions when he had contemplated resigning but withdrew. 'Angus made the mistake of putting himself under an obligation to Tiny,' recalls one director.

Yet even at that moment when Ogilvy could have acted on principle, he refused Spears's invitation to sign the resolution. Instead, after ending the conversation, he passed on the news of the coup to Ball. Rowland was shocked by Ball's telephone call. For the first time he understood the strength of the opposition. According to John Addey, the doyen of public relations for financial affairs at that time, who was at Hedsor Wharf, 'Rowland was bewildered, desperate and near to tears when the row broke.' Knowing who had signed, Rowland telephoned Elliott. At that moment, Elliott was still walking around Belgrave Square but had decided to sign.

Rowland telephoned the ninth director, Tom Prentice, the managing director of John Holt, in the country. The conspirators had planned to wait until Monday morning to obtain Prentice's signature. By Sunday night it was too late. Rowland's persuasion had worked. There would be eight signatures on the resolution, ostensibly a stalemate unless Sandys and Ogilvy could be persuaded to join the cause. But, in reality, there was already a majority because Rowland could not vote about his own future.

At 8.45 on Monday morning, Smallpeice called on Sandys in Vincent Square. The two men neither liked nor trusted each other, yet Smallpeice asked the chairman to negotiate Rowland's quiet resignation. 'I trust that you won't divulge the plan to Rowland,' added Smallpeice. Sandys was told that if Rowland refused to resign voluntarily, the Eight would demand his dismissal at the board meeting the following day. 'And we hope that you will remain as chairman.' Sandys did not demur. None among the Eight even contemplated that Sandys, a British statesman, would act other than in a proper manner.

To describe Rowland as bitter when he arrived at Cheapside that morning would be an understatement, but to describe him as recovering from temporary confusion would be accurate. His life's experience had not prepared him for the eventuality of a revolt by his friends. Yet as an invincible rebel himself, he understood and could judge better than anyone how to survive, retaliate and defeat a revolt. Hope, hatred and hunger for revenge radiated from his eyes. Overnight, he had, moreover, assembled his supporters, although for the moment both Roland Franklin and Du Cann officially pledged themselves as neutral.

When the Eight assembled in the boardroom, they felt victorious. Uniformly they believed that Rowland, keen to keep his transgressions hidden from the public and faced with a split board would, rather than force a vote, seek a quiet exit. Tiny, one speculated, might go to Kuwait and build a new business on his own terms. Fatally, the Eight, believing in decency, were unwilling to plunge the knife into their friend immediately. 'We didn't want to harm Tiny or Lonrho,' Percy would later say. But even to speak of the 'Eight' was to assume a unity which did not exist. Until that day, they had never sat together as a group.

Rowland sensed their lack of unity, their diverse interest in Lonrho and the absence of any instinct to kill. To Rowland, they represented provincials. They lacked ability and agility. They threatened to fire the first shot, albeit seemingly devastating, but seemed incapable of the follow-up. One by one he counted them off as worthless: 'Smallpeice, a humourless incompetent; Spears, unforgiving about the loss of Ashanti; Elliott, charming to everybody and loyal to none; Dalgleish, a nonentity; MacKenzie, a nice country man whose opposition was incomprehensible; Wilkinson, a paper merchant; and Gerald Percy, 'a man with many natural advantages which he managed to overcome. He's a dirty double-crossing rat who wants my job. Why not? It's a nice job.' Four Etonians against him.

'I don't need them,' he thought. 'They need me.'

The Eight looked at Rowland with blank expressions. None perceived his ruthless determination to survive. The outstanding negotiator was a consummate actor. He had fought too many battles and overcome too many adversaries to be cowed by this Establishment gaggle. Together, they had misjudged that he would fear public embarrassment. He had survived so many humiliations in his life that, in the ultimate battle for control of Lonrho, their threat was laughable. He had no fear of challenging the Old Order.

Rowland's priority was to win time. Roland Franklin told the board that Rowland had asked Keyser Ullman to dispose of his shares. The banker therefore proposed that due to the irreconcilable split and to avoid a public battle, Keyser Ullman should seek to negotiate a merger of Lonrho with another company. The prospective purchaser was Oliver Jessel who, like Goldsmith and Slater, was a young, speculative, industrial investor. Jessel Securities, although smaller than Lonrho, had a range of interests in minerals, sugar and agriculture throughout Africa.

The deal which Franklin quickly settled with Jessel was structured to avoid binding Jessel into making an identical offer to all shareholders. Rowland would receive £10.9 million cash for his 12.6 million shares and £1 million cash every year for eight years interest free. The price was 100 pence per share. Everything would be completed, Jessel and Lonrho's directors believed, by 23 March. Meanwhile, from his office, Rowland called John Cama, his solicitor, and John Addey, the publicist, to plan his counter-attack.

By early morning on Wednesday 21 March, the Eight realised that Rowland was refusing to resign. In anticipation of the board meeting the following day, Smallpeice sent Sandys a copy of the Eight's statement with the threat that if Rowland had not resigned by 10 a.m. the Eight would seek his removal by a resolution.

The ultimatum was immediately withdrawn. Franklin had told the governor of the Bank of England that Jessel would be buying Rowland's shares and Smallpeice was asked to delay the vote by twenty-four hours. He agreed, not realising that the first stage of Rowland's counter-offensive had begun.

Rowland and Addey had decided the strategy. Smallpeice would be identified as the ringleader, 'which we knew he wasn't,' according to Addey, and then he would be exposed as a ridiculous and compromised alternate to Rowland. The first stage of Rowland's plan unfolded at a board meeting on 22 March.

In his silky manner which inspired confidence and trust, Du Cann presented his committee's report about the secret agreements with Sandys. Unanimously, everyone agreed it was objective and honest. Lonrho's senior management, including Rowland, was condemned for 'casualness', 'irresponsible' behaviour and 'mishandling of formalities'. The board, Du Cann, Butcher and Ball confirmed, was not consulted and the minute books were falsified. The report was adopted. Then followed the sting.

Encouraged by the bankers who were still ostensibly neutral, Smallpeice agreed to propose a resolution adopting the report with a caveat that 'those involved had acted in what they considered to be the best interests of the company.' The 'ringleader' of the revolt against Rowland was compromised.

With that settled, the two bankers told the Eight that the negotiations with Jessel had not been finalised but were encouraging. 'Could we not defer the resolution to remove Tiny by seven to ten days,' urged Du Cann and Franklin, 'to allow the sale to be completed.' The Eight agreed. The new deadline was 3 April. No one was suspicious, including Jessel who, in his encounters with Rowland, was convinced that completing the transfer was a formality.

Indeed, Jessel even wrote enthusiastically to Sandys describing his company's success in Africa, his youthful management team and how, despite the obvious problems and burdens, he saw no problem in saving Lonrho. Under the Jessel plan, Rowland would resign immediately.

Out of his depth and relying entirely upon Du Cann's advice, Sandys shuttled between the factions as the independent messenger. 'He says that if he's removed Lonrho is bound to suffer,' Sandys told Smallpeice, 'and he would make sure that Lonrho suffered even more.' Rowland's threats escalated. 'He says that none of you will be allowed into Africa,' reported Alan Ball, 'and he says he will also arrange for Lonrho's assets to be nationalised.' The threats were sincere but the strategy was to win time.

At the end of March Roger Moss, the accountant, resigned explaining, 'I want nothing more to do with them.' Franklin asked Smallpeice for a two-day extension to the deadline: 'The negotiations with Jessel are taking longer than expected.' The deadline for Rowland's resignation became 5 April. On 2 April, the negotiations with Jessel collapsed. The official explanation suggested that Hambros, Jessel's merchant bank, refused to finance the deal, but to some it seemed an excuse. The Eight should have heeded one of Rowland's many homilies: 'An agreement is the basis for negotiation.'

Until then, Franklin had appeared as the neutral, honest broker. Several directors had been invited either out for lunch or to his country house to hear the same sermon: 'Tiny's a genius. He may be a fibber but he is skilful. You should not try to remove him, not least because the City's reputation will suffer if the row becomes public.' Franklin's seduction and attempts to split the Eight having failed, on 3 April, he threatened that if Rowland decided to call an extraordinary general meeting to protect himself, Keyser Ullman would support Rowland, 'with all the influence we can command'. Du Cann was equally committed to Rowland. Smallpeice, he believed, had blackmailed Sandys. 'It's very ugly,' he told the deputy chairman.

Battle lines had been drawn. At a fraught board meeting on 5 April, Sandys urged that he be given another opportunity to find an acceptable compromise. Once again the Eight prevaricated then gave Sandys thirteen days.

Within seven days, the Eight, still believing that Rowland would sell his shares, had found another buyer at 100 pence, the identical offer to Jessel's. The only condition was Rowland's resignation as chief executive but he could remain as a director.

With flippancy which revealed his growing confidence, Rowland rejected the offer demanding nothing less than 140 pence.

'I regret to say,' wrote Rowland, 'that I would not agree to sell my shares and leave Lonrho. I don't have to tell you what Lonrho means to me and I have never thought that I could consider an offer for my shares.' Instead, Rowland offered to buy the one million shares owned by the Eight for 140 pence and requested that they resign.

There was also a trap. On 16 April, Sandys told the board that his attempts at reconciliation had failed. The salvation however was a proposal to invest £8 million in Lonrho from the Zambian government and from Khalil Osman. Solemnly, Sandys repeated a letter from Franklin describing the offer, negotiated by Rowland, as of 'immense importance'. Rowland praised the inclusion of Zambian money: 'It would be a wonderful partnership with an African nation.' There were two conditions: the appointment of four new directors to represent their interests and a guarantee that there would be no changes in Lonrho's management. Instead of calling Rowland's bluff, the Eight woodenly rejected the idea.

Among Rowland's many qualities is his skill in scheming patiently. Successfully negotiating a deal is a masterly act of posture and gamble, and Rowland deserves an Oscar for his performance. That night, Rowland began playing for his professional life. In his mind, the eventual outcome of his battle was certain. He would win. The path to victory, however, was uncertain. Above all, he needed time and allies. He planned to gain time by prevarication, albeit disguised. He needed allies among the directors, but also from his employees and his political friends. Among the dozens of calls he placed that night were several to Lonrho executives across Africa. 'You'd never imagine what those bastards are doing,' he repeated. 'Come to London.' The objective, already formulating, was to stage a counter-coup from Africa.

The following night, 17 April, Rowland's African supporters began gathering at Hedsor Wharf. Rowland consoled himself with Udi Gecaga from Kenya, Tom Mtine from Zambia, Gil Olympio from the Ivory Coast, Khalil Osman from the Sudan and several other African friends. 'I always knew Gerald Percy was not to be trusted,' raved their host. 'I bet Jennifer put him up to it.' Rowland would become convinced that Percy's wife was the coup's ambitious instigator. Gecaga was impressed by Rowland's sangfroid. 'You don't stab a prince,' he smirked, 'You have to kill him.'

Rowland offered his guests a strategy for Africa. 'If you help me win the battle, I'll make Lonrho a private company and you can all be the principal shareholders – equal partners with me as part of revolutionary capitalism.' The assorted Africans were seduced not by the ideology but by the offer of a stake in Lonrho if they helped Rowland win the battle. 'The implication was that in return for helping Tiny, we would become rich,' recalls one of those present. The chance of gaining a serious fortune was sufficient to win their support.

Rowland asked each to obtain expressions of support for himself from their governments, if possible from the president. In the meantime, Rowland continued, his lawyers were looking for a nervous judge who could be convinced that Lonrho's assets in Africa would be nationalised if Rowland were deposed. 'We'll get an injunction to delay my dismissal,' explained Rowland. The reality, they all knew, was that no one in Africa would be concerned about Lonrho's fate. But judges in London, easily persuaded that they sat at the centre of the world's attention, would believe the fantasy.

That day, Rowland had also made a last attempt to tip the votes in his favour in a letter to Ogilvy. The tone was familiar. Effusive warmth cocooned by menace. Rowland complained that, despite Ogilvy's promise of support, he was now wavering and was even heard to complain that he had been 'compromised' in his dealings with Rowland. 'You and I know this is utter nonsense,' wrote Rowland and then reminded Ogilvy how the latter was precisely compromised. Namely the financial arrangements which were 'naturally private' but 'certainly not a shameful secret'. Rowland concluded with a final threat. If Ogilvy's support was not forthcoming, Rowland would fight his battle in open court. Ogilvy would later claim that he was blackmailed by Rowland 'but I sincerely didn't know that I'd done anything wrong.'

On 18 April, the Eight at last tabled their motion that Rowland should be removed. 'We finally realised that he would not go otherwise,' recalled Smallpeice. With Ogilvy suddenly taken to hospital, Rowland unable to vote and Sandys insisting that his chairmanship required that he remain neutral, the Eight had a clear majority over the remaining five directors. Yet, tactically, their strike was too late. Rowland's defence was in place.

The meeting would start at 2.30 p.m. At lunch, Smallpeice was told that Rowland was applying to a judge for an injunction to prevent his dismissal. Immediately, the Eight contacted their lawyers, Slaughter & May. 'Don't worry,' they were reassured by the experts, 'no judge will grant that injunction.'

In the boardroom, MacKenzie proposed the motion and asked for a vote. Sandys filibustered while, in a small room of the High Court, a Queen's Counsel argued that since his client was responsible for Lonrho's expansion, his removal would be 'disastrous for the company'. The directors calling for his removal, argued Rowland's lawyer, had not explained how they would manage Lonrho. The decision should be taken by the shareholders who risked 'colossal losses', at an annual general meeting. Since none of the Eight could be represented, Rowland's argument seemed convincing. The judge granted a temporary injunction forbidding Lonrho's directors to remove Rowland pending a full trial two weeks later. 'That judge should be promoted to the House of Lords,' smiled John Cama, blessing his good fortune.

That afternoon, John Addey, the proven public relations master of the vitriolic battle between Rupert Murdoch and Robert Maxwell for the ownership of the *News of the World*, summoned the press. It was the first indication of the turmoil within Lonrho's board. It was also the unveiling of Tiny Rowland who, until then, was unknown to the public. Businessmen in that era were not the glamorous icons described in best-selling autobiographies and Hollywood features and, more than others, Rowland had taken care to remain invisible to protect himself from the embarrassing questions about his past which had proved harmful in Rhodesia.

But Rowland understood that to win the battle, he 'needed to get his retaliation in first'. Addey's first charge to City journalists accused Smallpeice of incompetence. Having 'failed' at BOAC and Cunard, Smallpeice could not be trusted at Lonrho.

The contrast of images was indisputable. 'Stuffy' Smallpeice had served just thirteen months as Lonrho's non-executive deputy chairman while Rowland, the former Paddington porter had, within just twelve years, turned Lonrho's annual profits of £150,000 into £20 million and transformed a £1 million company into a £200 million multinational employing 100,000 people. Moreover, Rowland owned 10 million Lonrho shares while Smallpeice owned 1200. 'That indicates whose commitment is greater to Lonrho's fortunes,' puffed Addey. Lonrho's finances, briefed the publicist, were improving. Commodity prices were rising and the profits forecast was good. The rejection by the Eight of the Zambian/Osman £8 million offer proved their narrow-mindedness. Any doubters of Addey's promotion of Rowland were confounded by the intervention of Roland Franklin. At the same meeting, the banker declared that Keyser Ullman would resign if Rowland was dismissed.

The Eight had not anticipated the need for public relations, nor understood that, in the nature of their battle, virtue could not triumph over evil without proper packaging. Rowland's retaliation was demoralising. The next morning's newspapers proved his audacity.

Uniformly Rowland was extolled. An 'uncontrollable genius'; 'a brilliant deal maker on board a Mystere'; a 'merchant adventurer'; a 'swashbuckler'; 'a mystery who is not even listed in *Who's Who*'; and, 'a pirate: the kind of man who would walk into a revolving door behind you and emerge the other side in front. He feeds his cats with smoked salmon – typical of him too.' Others suggested that, 'the stories that surround Rowland are legend' and when Hollywood eventually sought to tell Rowland's lifestory, a 'powerful movie mogul will have to reincarnate Errol Flynn' to portray Rowland.

Unanimously salivating about the prospect, everyone predicted a hugely acrimonious public row. To most, the outcome did not seem a foregone conclusion. Since the 1971 crisis, all the City institutions had sold their Lonrho shares. Although Rowland owned 20 per cent of the company, there were still 80 per cent of the votes to win, nearly all owned by small shareholders. To protect themselves against Rowland's threatened action for defamation, the Eight relied upon winning their argument in the court hearings.

After reading the newspapers, Rowland was satisfied. At 10.30 a.m. Sandys walked into Rowland's office: 'Tiny, I have very grave news for you.'

'It cannot be all that bad, we have had plenty of bad news. What is the disaster now?'

'Angus has resigned.'

'I cannot believe it, Duncan, that he would do this to me.' Now Rowland understood why the previous night, he had been unable to reach Ogilvy on the telephone. Ogilvy's disloyalty was unforgivable.

Loyalty, Rowland would repeatedly assert, was the most important quality he sought from colleagues and employees, and his own virtue towards those with whom he worked. There could be no doubt that, in Rowland's terms, he was generous towards his employees and contacts in Africa. Whether his financial payments were bribes, investments in people, the means for manipulation and control or simply help to those in need was debatable but, as Rowland understood it, his generosity was to be returned with loyalty. In Ogilvy's case, Rowland determined that their financial relationship and friendship implied loyalty which overrode considerations of objective principle. The transformation of Lonrho had been a cabal among friends to dedicate their lives to his ideal of a commercial empire. Ogilvy was a member of the plot and to bale out was unpardonable.

Observing that Rowland was visibly distraught, Sandys left the office. *Sauve qui peut*, every man for himself, was the order of the day on the sixth floor. Devoid of courage and terrified of the publicity which the court proceedings due on 4 May were certain to provoke, Sandys began considering his own resignation. His principal concern was to avoid the publicity of his own corruption.

During that morning, Ogilvy issued a statement explaining that he had intended to resign at the annual general meeting because of 'other business commitments' but he had decided to bring forward his resignation because of the 'situation which has now arisen'. Ogilvy had obeyed an instruction from the Palace.

His reputation was now entirely at Rowland's disposal.

Sandys, whose reputation was also subject to Rowland's whim, also issued a public statement: 'I wish to confirm once again that in my capacity as chairman I have throughout endeavoured to play an impartial and unifying role.' Sandys pledged himself to continue working towards a compromise. The politician was desperate. Daily, Du Cann visited Vincent Square to comfort and strengthen a man terrified of public humiliation, bearing the cost of becoming indebted to Rowland.

Late that afternoon, Sandys spotted Percy in the corridor and beckoned him into the boardroom: 'I'm thinking of resigning.' 'That's the best course, Duncan,' agreed Percy, recalling the politician's partisan behaviour at the last board meeting. Without Sandys, the possibility of success for the Eight would improve. They were joined by Wilkinson. Looking quite pathetic, Sandys admitted that his position was 'intolerable' and asked for one guarantee. 'If I resign, will you keep my name out of the court hearings?'

'We'll do our best to avoid embarrassing you,' replied Percy.

Towards 6 o'clock, their encounter broke up. Percy and Wilkinson were convinced that Sandys would resign. Their hope of winning the battle had improved. Sandys returned to his office bearing little resemblance to the public's image of the robust politician. Within minutes Rowland appeared. With his back against the wall, the chief executive's threats were delivered with a calm, blunt menace. If Sandys thought that his reputation could be saved by resignation then he was mistaken. War had been declared and Rowland would act remorselessly: 'In open court, I'll defend myself,' he told Sandys. 'I have nothing to be ashamed of.' Sandys recognised the implicit menace: 'Are you putting pressure on me?' he asked Rowland.

'Think about it over Easter,' replied Rowland.

Three hours later, Sandys telephoned Percy: 'I haven't decided. I'm going to Portugal for the weekend to think it over.' To his disappointment, Percy detected a new tone. Sandys, like Ogilvy, was susceptible to Rowland.

There was little consolation for Sandys that Rowland's 'retaliation' was already materialising. A newly formed shareholders' committee had met Rowland and Ball for two hours and, claiming to represent one million shares, pledged their support for Rowland who 'generates profits and Smallpeice won't'. It was the birth of Lonrho's small shareholder movement which would support Rowland for the next twenty years.

The committee, led by Timothy Segrue, was offered unlimited facilities in Cheapside to promote their interests. On the sixth floor, they watched Rowland and his supporters working through the night, telephoning contacts throughout Africa, plotting their case. Among the staff committed to Rowland was Paul Spicer, originally recruited by Percy. Throughout the night, Spicer was on his knees collating press handouts for Rowland's propaganda. At the weekends, even his family would come to Cheapside to assist. His reward was to become Lonrho's spokesman.

The Eight resisted attracting similar support. Occasionally, they worked on Cheapside's fifth floor, but more usually from their own homes, or in a dark, draughty room in the Great Eastern hotel by Liverpool Street station. In every sense, in image and substance, they were the rebels while Rowland was in situ.

To demands for public explanations of their opposition to Rowland, Smallpeice and Percy just vacillated. Both feared writs for defamation from Rowland even though their allegations were accurate. But pleading sub judice in the midst of a public boardroom row suggested weakness. Nevertheless, background briefings, published in newspapers, about Rowland's 'secret payments' in the Cayman Islands sparked Rowland into retaliation.

'I am surprised', he told *The Times*, 'that there could be any suggestion that the dispute was caused by "secret payments".' Indeed, 'the payments', asserted Rowland, 'were known to and considered by the full board, a committee of which ratified the position. The accounts have been approved by the auditors without qualification on this point.' Another interview reported, 'Mr Rowland wishes to make it clear that there is no question of any such payment having been made to him.' Although disingenuous, this was true and won more supporters for Segrue's committee. For them, Rowland epitomised the best of capitalism. Profits and the reality of business in Africa dictated shady deals.

To the public, Rowland appeared cool and determined. In private, although unrepentant, he feared the publicity and tearfully lamented the desertion by Ogilvy. Late one night, after his resignation, Ogilvy sat with Rowland and Josie in their Park Lane flat. Over the past years they had shared many adventures and fun together. Rowland, the supreme egoist, could not understand why Ogilvy had abandoned his friend and the company. In fact, Rowland had become obsessed that Ogilvy's resignation was intended to destroy him. The departure was, he later said, 'timed to give me the *coup de grâce*'. Rowland never realised that Ogilvy resigned in an attempt to save himself. 'Why? Angus, why?' Rowland asked at 1 a.m. as they drank brandy. 'To avoid the publicity in court,' replied Ogilvy. Josie intervened: 'But Tiny will be dismissed. We'd have to leave England. He would be totally discredited.' Rowland was clearly moved that his wife, despite her simplicity, obviously understood the issue. Ogilvy, in contrast, was not impressed. Rowland's departure would be of benefit to everyone, he said, if he resigned quietly before the hearing in court. 'Get out Angus,' shouted Josie leaving the room, 'Don't ever come back again.' For differing reasons the two men were stunned. They drank more brandy and, like parting lovers, went together in a final search of a taxi to return Ogilvy to his princess. Even that search ended in failure. Rowland drove Ogilvy home.

Day after day, the dispute dominated the newspapers' front pages. The image of Rowland, a mysterious tycoon, living in a mansion or jetting around Africa in his private aeroplane to bribe African presidents, evoked shock and outrage. The only story which removed Lonrho from its prevailing press prominence was the revelation of a torrid sex scandal involving two ministers, Lords Lambton and Jellicoe, both accused of affairs with prostitutes which allegedly compromised national security. Their resignations coincided with revelations of corruption in local government involving Reginald Maudling, a senior minister and former deputy leader of the Conservative Party. The publicity about politicians' ethics, terrifying for Sandys, prompted the

Investors' Chronicle to praise Lonrho as 'a source of entertainment, not investment.'

In another attempt to end the argument, Sandys, encouraged by Rowland, invited Percy to his house in Vincent Square. The politician was finishing his breakfast. 'How much would you want to resign?' he asked, 'Would £100,000 do?' To Sandys, the boardroom row was clearly a clash of personalities and not principle. 'We could make it more,' Sandys added. He appeared surprised that his offer was rejected.

Sandys's last resort was to mobilise his wife Marie-Claire who was from French Alsace. In emotional telephone calls, she sought to persuade the directors to remove all references to her husband from their affidavits for the forthcoming trial. 'Your husband is ruining Duncan,' she accused Elliott's wife. Like other directors, Elliott refused to shake Sandys's hand thereafter. Most now accepted that Sandys had lied about the compensation, hence his fear of exposure. Sandys, who had proclaimed his impartiality, swore an affidavit supporting Rowland.

Rowland was also seeking an escape from open warfare in court. The leaders of the shareholders' committee, encouraged by Rowland, appealed to Smallpeice on 2 May to withdraw from the impending battle and await the annual general meeting due on 31 May. It was a crucial misunderstanding of the case, since it was Rowland who had initiated the proceedings. To their question, why had the 'Straight Eight' demanded Rowland's dismissal, Smallpeice squeaked unconvincingly that inaction would have been 'in dereliction of our duties as directors. We think we have a substantial case.' The shareholders, motivated by Rowland, condemned Smallpeice's refusal to explain as 'most regrettable' and gathered more supporters.

Yet among experts, the principles were clear: whether Rowland should be exempt from the implications of misleading his board and ignoring his responsibility to shareholders under section 184 of the Companies Act. The discussion of ethics in the City, such a passionate argument in the Eighties, was still in its infancy.

In the public's mind, the battle lines were blurred when

Rowland and the Lonrho directors began arriving at the High Court in the Strand just before 10.30 a.m. on 4 May. Technically, the hearing was to seek a continuation of the injunction to prevent Rowland's dismissal until the shareholders' meeting on 31 May. Sitting just a few feet from Smallpeice, Rowland was calm but he needed more time to organise his defence and, more importantly, find an escape from the inevitable but unwelcome publicity which his tactics had awakened. His lawyer, after thirty minutes' argument, won a temporary delay, allowing Rowland time to fire another shot.

On 5 May, Rowland dispatched to all shareholders the first of a succession of circulars which were characterised by his inimitable fluent style of an appeal from one shareholder to another – 'you and I as the shareholders' – deftly proclaiming bogus assertions. The boardroom argument, Rowland claimed, was about a clash of ideas about Lonrho's development in Africa and the Middle East. Lonrho's development in Africa, Rowland claimed, was 'quite unmatched by any other company'. Their dispute, he wrote, was about his ambitious plans for further expansion which were opposed by the Eight directors, and they should be removed.

Naturally, Rowland concealed more than he admitted. Compared to similar corporations like Inchcape, Mitchell Cotts and Booker McConnell who all operated in Africa, Lonrho's performance over the previous four years had been poor. Lonrho's share price had fallen from a peak of 300 pence in 1969 to 77 pence. Lonrho's profits had not improved since 1969 and dividends had fallen from £2.48 million to £2.43 million. In real terms, shareholders had lost money over the previous four years. The truth was concealed by a public declaration from the 'Lonrho shareholders' committee' giving their outright support for Rowland against Smallpeice. The Eight, comparatively disorganised, were unprepared to retaliate. Their moral stand was going by default.

Yet Rowland remained uncertain about the outcome of the battle. In a telephone call tinged with paranoia, he suggested that Ogilvy's shares in the annual general meeting would be cast against him: 'That's the end. You're a rat.' Ogilvy was nonplussed. Although his shares were owned by the family trust, he was certain that they would not be used against Rowland. Having reassured himself, he telephoned the news. Rowland was vitriolic and excited: 'You've let me down. I am absolutely going to crucify you and all your family.' Ogilvy slammed down the receiver. Rowland, he knew, had a perfect weapon. The £60,000 paid in Switzerland.

In a packed courtroom, on 8 May the trial finally started. Michael Wheeler QC, appearing for Rowland, sought an order that the board of directors did not have the power to dismiss Rowland. 'This case,' he told the judge, Anthony Plowman, 'is not concerned with the merits of the dispute between the directors and Mr Rowland.' The issue was whether the power to dismiss Rowland belonged to the shareholders. Wheeler sought to prove that, if Rowland were dismissed, Lonrho would suffer terminal damage and therefore the directors should be prevented from dismissing Rowland until the shareholders' meeting at the end of the month. To prove the damage which Rowland's pre-emptive dismissal would cause, he would produce dozens of affidavits from employees and African leaders testifying to his indispensability and importance.

Indicative of their maladroit understanding of the battle, the Eight had believed that Rowland would confine his arguments to the laws regarding the removal of a director. None had anticipated the avalanche of affidavits which Rowland had gathered testifying to his importance, which could not be challenged by oral cross-examination, and to the Eight's irrelevance.

The essence of the legal dispute did not interest the Africans to whom Rowland had appealed for support. Amid the explosion of publicity, they recognised only a power struggle. Rowland, they believed, was battling against malice, greed and spite. Despite Britain's poor relations with its former African colonies, Rowland was exceptional. 'I felt sympathy for Tiny,' recalls Ngethe Njoroge the Kenyan High Commissioner, 'because he was the underdog against the City and the Establishment.' Like so many Africans, Njoroge had over the previous years enjoyed Rowland's hospitality at the Dorchester and his friendship towards his family at Hedsor Wharf. Now was the time to return that support. Although Jomo Kenyatta could not be asked for support, the High Commissioner could testify on the government's behalf that Rowland's continued position was essential to Lonrho's survival in Kenya.

There were similar affidavits from the governments of Ghana, the Sudan, Zaïre and the Ivory Coast. But no one was more fulsome in his support than Kenneth Kaunda, Zambia's president, which was arranged by Tom Mtine, the forty-four-year-old manager of Lonrho's company.

Mtine spurned an advance from Percy and supported Rowland because 'Lonrho was Tiny'. Irritated that the Eight ignored the reality that their high incomes were unobtainable elsewhere, Mtine was blunt, 'Tiny does shabby deals for Lonrho's benefit, not his own. Tiny's working for Africa but the Eight are selfishly working for themselves. They wanted to take over to exploit his achievements but he was so far ahead that they did not understand him. I understood their case but there are many ways to skin a cat and they didn't need to stage a row.' Although Kaunda could not be persuaded to swear an affidavit, his staff, believing that they were encouraged by the president, swore convincing ultimatums.

Plucking at the affidavits, Wheeler read out a statement from Amock Phiri, the Zambian High Commissioner in London, which threatened the nationalisation of Lonrho's interests if Rowland was removed because, 'My government has had long experience of Lonrho under Mr Rowland and it has the most confidence in him.'

Another affidavit read by Wheeler testified that the government of Zaïre would emulate Zambia's policy, while Kamil Osman, the Sudanese, had sworn that Rowland's removal would 'endanger' existing and future Lonrho projects in Africa and the Middle East. Rowland, testified Osman, commanded respect among Africans and Arabs because he 'tried hard to understand the people' in that region. 'He is that unique European accepted by most African leaders in their homes on a family basis and to whom they can speak without reservation.' Significantly, but unremarked at the time, President Hastings Banda had refused to become embroiled.

Wilhelm Wilming, Rowland's long-suffering and faithful pilot, testified about his employer's energy and devotion to Lonrho's business as they dashed around Africa without sleep and snatched meals: 'I believe it to be impossible for most people to work the hours and to the extent that Mr Rowland does but he appears to thrive on it. It is astonishing and admirable how quickly people take to and trust Mr Rowland in Africa and the Middle East. . . I have been told and I believe that their confidence in him is because of his frankness and human qualities with which I have become so familiar.'

In combination, the evidence was a devastating propaganda coup confirming Rowland's allegation that the Eight neither understood Africa nor enjoyed its leaders' trust, which spoke for 96 per cent of Lonrho's business. Then Rowland attacked his fellow directors. Percy's reputation, he alleged, was 'lamentable' and unacceptable to African rulers upon whose goodwill Lonrho depended. 'I don't believe,' said Rowland in his melodious English accompanied by an engaging twinkle, 'that Sir Basil has ever visited Africa. Yet he wants to run the business.' It was a devastating denunciation; true albeit unjust. Smallpeice had been ill and, under Rowland's regime, was not allowed to travel beyond Cheapside. But Rowland's revelation alarmed shareholders that Lonrho without Rowland would evaporate without compensation.

On the second day, Samuel Stamler QC rose for the defence. The newly baptised 'Straight Eight' could have argued that they acted within their powers. But Rowland had shortsightedly provided them with a platform to launch a personal attack. Stamler could not rebut Rowland's success and importance in Africa; 'a paper tiger' was the best the advocate could muster to deride Rowland's testimonials. The Eight had not produced a single affidavit to prove their competence in Africa. But protected from defamation, they could vociferously justify their conduct which indelibly stained Rowland's reputation forever.

Smallpeice's affidavit, read out in a plummy tone by Stamler, was damning: 'the damage which has been done by the irresponsibility of Mr Rowland outweighs any benefit to be derived from his abilities and contacts. . . I came to the conclusion that Mr

Rowland was unfit by reason of his temperament and lack of commercial probity.'

The damnation went further. Rowland, he said, 'shows an utter intolerance of advice and criticism to the point of being unable to work in harmony with anyone who ventures to disagree with him. . . He is over-emotional and extremely ill-tempered and mercurial to such an extent that I and each of my co-defendant directors are of the opinion that he is not consistently capable of making balanced judgments.'

Sucking peppermints, Rowland sat impassively in the front row, occasionally speaking to his lawyers. He sat alone. Despite the welter of affidavits from Africa, it was notable that not one of the remaining five directors was in the courtroom.

William Wilkinson claimed that Rowland was financially irresponsible. In 1971, Rowland had ignored his warnings of the looming financial crisis and he predicted that the current £1.5 million overdraft would increase by the end of 1973 to £9 million. Rowland's ability in creating Lonrho was inadequate to the task of its management. 'There was', declared Wilkinson, 'a complete breakdown of the trust necessary for the running of a top management team.' Rowland, swore Wilkinson, resorted to 'extreme displays of rage which, on many occasions, have caused me seriously to call in question the state of his mental health'. In the front row, Rowland smiled, the only facial reaction to the personal onslaught during the courtroom hearing. As more affidavits from the Eight attacked him personally, his absences from the court became notable.

The scandal which dominated the headlines and questioned Rowland's probity forever burst on the third day. An affidavit revealed that Rowland was living 'rent free' at Hedsor Wharf because he refused to repay Lonrho £351,000 as required by Peat Marwick. The affidavit further alleged that Rowland, Ball and Ogilvy were using £3 million of Lonrho's money to finance the development of the Nyaschere copper mine in Rhodesia; the secrets of the Wankel deal; and it revealed that Rowland had encouraged African states to nationalise British assets and award Lonrho the management contracts.

The affidavit's sensational disclosure concerned Duncan

Sandys and the £130,000 payment in the Cayman Islands. *The Times* calculated that the amount equalled the accumulated wages over fifty years of a hospital worker. Smallpeice could justifiably claim that Rowland and Sandys had ignored the 'elementary standards of commercial propriety'.

Naively, Rowland had not anticipated the tidal wave of condemnation that swept across Britain that night. Rowland might have condemned the outrage as hypocrisy but he could not name another chief executive of a public company who had used funds in that manner. Yet he believed that he was maligned and misunderstood. Lonrho's shares, he told selected journalists, were valuable and the importance of Wankel was underestimated by the market. He had sacrificed all his social and family life for the good of Lonrho because he had been solely responsible for negotiations to expand Lonrho. Overnight, he threw caution and self-restraint to the winds. He launched a bitter battle of affidavits to defend himself and fulfil his threat to expose Ogilvy. The £130,000 'fair and reasonable' compensation to Sandys, declared Rowland, was 'approved after careful consideration by myself and Angus Ogilvy'. Both the Conservative Party and the Palace were tainted by Lonrho.

In popular jargon, Lonrho embodied the greed, avarice and dishonesty of the rich. Rowland's free home in Hedsor Wharf, his £1 million annual expenses, and his avoidance of British taxation which extended to the payment of a bill for 31 pence for Harrods pork sausages by Tweefontein United Collieries to avoid the suggestion that Rowland was domiciled in Britain, fuelled the scandal. 'Mr Rowland,' Stamler told the court, 'positively and intuitively misled his fellow directors, the auditors, the merchant bankers.'

For the first time, allegations by the Eight that Rowland was a 'dictator' and 'highly egocentric' struck home. Rowland's lame but revelatory reply was a sorrowful criticism about the 'number of harsh, thoughtless and unnecessarily heartless remarks' uttered by the Eight. Significantly, he never accused them of inaccuracy. But also, he did not surrender.

Through his African 'runners', one more testimonial was

obtained in questionable circumstances. A Ghanaian government official warned 'unequivocally and categorically' that any
boardroom battle in London could not 'interfere' with their
control of the Ashanti gold mine. There were also rumours
of a second testimonial by Bitwell Kuwani, the governor of the
Bank of Zambia, 'sworn' after meeting Rowland in Cheapside.
It threatened that Lonrho's assets would be nationalised if
Rowland was dismissed. No document was ever produced but
the newspaper headlines were memorable.

'A mailed fist in a velvet glove,' warned Rowland's lawyer. 'There is an unmistakable threat there [from Africa].'
Under close scrutiny, the threats were eventually disowned
by the African governments but Rowland's appeal was to the
shareholders who would be meeting in three weeks to decide
his fate. For them, the jewel of Lonrho's empire was threatened.

The court battle ended at 10.30 a.m. on Monday 14 May. In
a fourteen-minute judgment, Plowman rejected Rowland's bid
for an injunction preventing his dismissal. The Eight had won.
But instead of returning to Cheapside to vote for Rowland's
removal, the Eight prevaricated.

As they left the courtroom, Rowland threatened an appeal
which would last another ten days. Even if he lost, he warned
the Eight, they were liable for substantial costs. If he won
the shareholders' vote, Lonrho would not pay. The threat
was chilling. All eight men realised that despite the justice
of their case, many small shareholders believed the affidavit
evidence that Lonrho, without Rowland, was doomed. Unlike
their adversary, the Eight lacked confidence in their skill and
energy to marshal sufficient support for the decisive vote in three
weeks. The same brinkmanship which engineered deals throughout Africa persuaded them to seek a truce. That afternoon, the
judge was told that, following negotiations, Rowland would not
be removed before the annual general meeting.

Rowland turned the temporary ceasefire into another propaganda coup. 'I expected to be dismissed,' he beamed to journalists, 'until we were approached by the Eight. They realised at
the last moment that if I'd been dismissed, all Lonrho's assets
in Zambia would have been nationalised. They took fright and

didn't have the guts to sack me.' He added, 'There's been a great deal of cowardice in this battle.' The Eight were silenced, while shareholders, stoked by Addey, expressed their 'anger' that a damaging battle had been needlessly fought. 'We'd brought everything out in the open,' explained Smallpeice later. 'It showed our good faith. We were grateful for the opportunity.' Rowland could not resist another dig: 'Sir Basil is terribly interested in petty cash vouchers. He has no feel for Africa, never having been there as far as I know.'

That night in Downing Street, Edward Heath was considering his answers for prime minister's questions in the House of Commons the following day. Several questions were based on his forthcoming meeting with leaders of the Confederation of British Industry. He was negotiating Stage Three of the wage freeze with the trade unions and employers amid memories of a vicious coal strike in 1972 which was contrasted with the current uncontrolled property boom producing ugly images of 'whiz kids' and 'winklers' earning fortunes on the turn of a deal. Among the beneficiaries was Keyser Ullman and the secondary banks who were lending vast sums of other people's money to developers.

Heath might have been expected to avoid the Lonrho issue in the Commons with bland phrases. Indeed, there were good reasons to avoid any entanglement. Inevitably, the broad church of left wing ideologues would use Rowland as a political slogan for the greedy capitalist, breaking Rhodesian sanctions, and to earn profits by 'exploiting' the Africans. Moreover, Sandys, Du Cann and Ogilvy represented the Conservative Party and the Palace. But political savvy was not among Heath's more obvious qualities. His government had propagated a quasi-socialist atmosphere where profit makers were targets.

Three days earlier, at a private dinner in Perth during the Scottish Party Conference, Heath had exploded in a passionate condemnation about the laziness and failure of British management and industrialists to build the economy. As a puritan and self-made man, Heath was genuinely incensed by the revelations about Lonrho. They illustrated, he exclaimed to his audience, 'an ugly face of capitalism' which revealed the country's class distinctions and the failure of management.

His hosts, according to Douglas Hurd, didn't 'understand a word'.

For some Conservatives, Rowland's perks were no different from politicians' free trips. Many wealthy Conservatives drove Rolls Royces and inhabited large houses or company apartments and sought to avoid paying confiscatory income taxes. Businessmen could legitimately be paid abroad and the Conservative government had never proposed altering the law. For many Conservatives, therefore, Rowland was a maverick but not an outlaw.

But Heath had little sympathy for raw capitalism. Like so many in Whitehall and Westminster, he was puzzled how a businessman could earn so much, be so popular with those black nationalist politicians who first aimed their guns and then their invective against the British, and seemed so successful when the bulk of British industry was patently a dismal failure.

Heath might also have considered that politicians ignored their own conflicts of interest. Repeatedly, the two main political parties had refused to approve a compulsory register of interests for members of parliament despite evidence that senior politicians had lent their names to dubious and even corrupt businesses. Jeremy Thorpe, the former Liberal leader, was a director of a company which charged exorbitant interest rates, while Reginald Maudling, the former chancellor of the exchequer, had resigned after the exposure of his relationship with the convicted fraudster John Poulson. Heath had publicly condemned neither. To criticise Lonrho's directors for publicising their financial arrangements while politicians remained silent was hypocritical.

Finally, Heath might have considered that the criticism of Lonrho for breaking Rhodesian sanctions was also hypocritical. Ever since the Conservative victory in June 1970, even the pretence of maintaining sanctions had evaporated. During the Heath government, there would not be one meeting between ministers and oil executives to consider supplies to Rhodesia, although the government had a controlling interest in British Petroleum. One of the government's newly appointed directors to BP was Lord Greenhill who, aware of the conspiracy between Whitehall and the oil companies, recalls that no one in either Westminster or Whitehall ever discussed sanctions with him. Yet Lonrho was pilloried in the newspapers for financing the development of copper mines in Rhodesia.

The prime minister's objectivity was tainted by Lonrho's association with Duncan Sandys and Edward Du Cann. In formulating his attitude that night, he ignored that by condemning Lonrho and two senior Tories, he would also by implication cast an aspersion upon the 47,000 Lonrho shareholders, mostly Party loyalists, and the royal family. All were linked to Lonrho's sins.

Regardless of all those conflicting emotions and policies, the issue which Heath needed to address was simply Rowland's alleged dishonesty towards the Lonrho board. Instead, on entering the Commons that afternoon, Heath intended to join with the Labour and Liberal parties in condemning the 'dubious morality' of some boardrooms, blurring the essential principle that one could not tolerate corporate greed just to ensure Lonrho's survival.

Lonrho was raised as a supplementary question by Jo Grimond, the Liberal Party's elder statesman. Grimond asked Heath when he met the CBI to 'condemn unequivocally the sort of goings-on that we have all read about at Lonrho which are fatal to any counter-inflation policy? Will you also point out to the CBI that greed does not now seem to be a monopoly of the trade unions?'

In his carefully chosen words, Heath replied that Lonrho was not representative and that he should 'not exaggerate to the extent of saying that an incident of this kind is fatal to counter-inflation policy'. Then, with some vigour, Heath added the immortal phrase: 'It is an unpleasant and unacceptable face of capitalism but one should not suggest that the whole of British industry consists of practices of this kind.' The Commons continued its discussion about Stage Three without any further reference to Lonrho.

For a serving Conservative prime minister not associated for the remainder of his career with any other memorable phrase, Heath's remark was an astonishing and unprecedented condemnation of a British businessman. Lonrho and Rowland were tainted forever.

Rowland was surprised by the onslaught and admitted that he was 'hurt very much' by Heath's condemnation. In private he confessed his unhappiness that his wife Josie was pained. Considering Rowland's physical stature and his abrasive treatment of subordinates, some were puzzled by his sensitivity to Heath's criticism. The more perceptive understood that bullies are invariably either cowards or strangely vulnerable to the same invective which they dispense. But Rowland revealed a more serious weakness. Namely, he fundamentally misunderstood the nature of British politics, a flaw which would undermine his ambitions in Britain.

Instead of dismissing Heath as a failed politician, searching for any scapegoats as he led the country towards economic disaster, Rowland assumed the attack was a personal slight. In revealing his unworldliness about the antics of politicians who were more sophisticated than African dictators, Rowland failed to recognise Heath's predictable bid to win political capital. Instinctively, Rowland's violent reaction confirmed his image as a lifelong rebel. He would forfeit opportunities to transform himself, like other adventurers, into a pillar of the Establishment.

The Eight were naturally 'delighted' by Heath's condemnation, justifying their principled stand. Their enthusiasm was reflected by an editorial in *The Times*. Under a headline, 'Mr Rowland Must Go', the newspaper highlighted the Lonrho saga as 'a significant chapter in the development of British capitalism, raising a series of the most fundamental issues'. The principle, commented the newspaper, was whether Rowland's disregard for truth and honesty was compatible with the obligations imposed upon those managing a publicly quoted company.

Lonrho's shareholders were unimpressed. For many, Rowland represented a relief from Heath's capitulation to the trade unions and the slide towards socialism. He was a capitalist adventurer of a type Britain desperately needed. Those shareholders were therefore receptive to a new circular which Rowland issued to counter the accusations.

Written in an elegant, flawless style tailored for shareholders, from another shareholder who since 1961 had 'not sold a single share', Rowland's calm, even breathtaking distortion of past events revealed the qualities upon which his fortune was built since internment on the Isle of Man.

Portraying himself as the reluctant litigant, bolstered by the 'spontaneous' wave of affidavits, he blamed the Eight for resorting to the courts, ignoring that he had initiated the litigation. 'Their failure to give one valid reason for my removal', he wrote, 'was a pity' and the cause of 'much damage to the company'. His inspired bravura, undoubtedly composed with a wry smile and printed in enhanced typeface, added, 'I have come to recognise that it is essential to have a strong and independent Board.' Since he had never complained about the Eight until they had initiated his removal, it was an inadvertent admission of his own failure to manipulate the board or anticipate their challenge of his rule.

Selected quotations by the Eight appeared to support his own position. Wankel, he wrote, was bought 'despite strong opposition' and was worth double the price paid. He insisted that all the directors and Peats knew the 'precise terms' of the Wankel purchase 'on 28 March 1971', which was untrue. Hedsor Wharf's costs, he alleged, were not borne by shareholders, but he ignored that Peats had ordered his repayment of the money to Lonrho. Concerning Nyaschere he wrote, 'I personally have had nothing to do with the mine, its management or finance since UDI,' which would be contradicted by a subsequent inquiry. Finally, the Sandys payments, he claimed, were excused by a committee of the board led by Smallpeice, which was fanciful. One justifiable lament was that the failure to execute Peats's recommendations was caused by a 'clash of personalities'. Indeed, there was a row, but it was prompted by his own tactics.

All those inconsistencies were ignored in Rowland's lament that he could not rely upon the Eight who played with Lonrho 'like Monopoly', an argument which was cocooned in a humble appeal to shareholders for forgiveness: 'The Eight say that I am overbearing and intolerant. It is true that I feel strongly on some points and express myself strongly. Working intensively over long hours I may sometimes be tired, short tempered and even rude to my colleagues. I am sorry. But as the Affidavits from so many quarters show, I enjoy the loyalty of the Managers and others throughout the Group. An occasional breach of good manners among colleagues, although regrettable, should, I suggest, be weighed against the appreciable services I am rendering the Group.'

Rowland's conclusion was succinct and misleading: 'All the facts had been fully disclosed to the Board before the Eight acted. . . One would have expected them to make further efforts before acting suddenly and without notice. . . All the difficulties might have been avoided.' The circular was accompanied by a notice of an extraordinary general meeting, to be held contemporaneously with the annual general meeting on 31 May, where Rowland would demand the dismissal of the Eight.

Two days later on 17 May, the Eight published their reply. In contrast to Rowland's missive, it was noble – 'our duty was distasteful but necessary' – and accurate. But they addressed the wrong audience. While City practitioners sympathised with the Eight's complaints about Rowland's 'financial irresponsibility', 'dictatorial methods' and 'utter intolerance', Lonrho's small shareholders neither wanted nor could understand a lesson in corporate governance. Even the Eight's warning that Lonrho's two financial crises since 1969 would be followed by a third inclined shareholders towards Rowland who promised to save the company from collapse. In a dispute about money and honesty there should have been little scope for charisma and beauty. But Rowland's publicity had cultivated an image of the dashing buccaneer which contrasted sharply with that of the dismal bureaucrat and thereby mothballed the Eight's credibility.

A climax had been reached. The government announced that the Department of Trade would appoint two inspectors to inquire into Lonrho's affairs. With his eyes fixed upon the battle for survival, Rowland did not appreciate the implications of an independent inquiry into the Eight's complaints. Bravely, he announced, 'I welcome most warmly the minister's decision to appoint inspectors' who would be given 'every possible co-operation'. That day, Lonrho's shares fell to 64p but Rowland's confidence was strengthening.

In a deft switch of strategy, his next circular replaced spite with superficiality: 'I write to you about the future and real issues, whereas the Eight wrote about the past.' Lonrho's business, urged Rowland, was in Africa and, as the architect of that empire, Rowland urged it it was unrealistic to believe that the Eight could manage it better than its creator. Dismissing all the 'wearisome' allegations of his deceit as 'old complaints which have been well ventilated already', Rowland praised the soundness of his financial stewardship, endorsed by Roland Franklin.

Lonrho, the 'unacceptable face of capitalism', had become a divisive, debated topic in the media and parliament. Heath's phrase had cast the rebel as a pariah and outcast. Not surprisingly, in his fight for survival, Rowland found few allies among the City or political establishment. Desperately, he sought a new supporter. Addey needed a new angle for the Sunday newspapers. The only totem available was Sandys who, despite his recently tarnished reputation, remained an important personality in British politics.

In a statement written by Rowland, Addey and others in Cheapside but not by the politician himself, 'Sandys's statement', issued to newspapers late on Saturday afternoon, blamed Smallpeice for unnecessarily and singlehandedly provoking the row. For Lonrho's Conservative shareholders who read the account the following morning, their chairman's version was convincing.

According to Sandys, Smallpeice was asked on 12 March 1973 to list any 'specific complaints. . . But he declined to do so'. Instead Smallpeice 'began to collect signatures' for Rowland's dismissal. This, commented Sandys, caused him great surprise because none of the directors 'has at any board meeting during the past year expressed disapproval of any decisions taken by the chief executive [Rowland] or the manner in which he was discharging his duties'. On the contrary, wrote Sandys, on 15 September 1972 Smallpeice had written 'expressing entire satisfaction' with Rowland's reforms.

The image conjured by the Cheapside committee was of a maligned chief executive who, surprised by Smallpeice's sudden and uncompromising move for his dismissal, had been allowed no opportunity to 'reply to criticisms which were mostly of a very vague nature'. Sandys's statement was a masterpiece of distortion but as politicians through the ages have long discovered, the bigger the lie, the greater the credibility.

That night, Smallpeice was asked for his immediate comment. Instead of expressing outrage about the chairman's dishonesty, Smallpeice mumbled 'surprise' that Sandys was not impartial and criticised the 'construction of events'.

'Sandys has lied through his back teeth,' groaned Percy that Sunday, understanding Rowland's propaganda coup. Throughout that week, the initiative slipped towards Rowland, a notable achievement considering the substantiated charges which he faced. Brazenly, he emerged from the shadows to deny the charges.

The £130,000 payment to Sandys, he told ITV's *This Week*, was executed by Fred Butcher and 'done without my knowledge. . . I know nothing about it'. He added, untruly, 'I was never interested in South Africa at all.' 'When it is suggested that I have bribed my way into favour,' he told the *Daily Mail*, 'I regard that as an insult to the Africans with whom I have dealt. 'I'm not a capitalist,' he informed the *Sunday Express*. Hedsor Wharf, he told everyone, was necessary to reciprocate the entertainment he received from the kings and presidents in their palaces. 'After all,' he told a gathering of credulous journalists, 'when the Ruler of Kuwait recently came to London, he spent the whole weekend with his entourage at my house.' Rowland's account was true, as was his story that President Numeiry of Sudan and his whole cabinet had driven to Hedsor Wharf after dining in Buckingham Palace to spend the day with Lonrho's chief executive. Shareholders and businessmen were impressed, especially since the truth rankled with the inhabitants of Westminster and Whitehall.

Yet there was also human self-doubt. 'It's so utterly ridiculous,' he told BBC Television in an attractively shy manner, 'that sometimes I think the whole thing is a nightmare. I've made so many friends, I couldn't possibly give up my life with Lonrho – if I were sacked, I would have to start again.'

The remorseless efficacy of Rowland's campaign, which included housing African notables at the Sonesta Tower hotel to preach Rowland's importance to both the press and shareholders, justified Rowland's boast that Lonrho's growth was his singular achievement. Frustrated that propaganda rather than principle were swaying opinion, the Eight finally mounted their retaliation in the *Sunday Times*. Under the headline, 'Why Rowland is a liability', the article showed how Lonrho's share price was lower than the comparable international traders like Inchcape and Booker McConnell and the company's future was at risk. 'Now is the time to sack Rowland,' was the paper's conclusion.

Rowland was stung into reply. His final letter to shareholders on 22 May was sensitive, endearing and misleading. After accusing Smallpeice and even Percy, wrongly, of never visiting Africa, he wrote, 'I am distressed because you, as a shareholder, must naturally be deeply concerned that your share price has been knocked down so disastrously as a result of the recent Board Room row coming out into the open.' Then followed the *mea culpa* and a promise of self-improvement: 'Lonrho has been my sole interest over the last twelve years to the exclusion of all else.'

Rowland's letter was accompanied by a circular from the 'Lonrho shareholders' action group'. Nurtured by Rowland, the group had been chaperoned to meet bankers, brokers and Lonrho executives who sang Rowland's praises. Although unsophisticated, they were enthralled by the attention lavished upon them. If they could not go to Africa to push back the frontiers, they could at least support a man with the vision and daring to undertake that enterprise. Their support was unequivocal. 'We were greatly impressed by the intense loyalty to Mr Rowland,' they wrote, 'and his success in building the Company from small beginnings to a vast and prospering concern is incontestable.' Their backup of Rowland was total and they attracted the other small shareholders to their flag: 'This is one of those rare occasions when all Lonrho shareholders have the opportunity to show that it is their company and that they are demanding and exercising their right to control it.'

Two days before the shareholders' meeting, on 29 May, the board held a final meeting. Jim Butler presented the delayed half year's results. Pre-tax profits had risen from £8 million to £9.6 million while net attributable profits had risen from £600,000 to

£3.2 million. Late that night, the results would be leaked to the press.

'Tiny sat through the board meeting quietly triumphalist,' recalled one director. 'The proxy votes were in his favour.' During the following night, Rowland's jubilation grew. The count of proxies pointed clearly to victory, although to guarantee his success he had increased his stake to 22 per cent of the total shares issued. By dawn on 31 May, the count was completed: 4.5 million had voted against Rowland, 29.5 million votes endorsed his position. About 26 million voted for the dismissal of each of the Eight with 8 million votes for their retention. Rowland cast over 13 million votes. Victory would be announced at the public meeting which started at 2.30 p.m.

In anticipation of an enormous crowd, instead of the customary forty blue-rinse pensioners, Central Hall in Westminster, with a capacity of 2900, had been reserved. By lunchtime, in falling rain, a crowd of shareholders was standing in line. Overwhelmingly conservative, many from the shires rather than the cities, they were divided between those who were appalled by Rowland's business ethics and the majority who welcomed the opportunity to demonstrate their support for a brave businessman, representing the best of capitalism, a creator of wealth as opposed to the scroungers who sucked the wealth of the welfare state, maligned by a prime minister tilting the country towards socialism.

Technically, there were two meetings. The first was the annual general meeting to decide whether Rowland should be dismissed. The second was the extraordinary general meeting called by Rowland to dismiss the Eight directors. His quest for their removal was, Percy told journalists entering the hall, 'because we have had the courage to stand up to him'.

As they walked on to the platform, the Eight knew their fate. 'It was very disagreeable,' according to Wilkinson. How much easier and agreeable, they sighed, to have resigned weeks earlier and avoided the ridicule and unpleasantness of the public row. But all eight believed themselves to be honest, publicly minded citizens who placed duty above personal interest. If their audience, packed into the hall, had rationally considered why Lonrho's share price had fallen 60 per cent since September, they might have spurned Rowland. Instead, they flocked to a flag of hope and excitement.

Rowland had driven to Westminster after a champagne celebration at Cheapside. A roar, resembling that of a crowd of rowdy schoolchildren at sports day, greeted his entrance into the hall. Sixteen directors sat on the platform. In the middle sat Sandys. On his left was Smallpeice, wilting under the social and personal pressure, and the seven other anti-Rowland directors. On Sandys's right was Alan Ball, Rowland and the five remaining directors.

Sandys opened the meeting lamenting the controversy which unfairly besmirched Lonrho's 'high sense of moral responsibility'. The catcalls were silenced by his announcement of the count of proxy votes. As the hall erupted in cheers and boos, the Eight sat grim faced. Few directors are fired in public by the shareholders, especially for honesty.

Sandys called upon Rowland to speak. Dressed in a blue suit, white shirt and dark tie, he was heard in silence, some said charmed silence, as he reviewed the successful past and predicted a wonderful future. In what would become a noticeable trait, his speech was brief and disclosed only his desire to reveal nothing. Nevertheless, the faithful roared their approval. Thirty seconds of enthusiastic applause filled the hall as he sat down.

Smallpeice, who followed, was by contrast heckled throughout. In the thin, dry voice of a discredited official justifying the unjustifiable, his account of Rowland's misjudgment and the deceit which sparked the revolt was interrupted by jeers of 'resign', 'rubbish' and 'get out'. He did not look or sound like a hero but rather the personification of Britain's collapsing industry. 'He wantonly disregarded the decisions of the board,' intoned Smallpeice. 'Good thing too,' yelled an unimpressed shareholder. As he unemotionally battled against the insults to restate his reasons for his seeking the dismissal of the man just yards away, other directors opted not to speak.

Rowland sat expressionless, glancing around the hall without revealing his delight about his enemies' public humiliation. When Smallpeice finished, Sandys managed to lose his place in the agenda, ruled himself out of order and confused himself about

who had the right to speak. Amid his fluster, a shareholder
rose and, to laughter, in a voice which impersonated Sandys's
father-in-law, Winston Churchill, spoke inanely, epitomising
alternately either the stupid or the ugly face of capitalism. Like
a dried up Latin master who had long lost control of the class,
Sandys gazed absently around the hall and offered shareholders
the opportunity to question directors.

Asked why the Sandys payments were not referred to the
board, Butcher replied, 'It is difficult to say why.' Asked by a
shareholder if Lonrho was breaking sanctions against Rhodesia,
Sandys asked for another question. Asked whether Lonrho was
solvent, Du Cann rose and reassured everyone that no financial
crisis threatened the company. Wild cheers erupted, securing the
banker a fond position in Rowland's hierarchy.

From the rear of the hall, Sir Dennis Glover, a Conservative MP rose, 'The Percys have been raising rebellions
since the thirteenth century. They have never won one yet
and they never will.' Immediately the meeting degenerated into
a disorderly *mélange* of wild applause, catcalls, heckling, boos
and irrelevancies. Silently, Rowland was in total control. The
meeting ended. 'Thank you very, very much,' beamed Rowland,
shaking hands with well-wishers and even some of the Eight. 'I
don't regret doing what I did,' said Smallpeice having warmly
shaken Rowland's proferred hand. 'I realised with Mr Rowland's
large shareholding it was a long shot,' Percy commented, 'companies get the governments they deserve.' 'I'm delighted,' smiled
Rowland to the well-wishers as he left for another celebration at
Cheapside and then at Mr Chows, 'There are no hard feelings
and there'll be no recriminations.'

The defeated left the hall for a prearranged wake of vichyssoise
soup and salmon and Bollinger Special Cuvée at the Royal
Thames Yacht Club. Each was presented with an engraved
penknife by MacKenzie and signed the menu card as a memento.
They woke the following day to read of Rowland's announcement
that the Eight would not receive their contractual compensation:
'They won't get one penny.' The somersault did not surprise
Spears, 'The man's a cad.'

The universal reaction to Rowland's victory condemned

Lonrho's future to uncertainty. The *Sunday Times*'s post mortem was the most interesting. Rowland, the newspaper predicted, would be unable to replace the Eight with men of any reputation and Sandys would resign; Rowland would be unable to find new funds in the City or abroad when the inevitable financial crisis struck; there would be no major rise in the share price; Western Platinum had 'permanently damaged' Lonrho's future; the Wankel engine was the only certain success; and, unlike Slater Walker, First National Finance, Croda, Jessel Securities and Ralli International, whose earnings were 'many times greater than Lonrho's', Lonrho was doomed with Rowland. It is remarkable that each of those predictions was erroneous. All of those competing conglomerates crashed within the following twelve months. Lonrho shares would fall to 54 pence during that summer, a long way from their 316 pence high but only Lonrho survived because its assets, unlike those of its preferred competitors, were real.

The legacy of Rowland's victory influenced British corporate affairs for the next twenty years. The reform of Company Law – the redefinition of the responsibility of accountants and auditors and the creation of effective City watchdogs – which would have helped to settle the Lonrho row, was undertaken in the same perfunctory manner that initially had caused the Lonrho row and then allowed Rowland to win his battle.

Just before the meeting at Westminster Hall, Rowland had conceded, 'If I win, I will have to behave differently. I can no longer act as a one-man band.' Seizing upon this confession, others assumed that Rowland acknowledged the need to change his spots. They were proved to have misunderstood the nature of the man. Penitence does not feature among a rebel's qualities. Finally free of restraints in London, Rowland resuscitated the expansion of Lonrho's empire in Africa.

Seven
Resurrection

An unexpected telephone call late at night on 28 February 1974 in Nairobi was the first indication that Rowland's latest ambition was endangered. Udi Gecaga, recently appointed as the first African director of Lonrho in gratitude for his help during the 1973 boardroom row, was roused by his chief executive telephoning from Khartoum. He was told to meet Rowland the following day in Addis Ababa, the capital of Ethiopia. 'It's urgent,' snapped Rowland. 'We've run into some problems. I need your help.'

Over the previous weeks, Rowland had been negotiating with Nko Ekangaki, the secretary general of the Organisation of African Unity, to provide Lonrho's 'expertise' to the continent. The commodity was oil and Rowland's proposed scheme was as grandiose as any he had undertaken.

In the wake of the Yom Kippur war in September 1973, the price of oil had escalated in tandem with the rise of anti-western sentiments in the Afro-Arab world. Among the targets of that antagonism were the international oil giants. Always anxious to profit by befriending the underdog, Rowland proposed to the Organisation of African Unity that their member nations should shed their dependence on the western oil corporations and organise their own supplies from the Middle East. Lonrho would be pleased to serve as the broker and shipper. Its 'Shipping Division', namely the Watergate Steam Shipping Co which owned seven bulk ore carriers, would place its expertise at Africa's service.

Rowland was introduced to the OAU's Secretariat by Khalil

Osman, the Sudanese representative of Kuwait's Gulf Fisheries. Among Osman's close friends was Dr Mansour Khalid, the Sudanese foreign minister, and Rowland found little difficulty in recruiting the minister to promote Lonrho's cause within the OAU.

Rowland had next won the support of Nko Ekangaki who, as a national of Cameroon, represented political insignificance among the continent's powerbrokers. His weak status was matched by his questionable intellect and financial insecurity, a combination which Rowland found attractive.

Adopting his ingratiatingly charming posture, addressing Ekangaki repeatedly as 'Sir', Rowland had persuaded the official that Lonrho, as a service to Africa, would volunteer for no cost a survey of Africa's oil requirements. 'I love this continent,' he told the awed official. 'Africa has been very good to me,' he was fond of repeating as he presented himself as the 'honest broker' between Arab riches and African needs. 'It has given me so much and we want to do something in exchange.' The future, said Rowland, lay not in southern Africa but with thirty to forty independent African countries who would eventually find a common cause and form an immensely powerful bloc. 'I see a partnership between Western technology, Arab oil-money and African resources. I think that this is an unbeatable combination and one that I recognised years ago. It is here that the whole future of Lonrho should lie.' His dream was for Rhodesia, Angola, Mozambique and Namibia to be at peace. With his huge investments, he could, with Zambia's help, realise enormous profits. In the present case, Rowland's plan was to provide a link between the Arab oil producers and Africa's refineries.

To Ekangaki, the sentiments seemed wonderful, but he was naturally concerned about a European company's involvement. Rowland was reassuring. Lonrho's policy, he said, was absolutely pro-African and pro-Arab. He personally was the persecuted victim of colonial interests and accordingly, during the recent boardroom row, several African leaders and governments had publicly given him their support. Ekangaki had not seen an exposé in the *Daily Mirror* describing the conditions on the

Ceylon tea plantations where Lonrho's employees were housed in waterless hovels and paid low wages which could only be spent at the company store.

At an OAU committee meeting on 29 December 1973, Ekangaki sought permission to requisition an oil survey. His submission not surprisingly adopted Rowland's own phrases. Approval was granted and Ekangaki hired Lonrho as the consultant.

Nine days later, Ekangaki wrote to Rowland inquiring about Lonrho's interests in southern Africa. The Afro-Arab bloc had recently imposed an embargo upon oil deliveries to South Africa and the fight against apartheid was the single most important issue uniting the OAU membership. This was clearly a sensitive issue for Rowland.

In April 1974, Rowland flew to Rhodesia for twenty-four hours, visiting Inyati and Shamrocke. Potentially, if discovered by his Afro-Asian friends, the visit would have been embarrassing; also Rowland, since 1970, had been permitted by the Salisbury government to spend two days every month in the country. But by then Rowland had concocted an appealing formula. Lonrho's interests, he explained to Ekangaki were, 'historical' and administered 'by proxy as they were themselves banned from entering the areas because of their pro-African policy'. Embellishing the fiction, Rowland added that Lonrho had considered disposing of its southern Africa interests but was restrained 'by friendly African heads of state and governments' who advised that only 'the financial empires of the enemies of Africa' would benefit.

Ekangaki was satisfied and, in anticipation of the meeting on 28 February, Lonrho began quickly amassing information from the OAU's thirty-six members. Its progress was halted by General Idi Amin of Uganda. In a telegram to Ekangaki, Amin complained that the agreement with Lonrho was unlawful and Lonrho itself was 'widely known throughout Africa as being one of the leading imperialist and Zionist companies' which was supporting racist regimes to suppress nationalist movements.

Despite his exaggeration, Amin's outburst attracted support

from diverse leaders who, even to settle domestic disputes, found an advantage in joining the attack upon Lonrho. Naively, Ekangaki failed to identify the danger and alert Rowland. Instead, convinced that Lonrho had secured the contract to begin supplying oil to Africa, Rowland had already ordered two oil tankers. Indeed, he had remained in Khartoum in the belief that ratification was a formality which Ekangaki could effortlessly secure. The panic telephone call to Gecaga on 28 February was the first fissure in his plan.

When Gecaga joined Rowland by the pool of the Hilton hotel in Addis, Lonrho's chief executive was beginning to lose his customary cool demeanour. 'You know the foreign ministers here,' seethed the chief executive, 'settle the problems.' In the distance, the first shots were being fired in what became Ethiopia's savage civil war, an unfortunate omen.

Within twelve hours, Gecaga returned to Rowland, chastened by a succession of foreign ministers' blunt and even brutal criticisms of Lonrho. 'They've chewed my arse off,' he confessed. Lonrho's proposal had been abruptly rejected. Amin had even declared that Gecaga was prohibited from entering Uganda and Ekangaki was to be dismissed. 'We were all shaken,' recalls Gecaga. Rowland was crestfallen and unforgiving: 'It's all your fault. You didn't do your work. That's what I brought you here for.' The implication was clear. Gecaga had been expected to offer the foreign ministers inducements to win their support. A permanent frostiness crept into their relationship. Rowland would never again bless Gecaga as 'my successor'. Gecaga would later summarise, 'One has to know Tiny well to realise how nasty he is.'

Some weeks later, Ekangaki was seen in Cheapside. Desperately he sought an interview with Rowland. 'I need £2000 for my children's education,' he pleaded. 'Get that man out,' Rowland ordered an intermediary. 'He promised to deliver and he failed. I don't want to see him again.'

The African's forlorn plight was unimportant. The collapse of another project was not disastrous. 'Tiny's a good loser,' says Captain Wilming. 'We only talked about slimy Ekangaki for the next two months.' Lonrho's profits, boosted by the unexpected increase in prices of gold, copper and platinum, had in the previous three months risen by nearly 50 per cent. The merchants of doom in the City had been proved wrong and Rowland was currently finalising a deal which would stun his critics. His frequent visits to the Sudan and Kuwait were about to produce a spectacular success.

On Khalil Osman's farm outside Khartoum, surrounded by tribal dancing and music, Rowland had encouraged Sheikh Nasser to invest in Lonrho. Arab investment, Rowland calculated, would inject enormous funds, be an ideal passport to business opportunities in the region and would upset his enemies in the City. Osman had also encouraged his twenty-five-year-old employer to consider joining Rowland. Their recent co-operation, argued the former vet, proved the advantages.

The Kuwaitis, having studied Lonrho's sugar scheme for the Sudan, had agreed to provide some finance and the omens seemed favourable. The world price of sugar had reached a record £650 per ton which was boosting Lonrho's own profits. As with all commodities in the uncertain post-1973 era, the price spiral seemed to continue.

The site selected for Lonrho's scheme was barren scrub land called Kenana adjoining the White Nile. Tests had shown that, properly irrigated, the 80,000 acre site could initially produce 350,000 tons of sugar. The world's biggest sugar project was described by Rowland in a characteristically articulate phrase as a 'triangular project' – a combination of western technical expertise provided by Lonrho, Arab oil money and African resources. The expected cost was £130 million. Lonrho would own a 12 per cent stake, its Japanese partners 5 per cent, while the bulk would be Sudanese and Arab government finance. Lonrho would earn management and commission fees.

As Rowland danced and energetically played the bongo drums, Nasser was attracted by the notion that Lonrho would produce many more Kenana schemes. In the wake of restructuring a bankrupt shipping company in Kuwait, Nasser needed to utilise huge tax losses and Lonrho was a suitable vehicle for creative accountancy. On his return home, the Sheikh ordered Tom

Ferguson, a British economist on secondment from London, to investigate Lonrho.

Ferguson, an astute Scot, arrived to a warm welcome at Cheapside. Rowland was naturally effusive. Over the following ten days, Ferguson was given access to all the directors, accountants and auditors. Although there were dislikes, like the sycophants Spicer and Dunlop, Ferguson appreciated the unpretentious offices and the evidence that Lonrho's African subsidiaries were well managed and profitable. Unsuspecting, he was persuaded that the Kuwaitis would be counted as equal partners if they invested in Lonrho. Rowland's salesmanship of his dream of Arab oil money, African resources and western technology banished any doubts which the Scot might have harboured.

In November 1974, Lonrho announced that the Sabah brothers, Sheikh Nasser and Hamed, had bought 8 million newly issued Lonrho shares worth a total of £6.1 million. At 76.25 pence per share, compared to that year's low of 47 pence, Lonrho's fortunes were evidently recovering. Rowland had secured an unbreakable lifeline, obliterating his recent acknowledgement of criticisms.

As Rowland surveyed the condition of Britain he had reason to be pleased. The nation's economy had slumped during an energy black-out which reduced industry to working only three days every week. After his challenge to the miners collapsed, Edward Heath lost two elections and the leadership of the Conservative Party. The politician's humiliation mirrored the fate of Smallpeice who had failed to re-establish himself after Rowland's victory. The stock market had collapsed, counting Slater Walker among the casualties. Slater was heading towards financial ruin and an unsuccessful bid for his extradition. Other victims included Edward Du Cann's bank, Keyser Ullman, whose assets were wiped out by bad loans. Like Lonrho, the bank was under investigation by two inspectors appointed by the Department of Trade. Du Cann personally owed his bank over £1 million, indelibly influencing his political and financial status thereafter. The rise in oil prices and the apparent power of the Arabs terrified many. Only Lonrho seemed to be profiting from the new petro-dollars, alias 'oil gold'. There seemed a lot of truth in the Chinese proverb that if you stood patiently on the bridge across the river, you would eventually see your enemy's corpse float past.

The 1973 row had provided one enduring reward for Rowland. Building on the critical support from Kenneth Kaunda, he was drawn into an increasingly closer relationship with the president of Zambia. As the more virulently anti-British politicians around the president departed, Tom Mtine, Lonrho's chairman in Zambia, had secured Rowland unprecedented access to Zambia's vice-president and finance minister. To these, Rowland offered favours and encouraged them to speak in his support to Kaunda. Their vocal appreciation fuelled the cycle. None of Tiny's favours were more impressive and appreciated than the loan of his executive jet.

In an impoverished continent where airline connections between cities and nations were, and still remain, an occasional rather than a frequent and easy method of transport, Rowland's personal jet assumed importance beyond comprehension in Europe and America. Quite simply, African states were either too poor or technically unsuited to maintain a small plane for a president's use. Since few rich European and American executives worked in Africa, the sight of private jets flitting across the continent was a cause for comment. Hence the surprise when Kaunda greeted Bishop Muzorewa, then the leader of Rhodesia's nationalists, at Lusaka airport stepping off Rowland's jet. 'Tiny's very kind,' the Bishop told the president. 'A true friend of the Africans.' Soon after, Rowland also met the president: 'My plane is available for your use whenever you require.' The cost, £72,000, at today's prices, for a return journey from London to Lusaka, was ignored.

Confronted by the continued impoverishment of his country because of the war against Rhodesia and the patent futility of sanctions, Kaunda warmed to the man who shared his prejudices about British hypocrisy and voiced sincere support for African nationalism. Naturally, Kaunda knew that Lonrho was breaking sanctions, but that was not a cause for reprimand. Landlocked Zambia was also dependent upon continuing but unpublicised trade with Rhodesia.

Kaunda, however, was unaware of Lonrho's secret agreement with Dan Mayers to conceal the profits on the sale of Zambian amethysts through Blorg, the Liechtenstein company. In 1974, as the government's investigation got underway, Butcher was removing traces of any hidden arrangements whose exposure would add to Lonrho's embarrassment. Among those was the secret arrangement with Mayers.

In spring 1974, Butcher summoned Mayers. Instead of speaking in Cheapside, the two went to a nearby pub. 'Butcher was terrified,' recalls Mayers, 'that their office was being bugged.' Inside the pub, Butcher revealed that he was equally 'terrified' that Blorg, the company facilitating their tax evasion, would be exposed. 'We want to destroy the link between Blorg and Contango,' Butcher told Mayers. Lonrho's finance director proposed that Contango, the Liechtenstein company which was Lonrho's original holding company for its secret shareholding in Blorg, be liquidated. In an act of faith, Mayers's company Crystals would become Lonrho's trustee for its shareholding. According to Mayers, Butcher told him, 'In the climate of investigations, Lonrho simply could not stand such disclosures.' Among the embarrassments which the Lonrho director feared was a discovery that the inspectors appointed by the newly named Department of Trade and Industry [DTI] would unearth another taxhaven. As a precaution, Butcher burnt every relevant document.

Under Butcher's new arrangement with Mayers, the amethysts, mined in ever greater amounts, would continue to be shipped to Crystals, Mayers's company which was trading on behalf of all the partners. Mayers was also bequeathed the responsibility to dispose of the forty-ton stockpile of inferior-grade stones. Implicitly, Rowland trusted Mayers to reimburse Lonrho's share of profits. With that housekeeping chore completed, Butcher hoped that the deception against Rowland's most important African ally could be buried and forgotten.

Kaunda's and Rowland's ambitions in Africa were mutually dependent to a degree. Across Zambia's eastern border, in neighbouring Mozambique, the Portuguese were losing their bitter war against the Frelimo guerrillas, while across the western border in Angola, the guerrillas also fighting against the Portuguese had split between pro-communist and pro-western groups. In the vacuum bequeathed by the collapse of the British, French and Belgian empires, Africa had become a battleground between Soviet communism and western capitalism. In his search for trusted confidants and independent intermediaries, Kaunda found Rowland to be uniquely sympathetic concerning Zambia's isolation. From his office, Dennis Grennan, Kaunda's personal assistant, watched forlornly as Kaunda 'became convinced that Tiny was a good thing'. Flattered by the rich white tycoon's interest in himself and in Africa, Kaunda allowed Rowland to circumvent his government officials and establish direct contact for meetings at Rowland's convenience. For hours, Rowland would disappear inside the president's office, fresh with information from the presidents of other African nations, for private discussions about the *realpolitik* of southern Africa.

Among the first victims of Rowland's involvement with Kaunda was Vernon Mwaanga, Zambia's foreign minister. 'Rowland undermined my position,' recalls Mwaanga, 'by running Zambia's alternate foreign policy.' Mwaanga, an erudite hedonist with an unusual succession of marriages, had edited Lonrho's newspaper, *The Times of Zambia*, in 1972 without any interference from Rowland. After his appointment as foreign minister in 1973, Mwaanga noticed Kaunda's increasing respect for Rowland who, while boasting about his anti-Rhodesian credentials, was nevertheless in personal contact with both Ian Smith and John Vorster, the South African prime minister. Since Kaunda was desperately seeking a solution to Zambia's plight which neither Edward Heath nor Harold Wilson's second government seemed willing or able to negotiate, Rowland seemed a unique and trusted intermediary. 'Sometimes, I only realised what Rowland was doing after the event,' says Mwaanga. 'I protested to KK that it was wrong for a British businessman to represent Zambia, but I was ignored.'

Ever since Rowland's involvement in the Sudan coup and his bid for the OAU's oil supply, Rowland's interest in directly influencing African politics had grown. That interest had been augmented by the aftermath of Edward Heath's public interference in the boardroom dispute. Like the so-called front line states around Rhodesia, Rowland pleaded that he too was a victim of the British government and, for Lonrho's sake, sought an end to the illegal regime.

Rowland had taken his first significant diplomatic steps in 1974, after Jorge Jardim, Rowland's Portuguese associate, feared that Frelimo's bitter guerrilla campaign against the Portuguese would destroy his extensive investments. Knowing from other informants that Portuguese army officers were averse to continuing the murderous war, Jardim was introduced to Kaunda by Rowland to discuss Mozambique's future. Kaunda encouraged the Portuguese to grant their colony immediate independence. The advice was rejected but later, in one of their private conversations, the president passed on intelligence reports to Rowland identifying the terminal state of Portugal's resistance to the Mozambican guerrillas. In the belief that accurate information is a commodity to be converted into favours, Rowland used Kaunda's insight to prove his importance to the South African government.

In the war against African nationalism, the South Africans were Portugal's foremost allies. For Pretoria, the fates of Mozambique and Angola were critical to the survival of apartheid since an African government in Mozambique, backed by the Soviet Union, would inevitably support a nationalist war in South Africa itself. A new government might also stop the supply of Mozambique labour to South Africa's mines and interrupt the use of Lourenço Marques harbour. Hence, any accurate information about Mozambique's fate was of utmost interest in Pretoria.

By coincidence on 24 March 1974, Dr Marquand de Villiers, a fifty-three-year-old Pretoria lawyer, was in London for a family visit. A rugby enthusiast, de Villiers knew Sid Newman, Lonrho's South African director, who was also in London. De Villiers was invited to meet Rowland and Josie for dinner at the Savoy.

During the meal, Rowland realised de Villiers's importance. One of his golfing partners was John Vorster, the South African prime minister. Eagerly, Rowland passed on to the lawyer Kaunda's message.

Five days later, on 29 March 1974, three years after the warrants for Rowland's arrest for fraud had been issued, de Villiers was seated in the prime minister's office in Pretoria's Union Building. John Vorster was told that the Portuguese had 'thrown in the towel – capitulated' – in Mozambique. The surrender, said de Villiers, would occur within six weeks. Suspicious of the source, Vorster initially dismissed the authenticity of Rowland's information.

Three weeks later, de Villiers returned to the prime minister's office with further intelligence obtained by Rowland from Kaunda. Seated alongside Vorster was General Hendrik van den Bergh, the director general of the Bureau of State Security [BOSS]. The timetable in Mozambique, reported de Villiers, was clearer. The change of government would occur within two weeks. Protecting his own proprietary interests and ignorance, van den Bergh dismissed the intelligence. Two days later, on 25 April, the dictatorship in Lisbon was overthrown by a military coup and the leaders declared that the army would withdraw from Mozambique. Rowland's trustworthiness as an intermediary was established in Pretoria.

As a self-appointed broker, Rowland sought to arrange a meeting between Vorster and Kaunda, a Herculean ambition considering the history between the two leaders. 'Rowland and I were trusted,' recalls de Villiers, 'because we could not exploit the thing to our advantage and secondly, we could be repudiated by either party at any time.' Such was the faith of the two Lonrho executives that Vorster asked de Villiers to fly to London and brief Hilgard Muller, the foreign minister, about the proposed meeting. Muller was visiting Britain and no one else in the South African foreign service was aware of Rowland's brokerage. In recognition, Rowland was also invited on several occasions to Vorster's holiday home to discuss southern Africa. 'They got on well,' suggests de Villiers, 'Vorster trusted Mr Rowland as an honest broker but Mr Rowland never tried to ingratiate himself with Vorster.'

In the midst of these negotiations, Vernon Mwaanga met James Callaghan in Geneva. The British were hopelessly searching for solutions to Rhodesia's future. If the talks which Rowland was arranging materialised, Zambia's foreign minister knew that Kaunda hoped to persuade Vorster to withdraw South African officers from Rhodesia, to stop Rhodesian invasions into Zambia and to pressure Smith to start negotiations. All concerned knew that this was Rhodesia's last chance for a settlement before the outbreak of an uncontainable guerrilla war. In Geneva, Mwaanga revealed to the British Rowland's pivotal role in the peace process. 'They weren't very happy,' laughs Mwaanga. Their ire was directed at Rowland personally.

Rowland's relationship with Foreign Office officials which, over the following years, assumed a pattern of consistent warfare, was characterised by Rowland's unrestrained disparagement of Whitehall's diplomats. Although Britain had forsaken its empire, Rowland observed that the civil servants maintained a condescending and even arrogant attitude towards their former subject races. To his dismay, the Conservatives had been especially reluctant to challenge South Africa's racial policies or terminate the rebellion in Rhodesia. The new Labour government, despite its propaganda, was little different. Normally, his opinions would not have concerned British diplomats, but Rowland, through his own newspapers in Zambia and Kenya and in briefings to journalists in other countries, occasionally criticised British policies.

Ever since he withdrew his threat in 1968 to sue the British government for allowing the oil companies to break sanctions, Rowland had obliquely warned the government that, as an alternative tactic, he might reopen the pipeline. That attitude 'puzzled' the civil servants. After all, they reasoned, 'he was British yet had a close relationship to Kaunda'. Whitehall concluded that Rowland was 'letting his own side down'.

To relieve the strain, in 1974, Alan Campbell, a deputy under-secretary in the Foreign Office's Africa Department, arranged to meet Rowland for lunch at White's. Campbell had received cables from British embassies throughout Africa with complaints that Rowland's 'forward policy' was 'unhelpful' and 'coming across our bows'. Rowland's anti-British policies were, they reported, 'notorious'. To the most prejudiced, it occasionally appeared that Britain's rival in Africa was not the Soviet

Union, but Rowland. Campbell, who believed that Rowland's 'good' reputation was founded upon his assistance to African politicians, hoped to 'steer Rowland another way'.

Over an amicable lunch and an engaging discussion about Africa, Campbell sought to enlist Rowland's support. His guest misunderstood the suggestion. 'I'd be happy to act as a go-between on Britain's behalf with other governments,' replied Rowland, clearly intent on maximising his own influence. Campbell murmured: 'That's not quite what I had in mind.' The concept of Rowland, the uncontrollable entrepreneur and publicity seeker, as an emissary was risible. The ideal, countered the diplomat, would be regular meetings for an exchange of views to avoid fighting against each other. It was a genuine attempt to build bridges but depended upon Rowland returning with an offer which could be presented to the foreign secretary for approval. Instead, as the DTI inquiry progressed, the relationship between Rowland and British diplomats worsened. 'He became our totem figure,' recalls another diplomat. 'We worked our complexes out on him.'

Officialdom's bewilderment about the nature of Rowland was even shared occasionally by his closest advisers in Cheapside. On 12 June, Wilhelm Fuhrhop, aged ninety-five, died. Four days later, at the end of a boardroom lunch, Rowland casually announced, 'I've got to leave now. I'm going to bury my father.' According to Udi Gecaga, 'Everyone was very surprised. No one realised that Rowland's father was even alive. He'd never spoken about him.' Sixth-floor gossips suggested that Rowland had not mentioned his father's existence to avoid exposure of his true past or because of an unresolved argument. The latter theory was supported by the discovery that, in his last will, Wilhelm Fuhrhop had not mentioned his son. After peeling aside the layers of obfuscation and folklore which Rowland persistently wove either to disguise the truth or to satisfy his own fantasies, the reality of their relationship was quite mundane. The father was proud of his son but their relationship was unemotional and distant. The barriers which Rowland constructed to protect his past extended to his father, justifying the rumours that Fuhrhop had never seen his recently born grandson, Toby. The estrangement did not exist but the suspicions reflected the common perception of Rowland's desire to remove any obstacles to fulfil his ambitions. Rowland's absence of tenderness towards his father was evident in his own jocular account of his parent falling down the stairs and breaking a leg, 'rushing to hear the stock prices on the radio'.

During autumn 1974, Mark Shona, Kaunda's special assistant for political affairs, continued negotiations with Vorster through de Villiers. The prospect of preventing the war to overthrow Smith engulfing Mozambique improved as arrangements for a summit in December between Vorster and Kaunda were finalised. As a precursor, Vorster persuaded Ian Smith, after a succession of fraught negotiations in Lusaka, to release Joshua Nkomo and Robert Mugabe, the nationalist leaders, from detention and declare a cease-fire pending a negotiated peace.

On 25 August 1975, Vorster and Kaunda successfully manoeuvred Smith and the nationalist leaders to a summit in a railway dining car at Victoria Falls. In the brilliant setting, Rowland, firmly identified with the peace process, observed as the politicians undermined his efforts. Ian Smith, unwilling to grant majority rule, exploited the irreconcilable split in the nationalist movement and walked away from the chance of a peaceful settlement. Simultaneously, James Callaghan's counter-productive attempts to intervene, dubbed 'the winds of flatulence', exacerbated the tension. Guerrilla attacks intensified.

Robert Mugabe, a disciplined, uncompromising ideologue, travelled to newly independent Mozambique where, under Samora Machel, aligned to the communist bloc, he began building a guerrilla army. Mugabe's rival, Joshua Nkomo, returned to Lusaka to plot a settlement under Kaunda's patronage.

For Rowland, whose political and commercial fortunes were tied to an allegiance with Kaunda, there was no alternative but to support Nkomo, the pro-western candidate whose army was equipped by Moscow. Among Rowland's new employees was Vernon Mwaanga who joined Lonrho as a 'consultant'. 'I resigned as foreign minister,' recalls Mwaanga sardonically, 'because of Rowland. I could do the work better if I worked for Lonrho.'

Rowland's growing status in Africa reflected his unbounded confidence of success in Britain. Having shrugged off the residue of the boardroom row, Rowland had become a surviving member of London's maverick club of merchant adventurers. Like James Goldsmith, he had survived the crash and in 1975 could sweep up at bargain prices the assets of fallen heroes. Oliver Jessel's London & Australian General Explorations [LAGS] composed of anthracite, asbestos and gold mines in South Africa, an airline and other industries in other African countries, cost Rowland 25 pence per share against assets worth about 40 pence. He bought Lubok, Jim Slater's property company, and then lent Slater an initial £100,000 to establish Strongmead, a property business which helped Slater, a minus millionaire, to rebuild his fortunes. Lonrho bought Balfour Williams, a financing and confirming house, which would be stripped of its cash for further bids, and, most important of all, Lonrho bought the Volkswagen franchise, an investment which repaid itself within two years.

As in 1968, Rowland was enjoying a buying spree but with a particular difference. He was flush with money but there had been a price. To steer around the City's unwillingness to lend Lonrho funds and the company's inability to find a new merchant bank, between February and June Rowland had sold 28.1 million Lonrho shares to Gulf Fisheries of Kuwait for nearly £40 million, pricing Lonrho shares at 140p. The Arabs owned 28 per cent of Lonrho, while Rowland owned 16.5 per cent. The proportions were later altered to 22.3 per cent and 18 per cent. Initially, the two Sabah brothers and then, as an alternate, Khahil Osman became Lonrho directors. In the same year, a third Arab joined the Lonrho board.

During his travels in the Middle East, Rowland had met Roushdi Sobhi, an Egyptian lawyer. Sobhi introduced Rowland to Mohamed Al Fayed, an Egyptian operating out of Dubai, the Gulf state whose wealth had increased following the oil boom. At that stage, Rowland knew little about Fayed other than he had been married to the sister of Adnan Khashoggi, the Saudi businessman. In circumstances which were still unclear to Rowland, Fayed had separated from Khashoggi's family and established his own business as a middle man for British construction companies capitalising on the Gulf's new oil wealth and earning on his own admission between 15 and 20 per cent commission on each contract he secured.

Fayed had accumulated a 20 per cent stake in Costain, the British construction company which Rowland espoused as ideal for his tripartite vision. Rowland's first approach was in Fayed's Park Lane apartment. According to Fayed, 'He covered me with baloney about the triangular relationship between Arabs, Africans and Europeans and made me very excited.' In March 1975, Lonrho bought Fayed's stake in Costain in exchange for 5.5 million Lonrho shares plus £375,000 cash, a total value of £7 million. Fayed had bought the stake just before Christmas, from Slater Walker for £4.16 million. Buying a further four million Lonrho shares, Fayed became a Lonrho director and was appointed Lonrho's representative on Costain's board. According to Fayed, his relationship with Rowland was initially warm. Rowland never complained about the Egyptian but understood the nature of his new director. On a visit to Fayed's Park Lane penthouse with Udi Gecaga, Rowland cautioned the Kenyan not to drink anything. 'He's probably put something in it,' joked Rowland, glancing at a large album on Fayed's coffee table. It contained photographs of the most beautiful girls in striking poses. 'Very expensive,' Rowland muttered.

For the first time, Rowland was not Lonrho's major shareholder and, to his irritation, Tom Ferguson was wandering around Cheapside addressing the staff and urging that Lonrho should aggressively seek business in the Middle East. 'I used to own half of this company,' Rowland muttered to Basil West, the new finance director, 'and now I own less than the Arabs.'

West had arrived at Cheapside in May 1973, after the dismissal of the Eight. His introduction to Rowland was to watch the chief executive firing the secretaries who had worked for the Eight. 'He shouted "Get out" very roughly,' remembered the accountant recruited from the tranquillity of the Automobile Association by Peats.

As were his predecessors in the accounting department,

West was told by Butcher, 'We have no reporting organisation.' Butcher confessed to West that he would 'usually travel around Africa writing everything on a cigarette packet'. During 1975, West tried to improve his predecessors' accounting system which had established twenty-six reporting centres for Lonrho's operations in forty-one countries. West's efforts evoked a similar response to those of his predecessors.

Descending to his fifth-floor office and closing the door, Rowland said to West, 'We're not getting on. I'll give you £100,000 if you agree to go quietly.'

'I can't just leave,' replied West, a 'star' accountant from Oxford University. 'I gave various undertakings before coming.' West consulted John Cama, Rowland's lawyer. The following day, Rowland apologised and withdrew his offer. According to West, 'Cama had told Rowland it wasn't on.'

Rowland's response was to ignore West. On the sixth floor, he created an alternative accountancy department. Terry Robinson, a thirty-one-year-old accountant from Peterborough, was known as able, ambitious and a workaholic. The second accountant was Philip Tarsh, the son of a bankrupt Russian refugee who had managed Lonrho's Motor Mart in Kenya before returning to Britain with a considerable fortune. Tarsh had distinguished himself by negotiating the Volkswagen purchase which financed a substantial part of Lonrho's dividends for many years. Together they would sit at the Cheapside lunches and watch Rowland scathingly humiliate West.

Among those disenchanted by Rowland's style was Lonrho's new director, Mohamed Al Fayed. 'I thought I would contribute at board meetings but he wanted me to be a zombie. Everything had been arranged and agreed before we arrived. We were just expected to approve his figures and leave.' Among Fayed's early complaints was Rowland's use of Lonrho's money for his private ventures. 'I couldn't understand how he sent the Lonrho plane to collect someone's wife from Africa or pay for the education of African politicians' children. He was spending thousands on nothing. He told me it was all long-term investment which was necessary in Africa but I complained that I couldn't see any profits. He ignored me.' Rowland's confident resumption of his mercurial style coloured his attitude towards the DTI inspectors to whom, in May 1973, he had promised 'every possible co-operation'.

Allan Heyman QC, a Danish-born tennis enthusiast, and Sir William Slimmings, a senior accountant at Thomas McClintok, born in Fife, had established their offices near Finsbury Circus. Having seized Lonrho's files, they began an unusual investigation. Unlike previous DTI inquiries, there had been no suggestion of criminal fraud or a bankruptcy. On the contrary, Lonrho was thriving, prompting some to question whether the inspectors were seeking to unearth matters of particular public importance or were merely responding to the prime minister's spleen about Duncan Sandys's huge compensation payment which had erupted in the midst of delicate wage negotiations.

Ever since Robert Maxwell had launched a barrage of court cases to expose the intrinsic unfairness of a DTI inquiry, akin to a Star Chamber, those who were the subject of identical investigations complained about their helplessness. Denied access to any of the evidence upon which the inspectors based their questions, each witness could answer only the questions posed and not introduce issues which they considered relevant, although, in the secrecy of the hearings, witnesses could utter, unchallenged, any accusation. At the end, the inspectors exercised total discretion to decide what merited investigation and which areas should be ignored.

In Lonrho's case, not only Rowland's fate but also the fate and reputation of other directors depended upon the goodwill and fairness of the two inspectors. Responding to the inspectors' deliberate avoidance of confrontation, the witnesses occasionally exasperated the professionals' search for the truth. Yet overcoming bad memories, obfuscations and conflicting lies during their interviews, the inspectors were the first people to investigate properly the creation and management of Rowland's empire.

Fred Butcher demonstrated to the inspectors Rowland's magnetic grip upon employees. Swearing his oath on a Roman Catholic Bible, Butcher, the inspectors assumed, would be honest. Yet to their surprise, Butcher was initially unwilling to tell the truth, in order to protect Rowland. The board, testified Butcher, was told about the financing of Wankel but the evidence showed the contrary. Similarly, Butcher assumed the responsibility for Rowland's expenses, telling the inspectors that Rowland 'took no part in that discussion. . . He does not take a lot of interest in all these kind of things.' Again, the inspectors produced evidence showing the contrary. Twice during their questioning of Butcher, when his contradictions were exposed, the witness broke down in tears, evoking sympathy for his unswerving loyalty towards Rowland. In contrast, when Alan Ball was asked to explain his lies about the negotiations of Rowland's share options, he gazed silently at his accusers.

The examination of Sandys, who during the inquiry would become a peer, exposed a similarly faulty memory. 'I did not know all this was going to occur,' he asserted, referring to Butcher's 'unexpected' visit to discuss the compensation payments. Sandys denied that Butcher had written out their calculations during their discussion despite Butcher producing his notes to the inspectors. 'I think I borrowed one of Duncan Sandys's biros,' Butcher recalled, confirming that there was 'no beating about the bush' when Sandys demanded a higher price than Rowland anticipated. But when Sandys asserted that he initially consulted Edward Du Cann about the reasonableness of the £130,000 compensation, Du Cann testified, 'I knew nothing.'

Andrew Caldecott, the solicitor who resigned in 1971, explained the nature of a man who 'stormed out of the room' if a decision was not revised as he required: 'In practice you are dealing with a man who had completely converted what was a sleepy dozy company into something dynamic and who was a sort of tyrant and part madman to boot, but a brilliant one, and whose tyranny and madness had not become completely evident, and who was extremely persuasive, and who was extremely successful.'

Caldecott soon sensed that the inspectors were failing to understand Rowland: 'He keeps people on a string.' Heyman warmed to this explanation: 'Rowland's tactics,' asked the lawyer, 'were to make promises to people and sometimes fulfil them and make them dependent on him.' That, replied Caldecott, 'was absolutely cardinal policy, principle number one'. Caldecott also persuaded the inspectors that, even if Rowland denied knowledge of a decision, 'nothing could be done, without his either express or tacit consent.'

Naturally, the star witness was Rowland who, during their two-year inquiry, would be summoned about twenty times. The businessman's style was confident, provocative and initially friendly, anxious to convey to the two *ingénus* 'what this case is all about' and explain the 'fun' of transforming Lonrho into a multinational, multi-million pound conglomerate.

But whenever necessary, Rowland was also unforthcoming. Not once during those interviews did he ever admit that he might have been mistaken. When questioned about the original terms in 1961 for his entry into Lonrho, Rowland's memory was, the inspectors declared, 'poor'.

'Have you got any evidence?' Rowland asked the inspectors when challenged about a payment. 'If you tell me that is what happened on that particular day certainly I will confirm it,' he continued when the inspectors pressed for his version of events fourteen years earlier. 'It just goes to show,' concluded Rowland, 'that my memory is so bad.'

When questioned about the original option agreement, Rowland turned the tables, 'I would not have been directly involved, unless you have got documents or letters from me to the contrary.' Of course, as Rowland knew, the inspectors lacked any documents on that issue but they would conclude, 'We do not accept that Mr Rowland had as little to do with the matter as he makes out.'

Cross-examined about the secrecy and erroneous information which he gave the board about the Wankel engine, Rowland explained, 'I always assumed everything, my right to do as I pleased. . . I felt the whole show belonged to me.' Concerning the circular to shareholders on 8 October 1971 which described Rowland's acquisition of the patents as having 'the prior approval of the entire board', the inspectors decided that the board was 'deliberately misled by Mr Rowland' and the circular was 'improper and calculated to mislead'.

Few issues produced more suggestions of lies than the consultancy and compensations arrangement with Sandys. Rowland told the inspectors that he believed that he had told Percy and Elliott about the details 'at the end of 1971'. In contradiction, both insisted that they first heard in March 1972 and the inspectors reported, 'we accept their evidence'.

Nonchalantly, Rowland pleaded stupidity and blamed his unqualified subordinate: 'I am not a technician like Fred Butcher and it took a technician like Fred Butcher to negotiate it. . . The £130,000 is a complete blank. I did not work it out. I could not work it out. I do not know how we got to the £130,000.' But Rowland did concede that he was satisfied with the deal: 'I thought at the time this was super . . . very good for the company.' The inspectors would judge Rowland's account as 'extraordinary' and that Rowland was jointly responsible for a 'policy of concealment'. Rowland, they concluded, showed a willingness 'to withhold information from or to mislead the Board or shareholders which has been more than casual'.

Another critical topic was Rhodesia and Lonrho's observance of sanctions. The directors, especially Percy, were quite candid that the law had been flouted. Rowland, explained Percy, was a 'frequent visitor to Rhodesia' and there was constant telephone and telex contact with Kruger. The best Caldecott could say was that 'people turned a blind eye' to sanctions breaking.

But in the manner which characterised Rowland's attitude towards both the inquiry and his adversaries, Rowland denied outright any knowledge or control over Lonrho's activities in Rhodesia. Regarding the use of the Edmundian copper mine he said, 'I was not involved,' and added, 'I doubt very much whether any of the directors knew in London.' Rowland's profession of ignorance was not believed. The inspectors concluded that Rowland and the directors, contrary to the law, were in 'effective control' of Lonrho's Rhodesian operations.

The Shamrocke mine and its tripartite ownership aroused interest firstly because it involved breaking sanctions; secondly, because of a secret tax avoidance scheme via Canada and Switzerland between Rowland, Ball and Ogilvy; and thirdly because it seemed to give Rowland profits at Lonrho's expense.

Repeatedly, the inspectors asked the trio to clarify their deal. 'Mr Rowland,' they reported, 'was unable to explain the reasons for the . . . transactions and he referred us to Mr Butcher.' Later, the inspectors discovered that 'Mr Butcher was . . . unable to explain.' After some prevarication, Ball thought his share of the mine was not a gift but 'a loan'. Ogilvy, the inspectors discovered, was more forthcoming. Having explained the secret deal as a 'capital distribution' rather than a bribe, Ogilvy revealed Rowland's 'tirade' when he discovered in May 1973 that Ogilvy was no longer an unquestioning supporter: 'He said that he felt that I had behaved quite abominably and if it was the last thing he was going to do he was going to crucify me.'

When the inspectors re-examined Rowland and asked why he gave £120,000 to Ball and £60,000 to Ogilvy, Rowland uttered an incomprehensible reply and contrived humility: 'But it is so simple Mr Heyman, your mind is so clear, much clearer than mine.' Pressed further, he was not more forthcoming: 'My answer to that is: if I did, they deserved it and if I did not, it is just too bad.' That, replied Heyman, was 'no answer'. Rowland was blunt: 'It is my business. That is my answer.' Later, when asked whether the money was a gift, Rowland exclaimed, 'I am not Father Christmas; it is utter madness.' The inspectors would comment, 'Mr Rowland spoke to us at great length on this matter . . . without enabling us to understand any more about the transactions.' They would also conclude, 'We find it extraordinary that sums of this magnitude could be paid by Mr Rowland to Mr Ball and Mr Ogilvy without any of them knowing precisely what the payments represented.'

To Rowland, the inspectors were simply ignorant about business, naive about Africa and prissy about the task of winning friends and contracts. He believed that it was perfectly sensible to buy Hedsor Wharf to entertain African leaders and their entourages 'especially at weekends when most of them were sitting in hotel rooms or were at a loose end'. Similarly, he defended the purchase of the flats for directors as 'normal'.

Yet on the question of bribes, the inspectors showed themselves to be realists. Percy had provided the evidence of Lonrho's systematic payments to African leaders and Rowland was asked to provide his account from the British Linen Bank. Shocked by the inspectors' demand, Rowland prevaricated but then reluctantly complied.

After lengthy discussion, Rowland agreed that £836,499 were bribes and only under threat of court orders did he reveal the names of the recipients. The cheques, Rowland explained, although written against his own personal account to create a sense of obligation upon the individual African, were entirely for Lonrho's benefit.

After seeing the list of names, the inspectors understood Rowland's reticence. Famous African presidents, ministers and politicians featured prominently. The inspectors consulted the Foreign Office who advised that exposure would embarrass Britain's foreign relations. The civil servants urged that a veil be drawn over the bribes and would persuade the inspectors to disguise the issue under the heading 'special payments' made 'outside the UK'.

But Whitehall did not intervene to protect Angus Ogilvy, which was somewhat surprising considering the previous representations to protect the Palace. Ogilvy, by most accounts, was charming, outwardly honest and, on the best interpretation, naive. The test of Ogilvy's culpability during the inspectors' investigation was Ogilvy's knowledge about the development of the Shamrocke mine. Inevitably, their conclusions would be coloured by Rowland's explanations. On all the other issues, Rowland invariably had given versions of the same incident contradicting other witnesses, or had prevaricated and refused to tell any version. Whether he was deliberately lying was hard to fathom. But he displayed total candour about the extent of Ogilvy's knowledge about Shamrocke, for example: 'Everything. There was not a single thing that he did not know.' Ogilvy's protestations of ignorance, loudly derided by Rowland, did not convince the inspectors.

Again influenced by Rowland, the inspectors were unsympathetic towards Smallpeice. Rowland's exposure of the deputy chairman's own foreign earnings and his failure to master Lonrho's African activities, convinced the inspectors to reflect a common sentiment from both sides of the dispute that the tone of Smallpeice's threatening warnings to Sandys created 'an unnecessary degree of resentment', an injudicious disincentive to future whistleblowers.

Always forthcoming and never defensive, Rowland's reputation for getting in his retaliation first had paid dividends against Ogilvy and Smallpeice. But his appearance before the inspectors on 25 April 1975 was a watershed. Sensing that he would be criticised and irritated by the inspectors' interest in Lonrho's breach of sanctions, he feared that his company would be branded as a sanctions buster and a scapegoat for government failures.

By then it was common knowledge, according to Rowland, that many of Britain's leading manufacturers, the banks and insurance companies were committing the same crime. British Leyland was assembling Land Rovers in Umtali for the Rhodesian army; British Airways was selling tickets in Salisbury's Baker Avenue; Tate & Lyle had increased sales in Rhodesia; and Rowland had dispatched to the DTI a copy of an internal letter by Lucas showing their pricing arrangements in Rhodesia. Even under Val Duncan's supervision, Rio Tinto's operations in Rhodesia had expanded, and Duncan, far from being criticised, had been knighted and embraced by the Foreign Office as an adviser and by the Bank of England as a director.

Rowland began searching for any flaw in the proceedings which could be detonated to embarrass the inspectors. The two professionals, Rowland knew, intent on exposing Lonrho's Rhodesian operations, had sought evidence from both MI6 and BOSS, the South African intelligence agency. Heyman, he discovered, had been spurned during a visit to BOSS headquarters in Pretoria; while Heyman would deny receiving help from British intelligence.

The flaw which Rowland seized on was an alleged omission in the transcripts of a reference by Heyman about his visit to BOSS. What else, speculated Rowland in a trenchant letter, were the inspectors falsifying?

Calculatedly, Rowland's outburst began gently. After explaining why he sued the Eight in court – 'because I had nothing to be ashamed of' – Rowland accused the inspectors of wanting to 'kill' Lonrho. He, however, was the company's protector:

'Anybody who wants to kill that company has got to have a sub-machine gun, mortars, guns, all sorts of ammunition, because I'm going to protect it to the bitter end. Believe me, Mr Heyman, in me you have got somebody you have got to fight when it comes to Lonrho.'

Heyman was not shaken. Instead he smiled. Rowland's threats were uttered in a tone far removed from threatening an assault. 'You are really treating me,' said Heyman in return, 'as if I am some kind of hired assassin who is out to kill the company. You are threatening to use mortars and God knows what. I think you misunderstand the situation wholly.'

'No, I do not think I do,' responded Rowland unmoved.

The inspectors completed their report in October 1975 and, as required under the new regulations, submitted their criticisms to Lonrho for their comment. Unused to objective, professional criticism, Rowland was indignant that his version was not accepted, and, even worse, that he was accused of lying. Nothing new, he argued, which had not been investigated within four months by Peats, had been examined over two and a half years by the inspectors and yet the conclusions were dramatically different.

To reinforce his retaliation and, like other controversial businessmen, convinced that he was the victim of unjust persecution, Rowland embarked upon a succession of self-justifying letters to his lawyer, John Cama, alleging a widespread conspiracy and accusing his detractors of dishonesty. 'I have never abused my position as principal shareholder and executive,' he claimed, denying any 'benefit . . . at all' from the whole exercise involving Yeoman to execute his share options in 1966.

Rowland also wrote letters to both Cama and the inspectors impugning the honesty of other directors. Wilkinson was accused of duplicity on the grounds that he offered to withdraw his complaint about the Wankel deal 'motivated as it was', wrote Rowland, 'by a thwarted ambition and envy', if he could replace Percy. Wilkinson denied that accusation.

Ogilvy was accused by Rowland, in a secret letter to the inspectors, of serious financial impecuniosity prompted by threats of blackmail to his family. Ogilvy, who only discovered the letter's existence ten years later, was horrified that the inspectors might have been influenced by such poison.

To dispel the notion that he was either a pariah or an outsider, Rowland was grabbing at crumbs to disparage any criticism. Anticipating the inspectors' condemnation of Lonrho's trade with Rhodesia, Rowland published a telex, sent by Lonrho on 24 February to Nicholas Kruger in Salisbury. The telex conveyed a message to Joshua Nkomo from James Callaghan, the foreign secretary. Greenhill, telexed Rowland, would be visiting Ian Smith in Salisbury and would be pleased to see Nkomo. Kruger was asked to make the arrangements. To Rowland, the message revealed that the government, and especially Greenhill, was out of touch with the nationalists and relied upon Lonrho for communications. Publication of that message, Rowland hoped, would expose the government's incompetence and hypocrisy for condemning Lonrho's activities in Rhodesia. 'Even as I write,' he told Cama, 'I am handling further Greenhill mission messages.' According to the government, that was incorrect but, as anticipated, publication caused embarrassment.

That pugnacious counter-attack mirrored Rowland's insouciant style of managing Lonrho even during the inquiry, making the inspectors' work seem rather irrelevant.

By September 1974, having used Lonrho's and his own money interchangeably, Rowland owed the company £306,637. Technically, he had obtained approval from Lonrho's auditors, Fuller Jenks, a minor partnership whose income was heavily dependent upon the Lonrho account, for an improper exercise. They had agreed that Lonrho's dividends, which were payable to Shepton Estates in Rhodesia but blocked by sanctions, could be used to offset the money which Rowland had borrowed from Lonrho. Once Lonrho's activities were scrutinised, that offset was declared unsustainable.

On 12 February 1975, Lonrho's Finance Committee met to consider Rowland's debt to the company. Rowland, who had not kept proper accounts, was asked to submit expenses which everyone, including the accountants, agreed, to please their client, would equal the debt. The principal expense was Hedsor Wharf.

Butcher was responsible for settling Rowland's claim. Encouraged by Sandys to 'clear it all up', Butcher, in a nonchalant conversation, asked Rowland, 'How much have you spent on the house and furnishings?'

'Oh, £400,000–£500,000,' replied Rowland, pleased to delegate the problem.

Butcher arbitrarily decided upon £200,000 for the furnishings, an odd figure because the contents were insured for just £11,000.

Soon after that meeting, Butcher submitted that over seven years, between 1967 and 1974, Rowland's expenses totalled £307,471 – conveniently matching the amount which he owed Lonrho. The bulk of Rowland's claim was £294,000 for the running of Hedsor Wharf and £13,000 for entertaining. At a five-minute board meeting, Sandys, Ball and Butcher approved Rowland's claim. 'Nobody asked any questions,' recalled Butcher.

Rowland's accounts, however, suffered a fundamental flaw. Rowland had claimed for furniture, fittings and entertainment between 1967 and 1971, yet Hedsor Wharf was only bought in 1968 and occupied in September 1972. Rowland's claim for Hedsor Wharf was for furnishings and entertainment during three years when the house was either not yet purchased or was a building site. As Butcher would later admit, the claim was 'not necessarily correct, but it is a very good stab'. Slimmings' questioning of Butcher reduced the Lonrho director to tears. 'It was a Star Chamber inquiry,' recalls Basil West, Lonrho's finance director. 'Slimmings wanted to make trouble. He kept on talking about things I didn't understand. I was washed out.'

Butler's position and relationship with Rowland had become noticeably confused. Initially, the auditor told Butcher that a committee of the directors should vet Rowland's expenses. Yet in answer to the inspectors, Butler denied that the auditors had any role in the detailed vetting of Rowland's claim. The accountant argued that the directors had total sovereignty to decide whether expenses were justifiable and that auditors were powerless to demand proof of expenditure. Slimmings was outraged: 'We have this passing of responsibility,' complained the inspector. 'We are all left in a complete vacuum, are we not?'

Butler was unmoved. Heyman pressed Butler: 'It would not have taken even an uneducated mind like my own in accountancy matters to discover the whole thing really was not genuine.' Again, Butler was unimpressed. Checking the details of those accounts, he believed, was not an auditor's responsibility. His disdain for the inspectors' opinions was undisguised.

With the 1974 accounts complete, the Lonrho directors had to agree a statement for the annual report to describe the settlement of Rowland's debts. Robert Wright QC wanted the statement, in accordance with the Companies Acts, to be a straightforward admission of fault. With some emotion, Sandys, keen to avoid any mention, disagreed. Sandys was overruled. Rowland's debts were to be mentioned with the caveat that the practice would 'cease'. Wright's approved version was handed to Rowland on Friday 14 February. On Sunday morning, Rowland telephoned the lawyer at home. Rowland wanted to remove those words which were incriminating. Initially, Wright resisted but eventually agreed to a small change.

On Monday morning, Basil West arrived at Cheapside to find Rowland agitatedly complaining that he was, 'being treated as a schoolboy'. Rowland thrust Wright's draft at West with the incriminating sentences – three lines at the bottom of the page – crossed out. 'I have spoken to Wright,' said Rowland, 'These are the words which will go in.' West complied.

The 1974 report was published during the inquiry. To the inspectors' anger, the section about Rowland's expenses distorted the commission of a criminal offence. Summoned to the inspectors, Rowland insisted that Wright agreed to the version which appeared. For his part, Wright protested that his advice was ignored and contradicted by stealth.

After the inspectors complained, Rowland was asked to submit a new claim for expenses. It was an exercise in further contempt for the inspectors. Supported by Sandys, Du Cann and his appreciative directors, Rowland compensated for the reduced expenses for Hedsor Wharf by submitting a £57,000 payment to Stefan Klein. Earlier, Rowland had told the two inspectors that

Klein was not employed by Lonrho. The inspectors' surprise was met by Du Cann's smooth lack of concern. 'He [Rowland] is one of the most remarkable men I have ever met. It seems to me that if one goes on making life difficult for him – I don't see why he should go on living in this country at all.' Rowland, suggested Du Cann, 'lived his business. He would never fiddle his expenses. Look at his achievements.' The inspectors, he thought, displayed a lack of sympathy for a dedicated businessman. Butler had even recruited Sir George Bolton, a former deputy governor of the Bank of England, to become a Lonrho director and he, added Du Cann, approved the expenses. The inspectors were effectively snubbed. Having completed the correct legal procedures, the Lonrho directors showed they were answerable to the shareholders, not to regulators.

It fell to Du Cann, who believed that Rowland had been 'generous' in not claiming his proper expenses, to spend days ploughing through each of Rowland's receipts to check the claim: 'Honestly, you know,' Du Cann told the inspectors, 'you know truly – one makes the best judgment one can. I begin to wonder. . . You know. . . Can I share a reflection with you? I honestly begin to wonder why anybody should be a director of a company at all.'

The inspectors were unimpressed: 'We find it totally extraordinary . . . that the matters should have occurred whilst our enquiry was in progress' and that criticism extended to the auditors, lawyers and directors who had simply ignored the inspectors' concern about 'Rowland's unlawful accounts'. Rowland had asserted his total control over the company despite the investigation. His victory over the Establishment was total.

In their final report, the inspectors criticised Rowland's deliberate deception and concealment of information although they conceded that he believed he was acting in Lonrho's interests. Similar criticisms were directed at both Ball and Ogilvy. Both were accused of 'negligence'. The denial by Ogilvy of any knowledge about Lonrho's sanctions breaking was dismissed as untrue. Yet the inspectors suggested no reprimands for any of the directors, nor praise for the Eight for exposing the transgressions.

The only praise, paradoxically, was for Rowland: 'It would be wrong to conclude our report without acknowledging Mr Rowland's achievements. Lonrho as it is today is very largely Mr Rowland's creation. He is a man who has vision, negotiating ability, determination and personality in unusual measure coupled with unbounded energy to apply his talents. . . We believe that Mr Rowland has a great deal to offer Lonrho and its shareholders but his achievements will be all the greater if he will allow his enthusiasms to operate within the ordinary processes of company management.'

Queried about the paradox, they explained that theirs was a report to be handed to Ronald Cooper at the Department of Trade. While identifying Rowland's shortcomings for the government, it was also their duty to acknowledge Rowland's achievements. If he ignored their strictures, that was the nature of the man.

In the few weeks before the report's publication, Rowland strove to find some evidence whose potential publication would threaten to embarrass the government and therefore might persuade the DTI to reconsider publication. His ruse was the publication of a 200-page bound volume of his letters addressed to lawyers, civil servants and politicians during and just after the inspectors' investigation. Significantly, he did not publish their replies.

The letters, described by Rowland as 'often bitter, sometimes sarcastic, sometimes not,' were dispatched to H. C. Gill, a lowly official at the DTI's Companies Division. 'I felt annoyed when I wrote them,' wrote Rowland, 'and with good reason, but I was accurate.' The common theme in the letters was that the report, based on unreliable evidence, inaccuracies, every fragment of nastiness and prejudiced personal opinions heard in secret, 'is so larded with biased language and loaded remarks that it is impossible for me to stomach'.

Why were the inspectors, he queried, spending so much time in determining who paid for the curtains in Hedsor Wharf but ignoring Lonrho's annual expenditure of £750,000 on the Grumman II jet which he had bought in November 1974. 'I thought [Sir William] would pounce on this juicy bone in case

I had spent an overnight stop in Nice.' The two men, wailed Rowland, 'clearly lacked any understanding of the business world and of life within a billion pound corporation.'

In a reflection of Rowland's egocentric fury that the inspectors could accept any version other than his own, he vented his spleen about their 'amazing picture of Angus as helpless in my magnetic clutches'. These were the 'weedy afterthoughts' of the Eight and should have been ignored. Their scenario, he wrote, suggested that he had 'bought the Board' and acted in a conspiracy with a small group of directors. 'Angus, at the one time in 12 years when I personally needed his support, made himself scarce. If the inspectors are right in saying that I purchased him, then I believe that I may well have a case against him under the Sale of Goods Act 1893.'

The inspectors signed their completed report on 1 March 1976. Rowland still hoped to prevent publication. His weapon was a personal, handwritten letter penned by Ogilvy at Christmas 1975: 'My dear Tiny, Your letter was the nicest Christmas present I could have received and one which I won't forget. Friendship is not a thing that withers away overnight – certainly not as deep a friendship as we have had. If I were to have one wish for the New Year – it would be that this blasted business is over very soon and then we can all meet again and let's hope laugh! Do please give our love to Josie. Meantime a very very happy Christmas to you both, Yours ever, Angus.'

In the belief that he might cause a revision of the inspectors' criticism of his relationship with Ogilvy or even suppress the report's publication to protect Ogilvy and the Palace, Rowland sent a copy of the letter on 2 April 1976 to the DTI, 'I think,' he wrote, 'this makes a mockery of his pretence . . . that all his actions were attributable to his fear of "crucifixion" by me.' It did not serve that purpose. Instead it proved precisely what Rowland denied. Namely, the corollary of Rowland's feted generosity and loyalty was the ruthless exploitation even of private correspond-ence, which he had initiated, to further his argument. The publication of Ogilvy's letter reflected upon Rowland's rather than Ogilvy's character. Ogilvy, disliking rows and enemies, had forsaken the possibility of repairing his shattered City career but wanted to part on good terms. He was horrified when he saw how Rowland treated an act of friendship.

Three days later, on 5 April, Rowland fired another shot. On this occasion, he threatened the government that if the DTI's accusations of Lonrho's sanctions busting were exposed, then he would retaliate by describing how other British manufacturers, the oil companies and banks, supplied Rhodesia.

The situation in Rhodesia had changed dramatically. In March 1976, the government of newly independent Mozambique had closed the border, cutting off the oil supply route and providing another haven for Rhodesia's nationalist fighters. Lonrho's pipeline could only reopen after the fall of the Smith regime, which remained unpredictable. Within the Foreign Office, ministers and officials who knew about BP's and Shell's fictitious 'swap' arrangements, were quite prepared to repeat the untrue denials that the British oil companies were knowingly breaking sanctions.

Rowland decided to challenge the hypocrisy. He and Lonrho, he rationalised, had suffered losses by observing the law while the British government had knowingly tolerated those breaches. 'It is clear to everyone in Africa,' he wrote to the DTI, 'that British sanctions are and always have been meaningless formulae.' Simultaneously, news reports appeared, inspired by Lonrho, that the Foreign Office was urging the DTI to suppress the report to avoid embarrassing disclosures. In the House of Commons, Du Cann asked the government why Ken Flower, the head of Rhodesia's Central Intelligence Organisation, was allowed unrestricted entry into Britain. It was the opening salvo of Rowland's unceasing public war with Whitehall and Westminster, revealing that Rowland's understanding was not nearly as percipient as his grasp of African dictatorship. His war continued with increasing ferocity.

But contrary to Rowland's claim that the Foreign Office were seeking to suppress the report, the only lobby to prevent its publication on the grounds of national interest was Rowland himself. The trade minister, Edmund Dell, was unimpressed. Although he had been advised that, according to the inspectors, some of Lonrho's directors were subjects for criminal investigation and publication would be prejudicial to an investigation and trial, he recalls that, 'It was the sort of report which was politically impossible to withhold.'

With publication imminent and aware that he was unlikely to gain an equal chance on publication day to rebut the inspectors' criticism, Rowland masterminded an astute ploy to disarm his critics. Du Cann, as Lonrho's spokesman, would 'release' the company's criticisms about the report before its publication. A forty-four-page 'memorandum' from Lonrho and 200 pages of Rowland's letters would be distributed. A few journalists, trusted to read back their stories to Rowland before submission to their editors, would be allowed discreet access to the 'publicity shy' chief executive in his Cheapside office.

As a final gambit, Lonrho applied to buy Brentford Nylons, an employer of 1600 people, which in June had declared itself bankrupt. Consistent with the government's policy to spend public money to save jobs, the unions had sought assistance from the Department of Trade and Industry. To appear responsible and respectable, Lonrho applied through David Whitehead, its textile manufacturer, to save Brentford Nylons on condition that the Labour government advanced an interest-free loan. Since there were no other bids, the government's dilemma was compounded. Only a deal with Lonrho could avert the factory's closure. For £2 million Lonrho bought £5 million of assets, including a huge shed packed with redundant nylon looms. The political advantages for Rowland outweighed the fact that nylon was an unfashionable material. Negotiations began just as Edmund Dell, the minister of trade, was finalising arrangements for the report's publication.

The DTI report, Rowland was told, was to be published on 7 July. On the day before, while journalists were allowed to read embargoed copies of the inspectors' findings, Rowland released the 'sanctions' letter to the press which included details of how BP's and Shell's oil was transported by rail into Rhodesia, and summoned a press conference chaired by Du Cann.

The following morning's newspapers used Du Cann's vocabulary attacking the inspectors. 'Naive', 'sterile', 'no evidence of fraud', 'no suggestion of bribes', and 'reporting on matters which were of historic interest' complemented emollient headlines. 'Genius of Lonrho,' in the *Scotsman*; 'Tiny still one of the brightest stars in business' in the *Daily Telegraph*; and, 'The continuing rise of Tiny's empire' in the *Guardian* reflected Rowland's skilful presentation to the media. The myths, carefully contrived by Rowland himself – 'a mixture of James Bond, Cecil Rhodes and General Gordon' in the *Scotsman* – sat well with accounts which repeated his claims about the inspectors falsifying the transcripts, his victimisation because he opposed Ian Smith, and the alleged embarrassment of the Foreign Office because of his sanctions revelations.

As intended, his allegations were discomfiting for those companies named. 'This is absolute rubbish. There is no truth in it. Our links with Rhodesia ended with UDI,' a BP spokesman asserted. 'All our plants were taken over by the government. Mr Rowland's claims are nonsense.' A Foreign Office spokesman told newspapers, 'After investigation at the highest level we are completely confident that there is nothing in any of the allegations.' Senior Foreign Office officials began preparing a statement for the United Nations which concluded that on the basis of 'assurances given by Shell and BP' that there was 'no evidence of sanctions breaking by any British companies or individuals'. Rowland's bid to embarrass the government had failed.

There was however one redeeming report. The government announced that Lonrho had just been awarded a £4.9 million interest free loan by the Labour government towards the £9.8 million cost of taking over Brentford Nylons. Clearly the criticism had been discounted. 'This is political madness,' commented Arthur Latham, a left-wing Labour member of parliament, amid an outburst of Labour demands that the Lonrho directors should be jailed in Brixton, and the revelation by Brian Sedgemore that Rowland had telephoned his home and uttered threats to his wife. Dell's embarrassment titillated Rowland.

The operation to deflect the criticism did not please the Kuwaitis whose hope for a discreet investment had proved unrealistic. Both Sheikh Nasser and Tom Ferguson had been cautioned by Mohamed Al Fayed that Rowland was an unsuitable partner. The Egyptian had decided to leave Lonrho as the evidence mounted that Rowland regarded the company as his private fiefdom. 'I was afraid that my money would disappear,' complained Fayed. Rowland's personal expenses were costing the company millions and the income especially from Africa was, he believed, non-existent: 'I had entered a whorehouse and I wanted to get out.' Rowland agreed to a divorce. Fayed sold his Lonrho shares to Sheikh Nasser and bought back his stake in Costain.

To Rowland's irritation, the Kuwaitis now owned about 26 per cent of Lonrho. In retaliation and to cause their discomfort, Rowland embarked upon a sudden burst of investment in property, especially in co-operation with London & Westcliffe, managed by Harry Landy of the Israel-British bank. Rowland was attracted to Landy, a seedy character, on the principle that 'there's brass with muck'. London & Westcliffe proved profitable but the Israeli connection aroused the Kuwaitis' suspicions since there were also reliable reports that Rowland had made contact with David Kimche, the former deputy chief of Mossad, the Israeli intelligence agency, to aid Lonrho's activities in Zaïre.

To the Arabs, Rowland's intentions were obvious. With the worst over, he was set upon resuming his ambition to match RTZ and Anglo American. His criteria, they believed, were not profits but gross turnover. Lonrho, in 1975 a £600 million corporation with pre-tax profits of £63 million, had grown in 1976's published accounts to a £1 billion company with pre-tax profits of £93 million. But Ferguson, whose attempts to discuss strategy with Rowland were unsuccessful, suspected that the growth was the product of accountancy and not substance. 'It's hard to have a dialogue with him if he doesn't want one,' he commented after failing to discuss Lonrho's operational management with Rowland. 'He only wants to talk about the next deal.'

More pertinently, Rowland avoided all discussion about making Lonrho more acceptable to the City. Ferguson's nominees as non-executive directors were brushed aside. At board meetings, Rowland's decisions were rubberstamped. As Basil West, the financial director, discovered in his increasing isolation, the style was similar to that which had prompted the 1973 row.

'Rowland was going round the City to get financing without me,' he complains.

West's second complaint was Rowland's unrestrained bid for growth, including the demand that Lonrho's minority investments should be consolidated in the company's accounts to create 'a $3 billion' corporation. 'Peats agreed,' says West, 'but I believed that it contravened the rules of the Institute of Chartered Accountants and the idea was dropped.' West blames a 'lapse of standards' which followed a dinner for Rowland hosted by Leach and Butler. All Lonrho's remaining audits conducted by Deloittes were transferred to Peats.

For Rowland to succeed in the wake of the 1973 débâcle, required his recognition that dealing in London was different from in Africa. To neutralise Heath's epithet, as Ferguson and the Kuwaitis required, Rowland needed to make his peace with the City, the Conservative Party and the civil service. The traditional panacea would be to issue invitations to bankers, brokers and analysts to visit Cheapside for soothing reassurance. The antidote to the past antagonism with civil servants required charmed conversations with permanent secretaries. Reconciliation with the Conservative Party, which following Heath's disgrace was attainable, could be initiated by contributions to the Party's funds. But in each case, Rowland refrained from taking the initiative which would have rendered him acceptable.

That refusal irritated Ferguson and his Kuwaiti employers. In turn, Rowland was contemptuous of their criticism. He neither appreciated the existence of a stake in Lonrho larger than his own, nor did he consider the Arabs to be any different from the Africans, who were unsophisticated about business and inexperienced in negotiations. Both, he believed, could be charmed, flattered and, when necessary, ignored.

In April 1976, Maurice Hynett, Rowland's implant into Nigeria to invigorate John Holt, had transferred to Jordan en route to establish Lonrho Gulf, a new corporation with Sheikh Nasser as chairman and Rowland as deputy. On several occasions, Hynett and Rowland had celebrated in 'great jubilation' as they flew from Kuwait in the new Grumman jet convinced that Lonrho's profitable partnership was solid. But it suddenly soured. 'I was told by Ferguson that I wasn't welcome in Kuwait,' recalls Hynett. 'I was stuck in Cyprus and Tiny never spoke to me again. I'd done nothing but I was yesterday's man, labelled with the Kuwaiti failure.'

The discord began following a catalogue of setbacks at the Kenana sugar factory in Sudan, Rowland's first major 'greenfield' project, which he himself conceived. The scheme to build the world's biggest sugar complexes was by summer 1976 arousing hostility. Plagued by problems of completing a sophisticated development amid arid poverty, costs had nearly doubled, completion was delayed and more money was needed. Lonrho, criticised by the Kuwaitis for presenting a 'colonial concept', bore the blame for bad management. Rapidly, Lonrho's stake in Kenana was reduced from 12 per cent to 5.5 per cent, its management contract was terminated and finally its stake was further reduced to 3.36 per cent.

Rowland also had other grounds to be irritated by the Kuwaitis. The Sabah brothers, living in style at the Intercontinental and Claridges, were trading Lonrho shares. During the previous months a Palestinian employee was selling short the company from which they were obtaining price sensitive information. Rowland had misjudged his relationship with Arabs but failed to adequately analyse the cause.

Rowland, it appeared to Ferguson, did not understand that Arabs were consummate negotiators and dealers. Instead, he had judged the Sabah family as gullible because, persuaded by his charm, they had bought Lonrho shares and invested in Kenana. The Kuwaitis would complain of their irritation that Lonrho had failed to develop their collaboration. In reply, Rowland would complain about interference, a sharp contradiction to his 1975 report to shareholders which praised Lonrho's 'local knowledge and experience' in the Gulf. At the climax of their dispute, the two Kuwaiti-nominated directors resigned from the Lonrho board. Ferguson's intention was to find allies to mount a takeover bid for Lonrho. 'Tiny didn't understand that Arabs were different than Africans,' confirms Hynett.

Rowland was unconcerned by the Arabs' resignation. Their

purpose, to support Lonrho's finances in the wake of the 1973 row, had been served. Their departure was akin to the removal of an irritant, an obstacle to Rowland's political ambitions in Europe and Africa.

As Lonrho's divorce from the Kuwaitis materialised, Rowland resumed his hectic pace, crisscrossing Africa with Vernon Mwaanga, Zambia's former foreign minister. The Zambian had replaced Gil Olympio as Rowland's 'black ambassador'. A bitter dispute between Olympio and Rowland about commissions on contracts had culminated in a law suit in Paris. It was settled quietly in Olympio's favour. His row with Graham Beck over the Shamrocke mine was also settled as a victory for the South African. Rowland had argued with Stefan Klein as well after refusing to pay the agreed commission on the Wankel engine which had not proven to be the anticipated profit machine. 'You know, Tiny, you're oversexed,' Klein quipped after another disagreement about payments. Rowland was startled. Sex, as his friends knew, did not feature among Rowland's priorities. 'You like screwing people,' laughed Klein.

Mwaanga saw that, for Rowland, Africa was not just a place of work but also something to be 'screwed'. Selflessly, driving himself harder, often shivering from malaria, he hopped around the continent to expand Lonrho's sugar and agricultural empire, but the Zambian noticed a disturbing pattern. Lonrho was a trader and not a company which invested hard currency into African countries. Whether it was importing machinery and motors or producing minerals and foods, all the money invested locally was paid in worthless local currencies. Even loans were raised locally, invariably through the Standard & Chartered bank to whom Rowland had promised first refusal. Yet a percentage of the profits were remitted to Britain in hard currency. For struggling African countries, Mwaanga realised, Lonrho provided few benefits. 'Lonrho never put money in,' complained Mwaanga, 'it just took money out. But of course Tiny wants history to record that he made a big contribution to Africa's development.'

'These African leaders,' Rowland quipped to Mwaanga as they flew in the Gulfstream across the continent, 'are so corrupt that there's not a single one of them whom I could not buy.' The video film was stopped as Rowland continued speaking across the aisle: 'I pay for their wives, I pay for their cars, I pay for their hotels and they still don't do what I want.' As the rage subsided, the video was switched on. 'Don't tell anyone what I've said,' sighed Rowland. Back in London, Rowland revealed a contrasting policy to Basil West. 'Tiny,' says West, 'didn't want to have anything to do with bribes. He wanted to leave it all to local people to handle. We had to do it. It was the only way to get business done quickly.' But there was a new reality in Rowland's business approach in 1976 which he confessed to West: 'We'll have to get out of Africa and into hard currencies.'

Rowland's new strategy however was undermined by his own anger towards the British government, still successfully concealing the source of Rhodesia's oil. To describe Rowland as tormented about the criticism of himself and Lonrho would not understate his emotions. Investigated, judged, condemned and spurned by that single class which permeated Whitehall, Westminster and the City, Rowland's instinctive reaction was to seek further revenge. As in business, his approach was subtle. Unlike Maxwell whose blunderbuss against the DTI inspectors had proved counter-productive, Rowland understood the vulnerability of the British to the fatal understatement. His weapon was again the government's connivance in the illegal supply of oil to Rhodesia.

As the guerrilla war in Rhodesia intensified from bases in Mozambique and Zambia, the illegal regime's survival depended entirely upon the oil companies' supplies through South Africa. In Rowland's view, behind those thick granite edifices in Whitehall sat officials who, having passed a moral judgment upon him, deliberately tolerated the oil companies committing similar crimes in Africa. Protected from objective criticism by their arrogance and ignorance, their personal achievements, he believed, were minimal. Indeed, in Africa, their record was mendacious. During his trips around Africa, Lonrho's chief executive delighted in summoning British ambassadors to his hotel suite. Knowing that Rowland's access to heads of state was measurably better than their own, those British diplomats fortunate to receive the summons usually attended to receive a briefing about that nation's affairs. Yet officially, they still spurned his advice.

On 7 January 1977, Rowland sent Edmund Dell, the secretary of state for trade, a twenty-six-page letter. Tempered by wit and deft sarcasm and supported by incriminating documents, Rowland chronicled in extraordinary detail how BP and Shell had arranged to supply oil to Rhodesia, motivated by 'a fatal disease – greed'. Just as in his letter the previous year, the detail he provided about the monthly oil deliveries to Rhodesia was so precise, supplied by Jardim and Lonrho employees in Salisbury, that Dell was advised that Rowland had relied upon sources with access to Rhodesian government records.

The issue, Rowland explained, was why Lonrho had to bear the losses caused by the closure of the pipeline. The government's payments of £54,000 per month in compensation to Lonrho had ceased after six months. Rowland inquired why the inspectors, appointed to investigate Lonrho, had omitted to demand an explanation from the directors about their failure to obtain continued government compensation which by then would have totalled £6.4 million. 'I have always thought it odd', wrote Rowland, 'that the costliest and most peculiar corner of our business was left firmly alone. . . The inspectors did not even ask for an explanation.'

To Dell and his officials, Rowland's complaint was spurious and his motives were questionable. 'Rowland was a hate figure,' says Dell, 'not highly regarded in government circles, who was rampaging around causing problems.' DTI officials equated Rowland with Maxwell, as piqued by a critical DTI report. But unlike that of other suspected megalomaniacs, Rowland's campaign bore an offensive capability. 'In principle,' recalls Dell, 'I would not have believed Rowland to be a reliable source but his letter could not be ignored.'

Dell, who was an outright opponent of sanctions against South Africa, understood that Rowland possessed embarrassing information for a Labour government which presented itself as an ally of African nationalism. If Rowland's allegations were true, the socialist government would appear duplicitous and hypocritical. Rowland's letter was forwarded for comment to the Foreign Office and its minister, David Owen.

Unlike Dell, Owen was both an active campaigner against white racism in southern Africa and an abrasive cynic about civil servants' self-esteem. Distrusting his advisers, he forwarded Rowland's disclosures to the law officers and interrogated his officials about his 'open suspicion of past complicity and impropriety'. The tension between the minister and his 'exasperated' officials was ill-disguised. Once the files were moving between departments within the government machine, the conspiracy's future was imperilled.

Foreign Office officials, irritated by the sanctions, had endured several rows with the oil companies about their breach of British laws but had willingly convinced themselves that the companies' excuses, namely, compliance with South African regulations, were valid. Sanctions, they believed, were futile because many countries, not only European but also Arab and African, ignored their existence and their attempted enforcement had contaminated British foreign relations.

But those irritations were minor compared to the aggravation felt towards Rowland and Lonrho. 'We knew Rowland and Lonrho were breaking sanctions,' admits a Foreign Office official, 'but they were worse than the oil companies because Rowland was perceived as a maverick.' Rowland had become a peg on which Whitehall could hang its frustrations with Britain's attempts to find a settlement because 'he was not helping us'. Rowland's negative influence made him politically important.

Accordingly, Dell, while rejecting Rowland's complaints about the inspectors' report, assured Rowland that the oil companies would be asked to reply to his allegations. 'It will be necessary to make copies of your letter available to [the oil companies]', concluded Dell, 'I take it that you will have no objection.' Rowland of course did object.

Delighting in the irritation which he imagined the officials were suffering, Rowland refused permission for his letter to be shown to the oil companies: 'In no circumstances,' he wrote to the minister, explaining that sight of the letters would hamper Lonrho's proposed legal action to recover damages. Surely, he added petulantly, the government could use its own files.

Warming to his theme, Rowland included six pages of additional evidence to prove the conspiracy. His demand was for a DTI inquiry into the oil companies. 'It seems to me,' he wrote, 'that if Lonrho was of some interest to your Department, then companies which directly maintained an illegal regime in power for over eleven years, keep its military aircraft and helicopters flying, and literally fuel Rhodesia's entire economy, offer a much wider field in which to deploy your Inspectors. Your Department has had the powers and the information for almost a dozen years – why haven't they been used?'

The minister's answer was obvious, as was the rejection of Rowland's request for an inquiry, especially in view of his final taunt, 'I will be happy, under cover of total secrecy, to fill the Inspectors' ears with damaging and juicy morsels which no man in his right mind would utter in open Court, where he might be cross-examined. (No one is going to say that I have not learnt from the example set me by my former colleagues and acquaintances.)'

In a wry twist, Dell's officials, realising that they needed to await decisions by their Foreign Office colleagues, dispatched in reply to Rowland an extract from Hansard. A junior Foreign Office minister had told the House of Commons, 'I am generally satisfied with the observance of sanctions. . . Our record in this respect is second to none.'

Aware that he was winning, Rowland added to the humour: 'I felt that it was a bad swop to receive three pages of Hansard in return for key documents.' Owen, whose ambitions to be remembered as an outstanding foreign minister included an intention to launch a new initiative to end UDI, began contemplating an inquiry. The news that Rowland had passed his material to selected governments in Africa hastened Owen's resolve. Kenneth Kaunda, reported as feeling 'deeply shocked' and 'cheated' by British duplicity, had already lambasted a junior British minister, prompting a cringing apology from London. On Rowland's suggestion, Kaunda increased the pressure. The president announced that, like Ghana, he would also take legal action against Britain. Singlehandedly, Rowland was orchestrating the

British government's humiliation. On the eve of his departure to southern Africa, on 10 April 1977, Owen appointed Thomas Bingham QC to investigate all the government's records and report on Rowland's allegations. Despite newspaper reports, the announcement elicited limited reaction. The public, unaware of Britain's culpability, still believed that South Africa and France were responsible for supplying Rhodesia's oil. Bingham's secret hearings did not satisfy Rowland. His campaign escalated.

A public inquiry, he believed, where he could pose as the champion of nationalist Africa, would provide a forum for wreaking some revenge against Heath's damning judgment. Without fear of contradiction, he could demonstrate how Africa's plight had been worsened during eleven years 'due to the distrust' caused by the oil supplies. His target was Owen. In Africa, with Rowland's encouragement, both Kaunda and Nkomo attacked Bingham's 'secret inquiry' as a device for a cover up. In his own letter to Owen, Rowland claimed that the 'secret hearings' were 'a non-starter' because 'one man, sitting in camera, attempting to summon reluctant witnesses who have no obligation to appear, and expecting them to disgorge information in a way which can only damage their own careers would not overcome the inevitable intimidation and threats.'

Melodramatically and without any supporting evidence, Rowland told Owen that John Vorster, the South African prime minister, had issued threats. Allegedly a senior South African civil servant had passed the message, 'If Rowland continues to pursue the case against the oil companies, we will pull the trigger on him and prosecute Lonrho.' It was a fanciful embellishment which, in the wake of his management of the press the previous year after publication of the DTI's reports, showed that Rowland had mastered the skills of manipulating a campaign.

His first attack in public was an announcement on 31 May 1977 that Lonrho had filed a writ against thirty-three companies. The fifty-five-page statement of claim alleged that the oil companies, who had signed an agreement with Lonrho exclusively to use the pipeline to supply their Rhodesian subsidiaries, had used alternative means and thereby broken their contracts. In addition, by supplying oil, they had prolonged UDI and aggravated Lonrho's losses.

But it was the second strike which proved explosive. During the summer, Rowland had obtained a dossier of internal memoranda from BP's head office. Within the so-called 'Sandford File' were forty-one pages proving the company's illegal role in supplying oil to Rhodesia. Those pages revealed that George Thomson, the Labour minister, had learned of BP's illegality in February 1968.

The Labour government's embarrassment would be intensified, Rowland knew, if the history and data which he had hitherto passed in dribbles to Whitehall were published. The ideal newspaper was the *Observer*, respected and read in Africa. The most credible journalist was Colin Legum, the *Observer*'s Africa expert. There was however one problem. Rowland feared that his own reputation might undermine the credibility of the material. Accordingly, at Rowland's request, Jorge Jardim contacted Legum and handed over the damning proof of the conspiracy.

On 25 June under the headline, 'Oil chiefs bust sanctions', Legum launched 'Oilgate'. The government's embarrassment was palpable. Six weeks later, in a deft exercise to leave his fingerprints upon the source of the *Observer*'s exposé, Rowland invited D. I. Mellor, head of the Foreign Office section responsible for sanctions, for lunch. 'You can read the "Sandford File" said Rowland, 'but you cannot give it to Bingham.' Rowland left the restaurant, 'inadvertently' forgetting the file. By mid-afternoon, Foreign Office officials understood precisely the nature of their enemy and the nature of the war which he had undertaken. The officials also believed that Rowland had crudely calculated that his pre-emptive attack might deflect the government from prosecuting him for fraud.

Just after the completion of the DTI investigation, on 13 April 1976, David Tudor Price QC was asked to advise whether the inspectors' report revealed any criminal charges. Present at a meeting in the lawyer's chambers was a representative of the Director of Public Prosecutions and two officers from Scotland Yard, Deputy Assistant Commissioner James Crane, the head of the Fraud Squad and Detective Chief Superintendent Kenneth Etheridge, a senior Fraud Squad officer.

Etheridge had been investigating Lonrho ever since two Lonrho directors had confessed their fears to Peter Brodie, the Assistant Commissioner, in 1972. Initially, his investigation concentrated upon files delivered by the South African police and, subsequently, he began considering Duncan Sandys's involvement in currency dealings in the Cayman Islands.

Tudor Price told his clients that the DTI report revealed prima facie evidence of criminal offences. He advised that they investigate, first, a conspiracy to break the Rhodesia sanctions; second, the deal which allowed Rowland the option to buy Lonrho shares without revealing the terms to the shareholders, possibly a theft; third, the use of Lonrho money to develop the Shamrocke and Nyaschere mine, half owned by Rowland, Ball and Ogilvy, which was possibly conspiracy to defraud; fourth, the non-disclosure of the £130,000 compensation paid to Sandys and the Wankel acquisition, both possible thefts; and, fifth, whether the 'special payments' were bribes.

The lawyer emphasised the sensitivity of the undertaking. Besides Rowland, Ball, Butcher and Caldecott, both Ogilvy and Sandys might be accused of criminal offences. 'A list of their names,' cautioned Tudor Price, 'is sufficient to indicate the difficulties which may face a police enquiry.'

The investigation would be undertaken by Etheridge. In previous years, Etheridge, who investigated John Poulson's corruption, had achieved some unwelcome publicity in the tabloid press when, in 1972, the *People* had suggested that the policeman had enjoyed a holiday in Cyprus with James Humphreys, an infamous 'Soho porn king'. The revelations were not considered sufficiently serious to bar his involvement in the Lonrho investigation.

One month after meeting Tudor Price, Etheridge optimistically told the lawyer, 'it may be possible to . . . commence proceedings within a relatively short period.' But by October 1976, Etheridge had run into a major obstacle.

The 'special payments', he discovered, were paid in Britain

and, at a minimum, broke the Exchange Controls Acts. Similarly, the conspiracy to breach sanctions was an offence. Etheridge however realised that both offences involved not only Rowland but also Ogilvy. To continue his investigation, the policeman needed clearance from the DPP and Foreign Office since any prosecutions would not only embarrass Britain abroad but, more importantly, involve the royal family. He submitted a report.

Etheridge did not wait for an answer. Soon after meeting Tudor Price, he resigned from the police. In March 1977, at Rowland's invitation, he joined Lonrho as the company's security officer. Among his former colleagues, he was heard to boast, 'I'm the highest paid security officer in the world.'

Eight
Expensive Illusions

As one of London's surviving dealers, Rowland received a steady flow of propositions during 1977 from business acquaintances, all enthusiastically peddling 'situations' which, backed by Lonrho's status and money, could earn handsome profits. Among those calls in February was a tip that Sir Hugh Fraser, the forty-two-year-old son of the late Lord Fraser of Allander, was seeking a buyer for his 24 per cent stake in Scottish and Universal Investments Ltd.

SUITS, a conglomerate based in Glasgow and employing 4400 people mostly in Scotland, owned George Outram, publishers of two daily newspapers in Glasgow, the *Herald* and the *Evening Times*, and thirty-three weekly publications. Other SUITS' subsidiaries included a security printing company, a publisher of educational books, a textile factory, an international engineering business and Whyte & Mackay whisky. Most importantly, it also owned 12.5 million shares, or just over 10 per cent, of the House of Fraser, Britain's biggest stores group.

Instructions had been given by the Fraser family to Warburgs and N.M. Rothschild to find a purchaser for the shares. The family emphasised the need for both discretion and the friendly intentions of any prospective purchaser. The price was approximately £7 million in cash. Buyers were hard to find. Despite its increasing turnover, £61 million in the previous year, SUITS's profits were declining and in the deteriorating circumstances of Britain's financial and industrial condition, only a gambler could extrapolate any long-term advantages.

The situation was ideal for Rowland. The price was low, he

understood the management of a conglomerate and in his view a minority stake bequeathed control of the whole company. But most importantly, as a long-term investment, the earnings in sterling would fund Lonrho's dividends and tilt the balance away from Africa. 'It satisfies all the requirements to improve the quality of our earnings,' Du Cann reassured Rowland. SUITS was a harbinger of a new era for Lonrho. A major obstacle however was Warburgs. To overcome his detractors, Rowland decided upon a direct approach to Hugh Fraser. A minimum of research revealed that Fraser, whom Rowland had never met, was an ideal target for Rowland's brand of seductive salesmanship.

Born in 1936, Fraser had grown up obsessed by the contrasting influence of his domineering father and his weak, doting mother. Over forty-two years, Lord Fraser of Allander had expanded an empire, founded in 1849, to include over 100 stores. The climax of his career was the purchase in 1957 of John Barker in Kensington and, in 1959, of the Harrods group [including Dickins & Jones] which he described as 'the pearl in the crown'. Although all the stores varied in profitability, Lord Fraser had pioneered a formula of sale and lease-backs of the properties which had proved hugely advantageous. Having built or purchased a store, he sold the freehold to insurance companies and simultaneously bought back a long lease. Over the years, as inflation reduced the rents to peppercorns, Lord Fraser transformed his empire into Britain's premier stores group. To capitalise on his profits, Fraser had slightly complicated his company's ownership.

In 1948, the House of Fraser had become a public company. To mitigate inheritance taxes, Lord Fraser had simultaneously created SUITS, a private company, to own the family's remaining 50 per cent share of the Fraser group. Initially, 90 per cent of SUITS's assets were its shares in House of Fraser but that was reduced with further acquisitions.

In 1960, SUITS also became a public company but since the family retained 70 per cent of the SUITS shares, Lord Fraser continued to exercise complete control over House of Fraser despite owning by then a minority of the shares. Among his few but repeated edicts was the reassurance from his family that they would never sell their stake in SUITS. 'It is the key to everything,' he extolled.

During his father's lifetime, Hugh Fraser proved his skills as a retailer and as an employer. Starting as a £5-per-week counter assistant, he had learnt the business from the bottom. According to legend, he was even publicly chastised by his father, peering from behind a curtain, for ineptly wrapping a customer's parcel. The personal loyalty he won from the staff was one of the rewards of his training. But his father's authoritarianism was the seed of his weakness. To compensate for feeling insecure, lonely and plagued by an inferiority complex, Hugh Fraser surrounded himself with uncritical, beholden admirers. Preoccupied by business and the need to satisfy his father, Fraser suffered two failed marriages and a succession of distraught relationships.

On Lord Fraser's death in 1966, Hugh Fraser renounced the title – 'there was only one Lord Fraser', he explained – but sought to emulate his father in other ways. In the process, he risked his estimated £100 million inheritance.

Initially, Hugh Fraser bought a succession of other stores but the costs, the overwhelming work and his own personal lifestyle destabilised his finances. In October 1974, after the Monopolies Commission had blocked his planned sale of House of Fraser to Boots, Hugh Fraser sold 21.3 million House of Fraser shares, a 19 per cent stake held by SUITS, to Carter Hawley Hales, an American stores group. Carter nominated three directors on to the Fraser board. The sale was the first sign of Hugh Fraser's stress.

The second intimation of his problems was the uproar in the same month accompanying the group's purchase of the Army and Navy stores. The annual SUITS accounts failed to reveal a loan and concealed the sale by Hugh Fraser of a further 1.6 million SUITS shares. Fraser was criticised by the shareholders and censured by the Stock Exchange for his 'inefficiency and ignorance of financial matters'. Subsequently he was convicted and fined for the offence. Fraser's reputation suffered and among the reforms demanded by the City was the radical alteration of SUITS's management. Since the crisis occurred contemporaneously with the collapse of so many of the go-go property conglomerates, SUITS's share price slumped.

The unpublicised cause of Hugh Fraser's decline was his irrepressible addiction to gambling on the roulette wheel. As a regular and welcome visitor to London's casinos, Fraser frequently played two wheels simultaneously and, betting on 32 his 'lucky' number, was known to lose £500,000 in an evening. To John Patterson, his friend and personal assistant, Fraser mentioned his nightly misfortunes in the third person. 'The House of Fraser has lost half a million,' he would quip to Patterson in a manner suggesting that the money belonged to someone else. Patterson could see that his friend was excited by gambling, actually enjoyed losing, and was unrepentant about the forced sale of shares to settle his debts, but found the knowledge a heartbreaking puzzle which countless doctors, psychiatrists and psychologists whom he consulted could neither explain nor, more pertinently, solve.

Regularly it fell to Patterson to arrange with a local bank for the collection of tens of thousands of pounds in cash. Having packed the bundles into a briefcase, Patterson would visit a casino to pay the debts of his employer. The amounts were staggering and the flow continued unabated. The sale of shares and the loan in 1974 had been the first manifestations of those debts. Three years later, after much heartache, the family agreed to sell a further 24 per cent stake in SUITS to pay off Fraser's new accumulated gambling debts of £4 million.

To discuss the progress of that sale, Patterson visited N. M. Rothschilds one late afternoon in mid-February 1977, in the City of London. Patterson's conversation with the bankers was interrupted by a telephone call.

Speaking from his office at Barkers store in Kensington, Hugh Fraser's voice was unusually excited. 'John, I've just had lunch with this fantastic guy and he's just like my father. We don't need to look any further for a purchaser of the shares. I've agreed to sell to him.'

'Who is it?' asked Patterson.

'He's called Tiny Rowland.'

Patterson, having lived in Scotland, had only a vague impression of the personality whom Fraser had mentioned.

The lunch between Rowland and Fraser at the Dorchester hotel had followed a predictable pattern. Elegantly dressed and intoning impeccable English, Rowland had oozed flattery, philosophical vision and delicate assurances of a genuine partnership in the future and had cocooned Fraser's insecurity. The benevolent patrician was offering himself to Fraser as sympathetic to gamblers. Like so many Britons of his social position, Fraser was blind to his own fatal weaknesses, rendering himself vulnerable to Rowland's approach. Inversely Rowland, like so many foreign businessmen operating in Britain, understood that feeding the natives' self-delusion permitted outsiders to succeed at the expense of insiders like Fraser. By the end of his meal, Fraser's self-esteem had been rejuvenated and he shook Rowland's hand warmly on the deal. As he was a gentleman, that gesture was an irrevocable seal.

On 16 March, Fraser met the SUITS directors for a regular board meeting in Park Gardens, Glasgow. The day previously, he had assured Rowland that the board would raise no problems about the sale of shares. Without exception, he explained, they were loyal supporters. Keen to avoid unnecessary controversy, Rowland was gratified.

With a slight bluster, Fraser announced the sale to the four directors. His audience, according to Hugh Laughland, the forty-six-year-old Scottish chief executive, was 'left gasping'. Without any display of contrition, Fraser ignored their insistent demands for an explanation and recommended that they permit Lonrho to nominate three directors including Rowland as chairman. Laughland, appointed in 1974 after the censure of Hugh Fraser's management, led the opposition. Like all directors in a similar predicament, Laughland's instinctive reaction was to resist the unexpected threat to his own future. But having steadily improved SUITS's fortunes, he also suspected Lonrho's debts and reputation.

Unprepared for the opposition, Fraser rushed to telephone Rowland in London. Over the following hours, the incumbent chairman shuttled between the boardroom and his office to receive Rowland's guidance about the ideal procedure to secure the board's agreement. Eventually, Rowland asked to speak to

Laughland: 'I'm sorry that you cannot accept me as your chairman,' said Rowland.

'I've never met you,' replied Laughland who knew that there was no choice but to accede. Rowland's shareholding was the deciding factor.

Although his purchase of Fraser's shares was announced on 16 March, Rowland, with a conscious display of self-control, only flew to Glasgow one week later to attend a SUITS board meeting. Considering the controversy which ensued over the following decade, the announcement of the deal caused little public excitement. No one questioned where Lonrho obtained the cash, but according to Basil West, Lonrho's finance director, 'It was stripped from Balfour Williams.'

In trepidation, Laughland watched the jigsaw falling into place. On that first day, Rowland made three decisions. Flemings, the company's merchant bankers who had resigned, would not be replaced. Without the advice of a merchant bank, the SUITS board, said Rowland, was free of outside interference. Secondly, Rowland was appointed chairman with Fraser as his deputy. Fred Butcher and Tom Prentice joined as new directors. The third decision foreshadowed the future. Laughland's plan to sell the remaining 10 per cent stake owned by SUITS in House of Fraser was halted. 'I then realised,' says Laughland, 'that Rowland would want eventually to buy all of SUITS and use the company as a lever to get the House of Fraser.' Laughland's scepticism did not trouble Rowland. To him, employees, whether in Africa or Britain, were dispensable, powerless technicians subject to his total control.

Laughland's suspicions were self-fulfilling. By July 1977, four months later, Lonrho had steadily purchased SUITS shares on the market and owned 29.24 per cent, just below the amount where it would trigger a bid for the whole company. In the meantime, Rowland read SUITS's most confidential files and understood that the public share price undervalued the company. His deal with Hugh Fraser had been a bargain. The next step was not part of a masterplan but the inevitable consequence of the original deal.

In the summer of 1977, Rowland flew as usual to his house in

Acapulco, Mexico, via the United States. Among the stopovers
was Los Angeles where he met Phil Hawley of Carter Hawley,
one of America's biggest store groups, which held the 19 per
cent stake in House of Fraser. Gently, Rowland continued
a discussion initiated by Hawley in London to purchase the
American's shares. By early autumn, the sale was agreed for
£41 million. Since Lonrho's payments were staggered, only two
of Carter's nominated directors on the board of House of Fraser
would be immediately replaced by Rowland and Duncan Sandys.
The third Lonrho director would be appointed in May 1979.

Rowland announced the agreement as a *fait accompli* on his
return to London. For Basil West, it was 'the final straw'.
According to West, 'I didn't know about the deal. It was not
approved by the board when I was present. We needed £12
million immediately and we only had £4 million in the bank.'
West, often in trepidation of Rowland's 'Prussian fury', asked
where the money was to be found. 'Don't worry, it will turn
up,' assured Rowland. For Rowland, the accountant's niggardly
questions were boring and irrelevant. The outlook had rarely
been better. Within six months, with just a minority shareholding, he had placed himself in an unchallenged strategic
position to control Britain's biggest store group which included
Harrods.

With access to some internal accounts, Rowland gleaned the
hitherto unknown weaknesses of the House of Fraser. Harrods'
profitability sustained the declining value of the whole group.
The company was an ideal candidate for asset stripping.

The common controlling factor of both SUITS and House
of Fraser remained Hugh Fraser. Although the Fraser family
trusts owned only about 10 per cent of the House of Fraser
and 8.9 per cent of SUITS, the management's loyalty, dictated
by respect for Lord Fraser, still regarded his son, the chairman
of the House of Fraser, as the group's owner. But one factor
was irreversible. Although Rowland's position was dependent
upon Hugh Fraser, he had neutralised any hostile bid for the
two companies – other than his own.

Over the following months, Laughland rarely met Rowland.
While Hugh Fraser chaired SUITS's board meetings, Rowland

appeared only when, in Laughland's view, 'he had a message to give us'. The 'messages' invariably were to contradict Laughland's decisions. One of the most irritating communications was Rowland's insistence that SUITS settle an industrial dispute at the *Glasgow Herald*, contrary to Laughland's desire to withstand the wage demands. 'He was just roughing me,' recalls Laughland, 'to see how I'd react. I was resistant to his pressure. He soon realised that if and when he made his bid, I'd fight to the death. I wasn't going to be wooed over.'

By then, Rowland's acquisition policy had transformed Lonrho into one of Britain's biggest corporations. The addition in March 1977 of Dunford & Elliott, an engineering and steel group, added a further 6000 to Lonrho's 110,000 employees who were employed in 740 subsidiaries in forty-four countries. Half of Lonrho's £1.2 billion turnover was in Africa and the remainder in Europe and America. By any reckoning, its range of activities was striking. Leading producers of sugar, tea, wattle and sisal, Lonrho was also an important extractor of gold, platinum, coal and copper. It was involved in producing wine, textiles and tobacco. Throughout Africa, it owned a major network of franchises to sell cars and trucks; and possessed newspapers and transport companies. To improve hard currency earnings, Rowland had recently bought AVP, owners of the Metropole hotel chain, with five major properties in Britain. Although pre-tax profits in 1977 fell slightly to £90 million and Lonrho's loans doubled to £103 million, its share price was rising, disproving the 1973 predictions of crisis and doom.

During those expansionary years, Lonrho's management style did not alter. Rowland concluded the deal, often conditional upon the existing managers remaining, and passed on to search for the next prize. Lonrho's employees across the forty-four countries where the company operated rarely met their chief executive. Restricting himself to supervising the empire by glancing at balance sheets and conversations with trusted managers, Rowland seemed detached. But the corollary of his delegation to handpicked professionals was his explicit control of the empire.

The management style created an uneasy impression in London. Lonrho's offices in Cheapside, as uninspiring as the collective image of the board of directors, reflected a company shunned by most of the City's institutions and personalities. Bereft of the advice and ambassadorial services of a merchant bank, the company suffered because of Rowland's self-imposed invisibility. The principal cause of misgivings remained the accounts, which failed to explain in detail the remittances from Africa. Four years earlier, Rowland had spoken publicly about his love for and total dedication to Lonrho but the suspicion had hardened that the company was not just the culmination of his ambitions but rather a passport to enable him to undertake a personal, political agenda.

British diplomats in Africa had already noticed, 'Rowland was a shadow who kept crossing our path but never came near us.' Sir John Graham, a deputy under-secretary, who was attempting to negotiate a meeting between Ian Smith and Joshua Nkomo was among those most irritated. Graham's efforts, which were a marked shift from the recent British policy of avoiding any involvement in Rhodesia, were part of a new concerted effort by the West to prevent the escalating guerrilla war culminating in Soviet control of southern Africa.

In 1977, MI6 reports from many southern African and European stations mentioned Rowland's close ties with Nkomo. The author of that relationship was Kenneth Kaunda who supported Nkomo as leader of Zimbabwe's nationalist movement. Accepting Kaunda's analysis that Nkomo would be the first nationalist leader of the independent country, Rowland quite happily provided financial support for Nkomo and his entourage in their worldwide travels, while obtaining unusually lucrative concessions in Zambia. In return, he could hope for benefits in Rhodesia when the Smith regime ended. The alternative, a Soviet-sponsored Mugabe government, alarmed Rowland. 'We'll lose everything if the communists take over,' he repeated to Lonrho's directors.

Lonrho's substantial profits in Rhodesia aggravated those fears. Beyond the control of Desmond Krogh, the governor of the Reserve Bank, Lonrho under Kruger's management had accumulated enormous debts, was transfer pricing and was stealing foreign exchange. Summoning Kruger on several occasions, Krogh warned that the illegal activities should cease but laments, 'We couldn't get the proof.' Although Lonrho was condemned in Salisbury as a 'company without integrity', Kruger was personally excused as being merely 'His Master's Voice'. According to David Young, a Treasury official, 'Kruger's relationship with Rowland reminded me of the inscription on a native's tombstone I had seen in a British military cemetery in Bangladesh: "Well done you good and faithful servant." ' In Young's view, 'Nic was killing himself for Tiny' and Lonrho was not penalised because 'the company was loyal to UDI'.

Paradoxically, in London, the Bank of England quietly praised Lonrho's ability to remit dividends from Rhodesia through South Africa, justifying the retention of Rhodesian assets on Lonrho's consolidated accounts.

For John Graham and other British diplomats in Africa, the contradictions made Rowland 'a mystery. We couldn't understand his motives but suspected that they were commercial.' The conviction that 'money was involved' diverted the officials' attention from another of Rowland's motives. Supporting Nkomo had permitted Rowland to participate in the hectic negotiations to achieve a Rhodesian settlement and choose a moment when he might further humiliate his critics. For Rowland, revenge was as important as money.

At 3.40 p.m. on Thursday 16 October 1975, Rowland arrived at the State Department in Washington. Greeted by Ed Mulcahy, ranking second in the department's African affairs section, Rowland had been granted a rare opportunity to meet Henry Kissinger, having overcome the secretary of state's earlier protest to Mulcahy about his 'reluctance' to meet the businessman. One of the conditions of the meeting was that Rowland was never to disclose that it had occurred. Even the senior staff in the Department's African Bureau remained unaware of the meeting.

The visit had been arranged at the instigation of Kenneth Kaunda and the subject was the Portuguese colony of Angola, a country five times the size of Britain, rich in oil, diamonds and uranium, traversed by the British-built Benguela railway line, and, according to the CIA, a clear target of Soviet subversion.

In less than three weeks, on 11 November, the Portuguese would officially hand over government to Angolans. In effect, the Portuguese army, exhausted by colonial wars and disillusioned with the dictatorship in Lisbon, had revolted and abandoned any pretence of government. Four hundred thousand Portuguese had begun fleeing Angola in an airlift which would automatically reduce the country to chaos. The vacuum was filled, on the eve of their departure, by a murderous civil war which was funded and equipped by the Soviet Union, the United States and their surrogates.

Angola's guerrilla war for independence had been fought since the early Sixties, principally by three tribes marshalled into three armies. The most organised was the 'Marxist' MPLA, supported by the Soviet Union and Cuba. The second, the FNLA, initially supported by China, had more recently won the sympathy of the United States. The third, UNITA, was also originally supplied by China but Peking's sustenance had been switched to the MPLA, tilting diplomatic recognition from several African states towards the 'Marxists'. Rowland arrived in Washington to urge the Administration to give more aid to UNITA.

UNITA's leader was Jonas Savimbi, a charismatic, courageous and intelligent nationalist whose political allegiances remained ambivalent. Born in 1934 and educated by missionaries, Savimbi had spent eight years studying politics in Switzerland, guerrilla warfare in China and struggling for power in Egypt before returning to Angola in 1966 to build, with Chinese support, an army to defeat the Portuguese.

Over the ensuing seven years, Savimbi's hard-won victories had been tempered by the uncertainties of political support. By June 1975, the Soviet- and Cuban-trained MPLA guerrillas had succeeded in taking control over large areas of the divided country. Under pressure from Julius Nyerere, the socialist president of Tanzania, Chinese support for UNITA was evaporating and Savimbi turned to his neighbour, Kenneth Kaunda, an outright anti-communist, for patronage.

Only America, Kaunda knew, could balance the Soviet incursion. But Kaunda feared that the Nixon administration would ignore his argument. Five years earlier, he had visited Washington, not only as Zambian president but as representative of the fifty-four non-aligned governments in the OAU. Nixon had been 'unavailable' and Kaunda had returned home humiliated.

In April 1975, Kaunda had returned to Washington on a state visit and had met President Ford. At an unconventional White House dinner, Kaunda had publicly warned the Administration that the consequence of support for an apartheid government was a racial holocaust in southern Africa.

In private discussions, Kaunda warned Ford and Kissinger that the Administration should neutralise Soviet support for the MPLA by giving aid to the FNLA and UNITA. Both Americans knew that Cuban and Soviet advisers were aiding the 'Marxist' Angolans but the American secretary of state, renowned for his concern about 'geo-political forces', had displayed a notable lack of interest in the fate of Africa other than outrightly to support the white minority governments in southern Africa as a bulwark against Soviet influence. Kaunda's public reprimand had not encouraged Kissinger to consider reviewing his position despite the CIA's modest support to the FNLA's commander Holden Roberto, condemned by most as degenerate and drunk. Preoccupied by the imminent evacuation from Vietnam, neither American could concentrate on the fate of Angola, an unknown and strategically irrelevant country.

Three months later, in July 1975, as the MPLA's successes grew, Kissinger's opinion changed. In the months since the American ambassador in Saigon had fled from his embassy by helicopter, Kissinger had become susceptible to any argument that the communists, bolstered by their victory in South East Asia, would pursue their expansionism. Fearing that Angola would become a Soviet satellite after 11 November, the CIA intensified its supply of weapons, finance, advisers and mercenaries in a secret and illegal operation. The aid was principally destined for the FNLA but meagre amounts were also dispatched to UNITA.

That decision coincided with Rowland's agreement, at

Kaunda's behest, to supply a Hawker Siddeley 125 jet and two British pilots to Savimbi. The jet was ostensibly chartered by Armitage Industrial Holdings and based at Lusaka airport. Among the company's directors was Wilhelm Wilming, Rowland's pilot. Significantly, the expenses never appeared on Lonrho's published accounts. When asked about shareholders' interests, Rowland replied, 'If they don't like it, they can sell the shares.'

Rowland's emotional and financial commitment to Savimbi's victory, at Lonrho's expense, was nothing short of colossal. Lonrho, Rowland believed, would be guaranteed a pivotal role in the country's development once the Marxists were defeated.

Wilming's extended presence in southern Africa at Rowland's request was a public evincing of that conviction. Privately, observers noticed that Rowland and Savimbi were similar in both personality and character. There was a natural camaraderie between them when they met.

Regularly, in Lonrho's jet Wilming shuttled people, supplies and sealed packages to Savimbi's headquarters, and ferried Savimbi around southern Africa to meet government leaders to press his claims for support and recognition. While official British support was restricted by the pervasive financial crisis in London and the absence of any historic interest in the area, Rowland was convinced that his fortune would be earned if Washington could be persuaded to support his protégé.

On several occasions, Rowland was flown by Wilming to a Zambian airfield on the Angolan border to be transported by helicopter to Savimbi's jungle headquarters. 'I was Mr Rowland's bodyguard,' attests Wilming who carried a pistol and a rifle. After a few hours' conversation, the two Europeans would return to Zambia.

On 20 August, John Stockwell, a CIA officer, having visited Holden Roberto's headquarters, was flown in the Lonrho jet to Jonas Savimbi in Silva Porto. Stockwell, like others, was impressed by the conditions of travel. Plucked from Africa's heat and squalor and transported in air-conditioned luxury into the midst of a civil war, he was attracted to Savimbi's personality and organisation. On his return, Stockwell's recommendation that the Agency should also support UNITA progressed through the channels to Kissinger's office. Rowland took credit for that conversion.

With Angola's independence imminent, the war between the three tribal armies escalated. Accurate CIA reports that Cuban soldiers had been dispatched to Angola to combat UNITA's advances sealed Kissinger's theory that the fate of Zambia, Zaïre and even South Africa depended upon the defeat of Marxism in Angola. Overnight, Angola was declared another venue of superpower rivalry. In October 1975, in total secrecy, South African armoured columns, with air support and in liaison with the CIA, invaded Angola to support UNITA. In Washington, the director of the CIA was denying to Congress any involvement in Angola. The whole operation, including the presence of South African troops, was secret.

Kaunda, wanting to influence the war, responded to Rowland's offer of assistance. At a million dollars a month the provision of the jet to Savimbi was a small investment for Rowland if, on winning the war, Angola gave Lonrho access to its minerals. So, by design, Rowland was involved in a joint covert operation with the CIA in support of Savimbi against the Marxist government. Simultaneously, Rowland was also in partnership with MI6 who had supplied a Racal communications system to Savimbi. The equipment, addressed to UNIP, Kaunda's party, at Lusaka airport, was diverted on to Lonrho's plane to be transported into Angola.

Until Rowland arrived on the Gulfstream in Washington on 16 October, his sporadic attempts to build relations with the State Department and CIA had suffered limited success. Rowland was not a factor within the Department during the Seventies although he did enjoy individual relationships with diplomats. In Lusaka, Rowland frequently consulted with the ambassador, Robert Good, while in London, his point of contact was the Africa desk at the American embassy. But the only recorded meeting had occurred, at his own request, with Julius Walker in 1972.

Kissinger was naturally reluctant to consult with a foreign businessman about his unauthorised, secret operations. Rowland after all represented no one and was ignored in his own country.

It was a mark of Rowland's achievement that, despite those deficiencies, he was shown into Kissinger's office at 4 o'clock. The secretary of state listened for forty-five minutes to Rowland's monologue, saying little and committing the Administration to even less. Thrilled to be in the midst of a diplomatic mission, Rowland flew to Lusaka to report to Kaunda. The conversation proved inconsequential and subsequent events proved disastrous.

In December 1975, Congress compelled Kissinger to cease assistance to Savimbi and abandon the South African alliance. The CIA's intervention was unsuccessful. To Washington's embarrassment, the Marxists won a clear military advantage. By February 1976, Savimbi was defeated and retreated into inaccessible jungle, forgotten by the outside world but determined to rebuild his army. Two months later, Kaunda recognised the MPLA government. Most West European governments, anxious to placate the leaders of the African continent, followed suit. Rowland's personal commitment to Savimbi however continued. Although he temporarily withdrew the jet, a new plane was hired at Lonrho's expense in March 1976 to secure Rowland's stake when Savimbi eventually became leader.

America's intervention had suggested to Salisbury and Pretoria that Washington would not abandon Europeans in Africa to the Marxists. To be cast as defenders of white civilisation appealed to the Rhodesians; a perfect justification for their opposition to majority rule. But, within months, Kissinger had performed a *volte face*. In Lusaka in April 1976, on his first tour of Africa, Kissinger promised to support majority rule in Rhodesia. To achieve that goal, he urged negotiations rather than conflict. The spectre was that failure to concede to African demands would transform Rhodesia into another Angola. Hence, warned Kissinger, either Smith surrendered or he should be removed.

While not underestimating the problems, Kissinger felt that he was pushing at an open door. John Vorster, the prime minister of South Africa, was convinced that his country's survival depended upon a speedy and peaceful settlement in Rhodesia. Since the Smith regime's survival depended entirely upon South African support, Vorster was theoretically able to bring irresistible pressure upon the rebel regime. The major flaw in the *realpolitik* was Smith's obstinacy, duplicity and prejudicial conviction that the nationalists could never win a military war.

The problems facing Kissinger were considerable. The nationalist movement was bitterly divided – fragmented both by personality clashes and deep political differences. Although all the Africans insisted upon majority rule, they disagreed about the scale of violence needed to achieve independence. Leading the moderates was Bishop Abel Muzorewa, a unity candidate, who enjoyed limited support and lacked an army. In the middle was Joshua Nkomo, [ZAPU] a *bon viveur*, former trade unionist who was the 'father' of the independence movement. As an ideological carpetbagger, Nkomo believed in both the armed struggle and negotiation but was fundamentally weak because he led the nation's minority tribe, the Ndebele, living around Bulawayo in the west of the country. At the extreme was Robert Mugabe [ZANU], backed by the communists in Peking, a member of Rhodesia's largest tribe, the Shona, whose uncompromising creed was the armed struggle to overthrow the whites and the creation of a socialist state. Mugabe alarmed the West and Rowland.

The last hope for a peaceful settlement was launched in late 1975. Nkomo and Smith began discussions on a timetable which would lead to majority rule. At Rowland's expense, Robert Wright QC arrived in Salisbury to negotiate with the Smith government on Nkomo's behalf. Every night, Wright telexed a progress report from Lonrho House to the Foreign Office. But by February 1976, the negotiations collapsed. Nkomo reported to presidents Kaunda, Machel and Nyerere that Smith was insincere. Only a guerrilla war would liberate Zimbabwe.

While Nkomo, based in Lusaka, obtained military support from Moscow, Mugabe, supported by Peking, began operations from Mozambique. The combination of Rhodesia's military losses and its total dependence upon South Africa strengthened the coalition between Kissinger and Vorster to hasten majority rule in Rhodesia.

Kissinger manoeuvred Smith into a public declaration of support for majority rule but in September 1977 the agreement collapsed. Reluctantly, the British sponsored a conference for all the black nationalist factions and Smith in Geneva at which they faced recrimination from all sides for failing to accept their responsibilities in their colony. Had they wanted to make the choice, British Foreign Office officials would have been unable to judge which side loathed them most for their past behaviour and the evidence of their current importance. Inevitably, the conference collapsed.

In Rhodesia, Nkomo's and Mugabe's guerrillas fundamentally altered the political situation. Smith's retaliatory raids against Mozambique prompted Samora Machel to close their common border, cutting Rhodesia's access to the ports of Beira and Maputo [formerly Lourenço Marques]. Although troubled, Smith was convinced that his military could contain any threat and he remained confident that the West would not permit the destruction of its 'kith and kin'.

Kissinger's new interest in Africa sparked a demand for more information. Since neither the State Department nor the CIA had devoted sufficient resources to the area to satisfy that appetite, foreign service officers were encouraged to establish new contacts. Among those contacted by Bill Schaufele, an assistant secretary for African affairs, was Rowland. The businessman urged the Administration to support the end of Smith's regime. Although he credited Rowland's argument to be motivated by 'commercial profit not political beliefs', Schaufele recommended his successor, Ray Seitz, the political officer in the London embassy, to continue the exchange of views with Rowland. Seitz, who had been previously posted in Kenya and Zaïre, encouraged Rowland's developing relationship with Washington.

That emerging liaison coincided with the launch of a new Anglo-American initiative by David Owen. In mid-1977, Smith's predicament had noticeably worsened. Guerrilla groups were sweeping the country persuading many white Rhodesians to flee while the morale among those who remained plummeted. On 1 September, Owen arrived in Salisbury to negotiate with Smith but his intemperate display of contempt for Smith, mirroring the Rhodesian's dislike of Foreign Office officials, earned the minister only a dose of abuse. Once again, the peace-making efforts failed. It was an ideal moment for Rowland to take the stage and humiliate his critics.

Throughout the two years of their fruitless negotiations, Kaunda and Nyerere were united with Smith in their common scorn of British efforts. Rowland's revelations of the Labour ministers' conspiracy with the oil companies had fuelled the Africans' anger and drawn Rowland closer to Kaunda.

Regularly, Rowland would commute overnight from London to Lusaka, stopping only to refuel in Crete. Arriving at 10 a.m. after the eleven-hour journey, he would be driven directly to State House to ponder with the Zambian president the possible strategies to end the war. 'Not just an independent Zimbabwe,' explained Kaunda to Rowland, 'but Zimbabwe under Joshua.' Fearing the realisation of Mugabe's Marxist ideals across the border, Kaunda knew that only an early end to the war, before Mugabe's influence spread, could ensure Nkomo's presidency. Kaunda channelled his support towards Nkomo and encouraged Rowland to contribute help. Rowland was delighted to oblige.

For more than a year, Lonrho's office in London had provided airline tickets, hotel accommodation and expenses for Nkomo throughout the world. 'I was constantly travelling between Belgrade and Moscow, or New York and Havana, on tickets provided by this great capitalist,' wrote Nkomo. 'He knew where we were going but never discussed it.' In London, Nkomo usually stayed in a top-floor suite at the Royal Lancaster hotel. Rowland paid for the politician's food and clothes. On one occasion, Nkomo asked for his own credit card to 'that big store near Hyde Park'. Rowland whispered, 'He means the Outsize Shop.' In fact, Nkomo meant Harrods.

Lonrho's support extended to the war effort in Zambia. Twenty-four Land Rovers were provided to the ZAPU guerrillas. Nkomo had reason to be grateful. 'As I got to know Tiny I came to trust him. His charming wife Josie is Zimbabwean-born and Tiny became one of us. I began to regard him as a son-in-law, what we call the *mkweenyana*, one of the family by marriage.'

During the summer of 1977, as the Anglo-American initiative stumbled to failure, Kaunda and Rowland concluded that a personal meeting between the Zambian president and Smith might break the deadlock. With Kaunda's support, Rowland consulted the American government.

The Foreign Office had come to the same conclusion and, having consulted Kaunda, tasked Sir John Graham, based in Salisbury, to negotiate a meeting. By then, Rowland's diplomacy was underway.

Over dinner at the Ritz in Paris, Rowland outlined the proposal to Pieter van der Byl, the Rhodesian foreign minister. The advantage, Rowland explained to the obdurate racist, was to forestall Mugabe. 'You know the war's lost,' said Rowland with quiet persuasiveness, 'but we've got to protect the peace.' Although he trusted Rowland 'as much or as little as I trusted the Foreign Office', van der Byl decided that any offer of mediation was 'weighed' in Rowland's favour. A community of interest existed between Kaunda, Smith and Rowland to secure Nkomo's position in Rhodesia. All three knew that the only alternative was Mugabe's Marxism.

Smith had first met Nkomo in November 1974, shortly after his release from detention. The prime minister recognised that Nkomo, the founder of the independence movement in Rhodesia, was a moderate, pro-western protagonist who would retain his independence from Moscow. Van der Byl found Rowland's invitation tempting, 'I'll provide my jet to take you and Smith to Lusaka,' promised Rowland. 'No one will know.'

Rowland and Ian Smith next met on 24 September 1977 in the officers' mess at New Sarum, an airforce base outside Salisbury. Over tea and biscuits, Rowland explained to Smith that Kaunda wanted to negotiate a settlement personally. Smith had received several briefings about Rowland's mediation efforts from Ken Flower the head of CIO. Smith was unfazed by Rowland's past opposition to UDI: 'He was interested in his finances and I had wanted to save my country.' Smith needed a dialogue with moderate blacks and believed Rowland's assertion, 'I'm close to KK and I've persuaded him to come to a settlement.'

The following morning, Smith and two others were collected by Wilming. 'Smith came to the cockpit,' recalls Wilming, 'and saw I had some guns laid out. I explained they were for our protection.' In contact with military air traffic controllers in

Zambia, Wilming flew direct from Salisbury towards Lusaka. At a secluded position at the airport, the passengers transferred to a helicopter which landed on the lawn at State House. Kaunda was waiting. He had been told by Rowland who had arrived earlier that Smith wanted a settlement. In one of the earliest examples of Rowland's diplomatic style, each side was encouraged to believe that the other had initiated the meeting to present an agreement.

With Nkomo waiting in an adjoining room and Rowland walking in the gardens, Smith and Kaunda found themselves in a predictable *impasse* but eventually agreed that Nkomo was their favoured candidate and pledged to meet again.

Smith returned to Salisbury, grateful to Rowland for having initiated the contact. As 'an indication of good faith', James Chikerema, another of Rowland's favoured nationalist leaders, was allowed to return to Rhodesia. Chikerema was provided with a country house in Salisbury by Rowland. Although Rowland vastly overestimated Chikerema's political influence, he lived thereafter at Lonrho's expense, the only beneficiary of that summit.

Kaunda's pleasure faded after news of the summit leaked and Mugabe launched a bitter attack on the Zambian, exposing the ideological gulf between himself and Nkomo. Momentarily, Rowland's efforts seemed to have been in vain. Foreign Office officials drew comfort. 'Rowland', recalls Graham, 'kept moving our pieces on the chessboard just at the critical time.' As far as Rowland was concerned, Graham was not even a player. In any case, Rowland was momentarily diverted to play a more lucrative game.

During those months, Rowland had been assiduously cultivating Hugh Fraser, the unpredictable keystone to Lonrho's profitable future. Seventeen years after taking control of Lonrho, Rowland could finally visualise his dream as the owner of Harrods, purveyors to the Establishment. Building upon his stake in SUITS and the House of Fraser, Rowland would buy control and absorb both within Lonrho. Astride a considerable empire, he would expunge forever Heath's damnation, his apparent dependence on Africa and his uncertain status in Britain. He required just a little patience. Since a battle should be commenced only when the outcome is certain, Rowland's agents, especially Du Cann, were politely approaching the fund managers at the City institutions who owned blocks of SUITS shares. Gradually, they were being wooed.

In the meantime, Fraser was invited on several occasions to lunch at Cheapside. The routine for the Lonrho directors' lunch never changed. Duncan Sandys sat at the head of the table with Rowland on his right and the guest of honour seated opposite Rowland. Every director in the building attended the simple two-course meal which habitually became an unofficial board meeting where the company's affairs and prospects were debated, Rowland often silent, listening to the debate. Invariably, before Fraser's arrival, the Lonrho directors were urged to be 'on especially good behaviour'. Although after Fraser had left the meetings Rowland would contemptuously disparage his guest, in public the two were seen as close friends. 'I take the view,' commented Fraser with enthusiasm which some interpreted as hero worship, 'that once you make your bed, you lie on it, and my bed is 110 per cent with Tiny Rowland.'

Lonrho's final preparations for the SUITS bid were underway during March. Invitations to fund managers for lunch or to test-drive the new Volkswagen Golf were hosted by Rowland. His guests controlled about 30 per cent of SUITS shares. Their host was seeking acceptance but he delicately explained that his alliance with Hugh Fraser implied that there was no possibility of any opposition or an alternative offer.

The bid was formally launched on 4 April 1978. 'Lonrho has been helpful for SUITS,' said Hugh Fraser in support. The offer was to exchange five Lonrho shares for three SUITS shares. Since no cash was offered, Rowland needed to persuade the SUITS shareholders that Lonrho was a safe investment. So, anxious to appear acceptable to the City institutions, Rowland added that his offer was conditional upon the agreement of the SUITS directors. Technically, it was an unnecessary addition but Rowland wanted to portray himself as scrupulously fair and oblige Hugh Fraser's insistence that his team remain together.

Coincidentally, Laughland was visiting London when the bid

was announced. Throughout that 'uncomfortable year', Laughland had expected a bid but was unable to take any precautions. On Rowland's insistence, SUITS did not even have a merchant bank. Now freed from Rowland's constraint and steeled against allowing Rowland to 'snatch' the company, Laughland arranged that afternoon to meet Bruce Fireman, a thirty-four-year-old lawyer and merchant banker at Charterhouse Japhet, to discover whether he could oppose Rowland's bid. The omens seemed unfavourable.

Seated in a cramped office in Cheapside directly opposite Lonrho, Laughland explained to Fireman and George Willet, a corporate finance director at Grieveson Grant, SUITS's brokers, why he opposed the deal: 'He's getting the company too cheap, just for paper and he's going to take it away from Scotland.' Initially Fireman was unconvinced. Memories about SUITS's troubles under Hugh Fraser still lingered but the preliminary accounts produced by Laughland seemed positive. 'SUITS is worth a lot more than people realise,' Laughland exclaimed, 'but how do we stop him? He's got the shares.' By combining Lonrho's 29 per cent stake and the 9 per cent owned by the Fraser family trusts, Rowland required only another 12 per cent to win his bid.

Working through the night, Fireman discovered a possible strategy. Since Rowland had made the offer conditional upon acceptance by the board, Laughland should summon a board meeting. There were eight members of the board. Three were Lonrho directors who would be automatically excluded from voting. Of the remaining five, Hugh Fraser and James Gossman, his former personal assistant who would follow his employer's lead, would support Rowland. The decisive issue was whether Laughland could rely on the support of the other two directors to split the board against Rowland.

Overnight, hearing of Laughland's hostility, Rowland had bowed to Fraser's argument that Laughland and the two other SUITS directors would be compelled to support a more generous bid. Rowland raised his offer to exchange eleven Lonrho shares for six SUITS shares.

When the board met, Fraser, beguiled by Laughland's manner, called the vote on the offer. It was rejected by three to two.

Unknown to Fraser, Laughland and the bankers had persuaded Barrie Anderson, the fifth director, to oppose Rowland. Fraser looked 'startled'. The 'Straight Three', as they became known, had initiated a challenge, precipitating the acrimony which Rowland had hoped to avoid.

In public, Rowland disparaged the unexpected rebuff: 'We have never made an unsuccessful takeover bid.' He omitted any mention that all his previous bids had been accepted by the directors and that he was a virgin in fighting a contested take-over. Within days, the first hiccup arose.

Rowland's bid valued SUITS shares at 130p each. At great speed, Fireman had published an unusually cogent defence document which, based upon SUITS's unexpectedly high profits [up 44%], valued SUITS at double Lonrho's offer and urged fund managers to consider that since Rowland was so desperate to buy SUITS, he would pay a huge premium. Carefully briefing financial journalists to distrust Lonrho, the counterblast 'astonished Tiny by the ferocity of our attack'. City institutions became wary that Rowland might indeed be picking up his prize too cheap.

Before that missive was completely digested, Fireman launched a second front. The banker urged Laughland to embrace the Scottish aspect: 'Isn't there an argument that Lonrho would move SUITS' headquarters to London and so deprive Scotland of jobs?'

Donald Dewar, the eloquent prospective Labour member of parliament for Garscadden, was an eager recruit to lead the lobby on Whitehall not only to save Scottish jobs but also to preserve Scottish control over its businesses and newspapers. As Dewar stressed to Roy Hattersley, the secretary of state for prices and consumer protection, the issue was serious in Scotland and potentially could stem the loss of votes to the emerging Scottish Nationalist Party. The proof was a headline in the local *Daily Record* attacking an English company for dismissing Scottish workers.

Unexpectedly, Rowland had become immersed in a public battle defending not only the value of his bid and Lonrho's controversial status, but the integrity of the British Isles. 'You're trying to discredit Lonrho,' he accused the Straight Three, 'and are misleading the shareholders.' But the emotional arguments against moving control of Scottish newspapers to London were hard to counter since his ally, Hugh Fraser, had reneged on his father's commitment to protect the business from predators.

Takeover bids follow a prescribed three-week timetable. Twenty-one days after the details of Lonrho's bid had been formally published on 19 April, the offer would close. Within that period, it would be scrutinised by the Office of Fair Trading [OFT], an agency within the DTI, to decide whether the takeover would create a monopoly or was contrary to the 'public interest'. If either criterion applied, the OFT could refer the bid to the Monopolies and Mergers Commission for an investigation and report. For Lonrho, a referral would be clearly unwelcome. There would be delays and the stigma of intensive questioning.

Under Gordon Borrie, the OFT's director, the department's attitude towards Lonrho was shaped by the 1976 DTI report. 'We felt that Rowland was not the ideal man to take over a great Scottish company,' recalls one of the senior OFT officials. 'Lonrho's antecedents influenced our sentiments.' That bias was reinforced by a wave of visitors to Borrie and his officials. 'We feared that the Scots would make a nuisance of themselves if the bid wasn't referred.'

Borrie, the OFT's director for the following sixteen years under thirteen secretaries of state would, as much as anyone, influence Rowland's ambitions in Britain. Born in Croydon in 1931, the son of a solicitor, Borrie was a diligent, middle-class, grammar-school lawyer who epitomised Britain's meritocracy rather than its fading Etonian oligarchy. In the course of a successful university career as teacher of law, Borrie had co-authored the original study of the consumer and the law, a pathfinding textbook which demolished myths about the isolation of law and lawmakers from society. His applauded appointment to the Office of Fair Trading bequeathed him the power to police aspects of Britain's corporate activities, a challenge for a Labour Party supporter. But the context of Borrie's influence was the source of Rowland's growing antagonism towards the OFT and the Department of Trade. In essence, Borrie, conducting his activities in private, was personally and publicly unanswerable for his decisions despite their pervasive effect upon Lonrho's activities. Theoretically, Borrie's decisions were defended by the secretary of state in Parliament but, in practice, the extraordinary turnover of politicians passing through the office conferred upon the director general unusual discretion subject to the government's policy directives. Naturally, Borrie's discretion accumulated over the years.

The chances of a referral of the SUITS bid by Borrie to the Monopolies Commission were slim. After all, the takeover would not result in a monopoly and none of Lonrho's many former acquisitions over the previous two years had raised the suggestion of a referral. Only political expediency, camouflaged as 'the public interest' could trigger a referral and, like all politicians, Roy Hattersley was vulnerable to that argument from Labour politicians and trade unionists from Scotland.

On 10 May, the twentieth day after formal publication of Lonrho's bid, the Straight Three and Rowland were invited to meet Hattersley to argue the case about referral. Laughland and Fireman, the first visitors, wanted the bid 'kicked into touch to give us extra time to show how SUITS business was improving and play some political cards'. Laughland emphasised Lonrho's poor reputation and the detrimental effect of a takeover upon Scotland because control would be moved from Glasgow to Cheapside. The delegation left the minister's office pessimistic about the outcome.

Despite the warm weather, Rowland arrived in an overcoat. Suffering from an attack of feverish malaria, he sat hunched, shivering in his coat, opposite the minister. 'All he kept repeating,' recalls Hattersley, 'was a complaint that David Owen refused to meet him.' Rowland was preoccupied by Rhodesia. Politically, Hattersley had no sympathy for the businessman and Rowland succeeded only in confirming his prejudices. 'Let's do a deal,' suggested Rowland. Hattersley was puzzled. Rowland continued, 'If you let this bid through, I can mediate on your behalf with Ian Smith to end UDI.' Wide-eyed, Hattersley waited until his visitor had finished and bade him farewell.

Soon after he returned to Cheapside, Rowland heard that

journalists working for three national newspapers had been quietly told by a government official that, on 4 May, two officers of Scotland Yard's Fraud Squad had visited Cheapside with an order signed by David Owen requiring Lonrho to hand over documents connected to its operations which allegedly breached Rhodesian sanctions.

For Rowland, the coincidence of the leak with his visit to Hattersley was proof of a 'vendetta' co-ordinated between the DTI and the Foreign Office. Hattersley, he believed, was a political puppet whose decision on the SUITS bid would be dictated from the Foreign Office. In fact, the police officers who called were not from the Fraud Squad, but detectives who wanted documents for the Bingham inquiry which were already in the government's possession. Conveniently Rowland forgot how the raid also exposed his own attempted manipulation. Three months earlier, he had summoned the *Sunday Times* to announce that the DPP had decided not to take any legal action resulting from the 1976 DTI report. Under the front-page headline, 'Lonrho given the all-clear', Rowland had suggested that all Lonrho's problems had disappeared. That story was wrong and provoked the leak of the police visit to Cheapside on the day Rowland met Hattersley.

There was turmoil inside Cheapside that afternoon. Du Cann and others grieved that Lonrho was unpopular and how it was more convenient for a Labour government to order an inquiry rather than defend Lonrho. Rowland however remained cool. 'He likes to play games,' Du Cann once explained. Accordingly, that day Rowland summoned friendly journalists and challenged David Owen to 'discuss sanctions busting' in public. The foreign secretary, Rowland alleged, had 'personally' given an assurance that the criminal charges had been dropped. Asked to comment, the Foreign Office denied that Owen had ever dealt with Rowland or concerned himself with the prosecution.

The government's denial was not quite accurate. As Kenneth Etheridge, the former Fraud Squad officer, reminded Rowland, the decision whether to continue the criminal investigation into Lonrho for the payment of bribes and breaches of sanctions depended, according to Tudor Price, upon the Foreign Office. Moreover, Owen and Rowland had met, but events temporarily persuaded Rowland to withhold that disclosure until after the next round.

The following day, 12 May, Hattersley formally referred the bid for SUITS to the Monopolies Commission. Effectively, Lonrho's bid was frozen pending the investigation. Hattersley denied any pressure from the Foreign Office and insisted upon the legitimacy of his decision. The referral irritated Lonrho but in the context of a burst in Rowland's activities in southern Africa, it appeared a temporary blip.

By April 1978, Ian Smith, aware that without a settlement Rhodesia faced ruin, was prepared to recommence negotiations with the nationalists. Rowland offered to arrange another meeting and Smith accepted. Preliminary discussions were to be held in London. The central issue was to determine the conditions for Nkomo's return to Rhodesia as a potential leader.

Smith's emissary was Derrick Robinson, a former Special Branch officer and the deputy to Ken Flower. Born in Huddersfield, Robinson had first met Rowland twenty-five years earlier in Gatooma when the farmer had registered the theft of a suit with the local police.

Robinson was selected as an intermediary because twenty years earlier he had first met Nkomo as a special branch officer supervising the active black trade unionist. 'We understood each other,' recalled Robinson. More recently, Robinson had seen reports about Lonrho's assistance in the securing of a house for the Reverend Ndabaningi Sithole in Houghton Park, Salisbury and Kruger's payment of $7000 to settle ZAPU's expenses at the Ambassador hotel in Salisbury. Nkomo himself was dressed in fine-cut London suits boasting about the 'wine, women and song supplied by Lonrho'. Robinson's quiet contempt, as he spied other nationalist leaders enjoying Rowland's hospitality at London's Waldorf and Savoy hotels, turned to irritation. 'Rowland was paying and playing the field with our enemies but we took no action,' he lamented.

Ensconced at Hedsor Wharf with Sandys, Nkomo, and other nationalist leaders, Robinson noted the conditions for Nkomo's return. Also present was Brigadier Joseph Garba, the Nigerian foreign minister, an agreed intermediary. With Rowland in the chair, tactfully directing the discussions, everyone was optimistic about an agreement. Rowland found the role of powerbroker rather satisfying. Trusted and liked by the Africans, he was setting an agenda which had eluded Foreign Office officials and facilitated his own interests in increasing Lonrho's profits.

When the meeting terminated it was agreed that, to prevent misunderstandings, Robinson would travel to Lusaka to hear Kaunda's opinions personally. He would travel with Rowland. Their departure from Heathrow was jovial. 'Rowland grabbed my suitcase,' recalled Robinson. 'I protested but he laughed, "Don't worry, I got lots of experience at Paddington." '

As they flew to Africa, Rowland asked, 'I suppose you've got people watching me night and day.' Robinson's response was predictable: 'You're joking, Tiny. We've got more important people to watch and I haven't got enough men to keep watch on me.' In fact, the COI's surveillance had been exposed when a renegade officer offered Rowland the agency's tapes of bugged telephone conversations.

Robinson's report from Lusaka was positive. A meeting between Smith and Kaunda could go ahead. Simultaneously in Salisbury, Sir John Graham, on David Owen's instructions, was trying to negotiate with Smith for a plane chartered by the British government to fly him to Zambia. Once again, the Foreign Office was outwitted.

On 14 August 1978, Smith flew on Rowland's jet towards Lusaka. Awaiting him were Kaunda, Nkomo and Garba. At the end of their optimistic discussions, it was agreed that Smith would return the following week when Mugabe would be invited to join the agreement for an internal settlement. Rowland's own relations with the Marxist were strained. A few weeks earlier, Mugabe had visited Rowland in Cheapside. 'How much have you given to Nkomo?' asked Mugabe who had just arrived from Mozambique.

'It's my money and that's my business,' replied Rowland.

Mugabe had walked out in anger.

In Lusaka, Smith knew that Rowland, on Kaunda's insistence, had discriminated against Mugabe.

'Are you certain you can get Mugabe here?' Smith asked Garba.

'No problem,' replied the Nigerian foreign minister.

One week later, just hours before boarding the Lonrho jet, Smith was told that his return to Lusaka had been cancelled. Mugabe and his sponsor Julius Nyerere, irritated by Kaunda's secret diplomacy, opposed any discussions with Smith. 'This is Africa,' sighed Smith. Two weeks later, his harmonious relationship with Nkomo ended abruptly. A Rhodesian civilian Viscount airliner carrying fifty-six passengers had been shot down by Nkomo's guerrillas. Eighteen survived the crash but ten of these were subsequently murdered by the guerrillas. Smith launched a retaliatory bloodbath against Nkomo's guerrillas outside Lusaka. The dream shared by Rowland and Kaunda to slide Nkomo into power had disintegrated. On one of those rare occasions, Rowland did not hide his disappointment from Wilming. Sitting together in the Gulfstream's cabin, he confessed, 'It's a lost opportunity.'

Initially, Foreign Office officials took grim comfort from Rowland's failure. On Britain's behalf, Lord Carver, an austere and unappealing retired field marshal, was dispatched to Rhodesia to explore the possibility of a settlement. His mission's swift collapse was blamed by both the Rhodesians and African nationalists upon his personality and the futility of his proposals. As far as Rowland was concerned Carver's mission epitomised the absurdity of the Foreign Office and in particular David Owen. To expect an arcane soldier, dressed in uniform, to understand or command the respect of the Rhodesians of either colour was ridiculous. For their part, Foreign Office officials were content to shift the blame on to Rowland.

By then, Lonrho was paying a heavy penalty for Rowland's partisan involvement in Rhodesia's shifting alliances. In June, President Nyerere of Tanzania had nationalised all Lonrho's assets. Lonrho's eighteen companies trading in motors, tea, cotton and office supplies were valued by Lonrho at £15 million. In practical terms, they were worthless because they could not be sold for hard currency but their profits could be partially remitted.

Officially, Nyerere authorised the seizure as punishment for 'meddling' in Rhodesia's constitutional future and because Lonrho had 'undermined the freedom struggle in southern Africa'. Evidence for the latter, claimed Nyerere, was contained in the DTI's report on Lonrho's sanctions-breaking activities and expansion of trade in South Africa. After the disclosure of the second Lusaka meeting between Smith and Nkomo in September, Nyerere announced that his government would not pay any compensation for Lonrho's assets.

In normal circumstances, Rowland's quandary might have been embarrassing. Lonrho's shareholders could legitimately question why their chief executive had, for no benefit to the company, dabbled in vanity powerbroking and risked the company's assets. But since Lonrho's shareholders numbered only unquestioning admirers, Rowland was accountable solely to himself for the predicament and, by nature, Rowland rarely admitted a mistake. Instead, convinced that he was the victim of a Whitehall campaign, Rowland publicly blamed pressure from the British Foreign Office upon Nyerere for Tanzania's expropriation. There was no evidence to support his allegation and privately he admitted to Tom Ferguson, the Lonrho director representing Gulf Fisheries, 'It's a purely political decision prompted by Robert Mugabe who is backed by Tanzania and indirectly by Russia.' His public counter-attack inflamed his relations with Owen.

Coinciding with Tanzania's nationalisation, the government published on 19 September 1978 Thomas Bingham's investigation into the supply of oil to Rhodesia. The 500-page report confirmed Rowland's allegations that BP and Shell had broken sanctions. Theoretically, Rowland's vindication should have been a cause for celebration. Instead, since Bingham levelled the blame for the illegalities on minor employees and barely mentioned the senior civil servants and ministers who were parties to the conspiracy, Rowland rightly perceived the report as another Establishment cover-up. According to Rowland, even the report's preface which thanked Lonrho for supplying crucial evidence, was deleted on the Foreign Office's instructions. The whitewash was completed in parliament where an attempt by members to secure the release of Cabinet documents to expose the culpable senior officials was repulsed by the government. 'That shows,' Rowland complained, 'that once again the Establishment protect their own from the prosecution of crimes while revelling in superfluous criticisms about me.'

The time was ripe, he believed, publicly to challenge the Foreign Office. On 3 October, Rowland passed to *The Times* a letter which he had sent on the eve of Bingham's publication to David Owen. In essence, Rowland was openly accusing the foreign secretary of pressuring and of conspiring against Lonrho.

Owen's appointment in February 1977 had caused some surprise. At thirty-nine, he was not only one of Britain's youngest foreign ministers but was, according to his civil servants, probably the most arrogant, ambitious and abrasive minister whom they had served within their lifetimes. Contrary to their advice, Owen had agreed to meet Rowland in early June 1977 to discuss Africa because he shared Rowland's disdain for Britain's traditional diplomats and their record in Rhodesia.

Naturally Rowland was eager to seize the opportunity. He would be able to impress his opinions upon the government and be seen in Africa as a man of influence. Some would say that mere association with ministers flattered Rowland's self-esteem. In any event, during the course of their conversation, the two men also discussed the continuing *impasse* between Lonrho and the government.

Sixteen months later, on 18 September, Rowland's letter sought to remind Owen that in the course of their conversation, the foreign secretary had allegedly made two critical points.

Firstly, Owen assured Rowland that 'our [Lonrho's] own name would be cleared within weeks by the DPP'. Those were the grounds, claimed Rowland, upon which he had co-operated with Bingham since there was 'no basis to suspect that there exists any evidence' that Lonrho had breached sanctions legislation. Secondly, Owen had threatened that 'Lonrho would be one of the victims' if its litigation against the oil companies for compensation was not stopped.

Rowland alleged that because he had ignored Owen's warning and persisted with the litigation, the British government had harassed Lonrho: firstly, by dispatching police officers to Cheapside; secondly, by leaking their presence two weeks later on the most critical day of the SUITS bid; and thirdly, by colluding with the Tanzanians to nationalise Lonrho's assets.

By any measure, it was an astonishing letter but relatively easy to ignore since Rowland offered no evidence to substantiate his claim about Tanzania and was wrong to suggest that there was 'no basis to suspect' that Lonrho had breached sanctions. To the Foreign Office, Rowland seemed to be fixated by the belief that if something was repeated sufficiently often, it would become the truth. Alternatively, he convinced himself by his own repetition. Unusually, Owen's official reply outrightly accused Rowland of lying and distortion.

If by publishing the exchange of letters, Rowland hoped to embarrass Owen and his advisers, he failed. Despite an editorial in *The Times* claiming that 'the issues are of great importance', the Foreign Office declined all invitations to enter the fray and Rowland's anticipated public row fizzled out.

While others, throughout that exchange, viewed Rowland as a bully, he saw himself as the victim and not as the instigator of the dispute. Aggression, he believed, would protect him from Whitehall intimidation. In a form of self-protection that went as far as narcissism, he inflicted on others what he believed he was suffering himself. Psychiatrists describe the condition as projected identification. At that very moment, the victim of Rowland's harassment was Udi Gecaga, the Kenyan who was Lonrho's vaunted African director.

On 22 August 1978 Jomo Kenyatta died. During that night, some factions of his family had sought to prevent vice president Daniel arap Moi inheriting the presidency. They failed. As day broke, Gecaga knew that since Moi's supporters were enemies of his family, his value to Lonrho was diminishing. By lunchtime, he had already been dismissed as a director of Kenya Airways. 'I'm in trouble,' he told a friend. Rowland, he knew, believed political connections were critical to business success.

Only a few weeks earlier, Gecaga had seen the evidence of Rowland's spite and desire for revenge. On 24 May 1978,

Bruce McKenzie, Rowland's sworn enemy in Kenya, had been murdered in a spectacular fashion. While taxiing in his plane at Kampala airport to take off for Nairobi, McKenzie had received a radio message to delay his departure. An aide to President Amin drove along the runway and presented the Kenyan with a stuffed animal's head. 'A present from the president,' shouted the European with a grin. McKenzie's plane departed and exploded about fifteen minutes later. Amin had taken his revenge. Two years earlier, McKenzie had negotiated the permission for Israel to refuel their troop transporters in Nairobi en route to their daring raid in Entebbe where they would liberate the passengers of an El Al jet, held hostage by Amin. Despite that humiliation of Amin, McKenzie believed himself immune to reprisals and, during that fatal visit, was suspected of negotiating an arms deal.

Among the dead passengers on McKenzie's plane was Gavin Whitelaw, a director of Lonrho Exports. Whitelaw was also Fred Butcher's son-in-law. Rowland was understandably intrigued why a Lonrho employee was on board the aeroplane of his sworn enemy? Butcher, whose relationship with Rowland was strained by the unfair blame he had been forced to bear during the DTI inquiry, was targeted for Rowland's spleen. 'No one,' ordered Rowland, 'is allowed to attend Whitelaw's funeral. Those who disobey are to have their pay withheld.' Butcher was among the very few who disobeyed and was further ostracised. Kruger also protested. 'Nic hated Rowland's vindictiveness against Gavin Whitelaw,' recalls one of the Salisbury directors, 'and he was fed up with the bribes.' For six months, Kruger refused to take telephone calls from Rowland. 'He just put the phone down when Tiny called,' recalls the same director. Rowland passed messages to Kruger through Eileen, his wife.

The day following McKenzie's death, Rowland entertained Ngethe Njoroge, the Kenyan High Commissioner, to lunch. 'There is no reason to welcome anyone's death,' Rowland had said, but was understandably not grieving the departure of an unpleasant competitor. Kenyatta's death and the accession of Moi had curtailed Rowland's joy.

Gecaga was summoned to London to reassess Lonrho's operations in Kenya. Rowland wanted quickly to establish his allegiance to the new president and Charles Njonjo, the former attorney general who had been Bruce McKenzie's staunch ally. Gecaga, deemed to be an obstacle to the new diplomacy, was greeted accordingly.

Paul Spicer welcomed his friend with the suggestion that he should resign from Lonrho. Duncan Sandys ordered that the whole editorial team of Lonrho's Kenyan newspaper, the *Standard*, should be replaced by Moi's supporters. Rowland simply ignored his erstwhile protégé. Loyalty, as many discovered, was always owed to Rowland but the reverse remained strictly conditional.

Over the following days, Rowland repeatedly demanded Gecaga's resignation. The Kenyan declined except on his own terms which Rowland argued were unfavourable to Lonrho. Over the previous years, Gecaga had created three businesses – textiles, cars and a brewery – which were joint ventures between himself and Lonrho. In return for his resignation he wanted either to be paid for his share of the companies or be allowed to buy Lonrho's share. Gecaga's cool demand enraged Rowland: 'I made you,' he exploded in his small office, 'you think you can buy me out?' His audience, other directors, quivered silently. Only Gecaga looked steadily at his accuser. 'I could get you jailed for having stolen assets,' raged Rowland. The menace would be repeated several times. 'Sign the transfers!' Gecaga refused. But believing that Rowland's threat would be implemented, Gecaga fled to America.

The second major casualty of Kenyatta's death was Fred Butcher. Annoyed that Rowland had forbidden attendance at his son-in-law's funeral, stricken with diabetes and disillusioned about the implications of Rowland's understanding of loyalty, Butcher retired. Rowland did not lament his parting. Ever since Butcher had unilaterally organised a conference of Lonrho's African managing directors in Mauritius, Rowland's confidence in his financial adviser had declined. But among Butcher's unresolved legacies was the undisclosed financial relationship with Dan Mayers and the Kundalilla amethyst mine.

In April 1978, Rhodesian military raids into Zambia had

caused the mine's closure and then its destruction. Concerned about the future earnings, Zambian government officials queried Lonrho about the size of the stockpile of gems which, unknown in Lusaka, was worth about $1.6 million. Rowland was distressed. Hitherto, the secret deals with Mayers in Liechtenstein had been handled exclusively by Butcher. If the business was to continue, Rowland would become directly involved. The automatic self-incrimination was dangerous. So much of Rowland's political posturing depended upon Kaunda that it seemed foolish to risk everything on a small gem operation. Rowland therefore proposed to Mayers that they return the whole amethyst stockpile controlled by Blorg to Zambia and apologise for their mistake. According to Mayers, 'Rowland was going to President Kaunda and throw himself on his mercy, pleading complete ignorance of the events leading up to the formation of the huge stockpile. Mr Rowland assured me that he was confident that President Kaunda would indeed forgive him. If necessary he would offer to build another stadium.'

Rowland would dismiss Mayers's account, in a manner reminiscent of the Coronation Syndicate fraud in 1971, as 'fiction'. In Rowland's explanation, the whole operation 'was the brainchild of Mr Mayers and Mr Butcher'. He was totally ignorant, in every detail, of the amethyst business. 'The dealings were almost entirely between Mr Mayers and Fred Butcher . . . I was running 250 operational companies. Northern Minerals was one of the smallest and I was not running it. It was totally unimportant to us.' He intended to give an identical account to Kaunda. 'That was absolute nonsense,' according to Mayers. 'Nothing happened without Lonrho knowing.'

Mayers was alarmed by Rowland's proposal. 'That's mad and that's disreputable,' he told Rowland. While the amount of money to Rowland was comparatively minimal, Mayers's losses would be relatively substantial. Mayers rejected Rowland's plan and also refused to reveal the precise location of the stockpiles. Instead, Mayers proposed that they divide the stockpiles in proportion to their shareholding, 55–45. Rowland refused, but there was a dilemma. To remove any incriminating evidence, Butcher had burnt all the papers concerning Northern Minerals in 1974.

Rowland was therefore unable to understand any aspect of the business, especially the size and location of the gems stockpile.

On 29 November 1978, Mayers wrote a protective letter, incriminating Rowland in the venture, which was delivered to his erstwhile partner. To solve their disagreement, Rowland invited Mayers for dinner on 4 December. The American arrived at Rowland's apartment in Park Lane bearing a scroll containing a Chinese proverb: 'The tall tree catches the wind.' Rowland says that he suffered 'a sense of foreboding'. Rowland wanted to eat at the Berkeley hotel. Rowland maintains, disputed by Mayers, that after an hour's discussion Rowland and Josie agreed to eat at Poons, a bland Chinese restaurant in Covent Garden.

'Let's talk about Northern Minerals,' said Rowland picking up the menu.

'There is another Chinese proverb,' replied Mayers, 'let's not talk business on an empty stomach.'

'What are you talking about?' gritted Rowland. 'I am not here to discuss you and Aspen and your love life. We are here to discuss business.'

Rowland says that nothing was discussed. Mayers contradicts Rowland but both agree that nothing was settled. Nine days later, on 13 December, Mayers returned to Rowland's apartment for breakfast. Having accepted a cup of coffee, Mayers presented a letter and asked for Rowland's signature. Effectively, Mayers wanted a signed agreement that 'I had acted honourably'. Mayers's self-protection was naturally, from Rowland's point of view, self-incrimination. According to Rowland, 'I tore it up. I took him to the lift and said goodbye.' According to Mayers, Rowland 'went into a terrible fit of rage and when he read the letter, tore it up and swore he would use the full power of Lonrho to crush me. His face became contorted and flushed and his mouth full of foul language. In all my life I have never witnessed such uncontrolled and insane fury.' In contradiction, Rowland says, 'I never yell at people. It is not in my nature to yell at anybody.'

Nine months after Mayers disappeared, Rowland issued writs in Hong Kong, Geneva, London and Denver to freeze Mayers's assets and recover both the money owed and the stockpile of amethysts for their return to Zambia. Mayers admits that he was shocked but on reflection, 'I enjoyed fighting him and that annoyed him even more.'

In the helterskelter of Rowland's life, where several major and diverse disputes, projects, negotiations and dashed flights around Africa would occur simultaneously, while struggling with Mayer Rowland was also immersed in seeking to persuade Godfray Le Quesne, QC, the chairman of the Monopolies and Mergers Commission, that Lonrho's bid for SUITS was not contrary to the public interest. Over the following seven years, Le Quesne would, to Rowland's increasing annoyance, question Rowland's motives and proposals in four separate inquiries. Three involved the House of Fraser and the fourth was Lonrho's purchase of the *Observer*.

Born in 1924, Le Quesne was a Recorder and an appeal judge in the Channel Islands who was appointed to the Monopolies Commission in 1974. Under the Labour government, the Commission's duties were not simply to investigate the prospect of a monopoly, but to report upon the wider issues of whether the combination of two companies was in the 'public interest'. The criteria, which were clearly subjective and political, were further influenced by officials in both the Office of Fair Trading and in the Department of Trade and Industry.

By temperament and training, civil servants have little in common with self-made businessmen and they lack any natural rapport with mavericks. Their structured careers, established pay scales and inflation-proof pensions appeal to a different breed from that of a gambler who relies upon intuition and delights in his freedom.

Inherently, Rowland ignored rules and disliked government controls. Yet he was striving to operate in an era when a measure of intervention by the state into industry was still the accepted orthodoxy of both political parties.

Although Le Quesne would staunchly insist that the civil servants never sought to sway his decisions, he knew that they were at best cautious about Rowland and at worst deeply suspicious. Memories of the DTI's report about Lonrho were too fresh for the disdain and distrust harboured by most senior DTI officials to have evaporated. Contrary to Rowland's conviction, Le Quesne would deny a cosy relationship with the Department although he would incredulously assert that the Monopolies Commission was never used for political purposes. But regardless of his claims to impartiality, Le Quesne knew that Hattersley's motives were entirely political.

The SUITS hearings during the winter of 1978 were conducted in a conference room in Carey Street. Seven commissioners sat behind a mahogany table with about ten lawyers, accountants and secretaries seated behind. Facing them were Rowland, other Lonrho directors, their lawyers and accountants. On the tables were stacks of documents, duplicated twenty times, providing information on every aspect of Lonrho supplied by its bankers, lawyers, accountants and executives. The cost and disruption were enormous.

While Rowland could appreciate a political battle, he was perplexed why a judge without any proven commercial understanding should be empowered to decide what would benefit the shareholders of two companies. His prejudice was not assuaged when he met Le Quesne. The judge seemed to regard him as a mystery, as if there was something strange about his business affairs. How, mused Rowland, could a judge from the Channel Islands understand the nature of deal-making in Africa? Lonrho produced sales of £1.5 billion which ranked the company fourteenth in the UK corporate league, and there was still no respect. Rowland could never conceal his sense of grievance.

Bruce Fireman, the banker advising the Straight Three, shared Rowland's misgivings about Le Quesne, whose eyes were 'more closed than open'. In their submissions to Le Quesne, Hugh Laughland argued that Lonrho's finances were weak; that Lonrho was excessively dependent upon Africa; that Scotland would suffer if SUITS became English; that Lonrho wanted SUITS merely as a lever to buy the House of Fraser; and he emphasised Rowland's tarnished reputation. After their final session, Laughland suspected that his pleas were to no avail. 'The Commission's accountants,' complained Fireman, 'won't understand what we are saying.'

In fact, Le Quesne was intrigued by Laughland's analysis of

Lonrho's finances. The preparation of the company's accounts revealed Rowland's demands that his own requirements be satisfied rather than those of normal accountancy practices, especially with regard to Lonrho's debt. According to Laughland's calculations, Lonrho in 1977 had borrowings of £182 million which was 80 per cent more than the previous year. In 1978, its borrowings had increased to £222 million, while its shareholder funds were £80 million. Assessments by critical accountants suggested that Lonrho was probably bankrupt.

The puzzle, suggested Laughland, was Lonrho's treatment of its debts. In the 1977 published accounts, Lonrho's total debts were stated at £103 million. But in the 1978 accounts, the debts for 1977 were itemised at £87 million, a reduction of £16 million. The 1978 debts were even lower at £73 million. The accountancy according to Laughland was creative and quite startling.

Le Quesne asked Rowland to explain how Lonrho hoped to pay for SUITS and survive. Rowland explained that he had arranged a £50 million loan from abroad and expected 'substantial sums' from the litigation against the oil companies since he had rejected the oil companies' offer of £30 million to settle. In the event Rowland did not raise the loan, nor did Lonrho receive any compensation. On the contrary. Lonrho lost the case and paid all the legal fees, a record amount. At the time, however, Le Quesne accepted Rowland's assurance but he did recall Rowland on one issue.

In urging Le Quesne to prevent the Lonrho bid, the directors from the House of Fraser expressed their 'fear' and 'apprehension' that SUITS's anticipated 29 per cent stake in House of Fraser, controlled by Rowland, would mean that their company would effectively be controlled by Lonrho, a 'high-risk' company.

Le Quesne recalled Rowland. 'Are you planning to bid for the House of Fraser?' Rowland was equivocal: 'We are not considering a bid at the moment.' Rowland also dismissed the notion that Lonrho would seek to control House of Fraser because, he said, it was 'exceptionally well run'. Nor, pledged Rowland, would he influence its dividends policy.

To reinforce Rowland's assurance, Duncan Sandys had written to Le Quesne promising that Lonrho would not seek more than three directors on the House of Fraser board. Le Quesne concluded that Lonrho would not seek to 'fundamentally' influence House of Fraser.

In his final report, Le Quesne wrote, 'We accept that Lonrho has no present intention of bringing about a full merger with the House of Fraser.' But Le Quesne added that if Lonrho did bid for the group, 'a new situation would be created and . . . a further reference to us could, no doubt, be made.'

Just as the stock market closed on 3 March 1979, Le Quesne presented his report. Contrary to the expectations of the City, the Labour party and Rowland himself, Le Quesne reported that there were no grounds to prevent Lonrho's takeover of SUITS.

Although delighted, Rowland did not interpret Le Quesne's decision as evidence that the system was fair or that Lonrho was now acceptable to the City. He had won, he believed, because 'they' lacked sufficient reasons to pursue their prejudices.

Nevertheless, for the first time in six years, Lonrho seemed to be free of an official investigation. The DPP had announced on 3 November 1978 that no criminal charges would follow the DTI report. Rowland's supporters spoke of a 'watershed' and predicted less troubled times ahead. Others were less convinced. Among those was Bruce Fireman, the SUITS banker, whom Rowland telephoned that night to discuss the bid. 'We intend to continue the fight,' Fireman told Rowland.

Pending the outcome, Rowland had some housekeeping to complete. Ever since the Sabah brothers had resigned their position as Lonrho directors in 1976, the Kuwaitis had entertained the possibility of a takeover bid. With the failure of that strategy, they proposed to rejoin the board. As the largest shareholders, Gulf wanted to control Rowland's management, to increase the value of Lonrho shares and eventually recoup their losses. Tom Ferguson proposed to Rowland that Gulf appoint three directors on to Lonrho's board.

Rowland agreed to meet Sheikh Nasser in his Mount Street offices. For both sides, it was an important encounter. The Kuwaitis, outwitted and out of pocket, sought a respectable conclusion to the famous marriage of five years earlier. Rowland sought to remove the irritant of a larger shareholder than himself. 'I used to own 50 per cent of this company,' he would complain, 'and now I own less than 20 per cent.' At the end of their meeting, the Arab believed they had struck a deal. In exchange for three Gulf Fisheries directors on Lonrho's board, the Kuwaitis would support a rights issue, diluting their own stake, with which Rowland proposed to raise more money. An extraordinary general meeting was summoned to approve the issue.

Just as the Monopolies Commission report on SUITS was published, Tom Ferguson telephoned Rowland with the names of the three proposed directors.

'No way,' said Rowland. 'We haven't resolved compensation for the Kenana sugar project yet.' For Furgusson, that was a surprise but worse followed. 'And I don't like your three people.'

Ferguson understood that the Mount Street agreement was dead. The rights issue was approved, galvanising Ferguson to fight Rowland. To his dismay, trawling the City to find allies, Ferguson discovered that Rowland's ruthless reputation deterred every banker he approached. Without exception, even if they held Lonrho shares, the City institutions resisted his offer. 'They're too scared to fight,' he told Sheikh Nasser. Ferguson proposed himself and a colleague as alternative directors.

The battle burst into the open in an acrimonious exchange of circulars published in national newspapers. In a foretaste of countless whole-page advertisements directed at shareholders, the two sides exchanged insults in preparation for the annual general meeting. The issue was the appointment of two Kuwaiti directors to the Lonrho board. Rowland rejected their presence arguing that, 'The present members of the [Lonrho] Board have worked harmoniously together as a team with each member playing an important part and the Board cannot see how these proposed appointments would strengthen the team.'

At the shareholders' meeting, Gulf were outvoted but there was an interesting sequel to Rowland's dismissive argument against the Kuwaitis' request for representation. In similar circumstances one year later, Rowland demanded representation on the board of House of Fraser. That board rejected

Rowland's demand on grounds identical to those Rowland had used to rebuff the Kuwaitis.

Rowland had entered a new phase of life. The 'shy' businessman bounced to the other extreme and invoked public opinion to help him with his argument. The bold strategy, replete with contradictions and inconsistencies, was often undermined by the self-defeating blindness of its conductor's sentiments. The completion of the SUITS bid was the rehearsal for Rowland's emergence from the shadows to engage in public battles.

Cleared by the Monopolies Commission, Rowland published a new offer on 20 March, of one Lonrho share plus £1 in cash for each SUITS share. At 8 a.m. on Saturday, Rowland telephoned Fireman in his Highgate home. Rowland had every reason to believe that SUITS was finally won but feared Fireman's astute cultivation of the press. 'You can say whatever you like about my offer for SUITS,' warned Rowland, 'but if you attack the price of Lonrho shares, I'll destroy you.'

'But I must,' replied Fireman somewhat startled. 'You're offering Lonrho shares in part exchange.'

'Yes,' replied Rowland, 'but you mustn't say anything untrue.'

Unexpectedly, two days later, after the latest bid was published, Hugh Fraser announced that, on behalf of the family trust's 8.9 per cent stake, he opposed Rowland's takeover. Rowland, who had not quite understood Fraser's mercurial streak, was shocked. For the first and not the last time, the opposition to Rowland was directed by his erstwhile ally. All five SUITS directors now opposed Lonrho. Although delighted, Laughland feared that Fraser could quite easily switch again.

That night, Fireman was at the Berkeley hotel. Since it was one of Rowland's favourite restaurants, it was not a complete surprise that he spotted his adversary jovially entertaining a group of Africans. In retreat, Rowland kept up the same appearances as if he were in the vanguard. The conversation was polite but non-committal.

A few nights later, on 3 April, Rowland was back at the Berkeley. His guest was Hugh Fraser. Rowland sought to woo the gambler back to his side. The following morning it seemed that Rowland had failed. At a SUITS board meeting, Fraser agreed with Laughland that they should unite and fight. As the two men walked down the stairs, Fraser repeated to Laughland, 'I'm with you 100 per cent. I'm with you.' Twelve hours later, on 5 April, as he boarded a plane for Vancouver, Canada, James Gossman, Hugh Fraser's loyal fellow director, telephoned the *Glasgow Herald* and announced that Fraser had switched sides again. He would now support Rowland's improved offer of one Lonrho share and 115p in cash. Fraser never publicly explained his abrupt reversal. Privately, his friends suspected that Rowland had seduced the lonely Scotsman with temptations about their glorious future together.

Laughland finally accepted that his fight was over. The only challenge was to compel Rowland to increase the price and sweat before claiming victory. Fireman however was still determined to win. Rapidly he put together a consortium and £5.5 million to buy the shares owned by the Fraser family trust. While the family pondered Fireman's 195p cash offer, the banker urged all the institutions to reject Rowland's lower bid.

Among those whom he visited was Simon Garmoyle, the Warburgs banker and adviser to the House of Fraser. A defensive proposal, concocted by Fireman and Willet, proposed that Warburgs should establish a new company which would buy both SUITS and House of Fraser. Fireman dubbed his idea 'The Godfather deal', an offer that no one could refuse. Garmoyle's response was nonchalant. 'Rowland's next step,' warned Willet, 'will be to bid for House of Fraser.' Garmoyle scoffed, 'We can defend ourselves.' 'You do realise,' continued Willet, 'the gun is loaded, the trigger cocked and the finger is on the trigger?'

Garmoyle, a viscount who would become the sixth Earl Cairns on his father's death, was unimpressed.

Rowland was also uncowed. Hugh Fraser agreed to be bound by their latest agreement and formally support Lonrho, forbidding his family to take more for their stake than other shareholders. Rowland was still unable to find any other sellers of Fraser stock. On 3 May, when the Conservatives romped to victory, Lonrho had still only secured a tantalising 46.4 per cent of the shares, an ominous indication of the City's solid distrust of Rowland. Eight days later, Rowland raised the cash offer to 135p. By then 'The Hoover', an unidentified City operator who was picking up loose shares on the market, had accumulated a 4 per cent stake. Not surprisingly, he sold to Lonrho. Rowland scraped through.

On 10 May, Laughland gave up the fight and recommended that the remaining shareholders sell. Exhausted and despondent, he rejected Rowland's offer to remain as managing director: 'I'd told him from the outset that I'd never work for him.' Rowland, he felt, had walked away with a bargain although he had paid the equivalent of 216p per share compared with his original offer of 132p.

Lonrho's payment of £56.6 million for SUITS was indeed a bargain. Shortly afterwards, the company received an offer of £40 million just for the Whyte & Mackay distillery. Laughland's other predictions also proved correct. Contrary to the assurances Rowland gave Le Quesne, SUITS headquarters was moved out of Glasgow and Rowland began preparations to take control over the House of Fraser.

Nine
Misjudgments

The euphoria in Cheapside was flaunted. Sipping a spritzer, his legs on the desk, surrounded by his band of faithful directors, Rowland acknowledged their congratulations and spoke of his ambitions. Aged sixty-two, when most men would be planning retirement, Rowland was considering his potential as finally realisable. Despite occasional `attacks of malaria and asthma, Rowland had never felt healthier. A new age had dawned, not least because the Labour government and Rowland's enemies in the Foreign Office and DTI had been routed. With an annual salary of £225,000 and a further £4.4 million paid in dividends for his Lonrho's shares, Rowland wore his wealth as a badge of contempt for the little men who spurned his advice or impeded his enterprise.

Sheltered, deep in the background, were Josie and their four children. Three daughters, Plum, Louise, Anda, the eldest, and a son called Toby, were kept firmly beyond the limelight. The marriage had proved ideal. Devoted to her 'knight in shining armour', Josie provided whatever her husband required, guaranteeing, as far as possible, happy equilibrium. Visitors to Hedsor Wharf and later at their London house in Chester Square, were struck by the sheer unostentatious normality of family life. In notable frugality, Rowland was known to walk around the house switching off unnecessary lights and Josie rarely wore jewellery, not even a wedding ring. The only sign of ostentation was the multiplicity of telephone lines. Tiny loved the instrument and if an incoming call rang more than twice the caller would assume that Rowland was not at home. To some, Rowland lamented his frequent absences from home, which undermined his influence over and relationship with his children. Others believed that Rowland was still too preoccupied with his professional aspirations to pay more than lip service to parenthood. The isolation and ruthless requirement of loyalty in Cheapside were replicated in his home. Discipline, as in his own childhood, was strict and there was little evidence of family games. Rowland protected his children but unlike other empire builders eschewed cultivating his offspring to care for their inheritance or forge the notion of a dynasty. In a rare display of independence, Toby, contrary to his father's wishes that he should study German, travelled to Japan. But his son, Rowland had already determined, was unsuited to enter Lonrho. Otherwise, surrounded by an obedient family in Hedsor Wharf and sycophants in Cheapside, Rowland emitted an aura of solitude, even loneliness. In his evenings at home, he liked best to sit by the fire, listening to Mozart or Schubert, and read a book. Despite his anger and frustration with Britain and its natives, within the confines of his homes he was content to live in the country. Rowland's agenda laid him open to criticism. He gave the impression of being contemptuous of the company of others, with little interest in exciting affection, unless for expedience, in which case it could be bought. Singlemindedly he was tracking a vision which was made more possible by the new prime minister.

Margaret Thatcher promised in 1979 a fairer deal for business and a final settlement in Rhodesia. Naturally, Rowland would offer his services and, with Edward Du Cann's help, would now expect his advice to be accepted. This was an ideal moment to promote the new face of Lonrho, and Paul Spicer, who had assumed the mantle of company press spokesman, invited trusted journalists to Cheapside to record his master's voice.

Obligingly, the results complied with the desire. Under the headlines 'And suddenly, it's Shiny Rowland' and 'Rowland aims for the stars', Rowland enthused: 'Our aim is to become one of the five largest UK businesses over the next three years.' Lonrho, he believed, would be equal to the chemical giant ICI or Anglo American. These were the utterances of a man whose eagerness for glory ignored reality.

For among Rowland's assumptions was the conviction that the House of Fraser, of which Lonrho was the largest shareholder with a 29.98 per cent stake, could effortlessly be acquired because an alternative bid, instigating an expensive auction, was unlikely. Finding another £200 million to complete the takeover was, Rowland believed, not a problem. Lonrho could expect sympathy from the banks. The rewards would be enormous: prestige, a huge cash flow and assets which could either be sold or used as collateral for further loans.

The jewel was Harrods, the Knightsbridge store advertised as providing 'the world's most comprehensive range of merchandise and special services'. Harrods' pride was those idiosyncratic incidents which perpetuated myths and reputations. For example, in 1975, in response to a midnight call from Governor Ronald Reagan of California, the store promptly delivered a baby elephant six thousand miles away.

While the original purchase of SUITS shares had not been conceived as a strategic ploy to buy House of Fraser, Rowland's interest in the idea had developed as his relationship with Hugh Fraser revealed both the fragility of the family's control and the passivity of the company's management. By accident rather than by design, Rowland was positioned to acquire prestige and profits from an international symbol instead of obscure mines and motor franchises in Africa. Rowland admitted that attraction when he related an account of a conversation with Lopez Portillo, the president of Mexico. Rowland had planned a succession of projects in Mexico and after some effort secured an appointment with the president, whose approval was important. Portillo asked Rowland to describe Lonrho. Rowland recited Lonrho's African interests but watched forlornly as the president's interest dissipated. 'If I could have said "We own Harrods" then I wouldn't have had to go any further,' recounted Rowland in a devastating confession about his whole operation. But, given his anxiety to buy that passport to recognition, it was a telling indictment upon his limitations that he fell at the first obstacle which loomed.

On 19 October 1977, soon after the purchase of Hugh Fraser's SUITS shares, Rowland was invited by his new ally to meet twelve House of Fraser directors and senior managers. The occasion was a dinner at the Central hotel in Glasgow. In retrospect, it was among the most critical of the thousands of formal meals which Rowland had attended. Unfortunately, Rowland would only reflect upon its importance two years later.

Rowland was the guest of Scotsmen whose loyalty towards the Fraser family and especially towards the memory and philosophy of Lord Fraser was feudal. Although their stores were spread across the United Kingdom, the twelve who were directed from the company's Buchanan Street headquarters were uninterested in City of London intrigues and Whitehall machinations but proudly concerned about the well-being of their illustrious company.

Outsiders were not unknown to the board. The American retail chain, Carter Hawley Hale, then owned a 19 per cent stake and their three directors understood and had contributed to the business. This Glasgow dinner was the directors' first opportunity to get to know another new shareholder.

Convention dictated that Rowland's duty as a non-executive director was to attend board meetings and, in considering the interests of House of Fraser, to ignore any advantages for Lonrho. That evening in Glasgow, Rowland's hosts were understandably sensitive to discover whether he would abide by those rules.

Even before the first course was served, some in that room detected that their guest had misjudged the atmosphere. Rowland, who stepped into his jet more often than his hosts drove their cars, was clearly indifferent to their Scottish pride. Unusually, he displayed disdain rather than charm. These were mere employees, he thought, and badly dressed as well. 'Rowland thought that all of us were in Hugh Fraser's pocket,' recalls George Willoughby, the finance director. 'He didn't sense the vibes.'

The small talk petered as Winston Brimacombe, a director, asked Rowland, 'What are your plans?' Rowland prevaricated, refusing to confirm or deny whether he would eventually bid for the House of Fraser. The meal ended in disarray. Sentiment among the twelve after the dinner ranged between suspicion and outright antagonism. All agreed that Lonrho was unwelcome. 'It was a complete disaster,' recalled Willoughby.

Memories of that dinner sparked opposition from the House of Fraser board when Rowland bid for SUITS. Initially, the directors had considered a counter-bid for SUITS but were dissuaded by Hugh Fraser's enthusiastic endorsement of Rowland. But, just days after Le Quesne's report was published, their fears were confirmed. Rowland boasted publicly, 'Through SUITS we now have effective control of House of Fraser and that gives us control over £300 million of assets.' The effect upon the House of Fraser directors was predictable. Nevertheless, isolated in Glasgow from the realities of corporate warfare, they allowed Hugh Fraser to welcome Rowland's arrival on their board and assumed that business might continue as usual.

Within one month, their illusions were shaken. On 21 June 1979, Rowland protested about the continued use of Grievson Grant as House of Fraser's brokers and insisted that Carr Seebag, Lonrho's brokers, should be appointed. To placate Rowland, the board agreed that the company should employ two brokers. Rowland disagreed. At that point, on 18 October, Rowland encountered his old adversary, Warburgs.

Since their separation in 1971, neither Rowland nor the merchant bank had sought any reconciliation. On the contrary, during the 1976 Department of Trade inquiry, Rowland had even protested that the bank had actually forged a memorandum to justify their resignation retrospectively and he claimed to have evidence to suggest that Lonrho had lost money by accepting business proposed by Warburgs. But the mutual hostility might not have been resuscitated in 1979 had Rowland not introduced, at the outset, antagonism into his relationship with the House of Fraser directors. His confrontational insistence that Carr Seebag, an undistinguished broking house, should replace Grievson Grant, was a declaration of hostilities. By default, Rowland had galvanised the House of Fraser directors, unaccustomed to adversity, into seeking Warburgs' advice.

The two bankers consulted, both distinguished operators, were Simon Garmoyle and David Scholey. Neither professed a personal animus against Rowland but were mindful that House of Fraser was an important client and their directors 'were not streetwise'. Rather than depart from the looming conflict, they opted to continue as advisers. 'We felt that the other 70 per cent of the shareholders needed protection,' one of their team remarked. 'We'd had enough trouble with Rowland in the past and House of Fraser was a sensible client.' But if Rowland had avoided confrontation, the bankers' influence would have been limited.

To strengthen the board, Scholey recommended that Grievson Grant be replaced by Cazenoves and that in particular Michael Richardson and David Mayhew should advise the board. Since the Seebag broker assigned to House of Fraser appeared ineffectual, Rowland was suddenly faced with four formidable City operators. The battle lines were being drawn.

Warburgs' analysis of Lonrho's 1979 accounts showed a fall in pre-tax profits from £93 million to £84 million. Despite appearances, Lonrho's real profits, they discovered, had consistently fallen since 1976. Lonrho's admitted loans, despite the company's new accountancy practices, had practically doubled from £73 million to £137 million while their unconventional depreciation practice overstated Lonrho's assets by £195 million.

The discovery of the total of Lonrho's loans had been apparently by accident. For the first time, the Standard & Chartered Bank consolidated all their branches' lending to Lonrho's subsidiaries throughout Africa. 'They were staggered by the amount,' recalls Basil West, the finance director, who resigned before the Monopolies Commission completed the SUITS report. 'I went quietly,' says West, 'because of the way he bought Carter Hawley's stake in House of Fraser. It was the final straw.' For Warburgs, West's resignation and Rowland's refusal to appoint a new finance director prompted a resurgence of old suspicions. 'Whatever way we looked at Lonrho,' recalls one of the bankers, 'the company was shaky.' Rowland, the advisers realised, lacked the money to mount an unconditional bid for House of Fraser. For the moment, everyone was puzzled about his intentions.

Keeping the opposition guessing was a favourite Rowland tactic. His purchase of Dutton-Forshaw, the car distributors which included the Jack Barclay franchise selling Rolls Royces, for £23.2 million, was puzzling considering the new recession;

and the acquisition of Harrison & Sons, a security printer, for £1.9 million, defied analysis of any strategy other than unconditional growth.

Immune to criticism, Rowland was sure of his long-term game plan. Comforted by his regular telephone conversations with Hugh Fraser and their cosy lunches at the Dorchester, Rowland extracted extravagant assurances about their future joint management of the store group. Convinced that Fraser wielded similar dictatorial control to that he enjoyed at Lonrho, Rowland heard about Warburgs' unwelcome advice to the directors but accepted Fraser's boast: 'Everyone's loyal to me.'

Rowland's optimism about House of Fraser was matched by his anticipation of a peace settlement in Rhodesia. Forced by the increasing successes of the ZANU Patriotic Front's guerrillas over the Rhodesian army, Ian Smith had succumbed to an Anglo-American plan to resign in favour of a black transitional government. On 31 May 1979, Bishop Muzorewa became prime minister. The next stage was a conference at Lancaster House in London on 10 September to agree a constitution, a ceasefire and the timetable for a general election which would lead to majority rule.

Rowland, echoing Kaunda's choice, was anxious that Nkomo should become Zimbabwe's first president. Lonrho had survived in Rhodesia despite sanctions and Rowland's own overt sympathy with the nationalist African nations. With Nkomo as leader, he could anticipate a glowing future, even returning to make his principal home in Harare. The alternative terrified Rowland. 'If Mugabe wins,' he confided, 'Lonrho and all the West will lose all their investments in Zimbabwe. Everything will be confiscated and Russia will be the influential power.'

Since the Zambian and Mozambique economies had suffered catastrophically from Rhodesian military sorties, the pressure on both Nkomo and Mugabe from Kaunda and President Machel to accept the compromises offered by the British was intense. Rowland, like the Foreign Office, believed that Nkomo would win the elections and was assumed by most to have excluded Mugabe from his generosity to the delegations attending the Lancaster House negotiations. MI6 officers, monitoring all the delegations' communications, were convinced that Rowland was also supporting Mugabe. To some MI6 officers, Rowland's antics were bewildering. 'You can buy an African,' commented the agency's Zimbabwe officer, 'but how long will he remain bought?' Rowland's benevolence seemed destined simply to serve his self-esteem: 'A bugger who we could never miss noticing.'

For the Europeans, the unexpected announcement of the Marxists' outright victory on 4 March 1980 was, according to Ken Flower the chief of intelligence, 'cataclysmic'. In retrospect it is hard to understand Rowland's misjudgment. The Shona, Mugabe's tribe, were more numerous than Nkomo's tribe; Mugabe's election campaign was smoother; and the war had been won by Mugabe's rather than Nkomo's guerrillas. Mugabe's army, spread over the country, was positioned to intimidate the electorate.

Rowland was stunned by his own mistake. For fifteen years he had snubbed Mugabe. The realisation that he had completely misconstrued Rhodesian politics, the one nation where he professed to be an expert, was a bitter blow. Not only was his credibility in doubt but Lonrho's whole financial future in Zimbabwe was at risk. Despite Mugabe's articulate broadcast to the nation promising reconciliation and no recrimination, Rowland feared the worst. Yet, unlike so many white Rhodesians and British, Rowland had consistently opposed Smith's regime and genuinely sympathised with the nationalist struggle. In the art of building bridges, Rowland was not bereft of credibility.

Much depended on Herbert Munangatire, a journalist who had spent two years in detention with Nkomo. Although until recently a Nkomo supporter, Munangatire had smartly shifted his loyalties and proclaimed that since he and Mugabe were from the same village and school, he would naturally support his boyhood friend. Proffering a photograph of himself and Mugabe in 1963 at a meeting in Accra, Munangatire hoped that a critical interview with Mugabe, which he had published two years earlier at Rowland's request, would be forgotten. Hired by Lonrho as another 'runner', Munangatire obtained with pride a personal invitation for Rowland to attend Zimbabwe's independence celebrations. He flew to London to deliver the good news. But before his arrival, a telephone call from Mugabe's headquarters had cancelled the invitation. Rowland seemed philosophical. His worst fears that Mugabe would nationalise everything had already been partially allayed. On Machel's advice that the country's economy would collapse without the Europeans, Mugabe was stressing in interviews that the whites were secure if they remained. Munangatire returned home with instructions to buy the government's support for Lonrho.

News of Rowland's rejection by Mugabe fuelled the existing tension inside Lonrho House in Salisbury. Two Lonrho mine engineers had recently been murdered in a theft. The convicted murderer had been sentenced to death but, just prior to the hanging, was handed a razor to commit suicide. As independence day approached, Brian Thomas, the security officer in Lonrho House, effectively relinquished his responsibilities: 'Every political colour was running up and down the stairs looking for handouts.' In Rowland's absence, no one seemed to be in charge. Nic Kruger, calm but exhausted by the past decade, had withdrawn to his office. From their windows, Lonrho's employees watched shell shocked as gangs of youths, armed with machetes, hammers and clubs, roamed along Jameson Avenue, pulled down Cecil Rhodes's statue and celebrated the end of white rule.

Munangatire began to make approaches to the new government. The fuel, as Thomas observed, was money. 'Vast sums were given to Herbert, drawn from petty cash, for entertainment.' At both Meikles and the Ambassador hotels, Munangatire hosted lavish dinners and parties for hundreds of the new *nomenklatura*. Lonrho, he reassured everyone, one of Zimbabwe's largest private employers, was keen to co-operate in the reconstruction of the country. The company's huge reserves, accumulated in recent years, would be spent for that purpose. In meetings arranged for Rowland with every minister his past allegiance was not mentioned but he pointedly referred to his personal experience of imprisonment by the British to show his understanding of their struggle. Persuasively, Rowland spoke of the future and handed over money for rebuilding the president's old school in Katuma and for the construction of a hospital in the president's village.

Four months after independence in April 1980, Mugabe finally agreed to meet Rowland. Ian Smith, the former Rhodesian prime minister takes the credit for demolishing the barrier. 'Rowland came to ask my help and I agreed to speak to Mugabe. I told the president that it was in the country's interest that he should meet Rowland and he agreed.' When the businessman arrived in Harare, he was deliberately kept waiting. Their eventual encounter, in the former colonial governor's residence which had become State House, was unconciliatory. Cold and mannered, Mugabe irritated Rowland by preferring to delegate decisions rather than do as other African presidents and issue an order. As consolation, Rowland judged that he was not wholly at Mugabe's mercy.

Zimbabwe's financial future depended upon the oil pipeline from Beira. Although Rowland still feared that Mugabe might nationalise Lonrho's prize possession, its destiny was really controlled by President Machel because 90 per cent of the pipeline ran across Mozambique. Rowland's conundrum was how to approach Mugabe's mentor who, he assumed, would be antagonistic towards one of Nkomo's paymasters.

Rowland's intermediary was Alves Gomes, a Portuguese journalist who had sympathised with Machel's struggle and remained in Mozambique after independence. Rowland had met Gomes during the Lancaster House negotiations and asked the journalist, on his return, to test the water.

Although classified as one of the world's poorest nations, Mozambique has vast potential. Among its 300,000 square miles [three times Britain's area], the country boasts vast arable land, gold and diamond mines and a cornucopia of other natural wealth. But, during the previous decade, the economy had suffered dreadful destruction caused firstly by its war of independence; then in 1974, by the wholesale flight of all the skilled Europeans and the persecution of some who remained; and finally, during the later years, by systematic attacks undertaken by the Rhodesian military and Renamo, an anti-Machel group of Mozambique rebels organised and latterly financed by South Africa. Despite the end of the war in Rhodesia, Renamo guerrillas continued to receive support from Pretoria's military. The effect upon Mozambique's economy was gradually to compound disaster into catastrophe. In 1980, Machel's historic support from Moscow was insufficient to stem the financial haemorrhage. At the birth of the Reagan–Thatcher era, no western corporation would consider investing in a neo-Marxist state. Therefore, Gomes's inquiry about Lonrho's reopening of the pipeline was welcomed.

'I'm not interested in owning empty tubes,' responded Machel, who needed the foreign currency which an operational pipeline would generate. Yet, without Mugabe's agreement, Machel would not give formal approval. Since Mugabe was still unwilling to consider negotiating with Lonrho, Rowland gambled that he would reopen the pipeline without permission. With Machel's benign agreement negotiated through Gomes, Lonrho began refurbishing the pipeline, an investment which stood in stark contrast to the activities of other western corporations in nationalist southern Africa.

Rowland's second probe in southern Africa was Angola where Savimbi, contrary to all predictions, had recovered and was waging a destructive campaign against the Marxist government. But, bereft of western aid, Savimbi's fortunes were static.

Soon after the Conservative victory, Rowland had called on the Foreign Office to persuade its senior African experts that the British government should overtly support Savimbi. From the outset Rowland exuded optimism to John Sankey, a special counsellor on Africa, and Len Allasson: 'You'll see. Savimbi will be in Luanda by Christmas. You'll regret not recognising him.' The diplomats remained non-committal. Savimbi was a rebel and the civil war, they believed, was a tribal conflict which required reconciliation rather than the ideological war Rowland proposed. The officials discounted Savimbi's plea that he was fighting for an Angola rid of Soviet and Cuban advisers, which could hold free elections to determine its future. The proof was the Angolan government's offer to Moscow to extract the country's minerals, an offer the communists rejected, telling the

Angolans to deal with De Beers for diamonds and Gulf Oil for their petroleum since the Russians had a surplus of diamonds, oil and uranium.

For the diplomats, Rowland's arguments were suspiciously dictated by his own commercial interests. Peace in Angola with Savimbi in power would be good for Lonrho and the company's interests would be served if endorsed by the British government. 'He's gone for Savimbi because he's charismatic and anti-Marxist. He did not understand that Marxism in Africa was simply an anti-colonialist label.' To the Foreign Office, Rowland seemed to be influenced by propaganda disseminated by the Heritage Foundation in Washington, supporters of Ronald Reagan, who were identified with a conspiracy among South Africa's military to promote assassinations and warfare against left-wing governments. Savimbi, the Foreign Office believed, was associated with that group.

'Tiny is very good at backing the wrong horse,' the British diplomats agreed. Unspoken was the realisation that Rowland's support for Savimbi had been determined by Kaunda, which was just as maladroit as their support for Nkomo. 'We don't think the Marxist government is so bad,' Rowland was told. 'Traditionally British governments do not recognise politicians to show political approval but on the basis of recognising they are *de facto* in power.' Quite bluntly, Britain had no interests in Angola and, mindful of Britain's disastrous intervention in Nigeria's civil war, the Foreign Office was determined not to become publicly associated with a mess. Rowland was naturally dissatisfied and would return regularly to urge the diplomats to convert to his cause.

Rowland's argument, that Angola needed to be saved from communism, appealed however to Margaret Thatcher. The prime minister, distrusting the Foreign Office, sympathised with Pretoria's and Ronald Reagan's commitment to construct a bulwark against Marxism. In tune with the new wisdom, Thatcher lamented the West's pusillanimous reaction to the Soviets in Angola and appeared to connect the 'loss' of Angola with the recent Soviet invasion of Afghanistan.

In July 1980, Rowland organised a visit to London for

Jonas Savimbi. Naturally the guerrilla leader would stay at the London Metropole, the home of all Rowland's visitors. Savimbi's principal engagement was to address the right-wing International Institute for Strategic Studies to urge the rejection of any appeasement of the Soviets.

In anticipation of the visit, Edward Du Cann, by-passing the civil servants, had approached Thatcher and urged that she meet Rowland to discuss Angola. As chairman of the 1922 Committee, Du Cann had easy and regular access to the prime minister. In the early days of her administration, their relationship benefited from Du Cann's decisive support of her candidacy against Edward Heath and his regular reports about the mood in the Party which was initially restive about her ideological shift towards the market economy. Calling upon their friendship, Du Cann often persuaded Ian Gow, Thatcher's parliamentary private secretary, to insert documents supporting Lonrho into the prime minister's red boxes at the end of a working day.

For her part, Thatcher appreciated Rowland's contribution towards the completion of the Rhodesian negotiations at Lancaster House and, in the midst of reconsidering Britain's policies in South Africa, invited Rowland and Josie with the Du Canns for Sunday lunch to Chequers to hear a non-Foreign Office opinion. According to the Lonrho contingent, the meeting provoked Du Cann to marvel, 'Margaret regarded Tiny as extraordinary.' Rowland convinced himself that his arguments in support of Savimbi had been accepted at the highest level.

In London, Du Cann entertained Savimbi at a private dinner at the Savoy, at a huge reception at the Carlton Club and at a meeting for sixty politicians in the Palace of Westminster. Journalists, businessmen and politicians were urged to recognise Savimbi as a staunch anti-communist. Unfortunately for Rowland, Thatcher's interest did not translate into policy, but at least it appeared that he had finally declared peace with the government.

The probability that his dream of a matrix of Lonrho nations across Africa might be realised had never seemed surer to Rowland. His commercial interests would feed his political aspirations, and vice versa. By vaunting his political importance, developing his personal relations and spreading his generosity, Rowland had gradually paralysed objective criticism of his activities. His dealings in Malawi were typical of the way in which Lonrho contributed to African countries.

Ever since Lonrho had created a sugar industry in Malawi, Rowland's relationship with Dr Hastings Banda had flourished. With the president's agreement, Lonrho had expanded its sugar industry to 14,000 acres, had built a 5000-acre tea estate, developed cotton plantations, a textile industry and owned franchises for five motor corporations. In return, since Malawi was a one-party state and Banda the president for life, Rowland volunteered contributions to the president's favourite charities which included his political party. Despite his cultivated reputation as an enemy of corruption, Banda would take anything from Rowland and was one leader upon whose loyalty Rowland could always depend. 'Lonrho,' says Leslie Blackwell, Lonrho's local manager for twenty-two years, 'has a reputation as a soft touch in Africa because it has paid out so many bribes. No other company in Malawi paid out money in the same way. But, having started, Lonrho was too weak to stop paying.'

To an outsider, it would seem that the return on the effort was limited. Lonrho's accounts in Malawi consistently revealed that net profits were rarely more than 1 per cent of the turnover. The accounts, however, were never published. Blackwell's summaries were sent to London and never queried. 'What they did there, I know not,' he smiles, 'but no accountant ever came from Britain to check on the values which we assigned to our assets and machinery.' Increasingly, Malawi's Treasury officials like Julius Malange would ask Blackwell why the company paid barely any taxes or dividends. Blackwell would point to the company's charitable contributions which were set against tax. 'Lonrho's staff were treated with special care,' confirms a senior Malawi official. 'We would hesitate to attack Lonrho because we feared that Rowland would complain to the president.'

The truth, as Blackwell concedes, was that all accounts were consolidated in London, as with every other Lonrho operation in Africa. Transfer pricing was a standard practice in Africa to overcome restrictions on removing hard currency from the country. Invoices for Malawi's imports were dispatched from London by Lonrho Exports. Malawi officials were unable to scrutinise whether the actual payment was the same price as Lonrho registered in Malawi.

Within Malawi, Lonrho's factories enjoyed privileged monopolies. David Whitehead, the textile factory, produced expensive blankets. A senior civil servant summoned Blackwell and tried to persuade Whitehead to produce a cheap blanket for the masses. Blackwell explained that that would be unprofitable. 'You're incapable of producing cheap blankets,' expostulated the official, 'because you are inefficient and lack the machinery.' Prevented by the president from encouraging other textile manufacturers to invest in Malawi, the civil servant granted import licences for cheap Indian blankets. At Lonrho's request, President Banda ordered an investigation on all imports of cloth. Some licences were withdrawn.

Banda never protested. Enjoying a warm relationship with Rowland, he was delighted that Rowland took an interest in his country and that he dropped by in his Grumman jet to pass on the gossip from another president with whom he had just spoken. Banda's highest officials would often hear about Rowland's visits only after his departure. Presidents of other international corporations, bigger than Lonrho, would be greeted by unqualified refusals if they requested a conversation with Banda. 'I would just write a memorandum,' recalls one former presidential secretary, 'to record that someone wanted to come and his request was denied.' But Rowland basked in a privileged relationship with Banda which carried with it the bonus of lengthening Rowland's cast list of luminaries visited, so that on his return to Britain he could boast, 'I've met six presidents in the last five days.'

The visit to Blantyre would invariably encompass a similar call to Lusaka. No African president was more important to Rowland than Kaunda whose generosity had allowed Lonrho's operations in Zambia to become particularly profitable.

Tom Mtine, Lonrho's chairman in Zambia, had observed Rowland's developing relationship with Kaunda: 'The president liked Rowland's enormous knowledge through his social, economic and political connections. His visits were like an intelligence agent submitting his report. KK could always learn a lot from Tiny.' However, the reality of Lonrho's financial investments in Zambia was beyond the president's understanding.

Rowland's power in Zambia was awesome. Oliver Irvine, the senior partner at Coopers & Lybrand in Lusaka, had introduced De La Rue to the managers of the Bank of Zambia as prospective suppliers of a new issue of bank notes. Negotiations had progressed substantially when Rowland flew into Lusaka and drove directly to see Kaunda at State House. Harrisons, he explained, Lonrho's new security printing company, were perfectly placed to print the new notes. Although Harrisons was a minnow compared to De La Rue and was known only for printing postage stamps, Irvine's client lost the contract as he looked on helplessly. 'He just took the lot,' sighs Irvine whose partnership also lost all the accountancy contracts for Lonrho's subsidiaries: 'Rowland's a two-faced dog.'

The bulk of Lonrho's accountancy in Zambia was under the control of Peat Marwick. Operating under the Zambian Companies Acts, based on British legislation enacted in 1908, Peats were not required by law to register or publish any accounts. John Cruickshank, employed by Peats in Zambia for twenty years and now its senior partner in Lusaka, admitted that his firm 'did not gear our audit to investigate for bribes or ask questions which would reveal bribes because bribery is not common in Zambia'. Cruickshank is adamant, 'We have never seen any evidence of bribes, generosity or favours in Lonrho's accounts.' Even the extensive assistance provided by Lonrho for Nkomo in Zambia never appeared in any accounts submitted by Lonrho to Peats.

Unseen by Cruickshank and every auditor in every other country auditing Lonrho accounts was the file marked 'African Regional Expenses'. Jealously guarded by Lonrho's managing director and the senior accountant in Zambia, the file for 'special payments' contained the receipts for air fares, hospitality, hospital charges, educational fees and the other expenses which, with Rowland's specific approval, important Zambians and their families were granted.

Under Rowland's tutelage, the senior accountant would understand the requirement to 'move' those payments around the seventy companies and sixteen profit centres to minimise the tax payments and reduce the chance of exposure. An alternative device for avoiding taxes, details of which were outlined in a special file, was the dissolution of local holding companies. The effects of this technique, simple although questionable, were to shorten the chain of remittances passed back to Britain and to render the monitoring thereof more difficult for the officials at the local Central Bank. Otherwise, payments were juggled in London. The payment to a Zambian in dollars would be invoiced against another African country to extricate the hard currency, avoiding the use of funds in London. As in every African country, Lonrho could rely upon the relative ignorance of local Zambian officials.

The chance of discovery was further reduced by the subdivision of the African subsidiaries. While some were locally registered companies, others were directly controlled from London. The accounts for the latter were not submitted for audit in Zambia or any other African country. In Britain, they were consolidated beyond the sight of the curious.

Carefully concealed in those accounts were also the company's borrowings and the value of the assets. In Zambia, as elsewhere, Lonrho's accounts boasted valuable assets but since the buyers would pay in local, unconvertible currency, the assets were effectively worthless in British terms. Lonrho's valuation was based on 'trading accounts', colouring the credibility of Lonrho's proclaimed 'true' value.

Remittance of dividends in hard currency to Britain was and remains calculated as a direct percentage of the declared profits. Among the methods which Lonrho's auditors throughout Africa could utilise to augment those dividends was to lower the market value of the assets, which automatically increased profits, and verify that the practice 'is consistent with previous years'. Not only did that allow more hard currency remittances to be made, but it also bumped up the profits for the consolidated accounts in London.

Lonrho's employment policy, typical of its practices throughout Africa, was not beneficial to Zambia. Although Lonrho employed 10,000 Africans and was the country's largest private food producer, the company never promoted black Zambians to senior executive positions.

That policy particularly infuriated John Munthali who was employed for fifteen years in Lusaka as a Lonrho car salesman. On Lonrho's behalf, Munthali admits that he arranged bribes to the level of permanent secretary in the government to obtain contracts for cars and secured permission for foreign exchange allowances: 'I would give them lunch and dinner and then look after their needs. The actual bribe was paid by a white Lonrho employee. They didn't want me involved in those payments.' Munthali, in a manifestation of bias and *naïveté*, blames the company for introducing corruption into the country.

As the corruption intensified, Vernon Mwaanga, the former minister and Lonrho employee, was completing his autobiography. He sent a draft to Rowland. It included a description of the hectic Gulfstream flights across Africa and one of Rowland's more memorable monologues as he looked down on the parched landscape: 'These African leaders are so corrupt that there's not a single one of them I cannot buy.' At Rowland's request, Mwaanga removed the anecdote from the book. 'Bribes were not necessary in Zambia,' presumes Mwaanga. 'Other businessmen succeeded without paying them.'

The cost of falling out of Tiny's favour, as Mwaanga would discover, was already evident to Udi Gecaga. Over the previous two years, Gecaga had lived in America while his three joint ventures with Lonrho were managed by employees in Kenya. Requests for him to resign as a Lonrho director were rebuffed by his insistence, 'Let's first settle the exit package.'

In his absence, the directors passed a unanimous resolution dismissing Gecaga from the board. Since Gecaga was Lonrho's first and only black director, the public announcement curtly referred only to his 'resignation'. Gecaga's replacement, Rowland decided, would be the conventional 'runner' rather than another ambitious businessman. The candidate was Mark Too, a local businessman. Rowland's test of Too's suitability was simple. Sitting in Too's home in the Rift Valley, Rowland asked,

'Can you get the president on the phone?' Too dialled Nairobi and spoke to arap Moi, confirming rumours that Rowland was in the company of arap Moi's illegitimate son. Rowland appointed his new 'runner' as Lonrho's deputy chairman in Kenya. Too was provided with a suite at the Norfolk hotel and a flat in Nairobi, while his own haulage business could be expanded using Lonrho's connections and fuel. Too also wanted the stunning house at Eldoret in the Rift Valley owned by Arthur Morris, Lonrho's local managing director. When Morris left Kenya, Too's wish was fulfilled.

In Cheapside, the directors marvelled how, in each African country, Rowland's network could judiciously arrange the personalities, activities and profits of Lonrho's subsidiaries. But objective observers in London viewed his politicking suspiciously. In harsh terms, in winter 1980, Rowland's inscrutable diplomatic and financial arrangements in Africa could not disguise the truth that the company in Britain was reaching the limit of its borrowing facilities and facing another cash crisis. Attempts to talk up the share price collapsed when the news leaked that Lonrho's profits had fallen. Insufficient funds were being remitted from Africa and the drain of cash was accelerated when Rowland, in a maverick flourish, bought from Daniel Ludwig a half stake in the Princess chain of hotels.

The contrast between the two was notable. Ludwig, eighty-three years old, was a notorious recluse, misogynist and spendthrift. Since 1945, he had become one of the world's reputed billionaires by building ships, leasing tankers and prospecting for oil. His latest venture, the construction of a vast pulp mill in the middle of Brazil's Amazon rainforest, was souring when he met Rowland, whose fortune was estimated at a modest 80 million dollars. The financial Goliath was attracted by the pygmy's similar German origins, his offer of discreet friendship and political relationships, and the promise of joint mineral ventures in Africa. Rowland's charming self-salesmanship had overcome Ludwig's natural barriers to co-operation.

The price for a 50 per cent interest in the hotels was $81 million and 5 million Lonrho shares. Located in glamorous Caribbean locations, the chain had been inspired by Ludwig's conviction that American newly-weds would be prepared to pay for luxury honeymoons.

For Rowland, the venture promised a new source of hard currency to augment the cash flow, pay the dividends and tilt Lonrho further away from Africa. The incipient problem was the nature of the hotels, which were not the pristine investment Rowland imagined.

Soon after the purchase, Rowland flew with Josie from London to White Plains, New York, to meet the senior managers of the hotel chain. At the end of the day, Rowland impulsively ordered Wilming to fly to San Francisco. Without a reservation, they would stay the night at the Saint Francis hotel, part of the Princess chain. Arriving by taxi from the airport, Mr and Mrs Rowland checked into the hotel as normal guests. Wilming and the flight crew arrived separately. The following morning, Rowland summoned the unsuspecting manager. 'He told him,' recalled Wilming, 'that it was a seedy hotel with bad service. The manager's face dropped when he heard who Rowland was.'

Rowland's motives in spending $81 million on hotels were not entirely propelled by Lonrho's interests. Among the advantages of the purchase was the proxy granted by Ludwig to Rowland over the 5 million Lonrho shares to Rowland. Combined with Rowland's own stake, he now controlled about 17 per cent of the shares against 21 per cent by Gulf Fisheries. At that moment, the Kuwaitis, 'enjoying the heat of the battle', had renewed their sniping at Rowland's management. As so often, Lonrho's commercial interests were equated with Rowland's concern to keep control over the publicly owned company.

To weaken the power of Lonrho's largest shareholder and raise money, Rowland proposed another rights issue of 40 million new Lonrho shares. The proposal was opposed by Sheikh Nasser who, having decided not to buy his allocation, would certainly lose his pre-eminence. Formally, the decision would be taken at Lonrho's seventy-first annual general meeting on 14 March 1980 at the Grosvenor House.

Lonrho's 1979 annual report, presented at that meeting, emphasised for the first time Lonrho's development in Britain and America with unusually limited mention of Africa. In his bid to make Lonrho more acceptable to City investors, the ten pages of glossy photographs in Rowland's report portrayed five images of House of Fraser stores, suggesting they were part of Lonrho's empire rather than representing its 29 per cent stake, and two full pages of Princess hotels, ignoring the similar limitation of Lonrho's ownership. The report was more a statement of Rowland's intent, although his judgment was proving less astute than he assumed.

In those annual jamborees of the faithful, Rowland adopted a habitual performance. Sitting on the platform in front of the packed hall, he would remain calm and silent, a visible but not audible manifestation of the genius responsible for the transformation of the shareholders' company. But, by his occasional whispered instructions to his spokesmen, Edward Du Cann and Duncan Sandys, Rowland's authority was patently evident. On that occasion, as at other times, the interests of the shareholders were not synonymous with Rowland's. Sixty-eight million Lonrho shares remained unissued and the proposed 40 million new shares would further depress the price. Yet Sandys still proclaimed that Rowland was 'acting responsibly'. Tom Ferguson, the Kuwaitis' representative, felt that Rowland was acting exclusively in his own interests yet the shareholders enthusiastically endorsed Tiny. Ferguson's only consolation was that Rowland would personally pay £12 million for underwriting the issue, a signal of his anger towards his erstwhile partners and an unwelcome confirmation of why serious investors in the City looked askance at Lonrho shares. Lonrho was evidently still Rowland's personal fiefdom.

Among those voting for Rowland was Hugh Fraser. 'The Lonrho shares are the worst investment I have made', he said at the end of the meeting, referring to his 2.8 million stake. Over the previous weeks, their relationship had soured. 'I don't want Mr Rowland to bid for the House of Fraser,' added Fraser. Rowland's rejoinder suggested that a divorce was preceding the marriage: 'Sir Hugh Fraser is a charming man but a professional loser.' For, contrary to his warm assurances, Hugh Fraser had failed to 'deliver the board' to Rowland's requirements.

To describe Rowland's tactics in his pursuit of House of Fraser as conforming to a universal strategy would be both to exaggerate the skill of the architect and overestimate the substance of his manoeuvres. In essence, Rowland wanted House of Fraser but possessed insufficient money to launch a bid. Yet his assessment of House of Fraser was correct. The company's share price had hardly risen in fifteen years, its dividends and profits were low and the organisation of its business had hardly changed in two decades. Lacking the means to realise his ambitions, Rowland, in the crudest terms, was seeking to control the company without making a bid.

Gently, over lunches and dinners, Rowland had sought Fraser's support to increase the number of Lonrho directors on the House of Fraser board from the current two, himself and Duncan Sandys, to at least four. Rowland envisaged Fraser performing, like his assorted African politicians, as requested.

His ploy failed. At a board meeting on 24 January 1980 to fill three vacancies, none of Lonrho's nominees was considered. Rowland complained bitterly. Fraser's failure to obey was tantamount to a breach of loyalty. With the subtlety of a Sherman tank manoeuvre, Rowland's next target was House of Fraser dividend payment.

George Willoughby, House of Fraser's finance director, would demonstrate that he could match neither the personality nor the technical acumen of the brightest financiers of London. Reared in the Fraser mould, he epitomised the caution, honesty and loyalty which Hugh Fraser's father had impregnated among his staff. In February 1980, Willoughby proposed a dividend of 4 pence. Rowland, requiring a high dividend to show adequate earnings on his stake and to demonstrate House of Fraser's inadequacies, demanded 7.35 pence. Willoughby refused, arguing that the company should not pay more than it could afford. Rowland reduced his demand to 6 pence and stuck. On 18 March 1980, Willoughby and Hugh Fraser were invited to lunch at Cheapside. In the familiar dining room alongside Rowland were Terry Robinson and Philip Tarsh, the two accountants.

Although Rowland's directors would express amazement at Tiny's ability to switch his concentration from visions of Africa's future to the technicalities of boardroom warfare, in truth,

Rowland confused his relationships. During those early months of 1980, Rowland had become perplexed that, while politicians in Africa treated his opinions respectfully, a group of low-paid and comparatively impoverished directors at House of Fraser should deny his edict. The avuncular self-control, so evident in presidential palaces in Africa, was absent in Cheapside.

After short pleasantries, just as the meal was served, Rowland signalled the attack. Both Tarsh and Robinson accused Willoughby of incompetence. Voices rose, eyelids tightened and a bitter row erupted. Visibly excited, Fraser joined the developing slanging match: 'We're not paying more than we can afford. Lonrho is just a minority shareholder and doesn't control us.' Rowland appeared menacing: 'You've broken your word to me.' Fraser pushed back his chair: 'We're leaving. I'm selling my Lonrho shares.'

As his guests departed, Rowland was paralysed by paranoia. Fraser, he convinced himself, had even threatened at the climax of his outburst to drive straight to Warburgs, his bitterest foe. His delusion remained fixed. Neither Robinson nor Tarsh sought to correct their employer. The energy which had built the Lonrho empire, veiled by his fabled personality, had transmogrified into an uncontrollable rage against mere employees of a company in which he was the biggest shareholder. Insubordination was intolerable and it was imperative to Rowland to quash any opposition. Impetuously that afternoon he declared war against the board of House of Fraser. His implacable determination had taken a first step towards obsession.

The following day, Robinson requested a list of House of Fraser shareholders owning over 100,000 shares. The message was explicit. Rowland was considering appealing to other shareholders to oppose the board's recommended dividend. Five days later, Rowland delivered the message personally.

Interrupting a conversation between Robinson and David Milligan, House of Fraser's company secretary, Rowland warned that he would be launching a public attack against the board at the next annual general meeting. 'He is bullying us,' Willoughby told Fraser. The next day, 25 March, Rowland dispatched more threats. A telex demanded more directors for Lonrho and a bonus issue of shares. At board meetings, the two Lonrho directors began systematically voting against the other directors. Working hours were punctuated by irate telexes, abusive telephone calls and unreasonable demands from Cheapside. Finally, Rowland dispatched a circular to House of Fraser shareholders urging opposition to the dividend recommended by the directors. 'We were appalled,' says Willoughby. 'But it made us more determined.'

Since Rowland's high-profile confrontation coincided with his own battle against the Kuwaitis, the City institutions focused on Rowland, concluding that he was motivated by pique and impulse rather than strategy. 'His early mistake,' analysed by one Warburgs' banker, 'was failing to quietly visit the institutions who owned House of Fraser shares and suggest that everyone work together to improve the management. By declaring war immediately, everyone realised that he wanted to buy House of Fraser cheap.'

A storm of circulars erupted, transmitting Rowland's emotional accusations about bad management and his demand for a 6 pence dividend. 'Terrorism at its worst,' was one banker's reflection on Rowland's campaign to split the board. The House of Fraser directors were aware that, in the shareholders' vote, they started at a 29 per cent disadvantage and lacked experience to organise opposition. In the previous years, their annual general meetings had lasted at most eight minutes. Now they were faced with a fight for their own jobs. Helped by Simon Garmoyle at Warburgs and Michael Richardson from Cazenoves, they lobbied the institutions for support. Rowland would claim that Warburgs had taken oblique control of the board to defeat his honest campaign. 'The directors relied upon us,' admits a banker, 'but we were careful to give advice and tell them to make the decisions.'

By 18 June, as he flew to Glasgow for the shareholders' meeting, Rowland knew that his attack had been routed. He had failed to win support from City investors. Sitting on the platform, he meekly withdrew his motions and voted for the dividend he had so volubly criticised. 'I like to be on the winning side,' he explained, unaware that his lack of

subtlety had prompted his adversaries to erect a new barrier.

In one respect, Rowland's censure of House of Fraser had
produced results. The City fund managers had been persuaded
that House of Fraser management was weak. In unison, the
bureaucrats complained that Hugh Fraser was noticeably unable
to concentrate on business matters. 'Whenever we mentioned
figures,' recalls one banker, 'he'd change subjects.' Fraser
could concentrate on numbers only at the roulette wheel. Both
Garmoyle and Richardson were urged to appoint non-executive
directors to the House of Fraser board.

In the post mortem of the annual general meeting held at
Warburgs, both Hugh Fraser and George Willoughby were told
by the bankers, 'The institutions need reassurances.' In particular, their company needed a new chairman. To Willoughby, 'their
proposal was a complete surprise. Despite everything, Hugh was
holding the board together.' The feudal loyalty for the laird,
the cement which Rowland had spotted but so far had failed
to dissolve, temporarily united against the City.

A compromise was agreed. Fraser would remain but Warburgs' candidate, Professor Roland Smith would replace Rowland as deputy chairman. Smith, fifty-two, a hulking six-foot-four
professor of management science at Manchester University, had
successfully offered himself as a 'corporate doctor' to over twenty
companies. Considering that Smith was a medium-ranking businessman without any retail experience, the offer by House of
Fraser of £50,000 annually for two days' work a week was
attractive. Convinced by his own self-promotion that he was a
talented manager, Smith relished the opportunity to prove himself. He would be helped by Ernest Sharp, a former director at
Grand Metropolitan, who understood the business. 'We realised
that Smith knew little about retailing,' admits one of the bankers,
'but we thought he would be a good performer against Rowland
while Sharp could supplement his weaknesses.' To prevent
Rowland's interference, the actual management of the company
would be delegated by the main board to an executive committee,
chaired by Smith, from which Rowland would be excluded.
On that committee, Smith was empowered to overrule Fraser.

Rowland heard about Warburgs' putsch and his demotion by letter from Fraser on 5 August. Since he had admitted that Lonrho wanted to bid for House of Fraser, no one would believe his repeated insistence that he would abandon self-interest and act in the interests of House of Fraser. As a one-man operation, trusting no one, Rowland might have realised that his wariness would summon similar sentiment in others. He did not.

Having telexed his fury to Fraser, Rowland dispatched Paul Spicer to register his disapproval at that day's board meeting. Spicer's presence further antagonised the directors. 'He was despised by many,' recalls Willoughby. 'He was an absolute nothing and that reflected upon Rowland.' Smith was equally dismissive. 'Term-time in Manchester starts in October. I would like to see Lonrho off by then. I am not going to lose this battle.' In the face of an ultimatum, Rowland appeared powerless. But his irony never failed.

'Do you think you could arrange for Manchester United to play in Africa?' Rowland asked the professor, a director of the football team. 'You live in a fantasy world,' replied Smith. 'Just say it twice and you'll believe it's possible.'

Throughout that autumn, Rowland and Robinson sustained a continuous barrage against Smith and Sharp. 'That board meeting,' commented Sharp after a particularly acrimonious exchange with Rowland, 'was like Churchill's war cabinet with Goering and Goebbels sitting in.' The Lonrho intimidation was shameless. 'If you go ahead with this,' seethed Rowland during one telephone call, 'God help you.' A cascade of lawyers' ultimatums, demands for dismissal, rude telexes, caustic circulars to shareholders and divisive votes at board meetings was poured out by Rowland to unnerve the directors. Persistently he asked for sensitive financial information which would help assess the company's true value for a bid. Continuously he opposed Smith's recommendations to reverse the stagnant profits. Rowland condemned everyone on the board as 'stupid', a view which was somewhat shared by the company's advisers. Rowland's criticisms were correct but were ignored because of his motives.

Hence Rowland was still losing. The big professor, whom he now detested, lacked any weaknesses which could be exploited.

There was only one tactic, he believed, which could successfully reduce the company's value: the unity of the House of Fraser board needed to be irrevocably destroyed. His target was Hugh Fraser who, despite his weaknesses, remained the company's lynchpin. With brutal calculation, Rowland set in motion the entrapment and public humiliation of Hugh Fraser. The consequence, he hoped, would be the complete destruction of the House of Fraser board. On 2 December 1980, Rowland demanded an extraordinary general meeting to prevent the company selling the D.H. Evans store and buying back a lease. Shareholders would be asked to vote against a succession of the board's decisions which were the subject of Rowland's continuing disagreement. Roland Smith and his directors sighed. Innocently, they believed that the extraordinary general meeting, to be held on 20 January 1981, was just another ruse to unsettle them. The background was more sinister.

In November 1980, Rowland had been offered a speculative deal. Coral casinos had lost their gaming licence and five of London's leading clubs including Crockfords, Curzon House, International Sports Club and the Palm Beach were for sale. Since the chance of the Gaming Board renewing the licences was uncertain, the price for the clubs was low. As the owner of the Metropole hotel group, Lonrho bought the defunct casinos for £3.3 million and applied for licences.

At that time, Hugh Fraser owed money to many London casinos. Despite his earlier losses, his gambling had continued and among his creditors was Colyn Braun, the former Lonrho manager in Rhodesia and owner of the Knightsbridge Sporting Club. In late November, John Paterson, Fraser's personal assistant, had visited Braun to discuss an unpaid debt of £120,000. Anxious to stop Fraser's gambling, Paterson hoped that if he did not honour Fraser's cheques, the clubs would refuse to allow his friend to gamble. It was a desperate ruse which was not appreciated by Braun. After an unpleasant confrontation, which Paterson recalls included threats, they settled for £80,000 which was paid in cash. Soon after, Paterson complained to the Gaming Board. Eventually Braun lost his licence.

Fraser's debts were common gossip among London's casino

owners, but Braun, knowing about Rowland's special interest and irritated by his own losses, visited Cheapside and handed over photostats of Fraser's unpaid cheques. Rowland was left with the impression that Fraser owed hundreds of thousands of pounds around London's casinos.

During the weeks before the extraordinary general meeting, Rowland once again inundated shareholders with emotional circulars alleging bad management and promising continued interference. In reply, the House of Fraser board accused Lonrho of harassment and inconsistency. Fraser openly denounced Rowland, 'I am not a puppet on a string for Mr Rowland. I am a fighter and I intend to remain in control of House of Fraser.' With the help of Garmoyle's and Richardson's lobbying in the City, the board were assured that Lonrho's motions would once again be defeated. Rowland's terrorising seemed pointless.

Rowland dropped his bombshell the day before the extraordinary general meeting. In a letter to Fraser signed by Rowland and Duncan Sandys, House of Fraser's chairman was accused of being insolvent: 'When in 1977 the Lonrho Board resolved to buy Carter Hawley Hale's 20 per cent interest in the House of Fraser at 175p per share – a considerable premium – the Lonrho board relied on your promise that you would no longer gamble or visit casinos and that without such a promise Lonrho would not have bought into the company under your chairmanship.' The proof of Fraser's insolvency, wrote Rowland, were his unpaid gambling cheques. The institutions, concluded Rowland, would not have supported Fraser 'had they known that whilst you sat persuading them of the propriety of your cause, your own propriety was totally lacking. Hugh, I believe you have no right to continue in your office and you should step down now.' In a separate letter to the company's secretary, Rowland demanded that the extraordinary general meeting be postponed to deal with the crisis. Rowland believed that Fraser's ineligibility to continue as a director would scupper the board's support in the City.

'We were all shattered,' recalls Willoughby. Every director had known about Fraser's gambling but Rowland's letter was 'a huge collective blow'. Uniformly and naively, the directors were bewildered as to how Rowland could have obtained Fraser's cheques. Their initial suspicion that Fraser had lost the money at Lonrho's casinos was, regrettably, unsubstantiated. Fraser, they knew, was not insolvent, but no one guessed that he had lost nearly £10 million.

Legally it was impossible to halt the extraordinary general meeting. On this occasion, Rowland arrived early from Heathrow with his entourage to consult a team of lawyers about the various procedures which he could deploy. 'Everything was planned meticulously,' recalls Mervyn Greenway, Rowland's stockbroker. In Glasgow's Merchant House, the shareholders, carefully bussed in by House of Fraser but ignorant of the real drama, watched Fraser uneasily chair the widely publicised meeting. According to one eyewitness, 'Hugh was in an extremely nervous, excitable, shaky state . . . I think he was panic stricken about the possible exposure at the meeting in front of all those people, about the news of the bounced cheques.' Two places to Fraser's left sat Rowland. Quite noticeably, Rowland was barracking Fraser to unsettle his nerves. Nevertheless, Fraser decisively recommended that Rowland's demand to stop the D.H. Evans sale be rejected. The institutions agreed. 'Lonrho is conducting a war of attrition and is diverting the management's attention away from running the business,' commented Hugh Jenkins of the National Coal Board pension fund, an influential opponent of Lonrho who controlled 5.5 per cent of House of Fraser. Fraser was rewarded by an overwhelming vote against Lonrho. 'Never underestimate Tiny,' were Fraser's parting words. To the public, Rowland seemed unperturbed: 'This is only the second round. It is not the end. It is the beginning.'

Rowland's moment came at 2.30 p.m. after lunch. At a specially summoned board meeting in Buchanan Street, Rowland presented a letter which had been written in the previous two hours. In silence, watched by Rowland, the directors read copies of his demand for Hugh Fraser's removal. Embarrassed at the head of the table, Fraser feared that Rowland might produce more evidence. Equally fearful were his fellow directors who had rejected his offer of resignation to protect both the company and their jobs. After a pause, Rowland spoke: 'Hugh, you are unfit to serve as director let alone chairman of any public company, let alone a company like House of Fraser.' There was further silence. 'I therefore ask you to resign as chairman immediately.'

Fraser replied that the banks, by special arrangement, had been instructed to stop his cheques to prevent his gambling. The casinos knew about the arrangement. He was by no means bankrupt. His explanation stole some of Rowland's thunder.

From the middle of the huge, moulded rosewood table Roland Smith proposed an escape: 'I think that we need more particulars from Sir Hugh.' In the large, dark leather-panelled room the tension slackened. 'Perhaps Sir Hugh could give us a list of all his assets and all his debts?' Fraser agreed. The board meeting ended. Rowland had secured his initial purpose but unwittingly he had sabotaged his masterplan.

News of Fraser's gambling had been passed to Garmoyle and Richardson. Both believed themselves to be compromised. Before Glasgow they had reassured their contacts in the City institutions that the stories about Fraser playing in casinos with beautiful girls on either side and drinking champagne were exaggerated. Rowland's revelations, admitted Richardson, were 'bad news'. No one could have confidence in a chairman 'whose reliability to run the company was brought into question'.

Garmoyle and Richardson entered the boardroom after the historic meeting. Since Fraser had left the room, their task was easier. The two told the House of Fraser directors that the company was vulnerable to Lonrho's eventual bid unless Fraser resigned. Moreover, if the chairman did not go, Warburgs would need to consider its own position. 'You're talking about the most ruthless man in business,' said Professor Roland Smith, their adversary in mind, recognising that the board's survival depended on its City advisers.

While that discussion was underway, in another part of the same building, Rowland entered Fraser's office and found his victim standing beneath a portrait of Lord Fraser. Rowland spoke quietly: 'Hugh, I'm terribly sorry this has happened and I would like to think we are still friends and if you would like to meet me in London do please let me know.' Willoughby's subsequent interpretation of that moment was sinister: 'He had stuck the dagger in and now he was offering to pull it out.' Rowland later explained that he had been being pragmatic: 'I thought he needed a friend at that moment and I wanted to be that friend . . . I felt desperately sorry for him and I could not have cared less about his shareholding.'

Their conversation continued as they walked back into the boardroom together. The directors' 'amazement' was compounded when Fraser exclaimed, 'What a remarkable fellow Rowland is: do you know what he has just said to me – we should be able to sort these things out together Hugh. The problem is that you won't meet with me.' In unison, the directors exhorted him not to meet Rowland.

Rowland had inadvertently corralled the directors towards Warburgs, giving them the potential to form a strong camp of opposition. But there was still confusion at large and Rowland's victory hung rather vulnerably on his ability to exploit the crisis.

Rowland prided himself that, as an entrepreneurial clairvoyant, he could, by judicious dealing, profit from others' chaos. In the midst of the battle, pointing at the globe in his office, Rowland told his stockbroker, Mervyn Greenway, 'Your world is the Square Mile and my world is the real world. That's your problem.' In fact, the 'problem' was Rowland's confusion. The battle for the House of Fraser was within the Square Mile, not in Rowland's 'real' world. When he declared war against Warburgs and the City to buy House of Fraser cheap, he ought of necessity have set aside his 'real world' of African shenanigans, personality play-offs, Third World motor car franchises and fought by the rules of the Square Mile. Instead, denied the counsel of a merchant bank and feeding on his own anti-Establishment propaganda, Rowland flaunted his idiosyncrasies.

Two days after the denouement in Glasgow, on 22 January 1981, Rowland took the initiative. Fraser had agreed that they should meet secretly at the Marine hotel in Troon, near Glasgow. Rowland's dash from Paris to Scotland was delayed when the Grumman's windscreen was cracked by the blast of a DC-8's jet engine while taxiing towards Le Bourget's runway. In the breathing space provided by Rowland's and two other Lonrho directors' lateness in arriving at Prestwick, Willoughby tried to convince Fraser to include another House of Fraser director in the meeting. Fraser refused but agreed that Paterson, his personal assistant, could be present.

When the six sat down over coffee late in the afternoon, Rowland was grim faced. In a steely tone, he listed his complaints, accusations, threats and evidence to compound Fraser's humiliation. 'I'm going to expose your gambling,' said Rowland. 'I was the one who took you off the hook with your gambling debt . . . Your board are not going to back you. You know Warburgs. They're going to kick you off the board.' Fraser was unsure of himself. 'We're considering offering our House of Fraser shares by public tender,' said Rowland. A pause. 'We're thinking of advertisements in the newspapers.' The Scotsman's face fell. 'We'll call it, "The sale of the century".' According to Paterson, Fraser was worried about his mother whom Rowland had charmingly cultivated: 'He dreaded the thought that Rowland would reveal to her the gambling debts.'

As the four men watched Fraser's self-defence collapse, Rowland threw in a lifebelt. 'Of course, I'm at your service to help you Hugh. I'm doing it all for the good of House of Fraser. I want to help you and your father's great company. We at Lonrho think we can make the company better and we want to help you. And we want you to help us.' In amazement, Paterson watched as the slayer became the saviour. Rowland's offer was simple. If Fraser switched sides and supported the predator, Lonrho would forever support Fraser. Rowland would claim that contrary to intending to blackmail Fraser he 'wanted to forgive him'.

At the end of two hours, Fraser agreed once again to switch his loyalties. 'You can't do that,' said Paterson.

'I'm the chairman and I can do what I like,' replied Fraser.

'He's right. He's the chairman,' smiled Rowland. A handshake confirmed the reconciliation and the pact.

On the return flight to London, Paterson watched Spicer's hand creep upwards with a glass of white wine and toast his employer. In Paterson's briefcase was £40,000 in bank notes, another payment of a gambling debt due in London. Across the aisle he watched Rowland, whose eyes were glowing, raise his own glass. They were celebrating Fraser's downfall.

Convinced of his brilliance, Rowland had failed to appraise

objectively how others would interpret the reconciliation, a fatal blind spot in many ambitious men. The victor did not perceive that Fraser's destruction would make foes precisely of those whose support he still required.

Paterson drove from Heathrow to Barkers in Kensington, House of Fraser's new headquarters. His announcement that Rowland and Fraser were allies shattered the uneasy calm. Machiavellian plots and counter-plots were alien to the lives of managers of a store chain. A lunch was arranged with Fraser for the following day, Friday, 23 January.

As always, Fraser sat at the head of the table in the directors' suite. Around him, as usual, were his family's loyal employees. Only Smith stared with unconditioned disdain. There was a man, pondered the professor, who disappeared for ten days, reappeared with a suntan and chirped, 'I've been to Glasgow.'

Steadfastly, Fraser refused to explain his erratic behaviour and agreement with Rowland. 'If there is a dispute between House of Fraser and Lonrho,' asked Willoughby, 'would you support Lonrho?'

'Yes,' replied Fraser.

Scottish self-restraint muzzled any outcry. 'It was the turning point,' recalls Willoughby. 'Just numbness and disbelief. We'd been let down.' Fraser was again tied to Rowland's apron strings. Many suspected a secret deal had been struck in Troon.

In Cheapside, Rowland was finalising his plans. With the House of Fraser's management in visible disarray, it was the moment to strike. The prize would be cheap. A telephone call to Standard & Chartered bank secured agreement for a £200 million loan. He would announce his bid shortly. But first he would fan the flames. Summoning the *Sunday Times*, he chose his words to describe his relationship with Hugh Fraser with unusual care: 'We are now the best of friends and whatever happened in the past is forgotten. We are going to work together and are totally indivisible.'

As intended, Rowland's placatory reflections inflamed the House of Fraser directors. Over that weekend, they had agreed that Hugh Fraser would be deposed at the board meeting on Monday 26 January. Amid some melodrama, the twelve directors met on the Sunday night at the Grosvenor House to reassure themselves of their resolve. Rowland's interview in the *Sunday Times* steadied those who were wavering. Throughout that night, both Fraser and his mother telephoned the directors urging them to desist. Ultra-loyalists began again to falter but their doubts disappeared the following morning. Rowland and Fraser walked into the fourth-floor boardroom in Barkers together. 'Hugh looked so cocky,' recalls Willoughby. 'He thought he had a trump card in his hand.'

Watched by Rowland, Fraser firstly read Lonrho's badly typed ultimatum urging that he remain as chairman and then read a letter in which Lonrho was bidding for the House of Fraser and would offer 150 pence per share, compared to the market price of 117 pence. The silence was broken by Rowland: 'Our bid is conditional on Sir Hugh remaining as chairman.' Rowland did not savour the effects of his surprise announcement for long. There was an adjournment to consult Warburgs. On the directors' return, Rowland's bid was rejected. There was an unforgettable moment of tension as Fraser was asked: 'Will you resign?'

'No,' he replied emphatically.

Willoughby moved that Hugh Fraser be dismissed as chairman. 'If you continue,' threatened Rowland, 'I will call another extraordinary general meeting and withdraw my offer.' Gruffly, Smith took over the discussion as if there had been no interruption. But the excited confusion could not easily be suppressed. Phil Hawley of Carter Hawley offered a compromise. Fraser could be non-executive chairman while Smith was executive chairman. The proposal was rejected and the American broke his relationship with the board. 'You haven't treated Fraser properly,' said Rowland's ally. Within thirty minutes, Fraser was dismissed. Only Rowland and Spicer voted in his favour.

Fraser rose and, in a schoolboy, theatrical gesture, waved Smith into his chair. He was clearly convinced by Rowland's assurance that his absence would be temporary. Minutes later, at 12.25, amid startled shoppers, Rowland stood in Barkers' restaurant and told journalists that Lonrho was bidding £158 million cash bid for the remainder of House of Fraser, putting a total value of £226 million on the group. 'On securing House of Fraser,' he announced, 'Sir Hugh will be reinstated as chairman and, with the exception of three directors, the present board will be dismissed.' Fraser stood nearby smiling. Another casualty, continued Rowland, would be the real culprits: 'Warburgs will be flung out so fast they won't know what happened to them.' Rowland turned and walked back into the directors' suite.

Clutching glasses, the occupants stood shocked and discomfited. The funereal atmosphere appealed to Rowland. He had been bold. Willoughby returned from a telephone conversation with Michael Richardson. He had cried. It was the end of an era. Lunch was announced.

To everyone's surprise, Rowland not only walked into the dining room but quite pointedly sat in the chair reserved for Duncan Mair, one of the company's longest-serving directors. The trial of strength, the Blitzkrieg, assumed new dimensions. The directors' politeness was to be reciprocated with venom. Several eyewitnesses overheard Rowland tell Mair: 'I wish you the worst possible future in the House of Fraser.' In Rowland's view, these men were not protecting a company but safeguarding their own comfortable perks. The worst of all was Smith, a part-time nobody, whom he openly despised.

The media's billing, 'the most extraordinary takeover battle since the war', was self-fulfilling. Featuring not only a bitter public contest between Rowland and Professor Roland Smith, alias the 'unacceptable face of capitalism' versus the City, for control of the world's premier store, the newspaper accounts were spiced with sensational stories about Hugh Fraser's sexy twenty-four-year-old girlfriend and his accusations that Rowland had employed a private detective to expose his gambling. The bewildered House of Fraser directors became deeply pessimistic. Their company's profits were poor and, although the bid was condemned as 'derisory' by Smith, they were suffering exhaustion after months of argument. But Rowland had committed a crucial mistake. 'If he had bid generously,' admits Willoughby, 'instead of at the lowest level, we would have found great difficulty in arguing against the bid.'

Rowland was confident of success on the grounds that there

would be no counter-bid. Over the previous weeks, together with Robinson, he had committed unusual energy to finalising the 1980 accounts and the annual report to prove that Lonrho's shares were a sound investment and the company possessed sufficient funds. Indeed, Lonrho's results revealed 'record profits' which had risen 52 per cent to £119 million and a 'record' £2 billion turnover. Cash balances, he claimed, were at a record £108 million. Lonrho's debt, disclosed in the report as having risen from £137 million to £249 million, and considered by some accountants to be in reality £466 million, was naturally minimised. For the unprejudiced, Lonrho was a thriving and expanding conglomerate which, building upon its traditional African empire, had successfully diversified by investments in Britain and America. But Rowland had thought only of the battle, not about the strategy of a flanking movement to outwit his enemies. Accordingly, having half destroyed House of Fraser's board, he rested upon his laurels and watched his foe initiate the easiest defence. Warburgs advised the company to ask for Lonrho's bid to be referred to the Monopolies and Mergers Commission.

In his SUITS report in 1979, Le Quesne had repeated Rowland's assurance that Lonrho was not considering a bid for the House of Fraser. Le Quesne concluded his report expressly refraining from opining about the 'effect on the public interest' should Lonrho launch a bid. 'In such circumstances a further reference to us could, no doubt, be made.' Seizing upon that caveat, Smith began lobbying the DTI and the Office of Fair Trading to make a formal reference to the Commission.

The decision would be taken by John Biffen, appointed just days earlier as the secretary of state. Rowland hoped for fairer treatment from this Conservative trade minister than he felt he had received from Labour. Naturally, he turned to Edward Du Cann to smooth the way.

Performing a similar role to Rowland's African 'runners', Du Cann had become Lonrho's political fixer in Britain, the man who could relay the 'vibes' in Westminster and Whitehall for Rowland to analyse in infinite detail during the post mortems which followed any approach to a politician. But Rowland seriously misunderstood Britain's political nuances and overestimated Du Cann's ability to report accurately.

Arriving at Westminster in his chauffeur-driven Rolls Royce provided by Lonrho, Du Cann occupied an enviable office in the House of Commons, overlooking the Thames. Even the prime minister, located nearby, complained, 'Edward's office is bigger than mine.' Although Thatcher was duty bound to meet the chairman of the 1922 Committee, she, along with many others in Westminster who had noticed Du Cann's ostentatious lifestyle, was becoming suspicious of his standing.

Du Cann's personal accounts were under investigation by the Inland Revenue which would recover an estimated £400,000. Moreover Du Cann and other Keyser Ullman directors had borrowed huge sums from Keyser Ullman bank and a test writ for the recovery of £300,000 owed to the bank was finally settled by Du Cann as a preliminary repayment of the unspecified millions. Further tarnishing his reputation, a DTI investigation into the bank's collapse castigated Du Cann and the other directors as 'incompetent' for losing £21 million. The immediate financial pressure upon Du Cann was absorbed by Rowland as a mark of his eternal gratitude that the politician had raised £10 million in 1971 to save Lonrho. Mutual loyalty was the foundation of their relationship. Over the following years, as Du Cann's finances lurched repeatedly and peculiarly into debt, Rowland would lend the Lonrho director at least one million pounds. 'Tiny invested a lot in Edward,' complained Terry Robinson. Rowland reasoned that Du Cann, like Mark Too in Kenya and Tom Mtine in Zambia, could secure his access to ministers who wielded power.

Accordingly, when Du Cann asked John Biffen to meet Rowland for a conversation about the House of Fraser bid, Biffen, as an 'old colleague from the West Country', agreed. 'Du Cann', admits Biffen, 'still had status so I couldn't refuse his request.' Slightly formal and tense, Rowland arrived showing his customary deference towards politicians. Speaking with immaculate diction, he gently explained to the politician Lonrho's achievements in creating wealth. 'I'm very good at that, Minister,' repeated Rowland, 'but I need more tolerance, more consideration and more support.' In the interests of the nation, he had taken on Brentford Nylons and the steel mills, which continued to lose money. He now wanted some support from Whitehall and Westminster. Biffen, a 'dry' Tory with little faith in intervention, listened and smiled. Politically it was impossible to display any partiality but he was genuinely intrigued by the success of refugee businessmen in Britain although he wrongly perceived Rowland as a Jewish entrepreneur. At the end of forty-five minutes, Rowland and Du Cann departed hoping that they were better understood.

Biffen's ear was also filled with pleadings from Roland Smith, the trade unions and most of all by his own civil servants. The animus against Rowland within the DTI had crystallised, especially since the assurances of non-interference which Rowland had given Le Quesne during the SUITS inquiry had been flagrantly broken. Since there was no political advantage in rejecting the Department's pressure, on 27 February 1981 Biffen referred Lonrho's bid to the Monopolies Commission.

The announcement of the referral was drowned by the simultaneous publication of unexpected and therefore sensational news. Lonrho had agreed to buy the *Observer*, Britain's oldest Sunday newspaper. At sixty-four, Rowland had become a Fleet Street baron, the closest he would get to an honorary title, but nevertheless a huge advance towards the levers of influence. In theory, he owned an important focus of radical liberalism in Britain whose traditions were valuable to faithful readers around the world. In practice, his ownership was subject to approval by the government and a possible reference to Le Quesne at the Monopolies Commission.

Founded in 1791, the *Observer* had become a respected newspaper since its purchase in 1911 by William Astor, a New York property speculator who moved to Britain. In 1919, the newspaper's ownership and the Astor peerage passed to Waldorf Astor whose wife Nancy was elected Britain's first woman member of parliament. Their family home at Cliveden in Buckinghamshire, overlooking the Thames Valley and adjacent to Hedsor Wharf, became a magnet for a range of Britain's intellectuals, writers and politicians.

Under its legendary editor, James Garvin, the newspaper's circulation increased between 1905 and the early 1920s from 2000 to 200,000 but then went into a gentle decline. By 1942, Waldorf Astor's relations with Garvin, already strained by the editor's support of appeasement, broke completely. David Astor, his son, became editor.

Imbued with the atmosphere at Cliveden, Astor socialised with some of the finest of Britain's writers and journalists – George Orwell, Michael Foot, Sebastian Haffner, Jon Kimche, Donald Tyerman and Isaac Deutscher – socialists who supported a radical change in post-war British society. As the newspaper moved towards the left, Nancy Astor complained. To prevent a family split, her husband created a trust to own the *Observer* as a non-profit, non-partisan newspaper. The trust's statement of policy committed the newspaper to total independence and explicitly forbade any 'personal ties'.

The post-war years until 1956 were the *Observer*'s 'golden age'. Brilliantly reflecting the intense political and ideological debate dominating Britain, the paper increased its circulation to 568,000 and briefly overtook the *Sunday Times*.

Astor was magnetised by the pursuit of ideals, human rights and fine writing. Within the newspaper's offices in Tudor Street, he created an indulgent and generous atmosphere and was rewarded by selfless dedication to the newspaper by his recruits – Michael Davie, Colin Legum, Anthony Sampson, Edward Crankshaw, Nora Beloff, Andrew Schonfield and Samuel Brittan – who flourished to become legendary journalists. The *Observer*'s arts pages were equally memorable. Kenneth Tynan was the drama critic while Terence Kilmartin, the literary editor, commissioned some of Britain's most challenging reviewers: Philip Toynbee, Harold Nicolson and A.J.P. Taylor. Quite simply, the *Observer* was too important to be ignored both by those who sympathised with its ideals and by the targets of its criticism.

Astor's flaw was his distaste for the business of managing and selling his product. Like most idealists, especially the children of the rich, Astor had neither counted pennies nor worried about the technique of earning money. In the immediate post-war years, his amateurism could be ignored because government restrictions on newsprint, which limited the competition, concealed his meagre profits. But that changed in 1956 after the newspaper courageously denounced Britain's conspiracy with France and Israel to recapture the Suez Canal. Although the readership remained steady, advertisers withdrew to avoid association with the newspaper's politics. Astor declined to consider the cost of principles and relied upon the subsidy of the family trust.

In contrast, the *Sunday Times* was reorganising its commercial and marketing operations. As its success with heavily promoted book serialisations pushed its circulation beyond the *Observer*'s dreams, it was bought in 1959 by Roy Thomson, a Canadian who had mastered the art of making newspapers profitable.

In 1961, the *Observer*'s fortunes suffered another setback. The *Sunday Times* published Britain's first free colour magazine, revolutionising the Sunday market, and the *Sunday Telegraph* was launched. Reluctantly and slowly, Astor emulated his competitors but his lack of conviction was reflected in the product. In the Swinging Sixties, despite excellent reporting which drove circulation towards one million in 1967, the losses escalated. The profile of *Observer* readers, maliciously castigated as 'left-wing nigger lovers and central European Jewish intellectuals', did not entice the advertisers, while the economics of over-manned print presses for just one day's newspaper and the trade unions' blackmail aggravated the financial haemorrhage. Over the next nine years, the problems and the management stiffened into rigor mortis. Astor's citadel of writers serving an elite, by then anachronistic in a national newspaper, gradually disintegrated. In 1975, Astor accepted that his epoch was over.

Astor's prescription for his replacement was an 'organising' rather than a 'writing' editor. The ideal 'organiser' would be the journalist who understood every aspect of newspaper production and marketing, and who sympathised with every topic which the newspaper reported. The choice of successor was between Anthony Sampson and Donald Trelford. According to Astor, Trelford was an 'organiser'.

Trelford, then thirty-eight years old, had joined the newspaper ten years earlier as an assistant to the news editor. A graduate of Cambridge, he had served his National Service as an RAF pilot before editing the *Nyasaland Times*, owned by the Thomson Organisation, for two years. In 1968, Trelford was appointed the *Observer*'s deputy editor. To some, he was a swashbuckling, anti-Establishment personality who epitomised the newspaper's best traditions. Others saw a shallow, unimaginative technician, nicknamed 'The Jockey'.

Trelford's honeymoon period was brief. By September 1976, the losses and the fall of circulation to 665,000 compelled the Astor Trust to sell the newspaper. In secrecy, Astor and his legal adviser Lord Goodman began negotiations with Rupert Murdoch, the owner in London of the *Sun* and *News of the World*. The Australian's terms, implying that the paper would abandon its commitment to the political left, did not deter Astor who favoured an 'efficient Visigoth' rather than another idealist. To sabotage the negotiations, the prospect of Murdoch's ownership was leaked. 'Giving the *Observer* to Rupert Murdoch is like giving your beautiful seventeen-year-old daughter to a gorilla,' complained Clive James. In the orchestrated campaign in parliament and the media, Murdoch was pilloried and withdrew from the talks. In the ensuing mêlée, among those mentioned as alternative purchasers was Rowland but the suggestion was derided.

The *Observer*'s salvation was instigated by Kenneth Harris, one of the newspaper's feature writers, described by Astor as a 'cultivator of important people'. Through a mutual friend, Harris elicited the interest of Robert Anderson, the Texan chairman of Atlantic Richfield [ARCO] which ranked among the world's biggest oil companies. Like many self-made businessmen, Anderson's vanity was tickled by the prospect of owning one of the world's renowned institutions and the concomitant improvement of an oil company's image.

On 15 November 1975, Astor flew to Los Angeles and was impressed by Anderson's commitment to maintain the *Observer*'s principles. Within one week, Lord Goodman had negotiated that Anderson should receive 90 per cent of the newspaper for just one pound plus a guarantee to invest £3 million over the following three years by when he expected the paper to become profitable.

To celebrate Anderson's purchase, Goodman and Astor arranged a glittering dinner at University College, Oxford, for 150 of Britain's powerbrokers, including five Cabinet ministers and six other newspaper owners. They had cause for jubilation. Anderson's subsidy had dissipated the threat of bankruptcy and, furthermore, Anderson rarely interfered with the editor's decisions. 'An absolute godsend,' declared Trelford. Anderson also ignored the newspaper's commercial management. As the losses increased towards £8 million and the newspaper endorsed Labour in 1979 despite the 'Winter of Discontent', Anderson became disenchanted with his product and its creators. Having secured the final 10 per cent of shares from the Astor Trust, he secretly began contemplating a sale. His decision was finalised on 20 February 1981.

At a board meeting to discuss the newspaper's declining fortunes and the insoluble disputes with the trade unions, Anderson was humiliated by Goodman's rejection of Kenneth Harris, his nomination for vice-chairman of the *Observer* board, as 'totally unsuitable'. The following morning, Anderson met Rowland for breakfast at Claridges and offered to sell the newspaper. Within minutes of the proposal, Rowland agreed. He did not bother to consider whether he needed to consult his board or even what price Anderson required. The two men shook hands on the deal and Anderson flew back across the Atlantic.

Their introduction had been arranged by Daniel Ludwig in Acapulco where Rowland regularly spent his holidays. Their common interest was Rowland's familiar bait, the prospect of extracting oil in Angola. Rowland assured Anderson that when his protégé Jonas Savimbi won the civil war, ARCO's chance of gaining rights to prospect for oil in partnership with Lonrho would be guaranteed.

Rowland's interest in buying the *Observer* had been a regular topic between the two and had been repeated seven weeks earlier during Rowland's Christmas holidays. The attraction for Rowland was understandable. Under Astor, the newspaper had championed the rights of Africans and campaigned against

British colonialism and apartheid. The newspaper's particular heroes, Kaunda, Nkomo, Banda and Nelson Mandela, were, with the notable exception of Mandela, Rowland's closest supporters. Its impeccable reputation on the continent, Rowland hoped, would be transferred to its new owner and provide a passport to greater access and influence.

Naturally, Rowland was attracted to newspaper ownership by the same vanity, lust for power and certainty of a prestigious megaphone which had seduced Anderson. His recent attempts to be considered as a potential purchaser of the *Evening Standard* and *The Times* had been perfunctorily rejected. This opportunity to buy the *Observer* was unique, not least because the seller's principal desire for a quick and painless transfer excluded the possibility of any competing bid and avoided interminable negotiations with the employees. The agreed terms, $4.5 million in cash and 40 per cent of George Outram, Lonrho's Scottish newspaper subsidiary, a total of £6 million, were settled within one day. Rowland's feelings about the deal, in the midst of his takeover battle for House of Fraser, were identical to Trelford's five years earlier: an absolute godsend.

In the afternoon of 25 February 1981, Anderson telephoned Arnold Goodman at University College in Oxford. Few British lawyers in the post-war years have wielded as much influence as Goodman. As an adviser, mediator and friend to the royal family, politicians and the leaders of most aspects of British life, the 'Blessed Arnold' personified the unseen currents of power which flowed between the 'great and the good'. Many of his efforts, including his devotion over nearly twenty years to ensure the *Observer*'s survival, were unpaid.

The lawyer had enjoyed an amicable relationship with Anderson and, despite their recent disagreements, had been reassured by the Texan's repeated promises that he would never sell the *Observer*. He was unprepared for the news: 'I have some knowledge that might interest you. I have sold the *Observer* to Tiny Rowland. He'll call you within the hour.'

According to Goodman, he 'really was almost speechless. I virtually said nothing.' The shock of Anderson's moral betrayal overwhelmed the lawyer. 'He'd bought the paper for one pound,' complained Goodman, 'and sold it for £6 million. A bit cool.' That betrayal was compounded by delivering the newspaper to an individual who epitomised everything which the Astors and their senior journalists loathed.

There followed a telephone call from Rowland to Goodman: 'One thing which I do want is that you and Astor remain on the board,' soothed Rowland.

Goodman's reply was direct: 'Sir, not all the instruments of torture in the Tower of London would keep me on the board.'

'Well, think about it.'

Goodman was not contemplating a glittering dinner to celebrate Anderson's successor. Two years later, Rowland spotted Goodman at the Savoy Grill.

'I haven't heard from you,' said Rowland.

'Well, the post is slow,' replied the lawyer.

Astor was similarly horrified. Rowland's activities in Africa represented duplicity and avarice to the old editor. His motives, Astor believed, were obviously to exploit the newspaper's reputation on the continent. The reaction was similar at the newspaper. Running into the newsroom, Trelford stood on a table so that he could be seen and exclaimed, 'We've been sold.' Aware of Rowland's reputation and embarrassed by the secrecy of the deal, the editor could find nothing encouraging to say about the takeover. On the news agency wires was a statement from Sir George Bolton, Lonrho's eighty-year-old deputy chairman, who hinted that the newspaper would be transferred to Glasgow: 'I suppose there may be some editorial staff who would be having kittens tonight.' The director's vision was explicit: 'We always wanted a paper so we could really express the views of Africa and the Third World.' By nightfall, most *Observer* journalists were apprehensive about the 'unacceptable' businessman who either manipulated or despised the press.

That distrust was not reciprocated by Rowland. On the contrary, he had great faith in the newspaper, its journalists and the future. The excitement of owning the *Observer* transcended any reservations. He understood journalists, he told Trelford when they met in his office, and was looking forward to the

fun of competing with Murdoch and the other barons. He did
not conceal his intentions from Trelford. He hoped that the
Observer would support his plan for removing the Cubans from
Angola in exchange for the removal of the South Africans from
Namibia. There were obvious benefits for Lonrho.

At Trelford's suggestion, Rowland came to the newspaper's
offices the following afternoon to address seventy journalists.
In the neon-lit, dilapidated basement canteen, standing behind
a chipped formica table, Rowland gazed nervously at his newest
employees. Wearing a coat, surrounded by a blank-faced entourage, he stood uncomfortably, sniffing. By his side was Spicer,
to be distrusted according to one journalist because 'the seat of
his trousers is shiny'.

In Rowland's experience, most journalists, like his employees
in Africa, were anxious, insecure and grateful for work. His
favourite journalists, to whom he was readily available, were
thankful to be handed a story, ready for publication, and always
offered to read back their copy for his approval before submission
to their editor.

Some of the *Observer* journalists in front of him, he knew,
were different. John Davis, the city editor, had criticised his
House of Fraser bid as 'downright cheeky' and recommended its
rejection. In protest, Lonrho had withdrawn its advertising from
the newspaper. Anthony Sampson, the newspaper's columnist
and an old Africa hand, had denounced him on television the
previous night as unprincipled. Even Trelford had been objectionable and, in his own office, had stipulated that the editor
could not tolerate any interference.

Speaking to large gatherings appalled Rowland. He operated so much better in intimate twosomes. Yet he needed to
win these people's support. 'It's the one paper we've always
wanted to own in the UK,' he explained to justify his purchase, not recognising the clash of cultures. When asked about
the guarantees of editorial freedom from his interference, he
answered, 'Ask Dick Hall, not me. I've made it quite clear
there'll be no interference from the proprietors.' Hall had
edited *The Times of Zambia* for Rowland and would support
Rowland's protestations of his innocence in the matter of

non-interference although others would sharply contradict the editor's memory.

It was after Rowland had reiterated his enthusiasm to take on the *Sunday Times* that Colin Legum, the newspaper's respected Africa and Commonwealth correspondent, rose to reopen an old feud.

Legum had met Rowland before UDI in Rhodesia and had admired his genuine love of Africa and contempt for the white settlers. 'He was on the right side,' recalled Legum who had reported for the *Observer* from Africa since 1949. In 1976, Rowland passed to Legum the material for his scoop exposing the breach of oil sanctions. Legum understood Rowland's motives and was susceptible to the charm of a unique, anti-Establishment merchant adventurer responsible for beneficial, agricultural schemes in Africa.

But his vulnerability to those qualities was outweighed by his distrust of Rowland as a newspaper proprietor. Lonrho's activities in South Africa had violated the *Observer*'s support of sanctions; he constantly meddled in Africa's politics; and his treatment of individual Africans was, Legum believed, corrupt and unscrupulous. Udi Gecaga's fate in Kenya epitomised Rowland's treatment of his employees whenever a conflict of interest arose: 'I couldn't maintain my integrity as an independent journalist if my proprietor was Tiny Rowland,' he had told friends. Regardless of the purchase, he intended to retire.

'I've got three questions,' announced Legum, holding his lunchtime cigar close to Rowland. In the event only two were asked as the two men embarked upon a slanging match about Rowland's record in Africa.

Fixing his eyes on Rowland's sullen face, Legum sniped, 'Wouldn't your business interests in Africa affect the *Observer*'s credibility?' and he cited examples of Rowland's involvement in the Sudan, Angola, Uganda, Tanzania and Kenya. 'These were all highly dubious.' Legum had unsettled his reluctant sparring partner.

'Let me tell you something about Africa,' commenced the familiar monologue, reciting detailed information which Rowland would insist was uniquely gleaned from his privileged contacts. Africa was his domain and no one could know more. 'And in Tanzania, could I have counted on the *Observer*'s support?' snapped Rowland after describing Lonrho's plight after nationalisation. The obvious answer was 'No'.

In the eyes of Legum and the tight coterie of self-appointed guardians of the *Observer*'s conscience, Rowland had been defeated. To their satisfaction, Rowland departed, 'flushed, without his charm and in high dudgeon'. But they forgot that others in the canteen, with interests neither in Africa nor in finance, had ignored the acrimony and judged Rowland to be charming and the newspaper's only saviour.

Trelford concluded the meeting by reminding his staff that there would certainly be an investigation by the Monopolies Commission and speculated about other bidders. Even if he does win, said Trelford, 'you can rely upon me to keep Tiny Rowland out of tiny Trelford's editorial conferences.' Those still present voted. Overwhelmingly, the majority supported Rowland's bid provided there were editorial safeguards. Their newspaper's treatment of Africa was less important to them than their jobs. The reality was that Rowland would be no different from Murdoch and someone had to agree to subsidise the *Observer*'s losses. The officers were outvoted by the ranks.

Outside, one of Rowland's directors explained to Trelford that the transfer would be easier if he 'could find a way to get rid of Legum and Davis'.

'Over my dead body,' replied Trelford.

'That wouldn't necessarily deter him, Donald.'

Rowland had not anticipated the tidal wave of anger and outrage that erupted in Fleet Street. But he had considered the possibility of a reference to the Monopolies Commission. The legislation was to prevent a concentration of ownership of newspapers and safeguard the 'public interest', in particular 'the need for accurate presentation of news and free expression of opinion'. Rowland believed that the issue could not arise in his case. Lonrho's newspapers in Scotland were peripheral and, in the past weeks, the Express group had changed ownership, the *Evening News* had merged with the *Evening Standard* and Rupert Murdoch's purchase of *The Times* and *Sunday Times* had all been nodded through by John Biffen and the DTI. Murdoch's deal had not been referred to the Commission despite the new acquisitions guaranteeing News International over 30 per cent of the British market and the knowledge that Murdoch had distorted *The Times* and *Sunday Times* accounts to suggest the group was in danger of closing because of imminent bankruptcy. Emulating Murdoch, Rowland made his takeover of the *Observer* conditional upon no reference to the Commission.

But Rowland had misjudged the atmosphere and the state of patronage in Westminster. The country was battling through a recession and the government's ratings in the opinion polls were low and falling. Among the reasons why none of the three previous deals had been subjected to government review was the close relationship which all the proprietors, including Murdoch, strenuously cultivated with Conservative ministers and in particular with Margaret Thatcher. All understood that an appeal to the vanity of British politicians would be successful provided it was subtle but contained a realistic promise of support.

When Rowland returned to Biffen's office, accompanied by Du Cann, to discuss the *Observer* bid he offered nothing to the minister or to the Party in return for their sympathy. On the contrary, his mere presence surely guaranteed further controversy and problems. Across the ministerial desk, Rowland saw a politician who was vulnerable. Biffen had just suffered strong criticism for allowing Murdoch to bulldoze the *Times* sale through the regulations. To avoid criticism, Biffen had just referred Lonrho's bid for the House of Fraser to the Commission. Both Astor and Goodman were lobbying against Rowland. The government's popularity was plummeting. It was much easier to refer the *Observer* bid rather than face more criticism in parliament and in his ministry. As Rowland departed, Bill Beckett, the minister's legal adviser, sighed, 'Well, Secretary of State, I think we can now take our hands out of the piranha bowl.' Rowland's bid, agreed Biffen, should be decided by Le Quesne. The only problem was that, by the terms of the takeover, there would be no bid if there was a reference to the MMC.

Rowland was stuck and feared that he might lose the prize. Anderson, contemplating Britain's valuable oil and gas fields in the North Sea, would renege on the deal to avoid controversy that Goodman was instigating by publicly accusing the American of deliberate deception. Unlike Rowland, Anderson actually admitted his desire to be loved.

On 13 March, Rowland arrived in New York to seek Ludwig's help. In the British Airways first-class lounge at Kennedy airport, he urged Ludwig to persuade Anderson to stay onside because of the importance of the newspaper for Lonrho in Africa. He was already working on a solution, he reassured Ludwig.

On 20 March, just minutes before Biffen announced his decision refusing to allow the transfer of the newspaper, Rowland struck out. He believed he had delivered an audacious coup.

Anticipating that Biffen would reject his bid, Rowland announced that he had bought 50 per cent of the *Observer*'s shares in a personal capacity from ARCO's American subsidiary. Since he did not own any other newspapers and this 50 per cent share was registered in Delaware, there were no grounds for a Monopolies Commission investigation. The officials at the DTI, so scorned by Rowland for their incompetence and prejudice, were as he intended perplexed. Rowland had abandoned the original purchase and formed a partnership with Anderson to own the newspaper.

For the next forty-eight hours, Rowland observed the uproar of frustration with some satisfaction. Discriminatory rules, he believed, should be broken and he had ridiculed the government. The anti-climax was swift. The DTI's lawyers had joined the poker game. Lonrho's transfer of 40 per cent of Outram Press to Anderson, the government decided, would require investigation by the Commission since Anderson was a newspaper owner. Rowland's bluff was called. On 26 March, at Lonrho's annual general meeting, Rowland publicly retreated. Lonrho would bid for the *Observer* and allow a Commission investigation. His own deal was discarded. On 27 March, Biffen formally referred the bid.

For Lord Goodman and David Astor, Rowland's gymnastics proved his lack of reliability and that he was a 'suspect' and 'dubious' individual. How could the chief executive of a public company, asked Goodman, first make a bid on his company's

behalf, then insert himself instead of the company as the bidder, and finally reverse everything? When, asked Goodman,
did Rowland hold all the statutory board meetings? The lawyer
refreshed his memory. Among the inspectors' findings in the
DTI's 1976 report was their conclusion that Rowland showed a
'willingness to withhold information from or to mislead the Board
or shareholders which has been more than casual'. Goodman
anticipated that the Monopolies Commission would not trust any
assurance that Rowland uttered. But he had reservations. The
British, he had discovered, displayed great physical courage but
they were deficient in moral courage.

Since Goodman's and Astor's interests were essentially historic
and emotional, the real focus of resistance centred upon Trelford.
Although the Divine Right of editors to work without any interference from proprietors exists only in the realms of ideology,
the relationship between editor and owner is none the less
critical to a newspaper's success. While both share the ideal
of achieving acclaim and profits, they may not agree on the
newspaper's appearance and content, but like a marriage, their
partnership can succeed only with respect and concessions on
both sides. Trelford's instinctive worry was that Rowland might
not understand that journalism flourishes, and readership loyalty
survives, only if its authors are free to exercise their discretion
and skills. Did Rowland comprehend that *Observer* readers were
not interested in his propaganda but read the paper because they
trusted the journalists' reporting and judgments?

All the evidence suggested that Rowland, unlike Murdoch,
neither understood newspaper technology nor the chemistry
which spurred a diverse group of iconoclasts and individualists
to co-operate under abnormal conditions. The disparagement
of Rowland's suitability to own a newspaper was the crux of
Trelford's submission to the Monopolies Commission, but accurate information about Rowland's background was surprisingly
meagre. Despite the public's interest since 1973, the profiles of
Rowland which Trelford read simply repeated banal accounts of
an Anglo-German boy who had worked at Paddington Station
and then emigrated to Rhodesia to make his fortune. Indeed,
one of the lengthier profiles, published fifteen months earlier

by the *Observer*, concluded, 'The City and Westminster may not love men like Tiny Rowland, but they may very well need them.' Like all the other articles about Rowland, the piece was notable for generalisations and lack of hard-core information.

Trelford deployed his staff and correspondents in Britain and Africa to discover more facts to flesh out the most important story in the newspaper since its foundation. Their task was to fill the glaring gaps in accounts of Rowland's life between 1939 and 1961. Trelford hoped to print an account before Le Quesne completed his report within the statutory three months.

The hearings began in Carey Street. Among the seven other members was Alastair Burnet, the former editor of *The Economist* and *Daily Express*, whom the *Observer*'s senior journalists hoped would be sympathetic.

The principal objectors were a small group of senior journalists led by Astor. Their arguments against allowing Rowland's bid were based upon the DTI's 1976 report conclusions, the immorality of multinationals deciding the fate of newspapers and the conflict of interests raised by Rowland's activities in Africa which would motivate his destruction of the newspaper's independence.

In their evidence, both Colin Legum and Conor Cruise O'Brien told the Commission that it would be impossible to restrain Rowland's interference in the *Observer*'s coverage of Africa to protect his interests. Lonrho, they argued, 'very powerfully' according to one Commission member, was vulnerable because the African leaders would place pressure upon Rowland to intervene.

In his thirty-page submission, Trelford agreed. 'For Rowland to grant the *Observer* editorial independence would be to give one of his own companies *carte blanche* to damage the whole business to which he has devoted his life. It is as illogical as it is unbelievable.'

Trelford was motivated against Rowland because in the midst of the hearings he saw precisely what he feared. Lonrho placed a prominent advertisement in the *Financial Times* to welcome the president of Ghana on his first visit to Britain. That same week, the *Observer* published a report describing Ghana's 'poverty, corruption and mismanagement'. Under Rowland, Trelford wrote to

Le Quesne, the *Observer* would never be allowed to publish its report.

In unison with the other objectors, Trelford pleaded that Rowland was untrustworthy and his assurances were worthless although, curiously, in his arguments urging that the bid was 'against the public interest', the editor did not offer the information gathered by his journalists describing Rowland's suspicious activities between 1938 and 1948.

Trelford's fears were cast aside by Rowland. In a manner agreed by the Commission members to be 'most courteous and forthcoming', Rowland derided the evidence of his interference in *The Times of Zambia* as spurious. Producing Richard Hall, who testified that as an editor of *The Times of Zambia* he had enjoyed complete editorial freedom, and several Zambian journalists, Rowland certainly impressed Le Quesne. 'Your evidence won the day,' Rowland subsequently told Hall. To the Commission, Rowland had proved that either he did not interfere or, at worst, that the evidence was irreconcilable.

The conflict of interest was not, said Rowland dismissively, 'any real risk'. The *Observer* was not read widely in Africa, he claimed, and if a conflict of interest did arise, 'Lonrho would not impose any limits on the *Observer* whatever the cost.' Rowland's phrase 'whatever the cost' impressed most of the Commission who could not find overwhelming evidence in Africa or Scotland to suggest the contrary. Fortunately for Rowland, they were unwilling to consider the esoteric argument that anyone who sincerely believed in editorial freedom would eschew ownership of the newspaper. Yet Rowland knew that concerns about his interference would remain.

Rowland therefore proposed that he would accept a board of 'independent directors', appointed and remunerated by Lonrho, to supervise and guarantee the editor's freedom. To testify to the integrity of his concession, and to counter Goodman's criticisms, Rowland produced Lord Shawcross. The former Labour attorney general, City regulator and banker supported Lonrho's acquisition and Rowland's good faith.

As the verdict was awaited, there was unanimous agreement about Le Quesne, despite their division about the *Observer*'s fate. The chairman, they believed, was 'inadequate', a 'shadowy figure' and 'unimpressive'. Rowland's disdain for Le Quesne's supreme influence upon his fate was echoed by others who were also subject to the same process.

Le Quesne and his colleagues understood the disenchantment but they were merely fulfilling a statutory function. Since there was no evidence of monopoly, they were empowered to prevent the bid only if it was 'against the public interest'. To decide against Rowland upon that basis, Le Quesne believed, could apply only in 'wholly exceptional circumstances'. Therefore, although all agreed that Lonrho's ownership 'might' be against the public interest, they were unwilling to recommend that the bid be rejected. Instead they proposed that the sale be approved subject to Lonrho's ownership being supervised by six independent directors who would operate under specific guarantees and conditions.

Only one Commission member, Robert Marshall, a trade unionist who had worked in Africa, dissented on the grounds that, based on Rowland's past record and the DTI report, the safeguards would be ineffective. Le Quesne dismissed Marshall's fears: 'We believe that incidents and conduct such as the Inspectors criticised will not occur in the running of the *Observer*.'

Whispers about Rowland's success spread around London days before the formal announcement on 29 June. Astor's anticipatory complaint to *The Times* was doomladen: 'It is hard to see how that paper can avoid either being dead or unrecognisable within three years,' he complained. The MMC's safeguards, he lamented, were 'a farce'. The rejoinder was sent by Du Cann: 'By any yardstick, the Commission is an impartial and conscientious body.' It was an endorsement which he would soon regret.

Trelford was depressed. In an editorial, he condemned Le Quesne's report because 'it dodges all the awkward questions'. The Commission's reliance on independent directors was 'illiberal, unworkable and unacceptable'. Other newspaper editors agreed that Le Quesne's solution was 'muddleheaded and potentially dangerous'.

Few readers read Trelford's condemnation. On the first night of Lonrho's ownership, the unions caused mayhem and stopped work. Trelford's demands for more guarantees were ignored by Biffen who formally approved the sale.

For Rowland, the relief was enormous. During the hearings, he had even told Le Quesne that he was thinking of retiring. The lawyer understood that Rowland was exasperated by the treatment he received in Britain. The criticism, both from the journalists and elitists like Astor and Goodman, had fuelled his paranoia. All his critics had ignored the fact that the change of ownership of every other newspaper had raised identical issues. Murdoch's purchase of the Times group had caused an exodus of writers, some preferring to work for Rowland, but the Australian had not been investigated by the government. Lonrho, Rowland believed, was being persecuted.

Trelford's position now became, in theory, delicate. Having led the campaign against Rowland, he might have expected dismissal. But future employment prospects for forty-four-year-old ex-editors were dim. Moreover, despite his criticism, the Commission's stipulated protections forestalled any immediate demand for his resignation. Heading a delegation of journalists to Cheapside, Trelford aggressively listed his candidates for independent directorships. The result was stronger protection than the Commission had envisaged.

Under their agreement, the independent directors' approval was required for the appointment and dismissal of an editor, and they were to provide protection from any attempt to restrain his right to express an opinion or report news – even if it conflicted with the interests of the proprietor. The safeguards were 'subject only to a properly determined budget'.

As a survivor, Trelford understood the constraints. One of the stories which would not appear was the background material collected about Rowland by *Observer* journalists. Included were snippets from Rowland's security dossier provided by white intelligence officers working for Zimbabwe's new Central Information Office. Since 1961, Rhodesian intelligence officers had, with the help of MI5 and MI6 in Britain, compiled an unflattering profile of UDI's enemy. Among the morsels sent to Trelford were details of Rowland's membership of the Hitler Youth, his abrupt discharge from the army and his dubious mining deals before taking over Lonrho. That could no longer be published in the *Observer*. Some information had already been passed to other newspapers. The remainder he decided to keep as an insurance for the future.

Hitherto, inquiries into Rowland's life had failed because information had been sought only from Rowland himself and that was automatically refused. Steadfastly, he even rejected submitting an entry in *Who's Who*. Claiming the right to privacy, he had resisted all inquiries until approached by Charles Raw, a renowned financial journalist working for the *Sunday Times*. Raw's repeated requests had been parried until he mentioned that Rowland had been imprisoned in Barlinnie jail in 1941. Suddenly Rowland agreed to a meeting and, for the first time, described some of the circumstances surrounding his wartime internment. But in specific terms, Raw's published article, 'The missing wartime months of "Tiny" Rowland', while revealing many new facts, was influenced by the distortions and embellishments generated by Rowland. Successfully he glossed over the circumstances about his family's successive internments; his internment was described as normal for aliens rather than caused by his discharge from the army; he exaggerated his wealth in the post-war period; and most importantly, considering that he was a proprietor of a national newspaper, Rowland concealed his antipathy towards Britain in 1941. For the moment, he was saved further inquiries and embarrassment. Having forbidden his family and friends to speak to journalists, he hoped to avoid the inevitable consequence of newspaper ownership. But he suffered a distinct vulnerability. Among those who had sought to clarify the mystery of Rowland, a consensus emerged that a suspicious succession of puzzling contradictions ran through the enigma.

Rowland was surprised and hurt. He did not understand that one cause of his investigators' unease was his own distrust of people, including his directors. His secrecy and pugnacity propagated the mutual apprehension. Once again, he failed to perceive that the victory of a single battle could damage his overall ambitions. His own background would become a material issue in his battle for the House of Fraser. Hence he preferred to return to the shadows.

There was no celebration when he became the owner of the *Observer*. Uncharacteristically for a new proprietor of a national newspaper, he did not walk through the building or invite his senior staff for drinks to celebrate a new era and mould a relationship. On the contrary, he intentionally withdrew, aware that, had an event four weeks earlier and 4000 miles away been publicised, his ownership of the *Observer* might not have received the approval of the Monopolies Commission.

Ten
The Crazy Gang

By any account, the events on 4 June 1981 at Houston airport in Texas were bizarre. Just before noon, Rowland's Grumman jet landed after a two-hour journey from Acapulco. On board were Captain Wilhelm Wilming and a co-pilot, with Rowland, Josie and the stewardess in the cabin.

After Wilming parked the aeroplane and the Rowlands had driven to the city, Agent John Hensley of US Customs climbed on board to undertake a search. At the rear of the cabin, in their special rack, Hensley found three weapons: a Russian AK-47 automatic machinegun; a Thompson Commando Mark III semi-automatic rifle and a Colt Python magnum revolver. Wilming was unconcerned. At that moment he was completing, as usual, his Customs declaration form. Guns had been carried on the plane ever since he joined Lonrho. On some occasions, in Sudan and Angola, he had used them for self-protection. The procedure was always the same, even at Heathrow. If he was staying overnight, they were surrendered. Otherwise, supported by the licences issued in Germany and Switzerland, they remained on the plane.

In retrospect, Wilming has convinced himself that Hensley was acting suspiciously. On his radio, the agent was talking about the 'London and Rhodesia Mining Company', a name which had not been used for nearly twenty years. The agent was particularly interested in the AK-47 which had an ornately carved wooden butt. 'It was a present', protested Wilming, 'from Joshua Nkomo.' Originally it had been presented to the Zimbabwean by the Russians: 'I have it to protect Mr Rowland.'

Eight hours later, Hensley arrested Wilming on a charge of illegally possessing firearms. 'There is a secret agenda,' complained Wilming as he was incarcerated for the night. Even the Customs agents understood after they were ordered by the local prosecutor to seize the plane and imprison Wilming, that 'this was not a normal case'.

Rowland heard about the arrest that night. 'If you arrest Wilming, you must arrest me too,' he taunted the Customs agent. Hensley was baffled, especially as Rowland, in mounting anger, launched into cool monologue: 'I'm a personal friend of Alexander Haig, the secretary of state and of Ray Seitz, also in the State Department. And Duncan Sandys, the son-in-law of Winston Churchill, is one of my company's largest shareholders.' Dropping names is a familiar trait of Rowland's, but that evening in Houston more names per minute spilled into the atmosphere than ever before. Seitz had recently returned to Washington from London as the deputy executive secretary in the State Department's executive secretariat. Listening to the outpourings, Grant Northcutt, a second Customs agent, would later officially describe the offensive as a 'severe verbal caution'.

Rowland telephoned Haig himself but discovered that he was, within hours, flying to China. Switching tack, Rowland urged the agents to remain discreet and not to contact either Haig or Seitz in Washington. But by then, both agents were baffled. 'Someone in Washington', whom they suspected to be the CIA, was 'taking an interest' and Rowland again changed his approach: 'Give Alex a call. He'll clear it all up.' Rowland's friendly banter even included an offer: 'Come and see me when you leave government service.' Northcutt declined the offer.

The following day, Wilming was given $100,000 bail. Since the Grumman was impounded, he chartered a Lear jet for the party to return to Acapulco. From Washington, Seitz regularly telephoned Houston to urge Customs, according to Northcutt, to 'clear all this up'. Three days later, an order from the Justice Department in Washington ordered the plane's release. 'It appears', concluded the Houston Customs final report, that 'the State Department went to the Justice Department and got the case dismissed.'

In Mexico, Rowland reflected upon his fortunate escape from embarrassment. The suspicion lingered that if there was a conspiracy somewhere in Washington against him, there was also consolatory proof of friends in Washington, a remarkable contrast to his status in London.

Although Rowland's acquaintance with Alexander Haig remains uncertain because the State Department diary does not reveal any official meeting before the day of Wilming's arrest, Ray Seitz assured Rowland that the Reagan Administration was pledged to reverse Jimmy Carter's refusal to support Savimbi and save southern Africa from communism. The architect of America's new policy was Chester Crocker, a professor of African studies at Georgetown University, the newly appointed assistant secretary for African Affairs.

An able but austere academic, Crocker had considerable investments in South Africa which, on appointment, were placed in a family trust. For Crocker, the fate of both Angola and Namibia was the yardstick of Washington's commitment to prevent the colonisation of the continent by the Soviet Union. Unlike his predecessors, Crocker, handicapped by a cold personality, welcomed Rowland's offer of his services. Seconded by Seitz and Robert Frasure, responsible for Southern African Affairs, Crocker trusted the Briton as a 'major player' in Africa, unfettered by allegiance to a government, who displayed a reassuring penchant for clandestine diplomacy, guaranteed by the invisibility of any staff. 'His great strength was to get into his aeroplane and go anywhere at any time without going through channels with hundreds of approvals,' recall Crocker's officials who ignored Rowland's propensity for name dropping and his cultivated publicity. 'We liked to talk to him because it's not often we'd find a man who could be meeting one-on-one with four presidents in a week.' Rowland was a useful and intriguing source of gossip and information: 'It was curious that he was always on his own. There wasn't even an assistant when we met.'

Unlike the British, the State Department was impressed by his amoralistic, non-ideologue approach, appreciating that 'today's terrorist is tomorrow's president'. In Washington, no one looked askance at Rowland's use of his business as an instrument of political influence, and vice versa. As Rowland's battle with the British government developed during the decade, the sentiments of Crocker and the Bureau of African Affairs' senior staff warmed towards the rebel who, 'doesn't like being regarded as a pariah by the Establishment. We knew that talking to us enhanced his credentials.'

Invariably their meetings were in London where the Bureau of African Affairs maintained a twenty-four-hour information-gathering centre for the English-speaking countries on the continent. Consulting on a range of issues, the task force endorsed Rowland's importance, intensifying resentment in the Foreign Office where their explanation for the rebel's success confirmed the prejudice: 'The Americans aren't very good on Africa.' But the contacts in Washington afforded Rowland valuable prestige when he called on African presidents whose access to officials even at Crocker's level was limited.

So, contrary to strict guidelines against using foreign nationals, Crocker would ask Rowland to 'carry water', that is, pass messages to those with whom an American official could not directly speak. His reliability was judged to be 'fair'.

But contrary to the impression Rowland liked to create, Crocker's department would be his sole contact with the US government. CIA officers involved in African affairs during that decade deny any contact with Rowland. CSI-50/10, the CIA's Clandestine Service Instructions, forbids the Agency to deal with British nationals without British government approval. But bureaucratic regulations were not only the barriers to deploying Rowland's services. Added to these were the warnings from MI6. Crocker however was satisfied with their first conversations about Angola.

During 1981, UNITA's destruction of rail links, oil refineries and government offices in the Marxist government's zone had convinced Crocker to support Savimbi. In December 1981, Haig met a UNITA delegation and promised that the Administration would seek a withdrawal of the estimated 19,000 Cubans from Angola [the numbers would rise to an estimated 31,000], linked to the independence of neighbouring Namibia. For Rowland there was renewed hope that he had backed a winner. But Angola was an impoverished, war-torn Third World country whose future was totally irrelevant to Lonrho's profits. Rowland's delight at winning privileged access to Chester Crocker in 1981 was a grave misjudgment of the era by the businessman.

The early Eighties augured a glorious decade for capitalists. The Reagan–Thatcher economic boom galvanised the elite band of international players into exploiting their access to invaluable inside knowledge because the banks were desperate to lend their money. Small investors too, besotted by tales of mega-million earnings, were grabbing the coattails of the buccaneers of capitalism to share in the revelry of fortunes. All the major operators were deluged with offers of deals to earn on the turn – short-term gambles to buy and sell stock and currencies. Rowland spurned most of those offers. Although he lived to deal, Rowland was essentially a buyer of real assets. His distrust of paper merchants had saved him from the 1974 crash. Ten years later, that prejudice was a handicap. In those few years, dreams of unbelievable wealth were transformed into reality.

For example, in 1984 Rupert Murdoch earned $40 million profit by purchasing and selling an adversarial stake in Warner Brothers, the communications giant; and another $37 million profit in a similar 'greenmail' stake in St Regis Corporation, producers of paper and forest supplies. From newspapers, Murdoch earned $7.5 million from the sale of the New York *Village Voice* and $55 million profit after a management buy-out of the *Chicago Sun-Times*. Profits from those four deals, all on the periphery of Murdoch's mainstream media operations, amounted to more than half of Lonrho's pre-tax earnings in the same year.

Another British player, Jimmy Goldsmith, also squeezed early advantages in that new era. His purchase in 1982 of the American Diamond Match Corporation, a conglomerate with particular interests in timber, produced a notional profit of $500 million by the following year, double Lonrho's performance.

All three, Murdoch, Goldsmith and Rowland, possessed wealth which had been used to buy an image of respectable, family-loving citizens, but in substance they were amoral, shrewd pirates. In common, they could charm adversaries to serve their purpose in a manner which victims and critics castigated as manipulation.

Like Rowland, both Murdoch and Goldsmith refused to be encumbered by the other directors or be answerable to boards staffed by non-executives. But unlike Goldsmith and Murdoch, Rowland's propensity for boardroom dictatorship even precluded recruiting notably talented subordinates in Cheapside. In a reflection of his own weakness, he could not tolerate any competitor to his leadership and was too vain to appreciate the self-imposed disadvantages. Hence, while all three tycoons believed that the real profits were to be earned by going in the 'opposite direction' to the market and hesitated about partnerships with competing players, Rowland alone denied himself the quality of advice which could have realised his full potential.

For Murdoch and Goldsmith operated in America, the source of real wealth, not Africa. Through lack of skills, by temperament and by choice, Rowland was excluded from Wall Street, although not quite in the way he was isolated from the City. Symbolically, Rowland had placed himself as an outsider just when Murdoch and Goldsmith [and James Hanson] became the motors and beneficiaries of the Reagan–Thatcher revolution.

At that time, Rowland barely knew Murdoch and had fallen out with Goldsmith. At a dinner party on the eve of October 1974 election, Goldsmith bet Rowland £5000 about the outcome. Neither man now agrees about the terms of the bet and complains that the other failed to pay. Rowland has even threatened litigation against anyone who dares repeat Goldsmith's version. Since the details are both convoluted and uninteresting, they are best ignored except that the incident proved that Rowland preferred to rupture their relationship rather than settle. Two years later, to emphasise his antipathy, Rowland donated £5000 to *Private Eye* after the High Court ruled that Goldsmith could, most unusually, sue the magazine for criminal libel following the publication of an article questioning Goldsmith's honesty. Considering that Rowland, like Maxwell, would become one of the more litigious tycoons in Britain, hypersensitive to any criticism, the motives for his contribution were inexplicable other than to curry favour with the anti-Establishment and humour a potential critic.

The final rupture between Rowland and Goldsmith occurred in June 1977. Two months earlier, they had agreed to mount a joint bid for Beaverbrook Newspapers but Goldsmith had failed to produce £7.5 million, his half-share. Rowland offered to lend Goldsmith the money but the latter declined and literally disappeared. Rowland subsequently discovered that Goldsmith had sold his own Beaverbrook shares for a profit of £1.8 million to Trafalgar House, the new owners of the group. Arguing that it was a partnership, Rowland asked for a 50 per cent share of Goldsmith's profits. On submission to arbitration which included Jim Slater and Armand Hammer among the judges, Rowland was the victor. It is an ironic comment on British society that while Rowland was persecuted for his brand of capitalism, Goldsmith was knighted by Harold Wilson. Their attitudes towards Britain also bear ironic comparison. While Rowland disliked much about his adopted country in common with Murdoch and Goldsmith, they were by birth members of the very Establishment which they all feigned to condemn. Rowland was therefore exceptional. Not only was he outside the British Establishment and excluded from the world's financial establishment, but he was not even a member of the anti-Establishment establishment. Barred from the mavericks' club, in 1981, Rowland was digging into a clay pit, battling with a regulator in London. His chosen plight contradicted the boast that his future was planned five years ahead.

During the summer, Rowland continued his visits to Carey Street to be questioned by Sir Godfray Le Quesne. The Monopolies and Mergers Commission were undertaking their third investigation into Lonrho. The issue was the bid for the House of Fraser.

The relationship between the tycoon and the judge had not altered. The distrust was mutual. Rowland's accompanying entourage, especially Du Cann and Spicer, did not inspire Le Quesne's confidence either. For their part, the Lonrho team were as ever perplexed why the Commission never assembled as a complete team. 'Back at the dull mahogany tables of the Commission,' wrote Rowland, 'I found myself again seated opposite the familiar, tall, languid figure of Sir Godfray Le Quesne, rocking gently on his chair, with his hands clasped behind head and his eyes closed as he listened or slept through the hearings. He's been looking into us for four years and here, I thought, as I gazed by the hour and by the month at the hole in the sole of the leather of his shoe, and wondered why Lonrho's bid was in the hands of a man who couldn't organise his own shoe repairs.'

George Willoughby, House of Fraser's finance director, agreed, especially of the post-prandial sessions. 'In the afternoon it seemed sometimes like talking to a wall.' For his part, Le Quesne also complained that occasionally Rowland's attention seemed to have drifted away. But the process was more than a formality.

Only two years earlier, Rowland had assured Le Quesne that Lonrho was 'not considering' a bid for House of Fraser 'at the moment', and he denied that Lonrho would seek to control House of Fraser with its minority stake.

Lonrho's latest submission offered two explanations to remove Le Quesne's suspicions. Firstly, that the original promises were 'genuine' but because of probable 'misunderstandings on both sides', events had changed.

The second explanation was less credible. Lonrho's campaign against House of Fraser, said Rowland, was provoked by his fear of a conspiracy against him, masterminded by House of Fraser, Tom Ferguson of Gulf Fisheries and Graham Furgusson-Lacey, an unknown investor. Their plot, Rowland claimed, was a secret bid for Lonrho. Rowland had grounds to fear a bid. Tom Ferguson, the representative of Gulf Fisheries, was searching the City for partners who would lead a takeover and had been recommended Furgusson-Lacey as a potential partner. 'Tiny knew that it was not good to have a large block of dissatisfied shareholders,' explains Tom Ferguson, 'but he killed us off by calling Graham Furgusson-Lacey "a financial pygmy".'

In more reasonable terms, Lonrho's argument for approval of the takeover seemed unassailable. The company could afford to bid, albeit at a low price, there was no prospect of a monopoly and House of Fraser would benefit from new management.

For the defence, Roland Smith, supported by Warburgs, recited the 1976 DTI report's condemnations of Rowland and

provided a detailed diary of Lonrho's harassment in the boardroom over the previous months. Obliquely, the delegation from
the City disparaged the denizens from Cheapside: Rowland, a
password for unacceptability; Sandys, a discredited politician;
Du Cann, a financier under suspicion; Spicer, a universally
disliked nobody; and Lonrho, a company which could not even
hire a merchant bank for advice. Cumulatively, argued Smith,
the evidence proved Rowland's dishonesty and the unsuitability
of Lonrho's management of the store group.

Le Quesne's report was published on 9 December 1981.
Although he insisted that he had disregarded the bitter rows
and the allegations of harassment, his recommendation against
the bid suggested the contrary. He argued firstly that the merger would affect competition; and secondly that the takeover
was 'against the public interest'. The latter argument betrayed
symptoms of prejudice.

On loss of competition, Le Quesne quoted Lonrho's ownership of Brentford Nylons as a reason that the merged group
might refuse to sell other competing brands in House of Fraser
stores which 'might damage fair competition and be seriously
detrimental to some suppliers of House of Fraser'. Since sales of
nylon in Britain were minimal and hardly the choice of Harrods'
shoppers, Le Quesne's judgment seemed fanciful to some.

Le Quesne's main objection, the 'public interest', an objective phrase which could be utilised to match any purpose, was
explicitly directed at Lonrho's directors.

The continuing success of House of Fraser, explained Le
Quesne, was important to the British economy and would
be weakened if Lonrho, with no experience in retailing, took
over. Since most of House of Fraser's senior executives would
be dismissed, the group would be reliant upon fifteen Lonrho
executives which would lead to 'some overstrain and deterioration in the quality of decisions'. Age was Le Quesne's criterion.
Sandys was seventy-three, Sir George Bolton, the deputy chairman, was eighty-one, while Rowland, aged sixty-four, had
mentioned during the *Observer* inquiry that he contemplated
retirement. Lonrho's geriatrics, opined Le Quesne aged fifty-
seven, collectively threatened 'uncertainty and risk'. There was,

he concluded, 'at least a very real and substantial risk that the efficiency of House of Fraser would deteriorate seriously as a result of the merger and it would be detrimental to the public interest'.

The report was not unanimously supported. One Commission member, a businessman, argued that since Lonrho had success-fully produced good profits for its shareholders, the hostility of the House of Fraser board should not prevent a bid. His four colleagues, academics, a lawyer and a trade unionist, ignored commercial reality.

Unpredictably, independent public reaction condemned the Commission's recommendation as flawed, prejudiced and contra-dictory. Newspaper commentators surmised that the decision should have been taken by shareholders and not by 'a strange and shadowy body with ill-defined but sweeping powers'. According to the *Guardian*, Lonrho had received a 'disgracefully raw deal', while the *Sunday Telegraph* reported that the Commission's recommendation 'has met with a solid wall of criticism and contempt'. Rowland blamed the Establishment: 'They and the City don't like me and wish I would go away.'

On reflection, it was peculiar that Le Quesne could describe Rowland in glowing terms in 1979, approve the *Observer* pur-chase in May 1981 but, seven months later, disallow the House of Fraser bid. As Trelford 'puzzled', the Commission had decided that while Lonrho could own the *Observer*, it was unfit to own a department store 'on the grounds that a conglomerate based in Cheapside cannot exercise effective supervision over a stores group based in Knightsbridge'.

At the House of Fraser, Professor Roland Smith, 'delight-ed' by the report, offered the directors a glass of champagne to celebrate the reprieve. 'We thought it was all over,' says Willoughby. 'Everyone else who loses at the Commission just goes away. We didn't realise what was going to happen.'

Rowland resolved not to surrender: 'This is just another hurdle that we have to overcome. These are skirmishes. It's who wins the war that matters.' Publicly, his war was directed against Smith: 'The professor knows we are there and will see us in his dreams. He will need two Mogadon instead of one each night.'

But privately, he would even spread the story that Le Quesne had been summoned by the Duke of Edinburgh to Windsor and, over dinner, had been advised to find against Lonrho. The Duke, whom Rowland blamed for 'striking my name off the Buckingham Palace guest list', was, in Rowland's mind, intent on securing revenge for the embarrassment caused to Angus Ogilvy. The source of his conviction was Sir Robert Adeane's account of an encounter with the Prince on a subsequent shooting party. Adeane had been invited to Sandringham to brief the Prince about Lonrho and Ogilvy. Ever since, Rowland had extrapolated the Palace's antagonism towards himself. Le Quesne however, was known to have met Prince Philip only seven years later, in 1988.

Rumours produced by Rowland's fertile imagination were as prolific as rumours spread in the City about his intentions. Both fed upon Rowland's own conspiracies, real and imagined. Suspicions about him in the City after the Commission's report spread gossip that buyers, possibly Rowland's friends, were seeking 7 million House of Fraser shares following Lonrho's refusal to assure the Department of Trade and Industry that he would not mount a new bid.

Rowland's threat to keep his stake and continue the war unsettled officials at the Office of Fair Trading. Lonrho's refusal to accept the report caused confusion as officials sought a clause in the legislation which would deny Lonrho the right to contemplate a future bid. 'We realised', recalls one senior civil servant, 'that it was a lousy report and he could shoot holes through it.' The reference to nylon was 'ludicrous' and the emphasis on public interest was 'excessive'. The showdown terminated after four days of intense haggling. Retrospectively, Rowland snatched a qualified reprieve from the jaws of defeat.

In return for an undertaking not to buy more House of Fraser shares or to encourage other buyers to launch a new joint bid, John Biffen agreed that Lonrho could, in the future, be released from those undertakings and make a new bid if there were 'new circumstances'. The minister, an amiable but imprecise politician, believed the unprecedented phrase was meaningless and that Rowland would remain entrapped within the system.

Four months later, in early April 1982, Rowland ventured to break the blockade. In a letter to Biffen, Rowland requested a succession of meetings to review the Commission's report. Lonrho perceived a 'change of circumstances' and wanted, he wrote, to be released from its undertakings and make a new bid. In reply, Biffen suggested that Rowland should meet Gordon Borrie, the OFT's director general.

The relationship between Rowland and Borrie would become increasingly critical during the ensuing warfare. Two factors determined Borrie's reaction towards Rowland. Firstly, despite the radical changes promised by Margaret Thatcher, the Labour government's rules regarding monopolies, imposed upon the OFT, had not been altered. The philosophy that Whitehall should interfere in management in the public interest, even to the detail of managers' ages, remained binding.

Secondly, Borrie, like any other official implementing laws, naturally exercised his discretion to decide upon the inter- pretation of those rules. Regardless of public pontification, his discretion depended upon his personal attitude towards Rowland. Since the Eighties heralded unprecedented corporate activity, Borrie's importance grew in tandem with the volume of his activities and his visibility in public life. Executives working in the corporate, financial and legal professions sought opportu- nities to meet the director general at the endless succession of City receptions. In those circumstances, Borrie became infor- mally acquainted with men whose fate he could influence and he would make personal judgments accordingly. One man whom Borrie never met in the City's social village was Rowland.

To Rowland, City receptions were worse than irrelevant; they were to be disdained. Consequently, Borrie would never know or understand the Rowland who regaled presidents of corporations and nations across the world. Instead, on the innumerable formal occasions when they met over the months and years after the Commission's recommendation, Borrie was confronted with a polite, well-spoken millionaire whose manner belied his public reputation yet whose method of challenging the rules evoked suspicion of something sinister.

At their first meeting, Rowland was accompanied by Duncan

Sandys, Du Cann and Spicer. 'They weren't a pretty sight,' confesses an OFT official who saw through the gentle image. 'Not like the normal smooth merchant bankers. Rowland was red toothed and raw. Not an attractive quartet.'

The flaws in Le Quesne's report, said Rowland, were glaring. He proposed that, together with OFT officials, they scrutinise every paragraph to find a path for Lonrho to overcome the obstacles qualifying as a 'change of circumstances'. Aware that a 'public interest' argument in the management of shops was difficult to sustain, Borrie agreed that Rowland's complaint would be considered.

A crisis meeting was called in John Biffen's office although officials observed that the minister was keen 'not to make up his mind'. Playing for time was more convenient. The Monopolies Commission did not fit neatly into the new Thatcherite doctrine about the market economy and Biffen perceived that he would receive no gratitude for injuring Scottish myths and emotions about House of Fraser when the Nationalist challenge to the Conservative vote was increasing.

Sally Oppenheim, his junior minister, was more forthright. 'Harrods', she exclaimed, 'is a national asset which cannot be put at risk by bad management.' There was, she continued, a 'difference between the national interest and the public interest'. Her audience was baffled. Anxious to help, William Knighton, a DTI official nodded: 'Very interesting, Minister. I think it's what we might call a second order nuance.' No one understood the phrase but the ice was broken. Biffen agreed that his officials could now investigate the 'second order nuance'. It was best, he believed, to allow the argument to continue among officials and avoid entanglement with Du Cann. None of those present in Biffen's office saw any advantage in helping Lonrho.

Over the following months, Rowland and his advisers arrived at the OFT for two-hour sessions. 'I am available at any time,' smiled Rowland to the forlorn officials. 'We just couldn't see that it was worth the candle,' recalls a civil servant, 'but he knew our case was weak and he came back hard and began to win some sneaking sympathy.'

Rowland was unaware of any sympathy. In Cheapside, most

of his regular 9.30 a.m. meetings were dominated by House of Fraser. John Paterson, Hugh Fraser's personal assistant whom Rowland had hired when Fraser resigned from the board, watched bemused as the obsession, like a fungus, took root. Rowland's venom was directed in equal measure at the DTI officials, Roland Smith and Warburgs. Sometimes half of Rowland's day would be consumed by his agonising and the plotting of his tactics.

Absurdly coinciding with the departure of the British task force towards the Falkland Islands, Rowland's bellicosity resumed at House of Fraser board meetings. Terry Robinson and Paul Spicer, alternates for Rowland and Sandys, questioned, criticised and even pressurised the management to defend the company's poor annual results. Profits, in the recession, had fallen in the second successive year from £40 million in 1979 to £28 million in 1980. Rowland had cause to complain. A revaluation of the company's assets organised by Professor Smith suggested that the shares were worth 300 pence, yet the market price was only 150 pence, and that value was enhanced by the Lonrho bid.

Smith, complained Rowland in one of the regular circulars from Cheapside, 'has twenty-six other directorships and has spent £600,000 on very plush offices at the Army and Navy when that store is losing millions.' To reassert Lonrho's presence, in May 1982, an additional 283,000 House of Fraser shares were purchased, raising the stake to 29.9 per cent. Smith was defiant: 'They seek to wear us down drip by drip but they won't succeed.'

Rowland's complaints were justified but his messengers' behaviour provoked contempt, reflecting adversely upon Rowland himself. 'He is disruptive,' wrote one director to Rowland about Spicer, 'often ill-informed even on subjects of his own choosing and occasionally offensive.' That complaint followed a presentation to the board by Alec Craddock, the chairman of Harrods, explaining the proposed improvements of the store's famous food hall. 'Have you taken into consideration,' queried Spicer, 'that Sainsburys are opening a new branch in Cromwell Road?' The stupefied silence was broken by Craddock: 'I don't think that's a factor.'

Robinson was different. He was acknowledged to be intelligent. His lengthy letters and carping complaints, demanding the most detailed and secret information to fuel Lonrho's armour of criticism against the board, cast him in Willoughby's opinion as an unusual professional, willing to cause personal anguish to serve his master: 'We were an honest company and there were no skeletons to fish out. He was always trying to find ways to reduce our profitability which was contrary to a director's task.'

In the background, Rowland fumed privately and publicly against Warburgs, the suspected orchestrators of the campaign against Lonrho's bid for House of Fraser and, in his opinion, the source of Lonrho's problems. Ever since 1971, Rowland had ignored the fact that Warburgs had resigned after his refusal either to consult or accept the bank's advice before the liquidity crisis. Instead, a notion had germinated in Rowland's mind that Lonrho had been misunderstood and that a decade later it was again the victim of similar misfortune.

In April 1982, Rowland complained to David Scholey that Siegmund Warburg's public condemnation had been 'very hurtful' and 'the unkindest act . . . abandoning Lonrho when we were in difficulties' and urged him to desist from the 'vendetta'. But at that precise moment, the same bankers perceived Lonrho to be on the verge of a similar predicament.

Just one month after Rowland had talked up his company's shares, suggesting that profits would rise to £44 million, Lonrho's profits were in fact falling. In the first six months of 1982, pre-tax profits fell from £40.7 million to £38.5 million. In the previous two years, British earnings had fallen from £34.9 million to £22.2 million. Publicly, Rowland had preferred to emphasise Lonrho's 'record' turnover, but in an unusual accounting practice, Lonrho had included in its 'record' statistic a 29% proportion of House of Fraser's turnover. That accounted for £348 million of Lonrho's £1,440 million total. At the same time, Rowland bought another 5 million Lonrho shares to support the market price. The only factor which remained unchanged was Lonrho's high dividend. 'We pay a decent dividend,' Rowland disclosed, 'because I need the cash.'

Lonrho also needed cash. The stake in House of Fraser was

producing less in dividends than if the money were deposited in a building society, commodity prices were falling, and £52 million had been borrowed to buy the remainder of the Princess hotels. Rowland the deal maker was once again ignoring the value of financial prudence.

If Lonrho was to buy House of Fraser, it needed a loan. The money had originally been promised by the Standard & Chartered Bank but in late 1981 Du Cann approached Joseph Hirsh, an American financier, and began negotiating two twenty-year loans of $250 million and $1.1 billion. Du Cann's negotiations were not conducted on Lonrho notepaper but on behalf of West of England Development Co (Jersey) Limited, yet Du Cann did send Hirsh a copy of Lonrho's accounts. The negotiations terminated inconclusively and abruptly. Du Cann denied that his talks were connected with the House of Fraser bid but his denial coincided with Rowland's attempt to escape from two straitjackets. The first involved removing the Kuwaiti interest; the second was the sidestepping of the seemingly impregnable block to his bid for House of Fraser.

In April 1982, Rowland began negotiating with the Israeli government to establish a Lonrho presence in the nation's weapons industry. Simultaneously, he contacted David Kimche, the former deputy head of Mossad and the director of the Foreign Ministry, to consider future ventures in Africa. Rowland might have hoped that the publicity would trigger an official Arab boycott of Lonrho, forcing Gulf Fisheries to sell their remaining 15 per cent stake.

The threat coincided with another public struggle between Lonrho and Tom Ferguson, Gulf Fisheries' representative. Lonrho wanted to increase the company's borrowing limits from £976 million to £1.5 billion, allowing the company to take loans worth eight times more than its stock market valuation, an 'astronomic' amount according to the *Daily Mail* whose valuable sympathy for Rowland was ebbing. Gulf also condemned the notion arguing that Lonrho would just buy more companies and, on past performance, earn ever diminishing profits.

The increase in Lonrho's borrowing depended upon the approval of 75 per cent of the shareholders. In a succession of newspaper advertisements, Ferguson urged opposition to Lonrho's proposed changes in its rules at the forthcoming annual general meeting. To frustrate Ferguson's campaign, Rowland refused to allow Gulf access to a list of Lonrho's shareholders. In bizarre antics which again reflected adversely upon Rowland's complaints against the board of House of Fraser, the list of shareholders was eventually sent to Gulf on a Friday night by post in the expectation that its arrival the following week would be too late for Ferguson to dispatch circulars. That Friday night, 23 April 1982, Ferguson appealed to a judge to compel delivery of the list. An Order was issued, forcing Lonrho to search ignominiously through London's postal sorting centre to retrieve the package. Lonrho had good cause to fear Ferguson's opposition.

At the shareholders' meeting, Gulf defeated Lonrho's resolution. Visibly chagrined, Rowland suffered further retribution. Critics renewed their scrutiny and their criticism that his company was a lopsided shell, earning unremittable profits in Africa, losing money in Britain and incapable of creating original wealth. It was an attempt to overcome those weaknesses highlighted by the criticisms that had motivated Lonrho's handicapped quest for House of Fraser. 'There was no passion for Harrods,' according to Robinson. 'It was a simple cash operation.'

Rowland's Israeli negotiations had naturally evaporated but one reward of his visit was a chance meeting with Stanley Kalms, the managing director of Dixons Photographics. In the course of their conversation, Rowland mentioned that the *impasse* at House of Fraser might be solved by Michael Richardson, the stockbroker who had recently moved from Cazenoves to work as a merchant banker at N.M. Rothschild. Kalms agreed to ask Richardson to act as an intermediary.

Richardson was and remains an unusual animal in the City. Gregarious, smooth and shrewd, he was born in comparatively modest circumstances, was educated at Harrow, and after a short period with the Drayton Group, cultivated during the Sixties an image and clientele which was risky or rich, among them Robert Maxwell, to emerge as an exceptionally well-connected broker. Regarded as a City lion who marched to the sound of gunfire,

Richardson would ride to glory on the riches provided in the Thatcher era by privatisation and takeover bids. The career change in 1981 from broking to banking reflected his ambition to transform from a technician and tipster to rank among the financial world's elite. By then a prominent freemason in the Grand Lodge, Richardson offered Rowland a certain route to the heart of the City.

Richardson arrived at Rowland's Park Lane flat for lunch on 17 May 1982. 'Oh Michael,' gurgled Rowland, 'it's so marvellous to see you. You're the only one who can save the situation.' Similarly effusive, Richardson insisted that their conversation was exploratory and should remain confidential. Rowland agreed.

The banker inquired whether Rowland would sell his House of Fraser shares. Rowland refused but suggested that Rothschilds should become involved in a settlement. In the conversation which followed, the two men toyed with a compromise entailing Professor Smith's replacement by a strong but neutral chairman. 'Rowland was particularly angry with me,' Richardson would say, 'because I had chosen Smith to defeat Lonrho's bid.' Richardson mentioned the candidature of Christopher Soames, the Conservative politician, one in the banker's myriad of social friends. Rowland was enthusiastic. Over the following days, Richardson discussed the bank's possible involvement with Evelyn Rothschild but was informed that Lonrho was an unsuitable client. On relaying the news, Richardson was greeted with a tidal wave of invective. Out of a simple, private and unsuccessful discussion, Rowland constructed a gigantic conspiracy.

Rowland's indictment against Richardson was 'subterfuge' and he delivered his charge at a personal meeting with Lord Rothschild, a non-executive director of the bank. Victor Rothschild listened to Rowland's complaint and to Rowland's indirect offer to include the merchant bank in Lonrho's proposed Israeli activities. Curtly, Rothschild reiterated his cousin's lack of interest in any dealings with Rowland. The bankers expected the affair to end, although doubts at Rothschilds remained over Richardson's decision to become involved.

Rowland however saw the chance of further revenge. The

text of his private meeting with Richardson was leaked to newspapers and partially published in the *Daily Mail*. Convinced that Rowland had bugged the apartment, Richardson suspected that detectives hired by Lonrho had been constantly monitoring his movements. No evidence confirmed his suspicions. Feeding on Hugh Fraser's allegations that Rowland had hired girls to spy on his gambling, a wave of paranoia about Rowland's alleged dirty tricks spread to Warburgs. Specialists were summoned to check every office and telephone for bugging devices; letters were sent under special security; and guards were hired to protect personnel and their papers. No evidence was ever found of any espionage, but Rowland had successfully infected everyone involved in the House of Fraser battle with apprehension. 'We switched offices all the time,' admits a Warburgs banker, 'because we suspected that he would use those directional microphones from another building to eavesdrop. We were really afraid of him.' Security checks became a regular event. For the first time, gossip around London equated Rowland with unacceptable behaviour.

The fear of Rowland fuelled the desire to thwart his ambitions. Richardson had initiated a 'war chest'. Institutions were urged to buy House of Fraser shares as a long-term investment to prevent Lonrho either taking control by surprise or buying the company too cheap. Whenever blocks of House of Fraser shares were for sale, Garmoyle or Richardson would persuade 'friends' to acquire a stake. In Garmoyle's opinion, the operation was 'unique . . . I doubt if anyone else has really tried something on this scale before or since.' Rowland of course responded, deploying a ruse which startled Roland Smith and confounded officials at the DTI.

On 16 September 1982, Rowland wrote to Smith saying that Lonrho no longer intended to bid for House of Fraser because the share price was 'out of touch with reality'. Instead, Lonrho was demanding an extraordinary general meeting to approve the demerger of Harrods from House of Fraser.

Under a demerger, Harrods would become an independent company, entirely separate from the remainder of the group, creating the 'new circumstances', which would force the DTI to release Lonrho from its undertakings, would bypass the Monopolies Commission report, and allow Lonrho to bid for Harrods. Since the Knightsbridge store provided more than 50 per cent of House of Fraser's profits and the 110-store group had suffered its first trading losses, Smith was vulnerable both to Rowland's inspirational 'unbundling' concept and his guerrilla tactics which began the following morning. Staff arriving at Harrods received circulars criticising their manager, demanding his removal and encouraging their support for Lonrho.

Rowland's own explanation was published in *The Times*. Written in his inimitable style, the article, which started with the supplication, 'Now don't look bored', explained that the demerger would revitalise the group and produce better results. 'I do not mean to be unkind,' continued Rowland, 'when I say that the present part-time chairman is [not] suited for these tasks although he has been an enjoyable adversary in the fight to prevent us making a direct bid to shareholders . . . My favourite newspaper cartoon about the House of Fraser shows a dispirited shareholder opening yet another envelope and saying, "If only I'd had as many dividends as I've had circulars . . ." '

The proposed demerger was certainly attractive to City institutions disappointed by House of Fraser's poor earnings. To excite their interest, Rowland, Du Cann and other Lonrho directors toured the City with a convincing presentation of immediate profits if the demerger were approved. For the first time, Warburgs sensed that the initiative had shifted. Potentially, Rowland could win sufficient support to effect a cheap takeover.

Smith's bravura was also wilting. 'I don't think there is anyone like Mr Rowland,' he confessed. 'He is a very capable adversary and I don't think you could realise what it is like until you come face to face with the experience.' Nevertheless, Smith resisted the temptation to remove Rowland from the board. 'I like to know precisely where they are,' he explained.

Smith was exasperated by Rowland's timing. Each extraordinary general meeting cost £500,000 but, more pertinently, the directors had considered and rejected the demerger earlier because of tax complications. Smith was also puzzled because at their board meeting on 16 September Rowland had suddenly threatened: 'If allegations are made that I am acting in concert with other shareholders, a writ will be issued.' According to Smith, Rowland's threat came 'out of the blue'.

Rowland's threat was forgotten until 12 October. An anonymous postcard to Smith suggested that Rowland had a 'hand-in-hand' relationship with Geoffrey Musson, the manager of the Merchant Navy Officers Pension Fund. Rowland, the sender hinted, was involved in a secret plot.

Smith was intrigued. Eight days earlier, he had lunched with Musson. Over the previous four months, the fund manager had bought 5.3 million House of Fraser shares in nearly thirty separate transactions. His investment was particularly interesting because on 20 May 1982 the Fund had sold its complete portfolio of House of Fraser shares. Just four days later, the Fund began buying again.

During that lunch, Musson remarked that he had never met Rowland. Nevertheless, later that afternoon, Musson telephoned and announced that he had spoken to Rowland who agreed to dine with Smith to resolve their problems. The meeting did not materialise, but Smith became suspicious that Musson had been forewarned about Rowland's demerger plans. His suspicions increased when Musson complained about House of Fraser's management. 'That's odd,' retorted Smith. 'Then why have you bought the shares?'

The suspicions prompted Willoughby to hire a private detective whom he codenamed 'James Bond'. The first results established that Musson was both a friend and a neighbour of Terry Robinson, the Lonrho accountant. The second discovery was alarming. An inspection of the share register revealed that a German bank, Richard Daus, had bought 2.1 million House of Fraser shares between 24 September and 17 October. Not only were the purchases completed just after Rowland's demerger announcement but, unusually, payment for the shares was in cash, concealing the identity of the buyer. Despite repeated requests Daus refused to reveal, as required by statute, on whose behalf it was dealing. Willoughby's detective subsequently discovered that Lonrho had previously used the bank and that Rowland was friendly with its chief executive.

As the circular war ended in the days before the extraordinary general meeting, to be held on 4 November, Daus gave conflicting answers about the identity of the owner of the 2.1 million shares. Initially it was a Cayman Islands nominee and then Daiei, a Japanese store group. Daiei, associated with Jack Kato, a friend of Rowland's, however ignored all inquiries and did not register the shares. Afraid that the shares might be used in Rowland's favour, a Scottish court, at House of Fraser's request, granted an Order curtailing the voting rights.

Expecting a close victory, Rowland flew to Glasgow early on 4 November. Lawyers briefed his team in great detail but the meeting was an anti-climax. Warburgs marshalled the City institutions who, on the promise that a demerger would be considered by the board, defeated Lonrho's motion by a massive margin. Spicer, acting in his customary role as Rowland's mouthpiece, denied losing: 'We think this is bullshit. We do not think [Smith] won by a long chalk.'

Back in London, the House of Fraser board investigated the option of the Harrods' demerger and predictably rejected it. In turn, Rowland summoned another extraordinary general meeting for 6 May 1983, renewed the circular war, issued a succession of writs to protect his voting rights and began more effective lobbying of the City institutions.

At the extraordinary general meeting, a resolution opposing the demerger and expressing confidence in the board was passed by 65.6 million votes against 63.8 million. Rowland's defeat by just 1.8 million shares was tantalisingly close, confirming new support from some City fund managers. Rowland scented victory. In seven weeks, on 30 June, at House of Fraser's annual general meeting, there would be another vote on the demerger.

The prospect of Lonrho's victory prompted Smith to invite Rowland for peace talks. At their meeting on 12 May, Rowland demanded two more Lonrho directors on the board, that he should be deputy chairman and that the demerger be approved. 'That would give you virtual control of the company,' summarised Smith. It was so finely balanced, replied Rowland, that everyone taking a 10 per cent stake could take effective control. They parted without agreement, a prospect which did not trouble Rowland. For the first time, his confidence seemed justified.

Two days earlier, on 10 May, Rowland had lunched at the Ritz with Dr Ashraf Marwan, a son-in-law of President Nasser and the former chief of staff of President Sadat's private office. Marwan had met Rowland in 1971 when, among his other duties, Marwan was reputedly supervising Egypt's intelligence service. He was also a principal in Middle East arms deals and was a friend of Ahmed Gaddafadam, Colonel Muammar Gadaffi's security adviser. Marwan, who claims to have introduced Rowland to Adnan 'Mr Fixit' Khashoggi, described Rowland at that time as 'my best friend'. In 1987, Marwan classed Rowland, Asil Nadir and Robert Maxwell as the businessmen whom he most admired. All three have been accused of fraud.

During the 1970s, Marwan travelled with Rowland throughout Africa and the Arab world. At that time, Marwan noticed that while Rowland was 'loved' by Africans, he consistently failed to establish relationships with any Arabs except Libyans, who 'wanted to be loved', explains Marwan of that anomaly.

After leaving office in 1979, Marwan, who estimated his own wealth at £20 million, built a mixed network of companies. Among his purchases in 1980 was 40 per cent of Tradewinds, a cargo airline which Lonrho had bought two years earlier on Edward Du Cann's recommendation. Lonrho owned the remaining 60 per cent in association with a Liechtenstein-registered company whose director was Ahmed Gaddafadam, the Libyan intelligence chief. Over the following two years, Tradewinds declared losses of £6.9 million which were eventually paid off by Lonrho.

The airline's activities seemed unremarkable until in 1986 a cargo of weapons was seized which had been consigned from Miami to Libya and the Lebanon by two former CIA officers. The discovery of that shipment had coincided with the seizure of an illegal weapons consignment at Gatwick destined for South Africa and under the care of Kühne & Nagel, the German freight contractor, 50 per cent owned by Lonrho. Robert Dunlop eventually admitted that Lonrho had been aware of the shipment. The airline would also be used to transport American weapons from Morocco to Angola for Jonas Savimbi's army. Lonrho was exposed as a participant in the arms trade, which seemed further confirmed when in 1982 one of the Tradewinds' Boeing 707s was sold to St Lucia Airways, a CIA proprietary company run by Dietrich Reinhardt.

The losses and the unwelcome publicity disillusioned Rowland. 'Tradewinds', he admitted, 'was a disaster.' He was similarly unhappy about Marwan. 'In terms of business,' he sniped, 'Marwan is totally unreliable.'

That harsh judgment was prompted by Marwan's tactics in March 1983 when the Egyptian wanted to sell his share in Tradewinds and Rowland refused. Marwan leaked his intention to sell his stake to the Libyans. Rowland, hitherto 'unavailable', promptly telephoned. 'We would like to meet to solve the problem.' Their encounter was for lunch at the Ritz on 10 May 1983. By the end of that meal, Rowland had agreed to buy Marwan's stake. But a second subject of greater importance was also discussed. Namely, Rowland's demerger proposals for the House of Fraser.

Rowland was under a deadline. Within the coming seven weeks he needed to find more supporters to tip the balance in his favour at the annual general meeting. Naturally, anyone who bought huge stakes of House of Fraser shares and voted for demerger was a welcome friend. Since Rowland's battle to buy the stores group was a regular news item, it was natural that Rowland and Marwan should discuss the fate of the vote. Rowland explained to Marwan that anyone who bought the shares and voted with Lonrho would earn a good profit. 'Rowland cast that fly,' commented a subsequent investigator, 'and Dr Marwan swallowed it.'

Five days later, Rowland's cause received influential publicity. Jim Slater, whose fortunes had been restored entirely due to Rowland's generosity, contributed a regular column in the *Sunday Telegraph* tipping investors on profitable opportunities. On 15 May, Slater advised his readers that anyone who bought 1 million House of Fraser shares and voted for the demerger would be certain of a profit.

Four days later Dr Joern Kreke, a German who owned a

retail group, began buying 650,000 shares. Kreke employed the services of a Swiss lawyer, also hired by Rowland.

So when on 19 May, Dr Ashraf Marwan began a four-day buying spree of 2 million House of Fraser shares, he was joining a trend shared by others nebulously linked to Rowland. Significantly, Marwan, a novice investor in London, did not have a stockbroker. A request to one London broker to act for Marwan was rejected on the grounds of a conflict of interest since Lonrho was a client. The shares were instead bought by Derek Strauss of Strauss Turnbull, a broker who was known to Paul Spicer. The money was paid from an account of the Credit Suisse in Geneva.

Over those same days, Adriana Funaro, an Italian related by marriage to Mohammed Fayed, also bought 1 million House of Fraser shares. Funaro also channelled her funds through the Compagne de Gestion in Nyon to the stockbrokers Strauss Turnbull, a broker she had not used previously. Both Marwan and Funaro registered their shares abroad although both lived in Britain. Like Marwan, Funaro had not speculated on the London market before.

On 6 June, Jack Hayward, a well-known investor, who had met Rowland in the Bahamas, bought 545,000 House of Fraser shares and would buy another 1.5 million on a rising market over the following two weeks. Hayward paid about 200 pence per share, an investment of £4 million.

The rapid notification of those transactions startled David Milligan, the company secretary of House of Fraser. Ever since Musson's unusual sale and purchase of House of Fraser shares, Milligan had been alerted to follow all significant share transactions. The unforeseen purchase of large blocks of shares, all from abroad, followed by incessant telephone calls to the company's registrar to ensure that the new shareholders could vote on 30 June, was by any measure suspicious. In London, House of Fraser directors were speculating whether Rowland had organised a 'concert party', a group of sympathetic shareholders pledged to support Lonrho's resolutions who would profit from the inevitable rise in share price if the demerger was approved.

In the days before the annual general meeting, Lonrho had

organised that all those submitting proxy cards in support of the demerger should deposit them with their Glasgow bankers to be forwarded together to House of Fraser. On 28 June, Lonrho delivered boxes of proxy cards. Four cards belonging to Kreke, Hayward, Marwan and Furano were stapled together with a note on Lonrho paper: 'Attached to this letter are proxy cards for holdings that are not shown on the register in your possession as they are new holdings. These cards must be lodged with all the other cards.'

On 30 June, following his customary routine of early morning flights from London and final discussions with lawyers, Rowland arrived at Glasgow's City Hall obviously enjoying the problems which he had manufactured: 'I've got the Pacific to play in. The professor has only got the Serpentine.' But the calm image belied the nature of the battle. The predator had long forgotten the purely commercial benefits of the proposition. He had embarked upon a virility exercise where vanity demanded total success. The alternative had apparently become too awful to contemplate.

On the vote, Lonrho, with the support of the new share-holders, won the resolution for the Harrods' demerger by 4.7 million votes, or 53 per cent. But Rowland was deprived of his victory. Acting under Warburgs' advice, Smith had submitted a Special Resolution, opposing the demerger. The resolution required a 75 per cent vote to be defeated. The board, announced Smith, had won since the Special Resolution took precedence.

Rowland was suspicious and demanded to see the proxy cards. His banker's computation revealed that Lonrho enjoyed the support of 70 million votes. He wanted an explanation why so many votes had been disqualified. Mervyn Greenway, his stockbroker, marched into an ante-room adjoining the hall to investigate. 'I saw a teller and asked him why bundles of votes were uncounted. His face went bright red and he ordered us out. We had to leave. There was nothing else we could do.' Formally, Smith refused Rowland access to the counted votes. Rowland departed protesting that he had been cheated. Eventually, Rowland accepted that the vote was honest. For their part, Smith and his fellow directors suspected that Rowland had organised the four huge investments from abroad and was guilty of organising a 'concert party'.

Stories circulating in London tended to support their suspicions. On 11 July 1983 the *Sunday Times* published, under the headline 'Harrods: the sale that never was', Rowland's own account of the discussions one year earlier between himself and Michael Richardson. According to the article, Richardson had proposed that he could arrange with Warburgs Lonrho's purchase of the remaining 75 per cent of House of Fraser and the merchant bankers would remain as advisers. Smith, according to the *Sunday Times*'s version, would be removed and compensated with a knighthood and the chairmanship of a nationalised industry. He would be replaced by Lord Soames. The article ended with a homily about the honesty that Rowland had encountered when he had started work for a City broker called Kittle & Co in 1935. In truth, Rowland had started work with his uncle who owned a trucking business in the East End. The victims of Rowland's mischief-making noticed only the errors relevant to their own experience.

Richardson was deeply embarrassed and Rothschild was livid. 'He's taken the conversation we had and twisted it around,' complained Richardson. Some were unconvinced by Richardson's protests but others, in a saga which was dividing London, stepped forward to question Rowland's behaviour. Among the contributors was Robert Thornton, the chairman of Debenham stores, who recalled that during a lunch at the House of Commons in June 1983, Rowland had put forward a questionable deal to divide the House of Fraser.

A second informant was Rupert Murdoch. Meeting Smith at a reception, Murdoch related that at a lunch in February 1983, ostensibly to discuss the problems of Sunday newspapers, Rowland had unexpectedly suggested that the Australian should buy 5 per cent of House of Fraser with the promise that after the demerger was approved they would split the profits 50–50. Murdoch said that he had refused the proposition.

To Smith and Warburgs, the evidence of a 'concert party' seemed strong. Cecil Parkinson, the fourth DTI minister since Thatcher's election, was asked to order an investigation. He agreed. The second DTI inquiry into Lonrho started on 23 August 1983. Lonrho's bid for House of Fraser was partially 'kicked into touch'.

As an isolated incident, the diversion would have been unimportant, but Rowland's tunnel vision pursuit of his target was diverting his attention from Lonrho's declining fortunes. Pre-tax profits, according to the 1982 accounts, had fallen by 33 per cent in 1982, from £111 million to £73 million. Lonrho's final profits were a mere £19 million against a claimed turnover of £3 billion, a ludicrous imbalance suggesting that Rowland was interested only in the company's size and not its long-term strength, and that the accountants had been too creative in 1982.

The '£3 billion' turnover was artificial, drawing upon Lonrho's minority investments. Lonrho, which usually described 'turnover' as 'income', had exaggerated its activities. The following year the same turnover was 'restated' as £2.3 billion. Similarly, Lonrho's 'net current assets', described in 1982 as £295.5 million were subsequently 'restated' the following year as £88.9 million. The exercise was symbolic of Rowland's attitude. As the country emerged from recession, his unchecked grandiosity was distorting his judgment of true values.

The Conservative government had just been re-elected with a 142 majority. Rowland still hoped for good relations with Margaret Thatcher. They had last met on 16 May at a formal lunch in Downing Street for Samora Machel, in Britain for a two-day state visit. Thatcher's invitation had provoked considerable excitement at Cheapside, suggesting a decisive recognition of Rowland's special status in Africa and a change of attitude towards himself. Although, to avoid embarrassment, Rowland had asked the Mozambique authorities not to include his name on the list of invitees for the state dinner at Buckingham Palace – 'I don't like going there,' he had explained – the invitation to Downing Street, he reasoned, placed him, like Goldsmith and Murdoch, as a possible insider.

The accounts of that lunch are sharply contradictory. On their return to Cheapside, Edward Du Cann marvelled about Thatcher's welcome. But Rowland's subsequent version implied outrage about his treatment. Seated with Geoffrey Howe and

Joachim Chissano, Mozambique's foreign minister, Rowland related that he had been persistently questioned by the British foreign minister about Lonrho's investments in South Africa. It was, Rowland reasoned, a deliberate Foreign Office conspiracy to cause him embarrassment because Lonrho was Mozambique's biggest foreign investor. 'I'm not going back there again,' he told a fellow director. But reasoned analysis would suggest that Chissano would not have been irritated by Lonrho's activities since his country was itself dependent upon trade with South Africa.

Rowland had visited Mozambique for the first time five months earlier, in January 1983. His reception by Machel had been unexpectedly warm. 'So this is the monster,' laughed the president. 'I'm told you take over governments and countries.' Flattered that another African was acknowledging his contribution to the continent's development, Rowland showed his customary obsequiousness.

The arrangements for Rowland's arrival in Mozambique had been negotiated by Alves Gomes, the journalist who had become the president's confidant. Concerned by the country's plunging fortunes, Machel had asked Gomes to recommend investors in the country. Gomes mentioned Lonrho. 'If they're not with us,' reasoned Machel, 'they'll become our enemies. Invite him.' Gomes telephoned Rowland in Bourne End. Rowland flew into Maputo soon afterwards. A government limousine whisked him through the sprawling shanty towns of Africa's poorest nation to the gleaming marble palace which the Marxist president had inherited from the Portuguese. The presidential style appealed to Rowland. 'What can you do for us?' asked Machel. 'You must invest in Mozambique.'

The country's population was on the verge of starvation. Harassed by Renamo and the legacy of the twenty years' war, damage that was compounded by a drought, the country's agriculture had practically collapsed. Traditionally, British companies had invested in Mozambique's sugar and tea plantations and, despite its historic relationship with Portugal, Mozambique was attracted towards Britain not least because it was surrounded by former British colonies. That attraction had manifested itself during the Lancaster House negotiations when Thatcher and the Foreign Office had been particularly grateful to Machel for his decisive insistence that Mugabe remain in London and sign the agreements.

Three years later, Mozambique was a forgotten and abandoned nation. Other than Lonrho, no other European company or personality was interested in it. With his Grumman jet waiting at the airport, Rowland seemed to be a unique saviour.

In the midst of their discussion, Rowland embellished his image: 'Please accept a gift of maize seed from Lonrho.' He would arrange an immediate airlift from Kenya. Dispensing with an export licence, the $4 million consignment was flown from Lonrho's own farm. For the president, it was an overwhelming gesture which lent Rowland the stature of another head of state. His decisions could be implemented without reference to anyone else. Machel's reward was an immediate gift to Lonrho of two 20,000-acre farms, at no cost, producing citrus fruits, tomatoes, cabbages and cotton. Two more farms of 40,000 acres would be added later. In return, the president expected Lonrho's management to reactivate food production, develop Mozambique's gold mines and it would be allowed to operate an air charter company and own motor franchises. By any measure it was an astonishing deal reflecting Machel's desperation. Rowland left Mozambique correctly anticipating that Lonrho would become the country's largest investor.

The hidden agenda was the future of Lonrho's pipeline. Over the previous two years, Rowland had anxiously monitored the refurbishment which had cost $20 million. Mugabe's ideological desire to nationalise Zimbabwe's artery in collaboration with Machel in the interest of socialist brotherhood was thwarted by the continuing threat against Machel posed by the South African-supported Renamo guerrillas.

In October 1982, a Renamo group had blown up a pump station, disrupting the flow of oil. Realising that the Mozambique army was powerless, Rowland suggested, and Mugabe agreed, that Zimbabwean troops be deployed but the president's threat of nationalisation remained. On a return flight to Maputo, soon after his credentials were proven, Rowland suggested to Machel that his bankrupt country could earn hard currency by charging Zimbabwe for the use of the pipeline – albeit a meagre reward for the huge sacrifices during the independence war. 'I want to help Mozambique, Mr President,' said Rowland, accurately portraying himself as the nation's most committed investor. Machel was persuaded. Regardless of Mugabe's socialist brotherhood, the pipeline was to remain under Lonrho's control.

In Harare, the Zimbabwean president, the ruler of a sovereign country, was confronted with a *fait accompli* by the chief executive of a British company with a doubtful record. But Mugabe's initial reluctance to negotiate with Rowland was exacerbated by his anger that the proposed tariff for use of the pipeline was to be paid in hard currency. At 10 a.m. in Harare, Mugabe refused Rowland's terms. By 4 p.m., Rowland had flown to Maputo and returned to Harare to confront Mugabe with a signed agreement from Machel. The crisis had been solved on Rowland's terms.

On occasions, Rowland's power in Africa seemed genuinely awesome. Even Julius Nyerere, suffering a ban on international aid organised by Rowland, was compelled to negotiate compensation with Lonrho for the nationalisation of its assets. Across the continent, Lonrho was employing nearly 100,000 people. One man could claim to be the arbiter of their fate, but in reality Lonrho, compared to its rivals Inchcape and Anglo American, was becoming enfeebled both by its precarious finances and by the whims of its chief executive who, while feigning shyness, desired the acknowledgement and respect owed to the head of a £3 billion company. Circumstances that would have been avoidable had Rowland formulated a strategy, or understood the consequences of his own actions, were encroaching upon his ambitions.

The first omens did not obviously herald a cataclysm. In Angola, despite Rowland's apparent *rapprochement* with Margaret Thatcher, the Foreign Office ignored Savimbi's UNITA movement and encouraged British nationals to sell their expertise in mining and petroleum extraction to the Soviet-supported MPLA government. 'Africa would have to sort itself out,' recalled one Foreign Office expert. 'We weren't getting into another Biafra-type mess.'

In February 1984, a British trade mission to Luanda led by Malcolm Rifkind, then a junior Foreign Office minister, spoke of the good prospects for bilateral trade and promised that a British trade delegation would visit the country shortly.

The only British official to visit Savimbi was Sir John Leahy, head of the Foreign Office's Africa Department. In May 1984, Leahy flew to UNITA's headquarters to oversee the repatriation of British mercenaries captured fighting for the Marxist government. Leahy's trip, an embarrassment to the British government, had been preceded by a series of meetings with Rowland in London.

Once again, a Foreign Office official was exploring the possibility of co-operation rather than confrontation. For his part, Rowland was aware of Whitehall's culture of the smear and therefore cautious about – but none the less encouraged by – Leahy's approach to understand his policies.

Yet to the diplomat, Rowland's policies in Africa seemed unclear. Other than seeking to remove differences between warring African factions, Rowland wanted to influence British policies in Africa by winning access to ministers – 'the same that I enjoy with the State Department' – but his long-term object was undefined. Rowland seemed to be more interested in one-upmanship than the slow process of diplomacy. Conversations with Rowland resembled a boastful tally: 'I've just been to Africa for five days and seen six presidents. The State Department were very interested in what I discovered. So were the Germans.' To an extent, the Foreign Office, the butt of Rowland's derision, was also interested but before this latest tentacle of peace could begin to flourish, Rowland's relationship with Thatcher was abruptly pruned.

The blight was conceived at the *Observer*. Supervision of the newspaper had been delegated to Terry Robinson who, to some journalists, epitomised an accountant lacking the finesse and understanding of newspaper management. The *Observer*'s finances remained unreformed and negotiations with the print unions were moribund. Instead of reducing the unions' wages and restrictive practices, Robinson found he either had to succumb to their demands or that his trenchant opposition was undermined by Rowland's intervention and compromises. Robinson, according to Anthony Howard, the deputy editor, did not understand journalism. When told that the newspaper would contain a profile of Edward Heath, Robinson had inquired, 'What do you mean?'

Trelford's relationship with Rowland had been conditioned from the outset by his newspaper's inability to earn profits. Tainted by its Astor legacy, the newspaper had failed to attract the profile of readers which would generate more advertising and, although it was perceived by some as more respectable than the *Sunday Times*, the *Observer* remained an unadventurous and uncompelling purchase on Sundays. Symptomatic of Rowland's detachment, he rarely visited the newspaper's premises and, unskilled in newspaper presentation, he had taken little interest in his newspaper's development other than to discuss its contents with Trelford in general terms.

After the tumultuous introduction in 1981, Trelford appreciated that his personal future depended upon constructing a harmonious relationship with Rowland, not a difficult task for an ambitious journalist. Among his concessions after the takeover, Trelford 'gave' the expanded business section to the proprietor in exchange for keeping control over the main section which he deemed more important.

For his part, Rowland soon saw the back of his enemies. Conor Cruise O'Brien was marginalised and then resigned. John Davis, the City editor who had opposed Lonrho's acquisition of SUITS, was demoted. Similarly, William Keegan, the business editor who had given evidence against Rowland to the Monopolies Commission, was also demoted. The replacement was Melvyn Marckus, a reputable financial journalist with experience on many national newspapers. Marckus soon acquired the reputation, most unfairly in his opinion, of serving as Rowland's Trojan horse. Gossip claiming that Marckus routinely dined with Rowland on Wednesdays to discuss the section's editorial policy was untrue but, consistent with Trelford's concession, a substantial divide between the two parts of the newspaper had been formalised and Marckus did talk directly with Rowland on the telephone.

Some staff clutched at the straw that, since those changes, Rowland's interference had ceased. Perhaps, some pondered, their earlier judgment had been malign. Trelford knew better. He had seen the events in Kenya where, in the wake of an unsuccessful coup against arap Moi, the president had been criticised in the *Standard*, Lonrho's newspaper. On Rowland's instructions, following criticism of Lonrho in Kenya's parliament, the *Standard* published a fulsome apology, expressed support for the Moi government and announced the dismissal of the editor. The obsequiousness confirmed Trelford's own warning in 1981 that Rowland would not allow his newspapers to embarrass his financial interests in Africa. Indeed, Trelford had already given concessions to Rowland about the *Observer*'s coverage of Africa.

Since Colin Legum's retirement, Richard Hall had become the specialist covering the continent. Hall had supported Rowland's purchase and testified that Rowland would not interfere in the editorial content. His opinion changed on 8 August 1982 when Rowland telephoned Hall at home. The subject was an article published that weekend reporting that Moi's reign of terror was supported by the Reagan administration. Hall had already complained that his original report was 'edited almost to the point of blandness by Trelford'. He had not understood the reasons until Rowland's thirty-minute haranguing monologue, which included criticism of the *Observer*'s failure to support Reagan's anti-communism. 'Buying the *Observer*', concluded Rowland, 'was an error of judgment.' In Hall's opinion, Trelford was unperturbed by Rowland's complaints. Through *naïveté* or self-delusion, Trelford appeared to accept Rowland's increasing encroachment as the normal manifestation of a proprietor's anxieties. In the coverage of Zimbabwe, a country which was economically and emotionally more important to Rowland than Kenya, his interference had become particularly pertinent.

Ever since independence, Herbert Munangatire had wooed allies for Lonrho among government ministers. One of the few who were amenable was Edison Zvogbo, the minister of legal affairs. In January 1983, Zvogbo was invited at Lonrho's expense to visit London. Among Mugabe's ministers, Zvogbo had been vociferously anti-Rowland, but his attitude transformed after his wife Julie, a nurse, had been appointed a Lonrho consultant. Rowland would also lend money for the minister to buy a farm and negotiate an agreement to support the minister's new hotel chain.

Zvogbo arrived in Britain with his nephew, Godwin Matatu, an aggressive journalist whose critical articles for *Africa* magazine had irritated both Mugabe and Nkomo. To African politicians, Matatu was renowned as an alcoholic trouble-maker whose saving grace was his charm and intelligence.

One evening, soon after their arrival, the two Zimbabweans were invited to dinner at Hedsor Wharf. Matatu arrived drunk. As the Chinese waiter served soup, the journalist pushed his plate aside, plucked an apple and munched while gulping more wine. Rowland feigned amusement and continued talking to Zvogbo about the Beira pipeline. During the second course, Josie asked Godwin if he would like some meat. 'No thanks,' he replied with charm, 'I'm happy with wine.' Rowland continued speaking until interrupted by Matatu: 'I think the ladies should leave.' Josie obeyed.

In her absence, Zvogbo voiced his irritation of the West's critical coverage of Zimbabwe, a common complaint among Africa's politicians. On this occasion, Zvogbo made two proposals. He wanted to write an article for the *Observer* criticising his country's treatment by British journalists. Secondly, he proposed that the *Observer* should cease using the old-style, middle-aged, white journalists indelibly imbued with neo-colonialist attitudes to report about Africa and hire Matatu instead. His nephew, by then completely drunk but able to maintain a dignified pose, supposedly knew southern Africa and its new political leaders well.

The following day, Trelford agreed to publish a personal article by Zvogbo and was told that Godwin Matatu should be appointed the *Observer*'s Africa correspondent. The editor did not overtly resist Rowland's proposal, while Hall discovered the appointment only when he was travelling in Zimbabwe and was told by Zvogbo himself. Back in London, the journalist was reassured by Trelford. 'He'll soon blow up. This is not something for which I need to go to the limit, like Conor Cruise O'Brien's column.'

Matatu did not blow up. From Harare, he submitted through-out that year unsolicited articles about a wide range of African stories, undermining Hall and prompting the foreign editor to resign. For the first time, the threat to the *Observer*'s independ-ence surfaced in public. Accused of accepting Rowland's *diktat*, Trelford replied that Matatu was being used 'on his merits' but the revelation that Matatu's salary was paid by Lonrho, not the *Observer*, confirmed for many journalists the editor's impotence.

To smooth the waters and 'make people like Tiny', Trelford organised a conciliatory lunch, a rare occasion for Rowland to visit the newspaper. Accompanied by Du Cann, Rowland initially listened to Spicer's splenetic outburst against journalists and then to a manager's account of how Lonrho's appeasing intervention in a confrontation with the unions on a Saturday night had incurred permanent, costly knock-on expenditure. Lonrho's losses were accordingly escalating. By all accounts the atmosphere was tense but restrained. Towards the end of their meal, Rowland addressed his employees: 'We in Lonrho are one large family. We can't understand why you don't take a more robust attitude against the House of Fraser.'

The reply came from Adam Raphael, the political editor. 'With respect, that wouldn't work. People would see through it. As you know I gave evidence against you at the Monopolies Commission and to my surprise you haven't interfered. It wouldn't do any good to start now.'

Rowland's surprise transformed his sunburnt face into puce red. Du Cann and Spicer, accustomed to Rowland's uncon-trolled Prussian tirades, adjusted their countenances to images of terror. For the unsuspecting journalists, the explosion was 'gut-wrenching'.

'You've said too much, Mr Ruffles,' began the growl turning into a screaming onslaught. 'In that case I don't know why we bother to own the paper.' The tirade lasted ten minutes. Trelford, the newspaper's heroic defender, was silently embarrassed. Turn-ing to Anthony Howard, Rowland fumed, 'Tell me, can you give me one good reason why I should go on owning the *Observer*?'

'That's your problem, Mr Rowland,' replied the inscrutable deputy editor. For the Lonrho delegation, the outburst was no different from dozens of others, but the hosts anticipated immediate reprisals and dismissals arising from it. 'The rest of the world sees Tiny differently to us,' Du Cann would subsequently explain. At the newspaper, the Lonrho directors were thereafter called 'The Crazy Gang'. Their interference resurfaced on the eve of the 1983 election.

The Labour Party under Michael Foot was fighting a lamentable campaign against a united Tory government. Few businessmen in London supported a return to Labour's prescription of nationalisation and state control. Terry Robinson intimated his master's hope, consistent with his interference in Africa, that the newspaper would endorse the incumbents. Subsequent folklore suggested that the pressure for endorsement of Thatcher emanated from Edward Du Cann, hoping to be rewarded by an eventual honour and from Rowland, for his political and personal advantage. Du Cann would deny any involvement with the newspaper.

Robinson's motives were simply to transform the newspaper's fortunes. The new, separate Business Section had attracted an impressive volume of advertising and Robinson feared that if the *Observer* followed the *Guardian* as an outright Labour supporter, the potential profits from business readers would be lost. To Robinson's delight, there seemed little reason for the newspaper not to remain neutrally supportive of the government. The leading journalists were divided, Trelford was decidedly ambiguous and the Astor tradition, he believed, was to remain 'independent'.

Rowland, however, was becoming ambivalent about Thatcher. Despite his attempt to woo the prime minister, a few weeks earlier, in March, both Downing Street and Buckingham Palace had refused Kenneth Kaunda's request that Rowland be invited to the state dinners and lunches during his state visit. Rowland's presence would have been an acknowledged courtesy for a Briton enjoying such close relations with the Zambian president.

Strangely, even when Kaunda hosted a reciprocatory dinner for the Queen at Claridges, Rowland and Josie were relegated to a side table by the kitchen entrance with a group of comparative nonentities. One interpretation was that the Zambian did not want attention drawn to the principal benefactor of the president's favourite charities. Rowland blamed his discomfiture upon British officialdom and believed that the cause was still worth fighting. Hence his suggestion that the *Observer* should reconsider its traditional pro-Labour allegiance.

In a retrospectively irreconcilable conflict of accounts, the only certainty is that a debate occurred between Trelford and Cheapside on the eve of the election regarding the *Observer*'s endorsement and that the final decision was the editor's.

Towards the end of the last week before the election, an editorial conference, filmed by a BBC Television film crew, witnessed Trelford and Anthony Howard discussing and deciding that the *Observer* would oppose Thatcher. On the Saturday morning, Howard, a committed Labour voter, read the editorial leader opposing Thatcher. That evening, returning from a drink, Howard read the proofs and noticed that the leader had been replaced by an editorial supporting a Mark Two Conservative government. Incensed, he sprinted to Trelford: 'You can't do this. We went through agony for this.' Trelford was honest: 'Tiny insisted.'

In a moment of what Howard calls 'inspiration' he exclaimed, 'But the BBC filmed our editorial conference. If we change, we'll be exposed.'

'Are you sure?' asked Trelford.

'I saw them do it.'

'OK. Change it back.'

Rowland's hopes of further reconciliation with Thatcher were barely dampened by the *Observer*'s reiteration of its traditional stance although, during the remainder of the year, he was unable to forge closer relations with the new government. However his attempts were abruptly derailed in January 1984.

Under a prominent banner headline, 'The Son also rises', the *Observer* published a grave allegation. David Leigh and Paul Lashmar, both investigative journalists, alleged that Mark Thatcher had exploited his position since the 1979 election to earn huge fees as a consultant by manipulating his mother's influence to secure a £300 million contract in Oman for his client, Cementation International, a subsidiary of Trafalgar House.

The original impetus behind the story was Magnus Linklater, a senior executive at the *Observer*, who had been told that Britain's ambassador in the Oman was 'embarrassed' when Mark Thatcher had flown to Oman simultaneously with his mother in April 1981 and that the contract had been concluded soon afterwards. Linklater supervised the journalists' investigation.

In subsequent weeks, eleven more articles pursued the quarry. The prime minister eventually admitted that while in Oman she had been 'batting for Britain'. But otherwise, only her silence on whether she knew that her son was in Oman or that he was retained by Cementation provided the circumstances to arouse suspicion.

The public reaction to the allegations was venomous. The newspaper was accused of stooping into the gutter to attack the prime minister through her son. Other newspapers joined the fray. The lead was provided by Bernard Ingham, the prime minister's spokesman, epitomising Downing Street at its most rampant. Ingham's language on the telephone to Trelford was blue and sparking but, according to Linklater, 'Trelford was very supportive on a very unpopular story. He handled it courageously.'

Initially, Rowland was uninvolved but soon offered the journalists the services of Kenneth Etheridge. The former Fraud Squad officer provided a contact with information about Mark in Abu Dhabi but, according to Leigh, 'He was no use.' Rowland's attitude however was critical. 'At first he was benign,' recalls Leigh, 'but then he fanned the story.' In public, however, Rowland professed that although 'upset, I could not stop it.' While Lord Shawcross, an adviser to Rowland and an admirer of the prime minister, began a campaign to remove Trelford, Du Cann warned Rowland, 'She's very sensitive about the boy.' Equally sensitive about his own children, Rowland ignored the advice. 'He doesn't care about the consequences,' lamented Du Cann who failed to persuade Thatcher that Rowland had no part in the campaign. 'Du Cann couldn't smooth the ripples,' recalled Terry Robinson who watched Rowland's irrational delight about Thatcher's embarrassment obscure his long-term interests. Inevitably, the repercussions were considerable. For the Thatchers, the *Observer* was an 'enemy' and its proprietor was not 'one of us'. Not only was Rowland striking at the prime minister's most vulnerable spot, but Lonrho had conspicuously refused to contribute to Conservative Party funds in two successive election campaigns.

As the Mark Thatcher articles were concluded, on 9 April 1984, Trelford flew to Harare to meet and interview President Mugabe, an arrangement organised by Rowland. Trelford arrived in the wake of Mugabe's successful assertion of total control over the country. One year earlier, Zimbabwe's Fifth Brigade, an army group trained by the North Koreans, had been dispatched by the president to Matabeleland, Joshua Nkomo's tribal lands in the west of the country, to 'discover' evidence that his rival was planning a coup. When weapons were unearthed by the Brigade on Nkomo's farm, he was dismissed from the government.

Amid persistent harassment by the Fifth Brigade and fearing a murder plot, Nkomo fled Zimbabwe in March 1983 and eventually arrived in Britain. Rowland, anxious to avoid irritating Mugabe, suffered acute embarrassment. Despite his much vaunted pledges of loyalty, Nkomo's request for sanctuary was a liability, jeopardising Rowland's delicate mollification of Mugabe. Initially, the African accepted Rowland's condition of assistance: to remain closeted and silent at the Penta hotel.

Coinciding with Kaunda's visit to London, Nkomo broke his silence, claiming that the Fifth Brigade had perpetrated horrendous massacres in his homeland. His reward was to be ordered by Rowland to leave the luxury hotel and fend for himself in a dingy bedsit. 'I was very, very angry,' Nkomo would write in his memoirs. 'At the darkest moment of my life, the man I regarded as my friend withdrew his help and left me without either money or a place to live, at twelve hours' notice.' The blaring London newspaper reports, accompanied by photographs of Nkomo's squalor, threatened Rowland's olive branch in Harare. In a clear attempt to improve relations, Trelford arrived one year later to interview Mugabe.

The day before that interview, on 11 April 1984, Rowland had hosted a lunch for his editor at Lonrho House. Also present were

Neal Ascherson, the newspaper's feature writer, and the hastily summoned managers of Lonrho's operations around the country. It transpired that the latter had been invited to be an audience rather than guests, for they sat in total silence. Rowland's relationship with his employees implied torment. Even Trelford and Ascherson were silent victims of his intellectual invective as he expostulated opinions, insights and grudges which in normal circumstances would defy acquiescence but on that occasion required audible assent. His self-confidence in Zimbabwe was total. This was his country and he was the largest employer, empowered to pass judgment upon the world. Gadaffi, he announced 'is a mere retailer in death. The Americans are wholesalers.' Mentioning Angola, his face took on a glow as he outlined his dream of winning the oil concessions. At the end of the meal, the Lonrho managers were curtly dismissed. The two journalists also took their leave.

Outside Lonrho House in Harare, Trelford asked Ascherson, 'Is there any other story I could do while I'm here?'

'Well,' replied Ascherson, 'there's the war in Matabeleland.'

The massacres in the heartland of Joshua Nkomo's tribal lands had already been reported in the *Sunday Times* but the suffering caused by Mugabe's Fifth Brigade continued.

On Thursday morning, Trelford flew to Bulawayo with Godwin Matatu. The latter was not completely informed of the purpose of Trelford's journey. That night, while Matatu slept, Trelford was taken by Ascherson's contact to see eyewitnesses of the murders committed by Mugabe's army. Before Matatu awoke, the editor had returned to the hotel. Back in Harare, Trelford wrote a long account of the tragedy based upon his interviews with eyewitnesses which was telexed to London on Friday night.

Early on Saturday morning, Anthony Howard read the article. In graphic detail, Trelford had described the deliberate and brutal murder of hundreds of innocents by an army ordered by the government to undertake ethnic cleansing. One villager, quoted by Trelford, had watched his neighbours murdered by machine guns while their commanding officer, listening to a radio, leant against a tree. Trelford also described how two government soldiers forced a man to watch the beating of his wife and grandmother. One paragraph read, 'A dead baby was held up by a brigade major of the Fifth who told a village rally: "This is a dissident baby. This is what will happen to your babies if you help dissidents." He then dropped the tiny corpse into the dust.'

'The shit will hit the fan,' Howard told Trelford who had just arrived home from Harare. 'This is Lonrho country.'

Trelford seemed surprised. 'Why? Lonrho is quite broad-minded.'

Howard was puzzled but pleased. Trelford seemed intent on publishing the truth and would brave the consequences. The headline was 'Agony of a Lost People'.

After arriving in the office and supervising the article's lay-out, Trelford received a telephone call from Rowland who had already heard about the article from Robinson. 'You're trying to destroy my business in Zimbabwe,' commented Rowland.

'I have my job to do: to tell the truth as I see it.'

'You have your job and I have mine. You must expect me to protect myself,' said Rowland who urged Trelford to offset Mugabe's actions against the horrors perpetrated by Ian Smith's army. Trelford later reported that Rowland had threatened to close the newspaper 'because I won't be able to afford to keep them. You should think about the consequences.'

'I told him,' explained Trelford, 'that I was simply not prepared to talk on those terms.'

The eye of the storm which erupted in London on Sunday 15 April did not concern the grisly fate of the Matabeles but rather the fate of the newspaper's editor. Trelford had flown that morning to the Channel Islands for a holiday. According to Howard, 'Donald seemed taken aback when the row started.'

Before midday, Rowland received a telephone call from Harare. The nature of the government's complaint was predict-able as was Rowland's response. His unconditional apology to Mugabe was telexed while the president was publicly attacking the western media at a rally. Rowland's explanation accused Trelford of being, 'discourteous, disingenuous and wrong' for publishing a 'sensational' article using 'unsubstantiated material' and by taking 'advantage of his position as an editor' since the visit was arranged by Rowland. The telex was published, at Rowland's instigation, in the next day's newspaper in Harare. No one in Zimbabwe mentioned that corpses of victims had been found at the base of a gold mine owned by Lonrho.

Exactly three years after Trelford and other senior journalists had forewarned the Monopolies Commission about Rowland's irreconcilable conflict of interest in owning the *Observer*, the anticipated crisis had materialised.

Rowland's fury was compounded by the newspaper's falling circulation. In 1981, it had sold 886,000 copies but by 1984 circulation had fallen to 753,000, lower than when Trelford became editor. Lonrho's annual subsidy was estimated at £1.5 million. There was no sympathy for the newspaper among Lonrho's directors. Spicer, voicing the uncultured opinion, described the paper as 'a monster out of control, being paid for by us and our shareholders. It costs money to keep the *Observer* going and the people down there think they can do whatever they like.' Now the editor had placed the empire at risk. At Sunday lunchtime, editor and proprietor exchanged insults on BBC Radio.

Trelford was denounced by Rowland for spending a short time in Matabeleland to gather worthless evidence. Aroused from Guernsey, Trelford rebutted his employer's accusations as 'ludicrous', 'defamatory' and 'inaccurate'. Rowland's motives in denying the brutalities in Africa were blatant: 'Mr Rowland is simply acting to protect his business interests.'

Impulsive and, as so often, insensitive to the mood in Britain, Rowland dispatched a stinging rebuke to Trelford which was circulated to other newspapers before being delivered to Trelford. Rowland's menace, as usual, was cocooned in syrup: 'My dear Donald, I want to make it clear that there is nothing personal in this. I have enjoyed your company and looked upon you as a friend.' Having explained how Lonrho had always obeyed its undertakings to the Monopolies Commission and had subsidised the paper despite falling circulation under his editorship, he accused Trelford of behaving as if he were an owner-editor with a 'licence to lead the paper wherever you like'. That has 'considerably upset me'. Trelford was accused of distortions and failing to maintain expected standards by deceiving the Zimbabwe government and colluding with 'a very junior reporter from the *Sunday Times*' who produced the same story that day. Rowland suggested that Trelford return to Zimbabwe and, although 'the truth of these very sad stories is not an issue', he should revisit the area with a government guide.

In his published reply, Trelford aggressively rejected Rowland's offer and accusations and, referring to Rowland's acknowledgement that the massacres had occurred, challenged Rowland: 'Are you saying that I should have forborne to publish them because of the embarrassment it would cause to you and your company or to the Zimbabwe government?'

In cold print, the exchange appeared as a seminal confrontation between the objective value of truth and the pecuniary advantage of a company prepared to trade and profit with murderers. Yet even at the outset of this defence of editorial independence, a shadow was cast across Trelford's self-proclaimed purity. He had after all compromised about Hall and Matatu; he had allowed the Business Section to fall beyond his direct control; and, despite his original objections, he had willingly served a man and a company who were associated in Africa with fraudsters, arms dealers, bribers and murderers.

Rowland was naturally disinclined to dwell on Trelford's esoteric compromises. As soon as he encountered disobedience, he was roused into asserting his total control, allowing no hiatus for reflecting whether it was safe in the more sophisticated public arena to replicate the methods he favoured in Africa or within Cheapside. None of the sycophantic directors around Rowland dared caution that his treatment of Trelford would be watched by the inspector conducting the DTI inquiry into the 'concert party', and by Gordon Borrie at the Office of Fair Trading, and by officials at the DTI, the Foreign Office and in Downing Street. Not one of his highly paid directors pulled their employer aside to propose that if he wanted to succeed in Britain, he might be advised to keep a check on his impulsive behaviour. Everyone in Cheapside just sang in the chorus vilifying the *Observer* for wasting its subsidy. Such was the extent of the loyalty which Rowland commanded.

The dispute was referred to the independent directors for consideration on Tuesday, 24 April. Throughout that week, the row festered in public. The reputation of the 'unacceptable' Rowland, enhanced by his threat to reduce Lonrho's subsidy and refusal to pay the journalists, fuelled the criticism that he preferred suppressing editorial freedom to protect his commercial interests. Supported by all his journalists, Trelford gained stature as the crusader for press freedom. Rumours circulated, which Trelford did not discourage, that he was pondering whether to use the sensitive information about Rowland which had been gathered three years earlier. Suspicions of the file's existence reinforced his apparent defiance towards his employer. In an editorial on 22 April, Trelford urged the independent directors to protect the newspaper from a proprietor who accused his own newspaper of having 'knowingly written and published a "wrong" and "sensational" report'.

The challenge was well targeted. The independent directors could veto an editor's appointment and dismissal and protect his right to express an opinion, with one proviso: that the newspaper's budget should not be endangered.

To emphasise that ultimate power, Rowland invited Robert Maxwell to breakfast at Claridges. Rowland's unease before the Czech's brash, unsophisticated lust for fame and fortune was aggravated by the public's perception of their similarities. Two rootless, ambitious foreigners, unsuccessfully seeking social acceptance, were commonly associated in one breath as the 'unacceptable face' and the man unfit 'to exercise the proper stewardship of a public company'. Rowland for once ignored that disadvantageous image because he believed Maxwell could serve a purpose.

Deliberately, their meeting was well publicised and Maxwell rose to Rowland's bait. 'Tiny Rowland has told me,' Maxwell intoned, 'that we can do a deal if I am prepared to pay the right price. I am prepared to pay the right price.' In turn, Rowland extolled Maxwell as a 'super leader' which was precisely what no one wanted to hear. Unions, journalists and readers were all terrified of Maxwell buying the *Observer*.

'We had a good long chat,' Rowland smiled as he later stood on the pavement outside the hotel beside the grinning Maxwell, 'and Bob tells me that he is very keen to buy.' It seemed to confirm that morning's *Daily Mirror* headline, 'Maxwell set to buy *Observer*'. The photocall was Rowland's method of airing his threat. The independent directors, chosen according to Rowland 'at two in the morning by the Trade Department relying on a *Who's Who*', and whose annual salary he had threatened to reduce from £4000 to £1000, should not try his patience.

Rowland stepped into his Rolls Royce and sped off to Cheapside to meet the 'plastic gnomes' as he dubbed the directors. 'The one thing I haven't undertaken with the Department of Trade,' he would say, 'is to hang on to [the *Observer*]. I'm free to sell it. I have complete independence socially and financially. Nobody tells me what to do. That is my weakness and my strength.' From ten o'clock until three o'clock, the five directors listened to Rowland's monologue about the needs of Africa, their demeanour unimproved by Rowland's refusal even to offer a cup of coffee. But neither his threats nor his ruses worked. The directors judged against Rowland, criticising him for 'interfering' and for his 'inhibition' of Trelford. The protection provided by the Monopolies Commission had been effective.

This was an uncomfortable moment for Rowland. Challenged by his editor and condemned by the independent directors, he had manoeuvred himself into an exposed corner to be humiliated. Powerless to dismiss Trelford, he seemed equally incapable of imposing his view of how Africa was to be reported. His only sanction was finance and he announced that Lonrho would cease subsidising the newspaper: 'Trelford and the men of the *Observer* are on their own now.' Aware that the newspaper would be fatally incapacitated without Lonrho's money, Trelford moved swiftly to provide an alternative route for his employer.

Trelford's thoughts turned to his own position. The editor knew that Terry Robinson had urged his dismissal and had even presented Rowland with a replacement, Charlie Wilson. The determined Scottish journalist had been invited to lunch at Cheapside, but Rowland 'didn't feel comfortable' with an apparently independent spirit. By default Trelford had remained but, to his embarrassment, he could only sue for peace through Robinson.

The two met in a 'dingy workman's café' behind Cheapside. Over a tepid cup of coffee, the *Observer*'s editor sadly pleaded, 'I'm sorry. It was a mistake. I'll resign if you want.'

Robinson was delighted. Trelford's departure matched his precise desire. But the intermediary was bitterly disappointed. On hearing the news, Rowland's eye twinkled. With Trelford relenting, he had finally succeeded in 'breaking the man in'. The newspaper would now be edited by a man who had forsaken the fight and was prepared to obey his instructions.

A formula was agreed for the public row to be settled in public. By any measure it was a bizarre climax, revealing that the two men had more in common than was hitherto understood.

Trelford's published letter to Rowland paid tribute to the 'generous help' which Lonrho had provided and lamented the breach of the 'otherwise harmonious relationship'. Trelford continued, 'Should we not agree to differ on this matter, and respect our right to disagree? For my part I accept that you acted as you did, not out of a crude concern for your commercial interests as I originally suggested, but out of genuine personal conviction that the truth about Zimbabwe is more complex than I presented it. For your part, I hope that you will accept that I was honestly reporting the truth as I saw it.' Trelford concluded that the alternatives were stark: either resume the previous harmony or, if the 'mutual hostility' continued, he would resign.

Rowland replied, 'I support your editorship and I refuse to accept your resignation.' To the public, Rowland explained the row as a 'lovers' tiff'. Trelford explained the solders of their peace making: 'because we share three basic affections: for the *Observer*; for Africa; and for each other.' Trelford would soon afterwards be photographed with his family enjoying Rowland's hospitality in Acapulco.

Among the casualties of Trelford's campaign was Roy Hattersley, the Labour politician. During the row, Hattersley had, at

Trelford's request, outrightly condemned Rowland as a news-paper owner. His reward was a writ for defamation. 'He's on his own,' snapped Trelford after his peace treaty with Rowland. Hattersley had spent £4000 on legal costs with little prospect of victory when Anthony Howard telephoned on a Sunday morn-ing. 'Would you be prepared to take a call from Tiny?' asked the deputy editor.

'Sure,' replied Hattersley somewhat intrigued.

The telephone rang shortly after. 'Do you want to make up?'

'On what terms?' replied Hattersley cautiously.

'Come for lunch with my family so they can see you don't mean what you said.'

'How does that help?'

'Well if you break bread with me, my wife and children will know that you don't think I'm a rogue.'

Hattersley was anxious to retain some dignity. 'Well, when do you suggest?'

'Now.'

'I'm going to have Sunday lunch with my family and, in any case, I haven't got the means to get to Bourne End.'

'Well. You must come now because my son goes back to school tomorrow. I have had a car outside your house for three hours waiting to bring you.' Hattersley peered into the street and saw a Mercedes limousine parked outside.

'Why didn't you ring earlier?' asked the bemused politician.

'Because I couldn't find Tony Howard to telephone you,' explained the tycoon. 'But you must come today.'

'Well, I'll come for tea,' agreed the politician who replaced the receiver and watched the chauffeur in the limousine pick up the car telephone to receive his instructions.

At 4 p.m. the deputy leader of the Labour Party arrived at Bourne End. Tea and cakes were ready. Rowland and Josie were charming and three children were introduced, solemnly shaking hands. The conversation was suitable for a typical Sunday after-noon in England: politely inconsequential. For Rowland it was a pleasure to have a British politician in his own home, a fate which most others in his position might seek to avoid. Honour having been restored, Hattersley was allowed to depart in the chauffeur-driven car. As the limousine began to glide along the gravel, Rowland knocked furiously on the window and shouted, 'Don't let Maxwell take any credit for bringing us together.' An eccentric end to a Sunday afternoon at Hedsor Wharf.

Rowland's relationship towards the newspaper and its editor had substantially changed. Unperceived by his colleagues, Trelford had agreed to become more accommodating to his paymaster, not least because Lonrho's admitted debt had increased to £567 million and the 'Crazy Gang' in Cheapside had little affection for a trouble-making loss-maker which showed no loyalty in their battle for House of Fraser.

Ever since Rowland's victory at the extraordinary general meeting in June 1983, Rowland and Robinson had continued their harassment of Smith and the board. Every decision was questioned, accounts were investigated and Sandys even applied for a Court Order to prevent expenditure on the refurbishment of stores. 'Get your tanks off my lawn,' Smith told Rowland, reflecting the strain of continued resistance. Simultaneously, Rowland continued to batter officials at the Office of Fair Trading to release Lonrho from its undertakings. 'We thought they were a soft target,' explained Robinson. 'We thought we'd soon see a chink. But Warburgs kept them going.'

On 16 May 1984, Rowland launched his next salvo. He demanded that a resolution at the annual general meeting on 28 June should increase the number of directors to twenty-five, the majority to be approved by Lonrho. Considering that, in 1973, he protested that fifteen directors had been too many and had ever since refused to allow non-executive directors on Lonrho's board, his demand was pure expediency but, as a tactic, even Warburgs conceded, it was superb. For the first time, the banker's fortress was vulnerable because, with the support of Ashraf Marwan and Jack Hayward, Lonrho commanded a majority of shares. 'It's a cashless bid,' Smith protested and asked the OFT for a new inquiry to prevent 'creeping control'. Borrie agreed. Lonrho's manoeuvre was referred to the Monopolies Commission, to report by November. From Rowland came the demand that since there had been a 'change of circumstances', Le Quesne's inquiry should be expanded to re-examine the whole bid. Borrie refused.

Pending Le Quesne's report, Rowland bowed to the DTI's instructions to withdraw the resolutions to appoint twenty-five directors. Instead, he submitted one resolution calling for Smith's dismissal and the demerger of Harrods. With Lonrho's share of over 50 per cent of the votes, Smith's future was uncertain.

Smith's first defence was to postpone the annual general meeting until September and then visit Norman Tebbit, the fifth secretary of state at the DTI since 1979, and plead with the minister to issue an Order banning Lonrho's resolution. Tebbit was ideologically minded to refuse Smith's request. The second Thatcher administration was committed to destroying state controls over industry and to stimulating market control of the economy. Thrown on to the bonfire of controls were also the 'public interest' criteria in the terms of reference of the Monopolies Commission. That veto had become redundant.

Morally, both Smith and Warburgs were also weaker. One year earlier, a majority of shareholders had voted for a demerger. Using a technical ruse, Smith had ignored that vote, giving credibility to Rowland's argument that the chairman was simply sustained by an unholy alliance between City and the DTI. Steadfastly, Rowland refused to withdraw the resolutions which were certain to oust Smith.

In the House of Commons, Conservative MPs recruited by Du Cann joined in arguing Lonrho's case. For the first time, the DTI was compelled to compromise. In a deal negotiated on 4 July with Alex Fletcher, the minister for corporate affairs, Lonrho withdrew its resolutions in return for the expansion of Le Quesne's inquiry to reconsider the whole House of Fraser bid. For Rowland, it was a great success. 'Smith has been saved by the bell,' said Spicer. 'This should stop the Fraser board charging around like lunatics and messing with the assets.'

As Le Quesne began his fifth inquiry into a Lonrho bid, justifying Josie Rowland's quip that Lonrho was invented to be investigated, John Griffiths QC, appointed by the DTI to investigate the alleged 'concert party', was making little progress. The blame was attributed to the investigator and the nature of the alleged crime.

Born in Yorkshire, Griffiths had recently returned to Britain from Hong Kong, having served as Attorney General from 1979 to 1983. He had been fishing in Somerset when the summons to serve was delivered. His selection was peculiar since he had limited experience of commercial law in London and was unfamiliar with City practices and personalities. But in his apparent weaknesses lay the essence of his qualifications. Unlike most of London's commercial barristers, Griffiths had represented neither Lonrho nor House of Fraser and was therefore untainted by any conflict of interest. Moreover, he possessed some commercial experience from his practice in Hong Kong. But, unusually, the DTI decided that he should conduct his inquiry alone, without an accountant as a second investigator. That deficiency had proved a time-consuming handicap.

The second limitation was the nature of the alleged crime. To prove that Rowland had organised a 'concert party', Griffiths needed either a confession or documents to prove an agreement. Since Rowland instinctively committed precious little to paper, the chance of finding that evidence was slim. As Griffiths admitted to his friends, 'Rowland didn't need a specific agreement. All he needed to say was: "I'm going to make a lot of money once the Harrods demerger goes through. Anyone who buys the shares will make a fortune as well." '

Yet the circumstantial evidence against Rowland appeared strong. In the circumstances which had provoked the suspicions, five foreigners had within a few weeks bought 7.6 million shares and the Merchant Navy Fund had bought 5.35 million shares. All those shares were pledged to Lonrho and tipped the balance in the critical vote.

Not surprisingly, Rowland feigned a lack of confidence in Griffiths. Here was yet another lawyer investigating the world of the mega-rich and the mega-deal. 'Mr Griffiths,' Rowland addressed his interrogator, 'I meet a lot of people – a lot of rich people. It may surprise you.' The lawyer blinked. Rowland enjoyed suggesting that his adversary was naive. Compared to Rowland who was paying himself that year, including dividends, over £4 million, rising to £5.2 million in the following year, Griffiths was a pauper. But Rowland's deluge of verbosity hid genuine concerns. Rowland's doctor visited Griffiths to suggest that his patient was ill and needed to be harassed less. Griffiths dismissed the medical evidence as irrelevant. Rowland adopted another tack.

In December, Rowland argued that the inquiry's terms of reference required Griffiths to investigate all 'aspects of influence' on House of Fraser shares. Rather than simply investigate Lonrho, said Rowland, Griffiths should be aware that Warburgs and Cazenoves had organised a 'conspiracy' on behalf of House of Fraser in a 'defensive concert party' to prevent Lonrho's takeover.

In a letter to Griffiths, Rowland claimed that because of their 1971 argument, Warburgs 'made it impossible for a friendly feeling to enter the Boardroom of House of Fraser'. Lonrho had been victimised, complained Rowland, and its good advice ignored by Warburgs who 'have consistently refused to allow any reconciliation between House of Fraser and Lonrho'. Reconciliation in Rowland's terms naturally meant the capitulation of his adversary.

Warburgs, Rowland continued, had their tentacles in a wide range of investment funds and, like a puppet master, were co-ordinating a campaign in support of House of Fraser and against Lonrho. 'It is clear that Warburgs were engaged to repel Lonrho and to this end made every effort to marshal votes and that it consistently cast votes under its control, including discretionary control, against de-merger.' The conductor of the conspiracy, alleged Rowland, was Simon Garmoyle, who had persuaded the banks' investment fund managers to buy House of Fraser shares on behalf of clients and vote against Lonrho.

Although unable to provide any direct evidence to support his allegations, Rowland successfully dispatched the inspector on a marathon chase. Griffiths authorised the seizure from Warburgs' office of forty feet of files referring to House of Fraser, and read every page. He then questioned every fund manager.

Within Warburgs' files, Griffiths did uncover the evidence of the bankers discussing and planning the 'war chest' – the purchase and placing of House of Fraser shares in 'friendly' hands. But unfortunately for Rowland, in the crucial days between May and

June 1983, before the demerger vote which Lonrho was expected to win, Warburgs' fund managers actually sold the shares to take profits rather than vote on the crucial issue. Cazenoves' clients were likewise advised to take their profits. There was no evidence of a conspiracy against Lonrho.

However, six months after the investigation started Rowland's investigators had unearthed a morsel of derogatory information about Griffiths, upon which Lonrho hoped to destroy the credibility of the investigation.

Before returning to Britain, Rowland discovered, Griffiths had been embroiled in a controversy concerning the murder of a police officer. In an official report by a Hong Kong judge, Griffiths was criticised for a 'grossly misleading' statement issued at a press conference and for 'errors of judgment' in a telephone conversation. Regardless of Griffiths's explanations, he was, Rowland alleged, a tainted investigator.

Rowland's second criticism also attempted to undermine Griffiths's competence. During his inquiry in London, Griffiths had represented in court the National Coal Board Pension Fund whose director was a bitter opponent of Lonrho's bid for House of Fraser. Rowland could claim with a scintilla of justification that Griffiths suffered a conflict of interest.

On the basis of Griffiths's alleged unsuitability and complaining about the long delays in completing the investigation, Rowland submitted a lengthy summary of his suffering to Norman Tebbit, asking for the restrictions on Lonrho's bid for House of Fraser to be finally lifted. Those reading Rowland's plea were struck by the omissions, especially the disregard of his own responsibility for Hugh Fraser's resignation which had increased the board's reliance upon Warburgs. Yet there was a self-confident nonchalance within Rowland's concluding words: 'We are totally unconcerned as to the outcome of the Griffiths inquiry. We have nothing to hide and, for that reason, we have not asked for Mr Griffiths to be withdrawn from the case.'

Having applied the muck, Rowland left it to dry, or, as officials knowingly remarked, 'Tiny's getting his retaliation in first.' Yet those same DTI officials understood the strength of Rowland's case. Griffiths's investigation had lasted nearly a year.

Since he envisaged no conclusion until the end of another year, including many foreign trips, he was asked to write an interim report.

Griffiths's attitude towards Rowland was coloured both by Rowland's attacks and by the City's scions who had given evidence about their antagonist. Among the first to testify about Rowland's veracity was Michael Richardson who presented a conflict of evidence about their conversation in 1982.

Rowland argued that he had been deceived by Rothschild and produced supporting evidence from Robinson and Spicer. Both directors had claimed a 'vivid memory' of Rowland's contemporaneous report to the board of Richardson's offer. Yet Griffiths accused Rowland of lying: 'I did not find his evidence to be as believable . . . Mr Rowland, optimist that he is, whose wishes I believe often father his memory, [wrongly] believed that he had persuaded Mr Richardson and . . . thereafter Mr Rowland again acted true to his character as I see it: he caused his version of the matter together with his letter to Rothschilds to be given to the press.'

Griffiths's distrust of Rowland reappeared in his account of the encounter between Rowland and Rupert Murdoch in February 1983. According to Murdoch, Rowland had suggested that he buy 5 per cent of House of Fraser with the promise that after the demerger was approved, they would split the profits 50–50. Murdoch refused. In the aftermath of Murdoch telling Professor Smith about the offer, the account had reached Ivan Fallon of the *Sunday Times*. 'I rang Rowland and asked him to comment,' recalls Fallon. 'He went wild and shouted that it was "a total lie".'

Rowland also alleged to Griffiths that Murdoch was lying but the lawyer reported that, 'Mr Murdoch . . . gave me a compelling feeling that he was telling the truth. Mr Rowland did not.' Griffiths continued, 'In this inquiry Mr Rowland has been too often out of step with the evidence of others for this to be coincidence.'

With only scant details and no written evidence of a deliberate plot to form a 'concert party', the establishment of facts depended entirely upon Griffiths's cross-examination skills. By

Having pledged his own massive shareholding, Rowland was certain of victory at the shareholders' annual general meeting in May 1973. Despite Duncan Sandys's hopeless chairmanship, Rowland's success established a wide personal following among the army of Lonrho small shareholders.

Lonrho's lifeline after 1973 was provided by Sheikh Nasser Al-Sabah (*right*). The Kuwaiti was introduced to Rowland by Khahil Osman, a Sudanese vet (*second from left*). Initially enthusiastic about Kuwait's massive investment in Lonrho, Tom Ferguson (seated behind Osman and Sheikh Nasser) soon became disenchanted with Rowland's management and led an unsuccessful revolt.

In 1984, Donald Trelford's report in the *Observer* about the massacres in Zimbabwe provoked a public row with Rowland who threatened to sell the newspaper to Robert Maxwell.

On two occasions, Rowland sold his stake in House of Fraser to Mohamed
Fayed. His relationship with the Egyptian was as mercurial as with Sir
Hugh Fraser, a renowned gambler.

In the battle for House of Fraser, Rowland often flew to Glasgow. Among the regular passengers in the Gulfstream were (*from right*) Edward Du Cann, Robert Dunlop, Duncan Sandys, Mervyn Greenway, Paul Spicer, John Cama and Captain Bill Wilming.

Rowland's £20 million personal battle against Mohamed Fayed stemmed from derogatory information purchased from informants including Adnan Khashoggi, the Saudi arms dealer, and Shri Chandra Swamiji, and Indian guru.

Six Secretaries of State of the Department of Trade and Industry, targets of Rowland's wrath. (*Clockwise from left*) John Biffen, Leon Brittan, Cecil Parkinson, Paul Channon, Norman Tebbit and Nicholas Ridley.

Gordon Borrie, the director
of the Office of Fair
Trading, opposed
Rowland's bid to refer the
takeover of the House of
Fraser back to Godfrey Le
Quesne (*bottom left*), the
chairman of the Monopolies
and Mergers Commission,
who considered Lonrho's
various bids four times
between 1978 and 1985.

Jim Butler, the senior
partner at accountants Peat
Marwick, has remained
Rowland's staunch ally
since 1972, despite all the
revelations. Peats' accounts
have aroused considerable
controversy.

Rowland in Zimbabwe in 1992. From left, standing: Jack Kato and his
wife, Rowland's longstanding Japanese friend, Rowland's daughter Plum,
Eileen Kruger, Josie Rowland. Nic Kruger is seated on the right.

Lonrho's board in 1991. Standing, René Leclézio (*second from left*), Paul
Spicer (*centre*), Robert Dunlop (*third from right*), Terry Robinson (far
right).

Dieter Bock, Rowland's chosen successor, remains mysterious about his financial past and capability to manage Lonrho's African subsidiaries.

the end of the inquiry, very few admired his abilities. Griffiths, in his critics' opinion, was simplistic.

Griffiths cleared Jack Hayward as an honest investor in a speculative punt, while Adriana Funaro's explanation that she bought one million shares on the advice of Ali Fayed, acting purely after reading Jim Slater's tip, also satisfied the lawyer. Significantly, Mohamed Fayed, present at that interview with Funaro, told Griffiths that he was not interested in House of Fraser and never wanted to hear it mentioned again.

Griffiths also rejected the allegation made originally in the postcard of a suspicious relationship between Terry Robinson and Geoffrey Musson, the manager of the Merchant Navy Pension Fund. According to Griffiths, the two men met occasionally over eight years because their daughters attended the same school. 'I do not accept that there is anything unusual or sinister in [their] relationship,' commented Griffiths. 'It would be a sad day if the parents of two schoolfriends could not meet socially.' In 1992, when Robinson left Lonrho, Musson joined him as an employee in his new company. Musson was described as 'a friend of nineteen years'.

Griffiths's only culprit was Dr Ashraf Marwan, interviewed four times. Marwan told Griffiths that House of Fraser had not been mentioned at his lunch with Rowland. Rowland contradicted the Egyptian. Griffiths concluded that Marwan 'lied deliberately'.

Marwan claimed that he invested £4 million in House of Fraser shares after reading Jim Slater's tip in the *Sunday Telegraph*. It was 'just quick profit' he told Griffiths. Yet Marwan had admitted previously that he had never heard of Slater.

Griffiths's evidence of collusion between Marwan and Lonrho was the photostat of the Slater newspaper cutting which Marwan handed Griffiths to substantiate the pedigree of his interest. It was identical to the photostat produced by Rowland. Moreover, Rona Kelly, Rowland's secretary, confirmed that in the course of Griffiths's hearings Marwan had telephoned Rowland asking for the Slater cutting.

The evidence of collusion increased when, on 19 December

1983, Funaro sold 1.2 million House of Fraser shares while Marwan, on the same day, asked the same brokers, Strauss Turnbull, to buy 1.8 million House of Fraser shares. Ali Fayed, who arranged the sale, described the circumstances as a '100 per cent coincidence'. Griffiths disagreed: 'I find it almost unbelievable that it should be a coincidence.'

Griffiths would conclude that Marwan was 'not frank' because there was 'a closer liaison with Lonrho, and Mr Rowland in particular, than he sought to convey to me'. But Griffiths proceeded no further. His interim report, characterised by purple prose and angry rhetoric exposing his frustrations, was published on 10 August. 'I have tried when reaching my conclusions', he explained, 'to steer a course between the Scylla of ignoring the implications of the whole picture and the Charybdis of losing sight of the individual explanations because of an obsession with the jigsaw.' Nevertheless he concluded that, 'The story of the proud mother watching her son's platoon march past and saying, "Everyone is out of step with my boy" is in point: in this inquiry Mr Rowland has too often been out of step with the evidence of others for this to be a coincidence.' But he concluded that there was insufficient evidence to censure Rowland.

Everyone was dissatisfied except Rowland who, coinciding with the publication of Griffiths's report, issued his own publication identical in stylistic appearance. Entitled, 'Report by Lonrho to the ordinary shareholders of House of Fraser and Lonrho on the inquiry conducted by an inspector into the House of Fraser ownership', its vitriolic attack upon Griffiths accused the inspector of acting as a 'covert agent' of House of Fraser and Warburgs, causing Lonrho to be completely ignorant of the charges and the evidence. It was, complained Rowland, akin to 'a duel by battleaxes in a dark cellar'.

Rowland's anticipatory retaliation suggested a bad conscience, that he had feared conviction. Instead, the DTI did not ask Griffiths to complete his inquiry and never commented upon his findings.

Rowland's dismissal of Griffiths fuelled the propaganda war and won one new friend in the City. In June 1984, Robert Carpenter of stockbrokers Montagu, Loebel recommended Lonrho shares. The shares were trading at 131 pence but Carpenter claimed that their real asset value was 400 pence. Lonrho's sales were £2.3 billion and its profits £113 million. Carpenter forecast that profits for the year ending in September would be £145 million and rise to £175 million in 1985. In the event, the actual figures were £135 million and £158 million, but Rowland had found an admirer to promote his company and that was an achievement.

In Cheapside, Rowland was optimistic. Anticipating the final battle for House of Fraser, he published in a series of newspaper advertisements an open letter to the shareholders and the public. 'Lonrho's overall state of health,' wrote Rowland on 3 October 1984, 'is excellent . . . The financial year now starting will, I am convinced, show further improvement.'

Turning to House of Fraser, Rowland explained that he won 98 million votes to be re-elected as a director. Only 34 million voted against. He interpreted the large majority as a ringing endorsement of his campaign. Despite the controversy, he claimed, the investment in House of Fraser was profitable. Lonrho's 30 per cent holding was worth £71 million more than it paid, albeit that the share prices reflected the expectation of a bid, and Lonrho had received £25 million in dividends. The gross return over seven years, boasted Rowland, was 'a highly attractive 27 per cent per annum'. Everything was set, he concluded, to bid whenever the Commission lifted the restrictions. 'Whatever the obstacles put in the way of a bid, patient persistence will overcome them one by one.'

Every reader assumed that Rowland's seven-year dogged battle would continue. No one paid much attention to one sentence: 'We also have the option to sell our strategic holding and have recently been approached to sell by more than one buyer.' Everyone knew that Rowland was a buyer not a seller. But three weeks later that sentence assumed a real weight.

Eleven
A Fatal Relationship

On 1 November 1984, a brief announcement in the newspapers reported that the Monopolies Commission had been given an additional three months to complete its report. In a public statement Rowland expressed surprise: 'Neither the DTI nor the Monopolies Commission had the courtesy to inform us of this. We were left to read it in the papers. This was the first and last straw.'

In fact, Rowland had been told informally that the Commission was seeking an extension. 'We often ask for more time,' Le Quesne told an inquirer. Rowland's 'last straw', however, turned out to have been an exchange between Le Quesne and Du Cann during a meeting on 5 October. In Rowland's subsequent accounts of the House of Fraser saga, he would claim that the exchange was critical.

The circumstances are unclear because they do not appear on a contemporaneous transcript. Du Cann and Lonrho's advisers however had a firm recollection of Le Quesne's question: 'Why don't you sell your shares?' Later, on hearing Du Cann's report, Rowland would claim: 'As if a shutter had been opened, it became obvious that a sale was the very complete "change of circumstances" which the DTI required.' Subsequently, Le Quesne would be baffled about the importance placed upon his alleged question but Rowland proceeded to construct a scenario out of it.

The delay seemed to confirm an intimation which Rowland had received from a member of the Commission that Le Quesne, reluctant to reverse his earlier decision, wanted time to construct a rejection. Rowland had been advised that if the Commission again disallowed the bid, Lonrho might be compelled to sell the House of Fraser shares. In that event, not only the value of House of Fraser shares would collapse, but Lonrho's too.

Over the following days, while flying around Africa, Rowland fumed about the unjust treatment for which he had been singled out. At sixty-seven, he was finding that his ambitions were at best frozen. Meanwhile the financial markets in London were booming. Murdoch's News International had, in a brief period, nearly doubled in size; Maxwell had just bought the *Daily Mirror* with potentially huge profits and was still buying; while the Hanson conglomerate was hoovering up companies free from any government hindrance. In contrast he, Tiny Rowland, was stuck in a Whitehall quagmire which appeared to be thickening.

Rowland had never completely grasped why the human chemistry which smoothed his personal relations throughout Africa failed to succeed in London. Robinson was among the few in Cheapside who presented an explanation: 'He expected more of people in Britain than in Africa. His gifts in Africa were to help poor people. In Britain, it would be bribery.' Others, like Lord Hanson, called it contributions to Conservative Party funds. Indeed, when Rowland was asked for donations to a building scheme at Wycombe Abbey, his daughter Louise's school, the exchange had ended sourly. The visitor had suggested that Rowland's contribution of £5000 was 'not enough'. The donation, it was proposed, should be £100,000. Rowland tore up his cheque and withdrew his daughter from the school. Undoubtedly a principled act but an indication that Rowland was removed from the realities of commercial life in London.

Travelling in Africa, unremittingly fawned upon by politicians and his employees, Rowland was ill-situated to plot his tactics, especially since the insider's tip about the Commission's intentions was wrong. In consequence, Rowland was unaware that Norman Tebbit had, just recently, decisively limited the Commission's ability to interfere in the market. Le Quesne was required to report only on the issue of monopolies and no longer needed to consider corporate activity under the 'public interest' heading.

But Rowland, having denied himself the advice of skilled merchant bankers and informed stockbrokers, was isolated and excessively dependent upon Du Cann for intelligence about the thoughts of Conservative ministers. During that journey, therefore, operating under the illusion that Le Quesne's strictures were still as stringent, he hatched a plan to buy House of Fraser. Although he had received many offers to sell the shares, he decided that he would sell his stake to someone who lacked sufficient funds to launch a full bid and who would not qualify under the Commission's criteria as an acceptable purchaser.

Having no shares, Rowland envisaged that he would be released by the DTI from the undertakings he had given in 1981 and could launch a full bid including the repurchase of shares from his innocent warehouser. Because he was contemplating a bid of 380 pence per share, everyone would earn a profit. Moreover Lonrho would have sufficient cash to pay the forthcoming dividend.

The ideal warehouser would be Mohamed Fayed who had been telephoning his office. The Arab, in Rowland's estimation, was transparent. He understood precisely how this character, who seven years earlier had been a Lonrho director, could be manipulated. In Rowland's view, Fayed was at best a 'fifty man'. That is, worth at most 50 million pounds. He was wealthy, for example he owned a private jet, but Rowland knew little more about Fayed's background. Expecting to return to London on 28 October, Rowland told Robinson to clear the deal with the stock exchange. Naturally, it would automatically be approved by the board of Lonrho.

Fayed had been introduced to Rowland in 1974 and elected to Lonrho's board after the purchase of the Egyptian's Costain shares in March 1975. But by May 1976, the relationship had soured. Fayed had sold his Lonrho shares and Lonrho returned the Costain stake. Like the Kuwaitis who would finally sell their Lonrho shares in 1985, Fayed was another Arab who proved an unsuitable partner. The two had not seen each other for six years.

The circumstances of their reconciliation were, in retrospect, comical. At the end of 1982, Fayed had dispatched several hundred small leather diaries embossed in gold with 'Hotel Ritz,

Paris' to a cast list of the rich and famous whom he hoped might be potential guests at his new acquisition. Among the recipients was Rowland, whose gift also bore his own engraved initials. The package included two travelling bathrobes, marked with the hotel's name.

'Surprised' by the gift, Rowland telephoned Fayed. In the course of their conversation, they agreed to meet when Fayed was next in London. Unknown to Rowland, since his days in Lonrho, Fayed had metamorphosed into a more refined and ambitious businessman. In seeking to earn his fortune in the Middle East, Haiti, the United States, Brunei and France, the Egyptian had not concealed his ambition to win social acceptance.

His complete refurbishment of the Ritz in Paris had won accolades. An indication of his political and social adeptness was that he was to receive eventually the Légion d'honneur from Jacques Chirac for his contribution to Paris, a contrast to Rowland's relationship with British society.

Since their reunion in spring 1983, Rowland and Fayed had met for occasional breakfasts in Fayed's penthouse at 60 Park Lane. Rowland would walk the short distance from his apartment and afterwards be chauffeured to Cheapside. They discussed transport companies and oil concessions in the Middle East but no deal ever materialised.

Fayed also asked Rowland for a favour. He wanted to meet the Sultan of Brunei. A guru called Shri Chandra Swamiji, known as the Swami, who Fayed believed wielded some influence with the Sultan, had offered to arrange the introduction for $2 million. Fayed asked Rowland to investigate the thirty-four-year-old Indian guru's reputation in either Kenya or Zambia where he was known. At the time, the Swami wore a solid gold necklace, held court on a bed covered in tiger skins and was protected by bodyguards. By the time Rowland passed on the adverse reports that the Swami, earlier in his life, had been a scrap metal dealer in India and was the subject of police inquiries, Fayed had already paid a smaller fee and was in contact with the Sultan.

Situated on the northern coast of Borneo in South East Asia, Brunei is a tiny kingdom of 230,000 people whose dictator, blessed with considerable oil revenues, is dubbed 'the richest man in the world'. Owning more palatial homes scattered around the world than other mortals own shirts, the Sultan was a magnet for the world's wheeler-dealers seeking to sell planes, yachts, palaces or their services to help invest his estimated $24 billion fortune. One assessment in 1984 recorded that the Sultan possessed eleven Rolls Royces and Bentleys, seven Mercedes and four Ferraris. In 1992, he apparently owned 153 Rolls Royces. His first personal Boeing 727 included a jacuzzi from which, in emergency, the water could be dumped in less than eight seconds. The 727 was replaced by a lavishly decorated Boeing 747. His home, a palace of 1788 rooms costing an estimated $600 million, is bigger than the Vatican. The opulent lifestyle was, according to his dissatisfied courtiers, the product of a naive mind who was easily misled by avaricious vultures. Among those, Rowland would claim, was Fayed.

In the previous years, Fayed and his brother Ali Fayed had developed a relationship in London with Morgan Grenfell, the merchant bankers, who advised on the purchase of an office block in New York and the construction of three ships in Germany. The relationship ended in 1979 when Fayed used Lazards to buy the Ritz hotel. Until 1984, Fayed discussed several projects with Lazards, none worth more than £25 million. Between June and August 1984, at the same time as Fayed's frequent visits to Brunei, there was a huge influx of funds into Fayed's account at the Royal Bank of Scotland. Whereas the Bank's records from the early Seventies showed moderate transactions, Fayed has never satisfactorily explained the source of his new wealth although the Royal Bank believed that the money, which was transferred from Switzerland, did belong to the Sultan. The deposit of that money coincided with discussions between Fayed and Lazards' bankers about projects worth hundreds of millions and another meeting with Rowland.

On 28 June, Rowland and Fayed met for breakfast at 60 Park Lane. The possibility of Rowland selling his House of Fraser shares was mentioned. Strangely, just the previous day, Fayed had told John Griffiths, the DTI inspector, that he would never be interested in the company. Twenty-four hours later, Fayed discussed with Rowland the sale of his stake in House of Fraser. Rowland, however, remained non-committal and returned to Cheapside with a present from Fayed: a sex-aid device which Fayed had pulled from a draw. Rowland laughed as he showed it to his directors: 'He's mad about sex.'

Five days later, Fayed discussed the purchase at Lazards. The bankers advised that the success of his investment would depend entirely upon the attitude of Roland Smith and his directors. They issued one further caution. Fayed's success would also depend upon his ability to withstand public scrutiny about his background. That day, Fayed telephoned Rowland to suggest that they meet the House of Fraser board together. Rowland refused. Nevertheless, Fayed obtained a guarantee from the Royal Bank of Scotland of an £80 million loan if he bought Lonrho's shares.

Fayed's enthusiasm was dampened by a letter from Rowland sent by hand on 3 July: 'I have thought very carefully about your idea.' Rowland explained that he would only consider selling to someone who would make a complete bid: 'We have had so much loyalty and support from Lonrho and Fraser shareholders over the last year or two that it would be impossible for us to sell the shares while neglecting the effect on their holdings, if Lonrho accepted an individual offer.' Rowland reasoned that Lonrho's sale would depress the value of the shares because the market would assume that the possibility of a bid had evaporated. Therefore, 'the acceptable thing for us would be an offer to all the shareholders.' Taking Rowland's reply at face value, it was a model of probity, consistent with his normal caution towards dealing in shares.

Since the chance of a Lonrho bid for House of Fraser was unlikely, Fayed passed a message to Rowland through Dr Ashraf Marwan that he had sufficient funds at the Royal Bank of Scotland. In reply, Rowland repeated that he would only sell to a bidder for the whole company and told Marwan that he doubted whether Fayed had sufficient money. At this point, the contradictions in Rowland's behaviour began.

In evidence to John Griffiths, the DTI investigator, Rowland testified the Fayeds were rich: 'The Al Fayeds have huge joint interests and if you make enquiries, you will hear that when in London they conduct all their business from their Park Lane apartment, and know and receive numerous visitors every day from the City. They are extremely well known, and have brought well over a thousand million pounds worth of business to this country.' At the time, Rowland believed that the description served his purpose but the advantage was very short term.

Over the following weeks, Fayed had mentioned to Rowland that if he ever considered selling his House of Fraser shares, he would be an eager buyer. Fayed agreed with Rowland that Harrods, like the Ritz hotel, was an unexploited goldmine. Fayed had once made the offer in the lift at Cheapside. To his embarrassment, Rowland had laughed: 'You haven't got the money, Tootsie!' Fayed laughed because as an Arab he knew that the best deals required patience while the seller dangled the fruit to entice the buyers. Fayed believed that Rowland would eventually sell.

In mid-August, Fayed's preparations were interrupted by Lazards' resignation because of a conflict of interest. Fayed was livid. The same bankers were advising BAT on a parallel bid for House of Fraser. It was, he wrote to Ian Fraser, the bank's chairman, 'a complete betrayal of the duty which a financial adviser owes to its clients'. The bank was apologetic.

On the recommendation of the Royal Bank, Fayed transferred to Kleinwort Benson and was introduced to John MacArthur, a senior director. For MacArthur, aged fifty, it was 'just another normal deal'. As the deputy head of corporate finance at Kleinworts, MacArthur believed that he possessed 'lots of experience'. The two met on 28 August, five days after Fayed returned from Brunei where the Egyptian had been appointed an investment adviser to the Sultan. To MacArthur, Mohammed Fayed and his younger brother Ali seemed 'interesting and experienced people involved in big deals'. During their conversation, they spoke about their property and shipping interests in Europe, the Middle East and America, and their bank deposits in London, which underlined the assurance given to MacArthur from the Royal Bank of Scotland that the Fayeds had a large deposit.

Unlike every other client whom MacArthur had represented, the Fayeds were private individuals and MacArthur had seen only a limited selection of their bank statements. The regulations in London, weaker than in New York, would not require the Fayeds to reveal precise details about their wealth because their bid was wholly for cash and MacArthur was confident that the Fayeds could buy the House of Fraser shares using their own money. 'I have no statement of their consolidated financial power,' admitted MacArthur.

MacArthur's task was to guide Fayed through the City Code and the laws which established the rules for a bid. His overriding duty was to ensure that everything which was said was accurate and not misleading. He could expect that the reputation of Kleinworts would guarantee that his word would be trusted. Kleinworts at that time boasted its status as one of the City's most respected merchant banks, although it had been embarrassed by a lengthy internal feud which was resolved by the appointment of Michael Hawkes as chairman. A compromise candidate, Hawkes could not boast the most astute mind in the City. Nevertheless, Fayed was prepared for Rowland's approach when the latter returned from Africa.

On Monday 29 October, Rowland met Ashraf Marwan for breakfast in a Park Lane hotel. On Rowland's own admission, his commercial relationship with Marwan had been 'disastrous' but since his experience with the Kuwaitis he realised that he˙ needed help when negotiating with Arabs. During his absence, while he was planning his use of Fayed to warehouse the shares unwittingly, Fayed had telephoned both men several times. Even as they ate breakfast, Fayed continued calling, leaving messages. 'What does Tootsie want?' asked Rowland.

'Your shares,' replied Marwan.

'Has he got the money?'

'He says he has.'

They discussed the source and concluded that he must have borrowed funds from the Maktoum brothers of Dubai. With Rowland's agreement, Marwan telephoned Fayed from the hotel.

Marwan had first met Fayed in 1983. 'I didn't think much

of him,' said Marwan. 'He was a nobody whom I never even saw at the embassy.' Marwan thought that Fayed was worth 'at most 50 million pounds', the source of Rowland's own belief that 'Fayed was a fifty man'. Marwan returned from the telephone to tell Rowland that they were invited to Fayed's penthouse. Just before 11 a.m., the two men walked into 60 Park Lane.

On the eighth floor, in one of London's most spectacular homes overlooking Hyde Park, the Fayeds had created a palace. The walls, fitted with oak panels stripped from English castles, created a sumptuous atmosphere which removed any doubts about its owner's wealth. In Rowland's own description, 'between the potted orchids and the perfume-injected air, was the delicious smell of lots of money, and it attracted many, many influential visitors from the City and from politics.' Among them was Rowland himself, satisfied that the Fayeds were sufficiently rich for his intentions.

There were only fifty-five minutes for discussion. Marwan was due to fly by Concorde to New York that morning. Rowland's offer was simple. He would tolerate no haggling about price and no alterations to his timetable. He would sell 46.1 million House of Fraser shares for 300 pence each, and the £138 million would be handed over by Friday in cash. Lonrho's profit would be £80 million.

Fayed was delighted and added that he hoped to make a full bid for House of Fraser. Rowland smiled: 'You don't have enough money, Tootsie.' It was agreed that Rowland would return for breakfast on 1 November to settle any snags.

As Fayed escorted his guest to the oak door, Rowland believed that everything was going to plan. Fayed was also pleased. It was the beginning of a new era. As they waited for the lift, Fayed added: 'Tiny, I'll give you £100 million for your shares in Lonrho.' Rowland laughed: 'You haven't got that money, Tootsie.' Fayed added, 'And I'll pay you £5 million a year for five years if you continue to run Lonrho's Africa division.' Rowland laughed again. Long after the lift had delivered Rowland to the ground floor, Fayed was still smiling.

Later that day John MacArthur arrived to discuss the agreed deal and to persuade Fayed to employ a public relations adviser.

The purchase, MacArthur explained, would plunge the Fayeds into a 'high-profile situation'. Pleading their love of privacy, both Fayed brothers initially rejected the advice. Eventually they agreed and Brian Basham, summoned on his car telephone on London's Westway, was diverted to Park Lane.

Among the dozens of former financial journalists lured by higher income to cross the line and steer Britain's media away from embarrassing truths and towards the gloss which benefits their clients, Basham was one of the more intelligent, industrious and scheming consultants. Aged forty-one, the son of a London butcher and trained by John Addey, Basham could be relied upon for whole-hearted commitment to his paymaster. Eventually he would even admit, 'I'd work against Tiny Rowland for nothing.'

During their introductory conversation, Basham had no reason to doubt that the Fayeds fell easily into the category of one of the many Arabs crowding London's casinos and losing millions of pounds daily. For the same reason as everyone else in the City, including MacArthur and Rowland, the Fayeds were assumed to have the cash for the initial purchase.

At the end of their introductory conversation, Basham decided that, considering Fayed's bad English which was interspersed with frequent profanities, he would avoid press conferences and rely instead upon introducing trusted journalists for 'exclusive' interviews. He explained that he could be relied upon to 'control' everything. Everything was now in place for the deal.

As arranged, just before 8 a.m. on 1 November, Rowland returned to Fayed's flat in a good mood. Together they telephoned the Royal Bank to confirm their agreement. The bank was by then 'embarrassed' by the huge sums of money which Fayed had deposited. The exchange would take place the following day.

Unknown to Rowland, soon after his departure, at 11.30 Fayed drove to the Army and Navy Stores to meet Roland Smith for the first time. Instinctively, despite MacArthur's assurances, the professor was suspicious that Fayed was involved in a conspiracy or 'concert party' with Rowland. Considering the years of warfare, the professor reasoned that Rowland's proposed sale could not be straightforward. Smith however listened politely as Fayed outlined his plans and stressed that he would proceed only if he could count on the board's approval. 'We don't want any aggravation or controversy,' stressed Fayed.

House of Fraser's directors were summoned to come to London immediately. At 6 p.m., Mohamed and Ali Fayed returned to meet the board with an enticing introduction. Showing photograph albums of their renovation of the Ritz hotel and emphasising their love of Balnagown Castle, their home in Scotland, they extolled the virtues qualifying them to improve Harrods. Their audience's suspicions began to wane. 'It was a better atmosphere,' confirms Willoughby, 'than when we met Rowland at the Central hotel in Glasgow.' But there were still doubts. The board, asserted Smith, could not support a full bid until they had sufficient experience of the Fayeds.

At nine o'clock the following morning, Ali Fayed telephoned Rowland. Assured that everything was in place, Rowland was suddenly caught breathless. 'You are giving up the director-ships?' asked Ali.

'Certainly not,' snapped Rowland. 'The deal is cash against documents.'

'I only raise it,' continued Ali, 'because Kleinworts suggested it.'

'I'm dealing with the Fayeds and not Kleinworts. If you want we can call it all off.'

Rowland was agitated. His whole purpose was for Lonrho to retain its two directorships and wait for the DTI to with-draw the restrictions on Lonrho's bid. The Fayeds were cast as warehousers not principals. Despite the time, he telephoned Marwan in New York and remonstrated. Marwan, having paci-fied Rowland, quickly called Ali Fayed and urged him not to rock the boat. 'Ashraf, they must resign,' said Ali.

'Just complete the deal,' urged Marwan.

At noon, £138 million was transferred to Lonrho's account and the share certificates were handed over. Lonrho's dividend was covered. But by the end of the afternoon, Rowland's bitter feud with the Fayeds had begun. 'One telephone conversation broke their relationship,' says Marwan.

Barbara Conway was a *Daily Telegraph* journalist whom Rowland trusted faithfully to repeat his views in her newspaper. That afternoon, Conway telephoned Rowland and reported her conversation with Mohamed Fayed. The Egyptian, she told Rowland, was emphatic that the Lonrho directors would be leaving the House of Fraser board. Infuriated, Rowland telephoned Fayed who denied Conway's report. Rowland rechecked and called back. Fayed again denied Conway's report. 'You are lying,' said Rowland.

Rowland's fury increased as he realised that Fayed was contemplating a full bid. Worse than being outwitted, Rowland, who prided himself on 'reading people', was gripped by a panic that he had misjudged Fayed. His consolation was that Fayed, in his opinion, did not have sufficient money. Critically, he made no formal complaint to the DTI or OFT that he was the victim of deception or fraud. On the contrary, he remained temporarily silent.

Reports of their row not only dispelled Roland Smith's suspicions of a conspiracy between Rowland and the Fayeds, but finally provided the opportunity to rid the company of Rowland's interference. With Mohamed Fayed's encouragement, Smith wrote to Rowland that unless the Lonrho directors resigned, there would be an extraordinary general meeting to vote their removal. Rowland's resistance spread ambivalence about his intentions. Even Rowland seemed uncertain and that weekend he added more confusion.

Despite their instinctive loathing of journalists, the inhabitants of Britain's commercial and financial fraternity know that the swiftest and most certain means of communication of their intentions and reactions is through articles published in the City pages of the three quality Sunday newspapers. Every weekend, the City's doyens and those aspiring to become rich scrutinise those pages for information and nuances which could affect their fortunes.

In the wake of the sale to the Fayeds, Rowland clearly wanted to explain his motives and intentions. But by that time, he had argued with both Ivan Fallon, the City editor of the *Sunday Times*, and Ian Watson, the City editor of the *Sunday*

Telegraph. Both had supported Roland Smith in the battle. Instead of accepting their honest criticism, Rowland was infuriated by their lack of loyalty and gratitude for past kindnesses.

The *Observer* was therefore his only possible tribune. Until that moment, Rowland had confined his interference in the newspaper to coverage of Africa. Melvyn Marckus, the *Observer*'s City editor, had dined once with Rowland and spoken on the telephone but had not received any blatant directives. Grateful for Lonrho's support, Marckus had had his budget increased and his section expanded despite Trelford's Faustian pact with Rowland of partitioning control over the newspaper.

Effectively, Marckus was unprotected by the editor when Rowland telephoned on Friday, 2 November, to provide the quotations for an article about House of Fraser two days later. If neither Trelford nor Rowland understood that their use of the *Observer* to propagate Lonrho's arguments would undermine the newspaper's credibility, Marckus, on that first occasion, felt both impotent to refuse the proprietor's request and justified that Rowland's explanation was a genuine story.

In that Sunday's *Observer*, Rowland announced that the battle for House of Fraser was 'not over yet' and that he anticipated the possible repurchase of shares: 'It would depend on the price. We are a trading company. That means we are buyers and sellers.' Marckus's comment, based on Rowland's briefing, was self-deceptive: 'Lonrho's share sale and Mohamed Al Fayed's assurances to the Professor have clearly lessened hopes of an imminent full-scale bid for House of Fraser.' The belief that Fayed would not bid was contradicted by other newspapers.

A reflection of the confusion and ambivalence about the Fayeds within the *Observer* on that Sunday, was an article by Michael Gillard, a well-known financial investigator on Marckus's staff. Since early 1983, at Rowland's suggestion, Mohammed Fayed had been used as a source by Gillard for several stories about corruption in the Gulf. Invariably, Fayed was settling scores against a competitor. Gillard's acquaintance with Fayed helped his access to Fayed when the House of Fraser deal was announced. The investigative journalist described Fayed in an article on that Sunday as an, 'undisguised Anglophile whose old-established family has been doing business with Britain for more than a century. They started shipping cotton from Egypt to Liverpool.' Their fortune added Gillard, 'could be worth at least £500 million. They only smile when asked to put a figure on it.'

The journalists' confusion was compounded by their editor's own attitude towards Mohamed Fayed. Eight months earlier, Donald Trelford and his wife had stayed at the Ritz in Paris as Fayed's guests. In a subsequent letter to Fayed, Trelford thanked the Egyptian for his 'munificent hospitality at the Ritz'. Trelford promised to write a promotional article about the hotel and sought simultaneous advertising for his newspaper.

That weekend, the *Observer*'s benign attitude towards Fayed had not quite registered with the newspaper's proprietor. In his briefings, Rowland emphasised that all options remained open. 'Somehow I do not think,' he told the *Financial Times*, 'that Mr Mohammed Al Fayed will want to vote me off the board.' He added, 'You have only heard the beginning.'

At 9 a.m. on 6 November Rowland arrived at the DTI to see Alex Fletcher, the minister of corporate affairs. Having sold the shares, Rowland wanted to be released from the 1981 undertakings. Fletcher agreed to consult the Office of Fair Trading and also agreed that nothing prevented Rowland buying more House of Fraser shares. No one expected what followed.

The next day, Lonrho began buying House of Fraser shares. By 9 November, Lonrho owned 7 million shares. The sellers were Ashraf Marwan and Jack Hayward, who just one month earlier had been cleared of involvement in a 'concert party'.

Lonrho bought Marwan's shares through Strauss, Turnbull, the brokers who were favoured by Spicer and the brokers through whom both Marwan and Funaro had originally invested in House of Fraser. The coincidence switched the spotlight back on to Marwan. The Egyptian, who denied any knowledge of Rowland's new interest in the House of Fraser, insisted that he would not have sold his shares to Rowland if he had known that Fayed intended to bid for House of Fraser. The confusion was increased by Rowland's next call.

In a visit to Le Quesne, Rowland announced that he was still interested in bidding for House of Fraser. 'I am the second-largest shareholder,' he told the judge who had been 'very surprised' by Rowland's deal with the Fayeds. Lonrho insisted that the Monopolies Commission complete its investigation so it might be free to bid for House of Fraser. Any doubts about Lonrho's intentions were silenced by Lonrho's purchase of a further 3 million shares. Lonrho's 6.3 per cent minority shareholding, according to Mervyn Greenway, the stockbroker, 'blocked the Fayeds completing a takeover under section 209 of the Companies Act'.

Fayed and his advisers were surprised but not deterred by Rowland's re-emergence. In a show of unity, both Roland Smith and the Fayeds visited Le Quesne and emphasised their co-operation. Smith, whose salary would soon be doubled at the Fayeds' suggestion with a backdated bonus, proclaimed his conviction that the Fayeds were credible. Nevertheless, as a precaution, MacArthur was summoned by Elizabeth Llewellyn Smith, the deputy director general of the Office of Fair Trading, and asked to give assurances that the Fayeds had sufficient money to mount a full bid.

By this time, Mohamed Fayed had spread his hospitality. Alec Craddock, the Harrods manager, had been whisked to the Ritz in Paris and returned impressed, while all the House of Fraser board had been entertained in the Park Lane penthouse which Willoughby described as, 'outstanding, palatial. I'd never seen anything like the sheer quality.' Like Kleinworts, the directors assumed that the visible evidence confirmed the Fayeds' wealth.

On 16 November, MacArthur sent Llewellyn Smith a one-and-a-half-page list of the Fayeds' wealth. According to MacArthur, the Fayeds were 'leading shipowners in the liner trade', they 'owned' 75 Rockefeller Plaza in New York, the Ritz in Paris, they were bankers and were members of 'Middle East oil exploration consortia with major oil companies', and 'involved in many construction projects, particularly in the Middle East'. Among the Fayeds' construction contracts was an alleged $2 billion contract in Dubai for docks, a hospital and trade centre. Denied any independent means of investigation, Llewellyn Smith at that stage unequivocally accepted the banker's assurances.

Brian Basham, also relying upon the same draft by MacArthur of the Fayeds' wealth, provided selected journalists with background material to build up the image of the Fayeds. The result, published in most newspapers, was descriptions of the Fayeds as an old-established Egyptian family whose fortune was established a century earlier by their grandfather who grew cotton in the Nile delta which was exported to Lancashire. The brothers had attended British schools and been cared for by British nannies. The family's shipping fleet had survived Nasser's nationalisation. Their own wealth of about 1 billion dollars was based on 'widespread international interests' which included shipping, hotels, construction, oil, property and the Ritz hotel in Paris. Finally, they had enjoyed a long relationship with the Sultan of Brunei which dated back to their father. Unbelievably, the ownership of the Ritz alone would persuade the journalists about the Fayeds' enormous wealth.

Even Basham's account was exaggerated in newspapers but his clients, MacArthur and the Fayeds, did not correct the inaccuracies circulating about the Egyptians' wealth. Mohamed Fayed's reaction was pertinent: 'I have no comments on any reporter or journalistic hallucination or sensational writings. It is up to them.'

Reading the accounts, Rowland was struck by a rare foreboding. Had he misjudged the Fayeds? 'Where does their money come from?' he asked Du Cann. Rowland just could not accept the error of his own judgment that Mohamed Fayed was a 'fifty man'. He turned to Marwan for assistance to prove that the Fayeds could not have accumulated 1 billion dollars during the seven years since they had been Lonrho directors.

At that moment, Marwan was in daily contact with the Fayeds to mediate a dispute between themselves and a Swiss aircraft engineer. The engineer, Carl Hirshmann, claimed that Mohamed Fayed had interfered in a contract between himself and the Sultan of Brunei. To protect his claim of $48 million compensation, Hirshmann was physically detaining the Sultan's Boeing 747 as guarantee for payment.

In Zurich on 14 November 1984, Marwan obtained from Hirshmann the first evidence that Fayed held a power of attorney to use the Sultan's money. The source, wrote Hirshmann, was a Swiss bank. Marwan relayed the news to Rowland. 'Tiny went berserk,' says Marwan, 'because he thought that Fayed was a friend. He didn't like being cheated.' Immediately, Rowland flew to Switzerland to confirm the veracity of the witness.

Two weeks later, Marwan's relationship with the Fayeds cooled and then, amid considerable acrimony, fractured. His mediation attempts collapsed. Mohamed Fayed issued a succession of threats against Marwan who in turn issued a writ for defamation against Fayed. This was the critical point in the saga between Rowland and Fayed.

Marwan, in revenge, decided to help Rowland's campaign against the Fayeds and began deploying his contacts in Egypt and the Arab world to discover the background to the unknown businessmen and the source of their money. Rowland's original guess, that Fayed had borrowed money from Dubai, was forgotten. Having finally and reluctantly agreed to resign as a House of Fraser director, Rowland understood that Fayed was intending to bid for the whole company. As his masterplan collapsed, the architect went back to the drawing board to devise a melodramatic theory that would corroborate his suspicions.

During December, both Rowland and Marwan began telling selected journalists that the Fayeds were not buying in their own name but possibly on behalf of the Sultan of Brunei. Their evidence was said to be Fayed's recent acquisition of the Dorchester hotel which, within weeks, he resold to the Sultan for the purchase price. Barbara Conway wrote the story for the *Daily Telegraph*. The brothers sued Marwan and issued a public denial through Basham. But another event bequeathed greater credibility to the theory.

On 29 January 1985, the Sultan, accompanied by Fayed, visited Margaret Thatcher at 10 Downing Street. Britain was in the midst of a financial crisis which had been aggravated by the Sultan's decision to transfer the management of $5 billion worth of investments from London to New York. Thatcher sought to persuade her guest to transfer the money back to London. For his part, the Sultan was aggrieved by Britain's announcement that a group of Gurkhas, protecting his Kingdom, were to be withdrawn. By the end of the visit, the Sultan had agreed to return his billions to London and Thatcher agreed to reconsider the soldiers' deployment.

According to Rowland's melodramatic theory, the prime minister could not have helped noticing that the Sultan was accompanied by Fayed who had described himself at Heathrow's VIP lounge as the Sultan's 'Private and Personal Adviser cum Agent in London' and was presented in Downing Street as the Sultan's adviser. Again in the melodrama theory, Thatcher would not dare insult the Sultan by offending Fayed. However that hypothesis fails to take into account that, two months later, Fayed's close relationship with the Sultan was apparently abruptly terminated.

At the end of February 1985, Le Quesne submitted his report about Lonrho's bid for House of Fraser to the Office of Fair Trading. In effect, the lawyer contradicted all the conclusions he had uttered four years earlier. Lonrho's management, he reported, would not suffer the 'same danger of overstrain' as feared in 1981 and the effect on competition was not 'significant'. He recommended that since 'circumstances have changed', Lonrho's ownership, under Tebbit's new guidelines, was no longer against the public interest. Le Quesne's recommendation reflected what Professor Smith would characterise as a 'report with more U-turns than a London taxi driver performs in Oxford Street'. Borrie and other OFT officials sanguinely accepted Le Quesne's latest recommendation and it was submitted to the minister. Within days, the news leaked that Le Quesne's task was completed.

There was no jubilation in Cheapside. The stakes had changed considerably. The original 150 pence bid was clearly insufficient. A bid at £3 per share, a total cost of £460 million, was more than House of Fraser's value and beyond Lonrho's means. The company's debts had risen to at least £500 million. Nevertheless, Rowland's thoughts had moved in a different direction that overwhelmingly convinced him that he would win the battle. His frame of mind was based upon hope rather than fact.

He reasoned that since a British public company like Lonrho had been subjected to a rigorous inquiry by the Monopolies

Commission, it was inevitable that a Liechtenstein-registered, off-the-shelf company called the Alfayed Investment Trust, with three unknown Egyptian brothers listed as directors, would also be referred to the Commission to win permission to buy House of Fraser. Once the reference was announced, he believed, the share price would collapse and Lonrho could buy the store group cheaply.

Critically, Rowland's sources of information for that conclusion did not include the expertise of a well-connected merchant bank or anyone else who enjoyed an amicable relationship with Borrie or Tebbit. Instead, Rowland relied upon Du Cann, whose relationship with Thatcher had withered, and a gaggle of lawyers and brokers whose advice proved unreliable.

At Kleinworts, no one doubted that Le Quesne had cleared Lonrho's bid and that speed was essential. 'We can do it now, let's hit it,' urged MacArthur. On two issues, the banker was emphatic: 'Our bid will not be referred to the Monopolies Commission; and Lonrho don't have enough money to top our bid.' The pound had sunk to an all-time low of parity with the dollar. The Fayeds had more money in sterling than anticipated.

On 4 March, after securing Roland Smith's support, the Fayeds publicly announced their bid for House of Fraser at 400 pence per share, compared to the 300 pence they had paid Rowland. The Fayeds were offering £615 million – in cash. The news, the amount and the detail that the Fayeds could pay in cash, shocked Rowland.

By then, Brian Basham had been working overtime. Journalists automatically assumed that the super-rich Fayeds were an 'old-established Egyptian family enjoying long business links with Britain'. Rowland beseeched Marwan urgently to seek the truth about the fabulously rich pharaohs and the source of their money.

Ashraf Marwan finally found his best informant – Adnan Khashoggi, Fayed's former brother-in-law. At lunch, the Saudi middleman revealed that Fayeds were not members of an old-established family but the sons of a poor education inspector who lived in a squalid house in Alexandria. When they first met in 1953 in Jeddah, continued Khashoggi, Mohamed Fayed had been working as a salesman for Singer Sewing Machine Company at £10 per month. Khashoggi had employed Mohamed until he was dismissed after a dispute to become a manager of a laundry in Saudi Arabia. His wealth had been earned as a commission agent for British construction companies in Dubai. His shipping company had been bought from a Jewish family in Egypt but Fayed, according to Khashoggi, had defaulted on the payments.

By then, other inquiries by Rowland revealed that the Ritz hotel in Paris was fully mortgaged for £10 million; that the Fayeds did not 'own' a block in New York's Rockefeller Centre, but held a minority interest which was subject to a lease; and their 'fleet of ships' was just a few barges. The image evoked by MacArthur and Basham had proved erroneous. With all the adverse evidence, Rowland believed, there was no chance that the Fayeds would escape investigation by the Monopolies Commission.

On 5 March 1985, Rowland and Du Cann visited Alex Fletcher, the junior minister at the DTI. Since the Fayeds had bid, said Du Cann, 'we would expect a level playing field.' Lonrho should be released from its undertakings and given the chance to bid. Secondly, he warned his political colleague that the publicity about the Fayeds' wealth was untrue. Fletcher agreed to consider their arguments. By then, the DTI had received information from MI6 which disputed the Fayeds' claims.

The following day, at Rowland's request, Marwan wrote to both Borrie and Fletcher warning that the publicity promoted by Basham about the Fayeds' wealth was untrue. Citing as evidence a power of attorney, dated 23 August 1984 and signed by the Sultan, Marwan claimed that Fayed was acting on behalf of the Sultan of Brunei. Neither Fletcher nor Borrie was impressed. Their suspicions of Rowland were magnified many-fold by Marwan who five months earlier had been accused by John Griffiths, the DTI inspector, of lying. Even Rowland had told Griffiths, 'In terms of business, Dr Marwan is totally unreliable.' At that critical stage, Rowland's most reputable adviser and ambassador in London was Du Cann.

The pace was accelerating. On that same day, 6 March, Norman Tebbit had decided to publish the Commission report but to wait for another week before deciding finally whether to refer Fayed's bid to the Monopolies Commission. During that time, he would allow both sides to argue their case.

At that stage, Borrie's opinion of Rowland became crucial. Critically, during the previous weeks, he had lost trust in Rowland and Lonrho's directors and it was on his recommendation that Tebbit had delayed by one week the removal of the DTI's curb on Lonrho's freedom to bid for House of Fraser. Borrie reasoned that it would allow the Fayeds an opportunity to answer Rowland's allegations. Whatever the outcome, Borrie was certain that the Fayed bid would not be referred to the Commission, not least because he would not recommend that course.

Nevertheless, there was nothing to prevent Lonrho bidding for House of Fraser on condition that permission for the takeover would eventually be given by the DTI. Even Sir Jaspar Hollom, the chairman of the Takeover Panel, confirmed that position and possibility in a letter to Lonrho.

Attention was now focused on Rowland. He did nothing; not even buying House of Fraser shares up to the 29.9 per cent limit. He only repeated to all inquirers that since the Fayeds were a front for the Sultan of Brunei there should be an OFT investigation into the Fayed bid. Rowland's campaign did prompt Sir Alex Fletcher, the junior minister, to seek reassurance from both Professor Smith and MacArthur that the Fayeds 'have more than adequate funds of their own to finance the offer'. Both gave that guarantee.

Rowland also visited Fletcher on that Friday. He would later say that he was assured by the junior minister that Fayed could not bid for House of Fraser because it was 'a closed period. It would be against the rules.' Since that advice was legally wrong and no DTI official recalls that assurance, it is hard to conceive that Rowland entered the weekend believing that the Fayeds could not bid.

The weekend of 9–10 March was critical. The gossip reaching Rowland suggested that, in a pre-emptive move, the Fayeds would start buying House of Fraser shares when the market opened on Monday. Rowland hoped that his denigration of the

Fayeds would prompt the government to intervene. Inevitably, the weekend's news coverage would establish the atmosphere on Monday 11 March when both sides were due to meet officials at the OFT.

Basham had been working overtime to neutralise Rowland and MacArthur had helped. The banker told the *Guardian*: 'It is absolute nonsense that the money is coming from Brunei. It is coming from the Fayed family funds that have been accumulated over generations and been wisely invested.' MacArthur gave no indication that he had never requested or seen the Fayeds' accounts or evidence of their alleged wealth. Two Sunday journalists, brought to Fayed by Basham, also had no reason to doubt their interviewee.

In the *Sunday Times*, Ivan Fallon described the Fayeds' ancient wealth which was jeopardised by President Nasser: 'Fortunately their grandfather had begun investing in property in Paris and Switzerland eighty years ago and there was a major fleet of ships . . . Already wealthy when they left Egypt, the Al Fayeds have multiplied their fortune many times since.'

In the *Sunday Telegraph*, Ian Watson wrote, 'Kleinwort Benson . . . has had a relationship with the Al Fayeds for several decades. The bank will show Tebbit and the OFT this week that the Al Fayeds have about $1 billion of free wealth over and above the £615 million they have currently put on the table for House of Fraser. This is a lot more than the debt-ridden Lonrho could produce.' The Fayeds had enjoyed a relationship with Kleinworts not over 'several decades', but just for weeks.

But on Sunday, most important of all was MacArthur's appearance on Channel 4's *Business Programme*. Interviewed by John Plender of the *Financial Times*, MacArthur confidently stated that the Fayeds were worth 'several billion dollars'. The banker explained that the Fayeds' money had come from 'their own resources which stem from their family businesses going back several generations, founded in Egypt some one hundred years ago and since then developed outside Egypt post the Nasser period.' Although Plender cast doubt upon MacArthur's assurances, and especially upon the source of the funds, the cumulative effect of interview and press coverage on the OFT's officials inspired new confidence in the Fayeds and hardened suspicions about Rowland's motives. 'The interview,' MacArthur would subsequently admit, 'was a nightmare. I had no experience.'

Over that weekend, the most important newspaper for Rowland was the *Observer*. No one else in London would unquestioningly print his version, especially about the Fayeds. Talking to Terry Robinson, Melvyn Marckus had followed developments throughout the week. On Friday, he went to Cheapside to meet Rowland and Marwan. Only months later did Marckus and other journalists on the newspaper understand the magnitude of repercussions of that afternoon's events. Regardless of his own objectivity, Marckus appeared to become Lonrho's mouthpiece in the Harrods' battle and one of the eventual casualties was the collapse of the *Observer*'s credibility.

In Rowland's office, the Egyptian briefed Marckus about the Fayeds' real background and arranged for Marckus to speak on the telephone with Khashoggi for confirmation. At the end of the briefing, Marckus was stunned by the allegations that the Fayeds had lied.

Back at the *Observer*, Marckus, reciting the revelations, understood the conflicting pressure. 'All eyes are on you tonight, Marckus,' quipped a colleague unhelpfully. On Saturday, Marckus typed out his story which, as the morning passed, was read on the telephone page by page to Rowland by Anthony Howard, the acting editor that weekend. By the end of his writing, Marckus realised that Rowland was not pleased. Messages passed back by Howard queried why nine-tenths of the details supplied by Marwan and Khashoggi about the Fayeds had not been included. Rowland, it seemed, could not understand why his desires were not being met.

Trelford had absented himself that weekend from protecting his newspaper's independence and Howard was, Marckus would later complain, reflecting the office's poisonous partition, virtually 'saluting at his desk when Tiny rang', an allegation which Howard denies. Marckus's judgment was to follow the proprietor's arguments up to a point. All mention of the Fayeds' impoverished childhood in Egypt and Khashoggi's other material was excluded. 'I didn't know if Marwan was telling the truth,' explained Marckus to the subsequent inquiry, 'And I didn't realise that the credibility problem would last two years.'

In the published article headlined, 'The Bloody Harrods Battle', Marckus echoed Rowland's arguments and complaints about 'the bloodiest corporate war ever waged in the United Kingdom'. According to Marckus, Rowland feared that the Fayeds would launch a dawn raid for shares on the following Monday morning and he ruled out as 'absolute nonsense' a possible Lonrho raid. Instead, Rowland consoled himself that the government, impressed by his information about the Fayeds' links to the Sultan, would decide the outcome of the battle by referring the bid to the Monopolies Commission.

On Monday morning, fearing that the government might believe Rowland's allegations about his background and his lack of wealth, Mohamed Fayed issued a writ alleging defamation. Marckus, who believed his article to be 'objective' was, he told colleagues, 'surprised, astonished and furious. It's a gagging writ'. Having attempted to keep some distance from Rowland, Marckus was inspired by Fayed's writ to search for real truth and 'tended to drive the *Observer* somewhat closer to Rowland'.

As Rowland anticipated, at 8 o'clock on Monday morning, while the Fayeds sat in 60 Park Lane, brokers employed by Grieveson Grant began offering £4 for each House of Fraser share. There were no sellers. Everyone was holding back in the expectation that Lonrho would be making a rival bid and would force the price up. Fayed continued working with MacArthur and Edward Walker-Arnott, a senior partner at Herbert Smith, Fayeds' solicitors, to prepare their submission later that day to the Office of Fair Trading.

Early that morning, a letter from Rowland was hand delivered to Tebbit. Over seven pages, Rowland recounted his version of the Fayeds' impoverished background, their chequered career including allegations of corrupt deals with the notorious Papa Doc in Haiti, and an analysis of their wealth which he estimated to be a maximum of $150 million: 'Fortunes of the scale necessary to fund this bid . . . cannot be built up and maintained without public awareness.' Rowland urged that since the Fayeds did not possess one billion pounds, which was more than the value of British Airways, and the source was clearly the Sultan, 'it is the duty of the Secretary of State to intervene and prevent a prospective fraud.'

Ordinarily Tebbit would have referred the letter to his staff and especially Borrie, but over the weekend Du Cann had telephoned several times encouraging his colleague to take a personal interest. Tebbit was not as rigid as Borrie who, also that morning, received a letter from Du Cann. Lonrho's chairman asked that his company be immediately released from its undertakings not to buy more than 29 per cent of House of Fraser. Borrie did not reply. The minister however was minded to intervene if there was a fraud but not for other reasons. He would await the results of that day's meetings.

During those early hours, Rowland was pondering his reaction to the £4 offers on the stock exchange. The opinion from his fellow directors and brokers, echoing his own, was the certainty of a reference of Fayed's bid to the Commission. 'Unless you're prepared to top the Fayed bid, sell your shares and wait for the share price to crash with the reference,' was the advice which Greenway gave to Rowland. 'It's cast iron.' Their strategy was clear. When the Fayeds' bid was referred and the share price crashed, Lonrho would enter the market.

In Rowland's office, Terry Robinson agreed, although he would deny that they were certain about the identity of the buyer: 'There wasn't a name on the board and we had no merchant bank or broker giving us inside information.' Everyone around Rowland was convinced that, even if the Fayeds bought the shares, Le Quesne would reject the Egyptian's bid: 'They can't afford the holding costs for long,' everyone chimed to Rowland's tune. By selling, Lonrho would earn a further £16 million profit.

Just before midday, Robinson, obeying Rowland, gave the order to sell Lonrho's 6.3 per cent stake. It was the second time Lonrho had sold its shares and signalled to outsiders that it had finally abandoned the quest. But of course, Rowland intended the opposite, although he was blind to the consequences of the confusion he was causing. 'Tiny's a dealer and he's eccentric,' Du Cann judged when he heard the decision. In fact, Rowland was gambling and had broken the professionals' golden rule in the Square Mile: Only bet on certainties. By 1 p.m., the Fayeds owned more than 50 per cent of House of Fraser.

Rowland's thoughts were initially Machiavellian and became conflicting. Lonrho did not have £615 million and more to surpass the Fayeds' bid. Lonrho, he believed, could earn a further profit by selling its stake and buying back later. Although he would make subsequent protests that he was prevented from bidding on Monday 11 March because he was not released from his undertakings by the DTI, his complaints contradicted each other. Sometimes he would claim that he only received clearance when, 'Three hours later [after his second share sale] a junior official of the DTI sent a note uselessly releasing Lonrho from its undertakings not to bid,' while on other occasions, he would claim clearance arrived only on 14 March. In fact, he had received clearance the previous Friday from the Takeover Panel. The 'clearances' issue was significant only because the DTI's refusal formally to withdraw gave the impression that the government was deliberately placing Lonrho at a disadvantage to the Fayeds. That impression gained ground during Monday 11 March.

In mid-morning, Fayed and his advisers arrived at the Office of Fair Trading to meet Elizabeth Llewellyn Smith, the deputy director general. Over the weekend, the quiet, austere official says that she had become slightly sceptical of the Fayeds' claim and had prepared herself to pose critical questions. To satisfy the OFT, her visitors needed to provide assurances that the Fayeds' funds were acquired legally. She would later say that she was specifically not interested in the source of the money but she did want to know whether an unknown third party was involved. Others would say that knowing the money belonged to the Fayeds was 'of central importance . . . [because] the company's future might be uncertain if the unknown principal decided to change his mind'. In other words, to ascertain whether the Fayeds were, for example, a front for the Mafia.

The meeting was chaotic, not least because of Llewellyn Smith's docility and lack of questions. In contrast, her visitors were emphatic. In Fayed's presence, MacArthur repeated his conviction that they possessed assets worth $1.1 billion, 'including the Ritz hotel in Paris'. Stiffly in the course of his interview Walker-Arnott asserted, 'Herbert Smith do not take on cases which do not hold water.' Llewellyn Smith assumed that both MacArthur and Walker-Arnott were uttering those assurances because they had personally questioned and verified what Fayed told them. At no point did either banker or lawyer intimate that they were repeating parrot-like their client's claims without independent verification.

To their good fortune, Llewellyn Smith did not ask to see the accounts of Fayed's company which was buying House of Fraser, or request any proof that the Fayeds were 'leading shipowners in the liner trade', or that they actually 'owned' 75 Rockefeller Plaza, or that they owned banks and oil wells. Since the company was a tax-shell based in Liechtenstein, she might have insisted that its accounts were produced. By nature, she found it more convenient to remain silent and plead that she lacked the means to investigate the Fayeds' claims. Such was the reality of government supervision and regulation at the Office of Fair Trading.

Both City professionals were pleased with their performance and agreed to confirm their assurances in writing. 'We are . . . entirely satisfied . . . as to the accuracy of the instructions given to us by the Al Fayed brothers,' the lawyers would write. Fayed's submission would subsequently be condemned as, 'untrue, incorrect, seriously exaggerated or otherwise misleading'. Walker-Arnott's partner endorsed Fayed's submission.

Llewellyn Smith's slight and unproved doubt that the Fayeds had properly answered Lonrho's allegations was passed to Borrie. Until then, Borrie had contented himself with MacArthur's unsubstantiated two-page assurance sent in November 1984 that Fayed's independent wealth was one billion pounds. Since then, the director general had not sought any independent verification, for in Borrie's opinion, the Fayeds' background was totally irrelevant. As he told Tebbit, 'It's a cash bid and as long as the shareholders receive their money, the OFT has no further interest.' Llewellyn Smith's questions, Borrie felt, were simply to test whether the money was available. The OFT, he insisted, was not a court of morals.

Borrie's attitude to the situation was born of his mistrust of Rowland and his conviction that the allegations about the Fayeds' lack of wealth were untrue. Borrie did not believe that Kleinworts and Herbert Smith could be duped and that Rowland might be telling the truth. Accordingly, he recommended that the Fayeds' bid should not be referred to the Monopolies Commission.

To Borrie's surprise, Tebbit wanted to become personally involved; a mistake, the official believed. Tebbit would later claim that Rowland had misjudged government policy: 'If only Tiny Rowland could have read my mind at the time, he would never have sold out. I didn't care who owned Harrods or House of Fraser – I was only interested in takeovers on competition grounds, and there was no competition element involved.' But, by his actions, the minister effectively lobbied by Du Cann was concerned that he should not become the embarrassed victim of a fraud.

The following morning, 12 March, MacArthur, Professor Smith and the Fayeds were shown into the minister's office. Each of them repeated their assurances of the Fayeds' independent wealth and urged that the bid be allowed. In direct reply to Tebbit's questions, Mohamed Fayed endorsed MacArthur's estimate that his family's shipping interests owned forty liners. In fact, Fayed could be proved to own two cargo vessels.

As the Fayeds were led out through one door, the Lonrho delegation entered from another. Rowland's attitude towards the minister was complicated by his grievance against all Conservative politicians. While the deals proposed by Hanson and Murdoch were never stymied by reference to the Monopolies Commission, Lonrho, which enjoyed no political relationships, was hounded by the Conservative Party. 'Tiny thought it was corrupt and demeaning to pay the Party,' explained Terry Robinson.

Inscrutably, the minister sat listening to Rowland and his advisers arguing that Fayed was not using his own money. At one moment, according to Rowland, Tebbit asked, 'What does it matter who brings in the money, providing it's brought in?' Rowland summarised that attitude as 'Sod off Lonrho'. His evidence, conceded Rowland, might not be sufficient for a court of law but it raised questions which required investigation. Tebbit remained silent.

After the Lonrho delegation departed, Borrie sought to persuade Tebbit that no further inquiry was necessary. The minister however was suspicious. As an unusual precaution, Tebbit telephoned Michael Hawkes, the chairman of Kleinworts. Explicitly, the minister asked the banker whether the government could rely on Kleinworts' assurances about the Fayeds. Hawkes gave that assurance.

During the afternoon, two letters arrived for the minister. One from Rowland contained the address of the Fayeds' home in Alexandria and the location of their father's school. The evidence suggested that the Fayeds were poor, urged Rowland.

The second letter was written by Bernard Sunley, a building contractor in Dubai, who asserted that Fayed had produced 'contracts . . . worth in excess of £400 million' for the company. The circumstances surrounding Sunley's testimonial were suspicious. Among Tebbit's political interests was his own proximity to Britain's construction industry. Among the contributors to Party funds was Fayed. To the prejudiced, the links would seem sufficient to tip the balance.

The discussions which followed over the next twenty-four hours are subject to considerable conjecture and only Thatcher and Tebbit are privy to their content. In Rowland's opinion, the prime minister, mindful of Fayed's importance in the discussions with the Sultan earlier that year, gave a direct order to the secretary of state to clear the bid without a reference. Rowland also believes that Thatcher may have been sufficiently antagonised by the *Observer*'s allegations concerning her son to order Tebbit to ignore the doubts about the source of the Fayeds' wealth. There was one more event that excited Rowland.

Two days after Tebbit's interviews, on 14 March, President Hosni Mubarak of Egypt was invited to dinner at Number 10 Downing Street. One of the guests, sitting next to Carol Thatcher, was Mohamed Fayed. The invitation had been arranged by Gordon Reece, the prime minister's publicity adviser and a tenant of Fayed's in Park Lane. The justification for Fayed's presence was mysterious since he was not a prominent Egyptian. Thatcher would explain to Du Cann that the invitation was at the behest of the Foreign Office, an odd recommendation. Fayed was seen in animated conversation with Mubarak, a man he had never met before. In Rowland's opinion, Thatcher, having seen Fayed close to both the Sultan and the president, would have been persuaded to discriminate against Lonrho. These were the seeds of Rowland's conspiracy theory.

Later that day, Tebbit announced that the Fayed bid would not be referred to the Monopolies Commission. The battle for the House of Fraser seemed to be over. The Fayeds had achieved in ten days what had eluded Rowland for seven years. In private, Fayed boasted, 'The British government, they gave me House of Fraser in only ten days because they know who is Mohamed Fayed.' In public, Fayed said, 'I love Britain. I love your traditions and your history. And I like the way you do business. Ethics and morals count in Britain like nowhere else in the world.' Fayed even added that he had always wanted to own Harrods. Throughout his life, Rowland had never said a good word for Britain. On the contrary, he was contemptuous.

Tebbit's statement contained a hostage to fortune: 'In considering whether to make a reference . . . he took into account the statements made and assurances given by the Al Fayed family about the offer and their intentions with regard to the House of Fraser [and] the support given to those statements and assurances by Kleinwort Benson.' The politician had admitted that the source of Fayed's wealth was material.

In Cheapside, Rowland was stunned. 'I've been cheated by a crook,' he told his directors. 'I don't even want House of Fraser any more. I don't want someone else's mistress. I just want justice.' In fact, he wanted revenge. He declared war against Tebbit, Borrie and then against Thatcher. Engulfed by anger, he diverted against his enemies the energy which had transformed Lonrho's turnover in fifteen years from £1 million to £2.5 billion.

Twelve
War

Rowland's sparsely furnished office became a bunker; its inhabitant was plunged into a counter-offensive. Jettisoning common sense, Lonrho's chief executive embarked upon a hunt which was frenetic, erratic, costly and occasionally illegal. His objective was to prove a conspiracy: that Mohamed Fayed, lying about his past, had covertly used £615 million from the Sultan's fortune to buy House of Fraser with the collusion of Thatcher, Tebbit, their stooges and paymasters.

The goal was to persuade the government of the deception and that Fayed's takeover of House of Fraser should be referred back to the Monopolies Commission who could recommend a divestment order. The decision to make a reference could be taken only by the secretary of state for industry who in March 1985 was Norman Tebbit.

Rowland's crusade began as a propaganda war waged through an avalanche of accusatory letters and glossy brochures dispatched to a swelling mailing list; by personal visits to Gordon Borrie, politicians and successive secretaries of state; and in ceaseless articles published in the *Observer*.

Initially, Rowland had one independent ally in his quest. In May 1985, the *Financial Times* published an article doubting the Fayeds' claim of huge wealth. Written by Duncan Campbell-Smith, it was based on independent research. John MacArthur threatened a writ unless the newspaper published a retraction. 'We apologise for any embarrassment . . .' grovelled Geoffrey Owen, the newspaper's editor, who angered Campbell-Smith by endorsing all Fayed's claims about the source of his wealth.

Independent journalistic investigation into the Fayeds ceased. The prevailing sentiment against Rowland dictated that no other newspaper editor was prepared to consider his grievances sympathetically. Anyone daring to raise questions understood that the automatic response was a writ and wearisome expenses. Accepting Fayed's version, spooned out by the smooth Brian Basham with champagne at Harry's Bar or the Savoy Grill, was more palatable than the abrupt discourtesies hurled by Paul Spicer.

Effectively, the City, Westminster, Whitehall and Fleet Street found it more convenient to believe Mohamed Fayed and distrust Rowland. Their substantive motives were not merely antipathy towards the protagonist but an overriding sentiment that Rowland's complaint was unimportant. Rowland had twice willingly sold the shares to Fayed and the source of the Egyptian's money, most argued, was not an issue of principle considering that it merely concerned the ownership of shops. If Fayed was a liar, then he was no different from Rowland. The public, like their politicians and officials, felt that Rowland and Fayed deserved each other: a plague on both their houses. Alone, Rowland was committed to reverse the tide.

From the bunker in Cheapside, the occupant dispatched a letter to Tebbit which was a foretaste of unconditional war. Lonrho's shareholders, wrote Rowland, were entitled to know why Fayed's assurances were 'acceptable when those from Lonrho were not. . . Only the frankest explanation of the whole circumstances can satisfy us and it is no hardship for the same Civil Service who caused us months and years of delay, research and expenses to now spend some time explaining why the shelf bid from the Fayed brothers was so rapidly acceptable.' Ominously Rowland concluded, 'It will never be possible for our company to forgive and forget.' The letter was published on 2 June in the *Observer*.

The Rubicon at the *Observer* had been breached. Ever since the publication of his sympathetic article on 10 March, Melvyn Marckus had shifted closer towards Lonrho, partially the result of Fayed's writ which had impelled Marckus's dependence upon Lonrho for documents and evidence to formulate a defence.

The writ had also motivated Marckus to deploy his two best investigative journalists, Michael Gillard and Lorana Sullivan, to check Mohamed Fayed's wealth. 'It took Sullivan just a couple of days at Lloyds Registry of Shipping to prove that Fayed's claims to own a fleet of forty ships was untrue,' he told critical colleagues. Like most journalists, Marckus was intrigued by apparent dishonesty. But it was the telephone calls from Terry Robinson, urging Marckus to publicise Rowland's complaint, that finally entrapped and elevated the business editor to the forefront of the war against the government.

The first new evidence was collected by Ashraf Marwan. In Cairo, he obtained Mohamed Fayed's birth certificate which undermined the Egyptian's claims to a privileged childhood. A translator, supplied by Lonrho, helped the Business Section publish the details which, to Rowland's expressed disappointment, were not featured prominently. Fayed retorted that the certificate was a forgery, easily obtained by a former intelligence officer.

The next allegation was more substantive and sensational. A letter, supplied by Rowland, described by Marckus as 'the Sultan's power of attorney to Fayed', was the basis of successive articles between June and August 1985. The letter suggested that in August 1984, the Sultan of Brunei had advanced $1.5 billion to Fayed of which, in June 1985, $200 million was still outstanding. The money, according to Marckus, had been channelled through two Liechtenstein bank accounts. A letter with a similar explanation was also submitted in personal missives from Rowland to Thatcher, Tebbit, the Governor of the Bank of England, and the chairmen of the Stock Exchange and Takeover Panel.

The Sultan's reaction was negative. In an article in the *Sunday Telegraph* by Peregrine Worsthorne, a sympathiser of the Fayeds, the Sultan categorically denied that he had advanced the money to Fayed for the House of Fraser.

Rowland's setback was compounded. Bowing to his substantial pressure, Llewellyn Smith had asked Michael Hawkes at Kleinworts for an explicit reassurance that the Fayeds had used their own money, earned by their own commercial activities, to buy House of Fraser. Contemporaneous with the *Sunday Telegraph*'s article, Hawkes submitted to Llewellyn Smith a letter signed by the Sultan and supplied by Fayed, which denied that he was the source of the funds. The power of attorney, suggested Hawkes, was a forgery. Unfortunately for Rowland, the banker was correct. The credibility of the *Observer*, the journalist and Rowland began to slide as they discovered that their adversary was not a simpleton.

Desperate to find evidence establishing Fayed's source of money, in early September Marwan contacted David Coghlan, an expert in electronic surveillance. In Marwan's office, Coghlan was asked whether he could tap two telephones in Fayed's Park Lane home. In the course of their conversation, Marwan apparently telephoned Rowland three times to define their requirements. Coghlan undertook to examine the technical feasibility.

In September, Marwan reported to Rowland that he had dis-covered the most promising source of information in New York. Flying by Concorde, they were heading for the home of Adnan Khashoggi, a luxurious duplex apartment in Olympic Tower on Fifth Avenue. The Saudi's other guests were the Swami and his fellow guru whose assistance Fayed had sought some years ear-lier. By 1985, the Swami had, according to photographs, injected himself into the lives of Elizabeth Taylor, Richard Nixon, Imelda Marcos and other personalities who sought spiritual advice.

High above Manhattan's streets, the Swami revealed to Rowland that he possessed a tape-recorded conversation of himself and Mohamed Fayed which had occurred on 6 and 7 June 1985 when the two had met at 1 Carlos Place in London. The subject was the repayment of Fayed's debts to the Sultan. The conversation, said the Swami, was taped to convince the Sultan of Fayed's dishonesty and included an admission that the Sultan's money bought House of Fraser. Rowland's excitement was palpable.

At Khashoggi's invitation, the two men and a posse of assistants flew in the Saudi's DC-8, [housing four bedrooms and three bathrooms] to Toronto, Canada, to listen to the tapes. In Miller Gormley's house, Rowland, Marwan and Khashoggi listened intently but could understand only parts of the conver-sation. It seemed to be Fayed's voice but the quality was poor and some of their discussion was in Hindi. But, reassured by the Swami that Fayed did admit the source of the money, Rowland agreed to buy the tapes. The price, $2 million, was to be paid on 7 October on board Khashoggi's yacht, *Nabila*, in Antibes.

Rowland arrived with a banker's draft for the Swami drawn on Lonrho's account. The group posed for photographs. Everyone appeared amused. Khashoggi grinned because the guru had entrusted Can$86 million to his care for investment. Rowland was smiling because he thought that his hunt was completed. The Swami was laughing because Rowland had promised a further $3 million for documents which incriminated the Fayeds.

Back in London, Marwan asked Coghlan, the electronics expert, whether he could enhance the tapes' sound. Coghlan could not oblige but was instructed to start tapping the Fayeds' telephone lines.

Over the following weeks, Rowland spent hours deciphering his $2 million investment. One admission was audible. Fayed confessed to the Swami that his life was no longer peaceful and private. Rowland's campaign had forced him to use bodyguards, surround his home with barbed wire and drive in bullet-proof cars. With greater difficulty, Rowland believed that he could discern Fayed claiming to have a power of attorney from the Sultan for $10 billion: 'Everything I have is his.' Fayed also apparently boasted that his substantial influence with the British government had delivered Harrods, 'in ten days, because they know who is Mohamed Fayed for twenty-five years.' But Rowland searched in frustration to find the single sentence where Fayed precisely admitted that he had used the Sultan's money to buy House of Fraser. Instead of abandoning the charade of possessing the evidence, he continued to insist upon its existence.

Rowland's allegations, both in the *Observer* and in his letters, were neither showing progress nor getting reaction. His most important target was Gordon Borrie whom he was urging to investigate how the Fayeds had amassed their one-billion-pound fortune. Borrie, who had refused to conduct an inquiry before the bid and had hoped that Rowland would drop the affair, was naturally loath to undertake any action in the aftermath.

To provoke the official, on 11 October, Rowland visited

the Office of Fair Trading. Darkly, Rowland hinted that he possessed new evidence proving that Fayed had bought House of Fraser with a power of attorney for $1.5 billion provided by the Sultan. Inevitably, Borrie asked for the proof. Instead of revealing the existence of the tapes, Rowland mumbled and then raged: 'It's the OFT's duty to collect evidence, not mine. You made no checks before the Fayeds bought House of Fraser and you still refuse to make them. I'm not giving you my evidence. I don't trust you.' This was the excuse which Borrie desired. Protesting that his integrity had been impugned, Borrie scorned his persecutor: 'If you don't trust me, it's a waste of time carrying on. You had better leave.' The meeting was terminated. The rebel's unrepentant aggression was relieved, but the cause was deformed.

The theory of a conspiracy had taken a firm hold. In a letter to Borrie, Rowland threatened: 'My company intends to pursue a fair outcome, and to discover whether anyone, including yourself and those above you, acted with improper motives. As long as this remains undone, the title of your office, which I personally think you have disgraced, is a mockery.'

A copy was sent to Margaret Thatcher with a covering note predicting that allowing Fayed's takeover 'will prove to be a scandalous blot on your government's stewardship of the Department of Trade'.

A reflection of Rowland's anger glinted in New York. Freddie Laker, whom Rowland had embraced in February 1982 as a fellow victim and fellow rebel of the Establishment when the 'Skytrain' collapsed because of unfair pricing by British airlines, was close to finalising his litigation against British Airways for its participation in a cartel. For the British government, the settlement was a critical precursor to publication of the prospectus to privatise the airline, an important political milestone.

To annoy the government, Lonrho filed a suit in New York claiming $327 million damages incurred in its joint venture, the People's Airline, with Laker. Since that venture had been a twenty-four-hour hype in the aftermath of Laker's collapse and Rowland's unfulfilled public promise to compensate all Laker ticket holders, the writ in New York bore no chance of success.

But the irritation caused was considerable, especially to Nicholas Ridley, the minister of transport.

The quantum of aggravation he could provoke was Rowland's sole measure of his success. Tebbit had been replaced by Leon Brittan, the sixth secretary of state at the DTI since 1979. The new minister, Rowland hoped, would be more amenable to righting the injustice he had suffered. His lack of subtlety was impaled for all to see on his three-pronged assault of the DTI minister.

Sir Edward Du Cann, knighted during 1985, was calling in all his political favours on Lonrho's behalf. Despite his strained relations with Thatcher, he still sought the help of ministers and backbenchers by flourishing evidence to prove Lonrho's case. Mohamed Fayed's Swiss bank accounts, he alleged, revealed the sudden influx of funds from the Sultan. But when Elizabeth Llewellyn Smith requested more background material to substantiate the allegation, the politician could not oblige. Rowland never provided any proof that Fayed had used the Sultan's money.

Rowland's second approach was a letter to Leon Brittan alleging that Fayed was 'disgustingly anti-semitic'. Again, no evidence was provided. Three days later, Brittan told Rowland that Borrie would neither investigate the Fayeds nor reconsider the DTI's approval of the take over. 'One final point,' concluded Brittan, 'I would simply say that Sir Gordon Borrie enjoys my complete confidence.'

The campaign had reached an *impasse*. Coghlan's taps of Fayed's telephones had produced eighteen hours of irrelevant conversations. Rowland retained Carrattu International, private investigators, to produce material about the Fayeds, but in the meantime only a third method of attack remained, through the *Observer*.

Among City editors, Marckus was isolated. By November, he had written repeated accounts of Fayed's dishonesty which attracted writs but no other reaction. While he travelled to the Gulf, Gillard had collected evidence about Fayed's activities in Haiti, similar to that presented earlier by Rowland to Borrie, which alleged that in 1965, posing as Sheikh Mohamed Fayed, the Egyptian had defrauded Papa Doc's government and absconded with $100,000 belonging to the harbour authority. The allegation was strongly denied by the Fayeds, claiming that the evidence was unreliable.

In a melodramatic folly encouraged by Cheapside, Marckus published 'An open letter to Leon' in which, stressing his independence from Lonrho, he publicly offered to resign if the Fayeds had used their own money. 'I would like to think,' he concluded, 'that, should you be proved wrong, you would consider the same action.' The article, provoking mirth and predictable accusations of bias, had received Trelford's encouragement.

Ever since their reconciliation in 1984, the editor's relationship with Rowland had become closer. Although Trelford portrayed himself as an agile-minded operator boxing clever with Rowland to protect the newspaper from the proprietor's interference, his authentic attitude was revealed in a review of Richard Hall's biography called *My Life with Tiny*. Amid his general disparagement, Trelford commented: 'There is no great mystery about Tiny's background. He had the misfortune to be half-German and half-English at the time when the two countries were going to war. He and his parents chose England; his brother chose Germany. Had he been a Jewish refugee from Hitler, people would not think his origins as suspicious and want to keep raking them over.' Rowland, of course, had never decried his background or his plight. His concealment and distortion had been born of expedience and not lament. Inadvertently, Trelford had joined the chorus and was gradually espousing a policy of appeasement.

Just before Christmas 1985, Rowland summoned his editor. There was now certainty within Cheapside that the conspiracy against Lonrho was masterminded by the prime minister herself. The link with Fayed, Rowland believed, was Mark Thatcher. Trelford was shown letters sent by Rowland to Tebbit and Margaret Thatcher. Both letters emotionally alleged there was proof that Mark Thatcher had flown with Mohamed Fayed in a private Gulfstream jet to Brunei on 24 October 1984 and that the trip was linked with favoured treatment afforded to the Fayeds at Lonrho's expense. 'Why have you had anything whatsoever to do with Mohamed Fayed?'

demanded Rowland from the prime minister who deigned not to explain.

Rowland counselled his editor to consider Mark Thatcher's flight to Brunei in the context of other circumstances. In January 1985, Fayed was present when the Sultan visited 10 Downing Street; in March 1985, Fayed sat next to Carol Thatcher at an official lunch for President Mubarak; and in April 1985, Mrs Thatcher, in a visit arranged by Fayed, met the Sultan of Brunei and received a gold bracelet studded with diamonds and rubies. Now, Mark Thatcher, according to Rowland, 'was involved in a multimillion-pound building contract in Brunei' and Thatcher's and Fayed's 'names appeared on the Royal Guest Immigration Register'. It was not coincidental, summarised Rowland, that Tebbit had agreed to prolong the Monopolies Commission investigation into Lonrho just weeks after Mark Thatcher's trip to Brunei and had approved the Fayeds' bid for House of Fraser in March 1985.

Although Trelford confided to Anthony Howard that he was 'under pressure from Tiny' to publish the letters as a major story, his own behaviour acknowledged that he was compromising the *Observer*'s credibility, a consequence of the newspaper's losses.

In an unusual departure, Trelford decided not to involve any staff other than Marckus. Hints of Trelford's intentions began to leak late on Friday afternoon, 10 January. David Leigh, the *Observer*'s investigative reporter who had written the earlier allegations about Mark Thatcher, was particularly interested and, on Saturday morning, saw Trelford's draft. Alarmed, he approached Magnus Linklater, the managing editor of news.

'The Mark Thatcher piece is in my view journalistically unacceptable. It reads as though not only the information within it, but also the very wording, has been dictated by the proprietor.' Leigh warned that if they published it, Rowland would 'not achieve the results he wishes' and that the *Observer*'s reputation 'will be seriously, perhaps terminally damaged'.

Leigh criticised the failure to check, in the normal way, the allegations, especially with Rowland's sources. Unless that was done, urged Leigh, there was no protection 'from the charge that we were being used'. Linklater agreed. 'The investigation into Mark Thatcher had ceased to be purely journalistic but had been sucked into Rowland's campaign against the Fayeds. The story had gone off the rails. Donald, in my view, was over-influenced by Rowland and the apparent army of high-powered and glamorous contacts he provided.'

By then, outside in the street, a rumoured convoy of Rolls Royces and other limousines had gathered. Their passengers, including Rowland and Khashoggi, were said to be in the fourth-floor boardroom reviewing Trelford's work. Within the building, journalists were anxiously discussing how their integrity would be compromised. 'Unless we check, how do we know that Mark Thatcher wasn't in the Houston Astradome on the day in question?' asked Leigh. 'By lunchtime,' recorded Dick Hall in his diary, 'the newsroom was in ferment with people standing around in groups asking what could be done.'

Both Linklater and Howard complained to Trelford that the article was based on insufficient research and seemed oddly contradictory. Trelford had repeated verbatim Rowland's briefing and even added that the Thatcher–Fayed private visit to Brunei, 'has also been confirmed to the *Observer* by a senior official of the Brunei government'. But curiously, despite Fayed's alleged importance in Brunei, Trelford added that Thatcher had been introduced to the Sultan 'by a letter from the finance minister of Oman'. With Fayed's presence that would hardly have been necessary but it did, *post hoc*, justify the newspaper's earlier allegations against Thatcher's connections with the Gulf State.

Trelford waved aside his journalists' complaints as a 'demarcation dispute' but, to suppress the discontent, issued a defensive memorandum accepting Rowland's version of the House of Fraser affair: 'I happen to think he is right. . . Evidence was made available to me as Editor which would not have been made so available to any other reporter.' Lonrho's involvement, he wrote, could not be muted. 'We are a Lonrho-owned paper and everybody knows that. . . I am satisfied that Mark Thatcher's involvement with Brunei is demonstrably true.' With a rhetorical flourish his memorandum concluded, 'You may imagine that all the ethical and other considerations that are suddenly striking you have been with me for some time – and having considered them all very carefully, I am sure that it is in the *Observer*'s best interests to publish and be damned.'

Trelford's courage was nevertheless tempered when credit for the article, under the headline, 'Mark Thatcher's mystery trip to see Sultan', was bestowed upon an anonymous 'staff reporter'. Quoting the 'Jewish Press' in New York, Trelford had even added that Fayed was anti-semitic.

As predicted, Trelford's article did not spark outrage against the Thatchers, but backfired against Rowland and his abuse of the newspaper. The Sultan denied meeting Mark Thatcher; Fayed issued a writ; and the *Sunday Times* published a list of mistakes. Dissatisfied but resolute, Rowland confided to Anthony Howard, 'So far as I'm concerned, Mrs Thatcher and her son should both be in the dock at the Old Bailey.' The Thatchers were to be attacked with impunity regardless of the consequences to the *Observer*.

In the second week of May 1986, Rowland again invited Trelford to lunch. His other guests at Claridges were Khashoggi and the Swami, who was introduced to Trelford as a man who 'advises' kings, presidents and even Mrs Thatcher. Since their first meeting, Rowland had met the Swami on Khashoggi's yacht and at his homes in Spain and France. His reliance upon the Swami was, unknown to Trelford, conditional. Questioned about the guru in that period by an Indian journalist, Rowland commented, 'If people are foolish enough to allow themselves to be exploited, if people can't see through this badmash, then it's unfortunate. But as far as I'm concerned he has not exploited me. I'm old and experienced enough to take care of myself. But I must confess that I was not taken in by the Swami . . . for even one second.'

Yet the Swami was presented to Trelford as reliable. Rowland might have suspected the contrary but concealed his conjecture as he handed to Trelford proof that the Thatchers and Fayed were involved in a conspiracy.

The proof was an affidavit, apparently signed by the permanent secretary at the Brunei ministry of home affairs, which attested that Thatcher had visited Brunei with Fayed. The Swami, who obtained the document, confirmed to Trelford that the journey to Brunei did occur. In return for that evidence, Rowland had paid the Swami, in Khashoggi's presence, a further $3 million. In total, the Swami had now received $5 million from Rowland.

Confident of the document's authenticity but again writing in the guise of a 'staff reporter', Trelford published an 'exclusive' story under the headline, 'Mark Thatcher and guru clues to Harrods deal'. Trelford claimed there were three witnesses aware of the visit. Namely, the Brunei permanent secretary, a Brunei newspaper editor and the Swami.

The reckoning was swift. Fayed's lawyers flew to Brunei and India. Sworn affidavits from each of Trelford's witnesses, including the permanent secretary, testified that the *Observer*'s evidence was forged. 'The Certificate relating to an alleged visit of Mr M Thatcher . . . is an outrageous forgery. . . It is an absolute lie to suggest that I am the author of that document,' swore the Brunei permanent secretary. Trelford, who had apparently ignored the spelling mistakes, change of typeface in mid-paragraph and unusually illiterate language in the document, had been duped.

In July 1986, the *Observer*'s solicitors admitted that they lacked the evidence to prove that Mark Thatcher had ever met Fayed or travelled with Fayed to Brunei. Three months later, Lonrho demanded the repayment of $3 million from Khashoggi because 'value has not been received by Lonrho in the said transaction', and then sued for the return of $5 million from the Swami for the failure to deliver his promises. Finally, the *Observer*'s allegations of Fayed's anti-semitism, quoting a report in the Jewish Press in New York, were proven to have been planted by a friend of Rowland's. The *Observer* apologised.

Lonrho's nonchalance towards the *Observer*'s quandary raised a perennial question about the company's integrity: could it bribe, or invest in people, and remain honest within?

Inside Cheapside, there was no moral force to restrain Rowland. Indeed, regarding the other directors, he noted that they lacked his winning combination of charm, work ethic and ruthlessness. He concluded that they could not be trusted, especially for the succession, but he never thought twice about the fact that each had been personally selected by himself.

The same weaknesses which Rowland castigated among ministers and officials were present in his own boardroom. His personal success had been built on the shrewd exploitation of weaknesses but he was blind to the dangers which his activities caused.

Rowland's disdain for people and institutions was reflected by his visit a few weeks later to Colonel Gadaffi. It was shortly after the American bombing of Tripoli on 15 April and Rowland hoped to demonstrate his reliability as a friend to the only Arab with whom he still enjoyed any relationship. The punishment for Libya's patronage of terrorism and the threat of an embargo on American oil companies operating in Libya proved to Rowland that both he and Gadaffi were victims of the same enemy – contemptible hypocrites who enunciated a perverted morality to justify any deed. After uttering condolences and inquiring about the chance of taking over American oil interests should President Reagan's embargo be enforced, he flew south into Africa where he was idolised, not treated as a pariah.

When his mood eventually switched from anger to depression, Rowland resorted to more than symbolic gestures to express the hurt he felt he had received at the unjust hands of the British. Believing Lonrho's opportunities in Britain were doomed he decided the company should henceforth invest only abroad. In particular, in Germany, America and South Africa. Over the next four years, he directed Lonrho's profits and loans into an oil and gas joint venture with Bob Anderson, late of ARCO, into Ruhrglass, Krupp-Lonrho and apartment blocks in Germany; and into the further development of Western Platinum. During the Eighties, Lonrho invested about £1 billion. Just under half was spent in the aftermath of the House of Fraser fiasco. Nearly all was invested abroad based upon strategy coloured by anger rather than reason.

Hondo Oil & Gas, managed by Anderson and his son, was beyond any control by Lonrho and never fulfilled its expectations. The blocks of apartments in Germany were not an investment which could effectively be managed by an industrial conglomerate in Britain, while Western Platinum, the jewel in Lonrho's crown, absorbed more money than Lonrho could afford. Buffeted by the City's suspicions both of his accounts and of his crusade against the government, he was reverting to his image of 1973 – a maverick who could not raise money through a rights issue of Lonrho shares.

His reputation as an amoral, discreet individualist acted as a magnet to those seeking special favours, among them Adnan Khashoggi whose fortunes had dwindled as demand for his services failed to match his prolific expenditure. Having provided help for Rowland in the Fayed battle, Khashoggi sought a favour in return.

On Saturday 3 May 1986, Khashoggi led a strange delegation to meet Rowland at Crockfords, the gambling club. With the Saudi were Manucher Ghorbanifar, an Iranian who sought to emulate Khashoggi as an intermediary, arms dealer and intelligence source, and Amiram Nir, an adviser to the Israeli prime minister on counter-terrorism. The three men were immersed in a deal to sell weapons to Iran in exchange for the release of American hostages in Beirut. Their contact in Washington was Oliver North, an army officer directing covert operations in the National Security Council.

The three seated around the table with Rowland were hoping that they would be able, unbeknown to the Americans, to earn extra profits on the deal. Their prerequisite was a $15 million loan and 'some sort of umbrella company' to purchase weapons and spare parts to initiate the exchange. The fee was 7 per cent of the profits. Rowland was asked to provide that loan.

His response gave every impression of caution. Rowland would not want to become involved, he said, with any operation which was not approved by the American government. Nir assured him that the White House and in particular John Poindexter, the National Security Adviser, was involved although the knowledge was restricted to very few people. Rowland asked his visitors for time to consider their proposition.

Rowland's relationship with Khashoggi was warm but wary. The Saudi businessman had spent a large part of his fortune on women in the South of France. Rowland did not approve of vulgar womanising but he was attracted to men with weaknesses, especially if they were casualties of the business world and therefore vulnerable. Acutely, Rowland understood that Khashoggi, like Freddie Laker and Jim Slater, had in his heyday moved in powerful circles and still retained a network of contacts which could be useful to Lonrho.

Hence, the previous September Khashoggi had been introduced in Rome to Samora Machel after the president had enjoyed an audience with the Pope. Khashoggi, said Rowland, would help Mozambique attract Arab investment. Of course, nothing had materialised but both sides were grateful and the Saudi believed he could rely upon Rowland when necessary.

Khashoggi had already used Rowland's services for arms deals with Iran. In August 1985, he had borrowed $7.5 million to finance the purchase of 500 TOW missiles which had been bought from the Israelis and delivered to Tehran. Rowland would deny any knowledge of the deal but he held, as collateral for the loan, Khashoggi's DC-8, his yacht *Nabila* and his New York apartment on Fifth Avenue.

Khashoggi was however convinced when he left Crockfords with Ghorbanifar and Nir that Rowland would co-operate. For some time, Rowland had been interested to break into the lucrative Iranian market. There would be a subsequent meeting at Crockfords with Oliver North and Khashoggi to discuss the delivery of 'clean guns' for Iran through Mozambique. Khashoggi was taken in by Rowland's apparent interest in the discussions. For, increasingly, Rowland was becoming just as interested in diplomacy as in commerce. At sixty-eight he was stimulated by shuttling around Africa to broker political deals while delegating the mundane management of his business. Regularly he would wail to fellow directors, 'I've only got another three years,' revealing his neurotic conviction of a fatal illness and his impatience to establish a historic legacy. Still shunned by the Foreign Office, he found his most important ally in his African vision was the American administration, especially Chester Crocker. Nothing would be more gratifying than providing his services to the Reagan Administration but Khashoggi's involvement dictated caution. Restraining his impulsive interest, Rowland called on Robert Frasure, the officer at the American embassy in London who specialised in Africa. Rowland's 'innocent' check would accelerate the exposure of the plot to a wide audience.

Surprised by Rowland's query, Frasure passed the news to his ambassador, Charles Price. In turn, that same day, Price telephoned Michael Armacost, the under-secretary of state for political affairs who, on 3 May, contacted George Shultz, the secretary of state. Shultz, visiting Tokyo for an economic summit with the president, reportedly 'went bananas'. Until then, the State Department had been excluded from the operation to exchange arms for hostages. Simultaneously, Price also spoke to John Poindexter. Rowland's initiative in London would have profound implications for American politics, but the short reply relayed back to Rowland was to remain uninvolved. According to Shultz, 'I opposed dealing with people such as those identified in the message and said it would harm the President if the activity continued.' His fears were shared by Donald Regan, the president's chief of staff. 'When I heard the name Rowland involved in this,' Regan eventually explained, 'I was really concerned.' Asked whether Rowland was 'synonymous with syndication' Regan agreed that alarm bells [rang] saying, 'if Tiny Rowland is involved, my God, who else is involved?'

But at the time Rowland believed that his caution had been doubly rewarded. Khashoggi had failed to repay his original loan. To recover the money, on 15 January 1987, Khashoggi's DC-8 was grounded in Paris on the orders of a judge acting on Lonrho's request to ensure replayment of $15 million. The Saudi's DC-9, dubbed his 'spare plane', was also impounded and writs were also issued to secure the Manhattan apartment. 'Khashoggi's debt-bubble seems about to burst,' quipped Rowland referring to 'the great unbillionaire. He's a lovable person . . . but Khashoggi's day is past.' The Saudi's spokesman accepted the humiliation with grace: 'Mr Khashoggi still loves Mr Rowland very much. This is a slight hiccup, that's all.' The money would be repaid in kind, including the transfer of Khashoggi's luxury hotel in Kenya's Masai Mara, and the friendship resumed. Big players occasionally forget their anger.

A new twist had by then entered into the battle with the Fayeds. Independently of Lonrho, Peter Wickman, a former

Stern correspondent, had flown to Egypt to research the Fayeds' background. To his surprise, he discovered they had lied about their origins. His report, rejected for publication by Express newspapers, was seized by the *Observer* and published on 15 June 1986. Described in an article headlined 'In search of the fabulous Pharaohs', Wickman's journey through Egypt to find the roots of a rich family unexpectedly climaxed in a 'narrow, dark, unpaved lane' in the slums of Alexandria where the Fayed family was remembered for its poverty and the Fayeds' 'cotton rich' father was renowned for being 'kind to old ladies'.

Wickman was known as a reputable journalist and unlikely to be bribed by Lonrho. For the first time, there was independent corroboration of the allegations against Fayed. The article was distributed by Rowland to every member of parliament with a warning that, failing government action, Lonrho would pursue its case in the courts. Unfortunately for Rowland, his threats did not provoke fear.

Rowland began picking off individual critics, publicising his attacks in more widely circulated letters and brochures. One target in his propaganda avalanche was Eldon Griffiths, a Conservative member of parliament who had complained about Rowland's attacks on the Fayeds and misuse of the *Observer*: 'I had to look up "tergiversation" of course,' commenced Rowland's sarcastic rebuke, 'and found it meant "a turning away from a straight forward action" [*Shorter Oxford*], and was first used in 1570, and is now obsolete. It is a familiar term to you, but I assure you that no one at Lonrho has the faintest idea what it is; or how to practise it. I looked in the *Oxford Etymological Dictionary* as well and it was listed below "teredo", described as a "boring mollusc".' Financial journalists would also be targeted if Rowland judged that they were serving as Fayed's mouthpiece.

Brian Basham had escalated his entertainment of City editors to nights at the Ritz hotel in Paris. The influence of the generosity was questionable since those invited were already committed against Rowland, but even the suggestion that journalists could be bribed by hospitality paradoxically offended Rowland's sense of decency.

His fury was unleashed against the *Sunday Times* in particular: 'It is wrong to allow your Deputy Editor Ivan Fallon,' Rowland wrote to the editor, 'to repeatedly use your columns to butter the Fayeds up.' In the case of Kenneth Fleet, the City editor of *The Times* and a consistent critic since 1973, Rowland complained about his apparent support for the MP Peter Horden's promotion of the Fayeds: 'Please don't feel that you have put me to any trouble in writing to you. I am very happy to explain it as many times as are needed. Meantime, keep taking your anti-pomposity pills at least three times a day and always take a pinch of salt before you listen to Peter Horden.'

Newspapers, as Rowland knew so well, were vehicles of influence. Reading his arguments about the Fayeds printed verbatim in the *Observer* might not have convinced him that whatever was read was believed but seeing his unadulterated opinions in print calmed his anger. Owning another newspaper, he calculated, would reinforce the armoury and since the *Observer* had finally, albeit temporarily, produced a profit, of £1.2 million, he convinced himself that he had mastered the art of newspaper management.

In summer 1986, the newly launched *Today*, Britain's first colour newspaper, was struggling for survival. Eddie Shah, its founding owner and a folk hero among Conservatives for revolutionising newspaper production, had lost £11 million within the first three months. Shah's management was chaotic and, bereft of a solution, he was searching for partners. The proposition seemed ideal to Rowland. The negotiations were delegated to Terry Robinson who had become the only Lonrho director occasionally willing to tell Rowland unpalatable truths.

During a conversation at the Grosvenor House with Shah, Robinson assessed that the newspaper's monthly losses were £1 million. Thirty minutes after their meeting, Rowland offered to buy 35 per cent of the newspaper with Shah retaining the majority holding and remaining as chairman. 'I back people and I back ideas,' said Rowland, 'and I believe you will make it work.' Shah was delighted. 'I did not believe in Father Christmas until today,' he would say. Under the terms, Lonrho would pay £10 million for its stake and invest another £14 million cash in the newspaper.

That was the first mistake. The purchase should have been for shares, not cash. The second mistake was Robinson's underestimation of the chaos. The monthly losses were £3 million.

Costs were cut and Shah removed from the management, increasing Lonrho's stake to 90 per cent. In an attempt to find a party which would support Lonrho's battle with the government, Rowland agreed that the newspaper would be relaunched supporting the Social Democrat-Liberal Alliance. David Owen, leader of the SDP, was lured into reconciliation with Rowland, with the promise of Lonrho's financial support in the forthcoming general election.

Gradually within Whitehall and Westminster the realisation dawned that Rowland intended to sustain his criticism until the single question was answered: how did the Fayeds amass their fortune? His relentless demand for investigation was resisted until the unexpected configuration of three events at end of 1986.

Firstly, Leon Brittan, an implacable opponent, resigned amid a political maelstrom which unsettled the government. He was succeeded by Paul Channon, the sixth and weakest secretary of state for the DTI since 1979.

Secondly, there was a sudden rash of financial scandals. The unexpected arrest in New York of Ivan Boesky, the king of the arbitrageurs, had sparked an investigation into the Guinness takeover of Distillers. Separately, fraud was suspected in the stock market launch of Blue Arrow, an employment agency. DTI inspectors were appointed to inquire into both, suggesting that the City was inadequately regulated and that among other possible culprits were the Fayeds.

Thirdly, Rowland's lobbying, supported by a handful of sympathetic MPs, persuaded Sir Brian Hayes, the DTI's permanent secretary, to by-pass Gordon Borrie and summon Michael Hawkes. The Kleinworts banker was pointedly asked to list the independent sources for his assurance to Tebbit about the Fayeds' wealth. Hawkes admitted that he had relied solely upon a telex from a Swiss bank and the Sultan's denial on 23 October 1985 of any involvement in the House of Fraser purchase.

Hawkes's confession was unfortunate and unsettling. While

some DTI officials like Borrie adamantly urged that the source of the Fayeds' wealth was irrelevant since the shareholders had received the cash offered, others were sensitive to the accusation that Mohamed Fayed's alleged activities in Haiti raised the possibility of other dishonesties. But in common, all the DTI officials were loath to take any initiative which would disturb the status quo. Repeated ministerial changes had, even at the highest level, left a tidemark of complacency among officials with respect to their responsibilities for supervising Britain's corporate activities. Their consistent preference had become inactivity. They would be denied that choice by Rowland.

News of Hawkes's unsatisfactory reply leaked. To Rowland, it confirmed the conspiracy: Fayed had hired Gordon Reece to manoeuvre an invitation to Mubarak's dinner in Downing Street where he had impressed himself upon Thatcher, who in turn had ordered Tebbit to permit the takeover without any investigation.

His hypothesis was supported by Du Cann who was offended that after years of service to the Party his old colleagues ignored his pleas. 'I find it hateful and hurtful,' he told friends. 'I can't understand why they don't listen to me.' The only explanation, Du Cann speculated was 'Orders of State' – Thatcher and Tebbit had conspired.

Only a politician, Rowland knew, could overrule Borrie's negative approach. Writing to Channon, he urged that there were grounds for an investigation because the prime minister and Tebbit had 'flung aside the rules for a cheat'. He continued, 'No proper grounds for this decision have ever been put forward. It was a corruption of the Department of Trade to push it through, and a disgrace to ministers involved; a source of embarrassment which should not prevent an immediate inquiry.'

On his senior officials' advice, Channon merely acknowledged Rowland's letter in the hope that the tiresome man would eventually succumb to the government's indifference. But the unravelling Guinness scandal, embracing leading personalities and institutions in the City, reflected upon the ministry's incompetence and fed Rowland's aggression. In further personal letters, Rowland individually challenged Thatcher, Tebbit and others to sue for defamation if his allegations about their involvement in a corrupt deal with Fayed were not true. If investigations into Guinness could be launched so quickly, he commented to Channon, 'how ridiculous and hypocritical to [allow] political protection for Fayed who has lied his way into control of the House of Fraser. It seems difficult to imagine that, as an honourable person, you will want to be party to a cover-up – or even worse – an unsuccessful cover-up.' Rowland's ranting might have been further ignored had Ernest Saunders, the beleaguered former chairman of Guinness, not revealed to Rowland how the City's inner circle manipulated the same rules which for nine years had obstructed Lonrho.

Rowland met Ernest Saunders in Geneva, Switzerland on 6 April 1987. Anticipating criminal prosecution and destitution, Saunders was seeking friends and Rowland, always available to help the victims of the Establishment, whom he invariably bracketed as like-minded rebels, was keen to trade support for information. Having given Freddie Laker a well-paid position in the Princess Hotel group, he promised Saunders, another 'innocent scapegoat', employment with Lonrho once his problems subsided. One month later he would provide £250,000 surety for Saunders's bail.

In Geneva, Saunders explained how he had managed to overcome Rowland's two enemies, Le Quesne and Borrie, to clear the Guinness bid for Distillers.

Initially, the Guinness bid had been referred to the Monopolies Commission by the government, frustrating Saunders's ambitions. But instead of submitting to a long inquiry, Saunders revealed that, with the help of Gordon Reece at £4000 per month, the brewers' lawyers had informally huddled with Borrie and Le Quesne to discuss how they might overcome the reference. Le Quesne had suggested that, to avoid a concentration of whisky brands, Guinness should withdraw its bid and then sell its own whisky interests to another company. Afterwards, it might resubmit its bid.

Guinness followed Le Quesne's advice. With the government's agreement, the bid was withdrawn, the whisky brands, principally Haig, were sold to Lonrho at a fire-sale price, and a new bid was made for Distillers which was won after a fierce battle.

In his defence, Le Quesne would claim that he often held informal discussions to give potential bidders an opportunity to test the Commission's philosophy. But he could not cite a similar case where a bid was made, then withdrawn, then resubmitted and not referred to the Commission. That new bid, wrote Rowland, 'was the same dog wearing a Le Quesne-and-Borrie-approved collar, with a nice new dog licence from the Secretary of State.' In Rowland's terms, the huddled consultations with Le Quesne and the unprecedented events thereafter proved a conspiracy.

On his return to London, Rowland wrote again to Channon, repeating Saunders's allegations, and demanding an inquiry into the behaviour of Le Quesne and Borrie, the two officials who had allegedly tilted the regulations against him. Those two men, accused Rowland, 'without a constituency, who don't have to answer publicly for their decisions, who conduct all their meetings in private and who are virtually faceless . . . are the real originators of this scandal.'

Channon, as a member of the Guinness family, was placed in a dilemma by Rowland's accusations since his family had benefited by the increased value of Guinness shares. The department was also embarrassed because Sir Alex Fletcher, the former minister accused of tilting the playing field further against Lonrho, had acted as a paid adviser in the Guinness takeover battle. Against these accusations, combined with constant articles in the *Observer* about the Fayeds, Channon's resistance to Rowland's propaganda war collapsed.

On 9 April, Channon announced the appointment of two inspectors to 'inquire into the circumstances of the Fayeds' purchase of shares in House of Fraser in 1984 and 1985'. The inquiry, established under section 432 of the Companies Act, implied that there was a suspicion of an impropriety.

The excitement in Cheapside was not mirrored at the *Observer*. Depressed for some time that no other newspaper doubted the Fayeds, Marckus accepted that by then he had written too much. Channon's announcement was a hollow victory. The reputation of the newspaper was irredeemable.

Mohamed Fayed was certainly not pleased. The decision, he complained, 'cast a shadow on my dignity and my honour.

I can live without riches. I cannot live without a good name. A dog barked and the ministers listened.'

Having misjudged Mohamed Fayed in 1975 and again in 1984, in anticipating eventual victory once the DTI report was concluded, Rowland once again underestimated the Arab.

Since the takeover of House of Fraser, Fayed had assiduously cultivated the leaders of the Conservative Party whose treasurers in turn approached the Egyptian for support. In his bid to become the perfect Englishman, Fayed gave generously to charity and sought opportunities to be photographed with the royal family. But, behind the scenes, he was looking for a way to retaliate against Rowland's public campaign.

Just as Rowland was using ex-Chief Superintendent Etheridge and his agents to investigate the Egyptians, Fayed, on Basham's advice, recruited Richard New, a former investigator for Customs and Excise who in 1981 had become a private detective. New's brief was to unearth incriminating material about Rowland for publication. Accustomed to destroying any opposition, Rowland had not anticipated that an Arab could launch a similar counter-attack. It was apposite that among New's first discoveries was Dan Mayers, who had also withstood Rowland's onslaught.

In June 1986, Rowland's litigation against Mayers came to trial in Denver, Colorado. Rowland was suing Mayers for fraud, the return of the gems stockpile and $10 million. To bring the case to court, documents had been produced which disclosed the conspiracy against Zambia. Rowland however argued that he was ignorant of the conspiracy between Mayers and Butcher. 'I have come here on my private jet,' Rowland told the court, looking unusually pale, 'to bring this man Mayers to book' – despite a friend's warning 'not to get in a pissing match with a skunk'. But having rubbished his relationship with Mayers and claiming to know nothing of Blorg, the Liechtenstein company, Rowland quietly settled the case just before judgment. Lonrho recovered only a proportion of the forty-ton amethyst stockpile but paid Mayers his commission. Effectively, after a seven-year battle, Mayers had defeated Rowland.

Naturally, the Fayeds ensured that the *Sunday Times* heard

about the obscure case in Colorado. The prominent and successive articles in the newspaper highlighting Lonrho's conspiracy
to avoid taxes should have served a warning to Rowland but too
often he was dismissive about the influence of critical newspaper
coverage about himself.

Richard New's second discovery was Francesca Pollard, a
thirty-seven-year-old housewife who harboured a passionate
grievance against Rowland. Pollard alleged that Rowland had
helped her uncles, Harry Landy and Joshua Bension, after
they had stolen millions from the Israel-British bank. Until his
death in 1971, the bank had belonged to Pollard's grandfather.
In 1974, the bank crashed. Landy and Bension, both directors,
were convicted of fraud in London. Pending appeal, Landy was
allowed bail on a surety provided by Rowland whom he met in
1971 while negotiating Lonrho's purchase of the Wankel patents.
Eventually Landy was acquitted and was employed by Lonrho.

Pollard complained that her uncles had deprived her of an
inheritance under her grandfather's will. Without providing any
evidence, she claimed that there was a connection between the
Wankel deal, the Israeli bank's collapse and Lonrho's survival
of its liquidity crisis in 1971. But most pertinently, she condemned Rowland's employment of an alleged fraudster whom
she denounced for condemning her to poverty.

Pollard's first four-page glossy pamphlet, 'Therefore, I accuse
. . .', published in September 1986, was outrageously defamatory. Rowland did not issue a writ for defamation.

Unlike others in the army of Rowland haters, Pollard was
distinguished in her anger by emulating Rowland's tactics: the
pamphlet was mailed to politicians, professionals, bankers and
businessmen. Most unusually, Pollard regularly stood in Cheapside waving a placard denouncing 'Tricky Tiny' and 'Robber
Rowland' of fraud. Her success in attracting attention and even
interviews encouraged the Fayeds to pay Richard New to probe
into Rowland's life and Lonrho's accounts and contact Pollard.

Fayed's first serious retaliation was set for Lonrho's annual
general meeting on 19 March 1987 at Grosvenor House. Fayed
had commissioned Arthur Young, the accountants, to scrutinise
Lonrho's accounts, particularly those for 1986 which, as usual,

showed a consistent increase in pre-tax profits. A team of accountants analysed the published annual reports and travelled throughout Africa to scrutinise each subsidiary's returns. The result, despite frustrations, was rewarding.

Lonrho's accounts, the investigators discovered, did not reveal the earnings which were unremittable from African countries to London. Similarly, Lonrho disguised the amount of money available in Britain and the precise details of the company's valuation of its assets.

Arthur Young concluded that Lonrho's accounts 'give a misleading impression of the earnings and underlying performance of the Group; do not give the impression that dividends may effectively (at least it seems to us) be paid out of capital; contain valuations of assets on bases which are not adequately explained or disclosed, or possibly inappropriate and seem not to be fully realisable.'

Lonrho's profits, reported the accountants, 'give an unjustifiably favourable impression of their trading performance. Even taken at their face value, their trend of earnings is not especially impressive.' Three specific examples were highlighted.

Firstly, the sale of Reuters shares, which was an exceptional item, was included in trading profits to cushion a fall in profits. Secondly, Lonrho had wrongly excluded £20.2 million losses in the *Today* newspaper from its normal balance sheet and alleged that the newspaper's goodwill was worth £42 million although it had no profits and a falling readership. Thirdly, while profits from currency exchange deals were included in the normal balance sheet, currency exchange losses were treated as separate items. That, according to Arthur Young, 'represents a prima facie breach of the standard [accounting practice]'. Had the currency exchange losses been treated according to the standard, it would have had 'a devastating effect on the results for the year'.

The focus of criticism was on Jim Butler, the Peat Marwick auditor responsible for Lonrho's accounts since 1971. Ever since he ignored the complaints of the Straight Eight in 1973, Butler had authored or endorsed creative accountancy which permitted Lonrho's value, according to Arthur Young, to be 'very substantially' made up of revaluations of Lonrho's assets which were essentially guestimates. 'This is remarkable,' commented Arthur Young, 'because Lonrho had added, over the previous five years, well over £600 million to its own value.' Valuations were critical to Lonrho's accounts since 84 per cent of Lonrho's funds were based upon unsold revaluations, yet the company refused to reveal the names of those who had made those revaluations, a requirement under the Companies Act. In other words, the revaluations could well have been the product of Rowland's suggestions. Except for rising at the annual meetings to attest orally his responsibility for the accounts, Butler remained silent.

Arthur Young concluded: 'In our view, if Lonrho had followed the accounting practices adopted by most companies in each of these areas, it is likely that the Group profit and loss account balance at September 1986 would have shown a deficit of at least £100 million rather than a credit balance of £40.3 million.'

As usual, the 1987 annual meeting opened at Grosvenor House with adulation for Rowland, sitting silently as Du Cann, the company's chairman following Duncan Sandys's elevation to honorary role as president, read his report to what some unkindly dubbed a geriatric Nuremberg rally. Du Cann's reassuring manner, melodious articulation and adroit skills at handling the public were of considerable benefit to Rowland but his usefulness as a politician was questionable. Concern about his financial troubles had persuaded Du Cann to leave parliament at the approaching general election. His political efficacy, already diminished, would cease. Several Lonrho directors had counselled Rowland that the company needed another public image, but Rowland, convinced of Du Cann's abilities in public and reluctant to trawl through the City to find another obedient director, asserted his loyalty. Events that morning in Grosvenor House, orchestrated by Brian Basham and Royston Webb, the Fayeds' new in-house lawyer, upset Rowland's estimate of his chairman.

The national newspapers that morning displayed quarter-page advertisements showing that Lonrho's share price had historically outperformed the FT All-Share index. As a preliminary fusillade, the Fayeds announced early in the day their complaint to the Advertising Authority that shareholders would have been victims of a distortion. Over the previous twelve months, Lonrho shares had underperformed the market.

More substantially, scattered among the audience listening to Du Cann, were Fayed's proxies representing his 250,000 Lonrho shares. Hired by Basham, the solicitors and barristers were carefully briefed to challenge the accounts. After Du Cann had completed his report and deprecatingly cast a silvery wave towards 'the man to whom we owe this great success of record profits', he called for questions. One by one, Basham's lawyers raised their hands and articulately posed complicated but leading questions to explode both the joyous mood and the normal complacency that the accounts would be accepted unchallenged. Progressively the mood turned sour. Unable to answer the questions satisfactorily, Du Cann searched for genuine questioners.

His eyes fixed upon an elderly woman, dressed in hat and gloves, who timidly raised her hand. To Du Cann's surprise, she too was a Fayed lawyer whose question about the source of foreign profits and their remittability paralysed the chairman. These were issues which Lonrho never disclosed. 'Our doors are always open,' said Du Cann in Lonrho's defence. 'We publish so much information in our annual report. I am always struck by the number of compliments I hear on the annual report and on the quality of the illustrations.' The meeting ended with less euphoria than Rowland might have anticipated, but, as intended, the antagonism was deflected on to the chairman.

That afternoon, Arthur Young's analysis was submitted to the DTI and the Stock Exchange Council. The Fayeds would claim that the quantity of illustrations hid the paucity of the financial information. It was a gesture. In Britain, accountancy is a creative art rather than a precise science, and the regulatory agencies, unlike in New York, are staffed by third-rate bureaucrats. Accordingly, the Fayeds' submission was treated with a disdain similar to that which faced Rowland's retaliatory complaints to the DTI about Fayed's accounts.

Mohamed Fayed's finances were, according to Rowland, also puzzling. House of Fraser's debts had increased from £109 million in 1985 to £836 million in 1987. Moreover, since it had become a private company registered in Liechtenstein, the company, benefiting from 'Group Tax Relief' approved by Inland Revenue, declared no profits and, unlike in 1985 when it paid £20.3 million tax, for the financial year ending in 1986 House of Fraser paid no corporation tax. Rowland added a new twist to his campaign. Not only was House of Fraser not paying any tax, but the Fayeds, although resident in Britain, were allegedly not paying any income tax. By the constant repetition of Fayed's tax avoidance, Rowland believed he had gained a propaganda victory, but others had not forgotten his own refusal to declare his British domicile in 1973 to avoid British taxes and Mayers's case confirmed that Lonrho and Rowland also used taxhavens.

Recognising his own hypocrisy was not Rowland's strength. To avoid a repetition of the embarrassment at the annual meeting, Lonrho would apply to the High Court to disenfranchise Fayed's shareholding. The action was identical to House of Fraser's against Rowland, which he had so loudly condemned. Fayed recognised that, as more of Rowland's hypocrisies were exposed, Rowland's own allegations would be dismissed or ignored. Richard New was dispatched to unearth more embarrassing material.

Rowland was untroubled by Fayed's threat. The year 1987 proved Rowland to be among Britain's most consummate businessmen. Although certainly in the second division behind Goldsmith, Hanson and Murdoch, he had built a company, ostensibly based upon the cautious accumulation of assets, which weathered the great crash in October.

Unlike Hugh Fraser, who died in May of throat cancer, leaving £2 million of his £100 million inheritance, Rowland personally earned £7 million in 1987 in salary and dividends and he was saving his money. Seventy years old and quite distraught at Fraser's funeral, Rowland forbade any mention of age or death. Instead, discussion revolved around exciting new vistas which promised good profits.

In Germany, Lonrho had obtained more franchises to sell German machinery and motors in Britain and Africa. Combined with Kühne & Nagel and the Volkswagen franchise,

Lonrho, Rowland hoped, would be able to find more of the hard currency in Germany to pay the annual dividend. Considering his background, Germany might have seemed a natural stage for Rowland's operations, but surprisingly, his professional relationship with Germans was ambivalent. 'He was uncomfortable with Germany,' confirms Captain Wilming who, during their twenty-year relationship, spoke German with Rowland only on rare occasions in restaurants to avoid being understood. Even in formal discussion, despite his fluent German, Rowland often spoke English and evinced little pleasure travelling in Germany. While he admired the country's financial strength and moral determination, he criticised its pomposity, arrogance and inflexibility. 'I could never live here,' he would tell his fellow directors. 'I left of my own accord.' Yet he tried hard and successfully to impress Lonrho upon the Germans. Unusual in Germany, full-page advertisements were placed by Lonrho in financial newspapers and Rowland flew regularly to meet bankers in Frankfurt and Munich.

But there was a reluctance to formalise relations with the government. An invitation from Hans Dietrich Genscher, the foreign minister, was rejected. Rowland's loyalty was to Franz Josef Strauss, the Bavarian leader of the Christian Socialist Union and junior partner in several Bonn coalition governments. By all accounts, their relationship was close and, thanks to Strauss, Rowland spent much time socialising among the Bavarian 'chiceria'. Regularly, he flew to Munich for the Oktoberfest, the beer festival – a week of intense partying – a marked contrast to his avoidance of similar social events in Britain. Yet it was odd that a German with origins in the Protestant north should be so intimate with a Catholic politician renowned for his corruption, dishonesty and deceit. Consolation came in the form of introductions to the richest of Germany who admired his achievements. In the summer of 1987, Rowland's certainty of his invincibility and sheer professionalism was evident in two deals.

The first was to halt the haemorrhage of losses on *Today*, totalling £28 million in one year. That loss and a £6 million loss on the *Observer* combined to show finally that Rowland was unable to produce national newspapers profitably. The blame was placed upon underestimating the managerial inefficacy of Eddie Shah and the failure to recruit as editor David Montgomery from News International. In June, Rowland inquired of both Maxwell and Murdoch whether they would be prospective purchasers.

Murdoch and Rowland met on 13 June. Ever since John Griffiths, the DTI inspector, had accused Rowland of lying and the *Sunday Times*'s constant support of the Fayeds, the proprietors' relationship had soured. But Murdoch's payment to use *Today*'s presses to print the *News of the World* had mollified Rowland's self-esteem. Murdoch now offered a £40 million package for *Today*, paid over several years and subject to profits.

Soon after Murdoch left Chester Square, the secret deal unravelled. The initial cause was another article by Ivan Fallon supporting the Fayeds. In response, Rowland, casting a fly over the salmon pool, leaked his deal to ensnare Maxwell. The publisher of the failed London *Daily News* was seeking revenge against Lord Rothermere and calculated that if *Today* were revitalised he might harm the *Daily Mail*. Maxwell was also seeking revenge against Murdoch for twenty years of successive humiliations.

Maxwell's offer, £10 million in cash and £30 million in loan stock, was better than Murdoch's. On Saturday 28 June, the deal was announced and Murdoch believed he had lost. Chortling, Maxwell telephoned his rival in Aspen to offer the continued use of *Today*'s presses. During that conversation, Murdoch realised that the deal was still unsigned because Eddie Shah was haggling for the price of his final 10 per cent stake.

Over the following twenty-four hours, Murdoch flew to London while his managers contacted Rowland on board his new 164-foot yacht, *Hansa*, bought from Heinrich Thyssen, sailing in the Adriatic. For Rowland it was an ideal situation. He had ensnared Maxwell and now Murdoch followed, offering £38 million in cash, four times Maxwell's offer.

Terry Robinson, David Montgomery and representatives of News International started negotiating the final details at 7.30 on Monday morning while Murdoch was airborne over the Atlantic. Hearing the news, Maxwell angrily aborted the auction. But by

Wednesday, the deal was still uncompleted and Rowland, asking for more, pushed the buyer too far. Murdoch announced his return to New York. Just before he boarded Concorde, the second-division player accepted Murdoch's offer.

There was a final hurdle. As it would make him the owner of five national newspapers, Murdoch's latest purchase would naturally trigger a reference to the Monopolies Commission. By then, both Rowland and Murdoch understood precisely how to crush the paper tiger. Jointly they warned Lord Young, the seventh secretary of state at the DTI since 1979, that unless the transfer was immediately approved their agreement would be cancelled and Lonrho would close the newspaper. Young, whose principles would prove uncertain, capitulated without a gasp. In the parliamentary uproar accusing Young of breaking every rule to please a supporter whose newspapers had supported the Tories at the election, Rowland could only rue that he himself had not enjoyed that influence.

The second deal that showed Rowland's self-confidence was necessary to cover *Today*'s losses and finance the dividend. George Walker, the former boxer with a chequered past who had become a millionaire businessman, inquired in July 1987 whether Lonrho would sell its casino in Brighton. By then, Lonrho owned seven casinos for an investment of approximately £17 million. Rowland had never warmed to the business despite the high profits. Although he occasionally dined at Crockfords rather than his favourite Berkeley, he disapproved of gambling and feared that Fayed might 'push' girls into the clubs to provoke a scene which would terminate Lonrho's licences. Yet he could use the casinos to parade his diversity as when Robert Mugabe was sitting in his Cheapside office and he summoned the casino manager to report on the previous night's takings in front of the president. 'He did that to show Mugabe how powerful he was,' smiled an observer of the encounter.

Walker's offer to buy the Brighton casino was too ebullient for Rowland not to try an old trick. 'I don't think I want to sell Brighton on its own,' replied Rowland in a dry, unemotional tone.

'Well, how about selling the lot?' retorted Walker.

'What's your offer?' queried Rowland knowing that the fundamental mistake in negotiations is to be first in naming the price.

'A multiple of twelve,' offered Walker, referring to the annual profits. Rowland received £128 million for his original £17 million investment, which was valued by Lonrho at £65 million. One year later, Lonrho also sold Walker its whisky distilleries for £137 million. Within two years Walker was bankrupt and was later charged with theft. Lonrho would lose £5 million invested in Walker's bonds.

Lonrho, by contrast, appeared to be booming. The profits from Walker and a rising mineral market had financed the purchase of the remaining 50 per cent of Western Platinum for $75 million, despite a British government ban on new investment in South Africa. But most importantly, the profit had bought Rowland a breathing space and the money to pay the all-important record dividend. Historically, the high yield attracted shareholders. Combined with a record £3 billion turnover and stated profits of over £200 million, Lonrho's shares hit an all-time high of 334 pence. Unlike many other companies, Lonrho seemed a safe haven in the aftermath of the October crash.

In fact, Rowland's attention was concentrating upon the Fayeds and House of Fraser when the crash occurred. During a visit to Britain in that period by Nic Kruger, Lonrho's Zimbabwe manager, and his wife, both were struck how Rowland spoke of little else. After Sunday lunch at Hedsor Wharf, Rowland sat in front of the television and moaned about the injustice he had suffered. By four o'clock, both men had fallen asleep, exhausted by Rowland's anger against the government.

His anger was also directed against the two DTI inspectors who, six months after their appointment, appeared to have accepted Fayed's explanations that he was 'shy' about revealing his wealth. That sympathy, apparent at the inspectors' meeting at the Kensington home of Charles Riachi with Adnan Khashoggi, was reported to Rowland.

In front of John Beveridge QC, Rowland's lawyer working nearly exclusively for Lonrho, the inspectors proffered a colour photograph of a mansion in Egypt said to be the Fayeds' original family home to prove Khashoggi to be a liar and in Rowland's pay.

Beveridge's report prompted Rowland to dispatch a warning to the inspectors: 'Lonrho is not the subject of the inquiry nor are we defendants. We are witnesses. The basic cause of the Inquiry is the statements made by Fayed. . . They constitute fraud.' He continued, 'It is a perversion of the Inquiry to allow coloured photographs of houses allegedly owned by the ancestral Fayeds to be solemnly considered as evidence for the foundation of a world-class fortune.' Accompanying his letter was a glossy, seventy-eight-page booklet entitled 'Enter a different world, Harrods, created by Fayed.' Written by Terry Robinson, its detailed analysis alleged that the Fayeds' eight assurances in 1985 about the House of Fraser's future were bogus and broken. The accountant had been diverted to write propaganda to marshal Lonrho's case for damages from the Fayeds for their alleged calumnies. The sheer quantity of data Robinson had compiled compelled the inspectors to consider their own lack of resources to conduct an investigation. They employed no researcher and were denied a foreign travel allowance, a reflection of the importance of regulation in Britain.

Four weeks later, Rowland sent the inspectors another analysis. The fourteen-page breakdown of the Fayeds' wealth was based on research by an army of lawyers hired by Lonrho across the world to pry into government archives, unpublished accounts and valuations about each of the Fayeds' known assets. Lonrho's analysis showed the Fayeds' net wealth to be £43 million. Challenging the inspectors to strip away the Fayeds' 'lifeline' of secrecy and produce their own evidence of how the Fayeds' 'one billion pound fortune' was created, the inspectors were subjected to the same pressure which caused their appointment. Rowland had resumed his campaign.

To embarrass both Fayed and the Sultan, he distributed another glossy brochure. 'The Sultan and I' was the transcript of the conversation in Carlos Place between Mohammed Fayed and the Swami. Over 40,000 copies were sent to politicians, bankers, brokers, lawyers and Lonrho shareholders. Fayed swore an affidavit that the tapes were not authentic. In response, Rowland offered one million pounds to a charity if Fayed could prove it was not his voice. Although the tapes did not prove the financial relationship between Fayed and the Sultan which Rowland claimed, they did, in Rowland's opinion, prove Fayed to be a liar since the Eygptian's sworn denial of the tape's authenticity was, according to the DTI inspectors, apparently false.

Brochure writing had become a passion for Rowland. Late into the night, he would correct manuscripts at Chester Square and order the printer to deliver the proofs to his home for further scrutiny. The passion was unrewarded. His attack on the Sultan whose 'deferential use of titles is somewhat longer than the borders of Brunei' and whose 'conduct was disgusting' attracted limited support. Few believed his claim that the monarch was 'at the root of the worst fraud of the century'. Politicians and the public were unitedly not interested in an unimportant obsession. Rowland, the world declared, was just a bad loser.

By December 1987, Rowland's high-profile campaign to denigrate the Fayeds had persuaded the inspectors to question Fayed more closely, which influenced the Fayeds to withhold their full co-operation. In turn, the inspectors confessed their frustration since, without the Fayeds' help, they feared their investigation was impossible. Their appeal to Rowland to refrain from his public campaign provoked an intimidating rejoinder: 'The inquiry has been running silently for six months and must cause disquiet. . . After seven months, you still hesitate to believe that Mohamed Fayed has fabricated an identikit version of the background he would like to have. . . They can have no complaint about my circulars as there is nothing in them new to the Fayeds.' The inspectors, he concluded, should have used their powers to compel the Fayeds to deliver their bank records and completed their work in four months. Here was yet another example of Britain's amateur regulatory system.

To prove that only the supine remain silent, Rowland published another circular. Entitled 'A fool and his money', it alleged that the Sultan was angry that Fayed had not returned a loan of $900 million. The glossy brochure included photocopies of the 'Strictly private and confidential' letters from John MacArthur to the Office of Fair Trading. Rowland's 3000 readers could see for the first time MacArthur's glowing assurances that the Fayeds' wealth of 'several billion dollars' ranked them just behind the Queen in the league of Britain's wealthy.

Again, public reaction was muted, not least because Rowland did not provide any evidence that the Sultan had provided the money while the Sultan himself had gone to great pains to deny the allegation. Peregrine Worsthorne, one of Britain's more opinionated journalists, had flown to Brunei for what was billed as the Sultan's 'first-ever interview'. It was conducted in a 'most spectacularly vulgar edifice'. The Sultan, who was 'angered by many false reports', told the scribe that there was 'absolutely no truth' in Rowland's claims. Fayed, he said, had been given small amounts of money to cover expenses, but the power of attorney had been withdrawn within eighteen months.

That night, Trelford, alias a 'staff reporter', spoke to Rowland and published his employer's reaction: 'Is it not very strange that the Sultan should refuse to give evidence to the official inquiry, then choose a moment just before the report is due to make a statement on the matter to a selected journalist?'

Of course, it was not strange at all. Why should the 'richest man in the world' reply to the unsubstantiated allegations of a comparatively poor businessman? For Anthony Howard, the abuse of the newspaper's reputation was excessive. He resigned. But Rowland, aided by Trelford, pushed on regardless.

Weekly, Melvyn Marckus wrote about the Fayeds, repeating Rowland's allegations which he had investigated and endorsed. 'Surely this is of interest,' Terry Robinson purred regularly from Cheapside to persuade Marckus to devote another column to the saga. If Marckus prevaricated, Trelford would urge, 'Just do it for Tiny' or 'This is a story for Business to look at, don't you think?'

The insatiable search for new material to use against Fayed, which had caused Rowland to rely upon Khashoggi and the Swami, two outstanding showmen tantalising each other with grandiose assertions and unfulfillable promises, led Rowland in 1988 to Steven Martindale.

Born in Pocatello, Idaho, in 1942, Martindale was a dubious

Washington lobbyist and social groupie who, on the verge of bankruptcy, was retained in 1985 by the Swami to effect introductions to politicians and presidents.

In June 1986, Martindale had sworn an affidavit denying the authenticity of the Carlos Place tapes and had told his friend, the politician Eldon Griffiths, 'Tiny was being taken for a ride.' But two years later, by then a disgraced and undischarged bankrupt dying of AIDS, Martindale took £50,000 from Rowland, an indemnity against litigation and all his expenses including Concorde trips to London, to write *By Hook or By Crook*, a book in which it was described how, from an adjoining room in Carlos Place, he had heard Mohamed Fayed's taped conversation with the Swami. The tapes were, Martindale declared, authentic. Trelford serialised the book in the *Observer* despite its withdrawal by Century Hutchinson when the Fayeds sued for defamation.

Fayed's retaliation was swift and deadly. With some success, Richard New had assembled a chronology of Rowland's life which was accurate and unflattering. Published as a sixteen-page pamphlet entitled 'Fair Cop Fuhrhop', and subtitled, 'The True Story of Tiny Rowland', it was distributed as a letter from the vengeful Francesca Pollard.

For the first time, in dramatic form, 40,000 of the 'great and the good' read an exposé of Rowland's attempts to disguise and distort his past including his unsympathetic attitude towards Britain during the war, the perjury on his marriage certificate [his father was falsely named Rowland instead of Fuhrhop], and of Lonrho's tax evasion on the amethyst stockpile through Blorg. Adorned with a swastika on the cover, the pamphlet encouraged the reflection that Rowland's campaign to expose the Fayeds' dishonesty was the kettle calling the pot black.

On 25 March 1988, Rowland sat silently as usual for Lonrho's seventy-ninth annual general meeting. As usual, Sir Edward Du Cann praised Lonrho's financial strength, especially its diversity of operations. New oil refineries in America, he claimed, were profitable, investments in Ruhrglass and Krupp in Germany would prove profitable and a new shaft at Ashanti would increase production. Over the previous five years, said Du Cann, earnings per share had annually compounded by 36 per cent. Even Lonrho's British textiles and the *Observer*, he claimed, were 'highly profitable'. Growth and profits, he predicted, were set to continue for ever. The claims were as always criticised as unverifiable because, despite the tight financial controls organised from London over Lonrho's 700 companies and the demands that most earnings be remitted to London, outsiders suspected that the 'profits' were uncertain.

Turning to Rowland's campaign against the Fayeds, Du Cann forecast that the DTI inquiry would prove that they were guilty of making false statements and dishonesty: 'I cannot tell you how this matter will end except to say that as one who has supported the government's determination to protect investors against mismanagement or dishonesty while I was in the House of Commons for over thirty years I would expect the Department's report should be full and frank and, on the exposure of their guilt, it should insist on the disinvestment on the part of the Fayeds. Then justice will be seen to have been done.'

On 24 July 1988, the inspectors' report was delivered to the DTI. The secretary of state, Lord Young, a solicitor and property developer, was best known for Thatcher's quip about him: 'Other ministers bring me problems, David brings me solutions.'

Young's weakness was his lack of political experience and his dependence upon Thatcher's patronage. During his brief political career, Young sought, often unsuccessfully, to avoid unpopular decisions and offending his Party colleagues. In Rowland's case, Young knew that no advantage could be won for espousing Rowland against Fayed whom he, as a former chairman of the Conservative Party, had occasionally met.

Young had also met Rowland at Hedsor Wharf about ten years earlier. The dinner in the mid-Seventies, with the editor of *Ma'ariv*, the Israeli newspaper, was forgotten by Rowland. 'He was unreal,' Young recollected later, 'absolutely charming and dropping the name of every world leader.'

By 1987, Rowland had few illusions that Young would be more sympathetic than any of his predecessors. Earlier that year, the minister had ignored Lonrho's offer to buy the Rover motor company for a higher price than proposed by Professor Roland Smith, the new chairman of British Aerospace. Young announced that the tight timetable and advanced negotiations precluded Lonrho's offer but, to Rowland, the decision reflected the old prejudices.

The DTI report was handed to Young just before he boarded an aeroplane at Auckland airport, New Zealand, for the return flight to Britain. As Young settled into his first-class seat to spend the flight reading 'the yard-thick typescript', he was struck at the end of the first page by the inspectors' tone: 'They've bought Rowland's story.'

The inspectors, in their introduction, had sought to preclude that condemnation by explaining, 'We started our investigations with a predisposition not to trust' Rowland and Marwan. But by the end they had concluded, 'It was safe to rely on much of what those two witnesses told us.'

Initially, Mohamed Fayed had co-operated but, on the advice of Edward Walker-Arnott, the partner in Herbert Smith, the Egyptian's attitude towards the inspectors changed during their investigation. Without the benefit of the advice of a Queen's Counsel and relying upon Walker-Arnott, Fayed protested that the inspectors were going beyond their remit and then decided to withdraw from regular contact with the inspectors, to await their conclusions. Fayed intended at that time to answer all the issues. In the event, there was aggravated conflict. The inspectors, Fayed claimed, had refused to consider independent, professional valuations of his assets and had relied upon Rowland's informants about his alleged activities rather than conducting their own research. Finally, he condemned the inspectors for curtailing the period for his response. The inspectors' conclusions were good cause for his abuse.

Vitriolically, the lawyer and accountant demolished each individual claim by the Fayeds about their family background and the sources of their alleged wealth. 'The evidence that they were telling lies was quite overwhelming. But they were still determined to counter-attack and try to pretend that they were the innocent victims of some gigantic conspiracy against them . . . it was a false image and they knew it.' As the Fayeds'

alleged invective and hysterical attacks escalated, the inspectors'
suspicions hardened: 'We uncovered more and more cases where
the Fayeds were plainly telling lies.' The Fayeds' account, said
the inspectors was 'unreliable', 'untrue' and 'bogus'.

Kleinworts and Herbert Smith were also criticised for appearing to publish and verify facts which proved untrue. The professionals had, according to the inspectors, wrongly endorsed
whatever they were told by their clients: 'This unstructured
process of acceptance without critical inquiry was the dominant
feature of the events.'

'Mr Rowland and Lonrho,' the inspectors concluded, 'had
good grounds for feeling that Mohamed Fayed had treated
them very badly over the share sale. . . They were very angry
because they genuinely believed that the bid for House of Fraser
was being made on the basis of false representations.'

'We were told at the time of our appointment,' wrote the
inspectors, 'that an area of particular concern to the secretary
of state was the validity of the assurances given by the Fayeds
and their advisers in March 1985.' The inspectors' brief was
to prevent another minister being 'materially misled'. British
law, they continued, has 'frowned upon those who obtain or
attempt to obtain valuable benefits from others by dishonest
representation. Dishonesty causes honest people to act in a way
in which they would not act if they knew the true facts.' Since
Tebbit had based his decision upon 'the statements made and
assurances given by the Al Fayed family . . . and the support
given to those statements and assurances by Kleinwort Benson',
the inspectors assumed that the politicians and officials involved
would be shocked by their findings.

If the inspectors had concluded their report at that point,
David Young and his successors could not have escaped the
consequence of the report's conclusions. But the inspectors'
explicit trust of Rowland even extended to Marwan who, they
wrote, was 'wrongly' criticised by Griffiths; and to the *Observer*, which they believed was the victim of the Fayeds' 'attack on
its editorial independence and the professional integrity of its
journalists'. That sympathy led to the inspectors' bewildering
conclusion that the newspaper's articles about the Fayeds had

been 'written in an independent manner'.

Young could find further reason to doubt the inspectors' objectivity from their conclusions about the Fayeds' wealth. Since an expert declared the 'Carlos Tapes' to be genuine, the inspectors asserted: 'It is likely that the Fayeds used their association with the Sultan of Brunei and the opportunities afforded to them by the possession of wide powers of attorney from the Sultan of Brunei to enable them to acquire those funds.' But the Sultan had denied that possibility and the inspectors offered no proof to the contrary. Their blatant validation of Rowland's factual thesis animated Young against the inspectors' conclusions that it was wrong for the Fayeds to profit from their mendacity.

Young could only be relieved that the inspectors had failed to investigate the details of Rowland's more particular complaint about Tebbit's and Borrie's conduct. That fundamental defect allowed the minister to dismiss their report as a partisan comment upon a messy row between two mavericks. In Young's opinion, the inspectors had been supine to ignore Rowland's nefarious commercial motives in his two sales of House of Fraser shares and accept that Rowland was 'motivated by a sincere belief that the Fayeds were not telling the truth in very major respects'. The report, the minister concluded, was a hatchet job upon the Fayeds.

On his return to Britain, Young 'wanted to publish but I was advised that the report could not be published because it might prejudice the investigations by the Serious Fraud Squad and prejudice a fair trial'. The minister believed that the SFO's review would be speedy. As minister, he could have overruled that advice. Several DTI reports, including the 1976 Lonrho report, had been published while criminal investigations continued, without complaints of prejudice. But privately, Young agreed with his officials' regret that Channon had instigated the investigation. Young was not minded to tilt towards Rowland's interpretation of the 'public interest'.

Rowland was working to a deadline. After 22 January 1989, Young would be barred by statutory limitation from referring the Fayed takeover to the Monopolies Commission. Like a man possessed, Rowland preferred to kick down the door rather than rely further upon quiet persuasion. On 4 September, Rowland circulated a 185-page glossy brochure. Called 'The Hero from Zero, The story of Kleinwort Benson and Mohamed Fayed', it was drafted by Samuel Evans, an American lawyer who had represented Khashoggi, and completed by Rowland. Advertised in the national press, more than eighty thousand were distributed in English, French and Arabic, in a campaign which by then had cost Lonrho shareholders £20 million.

The barrage of brochures, rather than the arguments, persuaded Young to meet Rowland on 16 September. Accompanied by John Beveridge QC who sat opposite the minister, Rowland, according to Young, 'huddled in his overcoat, despite the mildness of the day, sat silent . . . brooding'.

Rowland's purpose was to urge Young to publish the inspectors' report which he had received two months earlier. All his experience of Young's six Conservative predecessors and of their officials suggested an unwillingness to publish a report which exposed the politicians and their officials as compromised fools. Yet Young interrupted Rowland: 'Before you say anything, I have decided to publish.' Asked when, Young replied, 'In a matter of weeks.'

Beveridge showed his relief but nevertheless used the opportunity, as briefed, to list Lonrho's achievements. The Fayeds, he mentioned, were only passing acquaintances of Rowland. Young interrupted, 'Surely Mohamed Fayed had been on the Lonrho board.' For Young, the past relationship between Rowland and Fayed was and would remain a crucial factor. Beveridge quickly passed on to other matters.

At the end of the meeting, Young mentioned to Rowland that they had met once before. Rowland had forgotten the occasion and asked, 'Why is the government prejudiced against Lonrho? I never receive invitations to government functions when Africans visit the country.' 'There was no real answer to that,' reflected Young considering the heap of anti-government brochures and *Observer* articles, 'so I bid him farewell.'

The following day, according to Young, he was told that the Serious Fraud Office would need more time to consider the report and publication would be prejudicial. The news was not passed on to Lonrho. Mohamed Fayed, however, was told and, realising that the inspectors' report was critical, suggested to the minister that it remain unpublished. The Egyptian hoped that Rowland's attention would be diverted, possibly permanently, towards his own survival.

On 5 September 1988, there was heavy trading in Lonrho's shares, pushing the price up 30 pence to 230 pence. The buyer was Asher Edelman, a forty-eight-year-old self-styled corporate raider from New York who targeted undervalued shares. By 23 September, Edelman's 6 per cent interest pushed Lonrho's shares up to 340 pence. Initially, the American's purpose was unclear. Either the buying was short-term speculation, or he envisaged a takeover followed by selling off the assets. Somehow it was appropriate that in the dying days of the frenetic Eighties, Lonrho, a company which epitomised uncertainty, should be the victim of speculation.

On the stock market, Lonrho was valued at £1.2 billion. British analysts estimated Lonrho's worth in a break-up at £2.25 billion. Rowland claimed Lonrho was worth nearly double, at £4 billion. The arithmetic was random. According to Bob Carpenter now of Kitcat Aitken, the Princess hotels were worth between £625 million and £700 million; the Metropole hotels £250 million; the Volkswagen distributorship £230 million; 50 per cent of Kühne & Nagel £130 million. Rowland's public refusal to meet Edelman pushed the share price higher which suited both Rowland and Edelman. 'We knew he wasn't serious,' recalled Terry Robinson.

Lonrho's unprecedentedly glossy, 112-page annual report reflected Rowland's customary optimism which, had it been subjected to realistic assessment, would have aroused more caution. The group turnover, Rowland claimed, was £5 billion, but in fact, Lonrho's was £3.6 billion. Rowland favoured including the turnover of companies in which Lonrho owned a minority share. Pre-tax profits of £273 million, up from £225 million, looked similarly healthy but half were earned in Africa where both the barrier on remittance and their soft currencies meant that Lonrho in Britain did not receive much of the money. The realisable trading profits were approximately £80 million after deducting extraordinary items. To raise the £87 million to be paid in dividends, Rowland had, in what had become a habit, sold assets. In 1989 it was the whisky distilleries and vineyards in France. Inevitably the real money available to the company was meagre and Lonrho's loans increased. In 1989, they reached a record £1.1 billion and the rising trend continued. Convinced that Lonrho's assets were undervalued, a sentiment shared by Rowland, Edelman had overlooked those unpalatable facts. But the American's interest, as Rowland appreciated, was speculative. A second predator was of greater concern.

At that moment, Alan Bond, a forty-nine-year-old brash, pudgy, British-born former signwriter who had emigrated to Australia in 1950 and become a legend in his lifetime, docked his 162-foot yacht *Southern Cross III* at Khashoggi's exclusive marina for the mega-rich in Antibes on the Côte d'Azur. Over the past twenty-five years, Bond had become a famous socialiser and folk hero who owned banks, energy resources, TV stations, the Chilean telephone system and considerable property and brewing interests including the highly profitable Castlemaine XXXX and Swan Lager brands. In the Eighties, Bond epitomised the glamour of Australian entrepreneurs, buying Van Gogh's 'Irises' for $54 million, winning the America Cup yachting race, and welcomed on his return home to Perth by a huge crowd.

Bond's arrival at Antibes coincided with Edelman's activities. Along the marina were yachts belonging to Robert Maxwell, Gerald Ronson and, by coincidence, *Hansa*, Rowland's 164-foot yacht, was on the adjoining mooring to Bond's.

Rowland was on his boat with Josie and his family. Remarkably, Rowland had changed little on the craft after its purchase from Thyssen, although it had been refitted near Bremerhaven. The few visitors to the boat remarked that the crew worked in Germanic fashion and recall Josie sewing labels on to the crews' garments. Compared to the buckets of champagne, endless gourmet food and partying nymphets on Bond's yacht, Rowland's offered more frugal fare, principally pistachio nuts, muesli and cold cut meat. Those who telephoned from London were occasionally surprised to be speaking to Robert Dunlop or even Paul Spicer. 'Why him on the yacht?' they would ask.

Bond and Rowland had previously met at the Scottsdale Princess hotel in Arizona. Bond, flying his private Boeing 727, had crossed the Pacific in weather which would have grounded the Gulfstream. Rowland was instinctively repelled by Bond's brash flaunting of his wealth and plane. 'Tiny didn't like big planes,' recalls Captain Wilming. 'Their meeting didn't last long.' The two had discussed participation in Britain's first television satellite. Lonrho later withdrew.

In Antibes, Bond sought to renew their acquaintanceship and sent several invitations to *Hansa*. For Rowland, the sun worshipper, it was an irritant but he eventually succumbed. Lying on the sun deck, he and Bond discussed business which led to a familiar Rowland wail: 'I don't know why I carry on in London. I'm an old man. I've just got another three years. All I want is the sun and my beautiful boat. Someone else should run my business.'

Bond had something else on his mind at that moment. He wanted to sell some of his empire and offered Rowland the St Moritz hotel in New York and a nickel mine in Australia. Rowland asked Terry Robinson to investigate and also to fax a report about Bond's business.

Robinson's speedy reply outlined that Bond's companies were valued on the stock exchange at just £350 million but the latest accounts showed borrowings of £3.2 billion rising to £4 billion, although his assets and profits had allegedly more than doubled in the previous year. Robinson concluded that Bond was bankrupt. Greed and self-delusion had driven the Australian to overestimate his own abilities and his empire was financially unstable. Nevertheless, according to Bond, Rowland suggested that he consider buying Edelman's stake in Lonrho.

Back in England, on Saturday 24 September, still in the midst of the Edelman excitement, Bond lunched with Rowland at Hedsor Wharf. Rowland would subsequently write to Bond that the Australian had invited himself, but Bond and more pertinently his girlfriend, Diana Bliss, whom he laughingly called 'an old friend of my mother', are certain the invitation was from Rowland. Both Bond and Bliss also recall Rowland's monologue about how, with advancing age, he was looking for a successor.

Prompted by those remarks, Bond asked whether he might help Rowland and buy a stake in Lonrho to stiffen the defences against Edelman. He believed in the company, said Bond, and offered to help Rowland against the American. Politely, Rowland declined.

According to Rowland, Bond replied, 'Right, I won't buy any Lonrho shares unless you ask me to.' By 22 October, Bond had paid £250 million for a 15 per cent stake in Lonrho, the same size as Rowland's, which included Edelman's shares. The talk was either of helping Rowland or removing Rowland. In Cheapside, Robinson admitted, 'Tiny's worried.'

One week later, Bond's stake had risen to 21 per cent. Even Rowland took note that Bond had just spent £300 million. Bond dispatched a letter to Rowland, 'By now you will have been informed that we have acquired some shares in your company.' Bond suggested that they meet when he was next in London. Clearly, as Lonrho's largest shareholder, he expected two seats on the board. 'What impertinence,' raged Rowland. Another call, according to Rowland, from the captain of *Hansa* in Antibes aggravated his irritation. Bond's captain had inquired when *Hansa* would be moving so that Bond's yacht could take the mooring. The implication was that Rowland should make way for Lonrho's largest shareholder. 'It was so embarrassing,' complained Rowland, probably apocryphally. 'It's such a small community down there, everyone must have heard about it. It was then that I decided to destroy him.'

Neither Rowland nor Robinson believed that Bond was making a bid for an undervalued company to sell off its assets. Bond simply lacked the necessary £2 billion. Instead, they calculated that he wanted to consolidate a proportion of Lonrho's assets and profits within his own company accounts. Similar to Rowland's tactics with SUITS and House of Fraser, Bond was buying a 29 per cent stake 'to get to know the company'.

A sign of Rowland's unease was his purchase of Lonrho shares, pushing the price up to 413 pence – a record compared to an adjusted high of 286 pence the previous year. Lonrho was suddenly a favoured stock. Bond's effrontery grated the sensitivity of a man unaccustomed to public humiliation by other dealers, especially when he was personally earning a salary of £1.02 million and £8.7 million in dividends. The predators ignored each other's vanity.

In a cocksure letter to Rowland on 2 November, Bond placed his hand in the piranha bowl and suggested that they should meet 'to take things forward to our mutual benefit'. Rowland snapped: 'I am sure it was an accidental implication of your letter that you and I should seek some personal mutual benefit – you don't know me very well.' It was signed, 'Very kind regards, Tiny XXXX' The letter was published in the *Observer* under the headline, 'Rowland Couldn't Give A XXXX'

As the City speculated about a bid at £5.50 per share, Robinson was completing a ninety-three page analysis of Bond's empire. The accountant concluded that the predator was 'technically insolvent' with debts of £6.5 billion and heading towards collapse. 'Is the pyramid structure on the point of collapse?' Robinson concluded. Rowland secured the loyalty of shareholders by trebling the interim dividend and authorised a share issue. The 12 per cent increase in profits depended on Volkswagen's sales in Britain because, despite Rowland's claims about 'plans for expansion' and 'increasing production', Lonrho's hotels, newspapers and mining interests were either losing money or stagnant. As usual, Lonrho's estimates of its value would be disputed and as usual Rowland's solution to Lonrho's liquidity problem was 'something will turn up'. Meanwhile he would continue enjoying his business diplomacy.

There is no disagreement that Robinson was tasked to destroy Bond by distributing his analysis. 'This is too important for Spicer,' he told Rowland. 'This needs a professional.' A beauty parade of four London public relations agencies was held at Cheapside. Hill & Knowlton won. While Robinson, trusted by City journalists, personally briefed each City editor over individual dinners at Cheapside or Howards hotel near Blackfriars, every major bank and broker throughout the world was approached by H & K's publicist.

The counter-attack released a tidal wave of criticism, investigations, subpoenas and allegations of fraud. Trawled in by the threat to his survival, Bond returned to London on 17 March 1989 for lunch with Rowland at Claridges to seek help to sell his

Lonrho shares. At the best of times, mercy and generosity were not dispensed by Rowland to enemies. Having arranged for the two men to be photographed for that week's *Observer*, Rowland dictated his quotation to be included as the epitaph for another of Basil Smallpeice's successors: 'I never bear a grudge. I share it with as many people as possible.' Bond returned to Australia while Rowland flew to Albania. By the end of the year, Bond's empire was in terminal decline. Two years later, he would be imprisoned but then acquitted in a retrial.

Bond's shares were sold, at a loss, to City institutions who, for the first time, had a financial interest in Lonrho. Rowland's stake in Lonrho would never be valued so high again.

In Cheapside, the image of Rowland as victor, supremely confident, the arbiter of the fate of people and nations, was indelible: 'He sits in the boardroom of Lonrho after lunch, immobile except for the occasional movement necessary to place a grape in his mouth and chew it,' wrote James Bartholomew. 'He is like a crocodile, steadily watching and waiting. He looks you straight in the eye. At any moment he may dismiss you as ill-informed or stupid. The jaws may snap. Meantime he listens and he tells you without hesitation or doubt what the facts are and how they should be interpreted. He takes a telephone call from America and asks the caller for information about the current standing of an Iranian middleman. During a call from India he casually refers to the fact that Adnan Khashoggi has been calling him every day. He will be seeing Rajiv Gandhi in a few days.' Unspoken was his lust to re-enact his destruction of Bond upon Mohamed Fayed.

As the delays on publication of the DTI report persisted, the *Observer* continued its weekly article to keep the issue alive and another glossy brochure was circulated containing a letter from Rowland to the Special Investigation Section of the Inland Revenue recommending the scrutiny of the Fayeds' financial status on suspicion that they were avoiding tax. Fayed's reply, that his status had been settled with the Revenue years earlier, was naturally unreported.

Rowland was kicking at a closed door. The collapse of Barlow Clowes, a medium-sized investment trust which had been defrauded of £113 million by its managing director, exposed the apathetic DTI staff as ill-qualified to regulate the nation's financial institutions. An inquiry would show that repeated warnings about Barlow Clowes's dishonesty had been wilfully ignored by DTI officials. The same collection of officials who shunned their responsibilities by quoting their reliance upon 'market forces' were hardly receptive to Rowland's complaints.

Gordon Borrie, having read the inspectors' report, was finally convinced that the Fayeds had lied about their wealth and in particular was struck by the allegations of Mohamed Fayed's fraud in Haiti. Although the same information had been presented by Rowland three years earlier, Borrie still regarded the DTI report as the first evidence of the Fayeds' dishonesty. But since it was Borrie who had advised Tebbit not to refer the Fayed bid to the Commission and, on his advice, Leon Brittan had ruled against a DTI inquiry, it was unlikely that the official would retrace his steps. It was Rowland after all who had twice sold his shares to Fayed, an action he had never sought to explain publicly. Rowland was not asking for justice with clean hands. The government was not at the disposal of businessmen to rectify their mistakes. Officially, Borrie's opinion was unchanged: 'The Commission does not exist to punish people for lying. The shareholders got the cash. Morality is irrelevant.' Unofficially, he wanted to avoid the horrendous prospect of unravelling the Fayeds' ownership and, more pertinently, admit that the Commission had been careless in accepting their assurances. Accordingly, on 22 November 1988, he recommended to Young that the takeover of House of Fraser should not be referred back to the Monopolies Commission.

That afternoon, Rowland led an eleven-strong delegation to Young to demand a reference. The sharp increase in House of Fraser's debts, a decrease in its profits and non-payment of taxes, argued Rowland, was further evidence of the Fayeds' deceit: 'The Fayeds' financial position is critical and possibly terminal.'

Uninterested in the Fayeds' finances and in the squabble, Young refused to be drawn. Personally, Young was grateful for Borrie's recommendation. There was no point in untangling the deal. No one, he argued, had actually lost any money and possibly Rowland even deserved his fate. Equally, he was unconcerned that the Fayeds had lied about their past. 'Many people lie about their history,' he said having read Francesca Pollard's sixteen-page circular 'Fair Cop Fuhrhop'. Rowland was also a liar. And even if the source of the funds, as an extreme example, had been the Mafia, the minister might have been unconcerned.

On 25 November, Young announced that he would not refer the House of Fraser takeover back to the Monopolies Commission. He added that the report would also not be published 'owing to inquiries by the prosecution authorities [which] indicate the existence of previously undisclosed material facts about the transactions'. Within his department, there was support for his decision. That, everyone thought, would end the affair.

At Harrods, Mohamed Fayed was delighted. He had derided Rowland's allegations about his finances. As a private company, House of Fraser was not interested in producing profits to pay tax. Unfortunately there had been exaggerations concerning his background in the accounts of their life, but that was Brian Basham's enthusiasm rather than their deliberate dishonesty. But that was all now irrelevant. 'Harrods will be in my family for a thousand years,' he smiled. 'I know that and so does Tiny Rowland.'

In January 1989, Rowland applied to the Divisional Court for an Order to compel Young to publish and refer the report to the Monopolies Commission. Lonrho's case was upheld. Mr Justice McCowan declared that the minister 'has no good reason' for refusing to publish. Young was ordered to refer the takeover to the Commission and to reconsider his decision on publishing the report. Rowland's euphoria was short-lived.

Young appealed, adamantly refusing to explain his decision not to publish the report. The Court of Appeal, consisting largely of Thatcherite appointees, had in previous years proved itself to be a protector of government powers and a declared enemy of whistleblowers like Peter Wright of *Spycatcher*. Repeatedly, it had denied itself the right to overturn a minister's fiat and not surprisingly was not interested in Rowland's complaint. The House of Lords confirmed that judgment.

But in one minority judgment, Lord Justice Watkins described Young's decision as 'irrational', adding, 'No reasonable minister could have reached the decision which he did.' Watkins also condemned the excuse of the SFO's explanation for the delay since it was 'fanciful to suggest that there would be interference with the gathering of evidence by the publication of the report'.

Rowland's frustration exploded. The whole Conservative Party, he was convinced, was part of a conspiracy. Not only were they suppressing the truth about the Fayeds, but individually they were attacking him. Tim Smith, an undistinguished member of parliament, asked the Solicitor General in the House of Commons, whether he would be 'recommending [*A Hero from Zero*] for the Booker prize for fiction?' He was rewarded by sixty thousand glossy brochures being dispatched to Lonrho's mailing list containing Rowland's demand that he explain why the inspectors had not accepted as factual all Lonrho's evidence? Since the inspectors' evidence remained unpublished, Rowland's riposte was ignored.

Both Edward Heath and Lord Chalfont also complained about Rowland's attacks on the Sultan whom they described as 'Britain's good friend'. In retaliation, each was made the subject of individual circulars. One vituperatively damned Heath as a protector of 'one fool and one fraudster'; while another castigated Lord Chalfont for defending the Sultan's practice of 'decades of imprisonment without trial'. The next target was Lord Young, personally accused of a conflict of interest.

In his evidence, Mohamed Fayed had told the inspectors that his enormous income in commissions from the British construction industry in Dubai included £40 million from Bernard Sunley. A critical letter dated 12 March 1985 from John Sunley for the use of the OFT asserted that Fayed had produced contracts worth 'in excess of £400 million'. The letter had been shown to Tebbit as evidence of the Fayeds' wealth and importance to Britain.

Eighteen months later, in October 1987, John Fryer, Sunley's managing director, had given evidence to the inspectors asserting that Fayed had procured contracts worth £200 million. Since Fryer had contradicted Fayed, the inspectors recalled Fryer in March 1988 and requested supporting evidence of the contracts.

Instead of more information, the inspectors received an obfuscatory letter, Fryer became terminally ill, and John Sunley personally returned to the inspectors accompanied by the same partner from Herbert Smith who represented the Fayeds. Sunley told the inspectors that all his records were missing. 'We wanted to shelter the Fayeds,' admits John Sunley. 'They were good clients and they had brought us a lot of good business.'

In summer 1987, Lord Young who had met John Sunley in his previous career, had agreed to become a member of the Lake Nona golf club in Orlando, Florida, under construction by Bernard Sunley. Among the other honorary members was Denis Thatcher, the prime minister's husband. Young knew that his name was solicited to promote sales and quite innocently sought to oblige a friend, failing to anticipate the ammunition he was providing one particular critic. One year later, on reading the inspectors' report that Sunley was associated with the Fayeds, the minister again had no qualms.

On 12 November 1988, the Lake Nona club was formally opened with a gala dinner. Young was not present. At about that time, Young announced that he would not refer the takeover back to the Monopolies Commission, nor would he publish the report.

Rowland had heard about the minister's relationship with Sunley and that the company had ceased to co-operate with the inspectors. What remained unclear was the background, although he spotted that Young's relationship with Sunley could be presented as a conflict of interest.

In February 1989, Rowland was telephoned by his lawyer in Germany. His representative revealed that three weeks earlier, on 20 January, Bernard Sunley had been sold to a Norwegian corporation and, promptly, it had been offered for resale. Intriguingly, on searching the Sunley offices, the Norwegians had discovered two files which contained the correspondence between John Sunley, the Fayeds, the DTI and the inspectors. Rowland, explained the lawyer, could have the files only if he bought the whole company. Lonrho paid the asking price.

Within the two files, Rowland read the handwritten notes of John Fryer and John Sunley recording conversations both between themselves and with Mohamed Fayed. Rowland believed that they revealed an agreement to mislead the inspectors about Fayed's payments.

One letter from Sunley to the OFT in March 1985 mentioned that the business was worth £400 million, while another letter to the Home Office in November quoted £250 million. But a telephone message from Fayed suggested that they quote '£500 million'. Rowland costed the contracts at £172 million. John Sunley would explain the discrepancies as due to variations of 'current worth' when the letters were written but, to the prejudiced eye, it seemed from Sunley's notes that the company was varying the value of the contracts to suit Fayed and that even the Fayed connections to some Sunley contracts were invented.

The final letter Rowland read was from the inspectors to John Sunley warning that his failure to explain the contradictory estimates would be reported to Lord Young.

Rowland's purchase of the company had been completed in secrecy. At break-neck speed he compiled a new brochure. The printer delivered the proofs to his home where, through the night he made final corrections. Called 'Birds of a Feather . . .', it was due for publication on 20 March.

John Sunley first heard about the sale of his erstwhile company that day. Telephoning Sir Edward Du Cann, he asked for confirmation of the rumour. 'Du Cann', recalls Sunley, 'assured me that Lonrho had no interest in Bernard Sunley. I naturally accepted his word.'

A few hours later, Sunley read Rowland's brochure. The commissions to Fayed, Rowland alleged, were 'illegal' because they broke Exchange Control regulations, precisely the offence which Rowland had committed twenty years earlier. Moreover, Rowland provided no evidence that the payments were illegal. Young was accused of 'dishonourable' conduct for failing to disclose his alleged friendship with Sunley. None of Rowland's brochures had caused much embarrassment – their main effect was to underline Rowland's obsession. 'Birds of a Feather' was no different.

Without official publication of the DTI report, Rowland realised, he would never be vindicated. But by then he had secured a copy. Ken Etheridge, Rowland's security director, had assiduously maintained his connections with his former colleagues at Scotland Yard. An officer was persuaded to pass Etheridge a photocopy of the report. Rowland's ecstasy on finally reading official vindication was offset by his anger with Lord Young and others who suppressed publication. Not once, as he read the inspectors' condemnation of the Fayeds, did he consider his own displeasure at other inspectors' arbitrary condemnation of himself in 1976 and 1984, and at their secret, unjust methods of collecting evidence and apportioning blame. His only thought was that finally he had a powerful weapon to bludgeon his enemies.

The next hurdle was to secure its publication and wide distribution. Rowland wanted to use the *Observer*. The only obstacle was whether the editor would completely renege on his commitment in 1981 to protect the newspaper's independence. Events over the previous weeks suggested that Trelford had become helpful in Rowland's campaign against the government.

Trelford's final capitulation had started on 21 January 1989 when he flew with Rowland on the Gulfstream to Tehran. Forlornly, Rowland was pressing the pariah regime to sign contracts for the exchange of African agricultural produce for oil but had discovered a race which was immune to his flirtation. According to Captain Wilming, 'It was terrible in Tehran.' Trelford was invited on the flight by Rowland's promise of an interview with Ali Akbar Hashemi Rafsanjani, the Iranian president. In the event, the interview did not materialise and Trelford published a tame substitute with the foreign minister causing suspicion that Rowland had once again used the newspaper to demonstrate his influence and obsequiousness to a potential customer.

Two other passengers travelled on Rowland's plane. Mahdi-al-Tajir a former adviser to the rulers of Dubai, employer of Mohamed Fayed and among the world's wealthiest men – precisely the type whom Rowland eagerly gathered around himself; and Wolfgang Michel, one of Rowland's many business contacts. During the journey, Michel told Trelford that he had compiled a dossier alleging a corrupt relationship between British

Aerospace and the Saudi Royal family which was the foundation of the Al Yamamah agreement, 'the arms deal of the century', variously estimated to be worth between £15 billion and £150 billion, an unprecedented contribution to Britain's industry and foreign revenue. Trelford agreed to read the file.

Three factors were not mentioned in their conversation. Firstly, that Rowland might have a commercial interest in undermining the Al Yamamah contacts because of his relationship with Dassault, British Aerospace's rival. In Kenya, Rowland had sought to persuade President arap Moi to abandon British Aerospace, the traditional suppliers, in favour of Dassault. One consequence of the Al Yamamah contract was Dassault's loss of a £15 billion order for planes from Jordan which British Aerospace's Tornado had won. Dassault was seeking to reverse the contract.

Secondly, Rowland might have wanted to embarrass both the British government and Professor Roland Smith, the chairman of British Aerospace.

Thirdly, Adnan Khashoggi, excluded from a deal which a decade earlier could not have been concluded without his services, might have been interested in redress.

One factor Trelford certainly did realise: Michel's investigations had been financed by Lonrho and Rowland had no moral scruples about investing in people who might be of service. Bribery in the Third World had previously not shocked Rowland and yet he had financed an investigation to expose the practice. Nevertheless, Trelford says, 'My curiosity as newspaperman was aroused.'

Trelford also knew that the *Observer*'s losses were escalating seemingly beyond control. Terry Robinson was urging his dismissal but Trelford could count upon Rowland's reluctance to dismiss a known employee – which would require his training of a new editor whose compliance would take time and effort to arrange. But Trelford understood that with that cosy niche came obligations.

Michel's thirty-page dossier was collected from Cheapside on 30 January and handed by Trelford to Melvyn Marckus, the first of seven *Observer* journalists to consider the story.

After reflection with two senior colleagues, Marckus rejected the material. He explained that there was a need for checks, that he and his staff were 'too busy', and that the so-called revelations were 'well-known'. In fact, a similar allegation by Michael Gillard some months previously had been publicly withdrawn in the following week's edition.

On about 4 February, Trelford offered Lonrho's file to Adam Raphael, an executive editor who, three days later, met Terry Robinson and Michel at the Berkeley hotel. Raphael says that he was 'not impressed with Michel's incoherent dossier' because of the lack of source material. But Raphael adds, importantly, that he had heard about the possibility of bribes from 'a senior Whitehall source'.

On 8 February, Raphael asked David Leigh, the newspaper's investigative reporter, to look through Michel's dossier. Leigh's response was adamant. 'I won't touch any Lonrho story. They are rarely what they seem.'

At this point, when four senior journalists had rejected the dossier, Trelford might have abandoned the story. Instead, on that same day, at Terry Robinson's request, Trelford wrote an unusually formal letter to Rowland. It started, 'I thought I should report to you, as chairman of the newspaper, on the progress we are making in our investigation into the Tornado contracts.' Some would allege that Trelford would feel compelled to report on that investigation only because Rowland ordered him to print the story. Trelford's denial, 'Mr Rowland has never instructed me to publish anything,' seemd at best questionable semantics.

Trelford's second paragraph however was controversial. 'My senior editorial colleagues and I are increasingly satisfied that the information we have received about irregularities in the contract arrangements, especially over commission payments, is authentic and raises issues of public importance that could cause serious political embarrassments to the government.' Firstly, two senior colleagues had told Trelford that they were not satisfied with the information; and secondly, Trelford seemed more interested in embarrassing the government than in considering the economic importance of the contracts for the country.

A third paragraph was similarly odd. 'I am putting my best reporters on to the investigation under the supervision of Adam Raphael, helped by Melvyn Marckus.' Yet the latter had already withdrawn his participation and Raphael's position remained ambivalent.

Trelford's letter, promising a published story within 'one month or so', therefore suggested that he was acting on Rowland's orders, which was contrary to the guarantees of editorial independence.

Once committed, Trelford asked Raphael to find other journalists to produce a story. But both John Merritt, a staff reporter, and Anthony Sampson, an expert on arms dealers, shunned the invitation. 'I pulled out because it was serving Lonrho's interests,' explains Sampson. 'The fact that Rowland was an arms dealer with commercial interests in the Middle East would damage my credibility and the story's.' Sampson nevertheless believed that the suspected bribes paid for the Al Yamamah contracts 'seemed quite correct' and an 'important issue'. By then, six journalists believed that Rowland wanted a bribes story in the newspaper for his own purposes.

Raphael therefore worked alone. Leigh, among the critics, would allege that Raphael was 'being leant on', while Raphael insisted he was following his professional instincts in undertaking the investigation.

Rowland offered more assistance. Trelford and Raphael were introduced to Khashoggi who, although ignorant about the specific deal, offered background colour about bribes to win weapons contracts.

During the research one important element emerged. Margaret Thatcher had personally negotiated with the Saudi and German governments to conclude the contracts. Her alleged connection with suggested bribes naturally excited Rowland. Unfortunately for Rowland, the published account failed to prove the payment of any bribes.

Under the front-page headline on 19 March, 'Thatcher in row over UK bill for Tornado deal', Raphael reported that the sale of eight Tornadoes to Jordan was in difficulties because 30 per cent of £45 million-per-plane price to Jordan, which was underwritten by the British government, comprised commissions or bribes. Moreover, since Jordan could not afford to pay for the planes, the British tax payer would suffer. 'But the Saudi deal is also haunted by charges that excessive commissions have been paid and that it has helped fuel a Middle East arms race.'

Inside, under the headline, 'Tornado Rip-Off', Raphael's first paragraph said, 'Billions of pounds of British tax payers' money are at risk in a series of arms deals that have transformed Britain into the leading arms supplier in the Middle East.' Over one complete page he suggested that huge commissions had been paid to secure Saudi orders worth '£150 billion' and, significantly, that Dassault described the loss of the contract in Jordan as 'unexpected, incomprehensible and catastrophic'. Great emphasis was laid by Raphael on an untraceable whistle-blower who, under a false name, denounced the Jordanian deal. Yet nowhere did Raphael either explain why 'billions' were 'at risk' or prove that any commissions had been paid.

The following week, the Jordanian order was cancelled, 'saving' Britain, according to Raphael, '£500 million' because the planes were sold at a loss to cover the bribes. Dassault was awarded the contract. Nothing more was written in the news-paper about the alleged commissions other than a report of a continuing National Audit Office investigation of bribes.

The publication aroused interest among readers but enor-mous controversy within the *Observer*. Led by Leigh, the accusation was made against Trelford of serving Lonrho's inter-ests by seeking to damage British Aerospace and Professor Roland Smith. Trelford condemned the complaints as 'lies, distortions and innuendoes'. The dispute was submitted to the independent directors for adjudication about the editor's obedience to the proprietor's wishes.

Five days later, on Good Friday, 24 March, Rowland summoned Trelford to Hedsor Wharf. Unwilling to continue suffering the government's malice, his voice tinged with excitement, Rowland hinted at possession of the DTI's report. Trelford had arrived anticipating that Rowland would risk a government injunction to prove the veracity of his campaign. Publishing the report in the *Observer* would not be straightforward. As soon as the first edition was seen, both Fayed and the government would obtain injunctions to stop distribution. The financial losses would be unrecoverable and the actual report would not be widely read, defeating the purpose.

Rowland told his editor that he wanted the DTI's report to be released at Lonrho's annual general meeting the following Thursday. 'Several million pounds of shareholders' money had been spent on the battle,' recalled Trelford, 'and he felt the shareholders were owed an explanation which the report could provide of how they had missed the glittering prize of Harrods.' It was agreed they would consider their tactics over the holiday weekend.

Their discussion resumed at Chester Square on Tuesday 28 March. In Trelford's subsequent published account of that discussion, Rowland and Du Cann insisted that copies of the report must be presented to the shareholders two days later and refused to wait for Sunday's edition. At that stage, Trelford could have agreed and allowed Rowland to issue shareholders with a Xerox copy or another glossy brochure. For, until then, Trelford had boasted that, despite the hiccups, he was protecting the newspaper's overall reputation until Rowland finally disappeared. Instead he claims that he wanted the report to be published under the *Observer*'s masthead. 'Partly to save his scoop, but also because he felt that the report's findings must be brought into the arena of public debate, he floated the idea of a special mid-week edition of the paper. He was particularly concerned to clear the *Observer*'s name which had been plastered with mud, mainly from the Fayeds, in the course of a four-year libel battle.'

If the choice really was Trelford's, then his decision was self-defeating because no one beyond Lonrho believed that a murky takeover battle for one hundred stores was an issue of paramount national importance. Hitherto, only the Business Section had been obviously influenced by Rowland's interference. To publish a special edition of the *Observer* to exonerate Rowland and Lonrho inevitably reflected upon the whole newspaper's credibility, painfully constructed over two hundred years.

Moreover, Trelford's published excuse was contradicted by those who worked with the editor during the week. The special edition, they suggest, was prompted by Rowland's directive. Faced with Hobson's choice, Trelford succumbed with little resistance to Rowland's orders and then, realising that he was compromised, assumed responsibility.

On his return to the *Observer* later that Tuesday, Trelford consulted Melvyn Marckus and Nick Morrell, the chief executive. In the course of their forty-five minute discussion, Trelford was excited: 'We've been to hell and back. We've been proved right. The problem of an injunction is less on a Thursday. And Tiny would like it for the AGM.' Since his audience did not represent the Astor tradition and were themselves already compromised, there was no opposition. In the aftermath, everyone agreed: 'I can remember the 'cons' for the special but what were the 'pros'?' The answer was Rowland's insistence and the editor's obedience. For many the decision would be the newspaper's nemesis.

In secrecy, throughout Wednesday, a handful of trusted journalists and secretaries produced the sixteen-page special edition. Under the huge headline, 'Exposed: the Phony Pharaoh', the subheading was the report's concluding sentence: 'The lies of Mohamed Fayed and his success in "gagging" the Press created a new fact: that lies were the truth and that the truth was a lie.' The opening paragraph was damning, 'The Egyptian Fayed brothers obtained Harrods and the House of Fraser, the biggest stores group in Europe, by fraud and deceit.'

'In Knightsbridge today, through the government's own negligence, crime is paying very well and cheats are prospering,' blasted the newspaper, having itemised the inspectors' merciless condemnation of the Fayeds, Kleinworts and Herbert Smith. Trelford, in particular, repeated the inspectors' criticism of Fleet Street's editors who unquestioningly repeated the Fayeds' lies. It was unforgivable, judged Trelford on the question of his competitors' courage, never to challenge the Fayeds' writs and allow their lies to multiply in the cuttings libraries of Fleet Street. But the main target of his criticism was Lord Young who had 'not acted in good faith. . . We believe he is party to a cover-up.' During that night 260,000 copies would be printed.

As Trelford's work progressed, Rowland sought to unsettle Young. In a letter, he recounted that Alan Bond had enjoyed a private meeting with the minister at the DTI. According to Bond, Young gave an assurance that his bid for Lonrho would not be referred to the Monopolies Commission, nor would his prospective ownership of the *Observer*. Rowland added: 'Your actions, in encouraging Alan Bond, were nothing more or less than comfort for Mohamed Fayed. . . Your classic manoeuvrings in this classic scandal of money worship will always give you much cause for regret.'

Young's office heard about the *Observer*'s special edition at 10 a.m. on Thursday 30 March. DTI lawyers began hunting for a judge, joined soon by the Fayeds. To the victims, it seemed natural that Lord Young and Mohamed Fayed should openly display their common cause for censorship.

Across the City, while newsagents were given the edition for nothing and allowed to keep the cover price, a ripple of excitement was released throughout the financial community. Even Rowland's enemies acknowledged his remarkable audacity. The man himself was sitting, silently as usual, in Grosvenor House listening to Du Cann reading his statement to adoring shareholders clutching the *Observer*'s special edition. To applause, Du Cann, whose annual salary that day was trebled to £408,558, demanded that the Fayeds be expelled from Britain.

As anticipated, at 11.55 a message was passed to Du Cann that an injunction was being issued. The confusion on the platform added to the drama and confirmed Rowland's complaint that Lord Young's sole interest was to throttle inevitable embarrassment.

But for the protagonists it was too late. In countless offices, the report was being faxed, photostatted and consumed. By any account, the publication should have caused an earthquake. Ministers, officials, bankers and lawyers were all convicted of disreputable conduct. Twenty-six years after his public humiliation by Edward Heath, Rowland had profoundly exposed the system which had sought to humble him. Some of the City's practices were proven to be at best inept and at worst dishonest.

Rowland might have expected the clamour for retribution and reform to sweep aside the culpable. But the same culture of inactivity which had allowed the transgression to occur four years earlier, and which had perpetuated it ever since, comforted those criticised with implicit guarantees of further inactivity.

Rowland and Trelford might have expected support in parliament or from other newspapers. But since *The Times*, *Sun* and *Daily Telegraph* had criticised the *Observer* for servility as a propaganda sheet for Lonrho and had never demanded the report's publication, their complaints were predictable. 'The *Observer* is guilty of an arrogant snub,' charged *The Times*, and Rowland had 'shown a level of contempt for his newspaper that is not much less than his contempt for the law'.

Anthony Howard's accusation that his former newspaper was being manipulated by its proprietor was hard for Trelford to rebut. There was no defence against the truth. Two weeks later, the *Observer* launched a new promotion campaign under the slogan, 'A different set of values. A different kind of paper'. The circulation continued to decline.

The focus switched to John Wood, the director of the Serious Fraud Office. According to Young, Wood had requested that the report remain unpublished while the police investigated the crimes. During those eight months, Wood established only that since House of Fraser shareholders had received more than the market price for their shares in cash, there were no victims. Not even Rowland. There was simply no fraud. The Fayeds' statements were not made under oath nor, under criminal law, were they material to the offer.

Nevertheless, as a knee-jerk reaction to the unpleasant spotlight, Wood dispatched two detectives to Cairo. Suitably dressed for the beach in Benidorm, the two officers sat in street cafés during Ramadan and two weeks later returned suntanned to Britain.

In London, the only noticeable effect of publishing the report was Lord Young's resolution to remain inactive. In 'Rowland v Her Majesty's Government', the defendant was determined despite the inherent contradictions in his defence. Young explained that while he would not publish the report because the inspectors 'clearly disclosed a wrongdoing' and he therefore could not risk prejudicing a possible trial, there was 'no public interest' to refer the bid to the Commission to investigate. Young would contradict himself again in his memoirs. 'In the end,' he wrote, 'the prosecuting authorities decided, as I always maintained, that there was no basis to launch a prosecution.'

The only trial at that moment was of Rowland and Trelford for contempt of court in publishing the DTI report. Eventually that would be dismissed and Rowland would claim £1 million for costs. But, for many journalists, that victory did not vindicate Trelford in his approval of the newspaper's use as a vehicle for Lonrho's shareholders.

Morale among some senior staff in the *Observer* was depressed. Trelford's permitting Rowland to use the newspaper as his complainant against the Fayeds substantiated the original fears in 1981. Some faith had been placed in the newspaper's independent directors who had succeeded in protecting Trelford over the Matabeleland massacre story in 1984. In April 1989, they adjudicated the 'Tornado' story.

In his defence, Trelford had asserted, 'I am not aware of any Lonrho commercial interests that were served by the Tornado stories.' The independent directors found in Trelford's favour but declared that the newspaper's image was 'tarnished' by its coverage of the Fayed saga. The journalists voted to accept the report. Leigh, infuriated by the 'whitewash', resigned.

Rowland emerged from the excitement to discover that nothing had changed. The only remaining target was Margaret Thatcher. Bereft of subtlety or mischievous humour, Rowland accused the prime minister of protecting the corrupt which included Tebbit and Young. The result, he asserted, 'could make Britain into Europe's dirty back door for fraud'.

In his second letter, accusing Thatcher of 'vindictiveness', Rowland presented a crisper image of a conspiracy. Rowland's informers had produced a letter from the Serious Fraud Office which discussed a 'settlement' with the Fayeds, involving, according to Rowland, the payment of over £50 million in undeclared taxes. 'You write to me that you "utterly repudiate" my attacks on the integrity of Tebbit and Young in this matter. They are certainly unable to repudiate it themselves.' While Lester Piggot, the jockey, had been imprisoned for non-payment of taxes, the alleged Fayed settlement made Thatcher 'a party to deception and protection of evil . . . you and you alone are keeping guard over the report, shielding a crook who is in the Sultan's shadow'.

Rowland's third published letter to the prime minister acknowledged that 'although you say my assertions are offensive, you cannot bring yourself to say they are untrue.' He continued, 'I understand clearly why you don't want to have the House of Fraser Report published. You got far too close for the comfort of the public to a crook.'

His explosions and his spleen were to no avail. On 7 March 1990, prompted by the DPP's decision that there were no grounds for a prosecution, the DTI report was finally published by Nicholas Ridley, the eighth secretary of state for Trade since 1979. The announcement was accompanied by Ridley's statement that he would not seek to disqualify the Fayeds as directors because it was not in the 'public interest'. For the first time, there was genuine uproar.

Since 1986, the DTI had sought to disqualify 1146 directors, many of whom were directors of private companies. Gordon Brown, the Labour politician, probed the impassive minister, 'He refuses to act where there is proven dishonesty and persistent dishonesty, [and] people are likely to ask, "when will he ever act to defend the public interest?" ' David Owen claimed, 'This is a litmus test about acceptable behaviour in business.'

Ridley was unfazed. No shareholder, he said, had lost any money and the inspectors' allegations had not been proven in a court of law. As backbenchers rose in the chamber of the House of Commons to demand that he explain the circumstances which *were* necessary for him to believe a director should be disqualified, Ridley sat serene as marble, assured of Thatcher's support. In Rowland's eyes, he represented the indolence, arrogance and ignorance which was driving Britain towards moral and financial bankruptcy. 'Sue him,' shouted Rowland convinced that the Fayeds were invulnerable because of their proximity to the Conservative Party. Beveridge hunted for any cause which would haul the minister to the court for a judicial review.

Among those who did pass comment was Tebbit. He admitted that it would have been a 'happier circumstance had everybody been perhaps a little more frank. . . But the question arises . . . does that actually mean that I should have referred the bid on the grounds that these men were dishonest?' A positive answer would have surprised the minister. Tebbit would receive a writ for damages from Lonrho while the Fayeds dropped all their defamation actions against Lonrho and paid the latter's costs.

'Only God can take House of Fraser from me,' exclaimed Fayed with a smile. Rowland remained in Cheapside brooding. For a man who claims to delight in problems, he had reached a dead end. For there was, to Rowland's outrage, no shame to be apportioned. Harrods even retained its Royal warrant. Two months after the report's publication, Prince Philip encountered Fayed at Windsor. Newspaper photographs showed them laughing together. Just days earlier the Prince had spoken at a meeting of the Confederation of British Industry. 'Nothing,' he said, 'corrodes a community more quickly or more completely than lying, cheating, corruption and double dealing.' Rowland naturally wrote to the Prince. Commenting upon his 'hypocrisy', he added, 'I hope you enjoy cosying up to this fraudster. . . Your behaviour is weird.'

Thirteen
Disenchanted Legacy

In early 1987, Rowland flew on his own initiative to Cape Town, South Africa. His target was Pik Botha, the foreign minister. Again on his own initiative, Rowland sought an opportunity to discuss Africa and 'offer his services'. Initially, Botha was wary but, knowing of Rowland's reputation among African leaders and his relationship with the State Department, he had become curious. Rowland's involvement in neighbouring Mozambique and Angola was of particular interest, as he had consistently avoided contact with Nelson Mandela's African National Congress movement, and his visit offered another opportunity to explore an end to South Africa's diplomatic isolation.

Jonas Savimbi's struggle had been made pivotal by the Reagan Administration to the future of southern Africa. Rowland had played a small part in persuading Washington of his protégé's importance and although Savimbi's alliance with South Africa had encouraged recognition of the Marxist government in Luanda, Rowland's continued association with the rebel would afford Pretoria a chance to participate in Africa's own mediation efforts directed from Lusaka.

In Mozambique, on South Africa's north eastern border, Lonrho controlled an estimated 40 per cent of the country's gross national product. That extraordinary statistic was based on the revenue from the oil pipeline, which after 1985 boasted an annual turnover of $20 million, although Lonrho's net profit for its 31 per cent share was a mere $0.5 million. That artery, along with the railway from Zimbabwe across Mozambique to Nacala, and the agricultural estates in Mozambique itself were targets of Renamo, the guerrilla group established by the Rhodesians in the late Seventies and later absorbed by the South Africans. Rowland's activities directly impinged upon Pretoria's own policies, more than they did on Angola's.

While the Zimbabwe government provided protection against Renamo for the pipeline, Mugabe refused to allocate soldiers for the railway, a vital route for 45 per cent of Malawi's exports which were produced by Lonrho. Delays in transport had a negative effect on the price of commodities with a finite shelf-life, as in the case of Malawi's tea, which would lose its freshness in transit.

In the absence of sufficient protection, Rowland negotiated with Machel in early 1986 that Lonrho would hire a private British security company, Defence Systems Limited [DSL], to guard the railway and the estates. Machel, whose affection for Thatcher had grown since their meeting in London, obtained British government approval of a £6 million loan from Lonrho to hire and arm seven former SAS officers and 600 Mozambican soldiers. 'We got the worst quality of soldiers,' recalls David Baxter, DSL's regional manager in Maputo, 'and they were fighting the worst sort of guerrilla action in the world.' The deployment began in August 1986.

By then, Rowland's relationship with Machel was, according to Alves Gomes, 'close'. Machel's son would be educated in Britain at Lonrho's expense. Among the other benefits which Rowland bestowed was a suitcase containing 1 million rand. The money was allegedly to finance the celebrations of Mozambican independence but few believed that suitcase's destination was not elsewhere.

Two months later, Machel died in an air crash. Mozambique's economy lurched towards the abyss as Renamo attacks increased. The instability in Mozambique was damaging Lonrho's investments in neighbouring Zimbabwe, Zambia and Malawi. None of those African governments was capable of launching a peace initiative to save their own economies. Devoid of civil servants and politicians with appropriate experience in shuttle diplomacy, they were also handicapped by their denial of any relations with South Africa.

The paralysis could be resolved only by a dedicated inter-mediary and Rowland's position was enhanced by the trust he had earned at the State Department in Washington. 'Tiny said that he was bored with business,' recalls one of Chester Crocker's aides. 'It had become a game. He wanted to do foreign affairs because he felt he could "bring peace in our time".' There were nevertheless reservations. Tiny, the Foreign Affairs Bureau agreed, 'dabbles in foreign policy'. He enjoyed acting the intermediary to move things along but was primarily involved in order to enhance his business interests. Although Crocker listened to Rowland, he never forgot that he was an independent businessman who could act without consultation: 'Tiny's a fascinating guy but, at the end of the day, State's dealings with him came to nothing. Our talks with him didn't change or influence anything.' But Pik Botha was impressed by Rowland's regular contact with the State Department, since both Lonrho and South Africa shared an interest in peace and, unlike Rowland, the South African was denied any possibility of discussion with his neighbours. The chemistry between the men warmed Botha to Rowland's style and his truthful, if harsh, assessment of South Africa's plight. On parting, Rowland agreed that he would contact the foreign minister whenever 'I think I might be of service'.

Rowland's unannounced agenda, to negotiate peace in Angola, Mozambique and the Sudan was, by any reckoning, ambitious. His diplomatic style – a mixture of professionalism, intrigue and bravado – would occasionally succumb to unrealistic expectations, displays of emotion provoked by disappointments and could even degenerate into farce, but above all it was unique. For good reason, no other American or European was attempting a similar feat. Firstly, because no one else possessed his depth of understanding, interest, sympathy and enduring relationship with Africa's leaders; and secondly, because by the late Eighties the mirage of African wealth had evaporated. Undermined by drought, starvation, disease, civil war, lack of education and corruption, the sub-Saharan continent's total gross national product [excluding South Africa] was less than Belgium's. Lonrho, swept along in the great vogue of the Sixties to overcome local suspicions of multinationals and invest in the dream of the Third World, had discovered that it was enmeshed in an increasingly ignored, insignificant and bankrupt continent. As an opportunity for business and investment, Africa had become both irrelevant and risky. Africa's leaders, accustomed to the flattering attention in the Sixties, had become unattractive to the superpowers. Desperately, yesterday's fêted guerrilla leaders were seeking high-ranking Europeans and Americans with whom they could assert their status in discussions about world affairs. In the absence of any other visitors, Rowland was the surrogate who would minister to their cause, someone who understood and sympathised with their problems.

During 1987 Rowland pursued his ambitions unobtrusively, shuttling between African presidents, listening to their grievances, seeking common ground and offering mediation. The font of Rowland's authority for those preliminary undertakings was Kenneth Kaunda whose unconditional trust of the Lonrho executive was revealed in the results of Rowland's interest in Zambia's amethyst trade.

In Lusaka, the Denver settlement with Mayers was reported as a vindication for Lonrho. 'I smelt something fishy,' Rowland told Tom Mtine, Lonrho's local chairman, 'and brought it out.' The 'victory' coincided with a noticeable deterioration of political conditions in Zambia. Kaunda, who had been formerly regarded as an honest, God-fearing Christian, was transforming the second republic into a tyranny. Among the beneficiaries was Rowland whose freelance diplomatic service was of increasing importance to the president.

In July 1986, just one month after the Denver settlement, Rowland agreed with Kaunda that Lonrho and the government should become equal partners in two companies, Kariba Marketing and Kariba Minerals, which would control Zambia's amethyst industry. Among the extraordinary benefits of the deal was the president's grant to Lonrho of a worldwide monopoly to sell Zambia's amethysts. Every Zambian amethyst miner was compelled to sell his raw gems at a price to be set by Lonrho.

Rowland's negotiations to win those rights had begun in 1984. In the six years since Lonrho's mine had closed, a German consortium had developed a new mine. In 1984, Lonrho provided evidence to the Zambian government that the Germans were falsely declaring the value of the exported amethysts – a crime identical to that committed by Blorg, Lonrho's subsidiary, in the 1970s. The German's licence was cancelled. The following day, Lonrho applied to the ministry of mines for that licence.

The application was considered by Dr Matthias Mpande, the newly appointed deputy minister. Trained in the United States and Canada, Mpande was of a new breed of intelligent and trained mining engineers which Lonrho rarely encountered in Africa. His departmental staff however numbered only three people and, according to Mpande, were ignorant and easily corrupted. Mpande refused Lonrho the licence and appointed an experienced gemmologist who in future could assess the value of amethysts which could be exported. The ramification was unexpected.

'I was constantly harassed by special branch,' recalls Mpande. 'They either queried my personal finances or offered me bribes. Kaunda realised that I was opposed to Lonrho.' Mpande resigned. Staff at the ministry were reassigned. The newly appointed 'chief mining engineer' was unqualified.

Mpande was 'furious'. Lonrho, he believed, had 'cheated' Zambia. 'The relationship between Tiny Rowland and African presidents is not really sincere and honest. I think it's really a colonial legacy. Like the relationship between the rider and the horse. The rider benefits.' Rowland's love for Africa, reasoned Mpande, was understandable. 'Africa has enriched him'.

Rowland negotiated the details of the monopoly with the president. His partner and chairman in Kariba was Francis Kaunda, the president's adopted son and the nation's second most important personality, who would later be investigated in connection with smuggling gemstones but without charges being brought. Their supporter was Doctor Ranganathan, President Kaunda's Indian guru who lived close to the head of state and mixed his spiritual with political advice, especially since gemstones wield significant influence within Indian mythology. Kaunda robustly condemned Rowland's critics as 'stupid'.

Under Kariba's articles of association, Rowland and Francis

Kaunda composed the quorum. The two men could agree anything. Mpande declared that to be 'a scandal'. The monopoly granted by President Kaunda was similar to a contemporaneous ten-year exclusive agreement granted to Lonrho for the export of Zambian cotton. To some, it was a sign of the president's *naïveté* that he granted Rowland such favours. Concurrent with his agreements with Rowland, the president had granted another European large tracts of land and diplomatic status to prove that oil could be produced from grass. To his critics, it seemed that the president believed Rowland also possessed powers to make heaven on earth.

Within weeks of the amethyst agreement, Zambian miners were complaining. Zambia's amethysts were by 1986 recognised as among the world's finest but the previous uncontrolled, massive extraction had depleted the country's stocks. The interruption of Lonrho's production after 1978 had encouraged other, albeit small, companies to begin mining. Those local Zambian miners were, under the new laws, bound to accept the prices which Lonrho offered. 'Kariba,' complained Eric Wightman, a Zambian miner, to the minister of mines, 'makes only a cursory inspection of the material before making a price offer without making any effort to grade the quality. We all believe that Lonrho's deliberate policy is to avoid any record of the grades and quality of amethysts bought in. Government controls are impossible.' Comparing Lonrho's prices for amethysts to those paid in other countries, complained Wightman, 'one realises on what a grand epidemical scale Lonrho is brazenly and immorally ripping off Zambia. We can with justification accuse them of economic treason for which they should be made to account.'

The world price for Zambia's amethysts was set at auctions in Idar-Oberstein, near Frankfurt. While Lonrho was offering miners $15 per kilo for low-grade and $90 per kilo for high-grade raw gems, the corresponding price the company obtained in Germany was $100 per kilo for low grades, and between $5300 and $35,000 per kilo for the medium to best grades. Local manufacturers, led by Arthur Yoyo, travelled to Europe, North America, Brazil and Hong Kong to establish that 'Lonrho was hiding its real profits from the government.'

The principal target of their criticism was Kaunda who, by 1987, was widely condemned as a tyrant. Critics, especially government ministers, were either dismissed and thereafter unemployable, or imprisoned on charges of treason. Rowland knew all of the victims. Most Zambians cannot recall that he ever protested about their fate. Among the casualties was Elias Chipimo, the former permanent secretary in the ministry of transport and High Commissioner in London, who publicly warned Kaunda to desist from tyranny. Chipimo's reward was his dismissal as chairman of Zambia's Standard & Chartered Bank, Lonrho's bankers, and a term of imprisonment. 'Tiny ignored my plight,' he recalls, 'to keep his position. He's a mercenary.'

Kaunda's critics among the gem miners in 1986 had initially gathered behind the new minister of mines, Pikson Chitambala, who also opposed Lonrho but was powerless since his ministry had been excluded from the original negotiations. According to Chitambala, Lonrho was exploiting the country by 'blatantly underpricing' Zambian amethysts and 'denying substantial foreign exchange earnings' to the country. The agreement with Lonrho, said the minister, 'has many defects and is not in the best interest of Zambia. . . It is very puzzling why [this] unfavourable relationship was adopted.' Chitambala particularly criticised Lonrho for failing to train a single Zambian in gemstone work, not least because 'Lonrho appears to have little knowledge themselves'.

To break the monopoly awarded by Kaunda to Lonrho, Chitambala issued a gazetted order in 1987 granting the exclusive right of foreign amethyst sales to a Zambian government agency. Chitambala was attacked both by Lonrho and by the president, who accused his minister of acting beyond his powers.

To settle the dispute, Lonrho agreed that a joint fact-finding mission with Zambian officials should visit the auctions at Idar-Oberstein and observe the sale of a particular consignment. The Zambians, led by Jim Lavender, a British-born civil servant, and the Lonrho delegation, including Ken Etheridge and Peter Kitchen, the company's gem expert, arrived in January 1988. For the Zambians, the two-day visit proved to be a depressing exposition. Lavender reported back to the minister that Lonrho's employees 'did not demonstrate any superior wisdom, experience or expertise in understanding the workings of the market', and their attitude antagonised the Zambians. 'No discernible consensus appears to exist which favours Lonrho's retention of a 50 per cent equal holding,' Lavender concluded.

Lavender's report was passed to Otema Musuka, the minister of commerce and industry. President Kaunda acted swiftly, without precedent and arbitrarily. In July 1988, when Musuka was abroad, Kaunda published an order in the government gazette permitting Lonrho to export unlimited amounts of amethyst without any price constraints. 'It was ridiculous and perplexing,' comments Mpande. 'It was a sign of Rowland's extraordinary influence on Kaunda.' Zambia had effectively granted the multinational – at the nation's expense – privileges and wealth which were starkly reminiscent of the colonial era. Annual losses to Zambia from smuggled emeralds were estimated at $250 million, and government ministers believed that a similar amount was lost by underdeclaring amethyst values. 'It is all our own fault,' lamented Musuka.

Undeterred, Musuka requested that Lonrho revalue its amethysts and, when that failed, demanded access to Lonrho's amethyst stores. Peter Kitchen, Lonrho's expert, guided the ministry's delegation around the company's storage areas. According to Zambian officials, 'the tour was a meaningless masquerade. Mr Kitchen only showed us low-grade material. He said the keys were missing to the sealed area containing the gems for export.' Musuka cancelled Lonrho's export licence. In retaliation, he was dismissed. 'A lot of people warned me,' he said later, 'when I started probing the amethyst issue that I was stepping on a "live wire", so I was not surprised when I was dropped.'

Kaunda's removal of the opposition extended even to Lonrho. On the president's orders, Tom Mtine, Lonrho's chairman in Zambia, was summarily dropped by Rowland in 1988 despite their twenty-five-year friendship. Mtine had criticised the new dictator. Kaunda's denunciation was particularly callous but, by his silence, Rowland endorsed that dismissal. In Africa, morality, loyalty or the odium associated with collaboration with dictators rarely influenced Rowland's activities. 'Tiny never even called me to explain,' recalls Mtine. 'There was a crisis in the country and I could do nothing.' For Rowland, the Zambian president was a vital ally whose patronage sustained Lonrho's profits.

The pattern was repeated identically throughout Africa. Lonrho's prosperity appeared to depend upon the favour of dictators with whom Rowland, exerting a particular combination of charm, profit-sharing, diplomacy and ruthless response to any challenge, formulated relationships that guaranteed Lonrho's survival. In his regular hops on board his Grumman jet from Harare to Blantyre to Nairobi, he affected a style which placed his personal services at the dictators' disposal but in return required their nations' economy to be available for Lonrho's benefit. Despite his age and concealing the weariness of endless obsequiousness towards men who governed nations but failed to fulfil their promises, Rowland was invariably greeted with genuine warmth. In contrast to British politicians, the leaders of Africa succumbed to the displays of personal interest visited upon them by Rowland as he flew across the continent, telephoning ahead to his 'runner' to announce his imminent arrival. This was the background of Rowland's relationship with President arap Moi who, with the help of Mark Too, had become a close partner.

Kenya's relatively strong economy and political stability rendered the country a potential powerbroker on the continent. Naturally there was a price. Rowland had paid a hefty contribution to Moi's favourite charities, including his university, and, on his trips to London, the president would receive a special discount at Anderson & Sheppard, the Savile Row tailors which Rowland had bought and which was managed by Josie. One consequence of their association was Moi's agreement that aspects of Kenya's foreign policy should be assigned to Rowland.

The tycoon's intervention was not welcomed by Basil Kiplogat, the senior official responsible for Kenya's foreign ministry since 1983. An unassuming, French-educated scientist and a former chairman of the National Christian Council, Kiplogat first heard from Rowland in early 1988. The subject was John Garang, the autocratic leader of the rebel Sudan Peoples' Liberation Army.

Over the previous four years, Kiplogat had, on his own initiative, developed a good relationship with Garang in a bid to negotiate an end to the civil war destroying Kenya's neighbour.

Garang had been born in southern Sudan and educated by Protestant missionaries. In the political turmoil of the early Sixties, he had fled to Kenya and then to Iowa in the United States where, in 1965, he had been awarded a degree in economics. On his return to Sudan in 1971, he had joined Anya Nya, the southern, Israeli-sponsored army and then received further training at the US Army Infantry School in Ft Benning, Georgia. He had returned home to become the southern army's director of intelligence. In 1981, following President Numeiry's promulgation that Islamic law was sovereign throughout the nation, Sudan had erupted in a civil war. Garang's Anya Nya units had revolted in support of regional autonomy within a federated state, an unlikely goal in a country of 562 ethnic groups divided between Islamic tribes in the north and Christians in the south. The war would cause millions of deaths, an equal number of refugees and the over-throw of Numeiry.

Garang's support depended both upon the CIA and upon Israeli weapons, training and the provision of logistics, including a strategically located airport. Through Israel, and in particular David Kimche, Rowland's interest in Garang grew as he recognised the region's economic potential. In particular, a swamp area where Chevron had invested considerable amounts in anticipation of extracting an estimated 5 billion barrels of oil. A desire to find out more about the area ruled by Garang motivated Rowland's invitation to meet the Kenyan foreign ministry official for lunch.

Kiplogat refused. 'Can we meet this afternoon?' asked Rowland. That invitation was also rejected. Although they had never met, Kiplogat had judged the businessman by his ruthless dismissal of Udi Gecaga in the aftermath of Kenyatta's death as unreliable and 'no good'. The Kenyan underestimated the foreigner.

At 2 p.m., Rowland was standing in Kiplogat's office asking the official to arrange a meeting with Garang in Addis Ababa.

Again, Kiplogat refused. The following day, Rowland flew to Addis and met the rebel leader, whose chances of victory and establishing a permanent peace were remote.

The following Saturday morning, Kiplogat was summoned by the president to his state house in Nakuru. To his surprise, Moi's guest was President Omar el Bashir, Sudan's new military leader. Moi explained that Rowland had telephoned that he would be flying with Garang to Nairobi. The rebel had agreed to negotiate an end to the civil war. Kiplogat was puzzled. With his four years' experience of the rebel, he did not believe that Garang was prepared for a meeting. By the end of the day neither Garang nor Rowland had arrived. President Bashir had come for only a day's visit but agreed to stay the night, so Kiplogat was dispatched to buy the head of state a toothbrush. The following day, Garang arrived but refused to meet Bashir. 'There's been no preparations, it's impossible,' he explained and departed. President Bashir also returned home.

Unembarrassed, a short time later, Rowland told Moi that Garang had repented and agreed to return to Nairobi for a summit to end the civil war. Rowland added that the presidents of Nigeria, Ethiopia and Zambia had also personally agreed to be present to guarantee the settlement. Again, nothing transpired.

In revenge, Rowland abandoned support for the rebel and a rival received the Briton's sponsorship. Iranian arms, shipped to Khartoum, were used against Garang while Rowland attempted to establish new business contacts in Tehran. 'Tiny was annoyed that his efforts had been ruined,' commented a Kenyan official. Eventually there was a reconciliation and Rowland ordered Lonrho's office in Zimbabwe to fund the manufacture of uniforms for Garang's army, provide an office in Harare for Garang's staff and support the rebel's family. Rowland would boast, 'I'm a card-carrying member of the SPLA. I'm number five in the hierarchy.'

'I'd make you number three,' Garang once told Rowland when they met in the Sudanese bush, 'but that would be too close to me.'

'Oh, I'm happy where I am,' replied Rowland.

The pattern of Rowland's diplomatic methods was established:

on the basis of a vague agenda, every leader was persuaded either by telephone calls or by personal visits from Rowland that every other leader was prepared for a summit to settle an issue. In that manner, ignoring his failure in the Sudan, Rowland won Moi's support to become involved in the prospective peace settlement in Mozambique.

Moi and Kiplogat had been convinced in 1988 that only Kenya, without any historic or political encumbrances, could broker the peace in Mozambique. Again, Kiplogat quietly undertook the footwork to establish the areas of agreement and disagreement. On his first journey, he consulted President Joaquim Chissano in Maputo. His second flight was to Frankfurt, Germany for a one-day meeting with Alfonso Dhlakama, the Renamo leader. Then began the shuttle diplomacy. While remaining in contact with Chissano, Kiplogat travelled four times by Land Rover and on foot through the Mozambique bush to Dhlakama's headquarters 'as a peacebroker'.

In mid-1989, Rowland intervened decisively. Alves Gomes, the Mozambique journalist who had introduced Rowland to Machel, was appointed Lonrho's chairman in Mozambique. Essentially, like Mark Too, Herbert Munangatiri and the late Tom Mtine, he was a 'runner' whose sole task, whenever necessary, was to smooth Rowland's access to the president. If Rowland arrived at night, Maputu airport would be especially opened for the Gulfstream. Rowland's meetings with President Chissano were less warm than with his predecessor but nevertheless productive. A £50,000 donation for the president to buy construction materials was gratefully received. One million pounds was handed over to the president's favourite charity. 'Did I make a good impression?' Rowland always inquired of Gomes when they left the president.

In August 1989, Rowland heard about Kiplogat's negotiations and urged Gomes to fly with the Kenyan to Lisbon to support Rowland's credentials so that he should be included in the process. One month later, on the evening of Friday 22 September, Rowland was closeted for two hours with Cavaco Silva, the Portuguese prime minister, explaining his relations with and assessment of UNITA and the problems in Mozambique.

Silva was clearly impressed because he complimented Rowland on his unbeatable knowledge and invited his participation.

On Rowland's initiative, Kiplogat flew to Pretoria in Lonrho's Gulfstream to brief Pik Botha and his senior official Rusty Evans about the peace talks. Between 11 a.m. and 4 p.m., in a guarded guesthouse, South Africa's isolation was terminated as Kiplogat successfully persuaded the two men that, while Renamo was taken seriously, there could never be a military solution but only a negotiated settlement in Mozambique. It was a remarkable achievement that Rowland was responsible for the first official meeting between Kenya and South Africa.

Building upon that success, in December 1989, Rowland delivered to South Africa another catalytic 'service'. At Rowland's instigation, Botha and Evans flew secretly to Nairobi to meet President Moi. Their discussions, which were conducted without the knowledge of either Kiplogat or the foreign minister, established their co-operation for peace negotiations in southern Africa. At Rowland's suggestion, Moi agreed that South African Airways could land at Nairobi once Nelson Mandela was released, a sign that their country's isolation would be further reduced. Rowland also instigated the negotiations permitting the airline to overfly the Sudan, allowing its first direct flights from Johannesburg to Europe across Africa rather than the circuitous route around the Atlantic coastline. 'Tiny did a lot of favours for us,' admits a senior South African official, 'and didn't expect any remuneration or favours.'

Effectively, Rowland was hijacking those aspects of Kenya's foreign policy of interest to Lonrho, just as, earlier, he had intervened in Zambia's. Soon after Botha's visit to Nairobi, Kiplogat was summoned to State House to discover Rowland ensconced with a ministerial delegation from Taiwan. The unannounced visit was a bid from the Nationalist Chinese to win recognition. In the expectations of business and loans from Taiwan, Rowland had assured the Taiwanese government that Moi would dispatch a return delegation. Only after strenuous debate was Moi persuaded that the consequent rupture with Peking would be expensive and damaging. The rupture of the initiative was an irritation. It also exemplified how the self-aggrandisement excited by Rowland's diplomatic forays and claims to a long-term strategy yoked Lonrho to losses in Mozambique from unprofitable businesses that should have been abandoned.

By 1989, the difficulties of managing the farms and exporting the agricultural produce in Mozambique were contributing at least £2 million every month to Lonrho's losses. The expiring DSL contract to protect the railways and estates had cost £6 million and there was no hope that Lonrho's loan to the government would be repaid. Secret payments to Dhlakama to desist from attacking Lonrho's assets had also failed to ensure protection. Replacing DSL's ex-SAS officers with Gurkhas had saved money but only a peace agreement between the Mozambique government and Renamo could stem Lonrho's losses. Steering South Africa towards a relationship with Moi was a breakthrough which Rowland believed might lead to an end of the war. To prevent further losses, speed was essential and Rowland was naturally anxious to accelerate the indigenous timetable.

Since Alfonso Dhlakama, the Renamo leader, had gradually grown to trust Kiplogat and the Kenyan initiative, Rowland perceived an advantage in intervening. His seemingly unlimited supply of money to feed and clothe the rebel negotiators who emerged from the bush shoeless and dressed in sacks, and the Gulfstream available for presidents and officials, supported his argument to the president that his involvement would be beneficial. Moi was also told that Herman Cohen, Chester Crocker's successor at the State Department, approved of Rowland's mission. Accordingly, during a visit by Dhlakama to Nairobi in January 1990, Moi telephoned Kiplogat: 'Come at 7.30 tomorrow morning to my office with Dhlakama.' The presidential summons, Kiplogat understood, implied Rowland's presence in Nairobi.

'Tiny was his normal, humble and charming self for those occasions,' when the two walked into the president's office. 'Your excellency,' said Rowland to the rebel leader, 'there are delegates in Blantyre who want to meet you to discuss peace. Allow me to fly you there on my plane.'

Dhlakama was resolute: 'Impossible. I can't negotiate without consulting my commanders.'

Rowland was undeterred. He believed that if Dhlakama were put in a room with others then, by magic, something would happen.

Accordingly, he broke the *impasse*: 'Well, your excellency, I know that you are returning to Mozambique, so allow me to give you a lift to Blantyre. Kiplogat can come as a guarantee for your safety and that there are no conditions.' The arrangement was blessed by Moi.

The three of them flew with Mark Too southwards watching a corporate video extolling Lonrho's achievements. Rowland felt content. The mere presence of the rebel leader was certain to accelerate negotiations. Some would criticise his ambitions as an expensive hobby, diverting his attention from Lonrho's commercial interests, but he prided himself on being a maker and shaker of governments, believing that willpower alone would ensure success. To his critics who complained that money was his sole interest, his peacemaking efforts proved that there was another agenda. Defining his political principles was impossible. He was certainly not a philanthropist, but there was something special encompassed in his deeds. From the plane, whose refurbished interior cost £3 million, he spoke by telephone in his normal code. Names were never used. Instead 'uncle', the 'doctor', 'our cousin' or 'my brother' were the ciphers to the subject. If Spicer was on the other end of the telephone in Cheapside, Rowland knew that he would be standing to attention. Airborne telephone conversations gave Rowland a frisson unknown to those merely worried about the mundane technicalities of normal commerce. As Rowland had no interests other than work, his dedication was all-consuming. This mission, he convinced himself, was history in the making.

At Blantyre airport, John Tembo, President Banda's secretary of state, was awaiting their arrival. As Rowland stood on the tarmac, Dhlakama stepped into a waiting car. 'Just clearing formalities,' he shouted as they sped away. Unperturbed, Rowland, Kiplogat and Too were escorted to a government guesthouse where three Mozambican and three Zimbabwean ministers were awaiting Dhlakama. It was noon.

Eleven hours later the nine men were still waiting. Dhlakama had disappeared. 'This is all Kiplogat's fault,' sneered Rowland. On the return journey to Nairobi, neither man spoke. Shortly afterwards, the magazine *Africa Confidential* published an account which denounced Kiplogat and accused the Kenyans of providing a haven for Renamo soldiers and weapons. The arms, it was revealed, were transported by Kühne & Nagel, the German transport company, 50 per cent owned by Lonrho. The civil servant, aghast at the accusations, guessed the source of the provocative article. The official peace negotiations were temporarily halted.

Rowland started to look for a solution in Angola instead. Jetting between presidents in Maputo, Blantyre, Harare, Lusaka, Pretoria and Nairobi, he sought to arrange, with Kaunda's blessing, that Savimbi's representatives would meet the MPLA leaders at a Sunday lunch in Kaunda's official residence. Convinced that Savimbi would be present, he also invited a delegation of South Africans. Rowland's and Lonrho's financial investment in Savimbi had accumulated into millions of pounds. In the expectation of the fortune which could be earned if the rebel were victorious, Rowland spared no effort in encouraging American support. On one occasion, he had refused to speak with Chester Crocker for months because Washington refused to supply Stinger missiles to UNITA and rejected his advice. But bringing the Americans, South Africans, the front-line states and Savimbi together in Lusaka would spell a major breakthrough for Rowland's diplomacy.

As the various representatives arrived for the elaborate lunch, Rowland behaved as a national leader, casting himself as a neutral referee to maintain the confidence of all sides, maintaining a sublime, even silent presence which avoided involvement in detail. But the meal passed without the prince. At the last moment, Savimbi had refused the invitation. Once again, Rowland's efforts and Lonrho's money had been expended to no avail.

The costly self-indulgence, albeit for a good purpose, was dependent upon Lonrho's continuing profits from the bedrock countries, the company's traditional roots. But over the years, Lonrho had evolved as a non-innovative corporation whose real profits were declining. With the exception of its sugar plantations and Western Platinum, Rowland had bought existing companies and responded to every offer with the question, 'And who's going to run it?' A pattern had been established in Africa whereby operations devolved total reliance upon the local European manager whose technical competence and efficiency were generally unassailable. The chief executive was summoned to remove obstacles which required political intervention. 'Tiny's tremendous,' enthuses a manager in Zimbabwe, 'because he pitches properly to the president to solve our problems.' But Lonrho lacked prestige.

Falling profits matched its tarnished image. In Zimbabwe and other African countries, Lonrho's managing directors, unlike Anglo American's executives, were not invited to sit on the boards of the major banks. Lonrho, because of Rowland's method of operations, was perceived as a political and secretive organisation, unquoted on the local stock exchange, excessively enmeshed in unsavoury activities at the presidential palace.

Yet as one of Zimbabwe's largest private employers, Mugabe decreed during the late Eighties that, rather than victimise the company, it was politic to forget past antagonisms. The president found that Rowland had proved to be a good friend, although he rejected outright an approach to honour Rowland for his services. Untainted by any allegations of malfeasance, Mugabe's explanation was emphatic: 'Lonrho has a reputation for buying governments and an honour would suggest that our relationship is close.'

The corruption, so rampant in Zimbabwe, running some laughed on autopilot, did not trouble Rowland. Despite Kruger's request that Lonrho cease payments, Rowland insisted that assistance to the company's friends should continue although all 'investments' above 15,000 Zimbabwe dollars were to be personally approved by him. The country, he told Kruger, was run by ministers and civil servants and their obstruction could be overcome only by presents.

Hence Lonrho's entertainment remained conspicuous. In

Lonrho House several employees were retained solely to entertain any available minister. Annually, Herbert Munangatire hosted a New Year's Eve dinner at Meikles hotel. In private Munangatire boasted to friends, 'I've given millions to government ministers and their courtiers.' Among the beneficiaries of his generosity was the daughter of Victoria Chitepo, the minister of tourism, whose psychiatric treatment in a London clinic was financed by Lonrho. For Rowland, it was an act of humanitarian altruism.

Politics and business, in Rowland's opinion, were synonymous. James Mocamba, a senior ruling party official, one of Rowland's business partners, co-operated with him to sell Zimbabwe Airways two Boeing 767s, a two-engined plane which many criticised as unsuitable for Africa. Over many months, Rowland personally lobbied President Mugabe on behalf of Boeing. Countering the arguments of those advocating the need for a four-engined, long-distance plane, Rowland arranged for the head of state to fly on a 767 from Washington to Seattle to defeat his critics. His successful salesmanship earned Lonrho a healthy commission. Mocamba was later Lonrho's partner in a hotel business.

But those who criticised Lonrho's investment policy were pointed to the case of Morris Nyagambo, a former minister of mines. In the course of negotiations for permits, Anglo American was asked by Nyagambo to pay for an irrigation pipeline on his personal farm. Anglo refused and in reprisal was penalised by ministry officials' refusal to grant licences. Lonrho would argue that by helping ministers, it avoided penalisation. But problems inevitably arose when the tenure of Lonrho's favoured politicians became precarious. That dilemma was particularly evident in 1991 in Zambia.

Food riots during 1990 prompted an army officers' coup. Although it was unsuccessful, Kaunda agreed to Zambia's first democratic elections since 1964. If Rowland had been dispassionate, he would have chosen that moment to reassess the loyalties, political realities and Lonrho's economic interests in the country.

Until that time, Lonrho had benefited from Rowland's privileged relationship with the president. Regularly at Lusaka airport, Peter Kitchen, Kariba's director, consigned a cargo

of amethysts on to a British Airways flight without allowing
Customs officers the right to inspect the stones. 'We have
exclusive rights,' Kitchen would say, 'so just sign the form and
don't interfere.' His explanation always proved successful. In
1990, reflecting Kaunda's declining control, the ministry of
mines asked Kitchen to provide a report on Kariba's activities.
The submitted result had been condemned within the ministry
as 'ignorant, confused, incompetent or covering up. . . I do not
think Mr Kitchen understands what he writes and perhaps even
less of mining and marketing.'

The small producers, losing colossal income owing to Lonrho's
low prices, agitated against Kitchen and Kariba, provoking Deb
Basuthakur, Lonrho's managing director, to summon Arthur
Yoyo, the chairman of Zambia's gemstone association, on 11
April 1990. Yoyo, a leader of the disgruntled amethyst producers, had publicly complained about Lonrho's extortionate
monopoly which he described as symptomatic of the company's
whole operation in his country.

'You're a liar,' Basuthakur accused Yoyo, 'fabricating and
distorting the truth. Everything you say about our operation
is rubbish. You are ungrateful about our efforts to promote
the gemstone industry.' Calmly, despite Basuthakur's threats
of legal action, Yoyo refused to withdraw his allegations. There
was, he knew, no remedy. 'It was the tragedy of the one-party
state,' he asserted. 'Everyone was intimidated from complaining
and Rowland, who was exploiting Zambia, had the president's
support.'

Instinctively, since his protector was in office, Rowland
ignored those criticisms. Convinced of his own influence and
that his prophecies would automatically be fulfilled, he even
dropped his withdrawn, self-deprecatory act. As the agitation
against Kaunda developed, Rowland tactlessly extolled the
president's virtues as a 'visionary, humane, and deeply caring
leader' while deprecating the president's opponents, including
Vernon Mwaanga, the former foreign minister, as, 'opportunists
and obstructionists. . . They have no following.'

On 31 October 1991, Kaunda was resoundingly defeated in
the elections. Mwaanga became foreign minister and refused

Rowland's request for an appointment. 'Zambia', he quipped, 'can live without Lonrho.' To repair the damage, Rowland telephoned Tom Mtine, removed by Kaunda in 1988 and ignored by Rowland ever since: 'A lot has happened. We should meet.' Mtine flew to London. Five days later he returned to Lusaka, reappointed as Lonrho's chairman, to defend his paymaster against a range of charges. 'Tiny has always been a target,' he smiles, 'and he just fights back.' Principle was not an issue for Mtine; he was grateful for the job.

Others sought revenge against Rowland, especially the amethyst miners. With Kaunda's departure, Mathias Mpande, Lonrho's previous scourge, was reappointed on 7 November as deputy minister of mines. His first orders were to prevent Lonrho's uncontrolled export of amethysts at the airport. Within one week of his order, Lonrho's controversial gemstone expert, Peter Kitchen, attempted his customary, uninspected dispatch of gems on a British Airways flight. On Mpande's orders, it was interrupted. 'Kitchen screamed,' recalls Mpande, who speaks in a quiet, scholarly tone, 'but our officers retained the gems.'

The following day Kitchen, and Lonrho's managing director, Deb Basuthakur, came to the minister's office bearing the permissions for export. 'I know your history,' said Mpande. 'Don't dangle your documents in front of me. Your monopoly days are over.'

Reality suffocated principle. Humphrey Mulemba, the minister of mines and an old friend of Rowland's, insisted that Lonrho should be given a chance to prove its interest in Zambia. The company was an important employer in Zambia, the minister argued, and with promises of reform, the row should be buried. The new government's only stipulation was that Lonrho should invest rather than remit hard currency. The effect of tighter controls upon Lonrho would be reduced profits in London, but that prospective discomfort did not detract from Rowland's notion about his company's indispensability in Africa, his personal invulnerability and his unique ability, born of forty years' experience, to outclass aspiring newcomers. That confidence was proven irrefutably in a challenge to his influence in Kenya.

The challengers were Nicholas Biwott, the minister of industry and Ketan Somaia, an Asian businessman who, equipped with his own Gulfstream, was seeking to emulate Bruce McKenzie's encroachment on Lonrho's businesses twenty years earlier.

Kenya had been a qualified success for Lonrho. The motor franchises selling Toyota, Mitsubishi, Massey Ferguson and Land Rovers had been profitable as were Lonrho's hotels, the Norfolk in Nairobi and the safari lodges in the Masai Mara. Expansion however demanded good relations with the government whose lubricant was bribery. Corruption in Kenya was endemic and insatiable. In Kenya, politicians expected to combine public office with developing their private commercial enterprises. Lonrho had donated 1000 acres to President Daniel arap Moi's favourite university. Symbolically, Moi's family owned the franchise for importing London taxi cabs, the finance house which monopolised the loans for those who wanted to join the profession and the insurance company which taxi drivers were obliged to patronise.

The opposition, increasingly vocal against corruption and the violation of human rights, was ignored by Rowland. When the editor of the *East African Standard*, owned by Lonrho, had been charged in autumn 1990 for 'publishing information likely to cause disharmony', Rowland had distanced himself: 'I have not seen the inside of the *Standard* since I bought the newspaper [in 1968].'

Biwott and Somaia's challenge had been expected soon after Ketan Somaia had visited Rowland in Chester Square in early 1991. The Asian had suggested that the two men might co-operate in Kenya. In return for Somaia's help with politicians, Rowland would offer assistance for expansion elsewhere in Africa. 'He had appointed himself,' recalled Rowland, 'the uncrowned agent for Kenya as far as I could see. Somaia sought to impress me . . . through his . . . understandings with . . . ministers in Kenya. I was very sad to hear what he said . . . it was staggering to hear how much he had amassed.' Rowland refused the offer.

Rowland had already tasted the president's inability to deliver on all his promises. In early 1991, Moi granted Harrison & Son,

Lonrho's security printers, the contract to produce a complete issue of new banknotes. But to Rowland's surprise, part of the contract was summarily withdrawn and De La Rue was awarded the contract for the two highest value notes.

Soon after, three contracts which Lonrho had expected to receive – for a sugar scheme, an oil pipeline and for printing new identity cards – collapsed allegedly on the direction of Biwott who, according to Rowland, 'has collected tens of millions in commissions, although not from us'. Simultaneously, Biwott was also lobbying to deny Lonrho and Mark Too, Lonrho's deputy chairman, the anticipated profits from the new relationship between Kenya and South Africa.

Rowland's counter-attack surfaced in the *Observer*. On 27 October 1991, the newspaper discussed the murder of Robert Ouko, the Kenyan foreign minister, which had occurred twenty months earlier in February 1990. The main suspect, according to the newspaper, was Biwott himself, 'widely known as the most corrupt of Moi's ministers with overseas cash hoards and investments said to total $200 million'. Kenya, claimed the newspaper, 'appears so morally bankrupt and commercially corrupt that . . . it is like Chicago in the Twenties, only here Al Capone is the mayor'. Ouko, alias 'Mr Clean', had apparently threatened to expose Biwott's alleged corruption and was therefore removed. Few doubted that Rowland masterminded the article despite his subsequent claim that, 'I am no more in a position to instruct the *Observer* to print [the article] than I could instruct them not to print such outstandingly relevant material.'

The Kenyan government's riposte, published in the London *Sunday Times*, was an interview with the vice-president, Professor George Saitoti. A 'very serious struggle', explained the politician, had erupted, casting serious doubt on Rowland's future in Kenya. Saitoti underestimated the substance of Rowland's authority in Africa.

In a formal statement, Rowland accused Ketan Somaia of being 'one of the . . . characters whose blatant statements, true or not, that he had ministers in his pocket, gave Kenya a bad name.' Rowland's words provoked the vice-president himself to summon a press conference and plead that he was not among

Somaia's recipients: 'I am not corrupt.' Shortly afterwards, Biwott was demoted and then charged with murder. The case was subsequently dropped due to lack of evidence. The *Observer* had once again served Lonrho's purposes and proven Rowland's supreme thesis: that Lonrho's fortunes depended not only upon his personal relations with the dictators but also upon his support for their continued survival. Nowhere was that immoral reality more evident than in Malawi.

In summer 1991, Julie Flint, the *Observer*'s Beirut correspondent, travelled to Malawi. For more than twenty years, Rowland's oldest patron and revered ally, Dr Hastings Banda, had, without international protest, incarcerated for unlimited periods his political opponents. The 'president for life', certainly aged over ninety despite an official date of birth given as 1905, relied upon John Tembo, his heir apparent, to rule the country. Flint's critical report about the 'tottering . . . desperately poor nation where tens of thousands of thin, ragged men run to work each day' which provided 'living proof that repression can work', described Tembo as 'cordially loathed by most Malawians'.

At first sight, the *Observer*'s unprovoked criticism seemed calculated to jeopardise Lonrho's investment in Malawi. Trelford had read the article before publication and had not intervened. Rowland was reported to be 'furious' and the following week the newspaper, admitting that it 'regrets any errors', permitted Tembo equal space to extol Malawi's enviable virtues.

Rowland's 'anger' confirmed his apparent sympathy for dictatorship. For years, Banda's critics had been tortured in the state's prisons. Their offences were simply to voice their opposition to dictatorship. Men and women would be incarcerated in abominable conditions where they risked death from malnutrition and brutality. Rowland's apparent connection in assisting Banda to suppress the opposition, and also in easing the succession for his protégé, John Tembo, at the expense of other claimants, was underlined by the unexpected arrival of John Beveridge QC and Andrew Nitch-Smith, a partner in Denton Hall, Lonrho's solicitors, to assist the Banda regime's prosecution of its opponents. The British lawyers' employment was arranged through Banda's office.

Rowland's support for Banda symbolised his fractured ideal.

Over the previous decade he had been revealed as a supporter of lost causes and losers in Africa. In Zimbabwe, Nkomo was powerless. In Angola, Jonas Savimbi remained a rebel. In South Africa, Rowland was a very late supporter of Mandela and the ANC. In Mozambique, he had little rapport with President Chissano. In Zambia, the electoral defeat of Kaunda reduced Rowland's influence throughout Africa. Across the continent, the pattern was familiar and repeated. Some believed that the loss of influence was caused by his inherent political *naïveté*, others recognised that Rowland, the benevolent dictator, found little rapport with the new swing towards democracy.

By 1992, Lonrho's strengths, achievements and imperfections had become a reflection of Rowland himself. His skill and diligence had produced an empire resting on moot morals and fragile finances. These two weaknesses coalesced in early 1992 when Lonrho's perennial liquidity crisis resurfaced in a particularly aggravated form. Rowland, whose life experience had unhesitatingly convinced him that businesses should emulate governments and deal with dictators regardless of their misdeeds, turned for salvation to Colonel Gadaffi. The agreement, in March 1992, to sell one third of the Metropole hotel chain to Libya, laid bare the financial and managerial shortcomings festering within Lonrho thirty-one years after Rowland's takeover.

The first indication of Lonrho's imbroglio began to emerge in August 1991. Buffeted by publicity about unpaid debts and dubious financial affairs, Sir Edward Du Cann offered his resignation as Lonrho's chairman in the wake of a report by the Official Receiver. In 1989 Homes Assured, a company providing finance to council house tenants to buy their homes, collapsed with £6 million losses. Du Cann was the company's deputy chairman. Two directors were charged with criminal offences. Fifteen years earlier, Du Cann had been condemned as 'incompetent' by a DTI inquiry into Keyser Ullman but not penalised. After the Homes Assured fraud, the DTI initiated proceedings for his disqualification as a director of any company, a prelude to his formal bankruptcy.

For some time, Robinson had urged Du Cann's removal but Rowland had reasoned that the effort to find a suitable replacement would be excessive. But on this occasion, to Du Cann's disappointment, Rowland agreed. Temporarily, Rowland became chairman while searching for a replacement in time for the next shareholders' meeting.

On the day that Du Cann's resignation was announced, Rowland was visiting Malawi to celebrate with Dr Banda the twenty-fifth anniversary of the Sucoma sugar plantation. At a cocktail party on the estate, Rowland heard René Leclézio, Lonrho's 'Mr Sugar', aged seventy-one, give a formal speech extolling the company's virtues. 'There's my new chairman,' exclaimed Rowland. His old associates suppressed their surprise. Although he had spent fifteen years on the company's board, Leclézio, a Mauritian who spoke English with a Hercule Poirot accent, knew little about international business, the City or British politics. All Rowland's criteria that Lonrho's chairman should represent an acceptable face and possess the ability to control the shareholders' meetings were absent. Leclézio did however possess one quality: he would save Rowland sleepless nights since he knew precisely what his master required.

Before his final decision, Rowland also approached David Owen. As a rebel, the politician seemed an ideal ambassador and their relationship had warmed with Lonrho's support for the SDP. But after further consideration, Rowland recognised that Owen's independence would prove too worrisome. Leclézio's appointment was announced in December 1991 just as, without warning, Lonrho's third major liquidity crisis erupted.

For some months, the public image had been perfect. City analysts, a breed who rarely travelled around Lonrho's empire in Africa but relied rather upon Spicer and Robinson for information, predicted that the company's profits would be maintained. Rob Davies at Shearson Lehman had forecast profits of £267 million on the basis of Spicer's assurance that Lonrho had sold its three basic metals, gold, platinum and rhodium, forward at advantageous prices.

Concealed behind the smokescreen was a critical rift between Robinson and Rowland. Throughout that year, Rowland's acknowledged pugilist among the directors had fallen out of favour with both Spicer and Dunlop. Neither admired Robinson's somewhat more independent spirit nor appreciated that, among City institutions, he was held in higher regard and credited for the fact that the ownership of the majority of Lonrho's shares had been placed with institutions rather than among small shareholders. Spicer's and Dunlop's distaste was encouraged by Rowland, who disliked Robinson's assumption that he was the heir apparent. 'There's another Gerald Percy,' Rowland told a Zimbabwean director. 'That's the devil's kiss,' replied his friend.

Robinson had returned from holiday in August to read in a speculative article in the *Financial Times* that he was Rowland's most realistic successor. At that moment, Spicer was with Rowland on the *Hansa*, lamenting Robinson's unreliability. Rowland appreciated his guest's comments. Like Dunlop, Spicer had cultivated the art of not only dressing like his chief but also adjusting his own countenance to mirror precisely Rowland's mood. If Rowland looked angry, so did both Spicer and Dunlop. And similarly, if Rowland laughed, both sought to please. Spicer had remained as a director, it would be said, by unquestioning loyalty; while others claimed that Dunlop retained his position by a combination of devotion and his wife's friendship with Josie. On the yacht, even Josie revealed that she also, automatically overprotective, reflected her husband's mood and opinions. Everyone knew how to keep Tiny happy, and if Tiny was irritated by Robinson's independence, then that dislike was cultivated.

On his return to Cheapside after the summer holidays, Rowland ignored Robinson's qualifications and appointed Philip Tarsh as chairman of the critical finance committee, replacing Du Cann. Two weeks later, Spicer and Dunlop were appointed Lonrho's deputy chairmen. Robinson had clearly been demoted. 'It was the worst moment of my career,' admitted a man who had served Rowland with total loyalty. Whisperers from Cheapside hinted that Robinson was too loyal to Rowland and had failed to steer the chief executive away from dangerous ideas.

Perhaps it was the evident antagonism towards himself in early September that persuaded Robinson finally to understand the company's past mistakes and undertake on his own initiative a strategic review.

Robinson's premise was that the company's indebtedness

was intolerably large and increasing. 'Lonrho is suffering from a negative cash flow,' he told Rowland. There were five major sources of losses: the absence of returns on the huge investment in the platinum mine in South Africa; the *Observer*; the huge and uncovered dividend payments; the overheads at Cheapside; and the cost of Lonrho's debt. The company was simply unable to pay off its debt which exceeded £1 billion despite Rowland's statement two years earlier that the company possessed £1 billion in cash and 'existing facilities'. Robinson's proposed remedy was to sell assets. The dramatic reduction of debt, he argued, would revive confidence in the company and allow Lonrho to purchase one major asset in Europe or America with money raised by a rights issue of shares rather than cash. In principle, he advocated a return to the philosophy which fifteen years earlier had prompted the purchase of SUITS and the House of Fraser.

Both his narcissism and his inherent distrust of independent-minded accountants prompted Rowland to reject Robinson's review. 'Don't worry, something will turn up,' he chided Robinson, reflecting his conviction that the German economy would painlessly absorb the costs of reunification and produce the required profits for Lonrho. Unwilling to contemplate that his wishful thinking might be wrong, he welcomed the opposition to Robinson on the board. 'I agree with the chief executive,' nodded Philip Tarsh.

By the end of 1991, Lonrho's spokesmen were predicting profits of approximately £250 million but, unknown to investors, Lonrho had lost nearly £700 million over the previous six years in foreign exchange. The company, suffering unsophisticated management of its treasury, had borrowed hard currencies to finance its African operations and had not hedged against devaluations and the decline of sterling. Consistently since 1973, Lonrho's accounts had boasted profits in Africa which could not be remitted while assets were sold in Europe to pay for the dividend reflecting the inflated profits. Ironically, in the same period Murdoch had earned substantial sums in currency speculation. The result of Lonrho's primitive financial management was a ballooning debt, stated in the accounts as £1.1 billion but, if extrapolated, had increased to £1.2 billion. The puzzle was the location of over £1 billion of the remaining profits which had allegedly been reinvested but were inadequately explained in the accounts audited by Peats.

In early 1992, after long discussions with Peat Marwick, whose fees would rocket inexplicably to £3.2 million, Lonrho's profits would be officially stated as £207 million, a fall from £273 million. But included in the profits was the sale of property worth £33 million and, most unusually, an additional £27 million from an accounting procedure which capitalised interest payments arising from the massive and unprofitable investment in Western Platinum.

Unexplained to outsiders, within Lonrho was a huge drain, sucking millions of pounds of profits. Officially, between 1985 and 1991, Lonrho had earned a total of £1501 million in pre-tax profits. £432 million had been paid in dividends. Interest payments on the bulging debt were costing over £100 million annually. The Advance Corporation Tax charged every year on dividends was reaching £80 million and could not be set off against non-existent British earnings.

There was also a gross imbalance in the company's revenues. Between 1986 and 1991, Lonrho's official income from Africa had amounted to just £115 million, yet it had invested £150 million in the continent, of which £89 million was in Western Platinum. Of its earnings 31 per cent was produced in South Africa and over 40 per cent in the remainder of the continent. The imbalance implied that Rowland had failed to address the major problem identified twenty years earlier by Peat Marwick, that Lonrho needed to improve its earnings in reliable, hard currency areas. Even where Rowland had invested in Britain and America, the accounts revealed uncertainty and poor management. The *Observer* was annually losing £14 million as sales and advertising fell, and Rowland failed to merge the Sunday newspaper with a daily to cover the costs. Lonrho's hotels were valued at £914 million but their profits were a mere £25 million. Setting aside the earnings from Lonrho's Volkswagen franchise, the operations in Britain had actually lost money. Either they were grossly overvalued or there was poor management. But the lessons and warnings were ignored on the sixth floor of

Cheapside. Precisely as in 1971, Rowland appeared unwilling to focus on the costs of Lonrho's perennial problem of imbalance, aggravated by the internal costs in Cheapside. Life was too comfortable for the directors to support Robinson's remedy.

Despite the spartan image of their headquarters, the seven directors paid themselves annually an average of £350,000; each was assigned a chauffeur-driven car and all enjoyed generous bonuses, pension rights and expenses. Rowland's annual salary of £1.6 million, his constant use of the Grumman jet at £2000 per hour and unlimited expenses, together with generous gifts to Lonrho's friends in Africa, annually contributed over £20 million to Lonrho's costs, considerably more than bigger corporations whose profits were not collapsing.

The requirement and the pressure to reduce Lonrho's debt was irrefutable. Rowland needed hundreds of millions of pounds as fast as possible. Denied access to traditional banks because of suspicions about the accounts, and disinclined to approach established corporations which would inevitably entail time-wasting complications, he listed individuals who might buy Lonrho's hotel chains for cash. Astonishingly, one candidate for a deal was Mohamed Fayed, who in 1985 had proven himself to have access to large sums of money.

Although Robinson had undertaken a blistering review proving that Fayed was bereft of funds, Rowland was convinced that the Egyptian could secure sufficient money from the Sultan of Brunei. Lonrho's bid to win compensation in the courts had fared badly. The huge costs and anticipated lack of rewards persuaded Rowland to seek a settlement. A deal to buy the Princess chain would compensate Lonrho and would fit in with the Sultan's considerable worldwide hotel operations. Rowland's approach was unusual.

On 31 October 1991, a man using the name 'Ostrich' rang Royston Webb, Fayed's in-house lawyer, claiming to be a friend of Richard New, the private detective. By that time, New had moved to Zimbabwe with his wife and was no longer employed by House of Fraser. 'Ostrich's' message was cryptic: 'I want you to meet someone whose identity I cannot divulge; to talk about a subject I cannot reveal.' Webb was intrigued, but rejected any meeting on those terms: 'Ring me when you can tell me what it's all about.' The voice he recognised was clearly Paul Spicer's.

The following day, after further comic attempts at disguise, Spicer admitted his identity and suggested that Rowland and Webb should meet at 5 p.m. on Monday 4 November at Claridges for tea. The topic for discussion was unclear but, in the midst of his melodramatic approach, Spicer revealed that Rowland had recently met Richard New in Zurich, Switzerland. Webb was no longer puzzled, but alarmed. To protect Fayed, he gave instructions to apply for injunctions against New, Rowland and Spicer.

Webb had good reason for suspicion. According to Rowland, New had approached Lonrho and suggested that Webb was 'pissed off' working for the Fayeds: 'New wanted a fee of £150,000 for an introduction to [Webb] and "if the outcome was satisfactory, a further £500,000 or 10 per cent of any financial arrangement, whichever is the greater".'

According to New, the approach had been from Rowland who offered £3 million in used banknotes if he could persuade Webb to defect. The proposed prize for Webb was £5 million. In return, both would disclose all Fayed's secrets. For Rowland even to consider paying so much money for the defections and to spend his time and effort on the strategy revealed the intensity of his preoccupation. To critics it suggested that Lonrho was financing his private battles but Rowland's justification had merits.

Webb, he believed, 'knew all the secrets and the full story'. His knowledge would not only reveal the source of Fayed's funds but would also be convincing evidence in Lonrho's trial for damages against Kleinworts and the Fayeds.

On 26 October, Rowland had flown with Josie to Zurich, the climax to several weeks of negotiations by Etheridge. As Josie poured wine and answered telephones in a suite at the Dolder Grand hotel, Rowland had sought to conclude an agreement.

Rowland's ploy to suborn Fayed's closest aides in the Harrods war had commenced earlier that year when he personally concluded a financial settlement with Francesca Pollard regarding her claim against her uncles. In return, in June 1991 Pollard had signed a four-page public apology circulated in an expensive brochure by Lonrho to the tens of thousands on the mailing list.

'I am conscious of the wrong I have done to R.W. "Tiny" Rowland,' she began, 'by the long and vicious campaign against him under my name.' Pollard continued that her whole campaign had been financed and organised by Mohamed Fayed. 'I hope my apology will help Mr Rowland to obtain an injunction against publication of the book which was shown to me in manuscript a short time ago.' The reason for her expensive recruitment by Rowland became more evident on Sunday 14 July 1991, nearly three weeks after the 'Apology's' publication.

The *Observer*'s front page, with Trelford's agreement, was dominated by Rowland's war. Under the headline 'Fayed's £100,000 smear campaign uncovered', Michael Gillard, the investigative journalist, uncritically reported Pollard's claims of receiving '£1000 or £2000 every month or so from Fayed's Park Lane address' and repeated her eyewitness account of Sir Gordon Reece advising Fayed not to embarrass the Conservatives before the 1987 election. Gillard did not compare Fayed's alleged £100,000 expenditure with the £25 million campaign orchestrated by his own employer.

A second front-page article, written by Trelford, concerned Farzad Bazoft, an Iranian journalist who had been arrested in Iraq while working for the *Observer* and executed as an alleged spy. Under the headline, 'Fayed's war on Lonrho may have doomed efforts to save Bazoft', Trelford conjectured that Fayed had forged Pollard's signature on letters to the Iraqi regime linking Lonrho with weapons supplies to Iran. Although the alleged letters were sent before the journalist's arrest, the editor speculated that in Baghdad, the link between Bazoft, the *Observer* and Lonrho's alleged supply of arms 'was bound to have influenced' Saddam Hussein's decision not to commute the death sentence.

Although Trelford's theory suffered from a lack of evidence, Rowland's purpose was served. With total credulity, Trelford quoted Pollard, a woman who had proven herself to be unreliable, that when Bazoft's execution was announced, Richard New had exclaimed in her presence, ' "What a good day!", and ordered a round of drinks.' New emphatically denies the allegation.

By any measure, both Trelford and Rowland had taken the battle against the Fayeds to a new level. Accompanying the newspaper's allegations was a writ issued by Rowland against everyone associated with the Fayeds, complaining of a 'conspiracy to injure'. On 10 September, the writ was served on New in Harare. It was the prelude to Rowland's next stage to seduce Fayed's cohorts to defect.

Soon after the writ was issued, Etheridge arrived in Harare from London. 'I considered,' testified New, 'that he was there to exert pressure on me in some way.'

The nature of the 'pressure' which persuaded New to fly to Zurich remains unclear but on Friday 25 October he met Rowland for two hours. The £8 million offer was 'all or nothing', said New. 'He seemed obsessed with his belief that I could arrange Mr Webb's defection and would become temporarily annoyed whenever I interjected saying that I could not possibly deliver what he wanted.' New flew back to Harare without concluding any agreement.

Rowland returned to London fuming. 'I've only got a few years of life left,' he exploded, revealing his anger about a situation beyond his control, 'and I've wasted my time on rubbish in Zurich.' Convinced that the initiative had come from New, and having concluded that Pollard was unreliable as a witness, Rowland's staff persisted in their interest.

New claims that he was approached by Barry Lundgren, Lonrho's local chief of security, an American national who had served in Ian Smith's army: 'Oh dear, if you've upset Mr Rowland I wouldn't make any plans in Zimbabwe now.' Lundgren was apparently acting on his own initiative. According to New, 'Lundgren made direct threats against me . . . and made clear that my days in Zimbabwe were numbered.' The threats included a fanciful notion that the Bazoft family was seeking revenge and New's expulsion from the country. New agreed to return to Europe to meet Rowland for further discussions.

On 4 November, New arrived in London. The previous day, the *Observer* had trailed Rowland's new twenty-six-page brochure, 'They Did It For Money'. Rowland claimed that both New and Royston Webb had authored 'murderous letters' which had compromised Bazoft's life. For different reasons, both the private detective and the lawyer were disconcerted.

The detective feared that he could neither rely upon Rowland to end the intimidation nor convince his former employers that he had not intended to defect.

The lawyer was amazed because, following 'Ostrich's' telephone call, he had agreed to meet Rowland that same day at Claridges to discuss, he anticipated, an end to the Rowland–Fayed war. Stung by the newspaper's allegations Fayed instead dispatched a private detective to photograph Rowland alone at the hotel. Webb did not arrive. The photograph was supplied to the *Mail on Sunday* accompanied by a story to embarrass Rowland.

Entangled in events beyond his control and enjoined with Rowland in an injunction issued by Fayed to prevent his further communication with Lonrho, New abruptly returned to Harare. He claims that the threats resumed and intensified within two weeks. The choice proposed to New was either to provide a full debriefing to Etheridge in Zurich for £2 million or 'an AK-47 would be planted in my house and "found" during a visit by the Zimbabwe authorities. Drugs may also be so "planted".' Fearing long imprisonment in an AIDS-infested jail, New and his wife fled Zimbabwe on the same day that the threat was issued. Through the night, he drove with his possessions to the South African border. In Pretoria, he swore a twenty-two-page affidavit about his experience. On 25 November, he sent the affidavit to Rowland from London. 'You are threatening a war which no one will win,' he wrote. 'Should I be assassinated or should any of the other threats against me, my wife or her family be implemented, I have made arrangements whereby such events will automatically trigger copies of my affidavit being distributed on a world-wide basis.'

Rowland received the affidavit that morning. New telephoned at 3 p.m. to secure his promise to halt the dialogue. The alternative, threatened New, was to file the affidavit in the High Court in London the following day. In their conversation Rowland assured New that he was 'safe' to return to Zimbabwe.

By then, Rowland had renewed his approach to Royston

Webb, Fayed's lawyer. Three days after the aborted meeting at Claridges, Rowland telephoned. Considering the history of the previous six years, Rowland's greeting was quirky: 'Long time no see. . . I thought I'd ring you and suggest that instead of meeting at Claridges you should come here and have a cup of tea with me, and a general chat; just you or bring anybody you like along with you.'

Webb's response was cautious but Rowland was persuasive that he sought an end to the feud: 'I've got nothing against Tootsie personally, except that he is fiendishly clever . . . the way he got hold of the company.' It was agreed that the two would meet at Claridges, although Rowland complained, 'I'm bound to feel outclassed.'

'Outclassed?' queried Webb.

'You're a barrister, and I'm just a chap who in normal circumstances would be a commissionaire or a waiter.'

Initially at their meeting, Rowland probed the possibility of a settlement of the dispute suggesting that Fayed pay £150 million in compensation; and then, with no forewarning, Rowland suggested that Fayed might want to buy one of Lonrho's hotel chains for cash. Speed was essential, stressed Rowland. Surprised, Webb agreed to consult Fayed.

Six days later, on 13 November, Rowland telephoned again. Webb turned on his tape recorder and told Rowland that Fayed was interested in continuing discussions about the Princess chain. Impatient, Rowland suggested that Fayed should fly to America the following day and conclude an agreement within the week. There were to be no 'professional appraisals' and no negotiations. In a later call, Rowland's price for 4200 rooms in seven hotels was $250,000 per room. 'That's dirt cheap,' he added. The £580 million was less than the £720 million valuation quoted by City analysts. Lonrho had poured money into the grossly over-valued asset.

The discussions ended in humiliation for Rowland. Fayed refused to buy the hotels but did own tapes of the telephone conversations between Rowland and Webb. They were published in the *Mail on Sunday*. To outsiders, the negotiations between Britain's most famous enemies were inexplicable. No one yet comprehended the pressure upon Rowland to mitigate Lonrho's debt. With the failure of those discussions, Rowland turned to another controversial partner, Colonel Muammar Gadaffi.

On 11 October 1991, Robin Whitten, a Lonrho director, wrote to the Libyan government, 'We are interested in expanding our activities in Africa and would like to discuss in what way we might co-operate with you.' Seven days later, Rowland confirmed that Lonrho would be interested in selling part of its hotel interests to the Libyans. The middleman was Adnan Khashoggi who in turn relied upon Mohammed el Obeidi, a Libyan with good contacts in Gadaffi's government. In return for a commission which Obeidi claims was 5 per cent, an invitation was arranged for Rowland to meet Gadaffi in Tripoli.

Gadaffi was under international pressure to surrender two Libyans suspected of placing the bomb on the Pan Am flight which exploded over Lockerbie in Scotland. Denied the old support of Soviet Russia, the Arab revolutionary's isolation had increased. His predicament was ideal for Rowland's political antennae to exploit. Quoting his friendships across Africa, Europe and with Ray Seitz, then the American ambassador in London, Rowland pitched, in his familiar self-deprecating act, a business proposition which sounded like a salvation offer to the Libyan. In return for Libyan investment in Lonrho, Rowland would not only use his enormous influence to improve Libya's understandable and justifiable case in the world, but would welcome a series of joint ventures combining Lonrho's expertise with Arab finance. The formula echoed a pitch familiar to the Sudanese and Kuwaitis from twenty years earlier.

Following the collapse of the Fayed negotiations, Rowland eagerly accepted the Libyans' proposal for a further discussion. On 26 November 1991 at the Le Laurent restaurant in Paris, Rowland met three Libyans employed by Lafico, the Libyan Arab Foreign Investment Company, a state investment organisation. In Khashoggi's presence, they discussed formalising his broad agreement with Gadaffi of a joint holding company for ventures in Africa. Rowland returned to London aware that negotiations with Arabs are time consuming and the necessity to reduce Lonrho's debts was paramount.

The urgency intensified on 5 December, the day Robert Maxwell's empire was revealed to owe over £1 billion stolen in a succession of frauds. In the ensuing hours, the spotlight swung fixedly on to Rowland. The 'tycoon factor', replacing the more endearing epithet 'rebel tycoon', cast suspicion on a company constructed upon secrecy and managed according to the idiosyncrasies of a single individual. Rowland's protest that his 92 million shares were unencumbered by debt was impossible to verify and his insistence that Lonrho's shares, at 120 pence, a six-year low and down from 300 pence in 1990, were undervalued, sounded hollow. Lonrho's finances appeared to rest upon sand. 'There's no justifiable reason' for the low price, protested Spicer. Since City analysts condemned Lonrho's published accounts as controversial and certain conclusive facts were still missing, the doubts lingered.

The truce broke on 6 January. That morning, Terry Robinson's resignation, a well-kept secret since Christmas Eve, was announced. A ripple of shock followed the news. Bereft of its qualified, independent-minded director, Lonrho seemed an increasingly shaky craft.

The blame for Robinson's departure was placed firmly upon Robert Dunlop and, in particular, Paul Spicer. Both directors, by popular judgment, were outclassed by Robinson and had combined to undermine the only person on the sixth floor who contributed original criticism of Rowland's decisions. But the feuds on the sixth floor had in fact been encouraged by Rowland's personality and style. Despite his generosity and protestations of loyalty, no one could hate with such dedication as Rowland. As Alves Gomes had noted, 'The atmosphere was terrible. There was permanent jealousy. Everyone was fighting, seeking Tiny's protection against someone else.' Even Captain Wilming had earlier decided that, despite their intimate bonds, he would also leave.

Wilming had become irritated by the cavalier attitude struck towards himself by both Spicer and Dunlop, but the deep-rooted problem was Rowland's intransigent refusal to believe that his era had passed. After 1986, it was no longer possible simply to jump into the Gulfstream at Heathrow and fly off. Departures had become dependent upon slots and that required pre-planning. 'He'd blow up when I couldn't do what he wanted,' laments Wilming, who had recently recorded a Country and Western record, 'Flying in the Air'. 'Tiny doesn't understand anything about mechanics except an on/off button. He thought everything was his to turn on and off.' Their arguments and the silences could last for two weeks until Rowland, a master craftsman at dismantling his own creations, signalled a resumption of their relationship. Wilming's departure, fiercely resisted by Rowland, was symptomatic of the ossification which was propelling the company towards a crisis similar to that in 1973.

At four o'clock in the afternoon of 23 January 1992, Lonrho's results were released and, for the first time, the company announced that the final dividend would be cut. In London and Johannesburg, where 13 per cent of Lonrho's stock was held, shareholders' disbelief turned to anger as they watched their shares fall to 110 pence. In New York, where Fidelity owned 5 per cent of the stock, the fund's managers were perplexed. In the City, analysts were livid. Their reputations, thanks to having regurgitated Spicer's whispers, were tarnished. For the first time, a new generation of City practitioners understood why, nearly twenty years earlier, the Straight Eight had revolted. Once again, City institutions complained about the absence of independent directors, the lack of information and the concealment of debt. One year earlier, Rowland had boasted in his annual report, 'Lonrho's unused banking facilities and strong cash position give us immediately available funds in excess of £1 billion to support further expansion without recourse to share issues.' Yet now, Lonrho was admitting debts of £1.1 billion and further analysis revealed debts of at least £1.4 billion. Similarly perplexing was Rowland's insistence that he had cut the dividend contrary to the advice of the Standard & Chartered Bank. If the bank considered the profits were healthy, it made little sense for Rowland to reduce the dividend which supported the share price. 'It's absolutely monstrous,' complained Euan Worthington at Warburg Securities. 'The episode has destroyed what support and trust the company had with the institutions.'

The 'tycoon factor' fuelled what Rowland himself called 'a

feeding frenzy' that he should resign. The annual general meeting was ten weeks away. Mindful that his annual salary of £1.53
million would be increased by £70,000, Rowland was asked if he
would stand for re-election. 'Re-election,' he laughed, 'are you
stark staring potty?' He was protected by Lonrho's Articles of
Association which precluded the re-election of Lonrho's senior
directors. 'I shall be here for another four or five years. I am
one hundred per cent fit and have no intention of giving up my
job. It is wrong for people to seek to hound me out.' To prove
his commitment he added, 'If ever there were a rights issue I
would underwrite more than £100 million. That is my faith and
commitment to Lonrho.' But deeper analysis of both Rowland's
and Spicer's explanations produced more confusion.

Spicer blamed the fall of earnings to £207 million on the
prices of the three metals which he claimed composed 40 per
cent of Lonrho's profits. But the price of rhodium had actually
risen from the 1990 average of $2700 to $4400 per ton in September 1991, covering the slight falls in the prices of other metals.
Something was amiss, especially when Spicer, in a moment of
frankness, announced, 'Everything is for sale, even my desk,' an
odd statement for a company which claimed to have earned £207
million in genuine profits. The unpleasant reality was that all
the newly purchased businesses like hotels and property flourished only in a buoyant economy. The certainty of the financial
problems was compounded by the ambivalence of the proposed
solution.

In a display of what he called 'housekeeping', Rowland began
selling bits of the empire. The much vaunted half share in
Kühne & Nagel, the freighters, went for £118 million; Scottish
and Universal newspapers was sold for £45 million; the British
franchise for MAN trucks was sold for £19 million; and George
Outram for £74 million. Rowland knew that compared to the
debt, those sums were peanuts and only confirmed Lonrho's
suspected weaknesses in Africa. Clearly, there were no buyers
of African assets at the values registered by Lonrho's accountants
and auditors.

The African empire raised awkward questions. In several
Lonrho offices across the continent, individual finance directors

could not understand why their company's consolidated profits were so low since their individual remittances to London were so high. Unanimously, they blamed the *Observer*, Rowland's expenditure on the Grumman jet, and the fancy salaries for the 'office boys' for the drain on the profits, but there were clearly other inexplicable losses in London related to the loans.

Even if the value of Lonrho's assets was questionable, these were nevertheless used as collateral against loans. How, asked individual accountants, did Standard & Chartered assess the security for their loans on African assets? The answer, according to Lonrho's accountants, was guarantees given by Lonrho in London against non-existent hard currency. Not only was that a potentially dangerous undertaking because of sterling's fluctuations, but a reversal of Lonrho's previously safe policy of never investing hard currency in Africa. The predicament was worsened, according to Lonrho's accountants, because the company's loans were, by then, 20 per cent higher than the values on assets assigned by the auditors. Just as in 1971, Lonrho was floundering beneath a huge debt.

The annual shareholders' meeting was just two months away and Rowland needed to reassure the City that the debts were being reduced. By then, only the Libyans could meet his needs.

On 7 February 1992, Rowland flew with Dunlop to Geneva for a two-day meeting at the President hotel to discuss the part sale of the Metropole hotel group. To entice the Libyans, he once again spoke about the wide range of other possible joint ventures throughout Africa and promised to use his network of presidential contacts to improve Libya's status in the world. No agreement was concluded despite the intense pressure on Rowland.

On 13 March, Lonrho shares fell by 17 per cent to 95 pence, the lowest since 1985. Calls for the appointment of independent directors were ignored and the following day the shares fell another 6 pence. The pressure grew. Five days later, on 18 March, just eight days before the annual general meeting, Rowland flew to Tripoli and began negotiating in earnest the sale of a stake in the Metropole group. According to el Obeidi, the middleman, the talks became a confrontation. The Lafico delegation demanded more than Rowland was willing to sell. His bluff, that they should obey Gadaffi and sign, aroused their anger. Once again, Rowland had equated Arabs with Africans.

Eventually, Rowland agreed to sell one third of the enlarged capital of Metropole group for £177.5 million cash. The whole group was valued by Lonrho at £393 million, proving that Rowland had won an impressive match. But the Libyans imposed restrictions. Their payment was to remain within the Metropole group; the Libyans had the right to appoint two directors to the board; and if the dividend could not be transferred to Libya because of sanctions, Lonrho could also not draw a dividend. According to el Obeidi, who started legal proceedings to recover his commission from Rowland, the secret annexes to the agreement granted the Libyans virtual control over the hotel chain's financing and management. That was unlikely. In effect the Libyans had invested too much money for an assurance of future intent. Even in his seventy-fifth year, the Master Salesman had proved his talents.

Once the agreement was signed, Rowland flew from Tripoli to Harare. The local British Airways manager watched with awe as the airport workers rushed to welcome the Gulfstream, bringing operations to a halt. Rowland emerged presenting ten-pound notes to his admirers before stepping into a Mercedes for the twenty-minute drive to Harare. In his old office, unchanged and still uncomfortable after thirty years, amid the remnants of the Rhodesia clique who built the company, he scoffed at the inevitable bad publicity. 'I'm not British,' he told his faithful clan, 'and I don't care. Gadaffi paid more than it was worth and the shareholders will be pleased.'

On his desk was the same white telephone that he had used thirty years earlier and the single framed photograph of the lanky, pipe-sucking young man with a double-breasted suit, next to his mother. The chairs were the same, and on a shelf were magazines published in 1973 reporting the boardroom row.

Not far away at High Noon, Irene Smith was still alive but senile. Faithfully, all her expenses were still paid from Rowland's unremittable director's fees. According to her nurse, occasion ally when aeroplanes passed overhead, she would amble to the window, look up, and murmur incoherently. Some believed she was saying, 'Tiny'.

During that stay, Rowland visited his old friend Nic Kruger, dying of emphysema. As both were sensitive about age and mortality, they avoided discussion about their illnesses.

Kruger was still devoted to Rowland but surprised that, despite his services to the 'Lonrho family', he had been rewarded with little corporate loyalty. He had heard that Les Blackwell's retirement after twenty-five years' service in Malawi had been ignored. 'Tiny said that I was a deserter,' explained Blackwell, 'and refused to speak to me.' When Kruger retired after thirty years, there was not even a boardroom dinner to honour his services. 'They'll give you a better send-off when you die,' complained his wife.

Shortly afterwards, Kruger passed on and his widow was proved wrong. Although Rowland and Josie flew to Harare and sobbed over the grave, other directors like Paul Spicer did not even send a letter of condolence. 'I expected at least a card,' sighed Eileen Kruger. 'I entertained Spicer so many times in my house.' Although she acknowledged that Lonrho's culture was 'quite unlike other major corporations', she was not alone in querying the meaning of Rowland's oft repeated phrase, 'the Lonrho family'. It would be put to the test on 26 March, Lonrho's eighty-third annual general meeting.

Rowland's agreement with Libya was announced just as the stock market opened. Predictably, there was uproar. Gadaffi's links with terrorism were proven and unforgiven. In St James's Square, opposite the former Libyan embassy, was a plaque commemorating the murder of a policewoman, shot by a Libyan diplomat. On that very day, the United Nations would consider imposing sanctions upon Libya for refusing to extradite for trial the two suspected Lockerbie murderers. Rowland was unapologetic.

'To me,' said Rowland, 'Gadaffi is a super friend. This is not the only deal we will do with him. We are already doing a joint venture with him for seventeen countries in every type of business. At my age I can say anything I like. Don't talk to me about morality and proper behaviour. I pay my taxes here . . . Gadaffi and Lonrho are a perfect fit.'

And there was a more pertinent observation: 'When the government permitted the Fayeds' bid, they said to me, "Who cares where the money comes from, so long as it comes into the country?" '

Rowland's justification in the *Observer* mentioned how many British companies including GEC traded with Libya, how Lonrho had 'never dealt in arms' and how the British government 'closed its eyes to the evasion of [Rhodesian] sanctions whenever it liked' for fifteen years, costing up to 50,000 lives. 'I think I've got a moral blind spot; I want to hear from anyone what their point of view is, and I don't like being told what my opinion ought to be. Governments renege on their opinions and alliances at the drop of a hat, and are unreasonable in expecting their citizens to fervently follow their latest ideas. . . Today's enemies are tomorrow's friends, I hope. In discussing and accepting the participation of the Libyan Investment Company in a hotel chain, with full attention to the law, and acting cheerfully and openly, I hope to give a lot of enjoyable annoyance to everybody. Wouldn't you?' Subsequently, Rowland would write another article attacking the United States for manipulating the United Nations to serve its own purposes against small nations like Libya.

Gadaffi's gratitude for Rowland's propaganda would be tempered by Lafico's disillusionment when Rowland's promised $300 million joint ventures failed to materialise. Although they had flown together around Africa, Denton Hall, Lonrho's solicitors issued a statement denying the claims of Omar Muntasser, the minister of finance, that Lonrho was committed to co-operation.

Those who would allege on the day of Lonrho's annual general meeting that Rowland had concluded the Libyan deal as a poison pill to forestall any takeover of Lonrho also misunderstood the conductor's motives. It was the Libyans who were trapped and no one, Rowland knew, was in a position to mount an unwelcome bid for a company whose control was vested in one man.

Since 1973, that one man's silent presence at the company's annual shareholder meetings thrilled a growing army of investors. Annually they made a pilgrimage to thank the man whose efforts had guaranteed them the high price of their shares and assured them of increasing dividends. For the first year ever, they received neither.

Each shareholder entered the Barbican Hall clutching an annual report which revealed record debts but provided no explanation. Although the meeting would start only at 11.30, the three tiers were filled to capacity some time before Rowland slowly and unobtrusively walked into the front of the hall.

The lights dimmed and a thirty-seven-minute film describing 'a year of celebrations at Lonrho's estates' burst on to the screen. Two images predominated. Firstly, the Kenana complex in Sudan, falsely portrayed as an important element of Lonrho's empire whereas the company's stake in the disastrous loss maker was less than 2 per cent; and secondly Rowland, proudly erect alongside Dr Hastings Banda at the celebration at Lonrho's Sucoma sugar estate. The combination of Lonrho's praise of both a soured dream and a harsh dictator reflected the absence of the customary annual triumphalism.

Rowland watched the film intently. He was of an age when dreams and aspirations merge with reality. When the film ended, he walked on to the stage. Behind him, forty of Lonrho's directors and employees were placed along the width of the stage to suggest that the company was not dominated by one man.

René 'Mr Sugar' Leclézio rose to deliver the chairman's report. As his appointment had been derided by the City as confirmation of Rowland's dictatorial style, Lonrho's share price had fallen. In retaliation, Leclézio attacked the press for a 'persistent and misleading campaign of hysteria'. The bathos of Lonrho's new spokesman was accentuated when the heavily accented voice quoted an old Arab proverb, 'Let the jackals bark, the caravan carries on.'

Quotations could not however explain why those on the stage should award themselves generous pay increases while over 2000 shareholders in the audience should suffer a loss of income. 'Will Mr Rowland stand up,' asked one shareholder, 'and tell us where are the other six directors on the board who could also do the deals to dispel the tycoon factor?' Rowland's head was already nodding 'no', when Leclézio replied, 'Tiny does not talk. He acts. And you have seen his act.' His great achievement that year, said Leclézio, was to secure peace in Mozambique. Unfortunately, the peace dividend for shareholders was unquantifiable. Unspoken was the certainty that Jonas Savimbi, reportedly murdering his own supporters, would lose his war and never repay Lonrho's huge investment in Angola.

'Isn't he past his shelf date?' asked another shareholder. Leclézio dismissed scattered suggestions that Rowland should retire: 'Mr Rowland is not an ordinary man. It is not easy to find a successor.' Tiny, the army was told, was 'fit and well' and would lead them into the next millennium, at the age of eighty-two.

The increase in directors' salaries, the litigation against the Fayeds and even the jet were questioned: 'If you accept Tiny, you accept the jet.' The debts, said Leclézio taking a cue card from one of the four assistants frantically scribbling behind, 'were around £850 million'. The figure was a surprise. With all the disposals, the debt had been assessed as £750 million, but in fact it had risen to nearly £900 million. For the first time, Jim Butler was questioned. Considering the failure of Maxwell's auditors, a shareholder queried Butler. 'Are you satisfied with the accounts?'

'Yes,' replied the auditor in one syllable and sat down. A marked man, thought cynics.

Leclézio's only promise was that the bad year would be repeated in the coming twelve months. Analysts at Phillips & Drew, Lonrho's joint brokers, reduced their forecast profits for 1992 by £25 million to £125 million, but the truth would be worse.

On 31 March, Lonrho was dropped from the FT-100 index. Sixteen years earlier, Rowland had predicted that Lonrho would rank among Britain's top five companies. Instead, his company was at the bottom of the Financial Times Index of Britain's top 100 companies and about to fall from its prestigious ranks. In December, Lonrho had been worth £1.5 billion on the stock exchange, half its value of two years earlier. By the end of January, its value had fallen to £790 million and was still sliding. To rank among the top five, Lonrho needed to be worth over £10 billion. The dream's disintegration scattered adverse consequences.

Soon after the sale to Libya was announced, Phillips & Drew resigned as a Lonrho market maker and broker. Lonrho's shares fell to 65 pence, valuing the whole company at £430 million, less than the Metropole hotel chain. Within one week the shares fell further to 59 pence. The fall might have continued had Genting, a Malaysian group, not bought over 5 per cent of Lonrho's stock, although no one could quite explain the reason. Rowland's personal fortune, based upon 83 million shares, had lost nearly £170 million in the past two years.

Like a downhill snowball, the bad news gathered momentum. Lonrho's half-year results announced in June revealed profits of £38 million, a 65 per cent drop from £109 million, and a steep dividend cut to 2 pence. Further sales worth £100 million were announced. The accounts were again puzzling. Having received £500 million in proceeds from the sales, the debt was reduced by only £192 million. Allowing for other debt consolidation, the company had lost a further £182 million in six months and yet the company was worth just £500 million on the stock exchange.

But Rowland promised that in the second half Lonrho would be 'back to normal' with total profits of between £100 million and £125 million. 'This is a year of good housekeeping for Lonrho,' said Spicer. 'We are cleaning up and climbing back.' City analysts echoed Spicer and predicted a better future. Rio Tinto, the company which thirty years earlier Rowland set himself to overtake and which was now worth about £6.5 billion, reported a rise in pre-tax profits in the same period to £295 million. The financial crisis inevitably sapped Rowland's influence. Robinson's departure encouraged more questions, albeit of a censored nature.

But the sales of assets aggravated Lonrho's problems. The decline of hard currency earnings reduced the company's ability to pay a dividend and to repay the loans which were supporting its African operations. The awful truth again resurfaced. Lonrho's African investments, so astutely accumulated, were unsaleable and therefore worthless.

'I'm tired,' Rowland told Robert Mugabe when they met in Botswana in August 1992. 'I just want to bring peace to Africa. I'm not so interested in business any more.' Mugabe, who had long suspected Rowland, finally warmed to his erstwhile critic. They were in Botswana as an overture to the signing of a peace agreement between President Chissano and Dhlakama, the Renamo leader, to end the Mozambique war. Before leaving Harare, Mugabe had read the five thick intelligence files on Rowland going back to the 1950s. They did not make pleasant reading but the president understood the mentality of their authors. Rowland, the old guerrilla leader knew, was an exceptional European. In his televised address after meeting both President Chissano and Alfonso Dhlakama, Mugabe praised Rowland as the man responsible for ending the war. Indeed, in the final moments when the agreement was to be signed in Rome on 17 August 1992, it was Rowland himself who flew to Africa to bring the reluctant rebel leader to Italy to fulfil his promises. To resolve a last-minute hitch, Lonrho's jet was dispatched to Portugal to bring Dhlakama's wife to the summit. From Rome, Rowland would travel to Sudan where he promised to mediate an end to another of Africa's civil wars. Unfortunately, the City of London had no interest in the fate of Mozambique or Sudan. Their preoccupation was Lonrho's debts.

By October, the pressure upon Rowland had become irresistible. Contrary to the most pessimistic predictions that profits would fall to £125 million, they would in fact be a mere £80 million, a 61 per cent fall, and the dividend would be just 4 pence instead of 13 pence in the previous year. Despite the Libyan funds and the other sales, Lonrho's debts were officially stuck at £947 million and there were other unrevealed debts in Africa. £447 million had to be repaid by mid-1994. Devaluation was costing the company at least £54 million and the motor franchises in Britain were losing money. The haemorrhage appeared unstoppable. While Jim Butler at Peats had valued Lonrho's assets at £1.33 billion or 204 pence per share, the stock market said the company was worth just one third of that amount.

The options were limited. Gencor, the South African mining company, had offered to buy Western Platinum, the world's third-largest platinum mine. The offer was rejected because, without the mine's regular income, Lonrho's future dividend payments would be imperilled. Indeed, without the platinum mine, Lonrho had no easily saleable asset.

A second option was further negotiation with Genting, the Malaysian investor. But since that would entail excessive revelations of Lonrho's finances, debts and secret arrangements to Genting's management, and also the sale of 75 million of Rowland's shares for £86 million, the option was rejected.

A third solution was to raise money by another share issue. But that raised a major problem. No bank would underwrite the issue and shareholders were unlikely to buy any more shares since even Rowland had dismissed the notion one year earlier as unnecessary. If Rowland, as in the past, were to underwrite a £100 million issue, he would risk a substantial portion of his personal fortune for a cause which might not be won in his own lifetime. Contrary to his promise one year earlier that he was prepared personally to underwrite his company's future, Rowland decided understandably to avoid the speculative investment.

On the eve of his seventy-fifth birthday, Rowland sensed his vulnerability. Although the stories about leukaemia and blood transfusions in Switzerland were nonsense, his fabled energy was indeed ebbing. Africa, he knew, could no longer provide Lonrho's source of wealth. The future lay in Germany, Eastern Europe and Russia. But he was simply too old to withstand the appalling climate and interminable bureaucracy of Russia to establish Lonrho's claims.

The solution was to find an investor who could temporarily relieve the pressure. The perfect candidate would be someone who could be persuaded that Lonrho was undervalued and that it would rebound when the recession ended. The ideal candidate would also not understand the business and therefore rely upon Rowland to continue the company's management.

Through friends in Germany, a nominee emerged: Dieter Bock, a fifty-three-year-old tax expert turned property developer, a chief executive of the Adventa group, who was searching for opportunities to invest his profits. Although he would be described as a billionaire with 'assets of between £500 million and £1.5 billion', there was no tangible evidence to establish his wealth precisely, except that he was a major investor in Cape Town's most expensive property development.

Indeed, to paraphrase Rowland only five years earlier about the Fayeds' unexplained accumulation of wealth, Bock's ability to augment an initial £10,000 investment in the mid-1970s to £1 billion was 'inconceivable . . . to be built up and maintained without public awareness'.

The German, another deal maker rather than manager, was encouraged to consider Lonrho, whose shares were languishing at 75 pence, as a bargain enhanced by the pound's recent devaluation. Since Rowland was keen to attract the German, their first meeting in Cheapside was characterised by the master's silky salesmanship, whitewashing Lonrho's losses in the two hotel chains, Metropole and Princess, and the Libyan 'poison pill' in a manner identical to that which had enticed the Kuwaitis.

'I've only got another three years,' he told the German, quoting his standard doomladen prophecy of the past decade. The recurring fevers convincing him of a terminal illness added plausibility to his tale of woe.

But to secure his signature, Bock set down unforeseen conditions. His investment was provisional upon Rowland's agreement, over a prescribed period, to sell his own 14 per cent stake. For the man who constantly boasted, 'I have never sold a Lonrho share', Bock's demand should have been resistible, but apparently Rowland found little difficulty in succumbing. If he was not prepared to invest his own fortune to support Lonrho, the pressure from the banks to repay the unsecured debts allowed little alternative. The consolation for Rowland was that Bock, without the chief executive, could not understand or manage Lonrho. Retaining control and enjoying the fun without any financial risk was the rationale behind Rowland's 'milestone' decision to sell his shares to another investor and ensure sufficient money for himself and his family in the future. A new twist was added to Rowland's final sentence in the 1991 annual report, 'Your board will always put the interests and protection of the shareholders first.'

For years, his associates had speculated that his refusal

to discuss his successor implied that after his death, his wife Josie, as the biggest shareholder, would faithfully supervise the continuation of the dream. Instead, he had guaranteed his greatest friend and admirer a simple life of luxury. To those aides, Rowland rationalised his decision by speculating the effect of his death on the share price. 'There would be a bear run and the share price would fall. With me out and a succession apparent, the air is clear for the long term.'

Under the agreement, Bock would underwrite half the issue of 200 million new Lonrho shares at 85 pence and also inherit Rowland's entitlement without charge. Since other shareholders would not pay above the 75 pence market price for the shares, Bock's stake was guaranteed. In parallel, Rowland agreed to sell just under half his 14 per cent stake, about 43.5 million shares, for 115 pence per share immediately and grant Bock both the right and the obligation to purchase the remainder at market price in three years or when Rowland ceased to be a director. Although in theory Bock was investing up to £169 million for the shares, the German was effectively underwriting only half the issue so Lonrho would receive only £85 million. A further £50 million would be paid to Rowland. Bock would therefore start with a 9 per cent stake which could rise to 25 per cent within the three-year period. His initial investment was £134 million for an 18.8 per cent stake. The mystery was why Bock should pay 115 pence for shares which were selling at 75 pence and still falling.

Bock explained that he had sought a vehicle for expansion into Eastern Europe and control of Lonrho was easily acquired by a deal with one man. Lonrho, he claimed, possessed the industrial experience which would secure valuable contracts in the former communist territories. The peculiarity of the explanation was underlined by Bock's refusal to become a Lonrho director before the rights issue was finalised. A cautious man, he recognised the danger of endorsing Lonrho's published accounts. It also invited speculation of secret understandings between Rowland and Bock concerning a buy-back agreement in the future. Ron Badger, one of Lonrho's financial directors who wrote the prospectus of the issue, announced his retirement soon after completing his work. Friends explained, 'He found the going and the strain too hard.' Badger joined the ranks of the many ex-Lonrho accountants.

The deal revealed the quintessential Rowland. In intellect, the tycoon was a car salesman whose ambitions were hampered by confused ethics. Much of what he had said in the past was untrue. He was a seller of Lonrho shares and he would act in his own selfish interests, taking 45 per cent more for his shares than their quotation, abandoning the other Lonrho shareholders to suffer the losses. He was unwilling or unable to convince Bock that there were no hidden factors in the company's accounts.

The deal also revealed how little he trusted his fellow directors. The details were disclosed only days before their announcement. 'I'm probably dying,' he sighed for the umpteenth time, provoking the familiar refrain: 'No, you're not, Tiny.'

'I'll clear out,' muttered the star.

'No, we need you very much,' rejoined the chorus.

The deal was announced on 9 December in conjunction with the sale of the Volkswagen franchise for a total of £124 million. The news was greeted as 'outrageous' by the *Financial Times* because other shareholders were denied a similar price; and as a signal that it was 'imperative for him to go at once', by the *Independent*.

Bock's greatest danger was the excitement spread by Lonrho about the 'chemistry' between Rowland and his new partner. Similar fervour had accompanied Rowland's previous 'lifeline' partners, the Kuwaitis, Fayeds, Bond and even Gadaffi. 'We are going to grow,' announced Rowland. 'I started Lonrho with four people and a cat. Today Lonrho employs 137,000 people. In two years, Lonrho will be employing 400,000 people.' The hyperbole never deflated. Rowland did not start Lonrho nor was there any possibility of its trebling in size by 1994.

Implicitly, Rowland had underestimated the effects of the recession upon Lonrho's hotel and metal prices and he admitted that Lonrho needed 'fresh capital . . . to continue expansion'. The company was contracting fast and yet more than half of Bock's money was destined for Rowland personally, not Lonrho.

Rowland's statement to shareholders gave a measure of

his audacity: 'I hope that you will accept as friends that the actions your Board has announced today have my strongest recommendation as being in the interests of shareholders. . . I do not believe that there is any unfair advantage since neither my company nor I has ever dealt in Lonrho's shares other than to buy them.' His last purchase had been to stave off Bond when he bought 4 million shares for £15.75 million at an average price of 380 pence. 'Believe me, it is only my age which occasions this.'

Few did believe Rowland. Bock seemed an unlikely partner. Lacking experience in any trade other than property, it was inconceivable that the German could manage the company's diverse African interests, especially in black Africa. Nor could anyone understand Bock's conviction that Lonrho, minus its debts, was even worth a total of £500 million. Since no outsider had ever penetrated Lonrho's financial secrets, the puzzle was to imagine how much Jim Butler had revealed to the German. The role of Peat Marwick remained as controverisal as before.

The reasons Leclézio gave for the sale further fuelled the doubts: 'These moves, together with the continuation of our policy of selectively selling underperforming assets, will enable the Board to return more quickly to its traditional policy of energetic development and selective expansion.' But Lonrho was selling profitable not 'underperforming' assets which contradicted the company's strategy. Leclézio's commitment that Lonrho would 'return to its African origins' was contrary to Rowland's own realism in seeing that the future was in Germany and Russia.

Seated at his polished desk in Cheapside, Rowland appeared unfazed by the inconsistencies. The narcissism and egoism shielded him from both self-reproach and others' criticism. Speaking interminably on the telephone to Africa, he occasionally forgot that, to most, the continent was either an area of famine and civil war or simply an irrelevant bore. For thirty years he had placed too great a faith in the positive results of his friendships with African presidents. Too late, he had realised that the continent was disintegrating. Akin to the consequences of the departure of the Romans from Britain, the continent was sliding back to its primitive past. Petrol stations were fuelless, roads were crumbling, telephone lines were stolen and not replaced, and even electricity was constantly interrupted. The clock was going back. Even when Lonrho had earned profits, the company had been unable to remit sufficient amounts to justify its investment. Even those profits which were remitted were depreciated by Africa's constant devaluations.

But Africa had served his principal purpose, namely, to provide the platform for his own ambitions. Fired initially by his thirst to avenge his past and subsequently by his enjoyment of power, Rowland prided himself on his achievements.

He had mediated negotiations during Rhodesia's rebellion; he had temporarily saved the regime of the Sudanese leader General Numeiry; he had attempted to channel Arab money into Africa; and he had sought to influence the civil wars in Angola, Mozambique and Sudan. Unlike any other European, he could fly from Cairo to the Cape and genuinely boast that he knew all the leaders of those nations over which the Gulfstream jetted. When he deigned to land, he would converse as an equal. Yet, just as the anticipated benefits to Lonrho had not materialised, the negative influence upon Rowland had been profound.

Vis-à-vis Europeans, Rowland found difficulty negotiating with his financial superiors and his political masters. Impatient with the consultations which both multinationals and governments undertake and with the imperfections of management by committee, Rowland had displayed bad judgment in his relationship with the City and the British government. The result, of his own making, was Lonrho's collapsing fortunes.

Rowland was the man who wanted to buy Rolls Royce and ended up with Jack Barclay, the Rolls Royce distributor. He had wanted to own Harrods but had controlled only 30 per cent of House of Fraser. In the previous decade, he had wanted to own *The Times* but had had to make do with the *Observer*. Above all, his desire was to nurture a rival to Anglo American but instead his love child had joined the sick-bay of stricken British companies, symbolised by the reluctant sale of the *Observer*.

By 1993, only 8 per cent of Lonrho's turnover was connected with mining and 4 per cent with agriculture. 60 per cent of turnover were sales of motors and general trade. Lonrho was a conglomerate of franchises rather than of invaluable assets which thirty years ago Rowland had declared it was his ambition to make it. The symbol of that failure was the quiet sale for 'nominal consideration' of the Wankel engine. Exactly twenty years earlier, Rowland had commended his secret purchase as the source of Lonrho's future profits. It was the triumph of personality and persistence over probity and percipience. The unravelling of Rowland's deal suggested that the conductor was masterminding a secret agenda which, to this day, has remained concealed. The public knows only that the original £12 million investment in Wankel, the equivalent with interest of about £80 million at today's values, has been lost.

During a pre-Christmas halt in Nairobi, Rowland confessed that his thirty-year quest to build a durable empire had faltered. Uncharacteristically, he had even produced a photograph of himself as a younger man with a Chinese girlfriend. 'We're going to move Lonrho to Germany,' he told his bemused African audience. In his seventy-sixth year, the conglomerate's architect appeared more depressed and uncertain than previously.

In common with every man blessed with exceptional energy, unique abilities and the requisite personality to effect his ambitions, Rowland suffered weaknesses. He suffered fools badly, yet gladly surrounded himself with that type in Cheapside. He well understood the need for financial management but was both impatient and unwilling to impose it upon his public finances. Ostensibly he pursued an altruistic vision in Africa but in reality he benefited more than anyone. Unlike other shareholders, in thirty years he personally earned at least £100 million from Lonrho, probably much more. His methods and morality were more akin to those of a car salesman than a member of the City establishment, yet he desired the respect accorded to the latter. His has been an extraordinary life of adventure and rebellion based upon instinct and anger. Initially, his egoism was richly rewarded, but the final result was the atrophy of a coveted empire. Instead of bequeathing the lasting monument of a resilient multinational corporation, Rowland's legacy is his image as a rebel tycoon, charming dictators and chastising regulators, with the final account of a dream built upon sand and secrets still to be revealed.

Notes and Sources

Introduction

The principal sources for this book were interviews with over three hundred and fifty people in Britain, Germany, France, Belgium, the United States and across Africa. Many people gave me access to their private papers and correspondence with both Lonrho and its chief executive. There were three reports issued by the Department of Trade and Industry and four reports published by the Monopolies and Mergers Commission. Many witnesses gave me the evidence and affidavits which they offered to both the DTI and MMC investigators and its officers. Naturally I used the voluminous newspaper and magazine coverage. I gained access to government archives in South Africa, Zimbabwe, Zambia and Sierra Leone.

The principal Department of Trade [DTI] reports referred to in the Notes by their date are:

Lonrho Limited 1976

House of Fraser plc 1984

House of Fraser Holdings plc 1988

The Monopolies and Mergers Commission [MMC] reports referred to in the Notes by their dates are:

Lonrho Limited and Scottish and Universal Investments
  Limited and House of Fraser Limited 1979

The Observer and George Outram & Company Limited 1981

Lonrho Limited and House of Fraser Limited 1981

Lonrho Limited and House of Fraser Limited 1985

In South Africa I was able to obtain the files of the Commercial Branch Investigation into Lonrho's offer to buy the minority shares of the Inyati mine. I have referred to these as the Fraud Squad Report.

Among the magazines referred to is *Property & Finance* [*P&F*], a Rhodesian financial weekly which is now defunct.

Since 1973, Mr Rowland increasingly issued his own publications to fight his cause. Initially, they were bound volumes of his letters to government officials, politicians and his lawyer. These are indicated in the Notes as, for example, 'Ltr Rowland to Cama'.

Latterly, as Mr Rowland's campaign against the Fayeds and the government developed, he issued a stream of glossy brochures. These are referred to by name.

In the course of the Lonrho boardroom dispute in 1973, all the parties submitted their evidence to the court by affidavit. These are referred to as, for example, 'Wilkinson affidavit'.

Evidence to the Monopolies Commission is referred to, for example, as 'Trelford evidence to MMC'.

The House of Fraser provided me with documents and boardroom minutes reflecting the internal dispute between the directors and the Lonrho representatives. These are referred to as 'House of Fraser Chronology' or 'Minutes'.

The most important source of information was the interviews with participants and eye witnesses. Inevitably, in a story such as this, the majority would speak only on the strict understanding that the conversation would not be 'on the record'. Most feared retribution from Mr Rowland. In respecting their wishes, I have not even alluded to confidential sources.

Book sources are referenced under author and page only. For fuller publication details see Bibliography

Chapter 1   *Metamorphosis*
Page 11   sporty nor sociable. Hilmer, Author interview
13   called Kittel & Co. *Observer* 14 Aug 1988
15   jail in Berlin. *Sunday Times*, 31 May 1981
                 a British passport. Cleminson, Author interview
16   headmaster was unwilling. Hall p.208
                 specific security restrictions. Anderson affidavit 4

July 1985 & Author interview

17   the Nazi regime. *Sunday Times* 31 May 1981
18   could not be done. *Sunday Times* 31 May 1981
19   was latrine cleaning. Anderson affidavit
with the authorities. *Sunday Times* 31 May 1981
20   as a security risk. Jack Cole, Author interview
bring your food. McCulloch, Author interview
Isle of Man. *Sunday Times* 31 May 1981
of his chores. Calderbank affidavit 1986
22   plenty of money. Hall p.211
string of damsels. Hall p.212
friends of Nazism. Karl Wehner, Author interview
anti-Nazi section. *Sunday Times* 31 May 1981
23   faintly embarrassed everyone. Joan Cole, Author
interview
25   and his internment. Cleminson, Author interview
book to me. Fallon p.40

Chapter 2   *A New Beginning*
Page 34   of unreleased gems. McKie, Author interview
make an arrest. Robinson, Author interview
38   farmer from Norton. Smith, Author interview
40   and last love. Ltr Rowland to Mercedes 23.11.57
Mercedes Official History
41   taking any decisions. Mercedes Official History
– archival document
42   enough to start. Sir Cyril Hatty, Author interview
43   from the bank. Milne, Author interview
45   organised by Beck. Hossy, Author interview
47   gold production increased. DTI 1976 p.9
a bit odd. Hatty, Author interview
49   a brilliant negotiator. Reynolds, Author interview
any successful strike. DTI 1976 p188
51   of Neville Chamberlain. R.B. Cockett, 'Ball
Chamberlain and Truth' *Historical Journal* 1990
arts in London. Sampson p.394
53   pocket £35,000. DTI 1976 p.7
stay with Lonrho. Hossy, Author interview

58	12.5 pence. DTI 1976 p.7
	he told Ogilvy. Jackson p.131
59	of my hands. Mayers, Author interview
60	bankrupt the company. Rowland Letters p.61
	needed three months. Abindor, Author interview
	copper was falling. £250 per long ton
61	was decidedly risky. DTI 1976 p.189
	with the public. DTI 1976 p.29
62	of Rowland's assets. DTI 1976 p.13
63	cut from you. Sampson p.396
	a partial secret. DTI 1976 p.24ff
64	your neck out. Sampson p.396
65	towards the newcomer. DTI 1976 p.78/91
	on a string. DTI 1976 p.69
	truthful and honest. DTI 1976 p.440
66	months after him. Eileen Kruger, Author interview
67	later that day. George Abindor, Author interview
	relationship with Rowland. *P&F* Dec 1962 p.43
68	a good purchase. *P&F* April 1962
69	Adams later admitted. Bednall statement 25 Feb 1962
70	and visiting directors. DTI 1976 p.405
	life gets boring. DTI 1976 p.27
	profiteering at Kanyemba. *P&F* Dec 1962
	especially non-executive directors. DTI 1976 p.436
	before board meetings. DTI 1976 p.358
	will to govern. Horne p.408
	and without conditions. Horne p.411
72	nature being undertaken. Welensky papers 29.11.62 Rhodes House, Oxford.
	real controlling force. Welensky papers 29.1.62
73	public relations officer. *P&F* Feb 1963
	situation is solved. *P&F* Dec 1963
77	was the boss. DTI 1976 p.435
78	estimated 69,000 tons. DTI 1976 p.14
	profit of £36,000. DTI 1976 p.15
	instead of £84,000. DTI 1976 p.15

risk and speculation. *P&F* Apr 63 p.47
and breathless expansion. *Financial Times* 14 Apr 63
79   such a withdrawal. *P&F* Nov 63 p.48
of the market. DTI 1976 p.9ff
80   Rhodesia for the cash. DTI 1976 p.90
the other shareholders. DTI 1976 p.23
84   as it advances. Hall p.18
86   beneath the surface. Hossy, Author itnerview
as absolutely balderdash. Rowland testimony Denver 1 August 1984 p.35
88   on an editor. Hall, Author interview
89   never interfere. Never. Hall p.29
kept his distance. Hall p.46
90   guaranteed from Mozambique. Bailey p.110/11 citing Jardim

Chapter 3   *A Decade of Dreams*
Page 92   post-war world. Bailey p.15
94   links with Rhodesia. Ltr Rowland to Gill 5 April 1976
three-month stockpile. Bailey p.121
95   and self-delusion. Wilson p.256
company in Rhodesia. DTI 1976 p.161
to discourage it. DTI 1976 p.162
within five months. Ltr Rowland to Dell 7 Jan 1977
96   the payments ceased. Bailey p.127
97   and later released. Bailey p.148
the melodramatic account. Smith, Author interview
recalled Colin MacKenzie. DTI 1976 p.133 & p.164
98   by Shepton Estates. DTI 1976 p.62. 1000 shares were registered in Rowland's name.
nature to emerge. DTI 1976 p.57
101   them a bribe. Arthur Winspear, Author interview
102   perks and pleasures. DTI 1976 p.67
of Rowland's options. DTI 1976 p.78

103   up the shares. DTI 1976 p.49
     had been declared. DTI 1976 p.49
     200,000 Lonrho shares. DTI 1976 p.70
     the legal requirements. Ltr Rowland to Cama 11 Dec 1975 p.44
     from Shepton Estates. DTI 1976 p.50

104   for our company. DTI 1976 p.58
     previous occasions, materialised. DTI 1976 p.58

105   the tax arrangements. DTI 1976 p.73
     total of £154,219. DTI 1976 p.51
     £62,000 of dividends. DTI 1976 p.73
     a complete hold. DTI 1976 p.77

106   to work together. *Daily Express* 1.6.73

107   into Banda's charities. Blackwell, Author interview

108   was never consulted. DTI 1976 p.400ff

109   18 per cent. *Accountancy*, October 1972

110   of the plant. Hall p.70

115   Christmas tree decorations. DTI 1976 p.451
     added is sancrosanct. DTI 1976 p.441

117   all the developments. DTI 1976 p.160ff
     to British diplomats. Bailey p.175

118   was absolute rubbish. *Financial Times* 7 July 1977
     for breaking sanctions. Bailey p.182, Bingham
     the cover-up. Bailey p.194 & p.199 Bingham
     effect upon Rhodesia. Bailey p.203

119   expected to resign. Bailey p.56, Rowland ltrs p.185

120   develop the mine. DTI 1976 p.95
     double by 1971. DTI 1976 p.103

121   Syndicate's other shareholders. DTI 1976 p.145.
NOTE: explanation in footnote DTI 1976 p.101
     one to another. *P&F* Sept 1971
     of Rhodesia's security. Barclay statement p.19
     in the mine. DTI 1976 p.102
     a criminal offence. DTI 1976 p.141/2 & p.147

123   non-resident in Britain. DTI 1976 p.407
     the increased expenditure. DTI 1976 p.409 & p.428

125   the utmost secrecy. Mayers affidavit p.6
129   ambassadors in Africa. Rowland press conference
               14.5.73

Chapter 4   *Eve of the Storm*
Page 132   to £135 million. Raw p.216
133   market recalled Slater. Slater p.106
134   information about Inyati. Fraud Squad Report p.20
               just been completed. DTI 1976 p.112
135   the remaining details. DTI 1976 p.110–111
               avoid being honest. Barclay statement p.20
               must be exerted. Bentley statement p.24
               Inyati be eliminated. Fraud Squad Report p.29
136   the girlfriend tonight. Bentley statement p.25
               and difficult reading. Bentley statement p.26
               the Inyati mine. Hossy, Author interview
               rand per ton. *P&F* March 1974
               risen six-fold. DTI 1976 p.116–17
               moment of idiocy. Hossy, Author interview
137   should withhold information. DTI 1976 p.119
               the shareholders' dissatisfaction. Fraud Squad
               Report p.42
               for the policy. Fraud Squad Report p.44
               South African shareholders. Fraud Squad Report
               p.48
138   interests of shareholders. DTI 1976
               profits from Inyati. Bentley statement p.30
139   enthusiasm among shareholders. Fraud Squad
               Report p.57–8
140   accepted the offer. Fraud Squad Report p.58 &
               Linklater's letter to Duncan Sandys in 1972 DTI
               1976 pp.145–169
               that excited suspicion. *Accountancy* Oct 1972
141   of financial information. DTI 1976 p.449
142   once or twice. DTI 1976 p.132
               oil to Rhodesia. Bailey p.217
143   not help matters. DTI 1976 appx 17 p.4
               our dressing gowns. Rowland, Author interview

144 stories were untrue. DTI 1976 appx 7
absolutely no truth in them. DTI 1976 p.599
an underwriting fee. DTI 1976 p.638
these absurd rumours. DTI 1976 p.600
been a knave. DTI 1976 appx 7 p.3
Lonrho about Rhodesia. DTI 1976 p.638–41

145 for private gain. DTI 1976 p.642–3
in the ground. Reynolds Author interview

146 contact of Rowland's. DTI 1976
owned by Lonrho. DTI 1976 p.281
worth £1 million. DTI 1976 p.243ff & p.260ff

147 paid by Lonrho. DTI 1976 p.277
half of any profits. DTI 1976 p.210
similar to Lonrho's. DTI 1976 p.194

148 then to Britain. DTI 1976 p.213
mine in Rhodesia. DTI 1976 p.235.

149 he did not know. DTI 1976 p.238
Rowland Mutual Association. DTI 1976 p.216
as very involved. *Observer* 20.5.73 article by
Charles Raw
South Africa at £46,000. DTI 1976 p.262
part of the action. DTI 1976 p.601–4
raise the loan. DTI 1976 p.221. The money
would be returnable in 1976.

150 gift or a loan. DTI 1976 p.226
received the payments. DTI 1976 p.222
separate occasions thereafter. DTI 1976 p.603
Rowland, Ball and Butcher. DTI 1976 p.283
per ton in March. DTI 1976 p.218
very nice idea. DTI 1976 p.418

151 Group Banking company. DTI 1976 p.419
these expensive houses. DTI 1976 p.418–19
group's legal adviser. DTI 1976 p.420
committee never convened. DTI 1976 p.423 16
December 1970.
buy Coronation shares. Technically it was through
Tweefontein Collieries which owned 62.2% of
Coronation Syndicate.

152	firm's biggest deal. Barclay, Author interview to its shareholders. Fraud Squad Report p.66 loans would be disastrous. Fraud Squad Report p.69 three days later. Fraud Squad Report p.69
153	for sanctions busting. Barclay statement p.14
154	Syndicate with Lonrho. Adams, Author interview
155	all the wrong reasons. Armitage to Butcher Report May 1970
157	motor trading and wine. Armitage to Butcher Report 27.8.70
158	out on its ear. *P&F* May 1971
161	in the 1970 accounts. Peat Marwick Report p.57ff
164	of the Libyan threat. Rowland, *Observer* 3 May 1992. are tomorrow's friends. *Observer* 3 May 1992 sanctions against Rhodesia. DTI 1976 p.170–1 under his control. DTI 1976 p.345
170	the Sudanese government. Cronje, p.182
171	sycophants and allies. DTI 1976 p.304 London and Johannesburg. *Daily Telegraph* 12.2.71 required bigger subsidies. Financial Situation Report June 1971 to Sept 72
172	secret from the stock market. DTI 1976 p.450

Chapter 5	*Deception*
Page 173	commented the *Sunday Times*. Raw p.350
174	which Lonrho would pay. DTI 1976 p.340.
175	fellow directors at Lonrho. DTI 1976 p.293 and Wilkinson affidavit.
176	desperate to sell. DTI 1976 p.296 we'll pull out. DTI 1976 p.295
177	20 per cent free ride. DTI 1976 p.340 (although strictly it was 18 per cent). of Rowland's good will. DTI 1976 p.300 to play with Wankel. DTI 1976 p.312
178	in better shape. *P&F* Aug 71

179   of DM36 million. DTI 1976 p.305
           no formal contract. DTI 1976 p.305 & p.307
           Wankel was not mentioned. DTI 1976 p.308
           Wankel deal was off. DTI 1976 p.309
180   could be illegal. Report by accountants Hock,
           Wiehahn & Cron: 'The unauthorised withdrawal
           of these amounts (R2,285,609.95) from Western
           Platinum Ltd.
181   pursue the right course. DTI 1976 p.310
182   to the board's endorsement. DTI 1976 p.316
           to play with Wankel. DTI 1976 p.312
183   flew to Kuwait. DTI 1976 p.320
           this difficult project. Wilkinson affidavit p.12
           finance Western Platinum DTI 1976 p.320
           recalled one director. DTI 1976 p.321
           same version to the board. Wilkinson affidavit
184   was DM64 million. DTI 1976 p.323
           for the DM36 million. Wilkinson affidavit 1973
185   people shied away. DTI 1976 p.312
           the uncontrollable Rowland. DTI 1976 p.324
           & p.452
           vendetta against him. DTI 1976 p.454
186   would never change. DTI 1976 p.457
187   clear up the mess. DTI 1976 p.327
188   ambassador thank you. Luttig's 'Top Secret'
           Report to Pretoria
190   the Israel-British bank. DTI 1976 p.325–6
           the financial crisis. Wilkinson affidavit p.21
191   It is very serious. December 1971 Financial
           Review
193   accept unpleasant facts. 1971 Lonrho Annual
           Accounts p.7
200   job said Rowland. DTI 1976 p.350
           to the other directors. DTI 1976 p.356–7
201   accumulated in Switzerland. DTI 1976 p.356–7
           whole unfortunate business. DTI 1976 p.350
           by the local governments. Rowland circular
           16.5.73; Smallpeice circular 17.5.73

202	have good potential. Rowland Ltrs p.77
	mine's entire development. DTI 1976 p.244
	misleading and . . . wrong. DTI 1976 p.245 & p.248
	would catch on to. DTI 1976 p.245
	by some as unprofessional. DTI 1976 p.245 & p.248
203	always so polite. Leach, Author interview
204	had complete confidence. DTI 1976 p.370
	appointment by some directors. DTI 1976 p.378
205	into the Cayman Islands. DTI 1976 p.370 & p.380
206	quibble about the price. DTI 1976 p.384
	less than £130,000. DTI 1976 p.379
	craning for this job. DTI 1976 p.383
	he wanted £130,000. DTI 1976 p.382
	without a chairman. Ltr Rowland to Cama 13 Dec 1975 p.52
	London and Overseas Services. DTI 1976 p.363
	the company's accounts. DTI 1976 p.363 & p.379
	not to inform them. DTI 1976 p.378
	could not be destroyed. DTI 1976 p.363
207	stand such disclosures. Mayers affidavit p.23
208	enlighten them further. DTI 1976 p.360
	£51,000 consultancy contract. DTI 1976 p.358
	the issue arose. DTI 1976 p.360 Smallpeice memorandum 14 March 1973
209	company recalled Smallpeice. Author interview and Smallpeice affidavit.
210	was at stake. Smallpeice DTI 1976 p.235
211	appointed a director. DTI 1976 p.461
	a profitable future. *Daily Mail* 18 May 1972
	vote of confidence. DTI 1976 p.466
212	the board's approval. DTI 1976 p.468–9
	suitable accounts staff. Moss, Author interview
	in Moss's reports. Ibid
	he could trust. DTI 1976 p.447
	extraordinary general meetings. DTI 1976 p.466

213   showing his approval. DTI 1976 p.466
            Rowland, Ball and Butcher. DTI 1976 p.466
214   by the information. DTI 1976 p.475 30.5.72
            continuing liquidity crisis. DTI 1976 p.468
215   misconceptions about my role. DTI 1976 p.468
            offer of resignation. DTI 1976 p.470
216   interest in Shamrocke. DTI 1976 p.250 15 June
            1972
            intended a sham. DTI 1976 p.252
217   I wouldn't agree. Beck, Author interview. Beck's
            action was settled in his favour in 1976.
            underneath the surface. DTI 1976 p.387
218   a public scandal. DTI 1976 p.388
            needed to be saved. DTI 1976 p.482
            God into Sandys. DTI 1976 p.482
            most almighty fall. DTI 1976 p.388, p.479 & p.482
            need to resign. DTI 1976 p.475
            of the fifteen directors. DTI 1976 p.394
            the £130,000 compensation. DTI 1976 p.388–9
            deny all knowledge. DTI 1976 p.390–2
            may say to you. DTI 1976 p.477–8
219   settled the question. DTI 1976 p.389 & p.483
            business he explained. DTI 1976 p.394
220   pay income tax. DTI 1976 p.415–17
            options were paralysed. Butcher memo 16.8.72
221   That was untrue. *Sunday Times* 18 May 1980

Chapter 6   *Conspiracy*
Page 223   Butcher over three weeks. DTI 1976 p.364
               payment to Sandys. DTI 1976 p.362
               about the arrangement. DTI 1976 p.364
               years with Lonrho. DTI 1976 p.265
224   accountants were astounded. DTI 1976 p.365
               muttered Butcher lamely. DTI 1976 p.365
               prepared to be accommodating. Leach, Author
               interview
               retrospectively by the board. Smallpeice p.237
225   management inadequacy. Wilkinson affidavit

lack of integrity. Smallpeice affidavit
I was pleased. Rowland Ltrs p.160

226 effort he complained. Smallpeice affidavit
228 for his actions. Spears affidavit
229 claim to the contrary. DTI 1976 p.605
230 a nice job. Rowland Ltrs p.169
233 basis for negotiation. *Sunday Times* 20.5.73
235 a shameful secret. DTI 1976 p.619
237 typical of him too. *Daily Mail* 27.4.73
to portray Rowland. *Daily Express* 29.4.73
238 on the telephone. DTI 1976 p.606
239 susceptible to Rowland. DTI 1976 appx 19
240 by secret payments. *Times* 30 April 1973
payment having been made to him. *Daily Telegraph* 30 Apr 1973
241 coup de grace. DTI 1976 p.607
drove Ogilvy home. DTI 1976 p.607 & Rowland, Author interview
244 down the receiver. DTI 1976 p.224
paid in Switzerland. DTI 1976 p.608
245 stage a row. Mtine, Author interview
246 become so familiar. Wilming affidavit
247 of commercial probity. Smallpeice affidavit
to £9 million. Smallpeice affidavit. *Sunday Times* 13 May 1973
248 of a hospital worker. *Times* 15.5.73
of commercial propriety. Smallpeice affidavit
fuelled the scandal. *Sunday Times* 3.6.73
251 understand a word. Hurd p.87
in British Petroleum. Bailey p.237
252 practices of this kind. Hansard 15 May 1973
253 by Heath's condemnation. *Midweek*, BBC TV 30.5.73
the most fundamental issues. *Times* 15 May 1973
254 money to Lonrho. DTI 1976 p.625 & Report by Peat Marwick 1972
255 every possible co-operation. 19 May Rowland circular

256   endorsed by Roland Franklin. 19 May Rowland
           circular
257   nothing about it. *This Week* 27.5.73
           whom I have dealt *Daily Mail* 22.5.73
           he informed the *Sunday Express*. *Sunday Express*
           1.6.73
           have to start again. BBC TV *Midweek* 30.5.73
258   the paper's conclusion. *Sunday Times* 20 May 1973
262   as a one-man band. BBC TV *Midweek* 30 May
           1973

Chapter 7   *Resurrection*
Page 264   realise enormous profits. *African Development*,
               Rowland interview June 1973
               given him their support. Cronje p.202
265   Africa would benefit. Cronje p.203
               suppress nationalist movements. Cronje p.208
270   stand such disclosures. Mayer's affidavit p. 23
272   discuss Mozambique's future. Martin p.126
273   party at any time. de Villiers, Arthor interview
276   winds of flatulence. Meredith p.171
281   showed the contrary. DTI 1976 p.321–2
               showing the contrary. DTI 1976 p.537–8
               at his accusers. DTI 1976 p.52–54
               compensation payments. DTI 1976 p.372
               to the inspectors. DTI 1976 p.374 & p.376
               than Rowland anticipated. DTI 1976 p.377
               I knew nothing. DTI 1976 p.390
               was extremely successful. DTI 1976 p.57
282   principle number one. DTI 1976 p.58 & p.69
               or tacit consent. DTI 1976 p.110
               case is all about. DTI 1976 p.66
               inspectors declared poor. DTI 1976 p.28
               memory is so bad. DTI 1976 p.30
               me to the contrary. DTI 1976 p.61
               as he makes out. DTI 1976 p.62
               show belonged to me. DTI 1976 p.314
               misled by Mr Rowland. DTI 1976 p.341

calculated to mislead. DTI 1976 p.325

283   accept their evidence. DTI 1976 p.358

to the £130,000. DTI 1976 p.380 & p. 382

for the company. DTI 1976 p.382

account as extraordinary. DTI 1976 p.383

policy of concealment. DTI 1976 p.397

more than casual. DTI 1976 p.629

contact with Kruger. DTI 1976 p.133

to sanctions breaking. DTI 1976 p.162

knew in London. DTI 1976 p.178

Lonrho's Rhodesian operations. DTI 1976 p.141

284   gift but a loan. DTI 1976 p.225

going to crucify me. DTI 1976 p.224 DTI 1976 p.218

is my answer. DTI 1976 p.222–3

is utter madness. DTI 1976 p.226

about the transactions. DTI 1976 p.227

the payments represented. DTI 1976 p.229

at a loose end. DTI 1976 p.408

285   outside the UK. Tudor Price Report.

hard to fathom. DTI 1976 p.606

did not know. DTI 1976 p.238

286   degree of resentment. DTI 1976 p.481–3

as a director. Ltr Rowland to John Cama 8 Dec 1975.

to be ashamed of. DTI 1976 p.607

287   comes to Lonrho. DTI 1976 p.655

responded Rowland unmoved. DTI 1976 p.656

share options in 1966. Ltr Rowland to Cama 11 Dec 1975 p.45

288   publication caused embarrassment. Ltr Rowland to Cama 15 March 1976 p.101

the company £306,637. DTI 1976 p.572

was declared unsustainable. DTI 1976 p.572–3

equal the debt. DTI 1976 p.580–1

289   clear it all up. DTI 1976 p.541

for just £11,000. DTI 1976 p.527, p.531–2

approved Rowland's claim. DTI 1976 p.542

questions recalled Butcher. DTI 1976 p.535
in September 1972. DTI 1976 p.523
very good stab. DTI 1976 p.533
vet Rowland's expenses. DTI 1976 p.517

290   are we not. DTI 1976 p.545 & p.552
was not genuine. DTI 1976 p.555
an auditor's responsibility. DTI 1976 appx 14
of Rowland's debts. DTI 1976 p.506
admission of fault. DTI 1976 p.574
any mention disagreed. DTI 1976 p.575
practice would cease. DTI 1976 p.513
in West complied. DTI 1976 p.567
a criminal offence. DTI 1976 p.562
version which appeared. DTI 1976 p.564
contradicted by stealth. DTI 1976 p.563 & p.571

291   employed byLonrho. DTI 1976 p.586
country at all. DTI 1976 p.588
his proper expenses. DTI 1976 p.515
company at all. DTI 1976 p.592
was in progress. DTI 1976 p.593
dismissed as untrue. DTI 1976 p.642–3
of company management. DTI 1976 p.659
me to stomach. Ltr Rowland to Gill 2 April
1976 p.176

293   stop in Nice. Ltr Rowland to Gill 2 April 1975
p. 175
Goods Act 1893. Ltr Rowland to Cama 31 Dec
1975 p.60
crucifixion by me. Rowland Ltrs p.180

295   impossible to withhold. Dell, Author interview
and Report by David Tudor Price QC 19 May 1976

296   of all the allegations. *Daily Mail* 7 July 1976
companies or individuals. 2 September 1976. Bailey p.43
embarrassment titillated Rowland. House of Commons 5 Aug 1976

300   to Africa's development. Mwaanga, Author interview

302   for an explanation. Ltr Rowland to Dell 7 Jan 77

303   complicity and impropriety. Owen p.291

304   they been used. Rowland to Dell 11 February 1977

second to none. Hansard 2 March 1977

for key documents. Ltr Rowland to Dell 30 March 1977

apology from London. Owen p.293 & Bailey p.65 & p.98

305   the oil supplies. Ltr Rowland to Owen 26 May 1977

and prosecute Lonrho. Ltr Rowland to Owen.

306   in February 1968. Bailey p.78

307   South African police. Rowland ltrs p.111

relatively short period. Report Tudor Price 19 May 1976

308   officer in the world. John MacNamara, Author interview

Chapter 8   *Expensive Illusions*

Page 320   in southern Africa. Meredith p.218

FNLA and UNITA. Bridgeland p.153

321   sell the shares. *Sunday Telegraph* 16.3.81

322   to support UNITA. Bridgeland p.572

transported into Angola. Bloch p. 193

326   never discussed it. Nkomo p.183ff

327   to a settlement. Smith, Author interview

328   Salisbury by Rowland. Flower p.184

329   with Tiny Rowland. *Sunday Times* 9 April 1978

331   unsuccessful takeover bid. *Observer* 7 May 1978

ferocity of our attack. Fireman, Author interview

333   some political cards. Fireman, Author interview

334   problems had disappeared. *Sunday Times* 12.2.78

338   indirectly by Russia. Ferguson, Author interview

339   criticisms about me. *Times*, 20.9.78

343   build another stadium. Mayers affidavit p.17

unimportant to us. Rowland testimony, Denver 1 August 1984 p.37 & p.3

344   sense of foreboding. Rowland testimony, Denver 1 August 1984 p.91

and said goodbye. Rowland testimony, Denver 1 August 1984 p.99

and insane fury. Mayers affidavit p.18

yell at anybody. Rowland testimony, Denver 1 August 1984 p.99

347   £30 million to settle. *Daily Mail* 27.2.80

348   House of Fraser board. Monopolies Commission Report 9 December 1981 p.27

with the House of Fraser. Monopolies Commission Report 1979 p.59

no doubt be made. Monopolies Commission Report 1979 p.61

Chapter 9 *Misjudgments*
Page 354 next three years. *Observer* 13 May 1979
355   about his whole operation. Fallon p.37
357   £300 million of assets. *Observer* 13 May 1979
358   by £195 million. MMC Report 1981 p.48
359   the influential power. Ferguson, Author interview. Rowland Ltr
360   of intelligence catacylsmic. Flower p.267
362   Rowland and he agreed. Ian Smith, Author interview
366   to stop paying. Leslie Blackwell, Author interview
368   a lot from Tiny. Mtine, Author interview
373   at Lonrho shares. *Times* 21 March 1981

2.8 million stake. *Times* 30 April 1980

378   lose this battle. *Sunday Times* 10 August 1980

God help you. House of Fraser Chronology 22 October 1980

380   Fraser's unpaid cheques. DTI 1984 p.212/3

around London's casinos. DTI 1984 p.225

control of House of Fraser. *Daily Telegraph* 13 Jan 1981

step down now. DTI 1984 p.209

381	the bounced cheques. DTI 1984 p.208
	running the business. *Sunday Times* 18.1.81
	is the beginning. *Times* 21 Jan 1981
382	brought into question. DTI 1984 p.215/6
	let me know. DTI 1984 p.217
383	about his shareholding. DTI 1984 p.217/8
	not to meet Rowland. DTI 1984
384	to her the gambling debts. Paterson, Author interview and DTI 1984 p.221
	wanted to forgive him. DTI 1984 p.225
391	a gentle decline. Astor p.76
	non-partisan newspaper. Astor p.121
392	European Jewish intellectuals. Astor p.240
393	than another idealist. Shawcross p.179
	of important people. Astor evidence to MMC 5.5.81
394	to become profitable. Astor p.282ff
	Godsend declared Trelford. Astor p.283
395	within the hour. Goodman, Author interview
	virtually said nothing. MMC Goodman evidence
396	A bit cool. Goodman, Author interview
397	benefits for Lonrho. Trelford evidence to MMC
	address seventy journalists. Hall p.142
	from the proprietors. Hall p.143
399	in high dudgeon. Legum, Author interview
	Trelford's editorial conferences. Hall p.144
	deter him, Donald. Trelford evidence to MMC
	free expression of opinion. Section 59(3) Fair Trading Act 1973
401	he reassured Ludwig. Trelford evidence to MMC p.13
402	more than casual. DTI 1976 p.629
403	well need them. *Observer* 11.11.79
	it is unbelievable. Trelford evidence to MMC p.25
404	subsequently told Hall. Hall p.156
	whatever the cost. MMC report p.40
	to suggest the contrary. MMC report p.72

405   wholly exceptional circumstances. MMC Report
           p.69
           running of the Observer. MMC Report 29 June
           1981
           were a farce. *Times* 4 July 1981
           and conscientious body. *Times* 6 July 1981
           unworkable and unacceptable. *Observer* 5 July
           1981

Chapter 10   *The Crazy Gang*
Page 410   not a normal case. Hensley Author interview
           and US Customs file
           got the case dismissed. Declassified Customs re-
           port
413   Chicago Sun-Times. Shawcross p.306/7 & p.320
415   by Harold Wilson. *Private Eye* 6 July 1979 No
           458
416   own shoe repairs. *Sunday Times* 14 Aug 1988
           events had changed. MMC Report 9 December
           1981 p.35
           secret bid for Lonrho. MMC Report 9 December
           1981 p.38
417   management of the store group. MMC Report
           9 December 1981 p.34
           suppliers of House of Fraser. MMC Report 9
           December 1981 p.60
418   but sweeping powers. *Economist* 19 Dec 1981
           disgracefully raw deal. 10 December 1981
           criticism and contempt. 13 December 1981
419   interest was excessive. Author interview
422   and occasionally offensive. House of Fraser
           Chronology
423   from the vendetta. Ltr Rowland to Scholey 22
           Apr 1982
           were in fact falling. *Standard* 7 July 1982
           I need the cash. *Standard* 7 July 1982
425   of Dixons Photographics. DTI 1984 p.82
426   Richardson was subterfuge. DTI 1984 p.74

to become involved. DTI 1984 p.80 and confidential information to the Author

427   initiated a war chest. DTI 1984 p.318
company too cheap. DTI 1984 p.318
before or since. DTI 1984 p.325

428   I've had circulars. 20 September 1982
face with the experience. *Daily Telegraph* 4 Oct
1982

429   writ will be issued. House of Fraser minutes
16.9.82
in a secret plot. DTI 1984 p.181
bought the shares. DTI 1984 p.195
with its chief executive. DTI 1984 p.246

430   won by a long chalk. *Glasgow Herald* 3 November
1982

431   whom he most admired. *Business*, Chris Black-
hurst March 1987
aware of the shipment. *Private Eye* 28 November
1986

432   is totally unreliable. DTI 1984 p.152
to solve the problem. DTI 1984 p.144
Marwan swallowed it. DTI 1984 p.176

433   Credit Suisse in Geneva. DTI 1984 p.135ff
London market before. DTI 1984 p.134ff
of £4 million. DTI 1984 p.122ff

434   all the other cards. DTI 1984 p.111
got the Serpentine. *Sunday Telegraph* 26 June 1983

435   divide the House of Fraser. DTI 1984 p.101
refused the proposition. DTI 1984 p.91

440   visit the country shortly. Bridgeland p.542
441   deemed more important. Hall p.161
442   dismissal of the editor. Hall p.166
error of judgment. Hall p.166
443   Cruise O'Brien's column. Hall p.180
445   of comparative nonentities. Hall p.175
448   at twelve hours' notice. Nkomo p.244
450   talk on those terms. Hall p.189
452   a government guide. *Times* 19 April 1984

454   and my strength. Colin Legum, *London Review of Books* 19 July 1984

on their own now. *Times* 25 April 1984

458   with the assets. *Daily Mail* 5 July 1984

460   Lonrho's takeover. DTI 1984 p.274ff

Fraser and Lonrho. Ltr Rowland to Griffiths 10 February 1984

against de-merger. Lonrho's leading counsel submission to Griffiths.

on a marathon chase. DTI 1984 p.281

read every page. DTI 1984 p.281

461   on the crucial issue. DTI 1984 p.288

to take their profits. DTI 1984 p.329

withdrawn from the case. Ltr Rowland to Jenkins 10 February 1984

462   given to the press. DTI 1984 p.87–89

a total lie. Fallon, Author interview

Mr Rowland did not. DTI 1984 p.97

this to be coincidence. DTI 1984 p.98

463   in a speculative punt. DTI 1984 p.132

it mentioned again. DTI 1984 p.75

not meet socially. DTI 1984 p.190

of nineteen years. *Mail on Sunday* 29.11.92

contradicted the Egyptian. DTI 1984 p.152

lied deliberately. DTI 1984 p.176 – albeit from 'misguided fear . . . that his investment was somehow unlawful under English law,' wrote Griffiths.

the Slater cutting. DTI 1984 p.166

464   should be a coincidence. DTI 1984 p.169/70

to convey to me. DTI 1984 p.172

with the jigsaw. DTI 1984 p.114

Chapter 11   *A Fatal Relationship*

Page 466   and last straw. *Observer* 4 November 1984

the DTI required. DTI 1988 p.87 & *Observer* 14 August 1988

468   his innocent warehouser. *Observer* 14 August 1988

telephoning his office. DTI 1988 p.87

with the stock exchange. DTI 1988 p.88

469   in contact with the Sultan. DTI 1988 p.66

470   Bank of Scotland. DTI 1988 p.283

belong to the Sultan. DTI 1988 p.285

in the company. DTI 1988 p.73

471   bought Lonrho's shares. DTI 1988 p.74

had sufficient money. DTI 1988 p.76; Marwan, Author interview

472   to this country. Fallon p.63

owes to its clients. Ltr Fayed to Fraser 16 August 1984

investment adviser to the Sultan. DTI 1988 p.83

473   their own money. DTI 1988 p.108

admitted MacArthur. *Business Programme* Channel 4 10 March 1985

474   and from politics. 'Hero from Zero' (circular) September 1988

Friday in cash. DTI 1988 p.88

Fayed was still smiling. DTI 1988 p.88

475   to 'control' everything. DTI 1988 p.91 & Basham, Author interviews

476   experience of the Fayeds. DTI 1988 p.92–5

deal urged Marwan. DTI 1988 p.94

477   lying said Rowland. DTI 1988 p.96

479   advertising for his newspaper. Ltr Trelford to Fayed 10 March 1984

in a concert party. DTI 1988 p.102

480   the Middle East. Ltr MacArthur to Llewellyn Smith 16 November 1984

481   image of the Fayeds. DTI 1988 p.447–8

up to them. DTI 1988 p.175

482   was a Swiss bank. DTI 1988 p.278

483   Agent in London. DTI 1988 p.287

485   the Fayeds' claims. DTI 1988 p.134

wealth was untrue. DTI 1988 p.129–131

is totally unreliable. DTI 1988 p.152

486   to finance the offer. DTI 1988 p.136

487　　　　Lonrho could produce. *Sunday Telegraph* 10 March 1985
　　　　　the Nasser period. DTI p.140

488　　　　about Rowland's motives. DTI 1988 p.457

489　　　　to the Monopolies Commission. *Observer* 10 March 1985
　　　　　closer to Rowland. DTI 1988 p.707

491　　　　undertakings not to bid. 'The Harrods Scandal', *Observer* 14.8.88
　　　　　third party was involved. DTI 1988 p.145
　　　　　change his mind. DTI 1988 p.165

492　　　　do not hold water. DTI 1988 p.144
　　　　　lawyers would write. DTI 1988 p.148
　　　　　or otherwise misleading. DTI 1988 p.462

493　　　　competition element involved. Fallon p.71
　　　　　that the bid be allowed. DTI 1988 p.148
　　　　　two cargo vessels. DTI 1988 p.201

494　　　　gave that assurance. DTI 1988 p.150

495　　　　wanted to own Harrods. *Daily Mail* 7.4.85
　　　　　by Kleinwort Benson. DTI 1988 p.152

Chapter 12　*War*
Page 498　　for the House of Fraser. 4 August 1985

499　　　　source of the funds. DTI 1988 p.160 & p.279
　　　　　was a forgery. DTI 1988 p.161
　　　　　banker was correct. DTI 1988 p.744
　　　　　the technical feasibility. Coghlan affidavit & Hansard 25 Apr 1989

501　　　　disgraced, is a mockery. Ltr Rowland to Borrie 29 October 1985
　　　　　of the Department of Trade. *Observer* 3 November 1985

502　　　　could not oblige. *Observer* 27 October 1985

503　　　　to the harbour authority. DTI 1988 p.623ff
　　　　　the same action. *Observer* 10 November 1985
　　　　　raking them over. *Spectator* 2 May 1987

504　　　　deigned not to explain. *Observer* 12 January 1986
　　　　　in March 1985. *Observer* 12 January/18 May 1986

as a major story. Howard, Author interview

505   contacts he provided. Linklater, Author interview
question asked Leigh. Hall p.230

506   consequences to the Observer. Anthony Howard,
Independent 19 January 1989
even one second. *Onlooker* 16 July 1986

507   editor and the Swami. *Observer* 18 May 1986
Fayed to Brunei. Ltr Turner Kenneth Brown
to Allen & Overy 4 July 1986
in the said transaction. Ltr Lonrho to Khashoggi
31 October 1986

509   7 per cent of the profits. Draper p.308
in the South of France. Kessler pp.234ff

511   the activity continued. Tower Commission Report
New York Times Special p.281
who else is involved. Iran Contra Hearings *Daily
Telegraph* 23 July 1987

512   as a boring mollusc. Ltr Rowland to Griffiths
21 June 1986

513   butter the Fayeds up. Ltr Rowland to Neil 4
May 1988
to Peter Horden. Ltr Rowland to Fleet 2 March
1987
today he would say. MacArthur Eddy Shah p.162

514   House of Fraser purchase. DTI 1988 p.163

515   an immediate inquiry. Ltr Rowland to Channon
18 Dec 1986

516   an unsuccessful cover-up. Ltr Rowland to Channon 4 February 1987

517   of this scandal. Ltrs Rowland to Channon 16
March 7 April

518   the ministers listened. *Sunday Times* 26 April 1987
match with a skunk. *Sunday Times* 29 June 1986
& Rowland testimony Denver 1 August 1984

522   underperformed the market. *The Times* 20 March
1987

525   10 per cent stake. MacArthur p.187ff & Shawcross
p.378ff

528   world-class fortune. Ltr Rowland to Inspectors 28 October 1987

529   inspectors apparently false. DTI 1988 p.289
       fraud of the century. Ltr Rowland to Heath 25 July 1988
       in four months. Ltr to Inspectors 8 December 1987

530   within eighteen months. *Sunday Telegraph* 29 May 1988

531   sued for defamation. June 1988

533   precluded Lonrho's offer. Young p.285ff
       and they knew it. DTI 1988 p.179 & p.537

534   plainly telling lies. DTI 1988 p.7/8
       of the events. DTI 1988 p.31
       of false representations. DTI 1988 p.542 & p.544
       in March 1985. DTI 1988 p.417
       being materially misled. DTI 1988 p.163
       the true facts. DTI 1988 p.5
       criticised by Griffiths. DTI 1988 p.592
       of its journalists. DTI 1988 p.695
       an independent manner. DTI 1988 p.706

535   acquire those funds. DTI 1988 p.13
       very major respects. DTI 1988 p.544

536   shareholders £20 million. Young p.281
       sat silent brooding. Young p.276
       on the Lonrho board. Young p.277

540   ask me to. *Observer* 6 November 1988
       to destroy him. Barry p.229

541   regards Tiny XXXX. *Observer* 6 November 1988

542   people as possible. *Observer* 19 March 1989
       Gandhi in a few days. James Bartholomew, *Spectator* 8 April 1989

543   and possibly terminal. 'A Financial Assessment' 5 September 1990

546   a lot of good business. Sunley, Author interview

547   contracts were invented. DTI Report appx 5 p.648

550   at best questionable semantics. Trelford comments on the report to the Chapel Committee p.3

552	investigation of bribes. *Observer* 30 April 1989
553	prize of Harrods. *Observer* 2 April 1989
555	cause for regret. Ltr Rowland to Young 29 March 1989
557	Commission to investigate. House of Lords 3 April 1989 & *Today* BBC Radio, 4 April 1989
	launch a prosecution. Young op. cit. p.284
	the Tornado stories. *Sunday Telegraph* 5 March 1989 & *Sunday Times* 7 May 1989 & Trelford Comments on the report to the Chapel Committee p.1 & p.8
	door for fraud. Ltr Rowland to Thatcher 27 June 1989
558	the Sultan's shadow. Ltr Rowland to Thatcher 19 July 1989
	to a crook. Ltr Rowland to Thatcher 11 August 1989
559	men were dishonest. Channel 4 TV 7 March 1990
	behaviour is weird. Ltr Rowland to Prince Philip 17 May 1990
Chapter 13	*Disenchanted Legacy*
Page 564	Africa has enriched him. Mpande, Author interview
	critics as stupid. Kaunda, Author interview
565	controls are impossible. Eric Wightman 17.3.89
	from the government. Yoyo, Author interview
566	relationship was adopted. Position Paper, P. Chitambala 22.2.88
576	only by presents. Eileen Kruger, Author interview
577	and don't interfere. Mpande, Author interview
578	mining and marketing. Ltr 21 February 1990 Nic Money, Geological Survey Department to Chiwenda, permanent secretary
	the president's support. Yoyo, Author interview
	have no following. *Finance* 1–15 November 1990 Nairobi
	live without Lonrho. Mwaange, Author interview

580   the newspaper in 1968. *Finance* 1–15 November 1990 Nairobi

he had amassed. Ltr Rowland to VP Saitoti, *Daily Nation* 11 November 1991

581   not from us. Ibid

outstandingly relevant material. Ibid.

Kenya a bad name. Ibid.

582   Malawi's enviable virtues. *Observer* 23 June 1991

malnutrition and brutality. Human Rights in Malawi, Report by the Law Society December 1992

589   is the greater. Ltr Rowland to Webb 11 November 1991

591   me in some way. New affidavit

in Zimbabwe now. New affidavit

592   return to Zimbabwe. Tape recording, New/ Rowland conversation

593   along with you. Ibid

594   Gadaffi in Tripoli. *Sunday Times* 9 August 1992

596   to share issues. March 1991 – Lonrho annual report

at least £1.4 billion. *Independent* 1 July 1992

with the institutions. *Sunday Telegraph* 26 January 1992

597   stark staring potty. *Independent on Sunday* 2 February 1992

to hound me out. *Sunday Telegraph* 2 February 1992

commitment to Lonrho. Ibid

598   Metropole hotel group. *Financial Times* 1 May 1992

Arabs with Africans. *Sunday Times* 9 August 1992

601   comes into the country. *Sunday Times* March 1992

Wouldn't you. *Observer* 3.5.92 and 28.6.92

nations like Libya. *Observer* 28 June 1992

604   and climbing back. *Independent* 1 July 1992

607   without public awareness. Ltr Rowland to Tebbit 11 March 1985

Bibliography

Bailey, Martin. *Oilgate*. Coronet 1979

Barry, Paul. *The Rise and Fall of Alan Bond*. Doubleday 1990

Bartholomew, James. *The Richest Man in the World*. Viking 1989

Blake, Robert. *A History of Rhodesia*. Methuen 1977

Bloch J. & Fitzgerald P. *British Intelligence and Covert Action*. Junction Books 1983

Bridgland, Fred. *Jonas Savimbi*. Coronet 1988

Booker, Christopher. *The Neophiliacs*. Fontana 1970

Cockett, Richard. *David Astor and the Observer*. André Deutsch 1991

Crocker, Chester. *High Noon in Southern Africa*. Norton 1992

Cronje S., M. Ling and G. Cronje. *Lonrho*. Pelican 1976

Draper, Theodore. *A Very Thin Line*. Touchstone 1991

Faith, Nicholas. *The Wankel Engine*. Allen and Unwin 1976

Fallon, Ivan. *Billionaire*. Hutchinson 1991

Fallon, Ivan & Srodes, James. *Take Overs*. Viking 1987

Flower, Ken. *Serving Secretly*. John Murray 1987

Hall, Richard. *My Life with Tiny*. Faber and Faber 1987

Harriman Ed. *Hack*. Zed Books 1987

Harris, Kenneth. *The Wildcatter*. Weidenfeld and Nicolson 1987

Horne, Alastair. *Harold Macmillan*. 2 vols. Macmillan 1988, 1989

Hurd, Douglas. *An End to Promises*. Collins 1979

Isaacson, Walter. *Kissinger*. Simon and Schuster 1992

Jackson, T. *The Drayton Group*. Charles Knight 1991

Jardim, Jorge. *Sanctions Double Cross*. Intervencao 1978

Kessler, Ronald. *The Richest Man in the World*. Warner Books 1986

MacArthur, Brian. *Eddy Shah*. David and Charles 1988

Martin, David & Phyllis Johnson. *The Struggle for Zimbabwe*. Faber and Faber 1981

Martindale, Steven. *By Hook or by Crook*. Century Hutchinson 1989

Meredith, Martin. *The Past is Another Country*. André Deutsch 1979

Morgan, Kenneth. *The People's Peace*. Oxford 1992

Mwaanga, Vernon. *An Extraordinary Life*. Fleetfoot 1982

Nkomo, Joshua. *Story of my Life*. Methuen 1984

Owen, David. *Time to Declare*. Penguin 1991

Raw, Charles. *Slater Walker*. Coronet 1977

Sampson, Anthony. *Anatomy of Britain*. Hodder and Stoughton 1962

Shawcross, William. *Murdoch*. Simon and Schuster 1992

Slater, Jim. *Return to Go*. Weidenfeld and Nicolson 1977

Smallpeice, Basil. *Of Comets and Queens*. Airlife 1981

Sylvester, Anthony. *Sudan Under Nimeiri*. Bodley Head 1977

Stockwell, John. *In Search of Enemies*. André Deutsch 1978

The Tower Commission report. Bantam Books 1987

Wilson, Harold. *The Labour Government 1964–70*. Weidenfeld and Nicolson 1971

Young, Lord. *The Enterprise Years*. Headline 1990

Picture Acknowledgments

Plate 1
Rowland in Hamburg, private collection; *Rowland at Churchers*, private collection

Plate 2
Peter Goosen, private collection; *George Abindor*, private collection; *Cyril Hatty*, private collection; *Rowland and Dan Mayers*, private collection

Plate 3
Rowland, Alan Ball and Ogilvy, Associated Newspapers; *Wallace, Adeane, R. and Beachcraft*, private collection; *Irene Smith*, private collection

Plate 4
Rowland and Banda, private collection; *Rowland and Mtine*, Associated Newspapers; *Tomo Kenyatta*, East African Standard; *Machel, Chissano*, private collection; *Kaunda*, Hulton Deutsch

Plate 5
Arrest warrant, private collection

Plate 6
Rowland, Thomson Newspapers; *Klein*, private collection; *Kruger*, private collection

Plate 7
Percy and Smallpeice, Elliot, Dalgleish, Gerber, MacKenzie, Thomson Newspapers; *Wilkinson*, private collection; *Spears*, Camera Press

Plate 8
Hedsor Wharf, Associated Newspapers; *Gulfstream*, John R Bater; *Du Cann*, *Ogilvy*, The Times

Plate 9
Shareholders, Sandys and shareholders, Press Association

Plate 10
Nasser and Osman, Associated Press; *Maxwell and Rowland*, The Keystone Collection; *Trelford*, private collection

Plate 11
Al Fayed, Associated Newspapers; *Hugh Fraser*, Donald MacLeod

Plate 12
Glasgow airport, Glasgow Herald; *Kashoggi and Swamiji*, private collection

Plate 13
Six secretaries of State of the DTI, BBC

Plate 14
Borrie, Financial Times by Ashley Ashwood; *Butler*, Financial Times; *Le Quesne*, BBC

Plate 15
Family and friends in Zimbabwe 1992, private collection; *Lonrho board in 1991*, private collection

Plate 16
Dieter Bock, Eric Roberts

Index